DREAMS OF POWER

African Studies Centre
Research Series
13/1999

DREAMS OF POWER

The role of the Organization of African Unity
in the politics of Africa
1963 - 1993

Klaas van Walraven

Ashgate

iv

Published by:

Ashgate Publishing Limited
Gower House
Croft Road
Aldershot
Hants GU11 3HR
England

Printed by PrintPartners Ipskamp B.V., Enschede

Cover illustration: The central panel of the stained glass windows at "Africa Hall", Addis Ababa. Courtesy of the Royal Tropical Institute, Amsterdam.

Illustrations:
page 214: *Die Burger*; page 250: *Révolution Africaine*; page 353: *Madagascar Renouveau*.

Research for this book was in part funded by two grants from the Netherlands Foundation for the Advancement of Tropical Research (WOTRO).

ISBN 1 85628 916 8

Contents

List of Tables

List of Figures

Preface and acknowledgements

A friend once thanked me in a paper he had written on the first All-African People's Conference for the encouragement I had given him by way of, what he saw as, my "Nkrumahist tendencies". It earned him an irritated response because, surely, I did not give others reason to belief that I was so naive about the feasibility of Osagyefo's Pan-Africanist ambitions.

Yet in a way my friend was right. For my interest in the OAU stems from a profound fascination with the paradox of a continent, where the seeds of discord are abundant, social and cultural cleavages are sharp and economic interests pitted against each other, but where many people nevertheless hold convictions about the need and possibility for African unity, frequently argue its case and to varying degrees attempt to work towards its realization — never mind the tremendous odds against it and the narrow margins of autonomy that Africans face in their struggles for a better future. In the context of these innumerable obstacles and difficulties this is a tale with an epic touch which no one can gainsay.

There are also few subjects so much governed by contradictions, surrounded by controversy and marked by ambiguities. Thus, when I had completed an interview at the Netherlands embassy in Addis Ababa I was brought back by the embassy's chauffeur to my temporary residence and we passed the OAU headquarters in Kirkos, one of the more plebeian districts of the Ethiopian capital. In a bid to kill the time I asked the chauffeur what *he* thought of the OAU. "I don't", he replied aptly, accompanying his answer with a broad grin on his face.

Africa and the OAU. This constitutes, indeed, a perplexing subject, as life on the continent is marked by huge social distances and Africans hold widely divergent views of the Organization. The discrepancies in African opinion are not only due to differences in positions and interests but — for reasons explained in this book — are also caused by the fact that the OAU represents the very epitome of Africa itself, and thus elicits and assembles all manner of wisdom, hope and frustration. It is therefore far from easy to ascertain the OAU's place in Africa — in fact as well as in thought.

This, however, is what I have intended to do. The purpose of this book is to show how the Organization of African Unity functions in the complex configurations of African politics. Special emphasis is laid on the ways in which this functioning is grasped by its officials and member states, as well as by Africans to whom the fruits of governmental privilege have been denied. As assessments of the OAU vary, it is imperative to unearth what specifically constitutes its rationale. This can only be culled from its ideological underpinnings, for international institutions do not have goals of themselves but only those assigned to them by the forces which control their existence. While constitutive treaties provide some clues as to their raison d'être, in the case in question these only amount to vague intimations of the intricate complex of forces, energies and aspirations driving the OAU.

Thus, in trying to conceive of the Organization of African Unity this book aims to reconstruct its ideological dimensions and provide fresh insights in African thought on issues of international politics. It is in this respect habitually forgotten that international organizations are much more than mere compilations of prosaic or tedious procedures and organs. They also serve as focal junctures that people, in and outside the corridors of power, employ for the expression of their ideas, the articulation of their visions and the experiencing of their dreams or nightmares about life in this world. It is, above all, these views and notions — obscure, jaundiced or concrete and articulate — that I have attempted to bring to the fore, as the role of the OAU in the political psychology of post-colonial Africa has, until now, received little to no attention.

In this I have especially tried to fathom the OAU from the perspective of *painfulness* which Africans sense, when confronted with the chasm between the aspirations embodied by the OAU and its impotence in the harsh world of power politics and, more generally, when they must face up to the dualism engendered by their own cosmology and the alien forms of international intercourse which to a greater or lesser extent were thrust upon them by the outside world. In order to make sense of these experiences Africans have coined various disturbing metaphors, around which this book has been structured. These key images have not been included in order to hold up to other people's ridicule what the OAU stands for, but to elucidate some of the apprehensions and anxieties Africans feel with regard to the OAU and the numerous issues, continental and global, with which it is concerned.

In fact, far from wishing to mock the OAU's ambitions and difficulties I must confess here to my own Pan-Africanist inclinations. As long as the texture of African societies continues to be seriously impaired by the uprooting forces of external penetration the logic of togetherness is, I feel, unassailable. So the OAU deserves thoughtful attention, while the dream of African unity remains, for better and for worse, a part of my own political landscape.

This book is therefore dedicated to the staff of the OAU's General Secretariat, who are the true heroes of this story. Here I wish to express my gratitude for the time they spent to receive me and answer my numerous queries, as well as for their willingness to engage in regular correspondence and forward to me valuable, additional documentation. As it would be a mark of conceit to assume that I could truly probe the psyches of those involved in Pan-African intercourse, it has to be stressed that this evaluation of the OAU, and its underlying mental complexes, is entirely mine and cannot be held against OAU staff.

I would further like to acknowledge the willingness of many of the personnel of African embassies in Addis Ababa to be interviewed for the purpose of this book. Their readiness to share their views and perceptions of the OAU with me was crucial for its realization. I also wish to thank A. Heldring, at the time Netherlands chargé d'affaires, for his co-operation in preparing the field, while I am grateful to George Groenewold for helping me to adapt as quickly as possible to life in the Ethiopian capital.

Although it is impossible to thank all the institutions in London and Paris where documents of, and relevant to, the OAU are stored special thanks must go to the staff of the newspaper section of the British Library in Colindale for coping with my insatiable demand for African press publications. I also owe a great deal to the library staff of the African Studies Centre in Leiden, for meeting during many years with my requests and for maintaining one of the best collections in African studies. My special thanks go to Koos van der Meulen, whose own views and research on the OAU have been of considerable support.

Among the many scholars who assisted me in bringing this project to fruition my gratitude goes, first and foremost, to Emile van Rouveroy and Alfred van Staden, both of the University of Leiden. Without their support this book would not have seen the light of day. Their advice on methodology, the theoretical perspectives informing the analysis, and the planning of fieldwork was crucial, while the importance of their intellectual criticism was only matched by their patience. I would also like to thank Martin Doornbos of the Institute of Social Studies in The Hague, Piet Kooijmans, now at the International Court of Justice, Robert Ross of the University of Leiden and Robert Buijtenhuijs of the African Studies Centre, for their comments on the Ph.D. thesis that lay at the basis of this book. I am indebted to Richard Fredland of Indiana University, for his willingness to share his insights on the OAU with me and I am grateful to Zdenek Cervenka of the Scandinavian Institute of African Studies in Uppsala, David Meyers of the University of North Carolina and Yassin El-Ayouty, formerly of the State University of New York, for their advice during the research stage.

Special thanks must go to the staff of the Netherlands Institute of International Relations 'Clingendael' for their patience and support during the final stages of writing. In particular, I would like to thank my colleagues in the research department for many stimulating discussions on questions that dominate in the world of international relations. I also wish to thank Stephen Ellis and Piet Konings of the African Studies Centre in Leiden for their insights and readiness to discuss with me the significance of the OAU in relation to other aspects of African politics. Dick Foeken and the African Studies Centre have obliged me for their assistance in getting the book ready for publication. I am indebted to Leontine van Dijl and Mieke Zwart who took care of putting the manuscript in the African Studies Centre housestyle. Last but not least, I feel indebted to all those friends and family, old and new, who through the years provided me with the moral support and humour that were needed to bring this work to completion.

Glossary[1]

Africa's international relations
encompass both the relations between African states and the non-African world and relations between OAU member states themselves (see also *extra-African relations* and *inter-African relations*)

African nationalism
the desire for liberation from European colonial rule by way of territorial self-government or independence, territorial autonomy and equality within a broader Eur-African framework, or racial equality between the African and European (white) populations in racially plural territories (see also *state nationalism*)

African politics
the continent's international relations and the domestic or internal political configurations inside the OAU's member states

African socialism
a generic category of various ideologies, which were influenced by Marxism but underplayed or denied the existence or significance of social cleavages in African society — as opposed to the importance of national unity and independence — and which rejected or resisted Marxism's atheist, and to some extent its materialist, aspects and stressed the importance of adapting socialism to African circumstances, often with reference to (pre-colonial) communal traditions

African unity
doctrine which may or may not be part of nationalist or Pan-Africanist ideology and whose meaning is context-dependent

alliance
the temporary or permanent coming together of certain states or actors to realize some common objective (synonym: *coalition*)

Anglophone member states
a category of OAU member states held to encompass all former British colonies, in addition to Liberia, Namibia, Ethiopia, Somalia and Eritrea but excluding Egypt (synonym: *English-speaking member states*)

balkanization
the decolonization and break-up by European colonial powers, with or without the help of their African clients, of their African territorial possessions into numerous, relatively small and weak, independent states

capability
resource or instrument with which actors seek to exercise power

---

1   This glossary only contains key concepts and involves definitions or descriptions as used or understood in this study. These do therefore not necessarily pretend general application or validity.

cartoon
graphical presentation of an ideological argument or statement

Central Africa
refers to the official OAU regional classification of member states (see Appendix D)

coalition
the temporary or permanent coming together of certain states or actors to realize some common objective (synonym: *alliance*)

collective good
a good which can only be supplied to all, and not just a few, actors of a system; the concept implies that no one can be excluded from its consumption, not even those that have not paid for it (synonym: *public good*; see also: *free rider*)

collective legitimization
dispensing of politically significant approval of the claims, policies and actions of a state by the membership of an international organization by way of debate, adoption of resolutions or informal means

collective security
a doctrine prescribing, by way of a collective defence strategy and structure involving all states, the protection of all states against all states wishing to commit aggression; it is only concerned with inter-state conflicts and presumes moral clarity of the concept and specific cases of "aggression"

colonialism
the system of formal and actual political rule by (metropolitan) European or white powers over African territories

compound stalemate
stalemate which occurs when disputants replenish resources and escalate their conflict until a new limit, and thus stalemate, is reached (see also *entrapment*)

conflict
incompatibility of goals or the violent expression of such incompatibility (synonym: *dispute*)

conflict management
reduction or transformation of conflict in less violent or (other) non-violent forms of interaction

conflict settlement
management of conflict or sometimes its resolution

consensus
a political procedure by which decisions are not taken by actual voting but by debate, which culminates in more or less general — and not necessarily complete — agreement, as formulated in the chairman's summary of deliberations or announcement that decisions stand adopted and in the absence of explicitly stated objections of most participants (see also *unanimity*)

conservative member states
pertains to a qualification or category of OAU member states that had some relevance up to the mid-1980s, yet was too complex, and to some extent too elusive, to allow for a precise definition (description in section 1.2)

conspiracy theory

articulating conspiracy theory represents a defensive way of compensating deprivation or a withdrawal from social interaction, by explaining one's problems as being caused by more or less identified (real or imaginary) political enemies

co-operation

points to the phenomenon of actors that adjust their behaviour to the actual or anticipated preferences of others through a process of policy co-ordination

core economies

economies, usually in the Northern hemisphere, which sell products with high added value to peripheral economies (see also *peripheral economies* and *semi-peripheral economies*)

decide/decision

with regard to OAU organs these terms refer to legally binding or not binding acts, depending on the context in which they are used and as determined by the contents of the relevant act

decolonization

process of terminating formal political control of a European metropolitan power or white settler-dominated government over an African country, leading to formal, internationally recognized, independence of, and/or African majority rule in, that country

dependence

a condition of being significantly affected by external forces, implying a relationship of subordination of one state or country to another, which negatively affects the former's development

deprivation

the distress that the human ego suffers when it cannot enjoy a certain value position that it demands

destructive conflict

conflict which becomes detached from its original causes and in which parties pursue maximalist options, involving a zero-sum situation marked by escalation

development

economic growth leading to structural changes in the economy

discourse

the construction of meaning as a social process through spoken or written dialogue

dispute

incompatibility of goals or the violent expression of such incompatibility (synonym: *conflict*)

doctrine

a specific contention or idea which is part of an ideology or which is synonymous for an (expression of) ideology

domestic conflict

conflict taking place inside an OAU member state (synonym: *internal conflict*)

dominant coalition

alliance of actors sufficiently powerful to enforce compliance by other actors with its preferred outcome of interaction

East Africa
refers to the official OAU regional classification of member states (see Appendix D)

elites
minorities that are set apart from the rest of society by their pre-eminence in the distribution of deference, authority, achievement or reward

enforcement action
some form of (non-)military activity in a conflict, which may legally only be undertaken or authorized by the UN Security Council and does not require the consent of the disputants (see also *peace-keeping*)

English-speaking member states
a category of OAU member states held to encompass all former British colonies, in addition to Liberia, Namibia, Ethiopia, Somalia and Eritrea but excluding Egypt (synonym: *Anglophone member states*)

entrapment
situation which occurs in the context of a compound stalemate and involves pressures on disputants, resulting from the costs of replenishing resources to pursue and escalate the conflict, to try and reach victory (see also *compound stalemate*)

extra-African relations
relations between African states and states/actors outside Africa

foreign affairs
synonym for foreign policy

foreign policy
a cluster of orientations, commitments to action and forms of behaviour pertaining to a state's relations with other states or external actors

Francophone member states
a category of OAU member states held to encompass all former French colonies and, in some contexts, also those of Belgium, but excluding Morocco, Algeria and Tunisia (synonym: *French-speaking member states*)

free rider
an actor which profits from the compliance by other actors with agreed rules of co-operation while not reciprocating in kind

French-speaking member states
a category of OAU member states held to encompass all former French colonies and, in some contexts, also those of Belgium, but excluding Morocco, Algeria and Tunisia (synonym: *Francophone member states*)

hegemon
a state that stands alone without equals at the top of the inter-state hierarchy of power and is more powerful than others in terms of the ability to control outcomes of interaction

hegemonic stability
refers to the situation in which co-operation between international actors emerges as a result of, and is dependent on, the domination of the international system by a hegemonic leader

hegemony
the consensual basis of a political system in terms of consent or acquiescence

ideology

(a set of) ideas, notions or concepts that purport to explain reality, prescribe goals for (political, social, economic, military, cultural) action to reform and alter, or preserve and defend, actual conditions and circumstances, and which provide criteria with which to legitimize such action

imperialism

refers to the historical process of European expansion, leading to the establishment, exercise and maintenance of different forms of control of countries or regions overseas, such as by direct political rule or indirect — f.i. economic — means (see also *colonialism* and *neo-colonialism*)

integration

an increase in the capacity of a political system, such as a state or a group of states, to solve common problems, often by way of — although not always to be equated with — some degree of unification among its actors through the establishment of common institutions

inter-African affairs/politics

synonym for inter-African relations

inter-African relations

a term which pertains to relations between (few or many) OAU member states (see also *Pan-African*)

interference/intervention

any act by one actor to exert influence over another actor, or articulation of a form of concern with regard to that actor, irrespective of legal connotations (*i.e.* wider than, and not to be confused with, the OAU's non-intervention norm as such)

internal conflict

conflict inside an OAU member state (synonym: *domestic conflict*)

international affairs/politics

synonym for international relations

international regime

sets of principles, norms, rules and decision-making procedures around which the expectations of actors in international relations (usually states) converge in a given issue area

irredentism

a particular form of secession or separatism, in which a socio-political, ethnic or cultural grouping aspires to be united with a neighbouring state and/or that neighbouring state expresses a similar wish with regard to that grouping, on the basis of (real or perceived) shared identities and/or historical grounds (see *secession* and *separatism*)

legitimacy

this concept is used as understood in political science and refers to the extent to which a system, rule or form of behaviour is considered and recognized as positive

leverage mechanism

the idea and effect that the large number of African states acts, through co-ordination of their behaviour, as an enlargement of the influence of individual African governments, and of the continent as a whole, vis-à-vis the rest of the world

marginalization

process involving Africa's declining significance or share in global economic development and/or military (strategic) respects, as manifested in various macro-economic indicators and/or attributed by non-African powers and interests

mediation

third-party intervention for the purpose of abating or resolving a conflict through negotiations

mentality

a notion which is wider than the concept of ideology as it also includes those mental realities which are unformulated, those that are apparently meaningless and those that are situated at the level of unconscious motivation

metaphor

technique of ideological reasoning through the creation of analogies, associations and comparisons with well known symbols, conditions or stories from other contexts

militant member states

pertains to a qualification or category of OAU member states that had some relevance up to the mid-1980s, yet was too complex, and to some extent too elusive, to allow for a precise definition (description in section 1.2; synonym: *radical*)

moderate member states

pertains to a qualification or category of OAU member states that had some relevance up to the mid-1980s, yet was too complex, and to some extent too elusive, to allow for a precise definition (description in section 1.2)

modern elite

used as synonym for petty bourgeoisie, implying some impermanence of social status, and involving the top stratum of post-colonial African society (see further petty bourgeoisie)

modernity

the concept that epitomizes the onset in world history of the modern era, as characterized by industrialization, faith in human progress and mastery over nature, and rapid development of science, technology and communications

nation

a concept that is difficult to define, but which is held to pertain to a people that (usually) lives in a definite territory, that possesses common cultural traits, language and/or racial characteristics, and which shares the conviction that it actually constitutes a single, exclusive and terminal community

nationalism

the desire to realize the freedom, welfare and integrity of the (existing or projected) nation by way of political independence or autonomy, usually articulated through, and tied to, the aspiration to establish a (nation-)state

neo-colonialism

refers to structures, relationships and attitudes, which were formed in the colonial period and which enable a former colonial power to continue to exercise indirectly a considerable measure of economic, political, cultural and other forms of control over the affairs of a former colony which enjoys formal and internationally recognized political independence

non-alignment

non-commitment to the world's dominant ideological blocs during the Cold War and preservation of the right and ability to judge world issues on their merits without undue external influence

non-governmental group(ing)

leading echelons of sections in Africa's modern elite that are denied access to governmental power and privilege but enjoy or aspire to elite status: political exiles, leaders and members of opposition parties and principal ranks of guerrilla movements

North Africa

refers to the official OAU regional classification of member states (see Appendix D and the categorization of *North African member states* — as opposed to sub-Saharan ones)

North African member states

Morocco, Algeria, Tunisia, Libya, Egypt (see also *North Africa*)

Pan-African (relations)

this term pertains to (relations between) all, or at least many, African states (in the latter case *inter-African* is its synonym)

Pan-Africanism

an ideology that is difficult to define because of its amorphous character, but which involves at least an aspiration to realize or recapture the dignity, freedom, autonomy and/or unity of Africans and/or of people of African descent

Pan-Africanist

pertains to the ideology of Pan-Africanism and is distinct from the term *Pan-African*

pan ideologies

ideologies that aim to promote the solidarity of groups which are (perceived to be) bound to each other by a shared language, culture, race, religion, nationhood and/or geographical area

peace-keeping

some form of military activity (as observation of cease-fires, separation of warring parties) in a conflict by a third party — usually an international organization — based on consent of the disputants (see also *enforcement action*)

peripheral economies

economies, usually in the Southern hemisphere, which sell products with limited added value, such as raw materials, to core economies (see also *core economies* and *semi-peripheral economies*)

petty bourgeoisie

top stratum of post-colonial African society, which enjoys elite status and encompasses businessmen, big agricultural entrepreneurs, professionals, traders, transporters, university-trained, civil servants, politicians, journalists (see also *modern elite*)

political process

the totality of patterns of interaction between actors

power

any form of influence that one actor wields over another

prisoner's dilemma

context of two actors which can decide to co-operate or not to co-operate, but which choose the latter option because of their ignorance about what the other actor will do, thus leading to a sub-optimal outcome in their interaction

propaganda

the deliberate attempt to control, influence or alter attitudes of others by communicating written, spoken or other symbols

public good

a good which can only be supplied to all, and not just a few, actors of a system; the concept implies that no one can be excluded from its consumption, not even those that have not paid for it (synonym: *collective good*; see also: *free rider*)

radical member states

pertains to a qualification or category of OAU member states that had some relevance up to the mid-1980s, yet was too complex, and to some extent too elusive, to allow for a precise definition (description in section 1.2; synonym: *militant*)

regional hegemony

regional inter-state ties based on domination and the creation of consensus by the hegemon's formulation and manipulation of norms, which in varying degrees legitimate its dominance in terms of the consent or acquiescence of other states in that region

rhetoric

the expression of words, ideas or arguments whose literal meaning differs from someone's real and unarticulated opinions

secession

refers to the aspiration of a socio-political, ethnic or cultural grouping to disengage from a post-colonial state, of which it was an official part since decolonization, in order to establish its own independent state (synonym: *separatism*)

self-determination

in the OAU this refers to the right of the entire adult population of the (post-)colonial state to freely determine — yet subject to the geographical framework of colonial partition — its political future, usually articulated through an aspiration to independent statehood and in principle only at the time of decolonization

self-reliance

a policy that has as its aim to enhance the economic autonomy of African states by an emphasis on endogenous and self-sustained development through (collective) self-sufficiency in various economic sectors

semi-peripheral economies

economies which are able to profit from declining wage-productivity in core countries and therefore operate between those and peripheral ones, standing between them in terms of product value, wage levels and profit margins (see also *core economies* and *peripheral economies*)

separatism

refers to the aspiration of a socio-political, ethnic or cultural grouping to disengage from a post-colonial state, of which it was an official part since decolonization, in order to establish its own independent state (synonym: *secession*)

side-payments
rewards which redistribute the net benefits of co-operation among actors to equalize inequities arising from their co-operation

social movement
several groups of individuals who represent a particular stratum of society and are activated towards realizing certain political, cultural or socio-economic objectives

Southern Africa
refers to the official OAU regional classification of member states (see Appendix D)

stability
the extent to which the characteristics of a political system, such as the forms and rules of interaction, the nature of its units and the system's boundaries, remain essentially the same

state capitalism
a development approach adopted after independence by most African states and marked by some willingness to work within established structures of the international economy, deliberate expansion of export production to finance importation of capital goods and, in general, the provision of a central place to the free market mechanism, yet together with the attribution of a key role to the state in the accumulation of surplus because of the relative dearth of private capital

state elite
top echelon of post-colonial African society exercising or representing central government power and consisting of the head of state, ministers, presidential advisers, party leaders, senior military officers, heads of departments and diplomats

state nationalism
African nationalism as articulated since decolonization

state socialism
development model pursued by some African states until the 1980s, marked by collectivization of several economic sectors, a high degree of central planning, varying attempts to revise the structures of the international economic order and of the role of their national economy therein, and considerable dependence on foreign development aid

structures of international relations
fundamental patterns of interaction between international actors

sub-Saharan member states
all OAU member states which are not part of the category of North African member states

subversion
the provision by a government of armed support or other forms of assistance to opposition groups in or from another African country

terms of trade
the average price of a country's exports divided by the average price of its imports

unanimity
a legal procedure — which does not exist in the OAU — by which decisions are taken by actual voting and all participants express themselves in identical fashion without abstentions usually precluding such full agreement (see also *consensus*)

uti possidetis
the norm, which in the OAU, involves the pledge by its member states to respect their inter-state frontiers as inherited upon decolonization
West Africa
refers to the official OAU regional classification of member states (see Appendix D)
zero-sum
refers to a context in which the interests of actors are strictly antagonistic and/or these actors perceive them as such

Abbreviations

AAPC	All-African People's Conference
AEC	African Economic Community
AEF	Afrique Equatoriale Française
ALF	Azania Liberation Front (Sudan)
ANC	African National Congress (South Africa)
AOF	Afrique Occidentale Française
CAR	Central African Republic
CCTA	Commission pour la Cooperation Technique en Afrique
CFA	Communauté Financière Africaine
CIAS	Conference of Independent African States
CMCA	Commission of Mediation, Conciliation and Arbitration
CNL	Comité Nationale de Libération (Congo-Leopoldville)
CNN	Cable News Network
CPP	Convention People's Party (Ghana)
EC	European Community
ECA	Economic Commission for Africa (United Nations)
ECCAS	Economic Community of Central African States
ECOMOG	ECOWAS Cease-Fire Monitoring Group
ECOSOC	Economic and Social Council (United Nations)
ECOWAS	Economic Community of West African States
EPLF	Eritrean People's Liberation Front
EU	European Union
FLN	Front de Libération Nationale (Algeria)
FNLA	Frente Nacional de Libertação de Angola
FPR	Front Patriotique Rwandais
FRELIMO	Frente de Libertação de Moçambique
FROLINAT	Front de Libération Nationale du Tchad
GATT	General Agreement on Tariffs and Trade
GDP	Gross Domestic Product
GNP	Gross National Product
GPRA	Gouvernement Provisoire de la République Algérienne
GRAE	Governo Revolucionário de Angola no Exílio
GUNT	Gouvernement d'Union Nationale de Transition (Chad)
IABL	Inter-African Bureau of African Languages
IAMO	Inter-African and Malagasy Organization
IMF	International Monetary Fund
KANU	Kenya African National Union
MPLA	Movimento Popular de Libertação de Angola

NATO	North Atlantic Treaty Organization
NFD	Northern Frontier District (Kenya)
NGO	Non-governmental organization
NMOG	Neutral Military Observer Group
NPFL	National Patriotic Front of Liberia
OAMCE	Organisation Africaine et Malgache de Coopération Economique
OAS	- Organisation de l'Armée Secrète (Algeria)
	- Organization of American States
OAU	Organization of African Unity
OCAM	Organisation Commune Africaine et Malgache
OMIB	Observer Mission in Burundi
OPEC	Organization of Petroleum Exporting Countries
OSCE	Organization for Security and Co-operation in Europe
OUA	Organisation de l'Unité Africaine
PAC	Pan-Africanist Congress (South Africa)
PAFMECA	Pan-African Freedom Movement of East and Central Africa
PAFMECSA	Pan-African Freedom Movement of Eastern, Central and Southern Africa
PAIGC	Partido Africano da Independência da Guiné e Cabo Verde
PANA	Pan-African News Agency
PDCI	Parti Démocratique de Côte d'Ivoire
PF	Patriotic Front (Zimbabwe)
PLO	Palestine Liberation Organization
POLISARIO	(Frente) Populár para la Liberación de Saguia el Hamra y Rio de Oro
RASD	République Arabe Sahraouie Démocratique
RENAMO	Resistência Nacional Moçambicana
SADC	Southern African Development Community
SADCC	Southern African Development Co-ordination Conference
SANU	Sudan African National Union
SG	Secretary-General
SIPRI	Stockholm International Peace Research Institute
SPLA	Sudan People's Liberation Army
SWAPO	South West African People's Organization
TANU	Tanganyika African National Union
UAM	Union Africaine et Malgache
UAMD	Union Africaine et Malgache de Défense
UAR	United Arab Republic
UAS	Union of African States
UDI	Unilateral Declaration of Independence (Rhodesia)
UN	United Nations
UNCTAD	United Nations Conference on Trade and Development

UNESCO	United Nations Educational, Scientific and Cultural Organization
UNHCR	United Nations High Commission for Refugees
UNIA	Universal Negro Improvement Association
UNITA	União para a Independência Total de Angola
UNOSOM	United Nations Operation in Somalia
UPC	Union des Populations du Cameroun
US(A)	United States (of America)
USSR	Union of Soviet Socialist Republics
WASU	West African Students' Union
ZANU	Zimbabwe African National Union
ZAPU	Zimbabwe African People's Union

*L'étude de ses rêves constitue, pour la connaissance
d'une société,
un instrument d'analyse dont on ne saurait
négliger l'efficacité*

Raoul Girardet, *Mythes et Mythologies Politiques*

Introduction, methodology and theoretical perspectives

1.1   Introduction

This chapter first discusses the objective of this study and how it came to be formulated. It then outlines the kind of sources that were used and the methodology that was adopted in the search for those sources. Part of this methodology is a classification of African states, which is discussed in the last section of section 1.2. The relevant theoretical perspectives are introduced in section 1.3. This is followed, in section 1.4, by an analysis of the phenomenon of ideology, which is a central concept in this study. This section includes a discussion of how ideology in general and the sources used in this study in particular, are interpreted. The last section explains how the concepts of Africa and the OAU are approached. It also outlines the limitations necessary for implementing the research objective; the structure of the overall narrative; and the way in which the sources will be cited.

1.2   Methodology

The research objective
The objective of this study is to determine how the Organization of African Unity (OAU) functions in African politics. The latter term is broadly conceived as encompassing both the continent's international relations and the domestic political configurations inside the OAU's member states.

In formulating this central research question we were particularly interested in finding out what inter-African co-operation by way of the OAU amounted to and how this could be explained. How and under which conditions would the Organization be able to realize its objectives and to what extent would the various cleavages marking inter-African relations, as well as the OAU's relations with other organizations, play a role in this? Answers to these inter-related queries are given in the course of this study.

Naturally, no researcher embarks on a study without holding certain initial assumptions that may colour one's perspective on the subject. It is therefore important to know what these assumptions were. Thus, it was presumed that the kind of co-operation embodied by the OAU could be related to the configurations of power at the national level, in the sense that the Organization functions as a platform for Africa's leaders and only reflects the interests of state elites rather than the aspirations of the mass of African peoples. It was thought that the OAU is to some extent able to structure Africa's international relations, both in terms of inter-African ties and relations with the non-African world, although it was not clear exactly how and to what degree. We also presumed that the ideology of Pan-Africanism constitutes a useful source of influence for the OAU which, it was held, forms an organization with a low degree of institutional development and limited legal powers. It was also thought that in the field of political co-operation the OAU enjoys more prestige than other African international organizations.

This study attempts to confirm and refine these ideas. Following the by now classical, seminal analysis by Claude[1] it was — and is — contended that four variables determine the OAU's functioning. These are the structures of Africa's international relations; the foreign policy objectives of the OAU's member states; the Organization's "resources" (financial, legal); and the OAU's objectives. It is contended that the first two variables are the most important, the other two being essentially off-shoots of Africa's international relations and the goals of member states. As Claude puts it, international organizations do not really have objectives of themselves, but only those that are attributed to them by the member states. However, he qualifies this by observing that international organizations are dualist in nature, in the sense that they are made up of member state representatives and the personnel of the organization's secretariat. The secretariat personnel to some extent embodies the organization's identity. It may have its own, different, objectives.[2]

These observations explain why it is possible that the nature of the OAU's objectives, and thus its role in African politics, are not undisputed. Its goals cannot simply be reduced to the formal aims inscribed in its Charter. This is especially so because this document was the result of a complex compromise and therefore excels in generalized formulations. The *real* objectives of the OAU can thus only be found by looking at what aims and roles are attributed to it by all its member states and, to a lesser extent, its secretariat personnel. It must be borne in mind that the whole purpose of an international organization with a large membership can be complex and may also change over time.

While international relations theorists agree that the structures of international politics exert greater influence on international organizations than vice versa, many contend that such organizations also affect international relations. If our principal aim is to determine how the OAU functions in African politics the question of its real objectives and, thus, its

1   See I.L. Claude, *Swords into Plowshares: The Problems and Progress of International Organization* (New York, 1964), ch. 1.
2   *Ibid.*

role therein, therefore assumes considerable importance. This importance is reinforced by the wide divergence in opinion among Africans on the issue of the Organization's role in Africa.

Thus, governmental presentations of the OAU as an heroic institution that waged war on white minority regimes alternate with lamentations over its impotence or positive evaluation of its role in global politics. Images of the OAU as the embodiment of Pan-Africanism are articulated by its Secretariat alongside awareness of its weak position vis-à-vis the member states. Non-governmental perceptions of the OAU as the incarnation of neo-colonialism, patron of Africa's state elites and defender of Western interests interchange with pleas for a "peoples OAU" and emphasis on the importance of an institution capable of defending the continent's interests against the rest of the world.

The variations in these assessments point to the use of different criteria with which the Organization is judged. In order to determine the function of the OAU in African politics one must therefore also find out what exactly constitutes its fundamental rationale. This can be gleaned from its underlying ideological basis or ground-work, as composed of aims and roles attributed by the majority of member states and, secondarily, its Secretariat personnel.

Thus, the central research question had to be re-phrased as follows: finding out how the Organization of African Unity functions, in an objective sense, in African politics, with special emphasis on how this is perceived by member states and Secretariat functionaries and, in this respect, the roles and objectives attributed by them to the OAU. With member states are actually meant the state elites, *i.e.* the top political leadership of those countries. A precise definition of state elites is given in section 2.2. Focus on state elites is justified by the fact that, in the OAU, only governments are represented and by the assumption that the Organization tends (or tended) to act as a protector of the narrow interests of those state elites. However, one can therefore not divorce the OAU's functioning from its role in the domestic order of member states. For this reason the revised research objective should also involve analysis of the OAU's roles as perceived by African non-governmental circles.

This study therefore aims at providing important building-stones for a systematic reconstruction of the OAU's ideological ground-work. Although various studies provide insights in its ideology, such a reconstruction has never been undertaken. In this respect it is noteworthy that most studies usually give an advance, rather general and superficial, assessment of the Organization's ideological foundations, on the basis of which their authors proceed to analyse and judge its functioning.[3] In attempting to reconstruct the OAU's ideological ground-work we hope to establish the role of the OAU in African political thought. This study being intended, above all, as a contribution to the field of African studies, this aim is supposed to yield insight in African political thought on questions of international co-operation. One can think here of perceptions of Africa's post-colonial set-up, its global position and the utility of international organizations to the management of the continental order.

---

3   See f.i. K. Mathews, 'The Organization of African Unity in World Politics', in R.I. Onwuka and T.M. Shaw (eds), *Africa in World Politics: Into the 1990s* (Basingstoke and London, 1989), p 34. While making a similar observation he makes the same mistake.

However, as can be seen in the revised central research question our reconstruction is set within the goal of determining the OAU's objective functioning in African politics. With regard to the latter's international dimension — *i.e.* Africa's international relations with the non-African world and the relations between member states (inter-African relations) — this study is undertaken in the framework of two international relations theories. Inter-African relations will be analysed from the perspective of hegemonic stability theory and Africa's relations with the outside world are assessed through the perspective of dependency theory. While various forms of criticism have been levelled against these theories this study will, as part of its principal objective, attempt to show that both do have considerable explanatory power.

The search for sources
Broadly, the sources for this study fall into three categories: documents of the OAU; African governmental newspapers and other government publications; and data obtained through interviews.

The importance to this study of OAU documents is self-evident. OAU documentation consists of public documents and documents intended for internal use by its organs. Public documents are resolutions; declarations; decisions; statements; official publications by the General Secretariat or any of its special or regional offices; treaties; charters; conventions; communiqués; and policy statements in the form of action plans. Documents intended for internal use are verbatim records of meetings by OAU organs that were held *in camera*; reports of the Secretary-General to the OAU's policy organs; memoranda; rules of procedure of organs; financial reports and statements; protocols; notes; activity reports; and briefs. Of all these types documents were collected. An overview is given in Appendix A, which also provides information on where they can be located.

Documents carrying the formal title of resolutions, declarations, decisions and statements represent official expressions of OAU policy. Usually they are, or are intended to be, of the greatest importance, whether in actual fact or in terms of perception and publicity profile. Although they constitute an enormous volume of documents, we therefore simply tried to collect as many as possible of them. As annual reports of the Secretary-General are rather voluminous overviews of OAU activities in various fields we collected examples from different points in time. Verbatim records were also collected. Unfortunately, after the 1960s the production of these documents became rare.[4] They consist of transcripts of tape recordings of deliberations by member state delegates at OAU meetings. Transcripts of the oral interventions of non-Anglophone delegates are always based on the simultaneous translation by interpreters. Some of these records, especially that of the founding conference[5] are a mine of information on the disagreements, cleavages and areas of consensus between member states.

---

4   See also C.O.C. Amate, *Inside the OAU: Pan-Africanism in Practice* (New York, 1986), pp xii-xiii.
5   Curiously, this record has rarely been used to the full. Amate, *Inside the OAU*, and M. Wolfers, *Politics in the Organization of African Unity* (London, 1976) are an exception to some extent.

With regard to other types of OAU documents, we collected material from every field of co-operation in which the OAU is known to engage because of the wide-ranging nature of the research objective. However, in view of the importance of co-operation on political issues and co-operation in the field of decolonization documents in these areas predominate. Most OAU documents collected are in English and some in French.[6]

The second category of sources — governmental newspapers and other government publications — consists of data which demand a more detailed discussion as to their nature and significance for this study and the research procedure followed. This will be given after treatment of the third category of sources.

This third category is made up of data obtained through interviews. For this field-work was undertaken in Addis Ababa, Ethiopia, in September and October 1989. Interviews were held with two groups of people: functionaries of the OAU's General Secretariat and diplomats of African embassies in Addis Ababa.[7] The data obtained are meant as a supplement to, and verification of, the other, written, sources, although they also contain interesting information that cannot be found in documents, such as on perceptions of OAU officials and makeshift budgeting practices.

The questions that were asked were mainly deduced from the fields of co-operation in which the OAU is and was engaged. Thus, questions were asked on the purposes of the OAU and its roles in specific issue areas; on institutional, financial and personnel matters, as well as working conditions of OAU officials and the relations between staff; on the nature and relevance of cleavages in inter-African relations; on relations with regional inter-African organizations, the UN, the Arab League, the Franco-African summits, the Commonwealth and the EU; and on the issue areas of conflict management, collective defence, decolonization, the functioning of the UN African Group, refugees, human rights and economic co-operation. Other areas of OAU concern, such as cultural and technical forms of co-operation, were ignored.

All interviews were conducted in English. Only one diplomat spoke in French. The maximum length of interviews was one to one and a half hour. None was recorded. One person explicitly disallowed it, while with most other interviewees we had the impression that answers would have suffered in frankness. Notes were therefore made during and after interviews. In rank selected OAU functionaries ranged from the middle to upper cadres of the professional grade. The highest official interviewed was an Assistant Secretary-General.[8] Member state diplomats had the status of ambassador, councillor and first secretary. On top of these interviews we had informal conversations with OAU functionaries below the professional grade, like secretaries, receptionists and clerks. Relevant information on interviewees, such as names, titles and dates of interview, is given in foot-notes and the list in Appendix C.

A substantial part of the sources used for this study is made up of material from African governmental newspapers or other governmental publications. However, this category also includes material on perceptions of, and roles attributed to, the OAU as

---

6   The four official languages of the OAU are English, French, Arabic and Portuguese.

7   The Netherlands chargé d'affaires was also interviewed.

8   An interview with the Secretary-General, though conceded, could not take place because of engagements on his part.

articulated by non-governmental circles. This material was selected from — if they existed — newspapers of opposition parties; tracts or diatribes written by political exiles and members of separatist movements; and letters written to the editor, although published in governmental publications.

In African countries government newspapers are usually the only, or at least a very important, mouth-piece for the articulation of governmental policies, including the area of foreign affairs. Their importance in this study is two-fold. First, they provide evidence on an aspect that is specially emphasized, namely the perceptions of member states with regard to the OAU and its functioning and the roles and objectives that these states attribute to the Organization. Second, African government newspapers provide information on matters that can often not be found in OAU documents. OAU resolutions often represent a general compromise which is usually adopted without voting on the basis of consensus. If it pertains to a conflict one will not find any condemnation of disputants, at least before the early 1990s. Thus, as verbatim records are often not available, one has to read these resolutions in conjunction with information on individual member state opinion, in order to trace disagreements and differences in interpretation.

The search for material from these sources took place as follows. First we took a particular member state and one of its governmental newspapers and selected a time-set as sample from the entire period covered by this study (1960-1993). As the choice of countries and time-sets was influenced by the availability of evidence, samples had a relatively random character. Within time-sets, which could cover any number of years, we focused on periods shortly before, during and after sessions of OAU organs, such as the Council of Ministers and Assembly of Heads of State and Government. Material was selected on the following criteria: its presentation and evaluation of OAU functioning in particular fields of inter-African co-operation; its discussion and appraisal of specific sessions of organs; its reference to OAU norms, principles, and attributed objectives; its appraisal of relations with other international organizations; and its reference to cleavages in inter-African relations. In this way we could collect evidence on member state views on particular problems, conflicts and crises.

With regard to the *form* of the material, priority was given to editorials as these tend to contain the most explicit presentation of opinions, attitudes and perceptions. The second category of material in terms of importance consisted of articles written by journalists of those newspapers themselves. Their significance would be enhanced if they contained appraisals, rather than mere factual presentations, of OAU functioning. A third category consisted of texts of member state speeches at sessions of OAU organs and published in their newspapers. The last category was made up of miscellaneous items, such as press communiqués and articles of foreign press agencies. In section 1.4 we discuss the way in which these sources are interpreted.

Although the selection of countries and time-sets depended to some extent on the availability of material, great care was taken to achieve a total set of samples that was as representative as possible. It was crucial to obtain a broad set of data because of the special nature of the OAU in the sense that it encompasses, with one exception, all the states of the African continent and its surrounding islands. It is therefore to a greater or lesser extent affected in its functioning by all countries, something that will be made

explicit in section 5.6. In view of the research objective it was also necessary to get data covering long periods of time. In addition it was vital to take into account the various cleavages that characterize inter-African relations and which were presumed to affect the OAU's functioning. These cleavages mark off groups of member states from each other. Sometimes they are at the basis of inter-African alliances, whether in terms of internal OAU issues or coalitions existing independently of the Organization. As will be made clear in the next section and following chapters, these cleavages have to a greater or lesser extent influenced the process of OAU decision-making. The cleavages in question are the following:
- the former fissures between radical and moderate-conservative states
- the division between North African and sub-Saharan countries
- the distinction between English- and French-speaking states
- the distinction between member states in terms of one of the continent's regions.
The next section provides definitions of these categories and information on the classification, in terms of these categories, of the various states.

The total number of countries from which data were collected was 33. This represents over sixty per cent of the possible total of countries from which material could have been collected.[9] However, this total ignores differences in time-set and volume of material, which for some countries was made up of numerous data extending over several decades and for others of only limited material covering one or a few years.

While material was collected from countries of all the above-mentioned inter-African categories, it should be realized that these categorizations are rather crude. In principle no two countries have exactly identical views on the whole gamut of foreign affairs, even if they adopt more or less similar postures in the OAU. Care was therefore taken to obtain data from several countries that were classified in the same category. An effort was also made to include all major countries — *i.e.* those that are relatively influential in inter-African politics. How much material was collected in terms of years for each country and inter-African category is shown in Appendix B.

Thus, in the North African category Algeria was — in terms of length of time-set — well represented. Others in this category were under-represented. In West Africa all major countries were covered well: Ivory Coast, Senegal and Nigeria, besides Mali. In view of their known OAU postures more material would have been justified for Guinea and Ghana. However, Ghanaian opinions and attitudes in the 1960s were richly covered in OAU documents and the writings of Nkrumah. From Central Africa data were obtained from most major countries. Abundant material was collected from Zaire for the 1960s and some later years. Less material, though in volume relatively extensive, was found for Angola and Cameroon, covering several years in the 1970s, late 1980s and early 1990s. Gabon was not represented in any samples, although its attitudes were sometimes articulated in data from Ivory Coast. With regard to East Africa most major countries were covered well: Kenya, Tanzania and (slightly less well) Ethiopia, Sudan and Madagascar.

---

9   The total number of countries is 54. This includes all members plus South Africa and Namibia, which (for long) were not members but were included in the research as they were targets of OAU decolonization policy. The figure includes Morocco, which withdrew from the OAU in 1984, and Eritrea, which became a member in 1993. The figure excludes Somaliland as its secession from Somalia proper has not been recognized by African states.

Uganda and Somalia were not or under-represented. For Southern Africa all major countries with the exception of Mozambique were covered well: Zambia, Botswana, South Africa and (slightly less well) Zimbabwe.

The abundance of material for some countries may reflect an active interest in OAU affairs. Examples are Algeria, Ethiopia, Zambia, Tanzania and Senegal. In our data certain countries known for their rejection of OAU policies were well or poorly represented. Ivory Coast, with its rejection of OAU South Africa policy, was well represented. Morocco and Somalia, which rejected the OAU's posture on colonial frontiers, were under-represented. Gabon was not represented at all, but is known to have had a foreign policy posture comparable to that of Ivory Coast. In the evidence many minor countries were not covered well or at all. Notable exceptions were Sierra Leone and Malawi, which have been known for their pro-OAU posture and rejection of OAU policy respectively. Isolated data were collected for numerous other small member states, such as Togo, Niger, Tunisia, Congo and several others.

In terms of total time-sets all regions were more or less equally represented, although Central Africa slightly less than the others. As we looked for data from the year member states achieved independence — excepting South Africa — evidence from Southern Africa did not go back further than 1964. Balance in total time-sets was also realized in terms of the fissure between radical and moderate-conservative states, as it was (more roughly) for the distinction between North African and sub-Saharan states and (more fully) for English-speaking and Francophone countries. However, if one would combine these categorizations one would find certain lacunae. For example, we found fewer material for radical states from Central Africa than for moderate-conservative countries of that region. Yet, in the course of research we found that postures on the OAU by radical countries from, say, West Africa, did not differ significantly from those held by radical countries from Central Africa. Similar arguments may be given with regard to other combinations of categories and resultant lacunae. Naturally, we do not hold that these categories are more than rough guidelines for the search of the gamut of African governmental perceptions or that, in consequence, the absence of material from certain countries in certain periods can be waved aside as irrelevant. Yet, the inclusion in all inter-African categorizations of several major states should compensate for this.

Finally, we found material for all years of the period covered by this study. The years 1960 to 1962 were included as part of the prehistory to the OAU. As work on this study commenced in 1988 research originally cut off in that year. However, in view of significant developments since then, both in African politics and the global context, it was decided to extend our time frame until the end of 1993. In many ways this year constitutes a good date at which to conclude the analysis. It marks three decades of OAU functioning and the introduction of a new mechanism for conflict management and new budgeting procedures. Moreover, at the time political events took place that carried considerable significance, namely independence for Eritrea and its admission to OAU membership and impending majority rule in South Africa.[10] Thus, additional research was done to cover the period up to 1993. Material from specialist magazines on topical African

---

10   South Africa was admitted in 1994.

developments[11] was added to evidence from African (governmental) newspapers. With regard to OAU documentation important documents were obtained in the field of conflict management.[12]

The classification of member states
In view of the importance that inter-African cleavages were and are presumed to have for OAU functioning and, thus, their role in the search for governmental newspaper material, it is important to provide a definition or description of the categories to which these cleavages pertain. A list of countries and the categories in which they have been classified is given in Appendix D.

For the purpose of this study the category of English-speaking states is defined as encompassing countries where English is *lingua franca* or one of those languages. It is therefore supposed to refer to the former British colonies, in addition to Liberia, Namibia, Ethiopia, Somalia and Eritrea.[13] While the English-speaking countries constitute, for the purpose of this study and in actual inter-African politics, a less clear-cut group than the Francophone states, section 5.6 will show that competition between English- and French-speaking countries has exerted some influence on OAU functioning. Francophone countries are defined as encompassing states where French is *lingua franca* or one of those languages. The category therefore refers to all former French colonies and, in some contexts, also to those of Belgium. However, the North African countries are deliberately excluded from the English- and French-speaking categories, as rivalry between Anglophone and Francophone states pertains principally to sub-Saharan Africa. While French is also spoken on the Seychelles and Mauritius they are included in the English-speaking category as they are former British colonies. Conversely, Cameroon is included in the Francophone category, although it is partly English-speaking.

The purely regional classification of states that is used here is the official one used by the OAU for internal institutional purposes, such as for achieving geographical balance in the composition of Secretariat personnel. The classification involves five regions: North Africa, West Africa, Central Africa, East Africa and Southern Africa. With regard to the distinction between North African and sub-Saharan states, North African countries are taken in this study to encompass the countries of the OAU's "North Africa" region: *i.e.* Egypt, Libya, Tunisia, Algeria and Morocco. Sub-Saharan countries are all others. Traditionally relations between North African and sub-Saharan states have been influenced by significant cultural differences. This has some relevance for the functioning of the OAU, which is discussed in section 5.6. Although one might contend that Mauritania and Sudan should be considered as belonging to Arabic-speaking North Africa, they have not been included in this category as in the OAU's regional categorization they are classified as part of West and East Africa respectively. In the interpretation of data that were found for Sudan it was realized, however, that some of the

---

11   Such as *Africa Research Bulletin*, *West Africa*, *Jeune Afrique*, *New African*, *Africa Confidential*, etc.

12   As will be indicated in the text some evidence was later also obtained through correspondence with OAU functionaries.

13   The last three are, of course, not really Anglophone countries. Yet, English is (also) used for the conduct of foreign affairs.

material may have more relevance as evidence for Arab-North African countries.

When studying Africa's international relations one comes across, up to the mid-1980s, a taxonomy of African states in terms of three rather vague political epithets or qualifications, namely "radical", "moderate" and "conservative". Radical states were also known by the synonyms "militant" and "progressive", while conservative states were sometimes dubbed, by their enemies, "reactionary". This study discards the use of the synonyms progressive and reactionary, although militant is used as a synonym for radical. If the categories of North African, sub-Saharan, Anglophone and Francophone countries, as well as most regional classifications, are fairly straightforward, the classification of states in conservative, radical and moderate groups has always begged a lot of questions. As they have nevertheless influenced inter-African relations and OAU functioning a detailed discussion of the nature of these categories is warranted.

In view of the features that radical, moderate and conservative states shared in common, both in policy and political behaviour, as well as the differences within these groups themselves, one may ask whether these qualifications really had any concrete significance. After all, as will be shown in chapter 2, all African states consider development a top priority and aspire to a more important role in international affairs. All of them try to preserve their integrity and security. All states supported the anti-colonial struggle in the dependent territories and most states have tried to diversify their political and military ties to one degree or another. In the past, most countries developed one-party regimes and in many the armed forces became a crucial political actor. Finally, during the 1970s and 1980s forces of civil society began challenging state authoritarianism in practically all countries.

Yet, there were also clear differences between radical, moderate and conservative governments, which assumed principal importance in the field of foreign affairs. Here we give a general description of these differences, while chapters 2 and 3 will discuss their foreign and domestic policy objectives in greater detail and the ideologies on which they were grounded.

We will first say something about the differences between radical, conservative and moderate countries as they appeared during the 1960s. Then we touch on the context in which these qualifications were introduced in inter-African politics. This is followed by a few remarks on the unstable nature of country identification in terms of these qualifications and the differentiation during the 1970s within the groups of radicals, moderates and conservatives themselves. Then an outline is given of the approach to the use of these qualifications in this study.

Countries that belonged to the radical tendency, as it came into usage during the 1960s, involved governments that favoured active assistance to liberation movements. These states were also more ready to demand fundamental changes in the international economic order and often favoured a state socialist model of development. Many radicals developed an explicit non-alignment policy, which entailed priority for the preservation of national independence, balancing of ties with East and West and a critical attitude towards foreign bases on African soil. It went hand in hand with a self-conscious and dynamic, if not impatient and vociferous, posture in international affairs.

The conservative states were less concerned with decolonization of remaining dependent territories. They exhibited a preference for diplomatic pressure on white minority regimes and were unenthusiastic about the granting of support to the armed struggle of liberation movements. They were generally more prepared to work within the structures of the international economic system and favoured a state capitalist model of development. Most had a strong predilection for close ties with the West in general or the former colonial power in particular. Their foreign policy behaviour was characterized by a pragmatic, quiet and low-key approach.[14] They were mostly Francophone countries, while the radicals were made up of different states. The moderate countries adopted policies and postures somewhere in between these two. They are therefore more difficult to pin down than the radical and conservative countries. Often they would side with the conservatives, but at times they would follow the position of the radical powers.

It is, then, obvious that these descriptions have an elusive ring around them. However, it is especially with regard to specific conflicts that they assumed concrete meaning. As shown in section 4.2, the distinction between radical, conservative and moderate states first appeared during the Congo crisis of 1960. In this conflict the radicals were the ones that sympathized with Lumumba. The conservatives were Francophone countries that gave support to Kasavubu, if not outright backing to Tshombe's secession, and the moderate powers were states that criticized UN policy in Katanga but did not back Lumumba. In most cases these labels corresponded more or less with the ideological orientations in domestic and foreign policy mentioned above.

However, this taxonomy did not always work full proof in explaining the "line-up", or grouping patterns, of states in subsequent conflicts or specific contexts of OAU decision-making. Countries could determine their behaviour on the basis of other criteria besides their general ideological outlook. Related to this was an at times complex differentiation of attitudes within these three categories themselves (see below). Moreover, a country's identification with one of these groups could change over time as a result of coups d'état or other internal developments. For example, after the coming to power of Muammar Qaddafi Libya aligned itself with the radical group, while during the early 1980s Sékou Touré's "radical" regime began to identify increasingly with the conservative powers.

With regard to the internal differentiation of these groupings, it should be realized that countries wearing the same label could differ considerably in their domestic policies. On foreign issues marked distinctions could be observed as well. This was especially the case with the moderate powers. Thus, during the 1970s increased internal group differentiation took place, with some moderate countries like Nigeria and Zambia articulating a self-conscious, independent foreign policy more or less similar to the attitudes of radical group members as Tanzania, Mali and Algeria. Among the radicals there appeared, by the middle of the decade, a small minority of governments that adopted more militant postures, inspired by versions of Marxist-Leninist ideology. Examples are Ethiopia, the Lusophone countries and Madagascar. Most of these developed close military and economic ties with the Eastern bloc, thus distinguishing themselves from other countries in the radical group.

The obvious question that therefore springs to mind is whether one should use this

---

14   See J. Woronoff, *Organizing African Unity* (Metuchen, NJ, 1970), pp 598-600.

three-fold taxonomy in the first place. Yet, in spite of the above the answer must be in the affirmative. The reason is that the qualifications involved refer to general ideological orientations that betrayed *actual* differences in foreign policies and often considerably influenced or determined postures to specific issues — notwithstanding exceptions. Although the qualifications acquired their most concrete meaning in specific situations it goes too far to argue that the composition of the groups to which they refer depended exclusively on the circumstances of a particular conflict.[15] These qualifications *did* influence, besides other factors, inter-African grouping patterns and OAU decision-making; to what extent and under which circumstances is shown in section 5.6.

Still, because of the internal group differentiation discussed above, as well as the fact that the three-fold taxonomy cannot explain the line-up of all member states at all times, some authors have argued for more complex classificatory schemes. However, these are sometimes also open to question as they contain their own anomalies. The problem is that all classifications depend to a considerable extent, though not entirely, on behavourial patterns in specific, past OAU decision-making contexts. The result is that another taxonomy generates its own deviants, whether in the past or the future.[16]

For example, the 1978 four-fold taxonomy by Cervenka and Legum lists Cameroon and Sierra Leone as belonging to the "second category",[17] which was supposed to vote together with Marxist radical regimes. Yet, during the Angolan and Western Sahara crises both lined up with the conservative and moderate powers. While this is realized by the authors in their argument that their first and second categories usually lined up on most questions "other than critical foreign issues", it is exactly these critical issues that matter in this study.[18] The subtle group configurations presented by Zang and Sinou also fail to explain certain anomalies, such as the line-up of Mauritania and the Central African Republic with countries calling for United Nations condemnation of the Stanleyville dropping.[19] Moreover, a more complex classification, with variously formulated identifying epithets, does not always relate clearly to alliance patterns in OAU decision-making.[20] For example, the implicit suggestion of Zang and Sinou that the North African powers acted as a group during the dialogue affair seems questionable.[21]

Thus, in view of the above we will retain the lump categories of radical, moderate and conservative groupings, yet as much as possible with reference to concrete examples

---

15   See in this vein L. Zang and D. Sinou, 'Dynamique des groupes au sein de l'OUA et unité africaine', in M. Kamto, J.E. Pondi and L. Zang (eds), *l'OUA: rétrospective et perspectives africaines* (Paris, 1990), p 162.

16   Z. Cervenka and C. Legum, 'The Organization of African Unity in 1978: The Challenge of Foreign Intervention', in *Africa Contemporary Record*, 1978-79, A27-29, recognize this by saying that particular issues will change voting patterns within their four-fold taxonomy. See in this respect their "category three".

17   "Radical nationalist, with serious aspirations to be non-aligned". The other three were (1): "Marxist radical"; (3): "nationalist with non-aligned aspirations"; and (4): "moderates and conservatives". *Ibid.*, A28.

18   *Ibid.*, A29. See on these crises further sections 6.3 and 6.4.

19   Zang and Sinou, 'Dynamique des groupes', p 148. See on Stanleyville ch. 8.

20   See f.i. categories 4-B and 4-C by Cervenka and Legum ('Organization of African Unity in 1978'), which refer to moderate states that believed in non-alignment and adopted anti-Soviet postures but lined up with categories 2 and 3 in OAU decision-making.

21   Zang and Sinou, 'Dynamique des groupes', p 152. See section 6.2.

of countries that were supposed to belong to them. Anomalies are also given whenever this seems relevant. This attempt at deconstructing these qualifications should make them more concrete, as well as expose the differentiation of viewpoints within these groups. Although no clear-cut dichotomy is assumed in inter-African relations this study usually refers to moderate and conservative powers together, as they often lined up jointly against radical countries. Finally, the actual classification of individual countries in terms of these categories is given in Appendix D.

1.3   Theoretical perspectives

Introduction
In this study more than one theoretical perspective informs the analysis. First of all, as Africa's international relations constitute the most important variable determining the OAU's functioning we must take recourse to at least two theories. These are hegemonic stability theory and dependency theory, which can clarify respectively the inter-African and extra-African dimension of Africa's international relations. While dependency theory to some extent elucidates aspects of purely inter-African politics it is contended here that its explanatory power is insufficient for the purpose of understanding all the intricacies of interaction taking place at this level.

Both hegemonic stability theory and dependency theory expose constraints in Pan-African co-operation, as embodied by the OAU. In the course of this study we discuss whether and to what extent these constraints can be overcome. This is done with the aid of other theoretical insights, namely regime theory; the game theoretical perspective on the relevance of reciprocity and number of actors in inter-state co-operation; and regional integration theory as articulated by Kothari and Guernier.[22]

In analysing the functioning of the OAU as such we take recourse, besides hegemonic stability theory and dependency theory, to explanations in terms of the domestic socio-political configurations of member states. In this respect we regularly refer to a perspective that the field of political psychology provides on the OAU.

The use of multiple theoretical perspectives is justified in two ways. First, it is warranted by the principal purpose of this study, which is to understand the meaning and functioning of the OAU and, through this aspect, contribute to the knowledge of African politics. As shown in the preceding section understanding the OAU's functioning in African politics also necessitates an appraisal of its role in the domestic order of member states. This dimension cannot be explained by the two principal theoretical perspectives used in this study, even if dependency theory may to some extent illuminate the workings of the political process at the sub-state level.

Besides its justification in terms of the principal objective our eclectic approach is legitimized by theoretical insights. While this study argues that hegemonic stability theory and dependency theory have considerable explanatory power, it will also show that, at some levels, they do not suffice. As is argued by Stein, international relations affect, but

---

22   R. Kothari, *Footsteps into the Future: Diagnosis of the Present World and a Design for an Alternative* (New York, 1974) and M. Guernier, *Tiers-Monde: trois quarts du monde* (Paris, 1980).

do not wholly determine, the behaviour of states, or rather, governments. It has in this respect been argued by Milner that theories of co-operation in international relations suffer from a neglect of the influence of domestic politics. The issue area of security, for example, is held to be considerably affected by the perceptions of national elites.[23] This study will show that this is especially the case in the African context. Explanations in terms of the sub-state level of analysis must therefore not be ignored.

Nevertheless, this does not mean that this study cannot provide a contribution to the academic debate on hegemonic stability theory and dependency theory. Before this can be done, however, the following sections must introduce the general arguments of these and some of the other theoretical perspectives.

Hegemonic stability theory and regional hegemony
Hegemonic stability theory posits that co-operation in international relations is only possible with the presence of one very powerful state or hegemon. Its foundations were laid by Kindleberger. He explained the severity of the great Depression by pointing to the inability of the United Kingdom, whose power was declining, to assume responsibility for stabilizing the international system of free trade. The United States, whose power was in the ascent, was unwilling to take over. There was thus a lack of one powerful state which could stabilize the international economy by maintaining a free trade regime.[24]

The provision of a free trade regime involves the supply of a so-called public or collective good. A public good is marked by the jointness of its supply and non-excludability. In its pure theoretical manifestation this means that, if the public good is supplied to one state, it is automatically supplied to all of them. No state can be excluded from its consumption, even if it has not paid for it. A state may thus profit from an international free trade regime upheld by others, while it does not adopt similar free trade policies: it becomes a "free rider" on the efforts of others. This can lead to states adopting an unco-operative posture so as not to be hurt by the defection or cheating of others while they themselves would co-operate. The public good may thus never be produced.[25] A variation on this so-called free rider dilemma is the "tragedy of the commons". Essentially this refers to a public good that is already in existence, but which is ultimately destroyed through collective inability to prevent free riding.[26]

These insights have been borrowed from Olson's (economic) analysis of the nature of public goods. In the anarchical context of international relations it is profitable for states to try and enjoy public goods while not contributing towards their cost. This behaviour

---

23   H. Milner, 'International Theories of Cooperation Among Nations: Strengths and Weaknesses', in *World Politics*, 1992, pp 488-495.

24   Ch. P. Kindleberger, *The World in Depression 1929-1939* (Berkeley and Los Angeles, 1973), ch. 14 and R.O. Keohane, 'The Theory of Hegemonic Stability and Changes in International Economic Regimes, 1967-77', in O.R. Holsti, R.M. Siverson and A.L. George (eds), *Change in the International System* (Boulder, 1980), pp 136-137.

25   M. Olson, *The Logic of Collective Action: Public Goods and the Theory of Groups* (Cambridge, Mass., 1965), ch. 1 and J. Gowa, 'Rational Hegemons, Excludable Goods, and Small Groups: An Epitath for Hegemonic Stability Theory?', in *World Politics*, 1989, p 309.

26   The commons refers to the public domain, such as free pasture land of which everyone has usufruct but which is destroyed by overgrazing and collective inability to limit its use. G. Hardin and J. Baden (eds), *Managing the Commons* (San Francisco and Reading, 1977).

cannot be simply condemned as malevolent, as it is rational as such to attempt to obtain these goods as cheaply as possible. Thus, the essence of Olson's so-called logic of collective action, and so of hegemonic stability theory, is not that states are unwilling to engage in co-operation. They are *unable*, through the lack of leadership, to achieve such co-operation: the structures of international relations preclude the generation or sufficient co-ordination of collective will for co-operation to emerge. It is even impossible to realize co-operation if all states would profit from it or have identical[27] interests and co-operation would thus achieve — in the totality of the system of international relations — optimal, rather than sub-optimal, outcomes.[28] Hegemonic stability theory says that one can only escape this scenario by way of a very powerful state. This hegemon must have an interest in producing the public good itself, even if this means that it has to bear the full costs. This occurs if the hegemon's capture of part of the public good outweighs the costs of its provision. This is the case if this state is of sufficiently large (economic, military) size.[29]

The theory has by and large two versions. The original one is linked with the area of free trade and predicts that, as the trade regime leads to diffusion of growth, the hegemon will gradually decline. This version thus assumes that the hegemon is benevolent: hegemony is beneficial to all, but the smaller actors profit more from the public good than the hegemon as they do not have to bear the costs of its provision. However, this is very hard to prove empirically.[30] The other version extends the theory's application beyond economics and holds that a hegemon is vital to the preservation of peace and security. This version does not emphasize the public goods aspect but argues that the hegemon uses its supremacy to structure international relations to its own advantage.[31] Moreover, it does not merely provide the public good (security, order), but it is capable to force other states to contribute towards its costs. In this coercive model the smaller states do not necessarily benefit more than the hegemon and the problem of free riders does not occur. The hegemon may enjoy some legitimacy in so far as the smaller actors receive net benefits. Both the benevolent model and the coercive version predict that states will be better off than if they would be without hegemonic leadership. They differ as to the distributive aspects of the advantages.[32]

Hegemonic stability theory thus posits that co-operation will only emerge if there is one state that is so influential that it can provide the public good itself or force others to conform. This hegemon provides unequivocal leadership, which is essential for states to agree to co-operation and guarantees that agreements are kept, rules obeyed and transgressors punished. Without such a leader one cannot expect any form of co-operation in international relations.

For the purpose of this study a hegemon is defined as a state which stands alone

27 In this vein R.O. Keohane, *After Hegemony: Cooperation and Discord in the World Political Economy* (Princeton, 1984), p 65.
28 Olson, *Logic of Collective Action*.
29 Gowa, 'Rational Hegemons, Excludable Goods, and Small Groups'; D. Snidal, 'The Limits of Hegemonic Stability Theory', in *International Organization*, 1985, p 581; and J.Q.Th. Rood, *Hegemonie, machtsspreiding en internationaal-economische orde sinds 1945* (The Hague, 1996), pp 43-53.
30 Snidal, 'Limits of Hegemonic Stability Theory', pp 581-582.
31 R. Gilpin, *War and Change in World Politics* (Cambridge, 1982).
32 Snidal, 'Limits of Hegemonic Stability Theory'.

without equals at the top of the inter-state hierarchy of power and is more powerful than others in terms of the ability to control outcomes of interaction.[33] However, it is difficult to operationalize this definition. One of the problems is that the theory has a rather generalized logic. Theorists are not agreed on the question of exactly how powerful a state must be to qualify as hegemon. Power is also relative to another actor, *i.e.* it is the differences in power between them that matter. One may contend that a hegemon must have the economic and military capability to unilaterally provide a public good and force all other countries to comply with agreements and rules.[34] However, there is no agreement on the proportion of the resources of power — *i.e.* capabilities — that such a state must command for this.[35] It is also unclear what kind of capabilities are crucial. Is it gross national product; financial reserves; capital goods; raw materials; technology; size and state of the armed forces or all of them? Moreover, the relation between capabilities and power is complex. Disposal of capabilities is a necessary condition, but not a guarantee, for the successful exertion of power. The American debacle in Vietnam is a good example.[36]

In this respect the motivation of the hegemon to behave as one seems important. It must be willing to use its capabilities for the provision of the public good and the enforcement of compliance with rules. Thus, it is sometimes argued that, even if there is a hegemon, its willingness is a necessary additional ingredient for international co-operation to emerge.[37]

One last element that appears relevant for the successful performance of the hegemon and, thus, the emergence of co-operation, is a certain legitimacy attributed by other states to its supremacy. The element of legitimacy is elaborated most explicitly in the concept of *regional* hegemony. With this concept one leaves the framework of hegemonic stability theory, although it involves rather similar arguments. The concept refers to inter-state ties based on domination and creation of consensus by the hegemon's manipulation of norms legitimating its dominance.[38] It resembles Gramsci's concept of hegemony, which refers to the consensual basis of a political system in contrast to more simply coercive domination.[39] Regional hegemony is not a static form of interaction but allows for various forms of influence. Ideally, the hegemon's use of force is occasional: it resorts to it if other means of influence fail. While it is prepared to violate the rights of other states, it does not always disregard them.[40] The concept thus refers to the ability of a state to

33   Stein, *Why Nations Cooperate*, p 182.
34   J.Q.Th. Rood and J.G. Siccama, *Verzwakking van de Sterkste: Oorzaken en Gevolgen van Amerikaans Machtsverval* (The Hague, 1989), pp 28-29.
35   Th. McKeown, 'Hegemonic Stability Theory and 19th Century Tariff Levels in Europe', in *International Organization*, 1983, pp 73-91 and S.P. Huntington, 'The US - Decline or Renewal?', in *Foreign Affairs*, 1988/89, 67, pp 76-96.
36   Rood and Siccama, *Verzwakking van de Sterkste*, pp 36-39.
37   Kindleberger, *World in Depression*, ch. 14 and Snidal, 'Limits of Hegemonic Stability Theory', p 585. Also P. van Ham, 'The lack of a Big Bully: Hegemonic stability theory and regimes in the study of international relations', in *Acta Politica*, 1992, p 30.
38   R. Iyob, 'Regional Hegemony: Domination and Resistance in the Horn of Africa', in *Journal of Modern African Studies*, 1993, pp 257-276.
39   W.L. Adamson, *Hegemony and Revolution: A Study of Antonio Gramsci's Political and Cultural Theory* (Berkeley, Los Angeles and London, 1980), ch. 6.
40   R. Lemarchand, 'On Comparing Regional Hegemons: Libya and South Africa', in R. Lemarchand

establish, maintain and change norms of regional interaction maximizing its own interests. Besides legitimacy the regional hegemon must dispose of other sources of influence. These capabilities can be military might, an economic base, a solid diplomatic network or a geographical location entailing superpower support.[41]

This study shows that hegemonic stability theory can explain several aspects of the OAU's functioning and that there is validity in the contention that co-operation depends to some extent on the presence of one very powerful actor. The evidence for this is presented by applying the theory of hegemonic stability *a contrario*, as there actually is no such powerful state in inter-African relations. In doing so we are aware that sweeping statements of the theory's ability to explain the link between power and international stability are unwarranted. As a hegemon's capabilities may not guarantee successful exertion of influence the link with stability is not self-evident.[42]

Still, this study argues that the theory does have explanatory power. It argues that African states are often not unwilling to engage in Pan-African co-operation but that absence of a state, that could pose as continental leader, precludes the generation or sufficient co-ordination of collective will to achieve co-operation or to make it more effective. However, it is also shown that in some cases this explanation does not suffice. This will take us to the nature of the domestic socio-political configurations of the OAU's member states.

In developing our argument on the validity of hegemonic stability theory this study attempts to confirm that a hegemon's willingness to use its capabilities for the provision of a public good and compliance with rules, is an additional condition for the emergence of international co-operation. This point will be argued with the help of the concept of regional hegemony.

With regard to this concept it will also be observed that, as in hegemonic stability theory, the degree of power that the hegemon must command to qualify as one, generates confusion. On this point this study argues two things. First, in the OAU's continental cadre the extent of influence exerted by Africa's most powerful countries is actually attenuated through the presence of numerous other states. Second, even in regional contexts these countries, some of which claim the status of regional hegemons, often face constraints with regard to the successful exercise of influence. Moreover, it is contended that in the concept of regional hegemony itself the power element is imprecise and that part of this is due to the fact that it imputes more legitimacy to the hegemon than seems warranted. This is true in the continental politics of the OAU, where any legitimacy for the status of would-be hegemons is consistently rejected, as well as in regional settings. This is clarified in the light of Scott's work on legitimacy. He distinguishes between acquiescence and genuine consent in the consensual element of hegemony.[43] Legitimacy

    (ed), *The Green and the Black: Qadhafi's Policies in Africa* (Bloomington and Indianapolis, 1988), p 169 and Adamson, *Hegemony and Revolution*, ch. 6.

41   Iyob, 'Regional Hegemony'.

42   Rood and Siccama, *Verzwakking van de Sterkste*, pp 36-39 and M.C. Webb and S.D. Krasner, 'Hegemonic stability theory: an empirical assessment', in *Review of International Studies*, 1989, pp 183-198.

43   J.C. Scott, *Domination and the Arts of Resistance: Hidden Transcripts* (New Haven and London, 1990), pp 70-76.

of dominance may thus be no more than acceptance of the inevitable.

Dependency theory

Section 2.4 provides an outline of the actual structures of Africa's international relations. Besides pointing out the absence of continental leadership and, more generally, the limited opportunities for the exertion of influence by African states in their mutual relations, it shows that their international position is marked by a high degree of dependence on the non-African world. Dependence can be defined as the condition of being significantly affected by external forces, implying a relationship of subordination of one state or country to another. This negatively affects the former's development.[44]

Thus, factors emanating from outside the African continent frequently affect the OAU's functioning. Often these exert influence while they remain in the background of the vicissitudes of inter-African co-operation. Sometimes they push themselves into the forefront, with the result that the link between extra-African conditions and the OAU's difficulties and opportunities becomes direct and explicit.

For these reasons dependency theory must inform our analysis. This theory holds that capitalism forms one single world system made up of "core" and "peripheral" countries. Core countries — principally in the Northern hemisphere — sell high-wage products to the peripheral economies. These are usually located in the Southern hemisphere and produce low-wage products, *i.e.* goods with limited added value, such as raw materials. The exchange of low- and high-wage products is unequal. Unequal exchange occurs if a peripheral worker must work many hours, at a given level of productivity, to obtain the product produced by a worker in a core country in a shorter period. In this way surplus value is drained away from peripheral economies, which causes underdevelopment.[45]

In these conditions international trade cannot be genuinely free, as its terms are unilaterally dictated by the core economies. The theory thus contends that international capital is the chief force in shaping the global division of labour. The major forces of change in peripheral countries are a function of the economic imperialism exercised by the interests of core economies. These arguments betray the strong influence that Marxism has exerted over dependency theory,[46] which was formulated with regard to the history of Latin America and later adopted by Africanists to analyse Africa's position vis-à-vis the Western world.[47]

The theory argues that peripheral economies are dualist in composition. One part of

---

44   After S.K.B. Asante, 'Africa and Europe: Collective Dependence or Interdependence?', in A. Sesay (ed), *Africa and Europe: From Partition to Interdependence or Dependence?* (London, 1986), pp 187-188.

45   See I. Wallerstein, 'Dependence in an Interdependent World: The Limited Possibilities of Transformation within the Capitalist World Economy', in *African Studies Review*, 1974, pp 1-26.

46   See W. Hout, *Capitalism and the Third World: Development, Dependence and the World System* (Aldershot and Brookfield, 1993), ch. 2 and *ibid.*, 'Centres and peripheries: An assessment of the contribution of dependency and world system theories to the study of international relations', in *Acta Politica*, 1992, pp 72-78.

47   A.G. Frank, *Capitalism and Underdevelopment in Latin America: Historical Studies of Chile and Brasil* (New York, 1967). African applications in P.C.W. Gutkind and I. Wallerstein (eds), *The Political Economy of Contemporary Africa* (Beverly Hills, 1976).

the economy constitutes a modern enclave, which originated as a result of imperial penetration and which is geared towards import and export. The class interests in this sector are tied to those of the core economies: a local (petty) bourgeoisie or modern elite formed through the alliance between the modern enclave and foreign capital. It therefore has an accommodating attitude towards the interests of core economies. As it has forged its most important alliance with foreign capital it is very weak vis-à-vis domestic forces. These are concentrated principally in the subsistence sector of the economy. This sector has institutions, a technology and a culture inherited from the past. It is influenced by the modern enclave, which causes disintegrative effects such as destruction of local artisanry by modern imports; investment of capital of the subsistence sector in the modern enclave; impoverishment of farmers; and migration to urban areas.[48]

Thus, dependency was originally conceived as a mechanical process in which the domestic structures of peripheral state and society are determined by their external links. This abstract and static version of the theory assumed that dependency permeats all aspects of life, denying the domestic dynamics of societies and ignoring the historical specificity of particular regions and processes of capitalist penetration.[49]

Various forms of criticism were levelled against the theory in this form. First, it was observed that in many Third World countries the economy is not simply marked by a rigid dichotomy between modern and subsistence sector. Second, the original version of dependency theory underestimated the role that is played by the state. Local factors in peripheral countries, such as political structures, economic inheritance and culture, are also important in determining the development process. This was later accounted for in more subtle versions of the theory. It was posited that domestic structures and their external links may have a dialectical relationship, in which domestic structures are not simply determined by these external ties. Their interaction gives the international system its dynamic nature. Domestic and external forces form a complex whole, whose structural links are rooted in coincidence of interests between the peripheral modern elite and foreign core capital. This implies a certain freedom of manoeuvre for the modern elite at the periphery vis-à-vis the external world, albeit a very limited one.[50] All dependent situations are specific and may change into new forms of dependence.[51]

However, while this admits of different degrees of dependence, the theory upholds the argument that the degree and nature of dependence will not change fundamentally as long as the alliance between foreign capital and the peripheral modern elite remains

---

48   See T. Smith, 'Requiem or New Agenda for Third World Studies?', in *World Politics*, 1985, pp 532-561.

49   G. Palma, 'Dependency and Development: A Critical Overview', in D. Seers (ed), *Dependency Theory: A Critical Reassessment* (London, 1981), pp 20-78 and A.Y. Yansané, 'Decolonization, Dependency, and Development in Africa: The Theory Revisited', in A.Y. Yansané (ed), *Decolonization and Dependency: Problems of Development of African Societies* (Westport and London, 1980), pp 3-51.

50   See Palma, 'Dependency and Development', pp 59-62; Smith, 'Requiem or New Agenda for Third World Studies'; and *ibid.*, *The Pattern of Imperialism: The United States, Great Britain, and the Late Industrializing World since 1815* (New York, 1981).

51   D. Fieldhouse, 'Decolonization, Development, and Dependence: A Survey of Changing Attitudes', in P. Gifford and W.R. Louis (eds), *The Transfer of Power in Africa: Decolonization 1940-1960* (New Haven and London, 1982), p 504.

intact.[52] Dependence can only be broken by dissociation from the world economy, for example by engaging in economic integration with other peripheral countries. The subtler versions of dependency theory argue that some countries leave the periphery but that they do not join the core. They become so-called "semi-peripheral" economies. They are able to profit from the decline in wage-productivity in core countries, yet they have little real power. They enjoy privileges through their exploitation of other countries on the condition that they help keep the capitalist system intact. Thus, their gains bind them to the system and reinforce it.[53]

This study does not go into the merits of arguments for or against the universal validity of dependency theory. Its principal purpose is more modest. It attempts to confirm, from the perspective of Africa, the contention in the theory's more subtle version that the modern elites in peripheral countries do have a restricted freedom of manoeuvre in their international (political, economic) relations. The OAU's formation is an example of this. If the behaviour of Africa's state elites would be strictly determined by their external links its establishment would have been superfluous.

This is not to say that the OAU is an expression of concrete resistance to the structures of the international economic order. Rather, this study argues that, while Africa's state elites have to some extent a stake in the preservation of these structures, their role in the international order is accompanied by a high degree of ambivalence towards the global politico-economic status quo. Even if they take, by sheer necessity and interest, an accommodating stand towards the interests of the core economies, it occurs amidst mixed feelings. It is this psychological dimension to the dependency complex, or the ideological insecurity[54] of peripheral modern elites, that also concerns us here. This dimension, as all non-economic aspects of dependency, hardly ever receives adequate treatment in expositions of the theory.

This dimension is at the root of a collective aspiration, through the OAU, to greater influence in the global order. That this aspiration was for long articulated through a modest attempt at enhancing Africa's influence in international fora, rather than by engaging in continental integration, does not contradict this. The limited nature of this effort is explained by the absence[55] of continental leadership and the crippling effects of dependence. Our explanation will, however, also refer to the structures of domestic socio-political configurations.

Regime theory and game theoretical perspectives
Our analysis in terms of hegemonic stability theory and dependency theory will expose certain constraints in co-operation as institutionalized in the OAU. An obvious question to be asked is whether anything can be done to alleviate these constraints.

---

52   See f.i. C. Leys, *Underdevelopment in Kenya: The Political Economy of Neo-colonialism 1964-1971* (London, 1975).
53   Smith, 'Requiem or New Agenda for Third World Studies'.
54   *Ibid.*, p 551.
55   Yet the history of the OAS shows that too much leadership can also hinder international co-operation. See f.i. M. Fortmann and J.Ph. Thérien, 'l'Organisation des états américains: un système de coopération en transition', in *Relations internationales et stratégiques*, summer 1994, pp 187-201.

Regime theory holds that in the absence of a hegemon co-operation is still possible.[56] It predicts that international regimes may facilitate co-operation by their mitigation of international anarchy and their assistance in the decentralized enforcement of agreements.[57] Regimes are sets of principles, norms, rules and decision-making procedures around which actor expectations converge in a given issue area.[58] They are more than temporary arrangements and must be distinguished from ad hoc agreements. The purpose of regimes is to facilitate such agreements. A regime is not an international organization as such, but refers to decisions of states to co-operate more or less permanently in the cadre of such an organization.[59]

Regime theory posits that regimes are likely to be created if optimal outcomes of interaction cannot be achieved through unco-ordinated calculations of self-interest.[60] Co-operation in regimes makes interaction between states cheaper: the totality of transaction costs incurred by realizing interaction with each other and the outside world decreases, as the regime provides a forum for establishing contacts and formulating common postures. As it encourages the linkage of issue areas and side-payments to balance the benefits of multiple deals, the opportunity for bargaining, and so for co-operation, is enhanced.[61]

One particular aspect of regimes is that, with their decision-making procedures, rules, principles and norms, they are held to reduce uncertainty between states about each other's intentions, policies and actions. Collecting information on these matters is a fundamental feature of the political process, in the course of which states incur costs. By participating in a regime they can improve their information while at the same time reducing the costs to get it. Obtaining information about each other is especially important if it pertains to mutual suspicions of free riding. By improving the information that states have of each other regimes can enhance the reciprocity in inter-state relations, both in terms of compliance with agreed rules and likely retaliation against those that violate them.[62] In this respect it must be observed that, as regimes encompass norms and principles, the behaviour of states engaging in regime-governed activity is affected by normative considerations that may go beyond calculations of narrow state interests.[63] These norms clarify standards of conduct, which in itself contributes towards transparency between states and therefore to potential reciprocity in inter-state co-operation.[64]

These contentions are tested with regard to co-operation among African states in the

---

56   Keohane, *After Hegemony*.
57   Milner, 'International Theories of Co-operation', p 475.
58   S.D. Krasner, 'Structural causes and regimes consequences: regimes as intervening variables', in S.D. Krasner (ed), *International Regimes* (Ithaca and London, 1983), p 1.
59   E.B. Haas, 'Regime decay: conflict management and international organizations, 1945-1981', in *International Organization*, 1983, pp 190-191.
60   D.R. Young, 'Regime dynamics: the rise and fall of international regimes', in Krasner, *International Regimes*, pp 98-113.
61   Milner, 'International Theories of Co-operation', pp 475-478.
62   *Ibid.*, p 475.
63   Krasner, 'Structural causes and regime consequences', p 3.
64   K.A. Oye, 'Explaining Cooperation Under Anarchy: Hypotheses and Strategies', in K.A. Oye (ed), *Cooperation Under Anarchy* (Princeton, 1986), pp 16-17.

OAU. It is argued that this regime does, indeed, affect the behaviour of states in their interaction with each other and the extra-African world in such a way that opportunities for co-operation are strengthened. However, it is also argued that these improvements are limited as the regime that the OAU provides is a weak one. This is caused by the main features of Africa's international relations, namely the complete absence of continental hegemonic leadership, the large number of states that characterize the African state system and intruding patterns of external dependence. In this context reference is made to the work done by Snidal and Rothstein.[65]

The theoretical possibilities for co-operation are further illuminated by the game theoretical contentions of Oye. He argues that countries compare the benefits of co-operation on the basis of agreed rules with the benefits derived from defecting from co-operation, *i.e.* cheating others by violating rules (free riding). The particular structure of the potential pay-offs emanating from these two alternatives — co-operation or defection — determines whether states engage in co-operation. It is therefore essential to influence this pay-off structure.[66]

Thus, Oye argues that, first, prospects for co-operation improve if states are made to realize that interaction is not a one time affair. The risk of retaliation by other states becomes more relevant if they are likely to meet in future. With interaction approaching an iterated game situation, rather than single-play conditions, the shadow of the future affects calculations about pay-offs of defection from, or compliance with, rules in the present. Reciprocity in compliance and retaliation is thus enhanced. Frequency of sessions of international organizations becomes important here, as they serve as vehicles of communication and (de-)legitimation of behaviour. The norms of a regime can therefore contribute to reciprocity between states and, so, co-operation. This is especially the case if states regard these norms as valuable in themselves. Such internalization of norms alters calculations of pay-offs in favour of compliance.[67] These contentions are tested with regard to specific contexts of co-operation in the OAU.

Another way to influence calculations of states is by involving fewer actors in a specific context. This can be realized by decomposing the issue area or differentiating procedures of co-operation. Such actor reduction tactics enhance reciprocity as the context becomes more transparent. Game theory postulates that, if the number of actors increases, prospects for co-operation diminish. Such contexts make it hard to identify all the different interests and anticipate the behaviour of all other countries. Relative anonimity goes up, probability of free riding increases and feasibility of sanctions is reduced. In such a situation reciprocity in retaliation can lead to the collapse of co-operation.[68] This study argues that in the OAU decomposition of issue areas or procedures of co-operation to achieve actor reduction do indeed contribute to more effective co-operation.[69]

---

65   See Snidal, 'Limits of Hegemonic Stability Theory', p 595 and R.L. Rothstein, 'Regime-Creation by a Coalition of the Weak: Lessons from the NIEO and the Integrated Program for Commodities', in *International Studies Quarterly*, 1984, pp 307-328.

66   Oye, 'Explaining Cooperation Under Anarchy', pp 4-11.

67   *Ibid.*, pp 11 and 16-17 and on the importance of reciprocity for co-operation also R. Axelrod, *The Evolution of Cooperation* (New York, 1984), ch. 9.

68   Oye, 'Explaining Cooperation Under Anarchy', pp 18-20.

69   The regional integration theories of Kothari and Guernier, which prescribe (continental) integration

Political psychology

Instead of concentrating on the activities taking place at the grass-roots level of African society this study focuses on the top political leadership of African states. Naturally, for the purpose of understanding African politics the importance of the various political movements originating in civil society cannot be gainsaid, but neither can that of the top brass.

The reasons for focusing on Africa's state elites were explained in the discussion of the research objective. The objective puts special emphasis on their perceptions of, and the roles and objectives they attribute to, the OAU. In reconstructing its ideological basis and thus establishing the OAU's role in African political thought as articulated by state elites, this study attempts to provide insight in the views of the continent's leadership on the utility of international co-operation to Africa and on the position of the post-colonial state and Africa's continental order in global politics.

It should be realized that the OAU provides an ideal opportunity for this. The principal reason is that it encompasses, with one exception, all of the continent's states. As argued in section 5.6 all of these countries, both the weak and powerful, to a greater or lesser extent affect its functioning. Because of this Pan-African membership and the fact that it is usually considered as Africa's most prominent organization in the area of political co-operation, it is seen as symbolizing the continent itself. As this study argues, the OAU is held, by Africans, to emblematize "Africa" and as having given this concept, probably more than any other institution, its most concrete, institutionalized expression. It therefore often is a reference point for overviews, criticisms and assessments of the various developments of the post-colonial era. Thus, while the OAU is not the only institution that gives insight in the ideas of state elites, its unique character provides a good opportunity for understanding some of their views.

For the same reason it dawned on us in the course of this study that an analysis of the OAU solely in terms of international relations theory missed certain crucial points. Looking at other studies of the Organization these lacunae are quite obvious.[70] It is as if these studies have taken the "mind" out of the OAU. Yet, if one looks at the primary source material this mind clearly thrusts itself upon the observer: it shows what kind of mental attitudes of elite Africans are at the basis of the Organization and partly explains why state elites have fitted the OAU with the ideological foundations analysed in this study.

This recourse to political psychology, while being related to dependency theory, can be seen from the perspective of the domestic socio-political configurations of member states. Its analysis is informed by some of the insights of Laswell. In his view "deprivation" involves the distress that the human ego suffers when it cannot enjoy a value position it demands. It may lead to two different reactions. Compensation by way of

---

as method to tackle constraints on co-operation emanating from external dependence, are discussed in section 8.3. This is justified by the fact that it involves a study of the OAU's extra-African links and its global role. These are mainly analysed in that part of chapter 8.

70   While many could be cited, the best examples are studies approaching the OAU from a legal-institutional perspective. See for a recent one f.i. P.F. Gonidec, *l'OUA trente ans après: l'unité africaine à l'épreuve* (Paris, 1993).

seeking power is likely if the person experiencing deprivation knows of others that are successfully wielding power. This is probable in the case of politicians. Another basic reaction to deprivation is withdrawal from social interaction, which may occur if deprivation is perceived as overwhelming.[71] In chapters 2 and following ones we will argue how these contentions can be applied with regard to African state elites in relation to the OAU. It is shown what kind of deprivation these elites experience, what causes it and how they respond to it in terms of OAU aims and roles — actual and attributed.

The above makes it imperative that we take Africa's state elites and their views on the OAU seriously. This must be the point of departure. As noted in section 1.2 most studies give an advance evaluation of the OAU's ideological ground-work before they commence their analysis. The result is usually a facile vilification of the state elites that compose the OAU. This makes it impossible, however, to *understand* their (socio-political) behaviour, actions and views and, thus, the objective functioning of the OAU and its meaning in African political thought.

Naturally, their behaviour often deserves to be vigorously denounced. Their privileged position in African society, their frequently callous indifference to the fate of their peoples and repressive forms of governance expose the extent of their responsibility for many of the continent's afflictions. Yet it is submitted that not all members of Africa's state elites are, quite simply, "pirates".[72] In certain respects, such as regarding their views on the continent's relations with the outside, non-African world, they do give reason for a sympathetic hearing, although with the necessary critical distance. Not all articulations of the OAU's ideological ground-work can be dismissed as insincere rhetoric. Much of this has to be taken seriously. However, this requires careful interpretation of the ideological foundations with which the OAU has been provided.

Similarly, as was already emphasized in the preface the views and perceptions held by Africans of the OAU are not presented in this study with the object to deride what the Organization stands for. Our intention is only to map some of the fears and anxieties of elite Africans about the world around them in order to understand the OAU's ideological ground-work.

---

71   *I.e.* when lost indulgences are demanded absolutely. See H.D. Laswell, *Power and Personality* (New York, 1948), ch. 3 and on the deprivation concept also T.R. Gurr, *Why Men Rebel* (Princeton, 1970), chs. 2-3. See on the importance of psychological factors in explaining ideology also R. Girardet, *Mythes et Mythologies Politiques* (Paris, 1986).

72   This is even conceded by Davidson, who presents them as such in his recent critique of the post-colonial state. See B. Davidson, *The Black Man's Burden: Africa and the Curse of the Nation-State* (London, 1992), pp 229, 243-265 and 311-312.

1.4 Ideology

The relevance of ideology

Ideology is one of the central concepts in this study.[73] It was previously argued that an international organization does not really have objectives of itself, but only those that are attributed to it by the member states and its staff. It was also noted that there has been considerable divergence in opinion on the OAU's aims and roles in African politics and that one therefore has to establish what its real objectives are. It was posited that these objectives can be gleaned from the OAU's underlying ideological ground-work as composed of aims and roles attributed by the majority of member states and its Secretariat personnel. Thus, the objectives and roles attributed to the OAU and related views and perceptions that member states and its staff have of the Organization, are considered as expressions of ideology. The same is true for non-governmental views of the OAU.

While it is contended that the OAU's ideology and actual functioning affect each other, the influence of this ideology as such on the Organization's functioning is restricted as ideology is, on the whole, determined by the infrastructural features of social life. This is explained in the next section.

The nature of ideology

Ideology refers to a complex phenomenon which is difficult to gauge. To a certain extent it is a rather elusive concept that is variously defined and is often surrounded by mis-understanding. This study uses the following definition: ideology constitutes in essence (a set of) ideas, notions or concepts that purport to explain reality, prescribe goals for (political, social, economic, military, cultural) action to reform and alter, or preserve and defend, actual conditions and circumstances and, finally, provide criteria with which to legitimize such action.[74]

Thus, it contains both descriptive and prescriptive elements.[75] The distinction between explanation and prescription is, however, difficult to make.[76] It involves a

---

73 Ideology as used in this study approaches the concept of "myth" as elaborated by Girardet, *Mythes et Mythologies Politiques*. Yet this concept is eschewed as many of the ideas in this study are intimately tied to more structured and mundane political goals and programmes of governments, for which the term ideology is more appropriate. While various notions on the OAU are very vague this still does not mean that the concept of myth is suitable, because this involves, in Girardet's terms, a more or less detailed *story*. Many of the functions of Girardet's myth are also similar to those of ideology as used here, while inclusion of Laswell's ideas on deprivation covers much of Girardet's emphasis on the psychological background of ideology.

74 See for various definitions R. Boudon, *The Analysis of Ideology* (Cambridge and Oxford, 1989), ch. 2.

75 See f.i. D.J. Manning, 'Introduction', in D.J. Manning (ed), *The Form of Ideology: Investigations into the sense of ideological reasoning with a view to giving an account of its place in political life* (London, Boston and Sydney, 1980), p 7 and T.J. Robinson, 'Ideology and Theoretical Inquiry' (in *ibid.*, pp 68-69).

76 See B. Crick, 'Philosophy, Theory and Thought', in *Political Studies*, 1967, p 52 and with reference to the African context J.A. Langley, *Ideologies of Liberation in Black Africa 1856-1970: Documents on modern African political thought from colonial times to the present* (London, 1979), pp 8-12.

practical, human activity aimed at explanation, the solution of problems and persuasion.[77] While its main force derives from its pretence of giving a plausible theory of reality,[78] ideology is not just correct or incorrect.[79] Above all, it aims at moulding and directing human action within a certain set of values and goals. Criticism which holds that ideology is not empirically verifiable misses the point, for its function is not merely to describe social reality but to help in its construction.[80]

This is even true in terms of its explanatory functions. In this sense the phenomenon of ideology may be viewed along lines more or less similar to the concept of "discourse".[81] This refers to the construction of meaning as a social process through spoken and written dialogue. Ideologies are systems of meaning through which reality is imagined. Such reality has to be imagined, as it needs recognition by the human subject.[82]

Ideology should not be seen in terms of comprehensive definitions, which only consider something as ideology if it involves a complex, holistic and closed system of thought that claims universal validity and is marked by explicit formulation, comprehensiveness, systematization and coherence.[83] Ideology encompasses more than that. It involves any notion or utterance with descriptive-prescriptive elements, however implicit, vague and inconsistent it may be and whatever level of abstraction, comprehensiveness and complexity is involved.[84] Even the most concrete, narrow and simple idea may be considered as an expression of ideology. As ideology constructs our consciousness there exist by definition numerous expressions of ideology, rather than one or a few.[85]

As an essentially social phenomenon its contents is affected by, and may change with, the conditions of social life. This inconstancy and interaction with the social context are part of ideology's fundamental features.[86] In this respect this study follows the materialist contention that ideology is by and large determined by the infrastructural conditions of society, *i.e.* the configuration of power relations between individuals and groups of individuals or the economic forces underlying socio-political life. In this sense we reject the contention of some discourse analysts that the whole of reality is discourse

77   Langley, *Ideologies of Liberation*, p 16.

78   Crick, 'Philosophy, Theory and Thought', p 52. A different emphasis in D.J. Manning, 'The Place of Ideology in Political Life', in Manning, *Form of Ideology*, p 86.

79   Boudon, *Analysis of Ideology*, p 19 ff.

80   This is missed by K.A. Appiah, *In My Father's House: Africa in the Philosophy of Culture* (New York and Oxford, 1992), ch. 2. See E. Voegelin, 'The Growth of the Race Idea', in *Review of Politics*, 1940, p 284. With reference to Africa J.A. Langley, *Pan-Africanism and Nationalism in West Africa 1900-1945: A Study in Ideology and Social Classes* (Oxford, 1973).

81   See also Crick, 'Philosophy, Theory and Thought', p 49.

82   D. Macdonell, *Theories of Discourse: An Introduction* (Oxford and New York, 1989), pp 1-4 and 24-42, which respectively discuss Foucault's concept of discourse and Althusser's work on ideology.

83   In this vein E. Shills, 'The Concept of Function of Ideology', in D.L. Sills (ed), *International Encyclopaedia of the Social Sciences* (no pl., 1968), vl. 7, p 66.

84   See f.i. P.H. Partridge, 'Politics, Philosophy, Ideology', in *Political Studies*, 1961, p 227 and in the African context C. Clapham, 'The Context of African Political Thought', in *Journal of Modern African Studies*, 1970, pp 2-3.

85   Macdonell, *Theories of Discourse*, pp 27, 33-34 and 37-38, which paraphrases Althusser.

86   See J. Dunn, 'The Identity of the History of Ideas', in *Philosophy*, 1968, p 88. Also Langley, *Ideologies of Liberation*, p 16.

or text. They argue that it is only ideas that exist, that it is ideas which create objects rather than vice versa and that objects do not exist outside discourse, *i.e.* if they are not spoken of.[87] A materialist perspective, however, points to the objectivity and modes of material existence.[88] Post-modernism, which has exerted strong influence on discourse analysis, is culturally reductionist and anti-Marxist in so far as it ignores the (re-)productive infrastructure of capitalism.[89] In contrast, this study sees ideology as the expression of the interests of groups and individuals and as constituting a connection between thought and social existence.[90] For this reason the influence exerted on the social order by ideology as such is limited.[91]

Yet, it should not be assumed that ideology derives directly from the infrastructural conditions of that order or that expressions of ideology are mechanically determined by someone's position in the social infrastructure.[92] This infrastructure determines what people can *not* do. While it considerably affects people in their relation to society, it does not dictate what people actually *will* do, say or argue.[93] Ideas originate in a certain social context, yet they still have to be understood by human beings. These are not deprived of thought merely because the ideas are located historically and socially.[94] The history of mentalities — a term that overlaps with, but is wider than, the concept of ideology as it encompasses unformulated, apparently meaningless and unconscious notions — rejects any mechanical reductionism. To some extent the relationship between the objective conditions of human life and the ways in which people narrate and live it is dialectical. The diffusion of ideas, for example, may involve a certain inertia.[95]

The interpretation of ideology

While this study focuses especially on the many perceptions that Africans have of the OAU's role and functioning, it does not follow the contention of some discourse analysts that there is not one reality but innumerable many, namely as many as there are discourses in human life; according to the relativist conception of post-modernism objective reality does not exist.[96]

This contention, which enjoys some popularity in anthropological research, is

---

87   See Macdonell, *Theories of Discourse*, pp 64-75, on the ideas of Hindess and Hirst.

88   Althusser posits from a materialist perspective the primacy of being over thought. *Ibid.*, pp 78-80.

89   *Ibid.*, pp 60-8 and B. Agger, *The Discourse of Domination: From the Frankfurt School to Postmodernism* (Evanston, 1992), p 291.

90   In this vein Langley, *Pan-Africanism and Nationalism*, p 7. On the complexities involved Boudon, *Analysis of Ideology*, ch. 6.

91   See also Partridge, 'Politics, Philosophy, Ideology', p 228.

92   Some definitions overlook this. F.i. J. Mohan, 'A Whig Interpretation of African Nationalism', in *Journal of Modern African Studies*, 1968, p 406 and L. Yablotchkov, 'L'évolution du nationalisme africain', in *Présence africaine*, no. 74, 1970, p 48.

93   As aptly observed by J. Lonsdale, 'From Colony to Industrial State: South African Historiography as seen from England', in *Social Dynamics*, 1983, p 71. On the complexity of the relation ideology - social context L.G. Graham, 'Ideology and the Sociological Understanding', in Manning, *Form of Ideology*, ch. 1.

94   Boudon, *Analysis of Ideology*, pp 73-74 and 97.

95   M. Vovelle, *Ideologies and Mentalities* (Cambridge and Oxford, 1990), pp 6-12.

96   See Macdonell, *Theories of Discourse*, p 73 referring to Hindess and Hirst, and Agger, *Discourse of Domination*, p 285.

categorically rejected here. While there may be as many different perceptions of reality as there are people, this study is based on the philosophical premise that there is only one reality, whose objectivity is grounded in the material conditions of existence. It is readily conceded that truth is not an easy thing to grasp, yet our position is that there is one, objectivized truth the search for which is an activity that political scientists and historians can justifiably engage in. That we only manage to find aspects of the truth and history is therefore regularly rewritten does not refute the premise of the existence of objective reality and, thus, of the relevance of research. It points to the obstacles that human beings have to overcome in terms of observation and the formulation of theory.

From what was said on the nature of ideology follows a particular interpretation of this phenomenon, which may be called "contextual reading". This rejects the approach by which ideology is interpreted in the abstract and separated from its socio-historical context. Such an approach is often followed by treatises on political philosophy or specialists looking for systematic presentations of political ideas. It is sometimes referred to as the "tradition of intellectualizing"[97] and to a certain extent neglects ideology's role in the social context.[98] Sometimes it involves facile comparisons with political ideas uttered in other contexts, simply on the basis of the use of the same kind of words.[99] It misses important points about ideology. Moreover, in so far as it entails a separation of the link between thought and material existence it is idealist philosophy that only favours those with an interest in the status quo.[100]

In contrast, contextual reading sees expressions of ideology in terms of the configuration of power relations and the (group of) individuals whose interests are articulated by such expressions. As ideology is by and large dependent on the infrastructural features of the social order, it becomes intelligible only in the context of a given historical experience.[101] However, as ideology is not mechanically determined by those infrastructural conditions one must never equate context with meaning. Insight in the causes of a particular articulation of ideology or the conditions in which it occurs does not necessarily lead to understanding of the point that its agent wanted to make.[102] If one confuses context and meaning the mind is taken out of politics:[103] following a position in between voluntarist and determinist conceptions of man's place in the social structure this study is based on the premise that human individuals do indeed exert influence on the course of history, even if their autonomy is very limited.

In interpreting ideology in context two other pitfalls must be avoided. To start with

---

97   A.A. Stein, *Why Nations Cooperate: Circumstances and Choice in International Relations* (Ithaca and London, 1990), p 184.

98   Two recent examples in the African context are Appiah, *In My Father's House*, ch. 2 and M.L. Ropivia, 'Critique des fondements conceptuels de l'unité politique de l'Afrique', in *Cahiers de l'IPAG*, no. 10, June 1990, pp 93-191.

99   See f.i. the remarks by R.W. Howe ('Did Nkrumah favour Pan-Africanism?' in *Transition*, 1966, no. 27-4, pp 13-15) on the Central African Federation.

100   See in this vein Macdonell, *Theories of Discourse*, p 76, on Hindess and Hirst.

101   See for this approach Manning, 'Introduction', p 4 and in the African context Langley, *Ideologies of Liberation*, p 19, both harking back to Mannheim.

102   Skinner, 'Meaning and Understanding', pp 38-49 and for the African context Langley, *Ideologies of Liberation*, pp 19-20.

103   Langley, *Ideologies of Liberation*, p 19.

the least obvious one: one should reject the overly relativist and cynical approach by which utterances are never taken literally. In its extreme form this approach holds that one cannot attribute sincerity to the agent articulating an idea. This idea would never be genuinely believed in by the agent himself, who would always mean something different from what he would say. In our view of African history, however, there is still room for sincere conviction. One regularly comes across individuals who, despite the narrow margins of African autonomy, passionately strive for justice and hold convictions about the need and possibility for change. Nkrumah is an obvious example, but so are the liberation movements struggling for independence in the Lusophone territories three decades ago[104] or some of the efforts of the early 1990s to realize political reform. Correspondence between self-interest and ideological convictions does not negate the sincerity of beliefs *per se*. While their expression in front of an audience is affected by considerations of what the agent wants his public to hear, this does not necessarily render these beliefs disingenuous.[105]

Naturally, very often one must not take utterances literally. The concepts of rhetoric and propaganda make this clear. Rhetoric can be seen as the expression of words, ideas or arguments whose literal meaning differs from someone's real and unarticulated opinions. Propaganda refers to the deliberate attempt to influence, control or alter the attitudes of others by written, spoken or other symbols, whose contents does not have to be (entirely) true or false to achieve that purpose.[106]

Yet, it is not always necessary to explain discrepancies between the literal and the real in terms of dishonesty. Thus, the use of metaphors is an important technique in ideological reasoning.[107] In contrast to what is the case with rhetoric and propaganda the person that argues metaphorically does not necessarily hide his real opinion behind the literal meaning of what is said. What is involved is the deliberate creation of associations, comparisons and analogies with well known symbols, conditions or stories from other contexts that are very powerful in terms of their emotive qualities. It constitutes a symbolic action whose object is to convince and mobilize on a point in another issue area that is also publicized to the audience for whom the metaphor is intended. It is argued by some that metaphor is the device *par excellence* on which the construction and attraction of ideologies rest.[108] This study will argue their central importance in the articulation of ideology and takes several painful metaphors, formulated by Africans with regard to the OAU, as the key to understanding its ideological ground-work.

In view of the above it must be concluded that there is no general rule for interpreting ideology in context. Nothing must be accepted at face value. The meaning of each and every utterance has to be established on a case by case basis.

Problems of interpretation specific to the sources
While it is difficult to gauge ideology in general, the explanation of ideology in the world of international politics seems even trickier. Thus, it was already argued in section 1.2 that

104   See Davidson, *Black Man's Burden*, p 296 ff.
105   This is admitted but still understated by Clapham, 'Context of African Political Thought'.
106   See f.i. K.J. Holsti, *International Politics: A Framework for Analysis* (London, 1974), ch. 8.
107   J.D. Rayner, 'The Use of Ideological Language', in Manning, *Form of Ideology*, p 107.
108   Boudon, *Analysis of Ideology*, pp 22 and 49, on Geertz.

OAU resolutions often involve a general compromise that is adopted without voting and usually lacks explicit criticism of the policies of member states. Close scrutiny of their language is therefore necessary and such resolutions have to be interpreted in conjunction with other material. Moreover, section 5.6 argues that OAU resolutions have multiple functions, such as announcing decisions to implement a particular policy; legitimizing or condemning events or actions; introducing or reaffirming norms and principles; translating a specific configuration of power reached by member states in their mutual interaction; or explaining away an experience of impotence. In each case such purpose affects the explanation of a resolution in its own way.

Another source that must be approached with caution is speeches that member states give at OAU meetings. Their propagandistic value is attested by the fact that they are regularly published, in full, in governmental newspapers. They serve a purpose in the realm of communication and exertion of influence vis-à-vis other states, as well as in the search for domestic and inter-African legitimation of national policies. If due regard is given to the kind of language and argument they contain, they are, however, an interesting source, especially for data on perception.

In section 1.2 it was argued that African government newspapers are an important mouth-piece for the articulation of governmental opinions. However, one could question whether government-owned or -censored publications should be seen as the expression of the governmental view *as such*. The definition of state elites that is given in section 2.2 does not include newspaper editors. This implies that the group forming the government and the one producing newspapers are at least not (fully) identical, so that the *étatiste* character of newspaper material is not self-evident. There is some spatial and political distance between both groups and the formation of opinion in government and the expression of views in government-controlled newspapers is not necessarily synchronous.

There are, however, good reasons for taking this newspaper material as expressive of governmental opinion. Various forms of control are exercised over government newspapers, which involves direct and indirect, as well as formal and informal, means. First, they are often fully government property. In many cases they are formal publications of the ministry of information or the ruling party and therefore articulate governmental attitudes. Sometimes this is reflected by the head of state being the official editor-in-chief or political editor of the paper concerned. The Ivorian newspaper *Fraternité* in the era of Houphouët-Boigny is an example. Even if they are not government-owned or do not constitute formal government or party publications, they are often littered with quotations from the head of state and the texts of speeches of, or editorials and articles written by, leading politicians. In those cases the link between government opinion and newspaper material is also direct and explicit.

Other material is produced by editors and journalists who are not part of the state elite but can be considered as members of the wider group of "modern elite" as explained in section 2.2. The texts they produce are usually censored beforehand or afterwards. The threat of post-publication censorship can also prevent divergence of the government or party line. Censorship can be exercised by actually checking material or by indirect means, such as manipulation of the supply of paper, ownership of the printing presses or licensing requirements for journalists.

Thus, one study on the African press during the early 1970s showed that, at the time, three quarters of daily newspapers were owned by the government or ruling party. Of the 34 countries studied almost half had a wholly government-owned press. Nearly sixty per cent exercised pre-publication censorship, including those countries where the press was fully government-owned. Seventy per cent exercised censorship after publication and aided newspapers financially. Almost half had licensing requirements for journalists and more than eighty per cent had legal means with which to punish journalists for criticism. Seventy per cent obtained material from Western press agencies through exclusive contracts. This ensured that information could be filtered and controlled, for example by channelling it first through the national press agency.[109]

The rise of multi-partyism and consequent liberalization of press regimes did, in principle, not affect our data as selection of newspapers focused on government publications.[110] One can therefore safely assume that the material used for this study by and large equates with *étatiste* opinion. This is also perceived as such by governments in other countries, which sometimes respond to its articulation by way of similar channels. This may, for example, result in the eruption of press wars.

In only a few cases control may at times not be sufficient for wholly equating material with government views. For example, one study of the press in Nigeria observes that it enjoyed relative freedom. It notes that the *Daily Times*, while (partially) government-owned, was sometimes critical of the government.[111] Another study concluded that control in Kenya was exercised in a lenient, indirect way.[112] This may be reflected in some of our material, as in Nigerian comment on the trade union metaphor and Kenyan reaction to the fall of Amin discussed in chapter 8. Similarly, section 8.3 shows that the lack of progress on continental integration drew criticism in Cameroonian and Senegalese sources. Yet, in these cases views were expressed in generalized terms, avoiding criticism of one's own government.

Awareness of foreign policy issues outside governmental circles is usually rather low. While this is even true in highly literate societies, it is potentially more underdeveloped in countries where sources for foreign policy information are controlled by government or autonomous ones are few and far between.[113] However, as the analysis of non-governmental views is part of the research objective, some opposition newspapers were included in the source material. Some of these, such as in Morocco, tow the government line on matters of foreign policy, while others do not. Appendix B provides a list of newspaper sources together with information vital to their interpretation.

One final word on African newspapers is in order. The importance attributed to them

---

109   See D.L. Wilcox, *Mass Media in Black Africa: Philosophy and Control* (New York, 1975). Also R. Buijtenhuijs and R. Baesjou, 'Center and Periphery News in Two African Newspapers: Testing some hypotheses on cultural dominance', in *Kroniek van Afrika*, 1974, pp 243-271.

110   See for more recent studies of the African media f.i. G.L. Faringer, *Press Freedom in Africa* (New York, 1991).

111   C.W. Ogbondah, *Military Regimes and the Press in Nigeria, 1966-1993: Human Rights and National Development* (Lanham, New York and London, 1994), p 115.

112   Buijtenhuijs and Baesjou, 'Center and Periphery News', p 252. Also Wilcox, *Mass Media in Black Africa*.

113   Holsti, *International Politics*, pp 382 and 387.

derives partly from the contention that it is here that one must look for ideological argument. In the mundane practicalities of African politics it is especially the notions and ideas found in these, often poorly written and published, newspapers that constitute the building-stones of African political thought, rather than the intellectualized expositions of, say, an Ali Mazrui.[114] These building-stones need not be phrased in subtle and stylized form or be coherent and systematized to perform a function in the conscientization of elite Africans about the day-to-day predicaments of their continent. To serve that purpose they may be quite rough and ready, contain hyperbole or at times be rather crude.

One particular manifestation of this is formed by graphical presentations of ideological argument — usually known as cartoons. These sometimes find their way in African governmental newspapers. Some of them convey messages in much more powerful and pregnant ways than is possible through writing. Although uncommon in most scholarly analysis of politics, some have therefore been included in this study. Justification for this lies in the interpretative purpose that they serve. Reference to them is made in the main text or foot-notes.

1.5   Concluding remarks

Deconstructing the central concepts: Africa and the OAU
In view of the subject of this study it is vital to realize that the meaning of the word "Africa" is not always self-evident or without its ambiguities. As the Sierra Leonean diplomat and poet Nicol once wrote:

> You are not a country, Africa,
> You are a concept,
> Fashioned in our minds, each to each,
> To hide our separate fears,
> To dream our separate dreams.[115]

Because of the many different historical, geographical, cultural and other features of this continent the concept of "Africa" is to a large extent a fiction of the imagination or at best an objective. This study is therefore not so much concerned with "Africa" as with African attempts to construct that "Africa". These efforts are analysed from the perspective of its *a priori* deconstruction. This deconstruction has been attempted by constant reference to the different actions, statements, ideas and policies of the OAU's various member states. Moreover, "Africa" is a concept that, indeed, occasions numerous ideas, dreams and aspirations among Africans. Some of these will become clear in the following chapters. In the conclusions and epilogue we assess to what extent (elite) Africans have, by way of the OAU, succeeded to construct "Africa" — and what kind of "Africa" they have constructed — from the diverse base that their countries and ideological perspectives constitute.

Similarly, international organizations often speak in different tongues. An analysis of

114   See on this also Langley, *Ideologies of Liberation*, p 3.
115   A. Nicol, 'The Meaning of Africa', in J. Drachler (ed), *African Heritage: Intimate Views of the Black Africans from Life, Lore, and Literature* (no pl., 1963), p 122.

the OAU therefore necessitates its deconstruction in terms of its various organs. Thus, it will be argued that the Organization's Assembly and Council have sometimes not seen eye to eye. Moreover, organs with limited membership such as the Liberation Committee, but also others,[116] have at times articulated policies and attitudes that differed substantially from the postures of the main policy bodies. However, for the sake of convenience we anthropomorphize our subject by speaking of "the OAU" when referring to the totality of its institutions, functionaries and member state governments. Also, while it was said that a regime is not an organization but refers to the decision of states to co-operate in its cadres, convenience demands discussion in terms of "the OAU regime".

The narrative: limitations and structure
Naturally, a study of the OAU's functioning in African politics, with special emphasis on reconstruction of its ideological ground-work, entails the risk of hopelessly widening the analysis. When processing our data it was therefore decided to narrow down the discussion to four major queries or issue areas. The study focuses, first, on the reasons for, and circumstances of, the OAU's formation. Then it concentrates on the internal functioning of the Organization. The third issue area concerns its role in the former struggle against colonial and white minority regimes. Finally, we analyse the OAU's role in the management of Africa's political order.

The subjects that are ignored are OAU concern with economic co-operation, cultural matters and co-operation in more technical fields. A systematic analysis of interaction with other organizations has been left out as well, although this dimension is partially integrated in the discussion of the above-mentioned issues. While the subject of economic co-operation gained in importance after 1980, its omission is justified by the fact that political issues have always been a major OAU preoccupation. This still holds true now, as since the late 1980s the Organization is putting renewed emphasis on the issue of conflict management.

Chapters 2 and 3 provide a necessary outline of Africa's political, social and economic structures and the general ideological dimensions that are part of these features. They focus on the patterns of interaction at the sub-state level; the process of foreign policy formulation; Africa's international relations; and the nature and manifestations of African (state) nationalism and Pan-Africanism. The OAU originated and functions in the totality of these dimensions and structures and must be analysed in the overall context that they constitute. These chapters are therefore of an introductory nature.

Research findings are presented in chapters 4 to 8. Chapter 4 focuses on the way in which the OAU was formed; the alliances that preceded it and the nature of their differences; as well as on the rapprochement that they found in the OAU and the ideological basis under-girding this. Chapter 5 analyses the OAU's legal and institutional features; the functioning of its Secretariat; the OAU's finances; and the nature of OAU policy- and decision-making. Chapter 6 first shows how the OAU's role in the anti-colonial struggle stemmed from its general ideological ground-work. It then analyses the diplomatic and military dimensions of its involvement in this struggle.

---

116   See f.i. on the (dissolved) Inter-African Bureau of Languages the brochure Linguistic Liberation and Unity of Africa (OAU Bill Publication 6, IABL, Kampala, 1985).

Chapters 7 and 8 deal with the way in which the OAU has sought to manage, in the widest sense, Africa's political order. It is shown how its rationale of conflict management stemmed from its general ideology. The patterns of settling inter-state disputes are analysed, as well as the more specific aspects of managing the continental order: OAU strategy towards domestic conflicts; the military aspects of managing that order; and the external dimensions of that management, in terms of the OAU's search for greater continental influence. The general conclusions of this study are presented in chapter 9 and the epilogue.

The citation of sources

Quotation of secondary sources follows the conventions of the *Journal of African History*. First references are given in full, subsequent ones in abbreviated form.[117] Documents of the OAU are cited according to the Organization's customs. Thus, regular resolutions, declarations, decisions and statements are quoted by their official code number.[118]

The complete title of a newspaper is not given if it is too long.[119] It can be found in Appendix B. Unless the name of the country of origin becomes clear in the title of the newspaper or the text it is quoted in brackets after the paper's name.[120] For the sake of brevity dates are given in abbreviated form and, if no further mention is made, newspaper material refers to an editorial. Thus, "*The Ethiopian Herald*, 3/7/80" refers to an editorial published in this newspaper on the third of July 1980. If it is not an editorial the word "article" is put in brackets after name and date of the newspaper.[121] If it is considered relevant, more specific reference is made in brackets to the nature of the non-editorial text, such as if it concerns speeches in an OAU organ. As most African newspapers are very small in size page numbers have been omitted.

In order to catch the full flavour of things the text contains numerous quotations. Those from non-English sources are given in the original, or in our translation so as not to slow down the flow of argument. Finally, most chapter sections have been given titles which were taken from, or allude to, expressions or metaphors subsequently quoted in the text. These refer to the central contention of our argument or parts of it. Their meaning will therefore become clear in the course of the text and their source is given where they appear in the narrative.[122]

---

117   However, if subsequent citation is rare it includes reference to the first note of full quotation for the sake of clarity. Page references are preceded by "p" or "pp".

118   For example: CM/Res.1073 (XLIV).

119   For instance: *l'Essor: La Voix du Peuple. Organe de l'Union Démocratique du Peuple Malien.*

120   For instance: *The Standard* (Tanzania).

121   Such as: *Dikgang Tsa Gompieno* (Botswana), 10/3/82 (article).

122   The title of section 6.2 does not derive from any quotation in the text. The source of the title of section 6.3 is given directly as the statement it refers to is not quoted subsequently.

2

The structures of African politics: domestic conditions, foreign policy and international relations

2.1   Introduction

This chapter provides an overview of the general context in which the Organization of African Unity operates. This context consists essentially of three different levels of variables: an array of domestic or "sub-state" factors; the national process of foreign policy formulation and decision-making; and the structures of Africa's international relations. One must pay some attention to the domestic conditions of African states, as the foreign policy process is influenced by both national and international factors. The process of foreign policy-making is an independent variable in its own right because it exerts separate influence on the fundamental interaction patterns between international actors[1] *i.e.* the "structures" of international politics. These structures of international relations and the foreign policies of states may be seen as the most important variables in the functioning of international organizations as the OAU.

The second section of this chapter is concerned with domestic factors. The third section pays attention to the foreign policy process and the fourth section is devoted to Africa's international relations. The analysis applies to the whole period covered by this study, *i.e.* the era of 1960 to the early 1990s, with an emphasis on the broader, longer-term developments.

---

1   See on interaction as determined by national calculations A.A. Stein, *Why Nations Cooperate: Circumstances and Choice in International Relations* (Ithaca and London, 1990).

2.2   Some general characteristics of African states

Introduction

Africa has over fifty formally independent states, each endowed with a myriad of cultural, social, political, economic and geographical peculiarities. It is therefore almost impossible to generalize about the sub-state level of Africa's continental order. Yet, it is necessary to provide some meaningful generalizations as space does not allow a detailed discussion of the intricacies of Africa's states and societies. One cannot circumvent the problem by simply focusing on one country, as the uniqueness of the OAU is that its functioning is to a greater or lesser extent influenced by all, or the great majority of, African states. However, following specialists in the field[2] it is submitted here that Africa possesses, especially as compared to other continents, some common political, cultural and socio-economic characteristics that justify some general remarks about African states. This section therefore provides information on some of their basic parameters: the economy; social stratification; the modern elite and its values; the institutions of state, party and the military; and, more generally, the changing relations between state and society.

Economy

African economies are characterized by underdevelopment. To a large extent, the population consists of peasants who produce food crops for their own subsistence or are, in whole or in part, active in the production of cash crops sold in the market economy. In 1988 63% of the economically active population was engaged in subsistence and commercial agriculture.[3] The dual nature of African economies does not present a dichotomy, however, because peasants are usually active in both sectors and can partly revert to subsistence farming if their activity in the market place does not reap sufficient benefits. Gross national product, a concept that refers only to the market economy, is to a great extent determined by the agricultural sector, which represented 41% of GDP in 1965 and 32 in 1988.[4]

While the export of cash crops forms an important source of government revenue, another source of government income is derived from the exploitation of mineral resources, with which several states are richly endowed. The level of industrialization is, with the exception of South Africa and a few relatively more developed economies like Zimbabwe and some North African countries, very limited. The proportion in GNP of manufacturing, *i.e.* products with higher added value, did not rise above fifteen per cent in 1960. Thirteen years later Africa's share in Third World industrial production reached only 0.6%.[5]

---

2   See f.i. J.F. Bayart, *L'état en Afrique: la politique du ventre* (Paris, 1989), pp 57-59.

3   *FAO Yearbook: Production*, vol. 43, 1989 (Rome, 1990), p 63.

4   Sub-Saharan Africa. From *World Development Report 1991: The Challenge of Development* (World Bank: Washington, 1989), p 209.

5   Both figures excluding South Africa. See J.F.A. Ajayi and M. Crowder (eds), *Historical Atlas of Africa*, (Harlow, 1985), map 71 and M. Cornevin, *Histoire de l'Afrique contemporaine: de la deuxième guerre mondiale à nos jours* (Paris, 1980), p 295.

Part of this state of affairs can be traced to the economic structures inherited from the colonial era. The colonial powers did not intend to industrialize their African territories, but kept them as cheap producers of raw materials and markets for Western industrial products. The development of infrastructure was almost exclusively tuned to this limited role of the colonial economy. Mining and plantation were under foreign control, as well as import and export and most intermediary trade.[6]

At independence, African economies were therefore highly dependent on price developments in the world market, as well as on aid and investment from foreign sources and trade with the former colonial power. The continent suffered large-scale poverty. Per capita income stagnated on average at 95 US dollars and life expectancy barely reached fourty years.[7] Health facilities were grossly underdeveloped and put under heavy strain by population growth and rapid urbanization: the continent's population grew from an estimated 281 million in 1960 to 363 million in 1970, while the urban community increased from 15.5% in 1960 to 20.8% in 1970.[8]

Thus, economic development became the primary objective of African governments. Although it is very difficult to generalize about the host of policies that have been pursued in this respect, one can say that up to the 1980s roughly two approaches were followed. Most countries adopted models that could be termed "state capitalism". This approach involved a central role for the free market mechanism, an expansion of export production to finance the importation of capital goods and an attempt to catch up with other capitalist countries. It was a reformist approach, because it did not imply a fundamental shake-up of the national economy, nor of the country's international role. As the majority of states had a lack of national savings, capital had to come from abroad. However, the state occupied a central place in the economy and in the accumulation of surplus, which was ensured through parastatal companies and Africanization policies. This was of principal benefit to the petty bourgeoisie, as opposed to urban workers and the mass of the peasantry. In these countries differences in wealth became generally very large, especially in the case of semi-peripheral economies.[9]

As argued in chapter 1, these operate between core and peripheral countries. They stand in between them in terms of value of products, wage levels and profit margins. Most African states consist of peripheral economies and only a minority of countries — such as Nigeria, Ivory Coast, Kenya, Algeria and South Africa — may be regarded as semi-peripheral.[10]

While most African states adopted models of state-capitalism, some countries, often peripheral ones, adopted a "state socialist" programme. In all versions of this model — which was generally pursued up to the mid or late 1980s — most economic sectors were

---

6   See f.i. A.G. Hopkins, *An Economic History of West Africa* (London, 1980), chs. 5-7.

7   Both figures for 1960 and excluding South Africa. See Cornevin, *Histoire de l'Afrique*, p 282 and A. Seidman, *An Economics Textbook for Africa* (London and New York, 1980), p 7.

8   *1987 Statistical Yearbook* (UN: New York, 1990), p 5. Figures on urbanization for sub-Saharan Africa only. *World Development Report 1991*, p 265.

9   See f.i. A.Y. Yansané, 'Decolonization, Dependency, and Development in Africa: The Theory Revisited', in A.Y. Yansané (ed), *Decolonization and Dependency: Problems of Development of African Societies* (Westport and London, 1980), pp 27-38 and T.M. Shaw, *Towards a Political Economy for Africa: The Dialectics of Dependence* (New York, 1985), pp 84-85.

10   Shaw, *Political Economy of Africa*.

collectivized, development planning was much more centralized and the accumulation of surplus occurred through state institutions. Concomitantly, attempts were made, with varying degrees of determination, to change the international role of the economy and challenge the structures of international exchange. However, as little foreign capital was available, many of these countries were dependent on foreign development aid. Countries like Tanzania and Guinea, but also Algeria and Angola, were illustrative of this approach.[11]

Thus, the state became a principal actor in all African economies. Moreover, while state capitalist countries showed greater willingness to play along with the capitalist system, at times they also expressed misgivings about the inequalities ingrained in the international economic order. Like some of the countries following state socialist models, they were sometimes willing to challenge this state of affairs, for example by trying to push up depressed commodity prices.[12]

While some economies, notably the semi-peripheral ones following state-capitalist models,[13] did better than others, after 1980 almost all countries fell in the grips of a severe economic crisis. International commodity prices underwent a sustained fall[14] and the continent's terms of trade therefore deteriorated significantly. While the value of its exports declined with a yearly seven per cent from 1980 to 1987, that of European, Asian and American products rose — and with it the price of African imports.[15] Africa's trade deficit increased threefold between 1981 and 1992, government revenues declined and by 1992 external debt stood at ca. 255 billion US dollars.[16]

Most governments therefore applied for assistance from the IMF and World Bank. These and other institutions like NGO's, as well as individual Western governments, responded by providing increasing amounts of aid. Thus, the sub-Saharan share of global official development assistance increased from 19.5% in the mid 1970s to 32% by 1989, as well as in real terms.[17] During the 1980s aid by NGO's increased from 600 million dollars to one billion.[18] Aid flows were, however, insufficient to compensate for the growth in debts. For example, by the early 1990s total African debt was ten times the entire Lomé III aid budget.[19]

Aid disbursement was increasingly tied to the adoption of IMF-inspired structural adjustment programmes. These dictated currency devaluation, trade liberalization,

---

11   Yansané, 'Decolonization, Dependency, and Development', pp 32-34 and Shaw, *Political Economy for Africa*, pp 84-86.

12   See also C. Young, *Ideology and Development in Africa* (New Haven and London, 1982), ch. 5.

13   For example, Ivory Coast, Botswana, Kenya, Gabon, Nigeria. See Shaw, *Political Economy for Africa*.

14   See J. Ravenhill, 'When Weakness Is Strength: The Lomé IV Negotiations', in I.W. Zartman (ed), *Europe and Africa: The New Phase* (Boulder and London, 1993), p 42.

15   P. Economou, M. Gittelman and M. Wubneh, 'Europe 1992 and Foreign Direct Investment in Africa', in Zartman, *Europe and Africa*, p 115.

16   A. Adedeji, 'Marginalisation and Marginality: Context, Issues and Viewpoints', in A. Adedeji (ed), *Africa within the World: Beyond Dispossession and Dependence* (London and Atlantic Highlands, NJ, 1993), p 4.

17   R.C. Riddell, 'Aid Performance and Prospects', in Zartman, *Europe and Africa*, p 140.

18   S. George, 'Uses and Abuses of African Debt', in Adedeji, *Africa within the World*, p 66.

19   Riddell, 'Aid Performance', pp 143-4 and I.W. Zartman, 'Introduction', in *ibid.*, *Europe and Africa*, p 6.

deregulation of price controls and severe cutbacks in subsidies. In most cases, however, full or partial state withdrawal from the economy did not stem decline. While some countries, like Ghana, began to perform better in terms of agricultural production and GDP growth, the debt issue remained a serious drag on development and structural adjustment failed to turn economies around.[20] On the contrary, African countries, both peripheral and semi-peripheral ones,[21] continued to decline in the global economic hierarchy. By the early 1990s this process had not yet been reversed. Thus, Africa's share in the global production and export of many natural resources has dropped; after the mid 1970s its share in European Community imports, together with that of Caribbean and Pacific countries, fell from eight to four per cent; and between 1970 and 1986 the share of manufactures in exports to the EC dropped by more than half.[22] This process of marginalization was reinforced by a stagnation and reduction of foreign private investment. During the 1980s numerous companies, especially British but also French ones and others, began to withdraw from various sectors of African economies, including mining.[23]

Thirty years of independence therefore resulted in an overall negative socio-economic record. While the rising expectations accompanying decolonization were in some cases met by a temporary boom in commodity prices, the 1970s brought both absolute and relative decline: growth rates decreased and turned negative in some cases; Africa's average per capita income stagnated at 190 US dollars; and for most countries total GNP did not rise above two billion.[24] Per capita food production also declined.[25] The third decade of independence only reduced living standards further. Per capita income decreased throughout the 1980s.[26]

The social effects of the economic crisis and structural adjustment were disastrous, especially in the more peripheral countries, such as war-ravaged Mozambique and in the Horn and the Sahel and, more generally, for the urban poor.[27] During the 1980s famine and malnutrition became more widespread, although structural adjustment was in principle supportive of agricultural production. Budget cuts threw people on the streets in their thousands and contributed to the decay of infrastructure, health care and education. The statistics are dire. For example, in the early 1980s Africa's average literacy rate stood at 36%, as compared to 57% in Asia, and infant mortality was 120 per 1,000 life births as

---

20   See S. Rasheed, 'Africa at the Doorstep of the Twenty-First Century: Can Crisis Turn to Opportunity?', in Adedeji, *Africa within the World*, pp 43-44; E.W. Nafziger, *The Debt Crisis in Africa* (Baltimore and London, 1993) and F. Tarp, *Stabilization and Structural Adjustment: Macroeconomic Frameworks for Analysing the Crisis in Sub-Saharan Africa* (London and New York, 1993).

21   Shaw, *Political Economy for Africa*, pp 34 and 63-64.

22   Ravenhill, 'When Weakness Is Strength', p 42.

23   W. Kühne, 'Looking South After the End of the Cold War', in Zartman, *Europe and Africa*, p 16 and Economou, Gittelman and Wubneh, 'Europe 1992'.

24   Only seven countries had a GNP above two billion dollars. Seidman, *Economics Textbook for Africa*, pp 92 and 164.

25   This contention is based on figures for developing, sub-Saharan Africa. Shaw, *Political Economy for Africa*, p 74 and Tarp, *Stabilization and Structural Adjustment*, p 12.

26   Adedeji, 'Marginalisation and Marginality', p 4.

27   In the late '80s 28% of sub-Saharans lived in urban areas and the continental population was ca. 610 million. *1987 Statistical Yearbook*, p 5 and *World Development Report 1991*, p 265.

opposed to 79 in Asia. By 1989 life expectancy was only 51, *i.e.* much lower than in Asian countries.[28]

Outline of social stratification

Stratification of African societies is extremely complex. As colonial creations, African states are culturally highly heterogeneous. Apart from small, kinship-based, social groups (often described as extended families, lineages or clans), some countries, such as f.i. Zimbabwe, possess a limited number of relatively large ethnic communities or identities. Many other states, however, encompass a host of smaller ethnic groupings of which none is able to dominate the post-colonial configuration of power. The presence of wider cultural complexes, linguistic cleavages, regional disparities, various religions and different ways of livelihood — such as that of nomadic and sedentary communities — complements this picture of cultural diversity.[29]

On top of this, African states possess a form of stratification along socio-economic lines. Apart from the petty bourgeoisie, on which more below, and the mass of the peasantry, most African countries have a usually small proletariat or working class and a group of permanent unemployed. The peasantry consists of a mass of small farmers that produce for the market and their subsistence needs. As pricing policies for long favoured the urban population, the poorer sections of the peasantry are vulnerable to immoderate extraction of their surplus by the state.[30]

Rich commercial farmers and prosperous plantation owners may be treated as members of the petty bourgeoisie. This social grouping is the most important in the context of this study as it occupies the central stage in post-colonial society. Apart from prosperous agricultural entrepreneurs, the petty bourgeoisie consists of small businessmen, such as traders and transporters; professionals; the university-trained; and property-investing civil servants, journalists and politicians. Until now, big private entrepreneurs have usually been very limited in number and most large businesses have been controlled by foreign capital or, especially up to the 1980s, the state. In view of the relatively low levels of foreign private investment in most countries, the concomitant importance of development aid and active state regulation of economic life, it is control of political power that provides principal access to economic wealth. The petty bourgeoisie is therefore to a greater or lesser extent dependent on state patronage.[31] To this purpose, there operates a complex of patron-client networks in which personal ties determine access to socio-economic rewards, in exchange for political support. In many countries

---

28   These reached 58 to 68. Shaw, *Political Economy for Africa*, p 111 and Tarp, *Stabilization and Structural Adjustment*, p 8.

29   See for descriptions of the concept of ethnicity and wider cultural complexes C. Young, *The Politics of Cultural Pluralism* (Madison, 1976) and J. Loup-Amselle and E. M'bokolo, *Au coeur de l'ethnie: ethnies, tribalisme et état en Afrique* (Paris, 1985).

30   See Shaw, *Political Economy for Africa*, pp 50-54; H. Cooperstock, 'Some Methodological and Substantive Issues in the Study of Social Stratification in Tropical Africa', in T.M. Shaw and K.A. Heard (eds), *The Politics of Africa: Dependence and Development* (London, 1979), pp 31-33; and for a controversial view on the peasantry G. Hyden, *Beyond Ujamaa in Tanzania: Underdevelopment and an Uncaptured Peasantry* (London, 1980).

31   Shaw, *Political Economy for Africa*, pp 35-50 and Cooperstock, 'Some Methodological and Substantive Issues', pp 28-31.

this control of resources has — closely tied up with the political manipulation of ethnicity — given rise to widespread corruption and informal sectors that provide opportunity for smuggling and black marketeering.[32]

Thus, the factor of ethnicity permeats many political and socio-economic issues, as well as the functioning and composition of state institutions and other forms of social and political organization. In the context of incomplete socio-economic stratification, ethnic identities provide a basis for group alignment in the struggle for resources or, as shown below, constitute a means of social protection in periods of economic contraction. Depending on the circumstances in each country, government policy ranges from proportional balancing of ethnic interests to outright discrimination of, and systematic favouritism to, different ethnic groups. Countries like Zambia have for long been an example of the former, while f.i. Liberia has been illustrative of exclusionary policies. Ethnicity is important in the allocation of budgetary resources, the provision of infrastructural facilities and job recruitment. The latter is relevant to the composition and cohesion of political parties, the military and civil service. Often the appointments to the government itself are evidence of the ethnic coalition or exclusion policies followed by African regimes.[33]

The modern elite

Because class formation is still in an incipient stage in many countries, this chapter refers to the different sections of the petty bourgeoisie as the "modern elite". The elite concept implies some social mobility and impermanence of social status.[34] Our study focuses on two specific sections in the modern elite. One is called the "state elite" and the other is collectively termed "non-governmental groups" or "groupings".

For the purpose of this study the state elite is held to consist of the top echelon exercising or representing central government power: the head of state, ministers, presidential advisers, party leaders, senior military officers, heads of departments and diplomats. This group is to a greater or lesser extent involved in the management of foreign affairs.[35]

The term non-governmental groups refers to that section in the modern elite that is denied access to governmental power and privilege but enjoys some, or aspires to, elite status: for example, the student corps and members of the modern elite of particular

---

32   See generally M.U. Ekpo (ed), *Bureaucratic Corruption in Sub-Saharan Africa: Toward a Search for Causes and Consequences* (Washington, 1979).

33   See f.i. D. Rothchild, 'An Interactive Model for State-Ethnic Relations', in F.M. Deng and I.W. Zartman (eds), *Conflict Resolution in Africa* (Washington, 1991), p 190 ff.

34   Elites may be defined as minorities set apart from the rest of society by their pre-eminence in the distribution of deference, authority, achievement or reward. After S. Keller, 'Elites', in D.L. Sills (ed), *International Encyclopaedia of the Social Sciences* (no pl., 1968), vol. V, p 26. See also G. Blanchet, *Elites et changements en Afrique et au Sénégal* (Paris, 1983), pp 99-100 and 120 ff.

35   Cooperstock, 'Some Methodological and Substantive Issues', pp 27-29 and S. Chodak, 'Social Stratification in sub-Saharan Africa', in *Canadian Journal of African Studies*, 1973, p 411. Those that are sent to occupy positions in the secretariats of international organizations as the OAU have similar status and background. Yet, for clarity's sake they will be referred to as distinct from the "state elites". See for a comprehensive overview of governmental structures and positions in African states Blanchet, *Elites et changements*, pp 92-94 and Cooperstock, 'Some Methodological and Substantive Issues', p 27.

regional or ethnic origin. In our study the term non-governmental groupings pertains to the leading echelons of these groups: *i.e.* political exiles; leaders and members of opposition parties; and the principal ranks of ethnically or regionally based guerrilla movements. These usually express critical views of the OAU, something that reflects their social background as modern elite section without access to state power.[36]

Before we discuss, in outline, the changing relations between the state elite and the surrounding society, some remarks must be made about the values of the modern elite as a whole, as these have a direct bearing on the foreign policies pursued by African states. The modern elite is very important as mediator between Western and, what is seen as, traditional values. During the colonial era members of the modern elite began articulating a marked ambivalence towards both traditional culture and the Western world. Many had enjoyed some colonial education, which inculcated Western values and condemned various traits of African culture. Admiration for Western technological capabilities was combined with an inferiority complex, created by an awareness of Africa's humiliating colonial status. Colonial education and a privileged economic position, as compared to the rest of society, resulted in a sense of alienation from one's traditional cultural background.[37]

However, frustrations over denied career opportunities, the realization of the fallacy of Western moral superiority and experiences with racism complicated these attitudes. This awareness led, especially during the 1950s, to a growing emphasis on (elite) African dignity and aspirations to equal status with the West. These objectives were articulated in the ideologies of nationalism, Pan-Africanism and different forms of socialism.[38]

Yet, attitudes towards traditional values remained ambivalent. Some aspects of tradition were rejected, some were idealized and others were merged with modern values. An example of the first is the critical attitude to the continued existence of chieftaincy, which was frequently looked upon as an obstacle to nation-building and socio-economic progress.[39] Among elements that were idealized figured the form of social organization in the pre-colonial era. A typical example of the fusion of modern and traditional beliefs is the political manipulation of witchcraft, which abounds in modern African politics.[40]

While the coming of independence mitigated the feeling of deprivation as experienced by the modern elite, it did not put an end to it. First, certain elite sections were excluded from government power or confronted with diminishing access to jobs and

---

36   See R. Buijtenhuijs, 'The Revolutionary Potential of Black Africa: Dissident Elites', in *African Perspectives*, 1978, pp 135-145. On African elites generally E.M. Bruchhaus (ed), *Afrikanische Eliten zwanzig Jahre nach Erlangung der Unabhängigkeit* (Hamburg, 1983); P.C. Lloyd, 'Introduction' and A.W. Southall, 'The Concept of Elites and their Formation in Uganda', both in P.C. Lloyd (ed), *The New Elites of Tropical Africa* (London, 1970), pp 53, 38-39 and 343-346; and a recent analysis by R. Weiss, *Zimbabwe and the New Elite* (London and New York, 1994).

37   R. July, *The Origins of Modern African Thought: Its Development in West Africa during the Nineteenth and Twentieth Centuries* (London, 1968), pp 460-466.

38   T. Hodgkin, *Nationalism in Colonial Africa* (London, 1956) and July, *Origins of Modern African Thought*, pp 466-472.

39   See f.i. K. Nkrumah, *Africa Must Unite* (New York, 1984 [1st ed. 1963]), pp 83-84.

40   See C.F. Fisiy and P. Geschiere, 'Judges and Witches, or How is the State to Deal with Witchcraft?: Examples from Southeast Cameroon', in *Cahiers d'études africaines*, 1990, pp 135-156 and E.A.B. van Rouveroy van Nieuwaal, 'Sorcellerie et justice coutumière dans une société togolaise: une quantité négligeable', in *Receuil Penant*, 1989, pp 433-453.

privileges. These people (the non-governmental groups) had every reason to articulate negative ideas about the state elite and its domestic and international policies. Economic contraction and the political manipulation of ethnicity only strengthened these antagonistic attitudes. The struggle over, and defence of, privileges and Western inspired lifestyles, both between elite sections and against society at large, merely intensified when economic conditions worsened.[41]

Second, the state elite itself has continued to experience feelings of deprivation, even though its position with respect to the rest of society has remained very comfortable. Deprivation has ensued from a continuing inferiority complex with regard to the Western world, as well as a sense of vulnerability to external (African and non-African) and domestic enemies: with regard to the latter it is shown below that the relation between state and society involves many (potential) conflicts and tensions. As argued in section 1.3 one basic reaction to deprivation may be, by way of compensation, a quest for power, especially if the person experiencing deprivation knows of others that successfully wield influence. For Africa's state elites the obvious examples to be emulated were, and are, their former rulers in the Western world. In section 2.3 we will look at the different postures to which this search for compensation gave rise in the realm of foreign affairs. The other basic reaction to deprivation, *i.e.* withdrawal, will be discussed there as well.

The growth of authoritarianism

While space does not allow a detailed exposition of the vicissitudes that have marked the relationship between state and society, some general remarks are called for. As was mentioned above, in practically all countries access to state power and economic wealth was to a greater or lesser extent curtailed. This occurred at various points in time, often already shortly after independence. Many factors were responsible for this. The widening gap between rich and poor, especially in some of the better endowed semi-peripheral countries, sharpened the conflict between the mass of the population and the modern elite. The latter tried to preserve its dominance by strengthening its inner cohesion and limiting the co-optation of other people. In most other countries diminishing resources and glaring gaps between expectations and realities led to a similar struggle.[42]

However, economic conditions do not explain everything. Like every social movement, the anti-colonial struggle carried in itself the seeds of domination by new rulers. Decolonization exposed contradictory social interests that had more or less been hidden during the struggle for independence. As any social movement, this struggle went in decline when there was no common enemy anymore to keep the nationalist front intact. Moreover, the growth of authoritarianism had much to do with the nature of the (post-)colonial state itself and the way it was introduced. The colonial state that preceded independence had been highly autocratic and the period of democratic government at the end of colonial rule had been brief. As it had grown out of external colonial forces, the state had been imposed on, and set up *against*, the various social forces in society, instead of evolving in continual conflict with it. It was the colonial powers that had forged the

---

41   See Lloyd, 'Introduction', pp 10-12 and Shaw, *Political Economy for Africa*, pp 42-43.
42   See Shaw, *Political Economy for Africa*, pp 99-102.

instruments of political control, which, with some exceptions, were inherited by Africa's nationalists relatively easily. Thus, the state was, upon independence, hardly embedded socially. Having few roots in indigenous political culture, society's political principles could not keep the state in check.[43]

Those with access to the state were therefore more or less freed from responsibilities towards society and could to some extent rely on external economic aid. Thus, the state elite could quickly develop totalitarian pretentions. With the concomitant expansion of a new bureaucracy, the state became, in a way, overdeveloped as compared to the society that had to bear it. However, in many cases it also remained a "soft" state, due to lack of political legitimacy, a limited economic base and the limitations on the actual control exerted over society.[44]

The role of the head of state was crucial in the process towards authoritarianism: while in some countries, like Ghana under Nkrumah and Tanzania under Nyerere, it was aided by the charisma of the incumbent leader, practically all countries developed some sort of leadership cult.[45] The degree of personalized control varied from country to country, with the highest level of individualized power, and its crudest exertion, in small countries with a marginal modern elite and underdeveloped institutions. Equatorial Guinea is an example.[46]

In all countries the bureaucracy was subordinated to the president, whose control of policy was augmented by the relative absence of constitutional checks and balances. Many former British colonies quickly departed from the Westminster model and Francophone states followed the example of the Fifth Republic: besides the usual responsibilities, the president often obtained emergency powers and, in the case of Francophone countries, legislative powers as well. Ministers would be responsible to the head of state, rather than parliament.[47] The latter lost much of its influence and the independence of the courts was to a greater or lesser extent circumscribed. The media were, with the exception of countries with a relatively free press such as Nigeria, put under tight control. Human rights were quickly curtailed by parliament or executive.[48]

The one-party state
In this context an important institutional development was the introduction of one-party structures. Its goal was to prevent forms of autonomous organization in society.[49] In

43   M. Doornbos, 'The African State in Academic Debate: Retrospect and Prospect', in *Journal of Modern African Studies*, 1990, pp 179-198; and J.F. Bayart, 'Civil Society in Africa' and J. Lonsdale, 'Political Accountability in African History', both in P. Chabal (ed), *Political Domination in Africa: Reflections on the Limits of Power* (Cambridge, 1986), pp 109-125 and 126-157.

44   Doornbos, 'African State in Academic Debate'; P. Chabal, 'Introduction: Thinking about Politics in Africa', in Chabal, *Political Domination*, pp 1-16; and C. Leys, 'The "Overdeveloped" Post-Colonial State', in *Review of African Political Economy*, 1976, pp 39-48.

45   Blanchet, *Elites et changements en Afrique*, pp 84-85.

46   Bayart, 'Civil Society in Africa', p 110.

47   A. Mahiou, *L'avènement du parti unique en Afrique noire: l'expérience des états d'expression française* (Paris, 1969), pp 95-97.

48   See B.O. Nwabueze, *Presidentialism in Commonwealth Africa* (London and Enugu, 1974).

49   Bayart, 'Civil Society in Africa', p 110 and A. Zolberg, *Creating Political Order: The Party Structures of West Africa* (Chicago, 1966).

most cases party organization took on highly centralized and hierarchical forms, which could reach down to village level. Mali's "Union Soudanaise" under Modibo Keita is a typical example. The structure of these parties often closely parallelled, and linked up with, state administration by way of overlapping membership. The party bureau, consisting of party chiefs and some government leaders such as the head of state, could exercise considerable influence over the council of ministers.[50] In most states, recruitment, functioning and control of the bureaucracy became heavily dominated by the party, leading to nepotism and the politicization of the civil service. The degree of assimilation to the state administration varied, as did internal party cohesion. Conflicts between party factions would in the final resort be settled by the party chief, *i.e.* the head of state, whose power put a check on party influence. Other organizations, such as women associations, youth brigades and trade unions, were often attached to, or fused with, the party structure.[51]

The military
The armed forces were, and often still are, another important institution in the state's attempt to control society. The role, size and structure of Africa's armies must be explained by reference to their colonial origins. As their main duty was to sustain European rule, they were the guarantor of internal, rather than external, security.[52] The infantry therefore constituted the largest part of the armed forces and this hardly changed after independence. Air and naval forces are, with the exception of South Africa, Nigeria and Egypt, still grossly underdeveloped. Africa's armies mainly consist of volunteers and suffer considerable technical, organizational and logistical limitations with regard to external defence, especially if compared to the military in other regions. While there are usually some elite forces like paratroopers and a gendarmery or presidential guard, these also have mainly domestic duties.[53]

Thus, although their external role is limited, African armies represent a powerful force within society. In many countries independence led to growth in terms of personnel and weaponry. Between 1966 and 1975, Africa's armed forces grew by 48% and paramilitary forces by 144%.[54] Although governments took measures to keep the military out of the political arena, the coup d'état in Togo (1963) already showed their limited effectiveness. By the mid-1980s, Africa had witnessed 47 successful military

---

50   Mahiou, *L'avènement du parti unique*, pp 291-300.
51   A recent analysis of one party rule in O. van Cranenburgh, *The Widening Gyre: The Tanzanian One-Party State and Policy Towards Rural Cooperatives* (Delft, 1990). Also M. Rambourg, 'Parti unique et administration en Afrique', in *Canadian Journal of African Studies*, 1968, pp 140-146 and G.M. Carter (ed), *African One-Party States* (Ithaca, 1962).
52   See C.E. Welch, 'The Roots and Implications of Military Intervention', in C.E. Welch (ed), *Soldier and State in Africa: a comparative analysis of military intervention and political change* (Evanston, 1970), pp 6-9.
53   See f.i. M. Janowitz, *Military Institutions and Coercion in the Developing Nations* (Chicago and London, 1977), pp 30-31 and 108-109 and W.J. Foltz, 'Military Influences', in V. McKay (ed), *African Diplomacy: Studies in the Determinants of Foreign Policy* (London, 1966), pp 70-72.
54   Figures exclude Nigeria and Egypt. Janowitz, *Military Institutions and Coercion*, pp 34-37 and 44-45.

interventions besides a host of failed attempts.[55]

While the weakness of civilian regimes in the face of economic problems is fundamental to an understanding of military intervention, its causes can frequently also be traced to corporate issues: complaints about rank, salaries and army resources and internal (social, ethnic) cleavages. In general, army intervention signifies the mere circulation of sections within the modern elite. Coups with a strong political, reformist programme as in Ethiopia and Sankara's Burkina Faso have been exceptional. Usually, economic contraction, lack of legitimacy and the failure to revitalize society make military regimes more authoritarian. While the military remains one of the most powerful institutions in society, its social and ethnic composition severely restricts its role as a stabilizing force.[56]

Civil society

During the last three decades, levels in repression have differed from country to country. In countries with a relatively autonomous business class, such as Nigeria, Kenya, Cameroon and Senegal, the state has been confronted with social forces that form an obstacle to uninhibited growth in the state's repressive apparatus. In countries where the state has been in full control of capital accumulation and this is used for patronage, such as in Zaire and Gabon, there have been fewer barriers to state coercion. Especially countries with very small populations and those where capital has been fully appropriated by the state, the degree of control could become proportionately greatest. The Central African Republic is a case in point. The crude forms of repression as exemplified in these one man dictatorships did not occur in countries with relatively well developed single parties. In this respect one may think of countries like Zambia, Tanzania and Kenya under Kenyatta, where these institutions could to some extent mitigate social conflict.[57]

However, during the 1970s and especially the 1980s it became increasingly clear that acquiescence to authoritarian rule had its limits. By then, authoritarianism had by and large only brought economic failure and political decay. In most cases, the state showed insufficient capacity to guarantee a take-off in development. In response, the various social forces that were excluded from governmental power and privilege were becoming increasingly defiant of the inroads made by the state. Africanists refer to these social forces with the term "civil society", a concept that applies to all those who are disenfranchised by the state: peasants, nomads, slum dwellers, members of specific ethnic groups, people in peripheral areas, as well as members of the modern, urbanized elite that are denied access to the state. Civil society alludes to the processes by which these social forces try to counteract state pressures.[58]

In Africa these processes have taken a bewildering variety of forms. Peasants

55   R.O.A. Ogunbambi, 'Military Intervention in Independent African States Revisited: A Review 1960-1983', in *Afrika Spectrum*, 3, 1984, p 293; Welch, 'Roots and Implications of Military Intervention', pp 6-14; and M. Benchenane, *Les armées africaines* (Paris, 1983), pp 75-128 and 214.

56   See T.R. Gurr, 'Theories of Political Violence and Revolution in the Third World', in Deng and Zartman, *Conflict Resolution in Africa*, p 153 ff and S. Decalo, *Coups and Army Rule in Africa: Studies in Military Style* (New Haven and London, 1976), ch. 1.

57   Bayart, 'Civil Society in Africa', pp 109-125.

58   See Doornbos, 'African State in Academic Debate' and Bayart, 'Civil Society in Africa'.

disengaged to a greater or lesser extent from the market economy by refusing to grow specific crops or reverting to subsistence farming. Declining agricultural productivity was matched by strike action in the urban areas. The strangle-hold of one-party rule was challenged by rising abstention rates at the polls and informal information circuits. Alternative forms of socio-economic organization appeared: different economic self-help groups, rural and urban collectives, but also more destructive enterprises as banditry. Religious revivals in the form of millenarian movements, Christian born-agains and Islamic "fundamentalism" took a firm hold. Social success at group expense was attacked by way of witchcraft. In many instances there was a renewed emphasis on ethnicity, as a form of protest and protection against state encroachment and economic stagnation.[59] In some cases the state itself disengaged to a greater or lesser extent from the surrounding society:[60] during the 1980s structural adjustment led to its withdrawal from several economic sectors, while in countries like Zaire, it shook off practically all pretence of performing normal governmental functions.[61]

Nevertheless, in several cases state elites were confronted with open, armed revolt. After the mid-1970s civil strife became more and more violent, partly as a result of increased arms procurement and foreign involvement. In the worst cases, such as Chad, Uganda, Mozambique, Ethiopia and Angola, perennial civil war took hold of the political fabric, taking ever higher tolls in life and uprooting millions of people.[62] In these cases, geographically peripheral areas such as frontier regions were naturally the first to slip from state control. These areas have always enjoyed some degree of autonomy, while the frontiers themselves are relatively permeable and thus provide ample opportunity for cross border traffic.[63] More widely, in many countries state sovereignty became increasingly precarious during the 1980s and early 1990s as a result of increased aid dependence; intrusion by NGO's and international financial institutions; and, in some instances, assumption of control by UN peace-keepers. In the worst cases, it almost amounted to recolonization.[64] In the wake of (near) state collapse, such as in Zaire, Liberia and Somalia, international recognition, bilaterally as well as through the OAU and the UN, began to form a principal guarantee of state survival.[65]

---

59 *Ibid.*; D. Rothchild and N. Chazan (eds), *The Precarious Balance: State and Society in Africa* (Boulder and London, 1988); W. van Binsbergen and G. Hesseling (eds), *Aspecten van Staat en Maatschappij in Afrika* (Leiden, 1984); and T.M. Shaw, 'Ethnicity as the Resilient Paradigm for Africa: From the 1960s to the 1980s', in *Development and Change*, 1986, pp 587-605.

60 Doornbos, 'African State in Academic Debate'.

61 C. Young and T. Turner, *The Rise and Decline of the Zairean State* (Madison, 1985) and J.C. Willame, *L'autonomne d'un despotisme: pouvoir, argent et obéissance dans le Zaïre des années quatre-vingt* (Paris, 1992).

62 See f.i. R.W. Copson, *Africa's Wars and Prospects for Peace* (New York and London, 1994), ch. 2.

63 See A.I. Asiwaju (ed), *Partitioned Africans: Ethnic Relations across Africa's International Boundaries 1884-1984* (London and Lagos, 1985).

64 D.N. Plank, 'Aid, Debt, and the End of Sovereignty: Mozambique and its Donors', in *Journal of Modern African Studies*, 1993, pp 407-430.

65 See on this aspect R.H. Jackson and C.G. Rosberg, 'Why Africa's Weak States Persist: The Empirical and the Juridical in Statehood', in *World Politics*, 1982, pp 1-24.

The rise of multi-partyism

However, state contraction does not necessarily lead to its collapse.[66] As there are relatively few forms of viable, institutionalized forces fully outside the state sphere, the revolutionary potential of civil society is not without its limits. Until the early 1990s, African states were still strong enough, for example, to prevent the secession of parts of their territory, with the exception of Somalia and Ethiopia.

Nevertheless, by the late 1980s increasing pressures of civil society combined with fundamental changes in the international context to put an end to single party rule. In the wake of the end of Cold War rivalry and Africa's continuing economic marginalization, Western countries formulated tougher conditions for the granting of aid: besides structural adjustment African states were asked to begin a process of democratization or at least a transition to a multi-party system. In order to understand the effects that these developments have had, until now, on Africa's international relations and, more particularly, the role of the OAU, a few general remarks must be made here.

The call for democratization has emanated mainly from urban sections of the modern elite: professionals, students, trade unions, but also representatives of universal churches.[67] As the peasantry has been less conspicuous, the struggle for a multi-party system to some extent by-passes the rural mass. Thus, at the polls abstention rates have often been very high. Moreover, in countries where the ruling party was defeated, such as in Zambia, prominent members of the modern elite have more or less managed to maintain their position. Their networks of patronage may be under economic pressure but they still enable them to exert great influence, even if the more narrowly defined state elite is replaced by a new political leadership.[68]

Recent political developments therefore provide a rather multifarious picture. In many countries, such as Benin, Madagascar and Niger, ruling parties and incumbent presidents had to make way for other parties. However, in some of these cases, such as Congo, the combination of economic constraints and multi-partyism did not contribute to political stability. Moreover, in other countries the ruling party managed to consolidate itself in the face of a divided opposition. Ivory Coast, Ghana and Guinea are examples. In some cases, the call for democratization led to total dead-lock between large sections of civil society and the state elite. Cameroon, Kenya, Togo and Zaire are typical of this.[69] In the worst cases the struggle between state and civil society degenerated in civil war, such as in Rwanda, Somalia and Liberia. Thus, in many countries the top echelons of central government — what we have termed the state elite — found themselves by the early 1990s embattled or paralysed.

---

66   Doornbos, 'African State in Academic Debate'.

67   See f.i. R. Buijtenhuijs and E. Rijnierse, *Democratization in Sub-Saharan Africa (1989-1992): An Overview of the Literature* (Leiden, 1993), pp 39-43 and J. Healy and M. Robinson, *Democracy, Governance and Economic Policy: Sub-Saharan Africa in Comparative Perspective* (London, 1992), pp 129-130.

68   See f.i. the special issue of *Politique africaine*, October 1991, vol. 43.

69   See for further details f.i. Healey and Robinson, *Democracy, Governance and Economic Policy*; J.A. Wiseman, *Democracy in Black Africa: Survival and Revival* (New York, 1990); S. Decalo, 'The Process, Prospects and Constraints of Democratization in Africa', in *African Affairs*, 1992, pp 7-35; and R. Buijtenhuijs and C. Thiriot, *Democratization in Sub-Saharan Africa 1992-1995: An Overview of the Literature* (Leiden and Bordeaux, 1995).

2.3   The foreign policy of African states

Introduction

Foreign policy can be defined as a three-phased phenomenon, consisting of a cluster of orientations, a set of commitments to action and forms of actual behaviour.[70] Its explanation is extremely difficult, because foreign policy is determined by a large series of domestic and international variables, whose interlocking relations and effects on foreign policy output cannot be estimated with great precision. An analysis of the foreign policy of several states only compounds the problem.

We will therefore try to present a general overview of the variables that determine African foreign policy without pretending to explain the exact intricacies involved. The analysis will first pay attention to factors as domestic political-economic weakness and the social make-up of the modern elite and, second, to features that may be deemed suprastructural in a Marxist sense: the process of decision-making, the role of particular personalities and other institutional factors. Although the first set of variables is responsible for the long-term features of foreign policy, particular foreign policy profiles are the result of interaction between these and suprastructural elements.[71]

This section will only focus on the domestic factors. International variables, which more than others determine the outcome of African foreign policy, will be analysed in section 2.4. As already noted, however, the structures of international relations do not fully determine foreign policy. As there is often no clear sight on the costs and benefits of a specific policy choice, situations allow for conflicting strategies. Due to domestic political influences and different perceptions, state interests can be assessed in various ways. The interaction between states is therefore not exclusively determined by the structures of international politics.[72]

Before an analysis of foreign policy variables the objectives of those policies will be presented. This will be done in broad outline, as many aspects are only valid for specific circumstances or were developed in relation to the OAU and are therefore analysed in later chapters. The goals of foreign policy can be divided into short-term objectives and longer-term orientations that betray a government's general attitudes to the external environment. The discussion is limited to this latter group of fundamental, long-term strategies.

Security as foreign policy objective

One of the most important foreign policy objectives is the protection of the security and integrity of the state and its state elite against both internal and external enemies.[73] Only a few countries have aspired, at one time or another, to territorial expansion besides the

---

70   J.N. Rosenau, 'The Study of Foreign Policy', in J.N. Rosenau, K.W. Thompson and G. Boyd (eds), *World Politics: An Introduction* (New York and London, 1976), p 16.

71   See the introduction to T.M. Shaw and O. Aluko (eds), *The Political Economy of African Foreign Policy* (Aldershot, 1984).

72   Stein, *Why Nations Cooperate*, ch. 7 (n. 1). Also K.N. Waltz, *Theory of International Politics* (Reading, Mass., and London, 1979), chs. 3-4.

73   D. Thiam, *La politique étrangère des états africains* (Paris, 1963), pp 59-63.

protection of state security. Libya, Somalia up to 1980 and Morocco are cases in point.[74] In section 2.2 it was shown that African states are highly vulnerable to domestic threats to their security. Section 2.4 will deal with their vulnerability to external challenges. These may emanate from outside Africa, but very often also from within the region or the continent itself. The ensuing sense of insecurity is compounded by a continuing inferiority complex vis-à-vis the Western world.

It is often argued by exponents of the realist school in international relations that, as international relations are characterized by the absence of one central authority, there are always risks to national security. States are therefore preoccupied with security issues and they are always sensitive to an erosion of their capabilities.[75] While other theorists contend that the realists exaggerate the security issue, it is admitted that the degree of fear for one's security varies greatly among states.[76] In the context of this study we are, indeed, concerned with a category of states for which, in the words of Grieco, individual *survival*, rather than economic well-being, is very often the key foreign policy interest.[77]

During the last thirty years, African governments tried to secure this foreign policy goal in several ways. First, most regimes developed policies of bilateral co-operation. For example, Ethiopia favoured a policy of defence co-operation with other African states to ward off any threats to its territorial integrity. Many Francophone countries consolidated their ties with France. Land-locked countries developed close links with litoral neighbours to secure their access to the sea.[78] Second, numerous normative principles were laid down in Africa's inter-state relations in order to guarantee state security. Respect for national sovereignty, political independence, territorial integrity, sovereign equality and non-interference in internal affairs are obvious examples. Third, many states enlarged their armed forces in an attempt to discourage possible enemies. The arms build-up of the last three decades in countries like Algeria, Ethiopia, Egypt, South Africa and Nigeria, responding to various domestic and external pressures, is illustrative.[79]

Naturally, the importance of state security as a foreign policy objective differs with country and time. During the early years of independence many regimes were rather inexperienced in the conduct of foreign affairs, leading to a general nervousness in inter-African relations and a spiral of alliances and counter-alliances. Later some countries developed a quiet, defensive foreign policy, whereas others embarked on a more activist,

---

74   O. Aluko (ed), *The Foreign Policies of African States* (London, 1977); Shaw and Aluko, *Political Economy of African Foreign Policy*; R. Lemarchand (ed), *The Green and the Black: Qadhafi's Policies in Africa* (Bloomington and Indianapolis, 1988); I.M. Lewis, *A Modern History of Somalia: Nation and State in the Horn of Africa* (London and New York, 1980), chs. 8 and 10; V. Thompson and R. Adloff, *The Western Saharans: Background to Conflict* (London and Totowa, NJ, 1980), part III.

75   See J.M. Grieco, 'Anarchy and the Limits of Cooperation: A Realist Critique of the Newest Liberal Institutionalism', in *International Organization*, 1988, pp 485-507.

76   H. Milner, 'International Theories of Cooperation Among Nations: Strengths and Weaknesses', in *World Politics*, 1992, pp 466-496.

77   In this sense Grieco, 'Anarchy and the Limits of Cooperation'.

78   See Aluko, *Foreign Policies of African States* and Shaw and Aluko, *Political Economy of African Foreign Policy*.

79   See f.i. W.L. Barrows, 'Changing Military Capabilities in Black Africa', in W.J. Foltz and H.S. Bienen (eds), *Arms and the African: Military Influences on Africa's International Relations* (New Haven and London, 1985), pp 99-120.

self-assured course in foreign affairs. Examples of the first are Kenya, Nigeria until 1966 and Ethiopia, while the foreign policy of Nyerere's Tanzania is illustrative of the second. By the early 1990s, however, national security and the survival of the state elite had in many cases again acquired top priority.

Moreover, as novices on the international scene, Africa's post-colonial states were, and are, intent on ending or modifying some of the (economic, political, military, diplomatic) inequalities ingrained in the international order. This interest in *reform* of the international system involves a desire to improve the status of Africa, its component states and, concomitantly, their state elites. It is shared by practically all African governments in their common capacity as weak newcomers to the international system.[80]

As individual states, however, their behaviour is often dictated by more direct, short-term security concerns. These entail an important stake in the *preservation* of the international system: in view of their security needs African regimes desire predictable state behaviour and orderly relations and they are to a greater or lesser extent prepared to collaborate with powerful countries in the Northern hemisphere, *i.e.* principal defenders of the present international order.[81]

The contradictory demands of immediate state security and mitigation of international inequalities are, however, two dimensions of one and the same security objective. In security issues elite perceptions play an important role.[82] As the perceptions of Africa's state elites about their international status are related to colonial experience[83] and awareness of the discrepancy in power between North and South, their (perceived) security hinges to a considerable extent on the question how the continent can achieve some sort of autonomy with regard to extra-African powers. It will be shown in chapters 7 and 8 that in the post-Cold War era this by and large still holds true.

Thus, African state elites have adopted certain psychological postures and, in relation to this, tried to realize some common, concrete foreign policy objectives, in order to compensate for the deprivation ensuing from their vulnerability to domestic-external enemies and their inferiority complex with regard to the Western world:
1. Many state elites have frequently articulated differen versions of conspiracy theory, which is a defensive, psychological way to either compensate for the deprivation suffered or, on which more below, withdraw from social interaction. It involves references to real or imaginary enemies. While these enemies are usually unidentified, references often allude to non-African powers, which are accused of fomenting and exploiting disunity among African states or threatening them with some hostile act. Although conspiracy theory betrays a sense of insecurity with regard to the external environment, it often points to domestic tensions as well.[84]

---

80 M. Ayoob, 'The Third World in the System of States: Acute Schizophrenia or Growing Pains?', in *International Studies Quarterly*, 1989, pp 67-79.

81 *Ibid.*

82 Milner, 'International Theories of Cooperation', p 490.

83 Ayoob, 'Third World in the System of States'.

84 See R. Girardet, *Mythes et Mythologies Politiques* (Paris, 1986), pp 48-57; J. Rogalla von Bieberstein, *Die These von der Verschwörung 1776-1945: Philosophen, Freimaurer, Juden, Liberale und Sozialisten als Verschwörer gegen die Sozialordnung* (Frankfurt, Bern and Las Vegas, 1978); and M. Zonis and C.M. Joseph, 'Conspiracy Thinking in the Middle East', in *Political Psychology*, 1994, pp 443-459.

2. Africa's state elites have persistently aspired to, an defended, equality of status with state elites elsewhere in the world.

3. Related to this, the continent's state elites have for long attempted to achieve concrete forms of multilateral co-operation, paraphrased as "African unity". This aim involves the reflection that the continent, united by inter-African co-operation, may function as a sort of "leverage mechanism". This mechanism can provide state elites with greater security and more influence than they exert individually, as well as enlarge the power of Africa as a whole vis-à-vis the rest of the world.

Following chapters will argue how these psychological postures and concrete objectives have found expression in the OAU, both in terms of its actual functioning and the roles attributed to it by state elites. In the course of this it will also be shown how the Organization sometimes facilitates the other basic reaction to deprivation, namely withdrawal from social interaction. It is submitted that in the context of the OAU this often takes the form of escapist constructs of reality. In this respect it should be realized that foreign policy provides state elites with access to the world of international diplomacy, whose attendant glamour can soothe psychological insecurity.[85]

Other foreign policy objectives

Another foreign policy objective is the realization of economic development. Up to the 1980s, two different strategies were, broadly speaking, followed to realize this goal: collaboration or confrontation with the structures of the international economic system. The majority of countries, following the state capitalist model of development, accepted the structures of the international economy, either whole-heartedly or by necessity. Only a few countries, usually following state socialist models, made some effort to change the international role of their economy and the nature of international economic exchange. Both strategies involved a search for investment capital or aid; diversification of trade flows; and attempts at economic co-operation with other African countries. Many countries in the first group quickly consolidated their links with the former colonial power or accepted their ties of dependence on Western economies. Gabon is a typical example. Countries in the second group, such as Ethiopia after 1974, Guinea, Angola and Mozambique, made vain attempts to obtain sufficient capital from the Eastern bloc.[86] Countries that accepted or developed close ties with Western countries were often considered as belonging to the group of conservative or moderate OAU member states. Those opting for close links with Eastern bloc countries were often perceived as belonging to the radical group.

However, most countries, whether more friendly to the West or to the East, had reservations about the functioning of the international economic order and at one time or another tried to push up prices for African exports. Many countries succeeded, to a

---

85   This contradicts an argument once made by R.A. Lystad, 'Cultural and Psychological Factors', in McKay, *African Diplomacy* (n. 53), p 118. See also the introduction to Shaw and Aluko, *Political Economy of African Foreign Policy*, p 8 and R. Good, 'State-Building as a Determinant of Foreign Policy in the New States', in L. Martin (ed), *Neutralism and Nonalignment* (New York, 1962), pp 3-12.

86   Aluko, *Foreign Policies of African States* and Shaw and Aluko, *Political Economy of African Foreign Policy*.

limited extent, to diversify their economic links, which meant diversification away from the metropolitan economies. Many embarked in this respect on policies of self-reliance and inter-African economic co-operation, though with different degrees of determination. Countries as Tanzania and Nigeria have been typical of this approach.[87] After 1980, a settlement of the debt problem became a major economic policy goal for virtually all countries. With the collapse of communism most of the policy differences between state capitalist and socialist governments diminished or disappeared. For most of them economic dependence, now especially by way of international financial institutions, remained a central concern.[88]

Up to c. 1990 another foreign policy objective concerned the attitude that should be adopted towards the conflict between East and West. The principle involved is called "non-alignment", which may be defined as the non-commitment to the world's dominant ideological blocs and the preservation of the right, and ability to judge, world issues on their merit without undue external influence.[89] It entailed an aspiration to greater political and economic autonomy and a minimization of security risks, for example by way of disarmament, denuclearization of specific regions and the peaceful settlement of disputes.

The pursuit of non-alignment led to co-operation with non-African countries in the wider non-aligned movement. However, interpretation of non-alignment differed from country to country. Many African countries, both radicals and moderates, tried to balance their economic and military ties with both East and West, while either maintaining strict neutrality towards, or reserving the right to judge on their merits, major international conflicts. Examples are Nigeria after 1966, Tanzania and Algeria. Several countries belonging to the conservative group, such as Egypt after 1972, Senegal and Ivory Coast maintained or strengthened their ties with the former colonial power and various Western states. Yet another group, consisting of Marxist-inspired regimes in the category of radical member states (f.i. Ethiopia after 1974, Angola and Mozambique), closely allied itself to the Eastern bloc. However, in most cases these different policies were all articulated as an implementation of non-alignment. Countries that did not pay lip-service to the principle, such as Ivory Coast, were an exception. Yet, when tensions between East and West began to diminish, such as during the early 1970s and late 1980s, the issue of military non-alignment lost much of its relevance and countries started to emphasize its economic component.[90]

The desire to end all forms of colonialism has been another foreign policy objective. African states supported liberation movements in various ways, which will be discussed in detail in chapter 6. However, the extent of support differed from country to country.[91]

87   See f.i. Aluko, *Foreign Policies of African States*; Shaw and Aluko, *Political Economy of African Foreign Policy*; Young, *Ideology and Development*, ch. 5; and A. Adedeji and T.M. Shaw (eds), *Economic Crisis in Africa: African Perspectives on Development Problems and Potentials* (Boulder, 1985).

88   See Nafziger, *Debt Crisis in Africa* and Tarp, *Stabilization and Structural Adjustment*, (n. 20).

89   After J. Okumu, 'Kenya's Foreign Policy', in Aluko, *Foreign Policies of African States*, p 158. Generally, G.W. Shepherd, *Nonaligned Black Africa: An International Subsystem* (Lexington, 1970), chs. 1-2.

90   Aluko, *Foreign Policies of African States*; Shaw and Aluko, *Political Economy of African Foreign Policy*; and D. Colard, *Le mouvement des pays non-alignés* (Paris, 1981), pp 127-141.

91   See for an effort to prove this by statistical means but yielding rather obvious conclusions V.B.

While some countries like Guinea, Tanzania, Mozambique and Angola, allowed liberation movements to use their territory as a basis for attack on neighbouring white regimes, other states like Kenya, Botswana and several Francophone countries were more passive in their support. Countries that actively supported the anti-colonial struggle often belonged, though not always, to the radical group. With the gradual disappearance of white minority and colonial governments, though, the objective of political liberation lost its priority and attention turned to the issue of economic decolonization.

Determinants of foreign policy: domestic weakness

An important domestic factor that influences foreign policy is economic underdevelopment. Section 2.2 has shown that, with some exceptions, national economies have remained weak, with little industrial development, poorly developed infrastructure, insufficient government revenue and a dominant agricultural sector whose food output does not keep pace with demographic growth. The weakness of the economic base, in combination with the precarious position of state elites, has important implications for political stability.

Together they have made the protection and consolidation of state security a primary foreign policy objective. Lacking sufficient economic and military resources, it becomes difficult to pursue an aggressive foreign policy towards other countries. Libya's record of foreign intervention, which was made possible by considerable oil revenues, is a rare exception. While some countries have faced domestic instability and external threats more than others, most governments have to adopt careful, defensive foreign policies to guarantee their own survival as well as minimal economic development. This does not negate the fact that states can harbour hostile intentions towards other countries. Economic weakness and potential instability, however, impose limitations on the choice of instruments with which those objectives can be implemented.[92]

Similarly, in the past most states could not afford active participation in the conflict between East and West. For many it became more profitable to try and play off one side against the other and reap greater economic benefits. Guinea in the Sékou Touré years is an example.[93] Yet, this non-aligned approach had its limitations. It depended on the seriousness of East-West rivalry, the strategic position of the country as perceived by the superpowers and the security needs of the state concerned. The sheer poverty of most African countries demanded the cultivation of relations with the West, which provided the bulk of aid and capital. The Francophone countries in particular had often little choice but to ally themselves with the former colonial power. Countries with serious security problems, like Zaire and Ethiopia, were also obliged to forge close links with powers in the Northern hemisphere.

At one level, anti-colonial policies were also related to the fear that colonialism formed a genuine threat to the military security of independent states, especially for countries sharing borders with European held territories. Even a country like Nigeria

Khapoya, 'Determinants of Support for African Liberation Movements: A Comparative Analysis', in *Journal of African Studies*, 1976, pp 469-489.

92   I.W. Zartman, *International Relations in the New Africa* (Englewood Cliffs, 1966), pp 87-105.

93   C. Rivière, *Guinea: The Mobilization of a People* (Ithaca and London, 1977), ch. 5.

could feel threatened by white minority regimes as they supported the secessionists in Biafra.[94] However, economic and military underdevelopment also meant that independent Africa could not risk direct, conventional warfare with the bastions of colonialism, but that it had to fight them with the more limited means analysed in chapter 6.

Determinants of foreign policy: the modern elite
The nature and social make-up of the modern elite provide another explanation for the foreign policies discussed above, as well as for some of the differences in these policies. For example, anti-colonial struggle as a foreign policy goal had a firm foundation in the nature and ideology of Africa's modern elites. Having originated through a process of decolonization, colonialism represented an insult to elite conceptions of honour and dignity.[95] The survival of pockets of colonialism sharpened the inferiority complex of many elite members. More narrowly, they called into question the equal status of the state elites with governments elsewhere in the world and emphasized their feelings of insecurity. While indignation about colonialism was closely bound up with the situation in dependent territories, support to the anti-colonial struggle served to legitimate the post-colonial order in independent Africa as well.

Some of the past differences in anti-colonial, economic and non-alignment policies must be explained by reference to the social make-up of the modern elite. For example, the top stratum of countries like Kenya, Ivory Coast, Zaire and Botswana is made up of prosperous members of the petty bourgeoisie. Although even they have at times expressed dissatisfaction about the inequalities in the structures of international exchange, they have important stakes in foreign trade, the extraction and export of mineral resources and plantation and ranching interests. The emergence of revolutionary regimes in neighbouring territories as a result of violent liberation struggles could have posed threats to international economic structures in ways detrimental to these elites. In its wake, the state elite could have faced potential domestic challenges to its hold on governmental power. Attempts to de-fuse those tensions and, concomitantly, more passive support to liberation movements and a more collaborative attitude vis-à-vis Western powers, were therefore fundamental to the protection of these economic and political interests.[96]

Similarly, more radical anti-colonial policies and, before the 1980s-1990s, attempts to restructure international economic relations and alignment with the Eastern bloc, can sometimes be explained by reference to the background of the state elite concerned. For example, the revolutionary origins of the state elites in Mozambique and Algeria resulted in warm military or economic contacts with the East and strong support for the anti-colonial struggle.[97]

---

94   O. Aluko, 'Nigerian Foreign Policy', in Aluko, *Foreign Policies of African States*, pp 171 and 186.
95   See f.i. J. Mayall, 'African Unity and the OAU: The Place of a Political Myth in African Diplomacy', in *Yearbook of World Affairs* (London), 1973, pp 126 and 133.
96   See for some of these countries, Shaw and Aluko, *Political Economy of African Foreign Policy*.
97   A. Ogunsanwo, 'The Foreign Policy of Algeria', in Aluko, *Foreign Policies of African States*, pp 25-30 and 33-38; and W.J. Schneidman, 'FRELIMO's Foreign Policy and the Process of Liberation', in *Africa Today*, 1978, no. 1, pp 57-67.

The process of decision-making: the presidential factor

There are several theories to explain the process of decision-making in foreign affairs. Examples are the "rational actor" model, the "cognitive" models and the "bureaucratic politics" model. Rational actor models postulate that a government behaves like an individual decision-maker, who acts on the basis of rational choice: when confronted with a certain problem, the decision-maker will look at alternatives, estimate their outcome and, on the basis of cost-benefit analysis, choose the policy that maximizes the fulfilment of his objective.[98] Yet, the basis of his choice does not have to be fully rational. The decision-maker may be faced with a lack of information about alternatives or outcomes and be forced to choose within a certain time limit. Given these constraints, he can only decide on the basis of subjective, or "bounded" rationality and, for example, opt for policies that are merely satisfactory, and not necessarily the best, for the realization of his objective.[99]

Other models therefore emphasize the role of perception in the process of decision-making. According to the cognitive theories decision-makers act on the basis of their *image* of objective reality.[100] Image and objective reality do not have to coincide. To gain insight in the operation of images of reality in the minds of decision-makers, some theorists have postulated the concept of belief system, which is a collection of personal views on empirical and normative issues.[101] Such a belief system acts like a filter when the individual perception of reality is constructed. Decision-makers are inclined to adapt or ignore incoming information if it contradicts previously held ideas.[102]

Some theorists argue that cognitive models can only play a secondary role as they suppose that the behaviour of governments is to a certain degree independent of individual perceptions.[103] Thus, several authors regard foreign policy as the output of standard operating procedures that limit the alternatives of politicians.[104] Others see it as the result of an internal negotiating process between actors with unequal influence. This

---

98   G. Allison, *Essence of Decision: Explaining the Cuban Missile Crisis* (Boston, 1971), pp 10-38 and R.B. Soetendorp, 'Analyse van buitenlands beleid', in K. Koch, R.B. Soetendorp and A. van Staden (eds), *Internationale betrekkingen: Theorieën en benaderingen* (Utrecht, 1994), pp 42-43.

99   See H.A. Simon, *Models of Man* (New York, 1957), pp 196-206 and Soetendorp, 'Analyse van buitenlands beleid', p 44.

100   K.E. Boulding, *The Image: Knowledge in Life and Society* (Ann Arbor, 1956), pp 5-6.

101   O.R. Holsti, 'Foreign Policy Formation Viewed Cognitively', in R. Axelrod (ed), *Structure of Decision: The Cognitive Maps of Political Elites* (Princeton, 1976), pp 18-54 and B.J. Verbeek, 'Cognitieve ideeën en internationale politiek', in *Acta Politica*, 1990, p 96.

102   R. Jervis, *Perception and Misperception in International Politics* (Princeton, 1976) and Soetendorp, 'Analyse van buitenlands beleid', p 48. Others claim that such an inclination depends partly on the extent to which their position of power is related to those incorrect ideas. See Verbeek, 'Cognitieve ideeën', p 99 and R.H. Lieshout and J.K. de Vree, 'How organizations decide: A systems-theoretic approach to the "behavior" of organizations', in *Acta Politica*, 1985, pp 129-155.

103   Soetendorp, 'Analyse van buitenlands beleid', p 49 and M.P. Sullivan, *International Relations: Theories and Evidence* (Englewood Cliffs, 1976), p 65.

104   See Allison, *Essence of Decision*, p 67 and Soetendorp, 'Analyse van buitenlands beleid', pp 50-52.

bureaucratic politics model emphasizes the power struggle between different groups and functionaries in a complex organization.[105]

The bureaucratic politics perspective has only limited relevance to the process of decision-making in African foreign policy. In Africa it generally approximates the situation described in the single or rational actor model in combination with insights of the cognitive theory.[106]

Zartman showed that the single actor model is applicable to the decision-making process as it evolved during the early 1960s. At the time decision-making became highly personalized and focused on the head of state. There were few institutional constraints that forced the president to reach decisions through a collective negotiating process. Foreign policy in particular was his natural preserve where other functionaries or institutions could not challenge his almost exclusive authority. Frequently, the president was his own foreign minister and in other cases the foreign secretary acted as his personal messenger who lacked an independent voice. Most decisions had to be taken by the head of state, even if it concerned very detailed issues. This meant that decision-making occurred on a serial and ad hoc basis, which slowed down progress and made long-term policy planning difficult. As the president was exclusively qualified in dealing with other heads of state, personal communication between presidents, with its attending travel and summitry politics, occupied an important place in foreign policy. In general, good inter-state relations depended to a large degree on personal friendships, which were sometimes inherited from shared experiences during the colonial period.[107]

While in some respects these features changed during the 1970s and 1980s, in others they remained the same. Ad hoc, serial decision-making and presidential concern with minute affairs were to some extent related to the underdevelopment and inexperience of the state elite. As many countries started multiplying their diplomatic ties, foreign ministries and the diplomatic corps expanded, taking minor issues away from the presidency. As the level of expertise in foreign affairs increased and several countries succeeded to formulate more articulate, coherent and long-term objectives,[108] foreign policy became more pragmatic and measured. Inter-state relations started to stabilize, although presidential friendships remained an important factor and the foreign minister continued to play a minor role.

Foreign policy in general continued to be dominated by the head of state, not only in small countries with limited economic and institutional development, such as Malawi, Niger and Djibouti,[109] but also in bigger or more developed countries where dictatorial

---

105 Allison, *Essence of Decision*, pp 144-148 and Soetendorp, 'Analyse van buitenlands beleid', pp 53-57.

106 C. Clapham, 'Sub-Saharan Africa', in C. Clapham (ed), *Foreign Policy making in developing states: a comparative approach* (Farnborough, 1977), p 88.

107 Zartman, *International Relations*, pp 53-54 and 65.

108 Ghana, Nigeria, Zambia, Senegal, Tanzania, Algeria, Angola and Egypt are illustrative in this respect. For more details, Shaw and Aluko, *Political Economy of African Foreign Policy* and Aluko, *Foreign Policies of African States*.

109 See C. McMaster, *Malawi - Foreign Policy and Development* (London, 1974), ch. 3; R.A. Higgot, 'Niger', in Shaw and Aluko, *Political Economy of African Foreign Policy*, pp 184-185 n. 7; and Ph. Oberlé and P. Hugot, *Histoire de Djibouti: des origines à la république* (Paris and Dakar, 1985), p 308.

powers guaranteed a near presidential monopoly. Somalia, Ethiopia and Zambia are typical examples.[110] In other countries, however, such as Angola, the growth of presidential power did not wholly eliminate the collegial factor or party autonomy, which had some effect on foreign policy formulation.[111]

In yet other cases the president had to balance and consult different group interests and could be termed a decision-"taker". He implemented a policy that was in some ways tied to domestic forces rather than the exclusive result of his personal choice. This was the case in countries with relatively extensive institutional and economic development or some semblance of democratic decision-making, such as Ivory Coast, Nigeria, Tanzania and Botswana.[112] However, even in these countries the president continued to dominate decision-making. In Tanzania, Nyerere enjoyed independence of action by his dual role of party chairman and state president. He could initiate many policies on his own, seeking approval by party and parliament afterwards.[113]

By the early 1990s, this state of affairs had not yet undergone many fundamental changes. While in many countries the process of democratization was derailed by, and led to the consolidation of, the incumbent president, in others a change in leadership was effected. However, it should be realized that in most political systems the conduct of foreign affairs eludes the same degree of parliamentary control as can be observed in domestic issue areas. Perhaps it is the very weak regimes, like Pascal Lissouba's government in Congo-Brazzaville, that must be careful to take account of domestic interest groups.[114]

To a certain extent, then, contents and style of foreign policy can be attributed to presidential personality. This implies that replacement of the head of state may cause considerable changes in foreign policy. The fall of Nkrumah led to an abrupt end to Ghana's Pan-Africanist objectives. The death of Kenyatta in Kenya led to an even stronger pro-Western stance because the new president had to consolidate his position.[115] The considerable degree of power that the head of state enjoys increases the relevance of his individual perceptions to the process of decision-making.[116] Thus, Sékou Touré's

110   Lewis, *Modern History of Somalia*, p 223; C. Clapham, *Transformation and Continuity in Revolutionary Ethiopia* (Cambridge, 1990), pp 32 and 232; and J. Pettman, *Zambia: Security and Conflict* (Lewes, 1974), pp 42-44 and 233.

111   See F. Soremekun, 'Angola', in Shaw and Aluko, *Political Economy of African Foreign Policy*, pp 29-30 and 52.

112   C.K. Daddieh, 'Ivory Coast', in Shaw and Aluko, *Political Economy of African Foreign Policy*, pp 125-126; S.S. Mushi, 'The Making of Foreign Policy in Tanzania', in K. Mathews and S.S. Mushi (eds), *Foreign Policy of Tanzania 1961-1981: A Reader* (Dar es Salaam, 1981), pp 5-15; and O. Aluko, 'Bureaucratic Politics and Foreign Policy Decision-making in Nigeria', in T.M. Shaw and O. Aluko (eds), *Nigerian Foreign Policy: Alternative Perceptions and Projections* (London and Basingstoke, 1983), pp 77-92.

113   Mushi, 'Making of Foreign Policy in Tanzania', pp 10-12. See for a different approach Aluko, 'Bureaucratic Politics', pp 77, 80-82 and 88-90 and W.A.E. Skurnik, *The Foreign Policy of Senegal* (Evanston, 1972), pp 256-295.

114   See f.i. *Africa International*, December 1993 - January 1994. See for a recent comparative analysis of African foreign policy T.M. Shaw and J.E. Okolo (eds), *The Political Economy of Foreign Policy in ECOWAS* (Basingstoke and London, 1994).

115   N. Chazan, 'Ghana' and V.B. Khapoya, 'Kenya', both in Shaw and Aluko, *Political Economy of African Foreign Policy*, pp 94-121 and 155-157.

116   M.G. Hermann, 'Effects of Personal Characteristics of Political Leaders on Foreign Policy', in

love for spectacular and dramatic gestures explains something of the style of Guinea's foreign policy, which under his rule frequently witnessed sudden twists in direction.[117] Libya's foreign relations have been equally subjected to the vagaries of its leader[118] and Ghana's determination in trying to implement Pan-Africanist objectives during the early 1960s depended entirely on the personal obsessions of Kwame Nkrumah. Nkrumah's example illustrates the degree to which individual misperception can play a role in foreign policy decisions. His persistent efforts to realize the idea of continental union ignored all signals of disinterest or opposition on the part of other African states.[119]

The process of decision-making: other institutional factors
However, the presidential factor does not explain everything, as the head of state does listen, or has to listen, to advice from certain people and institutions. We will finish this section by reviewing some of these groups and assess their influence on the decision-making process. An influential group of people are the advisors in the presidential staff, who constitute an important source of information and broaden the base of decision-making. Their freedom of manoeuvre is, however, difficult to ascertain. They may be relatives of the head of state or combine their advisory function with a diplomatic post in a metropolitan country. They may not only be nationals, but also exiles from other countries or Europeans. Membership by political exiles was a notable phenomenon during the early 1960s and could sour diplomatic relations and cause misperceptions in decision-making by distorted information. Expatriate advisors are relatively isolated within the political system and do not constitute a challenge to the authority of the president or upset a delicate ethnic balance in government. However, their presence may cause resentment among nationals.[120]

The cabinet or council of ministers may exert some influence on policy-making. However, in several countries the disintegration of the cabinet into smaller groups vying for presidential favour diminishes its influence, as does the infrequency of cabinet meetings. This influence may be greater in technical than important political issues.[121]

The influence of the party bureau may be greater, although this may now be a thing of the past. During the one-party era and especially in countries with elaborate party structures, such as Angola and Mengistu's Ethiopia, the bureau or central committee often played an important role in the formulation of foreign policy principles. It was also responsible for the maintainance of inter-party relations, which in some countries made it a crucial channel for international communication. In other states, however, the party became more subordinate to the presidency, as in Guinea, or the existence of several

---

M.A. East, S.A. Salmore and Ch.F. Hermann (eds), *Why Nations Act* (London, 1978), ch. 3.

117   L. Adamolekun, 'The Foreign Policy of Guinea', in Aluko, *Foreign Policies of African States*, pp 98-117.

118   See especially Lemarchand, *The Green and The Black*.

119   As his position was so closely bound up with, and legitimated by, Pan-Africanist action, these events confirm the hypothesis of Lieshout and De Vree (n. 102).

120   Zartman, *International Relations*, p 69. See for some examples, Daddieh, 'Ivory Coast', pp 122-123; and Pettman, *Zambia: Security and Conflict*, pp 43-44.

121   Zartman, *International Relations*, p 67. Examples in Aluko, 'Bureaucratic Politics', p 80; Mushi, 'Making of Foreign Policy in Tanzania', pp 10-12; and Pettman, *Zambia: Security and Conflict*, pp 45-46.

parties prevented assimilation to the state administration. Since the late 1980s, former single parties are facing considerable competition from new, rival parties. Their influence on the foreign policy process may therefore have diminished.[122]

The foreign minister often is a balancing political figure or trusted confidant chosen on political criteria rather than diplomatic expertise. He functions like a departmental chief performing administrative and technical tasks for the head of state and generally plays a subordinate role in formulation and execution of foreign policy. His position may be undercut by the use of other cabinet ministers in international negotiations and by the existence of a separate ministry of African affairs, as Ghana and Morocco had during the early 1960s.[123]

The foreign ministry itself was initially an underdeveloped institution which often started as a branch of the presidential office. As governments developed diplomatic ties, the ministry expanded. Although professional training improved, appointments to the ministry or foreign missions could, and still can, involve political and ethnic considerations.[124] While the ministry's role in policy formulation is not very great, its crucial task of collecting and processing information may provide it some influence, especially in larger, more developed countries. Nigeria is an obvious example.[125] As it is the nerve centre for the foreign missions, the ministry has an important role in the country's external communication, although several other ministries have independent access to the outside world. This may cause considerable problems of co-ordination.[126] After independence development institutions and parastatals increased international communication and during the late 1980s - early 1990s the growing influence of international financial institutions, UN peace-keepers and NGO's only compounded the problem.[127]

The influence of the diplomatic corps is therefore limited as well. It may affect the decision-making process by its supply of information, but all depends on whether or not diplomatic reports are given sufficient attention by those who can influence decision-making. Moreover, while the larger missions may be able to draw up thorough reports, the smaller ones are often preoccupied with basic administrative duties. The effectiveness of the diplomatic service, as well as the growth of a corporate identity, are undermined by the practice of sending special envoys to solve conflicts and the

---

122   For the one-party era Zartman, *International Relations*, pp 67-68 and 75-76; Mushi, 'Making of Foreign Policy in Tanzania', pp 5-8; Clapham, *Transformation and Continuity*, pp 84 and 233; Soremekun, 'Angola', pp 25-32 and 52; and Rivière, *Guinea*, p 144.

123   Zartman, *International Relations*, pp 66-67 and O. Aluko, 'Ghana's Foreign Policy', in Aluko, *Foreign Policies of African States*, pp 89-90.

124   See A.H.M. Kirk-Greene, 'Diplomacy and diplomats: the formation of foreign service cadres in Black Africa', in K. Ingham (ed), *Foreign Relations of African States* (London, 1974), pp 290-294 and S. Ojo, 'The Administration of Nigeria's Foreign Service, 1960-1980', in Shaw and Aluko, *Nigerian Foreign Policy*, pp 68-69.

125   See Aluko, 'Bureaucratic Politics'.

126   See Mushi, 'Making of Foreign Policy in Tanzania', pp 12-21 and Ojo, 'Administration of Nigeria's Foreign Service', pp 56-76.

127   See f.i. the case of Mozambique in Plank, 'Aid, Debt, and the End of Sovereignty' (n. 64).

appointment to mission posts of politicians or military officers whose domestic political position has become untenable.[128]

When in barracks the military do not constitute an important force in foreign policy-making, with the exception of decisions on arms purchases, defence agreements and inter-state crises in which the use of force seems likely. In general the army's major influence on foreign policy-making is its own weakness in external conflicts, which limits the choice of objectives as well as their manner of implementation. The foreign policies of military governments do not usually differ from those of their civilian precursor.[129]

While a relative lack of parliamentary control over foreign policy can also be observed in the Western world, the influence of African parliaments has in this respect been even more restricted.[130] The effects emanating from the rise of multi-partyism may, as was mentioned above, be rather limited. The role of public opinion in foreign affairs is in all parts of the world limited as well.[131] In Africa its influence was practically non-existent during the one-party era. However, even with the introduction of more liberal press policies, since the early 1990s, one should not over-estimate the role of public opinion. Low literacy rates and the complex relation between civil society and the state as a whole confine public opinion on international issues to sections within the modern elite.[132] This does not imply that domestic factors are irrelevant in foreign policy-making. Particular decisions may be effected by domestic pressures rather than the international environment. For example, the confrontation, in 1994, between the governments of Nigeria and Cameroon over control of a disputed peninsula had much to do with their precarious domestic position.[133]

2.4   The structures of Africa's international relations

Introduction
The approach in this section is state-centred, as states are the most important, although not the only,[134] actors in Africa's international relations. The analysis will show how the international system exercises crucial influence on the foreign policy of African states and, conversely, how their policies and actions influence, to a limited extent, the structures of their international relations. We will first assess their international relations with countries outside Africa, which are characterized by various forms of dependence. Then the structures of international relations between African states themselves, *i.e.*

---

128   On the development, size and structure of Africa's diplomatic missions, Kirk-Greene, 'Diplomacy and Diplomats', pp 279-319.

129   Zartman, *International Relations*, p 73; Shaw and Aluko, *Political Economy of African Foreign Policy*, p 375; and Foltz, 'Military Influences', pp 75-77 (n. 53).

130   See Zartman, *International Relations*, p 73 and for a specific example Mushi, 'Making of Foreign Policy in Tanzania', pp 8-10.

131   K.J. Holsti, *International Politics: A Framework for Analysis* (London, 1974), pp 381-387.

132   For an example O. Aluko, 'Public Opinion and Nigerian Foreign Policy Under the Military', in *Quarterly Journal of Administration*, Apr. 1973, pp 253-269.

133   See for example *Africa Confidential*, 15/4/94.

134   T.M. Shaw, 'The Actors in African International Politics', in Shaw and Heard, *Politics of Africa*, pp 373-382 (n. 30).

"inter-African" relations, will be analysed. This entails an appraisal of the distribution of power between them and the different sources of power that are relevant to the conduct of inter-African relations, with an emphasis on their more conflictual dimension. This is followed by an assessment of the possibilities of co-operation between African states and, in a broad sense, their actual patterns. We focus on those aspects that are specially relevant to the functioning of the OAU.

External dependence: the economic dimension
One of the most important characteristics of the international relations of African states, both peripheral and semi-peripheral ones, is the degree of dependence on the outside, non-African world. While the patterns of dependence have been changing, this has not resulted in a significant decline in the degree of external dependence. The nature of African dependence is primarily economic, but also extends to the military, political, cultural and social spheres.

The indicators of Africa's economic dependence are manifold.[135] Export commodities and the concentration of trading partners are of particular importance. The majority of states is dependent on the export of one or few agricultural products that provide little leverage in economic relations. Several countries, however, export important mineral resources and have attracted considerable foreign capital. This has stimulated growth and has enabled them to develop an influential role in regional relations. Examples are Libya, Algeria, Nigeria, South Africa and Zaire, but also Egypt, which has some manufacturing potential. Although these semi-peripheral states enjoy an influential position in inter-African relations, they are themselves dependent on regional exchange and extra-African markets. They are subject to external demands to adopt a collaborative approach towards foreign interests and remain vulnerable to fluctuations in international prices. The damage inflicted on the Zambian economy by falling copper prices is a good example. While European Union arrangements have cushioned against serious price fluctuations of African raw materials, their overall effects have been limited. European agricultural policies have also had depressing and destabilizing effects on international agricultural prices — and so indirectly on African economies.[136]

The possibilities for African cartels are limited by the influence that Western governments, multinationals and international financial institutions exert on African governments. In Southern Africa, the continent's major producer region of mineral resources, governments were for years controlled by collaborative white minorities. Nevertheless, several semi-peripheral countries enjoy greater leverage in extra-African relations because of their total share in the world production of important minerals. For

---

135   T.M. Shaw and M.C. Newbury, 'Dependence or Interdependence: Africa in the Global Political Economy', in M.W. Delancey (ed), *Aspects of International Relations in Africa* (Columbia, 1980), pp 58-59 and J. Adisa and A. Agbaje, 'Africa's Strategic Relationship with Western Europe: The Dispensability Thesis', in A. Sesay (ed), *Africa and Europe: From Partition to Interdependence or Dependence?* (London, 1986), p 137.

136   Ravenhill, 'When Weakness Is Strength' (n. 14), p 42 and O. Badiane, 'The Common Agricultural Policy and African Countries', in Zartman, *Europe and Africa* (n. 14), ch. 6.

example, with regard to chrome, uranium, gold, cobalt, platinum and diamonds this share ranges from thirty to seventy per cent.[137]

Europe remains Africa's chief source of dependence. Although British and French shares in the trade of their former colonies have decreased considerably since independence, France and Britain are still Africa's most important trading partners.[138] Bilateral trade ties have to some extent been replaced by dependence on the European Union as a whole, formalized in the Yaoundé and Lomé conventions. These arrangements have consolidated the continent's role of exporter of raw materials. Thus, EU preferences allow African countries to export 95% of their goods duty-free but block an expansion of the other five per cent, among which are certain crucial agricultural and live-stock products. Exports into Europe of manufactures are extremely low. Other EU arrangements have allowed relative preferential access of certain non-traditional products but not encouraged their global competitiveness. This has also been one of the effects of the Lomé Conventions.[139]

France and Britain have for long been the most important source of foreign private investment, which is concentrated in a limited number of countries like South Africa, Kenya, Zaire, Gabon, Nigeria and Ivory Coast. Britain and especially France also provide the bulk of Africa's development aid, although West Germany, the Scandinavian countries and, in some cases, Italy and Belgium, are important donors as well. European Union aid has also become progressively more important. More generally, during the 1980s official development assistance became the most important source of sub-Saharan Africa's total inflow of financial resources.[140] This did not keep pace with the growth in debt, however, and resulted in the near complete dictation of economic policy by the IMF and World Bank.

Relations between France and its former colonies have for long been much closer than in the British case. The Francophone countries are generally poorer than the English-speaking states and are tied to the former metropolitan power through an important monetary arrangement: most of them are united in the Franc zone, which involves a common, convertible currency, the CFA Franc. The CFA has a fixed parity to the French Franc and is guaranteed by the French treasury. At least up to the early 1990s, this arrangement entailed French protection against bankruptcy in return for the unhindered movement of capital, guaranteeing a near monopoly for French banking and commercial interests.[141] However, the importance of France's African interests has

---

137 Shaw and Newbury, 'Dependence or Interdependence', pp 46-49. Figures for 1981. A list of Africa's share in world mineral reserves and production in Adisa and Agbaje, 'Africa's Strategic Relationship', p 133.

138 O. Aluko, 'Africa and the Great Powers', in T.M. Shaw and S. Ojo (eds), *Africa and the International Political System* (Washington, 1982), table 1.

139 Zartman, 'Introduction', p 5 (n. 19); C. Cosgrove, 'The Impact of 1992 on EC-ACP Trade and Investment', in Zartman, *Europe and Africa*, pp 65-69; and Economou, Gittelman and Wubneh, 'Europe 1992', p 104 (n. 15).

140 67% in 1987. Riddell, 'Aid Performance', p 140 (n. 17). Also G. Arnold, *Aid in Africa* (London and New York, 1979), p 27 ff and Economou, Gittelman and Wubneh, 'Europe 1992', p 99.

141 B. Vinay, *Zone franc et coopération monétaire* (Paris, 1980).

somewhat diminished. In 1994, the CFA Franc was devalued, signifying a relative, though limited, French retreat from the African arena.[142]

The role of the United States has been minor as compared to European involvement. Trade, private investment and aid have been concentrated in a small group of countries like Egypt, Libya, Nigeria, Kenya, Ivory Coast, South Africa and Zaire. Soviet and Chinese economic aid have been much smaller, the Chinese-built Tazara railway in East Africa being an important show-piece. With the collapse of communism in Eastern Europe, the Russian role has diminished even further.[143]

While in terms of certain raw materials Africa is of considerable significance to other regions and countries, especially Europe and France,[144] it was noted in section 2.2 that this importance is diminishing. The European need for African products can in general also be satisfied by non-African economies without significant price increases. It should also not be forgotten that Africa represents a much smaller share in the external trade of Britain and France than vice versa. Interdependence between Africa and the outside world is therefore highly asymmetrical.[145]

External dependence: the military dimension
In the military sphere European dominance has been less clear-cut as a result of superpower rivalry. During the early 1960s and again from the mid-1970s the United States and Soviet Union actively intervened in regional conflicts such as the Congo/Zaire, Southern Africa and the Horn. The Americans developed important military links with Morocco, Egypt after 1973, Zaire, Ethiopia until 1974 and Kenya. The Russians gained influence through links with Somalia until 1976, Ethiopia (since 1977), Angola, Mozambique, Egypt until 1972, Guinea, Libya and Algeria. China and Cuba developed military ties with a limited number of states such as Tanzania, Angola and Ethiopia.[146] By 1980, the East European military presence in Africa totalled some 5,000 men, Cubans were some 35,000 strong and the United States had a substantial naval presence around the continent, including a rapid deployment force.[147] From the late 1980s, however, the number of East Europeans and Cubans began to fall sharply as a result of the Soviet collapse, as well as political developments in Namibia and South Africa. The Eastern bloc and the United States have possessed, at one time or another, important military facilities in Egypt, Angola, Kenya, Somalia, Ethiopia, Morocco and Diego Garcia.[148]

In spite of (former) superpower rivalry it must be noted that Britain and, especially, France enjoyed, and still enjoy, considerable influence in African countries, not only through arms supplies but also by the training of African officer corps, the retention of bases and direct military intervention. While after decolonization Britain strengthened its

---

142   See f.i. *Africa Report*, March-April 1994.
143   Shaw and Newbury, 'Dependence or Interdependence', pp 60-63 and A. Gavshon, *Crisis in Africa: Battleground of East and West* (Harmondsworth, 1981) pp 14 and 96.
144   G. Martin, 'Continuity and Change in Franco-African Relations', in *Journal of Modern African Studies*, 1995, pp 9-10.
145   Zartman, 'Introduction', p 5.
146   Shaw and Newbury, 'Dependence or Interdependence', pp 65-66.
147   Figures for military advisors and ordinary personnel. Gavshon, *Crisis in Africa*, p 175 and Barrows, 'Changing Military Capabilities', p 109 (n. 79).
148   See Gavshon, *Crisis in Africa*.

links with Kenya, Zimbabwe, Ghana and Malawi, France signed military agreements with a host of former colonies. These agreements entail military training, the supply of arms, the use of military bases and, if need be, armed intervention to defend state elites under threat.[149] Such intervention has occurred at least thirty times since 1963, of which nine operations took place between 1981 and 1994. Paris disposed, and still disposes, of bases in the Central African Republic, Chad, Djibouti, Gabon, Ivory Coast, Senegal and the Indian Ocean. By the early 1980s its military presence totalled some 15,000 men, which by 1993 had fallen to some 8,000. This excludes an intervention force of some 40,000 men which is stationed in southern France and can be flown in at a moment's notice. Together with the presence of a few hundred thousand French civilians spread over its former colonies this has made France into the dominant non-African power on the continent. The East European retreat after the late 1980s only enhanced its comfortable position.[150]

The West remained Africa's major arms supplier until 1976, when the Soviet Union started catching up. African arms imports reached record levels during the late 1970s. After a decline sub-Saharan arms imports picked up again during the second half of the 1980s. The collapse of communism did not halt the inflow of arms, as post-Cold War disarmament increased the number of potential suppliers and thus led to aggressive sales policies of Western and former Eastern bloc countries, as well as of industrialized countries in the Southern hemisphere like South Africa, Israel and Argentina, besides Iran.[151]

The continent's high degree of external military dependence has several implications for the development of inter-African relations. With the absence of any significant military industry, violent conflicts cannot easily be sustained without aid and armaments from outside. Domestic instability and inter-African tensions have therefore often been accompanied by external involvement, arms races and opposing alliances of African and non-African states. If conflicts continue for some time, increased dependence will be the result. The evolution from a bipolar world system towards a multipolar one enhanced the prospects for a diversification of extra-African ties. Yet, it also augmented, especially from the mid-1970s onwards, the sources of external penetration, increased international competition and intensified regional conflicts.[152]

External intervention does not simply occur because certain foreign powers wish to get involved, but results from the congruence of interests of African and non-African actors.[153] Non-African military intervention has always been a sensitive issue in inter-African politics. Yet, the relative absence of superpower involvement during the

---

149 Full-scale accords included those with Central African Republic, Gabon, Ivory Coast, Senegal, Cameroon and Comoros. Adisa and Agbaje, 'Africa's Strategic Relationship', p 142.

150 See f.i. Martin, 'Continuity and Change in Franco-African Relations', pp 12-14; E.K. Kouassi and J. White, 'The Impact of Reduced European Security Roles on African Relations', in Zartman, *Europe and Africa*, pp 28-31; and Gavshon, *Crisis in Africa*, pp 19, 175 and 297-298.

151 Gavshon, *Crisis in Africa*, pp 78-80; Foltz and Bienen, *Arms and the African* (n. 79), table 2.2; Kouassi and White, 'Impact of Reduced European Security Roles', tables 3.1 and 3.2; Kühne, 'Looking South' (n. 23), pp 20-21; and Copson, *Africa's Wars* (n. 62) , p 167.

152 Shaw and Newbury, 'Dependence or Interdependence', p 75.

153 T.M. Shaw, 'Africa in the World System: towards more uneven development', in Shaw and Ojo, *Africa and the International Political System*, pp 114-116.

decade of 1965 to 1975 was only partly the result of African non-alignment. The Americans could afford to work through their European allies and the Soviet Union preferred to challenge US interests in the Middle and Far East first. However, the 1970s witnessed increased acceptance of foreign troops by certain African states, as well as growing Soviet and American willingness to confront each other in the African theatre. Thus, the Horn and Southern Africa were transformed into major battle-grounds through a combination of domestic instability, proximity to strategic sea lanes and the latter's possession of important mineral reserves. After the early 1990s superpower involvement largely subsided, partly as a result of political developments in these countries themselves, but especially because of the end of the Cold War.[154]

Consequences of dependence for foreign policy
Thus, Africa is relatively powerless to prevent external economic, military and political penetration or, for that matter, disengagement. Yet, non-African influence is often limited too,[155] as the instability of African regimes may lead to sudden changes in foreign policy orientation and reduce the influence of a particular non-African actor. The quick demise of Soviet influence in Egypt after Sadat came to power is a typical example. Although the Francophone countries have preserved military, political, cultural and social ties with the metropolitan power, most states have tried to diversify political and military links, accepting military aid from East and West during the Cold War era. While relations with the West have remained dominant, diplomatic ties have in the past often been under stress due to colonial legacies and Western support for the white regimes in Southern Africa.

Nevertheless, the high degree of external dependence greatly limits the foreign policy options of African regimes. The perception of dependence may exert stronger influence on foreign policy than its empirical impact[156] because of educational backgrounds, foreign tastes and values, fatalism and lack of self-confidence.[157] In such a context, the glamour of foreign affairs provides state elites a psychological escape from reality rather than the possibility to implement a conscious choice. This partly explains why the vast majority of African states opt for a more or less collaborative approach in their foreign economic policies. In the past all attempts of countries such as Angola, Mozambique, Algeria, Ethiopia and Tanzania to confront the structures of dependence generally failed to achieve results. The pervasiveness of dependence, unwillingness to break all external ties and insufficient domestic reforms figure among the causes. Until the late 1980s, many of them depended on the Eastern bloc for military and economic assistance.[158] Yet, the end of the Cold War only strengthened dependence as the reduction

---

154   See R.A. Akindele, 'Africa and the Great Powers: with Particular Reference to the United States, the Soviet Union and China', in *Afrika Spectrum*, 1985, pp 125-151 and for a more recent analysis J. Harbeson and D. Rothchild (eds), *African International Relations* (Boulder, 1991).

155   See on this also Z. Laidi, *Les contraintes d'une rivalité: les superpuissances et l'Afrique* (Paris, 1986).

156   It is hard to measure precisely the effect of dependence on the freedom of manoeuvre. See S.M. Smith, 'Economic Dependence and Economic Empiricism in Black Africa', in *Journal of Modern African Studies*, 1977, pp 116-118.

157   Shaw and Newbury, 'Dependence or Interdependence', p 59.

158   See f.i. R.I. Onwuka, 'CMEA-African Economic Relations', in R.I. Onwuka and T.M. Shaw (eds), *Africa in World Politics: Into the 1990s* (Basingstoke and London, 1989), ch. 4.

of non-African powers on the scene removed the possibility to enhance one's autonomy by playing off one power against another.

Inter-African relations: economic and military aspects

The relations between African states themselves are more egalitarian. Ironically, dependence on non-African powers provides African states a degree of independence vis-à-vis each other. African governments put heavy emphasis on their formal equality, even if factual power disparities are considerable. At independence, the disparities in power between African states were not so obvious. In later decades, however, economic developments gave rise to considerable differentiation. Nigeria, Zaire, Algeria and South Africa became important actors in inter-African relations as they possess large populations, vast mineral reserves and/or, in the case of South Africa, a significant industrial base. Zambia, Angola, Ivory Coast, Egypt, Kenya, Libya, Senegal, Gabon and Zimbabwe may be regarded as economic powers of secondary importance.[159] Many of these countries serve as centres for regional economic interaction, which enables them to exert influence on their peripheral, often land-locked, neighbours.[160]

However, the extent of this influence may be limited by domestic instability, which has a disabling effect on the conduct of foreign affairs and allows other states to withstand pressure or even to interfere in the internal affairs of the semi-peripheral power. Angola, Nigeria at different points in time and Zaire are obvious examples. Moreover, the semi-peripheral countries are themselves dependent on their non-African allies. Contingent on their attitude, this may enhance or limit autonomy in inter-African relations.

Economic aid as a foreign policy instrument is only a viable option for some of the semi-peripheral countries. Negative economic sanctions may involve a closure of borders or mass expulsion of expatriates who are nationals of the target state. The effectiveness of border closures is usually limited, because frontiers are rather permeable and inter-African trade amounts to less than five per cent of total African exports due to the limited complementarity of African economies.[161] Yet, the resort to mass expulsions, usually by more prosperous semi-peripheral countries, can be very detrimental to the victim state.[162]

South Africa, Egypt, Ethiopia, Nigeria and Morocco have the largest armed forces on the continent.[163] Judging from their records of intervention, South Africa and Egypt must be ranked first in terms of external fighting capacity, followed by Morocco, Nigeria and Ethiopia.[164] Many African states have been involved, at one time or another, in arms races. These accompany regional tensions and greatly increase the intensity of warfare, as

---

159   Shaw and Newbury, 'Dependence or Interdependence', p 46. A list of their GNP's (figures 1970) in Seidman, *Economics Textbook for Africa*, pp 163-164 (n. 7).

160   See Z. Cervenka (ed), *Land-locked Countries of Africa* (Uppsala, 1973).

161   Economou, Gittelman and Wubneh, 'Europe 1992', p 116.

162   See f.i. O. Akinrinade, 'From Hostility to Accommodation: Nigeria's West African Policy, 1984-1990', in *Nigerian Journal of International Affairs*, 1992, no. 1, p 51 ff.

163   South Africa: c. 290,000; Egypt: 340,000; Ethiopia: 250,000; Nigeria: 133,000; and Morocco: 117,000. Figures early 1980s. On composition figures, see contributions in Foltz and Bienen, *Arms and the African*, (n. 79) pp 100, 142 and 174-175.

164   See *ibid.* for assessments of Africa's various armies.

illustrated by the Angolan civil war and the Ethiopian-Somali conflict of 1977-78.[165] For example, in 1979 the combined spending on arms by Egypt, Libya and Algeria totalled $4.4 thousand million. In the period 1976-80 Ethiopia obtained arms worth $2.3 thousand million, Angola for $950 million, Somalia $750 million and Sudan for $575 million.[166]

Nevertheless, as the history of Zaire and Ethiopia show, poor organizational capabilities, limited mobility and preoccupation with domestic conflicts reduce the external role of African armies. Subversion, rather than conventional warfare, is the dominant mode of military intervention: it is relatively cheap and easy to weaken neighbouring regimes by aiding political exiles that aspire to overthrow their own government. Guerrillas can be assisted with training, arms, finance and bases. If such rebellions succeed, the political pay-off is a friendly neighbour. However, the risks are considerable because a country's foreign policy may be tied to an unsuccessful cause, the presence of foreign guerrilla's may pose threats to national security and target governments may reply in kind. The complex alliances between central governments and liberation movements in the Horn of Africa during the 1980s are an extreme example.[167]

It has been frequently emphasized that Africa's inter-state frontiers are an important source of inter-state conflict.[168] As they were drawn by colonial powers that hardly took notice of local conditions, these borders partitioned hundreds of ethnic groups and cut across many wider cultural and economic complexes. Yet, while ethnic overhang and cross border traffic may become a cause of inter-African tensions,[169] boundary disputes have usually been caused by other sources of conflict, whether domestic or inter-African. Frontier disputes are often a pretext under which diverse issues are fought out or can be interpreted as international spill-over of different forms of domestic conflict.[170] Considering their arbitrariness, disputes over boundaries have been relatively infrequent. Among the causes one may mention disruption of domestic ethnic balance and the creation of precedents as a result of border revisions; international legitimation of colonial frontiers; and, in many cases, limited capacity for conventional warfare.[171]

Inter-African relations: other means of influence
If countries develop a stable, consistent foreign policy, implemented by an efficient diplomatic cadre, their influence may increase because other states will consider them as a credible and reliable actor. Tanzania and Senegal could be cited as examples.[172] Such

---

165   C. Legum and B. Lee, *The Horn of Africa in Continuing Crisis* (New York and London, 1979) and C. Legum, 'Foreign Intervention in Angola', in *Africa Contemporary Record*, 1975-76, A3-38.

166   Gavshon, *Crisis in Africa*, p 79 and Foltz and Bienen, *Arms and the African*, table 2.2.

167   Zartman, *International Relations*, pp 97-101 and the sections on Ethiopia, Sudan and Somalia in *Africa Contemporary Record*, 1986-87 and 1987-88.

168   See R.L. Kapil, 'On the Conflict Potential of Inherited Boundaries in Africa', in *World Politics*, 1966, pp 656-673. Kapil himself minimizes their destabilizing influence.

169   Examples in Asiwaju, *Partitioned Africans* (n. 63).

170   See J.B. Boyd, 'The Origins of Boundary Conflict in Africa', in Delancey, *Aspects of International Relations*, pp 159-189.

171   See generally S. Touval, *The Boundary Politics of Independent Africa* (Cambridge, Mass., 1972).

172   See T.M. Shaw, 'African states and international stratification: the adaptive foreign policy of

"prestige" may be enhanced by the quality of the political leadership. Presidential charisma may, in combination with personal ties with other heads of state, become an important channel through which influence can be exerted. The prestige of Haile Selassie in inter-African relations is a typical example. Especially during the 1960s this factor could, coupled with a strong reformist programme, attract a wide non-governmental following in other countries. The role of Ghana under Nkrumah, Tanzania under Nyerere and Egypt under Nasser are illustrative. To some extent this was related to the underdeveloped state of other means of power and inexperience in foreign affairs. Ghana could thus maintain an influential role that did not conform to its economic-military position.[173] However, the Ghanaian case also showed that such influence is relatively unstable as it depends on transitory conditions. During the last two decades these sources of influence have steadily diminished in importance.[174]

Closely related to the role of government ideology is the use of propaganda. Government newspapers and radio broadcasts are often used to articulate foreign policy statements, which may represent genuine government standpoints or consist of what a regime prefers to put across in an attempt to influence other governments.[175] However, during the single party era the flow of information could easily be controlled. Moreover, as noted in the preceding section foreign affairs generally fail to arouse the same degree of public interest as domestic issues and are less susceptible to public scrutiny. Just as the resort to a rupture in diplomatic ties, the use of propaganda points to some extent to the relative impotence of states to influence each other. Frequently, the use of propaganda degenerates into slander campaigns that merely increase existing tensions.[176]

Possibilities of inter-African co-operation
Generally, inter-state conflicts are related to high levels of domestic instability and rising inequalities between countries. However, the possibilities for one state to coerce another are slim, as the extent of influence that states wield is limited. Nevertheless, it is often contended that some semi-peripheral countries have the power to exercise leadership in Africa's regional, if not continental, relations. In this respect the concept of regional hegemony, discussed in chapter 1, is frequently used. States that have been mentioned as contenders for regional hegemonic leadership are Nigeria, South Africa, Libya and Ethiopia. One might also add Egypt, Zaire and Algeria.

Yet, one should realize that the extent of their influence is not without its limits. Claims to leadership by Libya and apartheid South Africa have always suffered from lack of legitimacy. Egypt and Algeria have always had to distribute their resources over the Middle Eastern and African theatres. By the early 1990s they were also seriously weakened by domestic instability, as has always been the case with Zaire. The end of the Cold War era could enhance the autonomy of regional hegemons, but in some cases it

---

Tanzania', in Ingham, *Foreign Relations of African States*, pp 213-233 and Skurnik, *Foreign Policy of Senegal* (n. 124 and 113).

173   Zartman, *International Relations*, pp 62 and 144-146.
174   Shaw and Newbury, 'Dependence or Interdependence', p 46.
175   On propaganda Holsti, *International Politics* (n. 131), pp 212-213.
176   Holsti, *International Politics*, pp 210-220 and Zartman, *International Relations*, pp 94-97 and 105.

also entailed the loss of vital superpower support. Thus, Ethiopia's position deteriorated significantly, as its influence could not offset the loss of superpower support to prevent its partial disintegration. None of the other contenders for regional hegemony has, at all times, been guaranteed of unreserved superpower backing. Even Nigeria's claim to regional leadership has always been disputed by other countries, notably Ivory Coast and France. It has also suffered, at one time or another, from domestic instability.[177]

Detached from its application in a regional context, the hegemon is defined, in hegemonic stability theory, as a state which stands alone without equals at the top of the international hierarchy of power and is more powerful than others in terms of ability to control outcomes of interaction.[178] It is thus obvious that the African state system lacks a continental hegemon. This has serious implications for possibilities of Pan-African co-operation. While it is often contended that, in the absence of a hegemon, co-operation is still possible,[179] it has also been hypothesized that, if the number of actors increases, prospects for co-operation diminish. Large numbers of actors increase the probability of cheating with regard to agreements and reduce the feasibility of sanctions against culprit states.[180]

However, one may argue that international regimes mitigate some of the negative effects emanating from large numbers of actors and thereby facilitate co-operation.[181] Yet in state systems characterized by lack of hegemonic leadership, large numbers of actors and intruding patterns of external dependence the resultant regimes, like the OAU, are themselves rather weak.[182] This will be shown in following chapters. This section concludes with a broad overview of the actual patterns that can be observed in inter-African co-operation.

Patterns of inter-African co-operation
Co-operation points to the phenomenon of actors adjusting their behaviour to the actual or anticipated preferences of others through a process of policy co-ordination. It can be tacit, without explicit agreement; negotiated in an explicit manner; or imposed by a stronger actor that forces others to adjust.[183] The actual patterns of bilateral and multilateral co-operation in inter-African politics have several dimensions. Here we will look at the

---

177   See also R. Lemarchand, 'On Comparing Regional Hegemons: Libya and South Africa', in Lemarchand, *The Green and the Black*, p 169 (n. 74); R. Iyob, 'Regional Hegemony: Domination and Resistance in the Horn of Africa', in *Journal of Modern African Studies*, 1993, pp 257-276; and E. Nwokedi, 'Le myth d'un leadership nigérian dans les relations inter-africains', in *Etudes internationales* (Quebec), 1991, pp 357-368.

178   Stein, *Why Nations Cooperate*, p 182 (n. 1) and I. Grunberg, 'Exploring the "Myth" of Hegemonic Stability', in *International Organization*, 1990, pp 431-477.

179   R.O. Keohane, *After Hegemony: Cooperation and Discord in the World Political Economy* (Princeton, 1984).

180   See f.i. K.A. Oye, 'Explaining Cooperation Under Anarchy: Hypotheses and Strategies', in K.A. Oye (ed), *Cooperation Under Anarchy* (Princeton, 1986), pp 1-24.

181   Milner, 'International Theories of Cooperation', pp 475-478 (n. 76).

182   D. Snidal, 'The Limits of Hegemonic Stability Theory', in *International Organization*, 1985, p 595 and R.L. Rothstein, 'Regime-Creation by a Coalition of the Weak: Lessons from the NIEO and the Integrated Program for Commodities', in *International Studies Quarterly*, 1984, pp 307-328.

183   Milner, 'International Theories of Cooperation', p 467 ff.

diplomatic, military and political ones. This final section only touches on them in a broad sense, as they will be studied in greater detail in the subsequent chapters on the OAU.

The configuration and intensity of inter-African co-operation can be gauged by looking first at the number and pattern of diplomatic missions that have been established in other countries.[184] Diplomatic interaction tends to be highest between neighbouring countries and between an African state and its former colonial ruler. Diplomatic representation at the UN and in other countries capable of dispensing aid is another priority.[185] The second level of inter-African activity, deduced from the number of missions established abroad, is the regional one. Here there are, in general, fewer diplomatic contacts between states in the same region than between neighbouring countries, although there are disparities between the different regions themselves. During the early 1970s interaction was highest among the states of North Africa, followed by those of Central Africa, West Africa, East Africa and Southern Africa. By the late 1980s these disparities had somewhat diminished as the rift between Egypt and its Arab neighbours had, at the time, caused a decline in North African interaction and the other regions had increased their own diplomatic exchange.[186] Inter-African relations have therefore to a limited extent become regionalized, a phenomenon that is accompanied both by opportunities for economic co-operation and fears of domination.[187] The most important regional powers like Nigeria, Algeria and Zaire are also the most active in regional interaction, although this dominance is less pronounced regionally than in continental patterns.[188]

Diplomatic interaction on a continental scale is the least intensive due to limited Pan-African economic integration. The phenomenal multiplication of states during the last three decades has made full diplomatic interaction impossible: in 1987 the total number of missions established in other African countries was 524 as opposed to a theoretical maximum of 2,450.[189] Those states that are the most powerful in economic or military respects or distinguish themselves in terms of leadership aspirations or ambitious foreign policies, are also the most active diplomatically. Thus, in 1975, Egypt, Nigeria and Zaire had each opened more than twenty missions in other African countries. They were followed by Ghana, Sudan, Algeria, Ethiopia, CAR and Liberia, who had opened between fifteen and eleven embassies.[190] By 1987, Egypt possessed 36 missions in

---

184   D.H. Johns ('The 'Normalization' of Intra-African Diplomatic Activity', in *Journal of Modern African Studies*, 1972, p 603) produced an overview of this for the year 1971. To reach a more comprehensive picture of these patterns for the last three decades we performed a similar analysis for one year in the later 1980s. We picked the random year of 1987 and based our tabulation on the annual reference guides *Africa South of the Sahara* and *North Africa and the Middle East*, 1988.

185   Kirk-Greene, 'Diplomacy and Diplomats', pp 286-287 (n. 124).

186   Based on figures for 1971 (Johns, 'Normalisation', pp 604-5) and 1987 (own tabulation). Disparities are partly caused by multilateral interaction and the number of states in one region.

187   Shaw and Newbury, 'Dependence or Interdependence', pp 66-68.

188   Based on figures for 1975 and 1987. Figures 1975 from D.H. Johns, 'Diplomatic Exchange and Inter-State Inequality in Africa: An Empirical Analysis', in Shaw and Heard, *Politics of Africa*, pp 279-281. Figures 1987 from own tabulation.

189   Figures own tabulation and excluding Western Sahara, Namibia and South Africa. See for reciprocity of exchange Johns, 'Normalization' and 'Diplomatic Exchange'.

190   Mention of CAR (Central African Republic) and Liberia and absence of others, as Senegal, Ivory

African countries, Nigeria 35, Zaire thirty, Algeria 29 and Libya 27. Thirteen countries had between eleven and eighteen missions[191] and eight countries had ten missions.[192] Given the financial constraints of most states, the lack of bilateral activity is partly compensated by interaction in international organizations. Thus, in 1987 28 countries, out of a possible maximum of 49, had established a mission in Addis Ababa, the OAU headquarters.[193]

Many countries also engage in military co-operation, in which the protection of state security against common enemies is a major objective. Examples of military alliances are the defence agreement between Ethiopia and Kenya; those between France and many of its former colonies and the defence protocol of the "Economic Community of West African States" (ECOWAS). Yet, there is often no automatic guarantee that signatories must come to each other's assistance. As such, many ECOWAS members have competing defence agreements with France, which provide better security against domestic enemies and semi-peripheral powers like Nigeria.[194] The Ethiopia-Kenya defence agreement was a relatively stable alliance directed against Somali expansionism, but mutual support was practically limited to the diplomatic field.[195] In general, the muddy world of subversion and counter-subversion makes the moral positions in inter-African conflicts far from clear. "Aggression" is an elusive concept, although it exerts some influence, as witnessed by the public condemnation of subversion. African peace is not indivisible, however, as many conflicts, especially domestic ones, are ignored by other states.

Finally, both in and outside the OAU African states tend to form various coalitions or alliances. An alliance or coalition is defined here as the result of the temporary or permanent coming together of states or actors to realize some common objective, whether or not in clear opposition to countries or other actors that remain outside their group.[196] Some have relatively stable, long-term objectives, such as the "Frontline alliance", which was formed to confront the white minority regimes. Other alliances represent more temporary, occasional groupings that dissolve the moment that their common objective has been attained. One could think here of countries forming a coalition for the sole

---

Coast and Tanzania, contradict the patterns of economic/political differentiation. Figures: Johns, 'Diplomatic Exchange', p 274.

191   Guinea: eighteen; Ivory Coast, Gabon : sixteen; Morocco: fifteen; Ghana: fourteen; Tanzania, Sudan: thirteen; Ethiopia, Somalia, Mauritania: twelve; Cameroon, Senegal, Zambia: eleven. Figures own tabulation (n. 184).

192   The remaining 23 had nine to zero missions. Own tabulation.

193   21 states had no missions, of which Angola, Madagascar, Tunisia, Somalia and Morocco are significant. The others were small countries: Benin, Botswana, Burkina Faso, Cape Verde, CAR, Comoros, Gambia, Guinea-B., Lesotho, Mali, Mauritania, Mauritius, São Tomé & Príncipe, Seychelles, Swaziland, Togo. Own tabulation.

194   See J.E. Okolo, 'Securing West Africa: the ECOWAS defence pact', in *The World Today*, 1983, pp 177-184 and P. Chaigneau, *La politique militaire de la France en Afrique* (Paris, 1984).

195   For some information, Aluko, *Foreign Policies of African States* (n. 74), pp 64, 144 and 161 n. 23.

196   See L. Zang and D. Sinou, 'Dynamique des groupes au sein de l'OUA et unité africaine', in M. Kamto, J.E. Pondi and L. Zang (eds), *l'OUA: rétrospective et perspectives africaines* (Paris, 1990), pp 137-138. For another definition O. Aluko, 'Alliances within the OAU', in Y. El-Ayouty and I.W. Zartman (eds), *The OAU After Twenty Years* (New York, 1984), p 70 ff.

purpose of opposing another OAU member in a specific dispute. For example, during the early 1990s an unlikely coalition of Ivory Coast, Libya, Burkina Faso and a few other countries opposed Nigerian intervention in the Liberian civil war.[197]

Some of these alliances form arrangements that are not formalized in institutional structures, while others appear in the form of membership of exclusive, rival international organizations. An example of the first is the former alliance of Frontline states in Southern Africa. Some of the more institutionalized ones are regional economic organizations like ECOWAS and ECCAS or various organizations formed by Francophone countries, like the former UAM and OCAM.[198] As will be shown in section 5.6, any of these alliances may have positive or negative effects for the OAU's functioning, depending on the degree of congruence of their objectives and the manner in which members use their alliance in relation to the Pan-African cadre.

Closely related to these alliance patterns are the cleavages that characterize inter-African relations. These are the former fissures between radical, conservative and moderate states; the dividing line marking off North African countries from the sub-Saharan ones; the distinction between Francophone and Anglophone states; and various regional divisions, that either pertain to institutional issues internal to the OAU or involve different sorts of coalitions existing independently of the Pan-African organization. Their influence on its functioning and, in particular, OAU decision-making, is also discussed in section 5.6, as well as subsequent chapters.

---

197   See Y. Gershoni, 'From ECOWAS to ECOMOG: The Liberian Crisis and the Struggle for Political Hegemony in West Africa', in *Liberian Studies Journal*, 1993, pp 21-43.

198   See f.i. D. Mazzeo (ed), *African Regional Organizations* (Cambridge, 1984) and K. van Walraven, 'Some Aspects of Regional Economic Integration in Africa', in *Hague Yearbook of International Law*, 1991, pp 106-126.

Some historical and ideological perspectives

3

3.1 Introduction

This chapter provides an introductory outline of African (state) nationalism and Pan-Africanism. Section 3.2 discusses the nature of African nationalism, both in its function as programme for the political forces of the 1950s and as official state ideology after decolonization. Some attention is given to the doctrines of African socialism, state capitalism and Marxism-Leninism, either of which became part of state thinking in connection with nationalist ideology. Section 3.3 attempts to establish what exactly is Pan-Africanism and section 3.4 analyses in what way it influenced, during the 1950s, the governmental ideology of Africa's emerging states.

It is readily recognized that the popularity of Pan-Africanism has always been restricted to sections in the modern elite, both in Africa and the Afro-American world. It is also conceded that, especially in retrospect, the relevance of the distinction between state capitalism, African socialism and Marxism-Leninism was relatively limited, as in all countries the state became a dominant economic agent and most of them later began to pursue free market policies. It is also acknowledged that African nationalism developed into a sterile state ideology, whose prime aim was and is to legitimate the dominance of the state elite, and that at present it elicits little, if any, support anymore among the mass of the population.

Yet, the focus on African (state) nationalism and Pan-Africanism is justified by their importance to the OAU. It is precisely because of its legitimation of the role of state elites that state nationalism is important to the OAU. The nucleus of the OAU's ideology consists of a combination of state nationalist ideology and several ideas and notions that find their origin in Pan-Africanism. It is also at the international level that African socialism, state capitalism and Marxism-Leninism assumed special distinctiveness. They provide a rough indication of differences in governmental views on issues in foreign affairs,[1] in the period before the late 1980s, and are therefore important to an under–standing of the OAU's functioning.

3.2   The nature and manifestations of African nationalism

Introduction

Nationalism may, in its simplest terms, be described as a desire to realize the welfare and integrity of the nation through the attainment and preservation of independence in a sovereign state. The concept of nation is more difficult to define. In theory, it refers to a people living in a definite territory, enjoying its own common language and culture and sharing the conviction that it constitutes a single, exclusive and terminal community.[2] Nationalism is essentially a modern phenomenon with its roots in European history. It followed on the fundamental changes brought about by the Industrial Revolution: this entailed the rise of the middle class, improvements in communication, rapid development of modern science and technology and faith in human progress and the mastery over nature; in short, the arrival of "modernity". It was only through the advent of modern colonial rule that this form of nationalism started to gain influence in Asia and Africa.[3]

At first sight it seems curious to postulate a resemblance between the nationalisms of Europe and that of twentieth century Africa, as the social make-up of European countries differs radically from the structures of African society. Yet, at one level of analysis there are fundamental similarities.[4] Colonial occupation created the channels through which capitalism could definitely start to penetrate the African continent. The introduction of modern science, technology and ways of communication; Europe's humiliating demonstration of military power; the formation of novel administrative structures; and the articulation of European cultural superiority all emphasized the need for an indigenous response. The people best placed to formulate an effective answer were the small Western-educated minorities, that slowly began to emerge as the result of colonialism's socio-economic impact. Their response consisted of calls for rapid modernization along Western lines. They pleaded for modern education, technology, science and economic development and articulated Western ideas on democracy, equality and "national" self-determination. These were to be realized mainly through Western models of political organization and, in most cases, the acceptance of the colonial territories as the framework of the new nationalism.[5]

---

1   See also the conclusion in C. Young, *Ideology and Development in Africa* (New Haven and London, 1982).

2   J.S. Coleman, *Nigeria: Background to Nationalism* (Berkeley and Los Angeles, 1958) p 422 and R.I. Rotberg, 'African Nationalism: Concept or Confusion?', in *Journal of Modern African Studies*, 1966, p 34.

3   R. Emerson, *From Empire to Nation: The Rise to Self-Assertion of Asian and African Peoples* (Boston, 1960), pp 188-190. A recent analysis in E. Gellner, *Encounters with Nationalism* (Oxford and Cambridge, Mass., 1994).

4   Coleman, *Nigeria*, pp 6-7; T. Hodgkin, *Nationalism in Colonial Africa* (London, 1956), pp 16-17; Rotberg, 'African Nationalism', pp 36-39; and Emerson, *From Empire to Nation*, pp 10-21.

5   R. July, *The Origins of Modern African Thought: Its Development in West Africa during the*

The European powers were to a greater or lesser extent successful in imposing the territorial element of the Western state, with its sharply defined boundaries and the legal concept of territorial jurisdiction.[6] Although at the end of colonial rule this process was far from complete, the introduction of a common administration, language and legal system, as well as increased intercourse and experience of common grievances within the same territory, created an element of territorial individuality.[7] The all-embracing nature of colonial rule led the Western-educated groups to conclude that, in order to be effective, one had to accept the new structures as the basis of political agitation. Demands had to be formulated in an ideological cloak familiar to the colonial power.[8] As independence in a sovereign nation-state had become, at least for the leading sections of Africa's modern elite, the symbol of the equality of peoples, it was not the state structure itself that was challenged, but those who controlled it.[9]

Social context

At a deeper level the differences between African and (West) European nationalisms were considerable.[10] Africa's social contexts involved, during the 1950s, various social movements. These interacted more or less peacefully, articulated different ideologies and were relatively amorphous.[11] They found organizational expression in a great array of institutions, such as political parties, trade unions, co-operatives, liberation armies, welfare societies, ethnic associations, separatist churches and millenarian movements.[12] It is hard to formulate a satisfactory definition of African nationalism, as all movements and institutions to a greater or lesser extent challenged (aspects of) European rule and nationalism formed, in essence, the aggregated, politicized expression of different social grievances. Nevertheless, if one would use the term "nationalism" for all forms of protest, the concept would be deprived of explanatory value.[13]

The fundamental objective of nationalism was the *liberation from colonial rule*. This sometimes took the form of an attempted, violent overthrow of European domination, such as in Algeria, Cameroon and — accompanied by more hybrid forms of nationalist

Nineteenth and Twentieth Centuries (London, 1968), pp 460 ff and A.D. Smith, *State and Nation in the Third World: The Western State and African Nationalism* (Brighton, 1983), pp 49-54.

6   Rotberg, 'African Nationalism', p 37 and Smith, *State and Nation*, pp 50-51.

7   J.S. Coleman, 'Nationalism in Tropical Africa', in *American Political Science Review*, 1954, p 412.

8   See on this forced necessity B. Davidson, *The Black Man's Burden: Africa and the Curse of the Nation-State* (London, 1992).

9   Rotberg, 'African Nationalism', p 37; Coleman, 'Nationalism', p 424; and Smith, *State and Nation*, pp 50-52.

10   J. Mohan, 'A Whig Interpretation of African Nationalism', in *Journal of Modern African Studies*, 1968, p 392. However, Davidson (*Black Man's Burden*) compares African and East European nationalisms.

11   Hodgkin, *Nationalism in Colonial Africa*, p 24 and I. Wallerstein, *Africa: The Politics of Unity. An Analysis of a Contemporary Social Movement* (New York, 1967), p 7.

12   Hodgkin, *Nationalism in Colonial Africa*, pp 24-25 and Coleman, 'Nationalism', pp 406-407.

13   As does Hodgkin, *Nationalism in Colonial Africa*, pp 24-25. For a critique G. Balandier, 'Contribution à l'étude des nationalismes en Afrique noire', in *Zaïre: revue congolaise*, April 1954, p 379 and Coleman, 'Nationalism', p 405.

ideology — in Kenya and Madagascar.[14] More often, however, nationalism's fundamental goal was paraphrased in a demand, through negotiations, for modern territorial "self-government" or "independence"; full autonomy and equality within a broader Eur-African framework; or racial equality between the African and European (white) populations in racially plural territories.

In many countries the urban environment became a focal point of the nationalist struggle. However, the rural areas played a significant part by their resistance to aspects of colonial policy as disease control in agriculture or anti-erosion measures.[15] Besides the grievances of urban skilled labour, there was the resentment of the innumerable unemployed, often young school-leavers or veterans, as well as of the mass of unskilled workers. Trade unions were often embroiled in labour disputes that involved conflict with the state. Sometimes this provided an important platform for nationalist politicians, as witnessed by the history of Sékou Touré's rise to power.[16]

It was modern political parties, however, that provided principal leadership to the nationalist movement. This gave nationalism an elitist character, as the parties were usually headed by members of the Western-educated groupings. Yet, in many cases the nationalist movement also depended on spontaneous, local responses, in which the party played a co-ordinative role, integrating resistance around the symbol of national independence. The history of nationalism in East Africa, which generally had a more radical tone than its West African counterpart, is illustrative.[17] However, most parties remained rather elitist and never developed into genuine "mass" parties. Even parties enjoying massive popular support, such as the "Tanganyika African National Union" (TANU) and the "Convention People's Party" (CPP), had community leaders, petty traders, landlords and local notables among their members.[18] In many other colonies the elitist basis of the nationalist leadership was even more outspoken, such as in Senegal and Ivory Coast.[19] The strength of party machinery also varied from case to case, with TANU, the PDCI, FLN and CPP as some of the better organized examples.[20]

---

14   R. Le Tourneau, *Evolution politique de l'Afrique du nord musulmane 1920-1961* (Paris, 1962), part IV; R. Joseph, *Le mouvement nationaliste au Cameroun: les origines sociales de l'UPC* (Paris, 1986), pp 218-233 and 350-354; D.L. Barnett and K. Njama, *Mau Mau from Within* (New York and London, 1966); and J. Tronchon, *L'insurrection malgache de 1947: essai d'interprétation historique* (Fianarantsoa and Paris, 1986).

15   Hodgkin, *Nationalism in Colonial Africa*, p 18; D. Austin, *Politics in Ghana, 1946-60* (London, 1964), pp 159-160; and J.M. Lonsdale, 'Some Origins of Nationalism in East Africa', in *Journal of African History*, 1968, pp 142-143.

16   B. Freund, *The Making of Contemporary Africa: The Development of African Society since 1800* (London, 1986), pp 202-208 and E.J. Berg and J. Butler, 'Trade Unions', in J.S. Coleman and C.G. Rosberg (eds), *Political Parties and National Integration in Tropical Africa* (Berkeley and Los Angeles, 1964), pp 342-366.

17   Lonsdale, 'Some Origins', pp 141-46; D.A. Low and J.M. Lonsdale, 'Introduction: Towards the New Order 1945-1963', in D.A. Low and A. Smith (eds), *History of East Africa*, vl. III (Oxford, 1976), pp 44-48; Coleman, 'Nationalism', p 408; and Freund, *Making of Contemporary Africa*, p 218.

18   Freund, *Making of Contemporary Africa*, pp 207-209; Austin, *Politics in Ghana*, pp 195-199; and J. Iliffe, *A Modern History of Tanganyika* (Cambridge, 1984), pp 523-37 and 542.

19   R. Schachter-Morgenthau, *Political Parties in French-Speaking West Africa* (Oxford, 1964), chs. IV-V.

20   Freund, *Making of Contemporary Africa*, ch. 9.

In general, support for the nationalist parties differed with time and place. They won massive and relatively early adherence in South Africa, the Gold Coast and the Maghreb, while the evolution of nationalist parties was rather tardy in the Belgian Congo and French Equatorial Africa.[21] Differences in social stratification, the duration and intensity of European rule, the presence of white settlers, as well as variations in colonial policy were responsible.

Objectives and manifestations

With some exceptions, like Cameroun, Madagascar and the North African countries, nationalist parties first articulated a demand for "self-government" rather than "independence". Even in the Gold Coast nationalists preferred a more gradual approach to a radical break with the constitutional order.[22] "Independence" was articulated relatively late in the process of decolonization, especially in the French colonies. In French Africa political activists faced tough opposition from the colonial authorities, as well as the influence of assimilationist sentiments and the issue of inter-territorial unity.[23]

African nationalism contained various ideas and values derived from the Western world. Apart from a strong desire to establish their own nation-states, modern parties articulated the call for the universal franchise. This was meant to tie the population to the nationalist cause and strengthen the struggle through the numerical preponderance of the "masses". It also pointed to, and enhanced, the superior legitimacy of the nationalists.[24]

In most cases, nationalists professed a strong desire for the ideals or the fruits of modernity. These were to eradicate Africa's dire poverty and bring economic prosperity. They would deliver the welfare state that Africa, too, deserved and needed in order to live a life in human dignity and in accordance with universal standards. These aspirations reflected the history of racial rejection of elite Africans, their personal frustrations and resultant sense of inferiority. However, in many countries, like the Belgian Congo and the Gold Coast, these ambitions were also related to an ebullient socio-political arena dominated by young upstarts intent on quick, personal enrichment. Their desires often had little to do with the ideals of development and much with the corruptibility of an emergent state.

On a wider scale, the aspirations to modernity reflected the mood of a society that was astir, excited and confident about a better future: as colonialism appeared to crumble relatively easily, the battle against poverty could surely be won in the foreseeable future as well. No doubt the best exponent of this optimism was Kwame Nkrumah, whose grand vision stressed the necessity of industrialization, agricultural reform and the introduction of modern science and technology.[25] Naturally, from the perspective of the

---

21   F.i. P. Walshe, *The Rise of African Nationalism in South Africa: The ANC 1912-1952* (London, 1970); Austin, *Politics in Ghana*; Le Tourneau, *Evolution politique*; Young, *Politics in the Congo*, ch. XII; and E. M'bokolo, 'Forces sociales et idéologies dans la décolonisation de l'A.E.F.', in *Journal of African History*, 1981, pp 393-407.
22   Generally, Austin, *Politics in Ghana*.
23   M. Crowder, 'Independence as a Goal in French West African Politics: 1944-60', in W.H. Lewis (ed), *French-speaking Africa: The Search for Identity* (New York, 1965), pp 15-41.
24   See also Smith, *State and Nation*, pp 51-54.
25   July, *Origins*, pp 469-472.

1990s one may doubt to what extent this was all appearance rather than reality. However, the decade of the 1950s was marked by widespread optimism about Africa's political and socio-economic future.[26]

African nationalism not only laid great emphasis on the realization of *freedom*, but also on the *dignity* and *equality* of Africa and its peoples vis-à-vis the rest of the world.[27] It was, with some exceptions as the North African countries and Somalia, based on a racial, rather than a national, consciousness. The cultural diversity of Africa's peoples and the relatively short period of territorial unity made a national identity a long-term objective, not something that actually existed in practice. In contrast, the common subjection to white rule created a sense of "African-ness" that formed the principal basis for political agitation.[28] Thus, in several cases nationalist ideology was interwoven with elements of Pan-Africanism, from which nationalism derived some of its ideas and concepts. Pan-Africanist sentiments, though, also complicated the nationalist struggle and became difficult to reconcile with nationalism after the attainment of independence.[29]

In the French colonies nationalism had to compete with assimilationist sentiments. Many African politicians had been educated in the best of France's cultural traditions and were conscious of their dependence on metropolitan assistance. The idea of a greater France, uniting metropolitan and African areas by their common acceptance of the French language, culture and ideals of freedom, equality and brotherhood, therefore had considerable appeal. While many tried to reconcile these sentiments with nationalist or even Pan-Africanist ideas, Houphouët-Boigny of the Ivory Coast for long declined to consider the idea of independence.[30]

Similarly, North African countries felt attracted to the slogans of Pan-Arabism. This ideology sought to unite all Arabic-speaking peoples on the premise that they constituted one Arab nation, that had been divided by European colonialism. Pan-Arabism also accompanied nationalist ideology in countries where only part of the population was Arab, such as Algeria and Sudan. The nationalism of all North African countries was more or less fused with forms of Islamic sentiment that stressed the belonging to a great "Dar al-Islam" opposed to the Western infidel. However, in Nasserite Egypt and Algeria Pan-Africanist sentiments were articulated too.[31]

---

26   J. Lonsdale, 'Political Accountability in African History', in P. Chabal (ed), *Political Domination in Africa: Reflections on the Limits of Power* (Cambridge, 1986), p 153. Yet, see R. Dumont, *l'Afrique noire est mal partie* (Paris, 1962).

27   Smith, *State and Nation*, pp 38-39 and 55-56; Coleman, 'Nationalism', p 424; and A.A. Mazrui, *Towards a Pax Africana: A Study of Ideology and Ambition* (London, 1967), pp 55-57.

28   Coleman, 'Nigeria', p 413 and B.O. Oloruntimehin, 'African politics and nationalism, 1919-1935', in A.A. Boahen (ed), *General History of Africa*, vol. VII: *Africa under Colonial Domination 1880-1935* (UNESCO: Paris, London and Berkeley, 1985), p 566.

29   Hodgkin, *Nationalism in Colonial Africa*, pp 181-182.

30   Crowder, 'Independence as a Goal', pp 306-310; E.J.Berg, 'The Economic Basis of Political Choice in French West Africa', in *American Political Science Review*, 1960, pp 404-405; and f.i. M. Crowder, *Senegal: A Study of French Assimilation Policy* (London, 1967).

31   See M. Kamel, *l'Arabisme: fondement socio-politique des relations internationales panarabes* (no pl., 1977); H. Djaït, *La personnalité et le devenir arabo-islamiques* (Paris, 1974); and G.R. Warburg and U.M. Kupferschmidt (eds), *Islam, Nationalism, and Radicalism in Egypt and the Sudan* (New York, 1983).

In most countries nationalism was mingled with, and complicated by, ethnic or other particularist loyalties. In colonies like Uganda, Togo and the Gold Coast more narrowly defined ethnic nationalisms weakened the supremacy of the modern nationalist movement. Especially in French Equatorial Africa, Nigeria and the Belgian Congo ethnic and regional factors exerted strong influence on the development of "national" parties and "nationalist" ideology.[32]

This eclectic nature of African nationalism was also reflected in the curious combination of traditionalist elements and the values of modernity. On the one hand emergent state elites tried to neutralize rival sources of political power. This entailed hostility towards chieftaincy and the survival of ethnic loyalties — notwithstanding their own ambiguity in this respect. Hence, these social structures and sentiments were criticized as forms of "feudalism" and "tribalism" standing in the way of social and economic regeneration. On the other hand many nationalists responded to the humiliations of colonial rule by idealizing the virtues of African civilization. They took pride in Africa's pre-colonial states and empires, extolled the resistance of their forbears and emphasized African achievements in philosophy and the arts. Specific virtues were attributed to the African, such as sensitivity and human solidarity, and these were set against examples of what was seen as European depravity. Sometimes these ideas were expressed in the concepts of "African Personality" and "Négritude" discussed in the next section.[33]

State capitalism, African socialism and marxism

With independence drawing nearer, nationalists had to think seriously about the management of their society and economy. Several felt attracted to socialist ideology. Capitalism was perceived to be intricately linked to imperialism and colonialism. Moreover, it was sometimes feared that a free market economy would generate insufficient capital, while several nationalist leaders aspired to reform their country's role in the international economic order. Francophone politicians in particular were, before independence, strongly influenced by Marxist thought as a result of their contacts with French communists and socialists.

However, in most cases the dominant parties articulated an ideology that was not socialist in a truly Marxist sense. Seeking to strengthen the struggle for independence, they considered themselves as mass parties representing the entire "nation" rather than a specific "class". With Africa's social stratification differing from that in the West the existence of classes was often denied altogether and, with it, the necessity of class struggle. Some concluded that the context of African societies was ill-suited to Marxism's European foundations, whose domination, moreover, one tried to escape. The atheist dimensions of Marxism were rejected, as were to some extent its materialist aspects. Socialism had to be adapted to African circumstances and rooted in African culture.

---

32 See M'bokolo, 'Forces sociales', pp 406-407; Coleman, *Nigeria*; Freund, *Making of Contemporary Africa*, pp 222-223 and 228-230; R. Cornevin, *Le Togo: des origines à nos jours* (Paris, 1988), pp 293-306; and Austin, *Politics in Ghana*, p 265 ff.

33 July, *Origins*, ch. 22; T. Hodgkin, 'A Note on the Language of African Nationalism', in K. Kirkwood (ed), *African Affairs, no. 1: St Antony's Papers, no. 10* (London, 1961), p 24; and Hodgkin, *Nationalism in Colonial Africa*, pp 173-178.

Africa's communal traditions were in this respect regarded as an appropriate basis. They were, however, blown up out of all proportions, leading to a perverted picture of "traditional" Africa.[34]

These ideas became known as "African socialism", a generic category containing numerous variations on the above-mentioned theme. After independence, several governments tried to implement different versions of this programme, whether or not under the name of African socialism. Examples are Nkrumah's "consciencism", Modibo Keita's socialism "founded on African realities" and Guinea's "socialist path" under Sékou Touré. However, in all cases its official aims were never realized. The private sector either dwindled or resisted its introduction.[35]

The same conclusion could be drawn for Nasserite Egypt, FLN-dominated Algeria and Nyerere's Tanzania, where ambitious nationalization programmes led to massive bureaucracies with more or less totalitarian pretentions. Usually, the version of socialism that was practised hardly depended on autonomous social forces but was contingent on the whims of a single leader or a narrowly defined group with access to government.[36]

Some countries later rejected African socialism as an aberration and accepted Marxism-Leninism as official ideology. Even here, however, nationalist elements fused with Marxist views and economic programmes often differed from the tenets of Soviet orthodoxy. Thus, national liberation formed an important element in the ideologies of FRELIMO and the MPLA, while national integrity constituted a crucial priority for Mengistu's Ethiopia. The scientific socialism that was preached during the 1970s and 1980s in Madagascar and Somalia was reconciled with specific national, cultural dogmas. The introduction of Marxism-Leninism was, with the exception of the Lusophone countries, related to the search for legitimacy by military governments that wished to distinguish themselves from the regimes they had toppled. The social basis of this ideology was, at least originally, made up of the urban young, the intelligentsia and professionals. Class analysis was therefore usually absent or perverted, as in the case of Somalia and Benin. The prime target of these governments was colonialism and its remnants, rather than capitalism *per se*. In Benin and Congo-Brazzaville foreign capital was left untouched. Even where large-scale nationalizations took place, as in Ethiopia, Madagascar and Mozambique, foreign private investment was, of necessity, welcomed.[37]

After independence most countries adopted programmes of state capitalism.

---

34   K.W. Grundy, 'The 'Class Struggle' in Africa: An Examination of Conflicting Theories', in *Journal of Modern African Studies*, 1964, pp 379-393; Young, *Ideology and Development*, pp 97-99; the introduction to W.H. Friedland and C.G. Rosberg (eds), *African Socialism* (Stanford, 1964), pp 3-9; and Hodgkin, 'Language of African Nationalism', pp 29-40.

35   C. Legum, 'Socialism in Ghana: A Political Interpretation'; C.F. Andrain, 'Guinea and Senegal: Contrasting Types of African Socialism'; and K.W. Grundy, 'Mali: The Prospects of "Planned Socialism"', all in Friedland and Rosberg, *African Socialism*, chs. 8-10. See also Young, *Ideology and Development*, pp 151-182.

36   Young, *Ideology and Development*, pp 103-141; P.J. Vatikiotis, *Nasser and His Generation* (London, 1978), ch. 11; and O. van Cranenburgh, *The Widening Gyre: The Tanzanian One-Party State and Policy Towards Rural Co-operatives* (Delft, 1990).

37   Young, *Ideology and Development*, chs. 2-6 and contributions in C.G. Rosberg and T.M. Callaghy (eds), *Socialism in Sub-Saharan Africa: A New Assessment* (Berkeley, 1979), pp 174-372.

However, since these were equally nationalist in nature they encouraged the growth of a national capitalist elite, which in the context of a relative dearth of private capital led to a sizeable public sector as well. Most countries practising state capitalism did not feel the need for an explicit formulation of its ideological underpinnings. Its implementation took place under various headings, such as "pragmatism" in Nigeria, "humanism" in Zambia, "authenticité" in Zaire, the uncamouflaged "state capitalism" in Ivory Coast and even "African socialism" in the case of Senegal and, for some time, Kenya.[38]

Whatever policies were adopted, economic constraints and regime competence had a strong influence on their outcome and reduced the relevance of ideological preference. Thus, it was in the field of foreign policy that many of these regimes could behave in a more orthodox manner.[39] The differences in the above-mentioned policies were partly responsible for the cleavage between radical and moderate-conservative member states.

State nationalism

In view of its diffuse and composite social basis, it is not surprising that the transition to independence strongly affected the character of African nationalism. In section 2.2 it was shown why and how decolonization was followed by a growth in authoritarianism. African nationalism provided legitimacy to this process, if only in the eyes of the state elite. During the struggle for independence the doctrine of national unity and appeals for self-sacrifice had been ideal instruments with which to induce the masses to follow the nationalist leadership. The same principles could be easily linked to the consolidation of the new state elite by pointing to the need to strengthen national independence and stimulate economic development. The notions about a classless society, the denunciation of "tribalism", the manipulation of ethnicity and the romantic interpretation of pre-colonial communalism could all aid in the mystification of social contradictions, the centralization of power and the stifling of opposition.[40]

The modernist origin of nationalism and its articulation in Western languages gave it an exclusionary and alienating character, setting the state elite apart from the populace.[41] State bureaucracies formulated ambitious development policies, even if these were to remain largely rhetorical and ineffective.[42] Their weakness led to a strong emphasis on the symbols, rather than the intrinsic values, of modernism, which could make an impression on the greater mass of the population living in more traditional settings.[43]

Other elements that helped in this process were traditions of despotic leadership, an

---

38   Young, *Ideology and Development*, ch. 4; Andrain, 'Guinea and Senegal'; and A. Roberts, *A History of Zambia* (London, 1976), pp 246-247.

39   Young, *Ideology and Development*.

40   L. Yablotchkov, 'L'évolution du nationalisme africain', in *Présence africaine*, 1970, no. 74, pp 46-60; Y. Person, 'Les contradictions du nationalisme étatique en Afrique noire', in K. Ingham (ed), *Foreign Relations of African States* (London, 1974), pp 239-257; E. Hobsbawm and T.O. Ranger (eds), *The Invention of Tradition* (Cambridge, 1983); and Y. Benot, *Indépendances africaines: idéologies et réalités*, 2 vls. (Paris, 1975).

41   J.F Bayart, *L'état en Afrique: la politique du ventre* (Paris, 1989), pp 220-222.

42   T. Callaghy, 'Politics and Vision in Africa: The Interplay of Domination, Equality and Liberty', in Chabal, *Political Domination*, p 35.

43   A. Schwarz, 'Mythe et réalité des bureaucraties africaines', in *Canadian Journal of African Studies*, 1974, pp 255-284.

emphasis on personalized authority and the tendency to sacralize political power. Psychological coercion through manipulation of charms and witchcraft often induced the populace to attribute magical powers to the state.[44] Heads of state were deliberately portrayed as traditional chiefs, who as head of the family stood in contact with the ancestors and acted as intermediary between the living and the dead. This conferred authority on the chief and sacralized his power, making him the incarnation of the unity and values of the group.[45] As such, in the post-colonial order heads of state became the symbol of the "nation", but without the constraints of pre-colonial constitutional principles. They actively encouraged allusions to sacrality, as exemplified by Nkrumah's adoption of the title "Osagyefo", meaning redeemer or saviour.[46] Speaking in paternalistic language to their flock, they sought to enforce a degree of social control as in a family. This entailed the use of terminology derived from kinship.[47]

Nationalism thereby ended up in preserving the status quo. The state became its principal reference-point, serving the interests of an elite that had monopolized the main channels of its articulation. Emphasis was put on territorial integrity and sovereignty. The liberation of the masses was supposed to have been fulfilled with the attainment of independence. Thus, since decolonization the nationalist ideology is usually referred to as "state nationalism". Naturally, the extent to which it evolved into a negatively oriented, conservative and sterile ideology differed from country to country. Yet, by the late 1980s its fallacy was exposed in many cases, giving rise to fierce struggles against state elites.[48]

3.3   The nature and manifestations of Pan-Africanism

Introduction

"Pan" ideologies are ideologies that aim to promote the solidarity of groups which are bound to each other, or perceived to be so, by a shared language, culture, race, religion, nationhood and/or geographical area.[49] As they wish to unite broad groups of people, who may only have one or two characteristics in common, they are designated with the Greek word *pan*, meaning "all". They involve a wide variety of ideologies and are usually described as social movements. However, as the social basis of Pan-Africanism has always been rather limited, it will be approached as a form of ideology.

Pan ideologies are a modern phenomenon that originated as a reaction to the same socio-economic upheavals that stimulated the rise of nationalism. They generally formed

---

44   B. Asso, *Le chef d'état africain: l'expérience des états africains de succession française* (Paris, 1976), pp 210, 81-83, 170-173 and 198-200 and J. Vansina, 'Old and New African Political Traditions', lecture at post-doctoral course on African studies, African Studies Centre: Leiden, 9 June 1992.

45   Asso, *Chef d'état africain*, pp 22-33.

46   See f.i. K. Bediako, 'Christian Religion and African Social Norms: Authority, Desacralisation and Democracy', pp 11-12; paper delivered at African Studies Centre: Leiden, 2 April 1992.

47   Bayart, *L'état en Afrique*, pp 220-221.

48   See Davidson, *Black Man's Burden*.

49   See H. Kohn, 'Pan-Movements', in E.R.A. Seligman (ed), *Encyclopaedia of the Social Sciences* (New York, 1958), vl. 11, p 544 and F. Kazemzadeh, 'Pan Movements', in D.L. Sills (ed), *International Encyclopaedia of the Social Sciences* (New York and London, 1972), vl. 11, p 365.

the expression of a desire for social and economic modernization, cultural regeneration and political self-determination, as articulated by groups which had been most exposed to the influences of modernity. Such groups often represented new elites that were thrown up as a result of contact with a foreign, occupying power. This contact created divisions between those elite members that wished to preserve the old and those that favoured innovation, with usually an intermediate group aspiring to a combination of traditional and modern elements. Pan ideologies often reflected these contradictions in a confusing eclecticism.[50]

The most important pan ideologies are "pan-national" ones, which aim at uniting people of common language, culture, ethnicity or racial stock and can be seen as an extension of nationalist ideology. Pan-Africanism is a good example. They derive much of their strength from struggles for national or racial emancipation. However, all pan ideologies are rather marginal, often transient phenomena. They are highly elitist as compared to nationalism, which usually has a broader appeal.[51]

It is hard to give a satisfactory definition of Pan-Africanism. It is made up of several orientations and doctrines. Its contents has been articulated by innumerable spokesmen and institutions and its meaning has varied with its geographical distribution and the stages in its history. A precise definition is therefore not given. Instead, this section describes the essence of this amorphous phenomenon, followed by an outline of major orientations and stages until 1945. Emphasis is laid on the more political concepts and notions, especially those that were to play a role in later days.[52]

Essence and social context

Pan-Africanism is a collection of ideas and emotions that originated among (descendants of) enslaved Africans in the Western hemisphere.[53] The blacks of this diaspora slowly began to regard "Africa" as a disinct entity, which was a key step in the evolution of Pan-Africanism. Acculturation and social alienation in their new environment, physical separation from the African continent, limited knowledge about the land of their origins and, consequently, a romanticized image of Africa, were crucial to the development of this idea.[54]

After the abolition of slavery, black Americans and West Indians[55] still faced many obstacles to social advancement, such as lack of political liberties, discrimination and the rise of racist ideologies. Contingent on their chances of social acceptance — which usually depended on the degree of skin pigmentation — their responses varied from

---

50   Kohn, 'Pan-Movements', pp 544-545; Kazemzadeh, 'Pan Movements', pp 365-366; and I. Geiss, *The Pan-African Movement: A History of Pan-Africanism in America, Europe and Africa* (London, 1974), pp 5-6 and 430.

51   Kohn, 'Pan-Movements', pp 544-545 and T.O. Lohata, 'L'idéologie panafricanisme', in *Le Mois en Afrique*, Febr.-Ma. 1987, nos. 253-4, p 161.

52   Also, Geiss, *Pan-African Movement*, ch. 1; American Society of African Culture (ed), *Pan-Africanism Reconsidered* (Berkeley and Los Angeles, 1962), pp 12-13; and P.O. Esedebe, 'What is Pan-Africanism', in *Journal of African Studies*, 1977, pp 167-187.

53   After C. Legum, *Pan-Africanism: A Short Political Guide* (London and Dunmow, 1962), p 14.

54   Geiss, *Pan-African Movement*, pp 20-27.

55   Both are also referred to as Afro-Americans. Francophone West Indians are also referred to as French Antillians.

efforts to obtain equal rights in Western society to ideas about re-emigration to the old continent. It was hoped that a physical or spiritual return to "Mother Africa" could provide a more hospitable environment or boost self-confidence. The foundation of Liberia formed one of its concrete results.[56]

Afro-American thinkers emphasized that black people should unite on the basis of, what they postulated to be, a fundamental, racial[57] solidarity, in order to work for their prosperity and freedom. They claimed that Africa was a cultural unity and the homeland for all Africans and people of African descent, even if the latter did not contemplate a physical return. Both groups were said to belong to one homogeneous people. Africa's cultural values, its past and future were idealized in reaction to white prejudice and an attempt to formulate a model of reform for the present. For long these ideas remained a set of unclear dreams and visions, whose objectives were often irrational and ill-defined. Pan-Africanism is an emotional outcry against the humiliations of slavery, discrimination and colonialism. It represents a demand for justice and reaffirms black *dignity*, which is one of its key concepts. Its inarticulate nature owed much to the difficulty activists had in obtaining a proper education and to the continuation of racial oppression. As shown below, Pan-Africanism involved several continents. It was therefore hard to find one common objective that took account of the diversity of conditions black people faced. This problem was compounded by poor communication and, concomitantly, limited knowledge of Africa in the Western hemisphere.[58]

Pan-Africanism developed into a triangle of influences between Africa, Europe and the New World. From the late eighteenth century onwards, ideas were exchanged between black Americans and West Indians; the minorities of Western-educated Africans in the coastal regions of West Africa and later from Southern Africa; and Afro-Americans and Africans who journeyed to Europe. The dominant contribution to Pan-Africanism came from black Americans from the United States and Afro-Americans and Africans from the British West Indies and British West Africa. British colonies had a tradition of political decentralization and relative freedom of expression, which made the formulation of Pan-Africanist demands easier than in the assimilationist framework of the French empire.[59]

Through extensive travel and exchange of ideas Pan-Africanists evolved into tiny heterogeneous and cosmopolitan communities, which developed broad political horizons and tried to internationalize the significance of local conflicts. This compensated somewhat for their marginal social basis. They belonged to a small Western-educated elite

---

56   P.O. Esedebe, 'Origins and Meaning of Pan-Africanism', in *Présence africaine*, 1970, no. 73, pp 111-127 and Geiss, *Pan-African Movement*.

57   On the race concept J. Ki-Zerbo, 'Editorial Note: theories on the 'races' and history of Africa', in J. Ki-Zerbo (ed), *General History of Africa*, vl. I: *Methodology and African Prehistory* (UNESCO: London, Paris and Berkeley, 1981), pp 261-269 and K.A. Appiah, *In My Father's House: Africa in the Philosophy of Culture* (New York and Oxford, 1992), ch. 2.

58   Geiss, *Pan-African Movement*, pp 5, 27 and 425-426; Legum, *Pan-Africanism*, p 15; J.A. Langley, *Pan-Africanism and Nationalism in West Africa 1900-1945: A Study in Ideology and Social Classes* (London, 1973), pp 3, 8, 12 and 372; and Esedebe, 'Origins and Meaning', p 125.

59   Langley, *Pan-Africanism*, pp 1-2 and Geiss, *Pan-African Movement*, pp 12-14.

and included lawyers, doctors, journalists, students, clergymen, as well as printers, clerks and trade unionists.[60]

The petty bourgeois character of this community was reflected in the contents of Pan-Africanism, which was usually preoccupied with constitutional action and issues. Pan-Africanism articulated Western ideas on national self-determination, democracy, modernization and equality. These were held to be valid for all peoples of Africa and African descent. As nationalist ideology and Pan-Africanism were the embodiment of a racial[61] consciousness they had largely identical objectives. Thus, they were almost impossible to distinguish. The scope of their geographical application might differ, but their protagonists hardly experienced contradictions between their messages until well after World War II. As such, Pan-Africanists were usually also (proto-)nationalists and vice versa. Moreover, in Africa itself the difference between territorial nationalism and Pan-Africanism remained initially rather vague, as territorial individuality was at first still underdeveloped.[62]

Besides glorifying Africa's past and culture, nineteenth and early twentieth century Pan-Africanist spokesmen also called for economic uplift and cultural regeneration. Attempts to introduce educational facilities therefore formed an important activity. Africa itself should be modernized in every respect and be familiarized with the concepts of modern education and the message of Christianity. Its "redemption" should be worked for strictly in the interests of black people. The rallying call was therefore "Africa for the Africans", whether those "at home", *i.e.* the peoples of Africa, or those "abroad" — the Afro-Americans. The latter should have a pioneer role. As many of them travelled to West and Southern Africa to work as missionaries, traders, artisans, journalists and lawyers, or were stationed there as soldiers or officials of coastal colonies, they were the paradoxical forerunners of European colonialism.[63]

Thus, many Afro-Americans, as well as some Westernized West Africans, developed an ambivalent attitude towards the African continent. Many Afro-Americans had been acculturated in the Western world and were estranged from African society. Most of them did not wish to return and for those that did, a visit to Africa often led to disillusionment. During the nineteenth and early twentieth centuries, several Afro-Americans articulated Western racist views of Africa. The tensions generated by this were to hinder Pan-Africanism's development into a coherent ideology.[64]

---

60 Geiss, *Pan-African Movement*, pp 425-426; D.E. Apter and J.S. Coleman, 'Pan-Africanism or Nationalism in Africa', in American Society of African Culture, *Pan-Africanism Reconsidered*, p 85; and Langley, *Pan-Africanism*, p 10.

61 Yet see M.L. Ropivia, 'Critique des fondements conceptuels de l'unité politique de l'Afrique', in *Cahiers de l'IPAG*, no. 10, June 1990, pp 93-191.

62 July, *Origins* (n. 5) and Oloruntimehin, 'African politics and nationalism', p 566 (n. 28).

63 Geiss, *Pan-African Movement*, ch. 1; Legum, *Pan-Africanism*, pp 22-23; and G. Shepperson, 'Notes on Negro American Influences on the Emergence of African Nationalism', in *Journal of African History*, 1960, pp 301-303.

64 Geiss, *Pan-African Movement*, pp 28-29 and Legum, *Pan-Africanism*, pp 108-110.

Objectives and manifestations

Organizations articulating Pan-Africanist objectives were on the whole rather ephemeral and poorly financed institutions. They were preoccupied with collecting information about events elsewhere in the triangle and often had to limit their activities to the issuing of demands and declarations.

During the nineteenth century Pan-Africanist ideology was also taken up by West Africans. One example is James Africanus Horton from Sierra Leone, who pleaded for modernization of West African society on European lines.[65] In contrast, Edward Wilmot Blyden, a West Indian who emigrated to Liberia, formulated the concept of African Personality. This was set against Europe's materialism and contribution to science and technology; consisted of strongly idealized African values; and tried to encourage self-confidence among blacks and elite Africans.[66]

From 1900 a substantial part of Pan-Africanist activity started to shift to Europe, especially to England and France. A "Pan-African Conference" in London called for equal rights and opportunity for all black people and the granting of autonomy to the British colonies in Africa and the West Indies "as soon as possible". With only a few Africans present, the majority of delegates were black Americans and West Indians.[67] It was during this conference that the term "Pan-African", from which "Pan-Africanism" derived, appeared in political vocabularies.[68]

After World War I W.E.B. Du Bois, an Afro-American professor and civil rights activist from the United States,[69] started a series of "Pan-African Congresses" to press demands for racial equality and colonial reform. At all the gatherings blacks from the United States and the West Indies were in the majority. They also attracted some French Antillians and Francophone Africans. However, the latter were, like the "assimilados" of the Portuguese empire,[70] strongly influenced by the assimilationist forces of colonial rule. This became a source of friction with English-speaking Afro-Americans and Africans. The Du Boisian Congresses only condoned constitutional means and pleaded for self-government for African and West Indian colonies, either by stages or directly; the extension of the franchise; an end to discrimination and colonial exploitation; and economic development to the benefit of all Africans and Afro-Americans.[71]

---

65   C. Fyfe, *Africanus Horton, 1835-1883: West African Scientist and Patriot* (London and New York, 1972).

66   July, *Origins*, ch. 11; Esedebe, 'Origins and Meaning', pp 121-125; H.R. Lynch, *Edward Wilmot Blyden: Pan-Negro Patriot* (London, 1967); and P.F. de Moraes Farias and K. Barber (eds), *Self-Assertion and Brokerage: Early Cultural Nationalism in West Africa* (Birmingham, 1990).

67   Geiss, *Pan-African Movement*, p 182.

68   Geiss, *Pan-African Movement*, ch. 10 and J.R. Hooker, *Henry Sylvester Williams: Imperial Pan-Africanist* (London, 1975), chs. 3-4. Text main resolution in J.A. Langley, *Ideologies of Liberation in Black Africa 1856-1970: Documents on modern African political thought from colonial times to the present* (London, 1979), pp 738 ff.

69   D. Levering Lewis, *W.E.B. Du Bois: Biography of a Race 1868-1919* (New York, 1993) and P.S. Foner (ed), *W.E.B. Du Bois Speaks,* vl. 1: *Speeches and Addresses 1890-1919* (New York, London and Sydney, 1986) and vl. 2: *Speeches and Addresses 1920-1963* (New York, London and Sydney, 1986).

70   See E. dos Santos, *Pan-Africanismo de ontem e de hoje* (Lisbon, 1968), pp 121-123 and 131-132.

71   Geiss, *Pan-African Movement*, ch. 12; Langley, *Pan-Africanism*, pp 63-87 and 375-9; Legum, *Pan-Africanism*, pp 133-4; and G. Padmore (ed), *History of the Pan-African Congress* (2nd ed.:

Marcus Garvey, a black journalist and printer from Jamaica, articulated a more radical message. He formulated grandiose plans to contribute to Afro-American self-confidence and race pride. He pleaded for a physical or spiritual return to Africa and programmes of economic self-help. To this end he founded the "Universal Negro Improvement Association" (UNIA), of which numerous branches sprang up in North America, the West Indies, various parts of Africa and Europe.[72] From his base in Harlem, New York, he dreamt of a "United States of Africa" and had himself elected as the provisional president of a continental government in exile. As with all pan ideologies, Pan-Africanism involved notions of inverted imperialism.[73] Garvey's influence in Africa was greater than that of Du Bois. Certain sections of the modern elites welcomed his ideas on black capitalist enterprise and his assertions of racial pride, but were hostile to his ambition of a large black empire in Africa. Garveyism strongly influenced later activists like Nkrumah.[74]

A less populist note was struck by the "National Congress of British West Africa", which was an outgrowth of the Gold Coast nationalism as exemplified by Kobina Sekyi and J.E. Casely Hayford. These belonged to a conservative elite that expressed limited demands, such as local self-government, extension of the franchise and an end to discrimination. The Congress paid lip-service to the idea of a united West Africa to be realized through a British West African federation with dominion status. There were no political contacts with French West Africa.[75] The Congress did establish links with the "West African Students' Union" (WASU). This group spread new ideas in British West Africa and its headquarters in London became a hot-bed of nationalist activity, as would its French counterpart in Paris after 1945.[76]

Before World War II there were numerous activists in France who also articulated Pan-Africanist objectives, such as Louis Hunkarin and Tovalou-Houénou from Dahomey; the Senegalese Lamine Senghor; and Tiemoko Garan Kouyaté from Soudan (Mali). Many of these had contacts with communist groups and English-speaking activists like Garvey and the WASU group. Their "Ligue de Défense de la Race Nègre" at one time demanded independence and a black state comprising the whole of Africa and the West Indies.[77] Most French Antillians were less radical but adhered to the concept of

---

London, 1963 [1st ed. 1947]), pp 23-24.

72   E.D. Cronon, *Black Moses: The Story of Marcus Garvey and the Universal Negro Improvement Association* (Madison, 1955).

73   Kohn, 'Pan-Movements', pp 547-548; Kazemzadeh, 'Pan Movements', pp 367-368; Geiss, *Pan-African Movement*, pp 279-280; and an example in J.E.C. Hayford, *Ethiopia Unbound: Studies in Race Emancipation* (2nd ed.: London, 1969 [1st ed. 1911]), p 91.

74   J.A. Langley, 'Garveyism and African Nationalism', in *Race*, 1969, pp 157-172; R.L. Okonkwo, 'The Garvey Movement in British West Africa', in *Journal of African History*, 1980, pp 105-117; and Geiss, *Pan-African Movement*, p 280. For Garvey's writings, R.A. Hill (ed), *The Marcus Garvey and Universal Negro Improvement Association Papers* (Berkeley, Los Angeles and London, 1983-90), 7 vls.

75   Langley, *Pan-Africanism*, chs. 3-6.

76   Geiss, *Pan-African Movement*, pp 297-304; P. Garigue, 'The West African Students' Union: A Study in Culture Contact', in *Africa*, 1953, vol. 23, pp 55-69; and C. Diané, *Les grandes heures de la F.E.A.N.F.* (Paris, 1990).

77   Ph. Dewitte, *Les mouvements nègres en France 1919-1939* (Paris, 1985), chs. 2-5.

Négritude. Although its proponents did not explicitly formulate Négritude as part of Pan-Africanism, it contains sufficient similarities to regard it as one of its (cultural) manifestations.[78] In the assimilationist context of French colonialism the search for one's "Africanité" became an effective weapon against the modern elite's sense of inferiority and alienation. Négritude therefore laid great stress on African cultural values. While in the English-speaking world it was to evoke sharp criticism, for many Francophones Négritude meant a cultural rediscovery and a boost to political consciousness.[79]

Radicalization

While in European and American cities, Afro-Americans and Africans made contact with abolitionists, philanthropists, Fabians, liberals and Marxists. They also got to know nationalists from Asia, which encouraged incipient notions of Afro-Asian solidarity[80] and, through the influence of Mahatma Gandhi, ideas on non-violence and civil disobedience. Men like Ho Chi Minh helped to spread more militant, Marxist views. Inspired by communist front organizations and the Comintern blacks participated in communist activities. Examples are Jomo Kenyatta from Kenya, I.T.A. Wallace-Johnson, a trade unionist from Sierra Leone, and George Padmore, a journalist from Trinidad.[81] Their consciousness was also stimulated by the Italian invasion of Ethiopia, a country revered as a symbol of black independence. Italy's onslaught and Europe's muted reaction to it therefore aroused deep emotions among black activists.[82]

However, relations with Marxism remained difficult. Some communists tended to criticize nationalism, provoking tensions with, and divisions among, those who mainly articulated Pan-Africanist ideas. Most of these broke with communism after the mid-1930s, partly as a result of a sudden shift in Soviet policy. It was felt that European communism was an untrustworthy ally and that Pan-Africanist objectives should not become subordinate to it. A coalition with communism would also lead to persecution by the colonial powers. Moreover, a racial analysis, rather than one based on class, seemed more appropriate to the liberation of black peoples. These ideas were best articulated by George Padmore. They reflected the petty-bourgeois base of Pan-Africanism, encouraged the growth of African socialism in later decades and bore the risk of entrenching elite interests.[83]

---

78   Differently Ropivia, 'Critique des fondements conceptuels'.
79   J.L. Hymans, *Léopold Sédar Senghor: An Intellectual Biography* (Edinburgh, 1971); Ch.A. Diop, *l'Unité culturelle de l'Afrique noire: domaines du patriarcat et du matriarcat dans l'antiquité classique* (Paris, 1959); and Legum, *Pan-Africanism*, pp 92-104 and 212-220.
80   See K. Mahmud, 'A Short Biography of Duse Mohhamed', in *Nigeria Magazine*, 1986, no. 4, pp 83-92.
81   Geiss, *Pan-African Movement*; Dewitte, *Mouvements nègres*, ch. 3; and J.R. Hooker, *Black Revolutionary: George Padmore's Path from Communism to Pan-Africanism* (London, 1967).
82   Langley, *Pan-Africanism*, pp 327-346. Also S.K.B. Asante, *Pan-African Protest: West Africa and the Italo-Ethiopian Crisis, 1934-1941* (London, 1977) and J.E. Harris, *African-American Reactions to War in Ethiopia 1936-1941* (Baton Rouge and London, 1994).
83   Geiss, *Pan-African Movement*, ch. 16; Legum, *Pan-Africanism*, pp 104-107; Wallerstein, *Politics of Unity* chs. 1, 2 and 11 (n. 11); and G. Padmore, *Pan-Africanism or Communism? The Coming Struggle for Africa* (London, 1956), ch. 16.

World War II altered the circumstances for Pan-Africanist co-operation. The war was officially being fought for democracy, against racism and for self-determination, as exemplified by the "Atlantic Charter". This document had a strong effect on activists, many of whom began to articulate the objective of independence more explicitly than ever before. In Manchester in October 1945, they organized the Fifth Pan-African Congress, which included delegates representing Liberia, Gambia, Gold Coast, Nigeria, Sierra Leone, South Africa, Nyasaland, Tanganyika, Kenya and Uganda.[84] Francophone activists were absent due to transport problems and the constitutional preoccupations of the French empire.[85] Nevertheless, for the first time most Pan-Africanist tendencies were present. Trade unionists, student leaders and modern nationalist parties like the South African ANC and the "Nyasaland African Congress" sat side by side with conservative elements from the Gold Coast, the UNIA, Du Bois and a more radically inclined group led by George Padmore and Kwame Nkrumah. There were also other future African leaders like Jomo Kenyatta from Kenya and Obafemi Awolowo from Nigeria.

Two general resolutions betrayed the influence of Padmore and Nkrumah and affirmed the right to self-determination, while emphasizing that political liberation was the first step to economic emancipation. They recommended non-violent methods of struggle, yet conceded that Africans had the right to use force as a last resort. African issues received greater attention than ever before. Central and North Africa, East Africa, West Africa, Ethiopia, Liberia and South Africa and some of its neighbours were covered in separate resolutions. The Congress called for an end to colonialism, articulated in terms of self-government, the franchise and "complete and absolute independence".[86]

The explicit, sharp demand for political rights underlined Pan-Africanism's evolution. Attention focused on clear-cut aims couched in uncompromising language. By 1945 Pan-Africanism was therefore more radical than most manifestations of nationalism. It presented itself as an ideological stimulus to, and cadre of, the emergent nationalist struggle.[87] However, its weaknesses were also obvious. Its internal divisions; absence of encompassing institutionalization; distribution over wide and disparate areas; limited communication between French- and English-speaking activists; and domination of Pan-Africanism by the latter, all restricted its impact. While it derived strength from the sentimental appeal of its ideas, this also entailed weaknesses. There was an uneasy combination of modernity and romanticism. Thus, some of its concepts remained relatively inarticulate.

---

84   List of delegates in Padmore, *History*, pp 71-73.
85   E. Charles, 'Pan-Africanism in French-Speaking West Africa, 1945-1960', *Boston University African Studies Center Working Papers*, no. 59, p 2 and Geiss, *Pan-African Movement*, pp 385-404.
86   Text of resolutions, Congress messages and abbreviated minutes of proceedings in Padmore, *History*, pp 8-10 and 27-67.
87   Geiss, *Pan-African Movement*, pp 404-408 and Langley, *Pan-Africanism*, pp 355-356.

3.4   An outline of Pan-African co-operation 1945-1960

Introduction

With the onset of decolonization the focus of Pan-Africanist activity shifted to the African continent. Manchester had made the fulfilment of the nationalist dream the first priority. However, when independence seemed imminent, the priorities of Pan-Africanism changed again. With the realization of the nationalist ideal, the political unification of the continent became a principal objective. The shift towards a pan-continental emphasis and solidarity with non-negroid North Africa can be attributed mainly to the views of Nkrumah and Padmore.[88]

Yet, during the 1950s the nationalist struggle achieved such momentum that Pan-Africanism and nationalism evolved into opposing forces, with nationalism gaining the upper hand. Political liberation of the colonial territory constituted the most practical strategy for the nationalists because, with some exceptions, the colonial powers did not accept any structure other than the individual territory as basis for the devolution of political power. Technological impediments and great diversity in political conditions made larger-scale mobilization extremely difficult. The colonial territory provided a more solid social base for political activists, which firmly tied them to local interest groups. The nation-state symbol itself also formed a powerful attraction. Decolonization reinforced this process as it led to the entrenchment of new elites that needed the state apparatus to consolidate their interests.[89]

Furthermore, the extent to which people were fully committed to Pan-Africanism should not be over-estimated. As a set of modernist doctrines of non-African origin Pan-Africanism was not the ideology of the African populace, for which it constituted a relatively incomprehensible abstraction.[90] While for many of Africa's modern elites Pan-Africanism exerted a sentimental appeal, this did not necessarily add up to an acceptance of its Nkrumahist conception. Pan-Africanism had no official ideologue and did not form a systematized body of ideas. This enabled everyone to pick one's own concepts and interpret them at will. Thus, ideas like "unity", "African Personality" and "Africa for the Africans" were sufficiently attractive and vague to be articulated by many of Africa's emergent elites. Even those people that did not seriously believe in Pan-Africanism were to use its rhetoric, as many of its notions enjoyed popularity despite, or because of, their mystifying contents.

The best example is the doctrine of (African) unity. While it may also be related to nationalist, or even more traditionalist, ideology, the concept has always been closely bound up with Pan-Africanism. Yet, unity is an abstract term that has no meaning unless related to specific objectives, problems, interests or enemies. It is these that provide it with contents and make it come to life. Concomitantly, attitudes to unity depend on the

---

88   Lohata, 'L'idéologie panafricanisme', p 153 (n. 51).
89   Apter and Coleman, 'Pan-Africanism or Nationalism', pp 89-103 (n. 60).
90   T. Yannopoulos, 'Aliénation idéologique et unité africaine', in *Problèmes actuels de l'unité africaine: colloque d'Alger (25 mars - 12 avril 1971)*, (l'Université d'Alger: Algiers, 1973), pp 490-492.

question to which particular goal it is meant to contribute or against which particular enemy it is to form a front.

During the struggle for independence the concept of (African) unity depended on the shared interest against colonial powers. After decolonization, however, its meaning became less clear. In foreign affairs it came to be related to a host of different issues as the perception of priorities and dangers varied. Yet, in almost all cases African governments adhered to the notion of African unity because their vulnerability made international co-operation a *sine qua non* for the consolidation of the state. Even the Francophone states articulated the concept of African unity, although in their case it was also tied to the co-operative framework of the former (colonial) inter-territorial federations in West and Equatorial Africa (AOF and AEF). So unity could also paraphrase Eur-African co-operation with the metropolitan power, emphasizing the complementarity and interdependence between the two continents.[91] This was contradictory to, or at least had an ambiguous relation with, the dictates of Pan-Africanism. The latter principally aimed to promote the *autonomy* of Africans. The term Pan-African must therefore be distinguished from Pan-Africanist, as not all Pan-African co-operation formed an implementation of Pan-Africanist ideology.

Conference of Independent African States — Accra, April 1958
Nkrumah, however, was a convinced Pan-Africanist. Regarding himself as the Osagyefo or saviour, he argued that political unification and a common defence policy, as institutionalized in a "Union of African States" and "Union Government", would prevent outside powers from exerting influence on the continent. Economic development called for large amounts of capital that could only be realized through the pooling of resources, thereby necessitating the establishment of a central, Pan-African institution. Political unification would also strengthen the continent's influence on the world stage. As such, Nkrumah was strongly attached to a continentalist notion, whose attraction lay in a vague assessment of the continent as a source of enhanced power. Although initially entertaining the idea of regional integration as a step to continental unity, he later rejected this strategy and aimed at the immediate establishment of continental government.

With the realization of an independent Ghana, Pan-Africanism therefore attained a base in Africa itself. With the aid of Padmore, Nkrumah organized a "Conference of Independent African States" (CIAS) in Accra in April 1958. It was attended by all the independent African governments, *i.e.* Ghana, Liberia, Ethiopia, Egypt, Tunisia, Morocco, Sudan and Libya. While most did not go as far as Nkrumah in their attitudes to inter-state co-operation, the meeting exemplified a gradual realization of some common continental interests. In the words of the conference, they wished to assert their distinctive African Personality, which would speak with one voice in international fora like the United Nations. This could be achieved by establishing a "fundamental unity of outlook on foreign policy".[92] An important goal of such a policy would be the

---

91   G. Martin, 'Africa and the Ideology of Eurafrica: Neo-Colonialism or Pan-Africanism?', in *Journal of Modern African Studies*, 1982, pp 221-223.

92   See *Conference of Independent African States: Declaration and Resolutions* (Government Printer: Accra, n.d.), pp 1-4.

preservation of national independence and territorial integrity, prevention of interference in internal affairs and peaceful settlement of inter-state disputes.[93]

Decolonization was an obvious topic for discussion. Although by 1958 there could be some confidence about the arrival of a new era, it was also clear that in many cases colonial powers had to be pushed in making concessions. South Africa, which had turned down an invitation to attend, came in for sharp criticism. Delegates pleaded a time-table for decolonization of remaining dependent territories and recommended "all possible assistance" to the struggle of the dependent peoples.[94]

However, an Egyptian proposal to give military assistance to the FLN, which was fighting the French in Algeria, was defeated. Still, the conference argued that the FLN be recognized as the party with which France should negotiate, thereby creating a line of confrontation with the French that was to place the Francophone territories in a awkward position. The Palestinian question also proved difficult. The sub-Saharan states had good relations with Israel and did not wish to be drawn into the Middle Eastern dispute. The Arabs agreed that the CIAS conference was not the appropriate forum at which to deal with the issue and decided not to push the matter.[95]

The economic resolution showed careful searching for common ground. It spoke of the possibility of an eventual African common market, but also argued that co-operation should not affect national independence. Although incorporation of dependent economies into the economic system of the colonial powers was questioned, the linkage of the Francophone territories with the European Community was not mentioned. The need for foreign aid and capital was readily admitted and not considered, in principle, contrary to African autonomy. The resolution therefore spoke of strengthening co-operation with UN Specialized Agencies and the "UN Economic Commission for Africa" (ECA), which was to be established shortly in Addis Ababa.[96]

An important principle for foreign policy was to be Africa's non-alignment vis-à-vis the world's power blocs. The conference called for abstention from defence arrangements serving big power interests. This attitude was to cause problems in the future, especially for the Francophone states with their defence accords with France. The attending states also condemned atomic tests, notably those by the French in the Sahara, and called for conventional arms reductions among the great powers.[97]

Some of the above-mentioned principles had already been formulated at the conference of Asian and African states at Bandung in 1955. One figure that tried to play a prominent role in Afro-Asian affairs was Nasser. As a Pan-Arabist he dreamt of unifying all Arabic-speaking countries, besides the liberation and coming together of the African continent and greater co-operation in the Islamic world as a whole. Egypt should become the focal point of these three "concentric circles" and form the main headquarters of the struggle against colonialism.[98]

---

93   Resolutions No. I and V (for source preceding note).
94   Resolutions No. II and IV.
95   Resolutions No. III, VII and XII. See also C. Legum, *Bandung, Cairo & Accra: A Report of the First Conference of Independent African States* (Africa Bureau: no pl., 1958), pp 17-20.
96   Resolution No. VIII.
97   Resolutions No. I and V.
98   G. Abd El-Nasser, *The Philosophy of the Revolution: Book 1* (no pl. or d.), pp 69-73.

Nasser therefore came into competition with Nkrumah for the command of Pan-Africanism's struggle for unity and liberation.[99] There were also cleavages between the North African and sub-Saharan states as a whole. The North African countries generally favoured a stronger line against colonialism than the sub-Saharan states. Ghana was ostensibly in favour of the tactics of "positive action", *i.e.* civil disobedience. Nasser's closer links with communist countries met with distrust too. The sub-Saharan states also resented North Africa's ambivalence towards "black Africa". This found expression in a tendency to emphasize its Arab identity; the priority given to links with the Middle East; and paternalistic attitudes to black Africans.[100]

However, at the CIAS conference countries from both north and south of the Sahara expressed fears over leadership ambitions, whether those of Egypt or Ghana.[101] Delegates knew that Nasser and Nkrumah did not hesitate to appeal, over their heads, to non-governmental groups in order to win converts. During the coming years opposition elements from independent African states were to flock to Cairo and Accra, besides members of liberation movements in dependent territories. There they found political and material support in their struggle against colonial powers or African governments.[102] Pan ideologies provide an ideal cover for such activities. They can be easily turned into a vehicle for expansionist ambitions, as they may themselves contain allusions to imperial ideas.[103]

The question of how to continue inter-African co-operation created controversy as well. A Ghanaian proposal for a permanent secretariat did not get unanimous support. A compromise involved the decision to constitute the African ambassadors at the UN into an informal machinery to co-ordinate matters of common concern. Thus, from Nkrumah's perspective the results of CIAS were far from radical. Yet, it marked the emergence of Africa as a diplomatic bloc, at the UN if nowhere else. Even the old states of Liberia and Ethiopia, with their conservative leadership and traditions of political isolation, were prepared to enter the new, more self-conscious mainstream of inter-African politics.

All-African People's Conference — Accra, December 1958
Before the CIAS took place, it had been decided to hold a separate conference for non-governmental groups. The decision to distinguish between these and the state elites set a trend that was to become a continuing source of friction in (inter-)African politics. However, in December 1958 Padmore organized the first "All-African People's Conference" (AAPC) in Accra in an attempt to provide a more popular basis to Pan-Africanism and stimulate the struggle for independence in other territories. More than 200 delegates of nationalist parties from all over the continent were invited, including future statesmen as Patrice Lumumba, Tom Mboya, Hastings Banda, Julius Nyerere and

---

99   Legum, *Bandung, Cairo and Accra*, pp 6-9 and 27.
100   W.S. Thompson, *Ghana's Foreign Policy 1957-1966: Diplomacy, Ideology, and the New State* (Princeton, 1969), p 8 and H.F. Strauch, *Panafrika: Kontinentale Weltmacht im Werden? Anfänge, Wachstum und Zukunft der afrikanischen Einigungsbestrebungen* (Zurich, 1964), p 78.
101   Strauch, *Panafrika*, p 84 and Thompson, *Ghana's Foreign Policy*, p 33.
102   On Ghana Thompson, *Ghana's Foreign Policy*, pp 221-245 and on Egypt f.i. V.B. Thompson, *Africa and Unity: The Evolution of Pan-Africanism* (London and Harlow, 1969), pp 72-73.
103   Kohn, 'Pan-Movements', p 545. See also K. Haushofer, *Geopolitik der Pan-Ideeen* (Berlin, 1931).

Kenneth Kaunda. As governments were not represented, the AAPC struck a much more militant note than the CIAS.[104] Through the contacts and finance its platform provided, it greatly encouraged nationalist leaders. The timing of the conference and the euphoria and publicity surrounding it, stimulated the excitement and confidence that characterized the political atmosphere in much of Africa.[105] Thus, with CIAS and the AAPC the Osagyefo had managed to occupy centre-stage in Africa's struggle for liberation.

Nevertheless, at the AAPC many of the above-mentioned tensions and disagreements came to the surface again. Some delegates managed to get a reference accepted to respect for human rights in independent African states, which was an early hint to the difficult position of opposition parties.[106] The resolutions also betrayed some features that Pan-African decolonization strategy would develop in the coming years. It was noted that liberation of a territory was the responsibility of the people involved, which should fight with a united front. However, the conference decided that the independent states should help with a diplomatic and economic boycott of culprit regimes and a financial fund. It also paid lip-service to the idea of a legion of volunteers that "were to protect the freedom of African peoples".[107]

The AAPC also articulated the ideal of Pan-African unification, albeit in hazy terms that pointed to disagreement among the delegates. Closely related to unification was the call for the abolition of "artificial frontiers". Africa's independent states were asked to find solutions to this problem based upon "the true wishes of the people".[108] The idea of the artificiality of territorial boundaries was linked to the concept of "balkanization", which as the antipole of African unity was feared by many African leaders, especially the more militant ones. Nkrumah, Nyerere, Touré, but also Senghor, referred to the break-up of the Habsburg and Ottoman empires and their replacement by weak Balkan states as a negative example for Africa's future. Many regarded decolonization into the present territorial structures as a form of balkanization, master-minded by colonial powers intent on preserving their dominance. Portrayed as the primary tool of "neo-colonialism", on which more is said in section 4.2, it may be seen as a specific form of conspiracy theory. Whether such colonial activities were real or imaginary — and notwithstanding the divisive behaviour of African politicians themselves — the focus of balkanization on the perceived smallness of African states pointed to an awareness of weakness and vulnerability regarding the new territorial units.[109]

However, in some cases reference to balkanization reflected disputes over the future of UN trust territories, the colonial federations of French Africa and the East African

---

104   See f.i. 'Speech by the Prime Minister of Ghana at the Opening Session of the All-African People's Conference on Monday 8th December, 1958', in *All-African People's Conference: News Bulletin*, vl. 1, no. 1, p 7.

105   Thompson, *Ghana's Foreign Policy*, pp 61-62.

106   E.S. Munger, 'All-African People's Conference', in E.S. Munger, *African Field Reports 1952-1961* (Cape Town, 1961), pp 81-83.

107   See Resolution on Racialism and Discriminatory Laws and Practices and Constitution Adopted for Permanent Organisation in Legum, *Pan-Africanism*, pp 224 and 234 and C. Hoskyns, 'Pan-Africanism in Accra', in *Africa South*, 1959, no. 3, p 73.

108   Resolution on Frontiers, Boundaries and Federations in Legum, *Pan-Africanism*, pp 229-232.

109   B. Neuberger, 'The African Concept of Balkanisation', in *Journal of Modern African Studies*, 1976, pp 523-529.

colonies. In these territories the geographical scale on which the new political order should be organized seemed open to question.[110] In other respects the reference to artificial frontiers reflected expansionist designs, as it opened the door to countries like Ghana to support irredentist claims articulated in neighbouring states. Thus, sentiments among the Ewes in Ghana, British Togoland and French Togo to unify their people across territorial boundaries were used by Nkrumah to call for integration of French Togo with Ghana, on the pretext that artificial frontiers should be removed. This soured relations with the future Togolese government. His attempt to challenge Houphouët-Boigny by proposing to unite the Sanwi in Ivory Coast with the Nzimas in Ghana, their relations and Nkrumah's own ethnic group, did not foster his relations with the Ivorian leader.[111]

Co-operation among Francophone countries
French Africans had been grossly underrepresented at the AAPC. Many of them, notably from government parties, had declined to accept an invitation. At the time they were preoccupied with several issues complicating the struggle for self-determination. Realization of independence was no easy task as a result of France's intransigence and the hostility of some of its local allies as Houphouët-Boigny. It was made even more difficult by the question of how independence could be harmonized with continuous links with the metropole. This was of vital importance to French Africa's economic survival. The desire to preserve some federal structure between the different territories formed an additional complication. However, the colonial federations of French West and Equatorial Africa broke up under the weight of conflicting territorial interests, personal and ideological squabbles and France's desire to consolidate its influence by associating with individual, relatively weak territories.[112]

While many Francophone politicians aspired to some co-operation among themselves, Pan-Africanism rarely formed its ideological inspiration. Anglophone and Francophone activists managed to establish irregular contacts and numerous young militants, especially students and from opposition parties, articulated the objectives of immediate independence and unification. Yet, Pan-Africanism had few serious adherents in government circles. Among those holding power Sékou Touré of Guinea was its most outspoken protagonist. Enjoying a secure territorial base, he also withstood the French by achieving independence outside the new framework of Franco-African co-operation. Modibo Keita of Mali articulated the objective of political unification as well, though to a lesser extent than Touré. The latter became a friend of Nkrumah, although like Keita he was a more realistic, calculating politician.[113] A grander Pan-Africanist programme,

---

110   Munger, 'All-African People's Conference', pp 81-83 and on the Cameroons C.E. Welch, *Dream of Unity: Pan-Africanism and Political Unification in West Africa* (Ithaca, 1966), chs. 4-5.
111   Thompson, *Ghana's Foreign Policy*; Welch, *Dream of Unity*, chs. 2-3; and Legum, *Pan-Africanism*, p 255.
112   W.J. Foltz, *From French West Africa to Mali Federation* (New Haven and London, 1965), ch. 6 and W.A.E. Skurnik, 'France and Fragmentation in West Africa: 1945-1960', in *Journal of African History*, 1967, pp 317-333.
113   Generally Charles, 'Pan-Africanism in French-Speaking West Africa', (n. 85) and on Touré and Keita, Legum, *Pan-Africanism*, pp 66-67 and 77 and Welch, *Dream of Unity*, pp 293-298. Also S. Touré, *Expérience guinéenne et unité africaine* (Paris, 1959).

comparable to Nkrumah's, was articulated by Barthélémy Boganda, the charismatic leader of Ubangi-Shari, who aspired to the creation of a "United States of Latin Africa". Yet, besides the name he gave for this purpose to his own territory, the "Central African Republic", nothing of his plans survived his premature death in 1959. Finally, Senghor held Pan-Africanist ideas as well. However, his cultural and philosophical inclinations diminished their political relevance, while he combined them with a strong desire for close relations with France.[114]

Until 1960, the most concrete outcome of Pan-African co-operation between Francophone countries was the federation between Soudan (Mali) and Senegal. Named the "Fédération du Mali", as a latter-day resurrection of the ancient empire, it possessed a federal party, executive and parliament, as well as integrated economic institutions. It was originally intended to comprise all of French West Africa, but after French and Ivorian pressure Upper Volta and Dahomey declined to participate. Shortly after independence (1960) the federation broke up when Senegal decided to secede, with Soudan retaining the name of Mali. Differences in economic policy, contradictory views on international co-operation, personal rivalry between Keita and Senghor and French-Ivorian animosity figured among the causes.[115]

The break-up of the Mali Federation proved a negative example for future supra-national initiatives. It represented a victory for Houphouët-Boigny, who had successfully tried to win back some of the initiative in West African relations by shifting his criticism of Pan-African co-operation as such to the form it should take. In May 1959 he founded the "Conseil de l'Entente" with Upper Volta, Niger and Dahomey, involving a customs union and an Ivorian commitment to provide financial assistance to the poorer members. The Entente formed a loose structure as it had no integrated, central institutions. With French blessing it aimed at co-ordinating national economic, political and military policies. As the nucleus of the later Brazzaville group, its inter-governmental framework was to set an important trend.[116]

Other initiatives in co-operation

Early attempts at greater unity between Morocco, Algeria and Tunisia and the integration of Egypt and Syria ended in failure. Relations between the Arab countries were dominated by numerous rivalries and conflicts.[117] Before 1960 there were two other initiatives in regional co-operation that deserve mention. In November 1958 Ghana and Guinea proclaimed a union between themselves, to which Mali, after the collapse of the federation with Senegal, acceded as well. This "Union of African States" (UAS) condemned exclusive co-operation between countries in the same colonial language area

---

114   L.S. Senghor, *Nation et voie africaine du socialisme* (Paris, 1961), part 1 and on Boganda, P. Kalck, *Central African Republic: A Failure in De-Colonisation* (London, 1971), pp 101-103 and Strauch, *Panafrika*, pp 193-194.

115   See G. Dugué, *Vers les états-unis d'Afrique* (Dakar, 1960), part III and Foltz, *From French West Africa*, pp 187-188.

116   Strauch, *Panafrika*, ch. 24 and V. Thompson, *West Africa's Council of the Entente* (Ithaca and London, 1972), chs. 1-2. See on the difficulties facing co-operation in French Equatorial Africa f.i. F. Wodie, *Les institutions régionales en Afrique occidentale et centrale* (Paris, 1970), chs. 2-3.

117   Strauch, *Panafrika*, ch. 22 and H.A. Hassouna, *The League of Arab States and Regional Disputes: A Study of Middle East Conflicts* (New York and Leiden, 1975).

and considered itself as a "higher and more healthy conception of African unity". Initially it was regarded as the nucleus of a future union of West African states and later, on Nkrumah's insistence, of a future United States of Africa. Its objectives were to pool resources, harmonize domestic and foreign policies in order to enhance the liberation of the continent, and consolidate independence. Alignments with non-African power blocs or foreign military installations would not be condoned. A common defence policy would have to deter aggression against any member state.[118]

The significance of the UAS lay in its breakthrough of the language barrier in West Africa and its advocacy of political unification. It was, at least originally, inspired by Nkrumah's fascination with the American federal system, while as a nucleus of the future Casablanca group it articulated a more radical anti-colonial message. Nevertheless, the UAS never evolved into a real union as each member was supposed to preserve its individuality and its institutions consisted mainly of the heads of state assembled in conference. The UAS was instrumental in helping Guinea and Mali to survive French hostility, but as Ghana did not share borders with them they were unlikely candidates for integration. As the UAS depended on co-operation between three headstrong, charismatic personalities, it began to disintegrate when Touré and Keita consolidated their rule. While all three countries possessed constitutions that foresaw the possibility of a partial surrender of sovereignty, Mali and Guinea became progressively less interested in unification. The UAS was therefore to disappear quietly after the formation of the OAU.[119]

A more modest approach was followed by the "Pan-African Freedom Movement of East and Central Africa" (PAFMECA, 1958). This loose grouping of political parties wished to co-ordinate activities to accelerate liberation from colonial rule and enhance economic development by regional unification. While formally it was a participant in the larger AAPC, it was an autonomous organization with a secretariat in Dar es Salaam. Dominated by the towering figures of Julius Nyerere and Tom Mboya, Pan-Africanism was explicitly recognized as its ideological basis. Its name later changed into PAFMECSA when it accepted political groupings from Southern Africa. PAFMECSA challenged the dominant position of Nkrumah and Touré in Pan-Africanist co-operation and propounded the view that continental unity should be realized gradually through regional federations. It was to play an important co-ordinative role in the struggle against colonialism until the formation of the OAU led to its demise.[120]

General patterns of Pan-African co-operation before 1960
Thus, even before the majority of states achieved independence Pan-African co-operation had become a notable feature of Africa's international relations. It originated from a desire by nationalists to establish contact with each other and as such helped to build confidence and contributed to their struggle against colonial rule. Its evolution also marked the gradual realization that, once independent, African governments had some common

---

118   For texts of relevant documents, Legum, *Pan-Africanism*, pp 160-161, 175 and 183-186.
119   Welch, *Dream of Unity*, ch. 7.
120   R. Cox, *Pan-Africanism in Practice. An East African Study: PAFMECSA 1958-1964* (London, 1964).

interests, among which was the eradication of colonialism. However, the struggle for independence depended primarily on territorial forces, which, as in French Africa, could even be hindered in that objective by the search for unity.

Before 1960 alliance structures were fluid and nervous as countries were testing the degree of their power and searching for their natural partners. While frequently couched in terms of Pan-Africanist concepts, only a few initiatives in co-operation were more or less based on, or inspired by, Pan-Africanist ideology. Non-governmental groupings and initiatives, often in alliance with some radical government, still played a notable part in Pan-African co-operation and gave the drive for unity a more populist streak. Yet, there were early signs of friction with newly established governments, which were in the process of discovering common interests. Nevertheless, despite numerous conflicts, the political atmosphere was still full of confidence that a new era was dawning. The dominant mood was that independence and some sort of unity would provide a more dignified political life and accelerate socio-economic progress. In the grander visions an independent, united Africa stood on the verge of being catapulted to prosperous heights, which would deliver it all the fruits of modernity.

The formation of the
Organization of African Unity

4

4.1 Introduction

1960 was "Africa Year". Over fifteen countries became formally independent, most of them Francophone colonies. They were admitted to the UN, thereby substantially strengthening the African voice in the world body. The rapid progress of decolonization contributed to the euphoria of the preceding years, which were so full of confidence that the continent could expect a bright future of freedom and prosperity.

However, the emergence of so many political actors strengthened the fluidity and nervousness that had characterized inter-state relations before 1960. In section 4.2 we will argue that inter-African relations became, during the following two years, highly volatile and sensitive to incidents and misunderstandings that easily soured the political atmosphere. The common ground on which the independent states had managed to find each other before 1960 rapidly vanished, mainly as the result of two violent conflicts, the war of independence in Algeria and the decolonization of the Belgian Congo.

Nevertheless, the opposing alliances to which this gave rise were themselves rather unsettled. Section 4.3 will discuss why and how these cleavages gave way, by 1963, to a new patterning of inter-African relations. The last three sections of this chapter will show how this led to some sort of rapprochement by way of the formation of the Organization of African Unity. An analysis will be given of the nature and extent of the various centrifugal and centripetal forces, which provided impetus to contradictory tendencies to fragmentation and co-operation. In the process, the ideology underlying the formation of the OAU will be discussed.

4.2 The emergence of inter-African cleavages 1960-1962

Introduction
Chapter 1 discussed the nature of the groups of radical, moderate and conservative states and the cleavages that separated them. This section shows how these groups originated and how their identifying qualifications became a part of inter-African politics. Moreover, the differences between the specific alliances to which these qualifications gave rise between 1960 and 1962 will be studied in great detail, as these have often been mis-understood and misrepresented in the literature. This section is therefore a necessary contribution to setting the historical record straight.

After 1960 Ghana gradually lost the initiative it had enjoyed in Pan-African co-operation. The limited size of its national base, the multiplication of states and resentment of the support that Nkrumah provided to opposition groups from various countries resulted in an increasingly anti-Ghanaian environment and a decline in Ghana's influence. Nigeria in particular developed a bitter feud with the Osagyefo, as its conservative government considered that Africa's most populous state was entitled to assume the leading role in the continent's international relations. It resented the forceful dynamism of the Ghanaians and their support to Nigerian opposition elements.

Conference of Independent African States — Addis Ababa, June 1960
Thus, at the second Conference of Independent African States (CIAS) the Nigerian delegate launched a slimly veiled and rude attack on Nkrumah, who was absent from the meeting. While thanking African leaders that had contributed to the "Pan-African movement", he warned that "if anybody makes the mistake of feeling that he is a Messiah who has got a mission to lead Africa, the whole purpose of Pan-Africanism will ... be defeated. We all can recall what Hitler thought and did in Nazi Germany and what that meant to the whole world".[1]

Despite some disagreements, the second CIAS admitted the FLN's provisional government of Algeria (GPRA) as a full member to the conference. A delegation from Cameroon was also accepted, in spite of the fact that a radical exiled opposition party, the "Union des Populations du Cameroun" (UPC), was still supported by countries like Ghana and Egypt in its struggle against the government of President Ahidjo.[2] Yet, the conference adopted a tone that was much sharper than anything later to be used by conservative countries. At the time, many of these were not yet independent and therefore not represented at the CIAS.[3] Notably the Francophone countries, most of which were under conservative leadership and assumed independence in the latter half of 1960, were

---

1   Statement of the Leader of the Nigerian Delegation, the Hon. Y.M. Sule, at the Second Conference of Independent African States, Addis Ababa, June, 1960 (extracts in C. Legum, *Pan-Africanism: A Short Political Guide* (London and Dunmow, 1962), pp 172-174.

2   *Afrika Informationsdienst*, no. 16, 1960, pp 193-195 and I. Wallerstein, *Africa: The Politics of Unity. An Analysis of a Contemporary Social Movement* (New York, 1967), p 40.

3   Differently Wallerstein, *Politics of Unity*, pp 40-42 and I.W. Zartman, *International Relations in the New Africa* (Englewood Cliffs, 1966), p 27. Colonies with fixed independence dates were invited. Nigeria and Somalia attended. Madagascar, Congo-Leo., Mali and Togo did not. Wallerstein, *Politics of Unity*, p 40. List of observers in *Ethiopia Observer*, August 1960, p 282.

intent on maintaining collaborative structures with the former colonial power and the West in general. They therefore shied away from the uninhibited rhetoric that several states used at international conferences and that characterized the revolutionary atmosphere of the times.[4] In the volatile context of inter-African relations, the rhetorical tone in foreign affairs developed to some extent into an issue of its own, separate from the differences in interests that it reflected. It was capable of souring the relations between different countries.

The huffy mood at CIAS was influenced by the grim state of superpower relations, the Algerian war, recent nuclear tests that France had undertaken in the Sahara and the impending Congo crisis. Apart from resolutions on colonialism, the conference criticized "colonial penetration through economic means". While not explicitly mentioning the concept of *neo*-colonialism, it did refer to foreign companies and "agreements and pacts with foreign Powers" restricting "total independence". CIAS also urged the leaders in dependent countries to resist any "balkanization".[5] These statements referred to the Francophone states, which were negotiating co-operation agreements with Paris, in some cases agreed to the presence of French troops and had allowed the break-up of the colonial federations of French West and Central Africa. In another resolution CIAS expressed veiled criticism of the association between the Francophone economies and the EC.[6] Yet, it failed to agree on how to institutionalize co-operation. It decided only to continue the informal group of African ambassadors at the UN, as formed by the first CIAS in 1958.[7]

The Congo crisis and inter-African relations

A week after the conference, the Belgian Congo obtained formal independence and plunged into a crisis of cataclysmic proportions. For some time it would make the implementation of the various plans for continental co-operation impossible, as Africa's states became deeply involved in attempts to quell the crisis or supported one Congolese faction against another. International involvement became so intense that the crisis grew into a full-blown Pan-African conflict. In the course of this, the struggle in the Congo developed meanings that differed, and were to a certain extent distinct, from the perceptions as they obtained within the Congolese arena itself.

Congolese politicians had been badly prepared for the rapid march towards independence that the Belgians had set them on. The political bloc led by Patrice Lumumba, Congo's first prime minister, came closest to developing a nationalist ideology. It advocated a centralized, "unitary" constitutional structure, which at independence was still in a provisional state.[8] The Lumumbists achieved a country-wide

---

4   See, for example, the speech of the Somali delegate at the 2nd CIAS quoted in *Ethiopia Observer*, August 1960, pp 298 and 310.
5   Resolution on the Eradication of Colonial Rule from Africa: Means to Prevent New Forms of Colonialism in Africa.
6   See further below. Resolution for the Creation of an Organization for African Economic Co-operation and *Afrika Informationsdienst*, no. 16, 1960, pp 193-195.
7   Resolution on the Promotion of African Unity; Resolution on the Future Status of the Informal Permanent Machinery of the Independent African States; and *Ethiopia Observer*, August 1960, pp 287 and 291.
8   C. Young, *Politics in the Congo: Decolonization and Independence* (Princeton, 1965), p 516.

audience and tried to implement nationalist policies, although they had their electoral stronghold around Stanleyville in the north-east of the country and did not hesitate to play on ethnic loyalties.[9] Lumumba was the only Congolese with charisma comparable to other nationalist leaders like Touré and Nkrumah. His nationalism at times contained a radical, populist tone, besides some Pan-Africanist sentiment, that earned him allies among the more militant independent states such as Egypt, Guinea and Ghana.[10]

His greatest rival was Joseph Kasavubu, who had his stronghold in the region around the capital Leopoldville. He articulated a belief in federalism, which was an outgrowth of strong ethnic (Bakongo) pride and fears of domination by other ethnic groups. After independence Kasavubu became president and established an uneasy alliance with Lumumba.[11] In the course of the conflict, he managed to find allies among the more conservative African states, especially the Francophones. These were inclined to follow France's position on the Congo and did not find it difficult, from their own experience with the break-up of the French colonial federations, to justify a federal formula for the country. They also felt at ease with the pro-Western tone that the group around Kasavubu increasingly adopted as the conflict internationalized. As the crisis developed international dimensions, labels like "radical", "conservative" and "moderate" gained limited relevance.

In the southern province of Katanga, the prosperous mineral-producing area of the Congo, Moise Tshombe had built up a regional following, especially among Africans that feared domination by the Luba people in their province and among the large European community. The latter had traditionally resented rule from distant Leopoldville and worried about the rapid withdrawal of Belgian suzerainty. At independence Tshombe became provincial president and at best favoured a loose federal structure for the Congo. However, what he really wanted was secession of Katanga.[12] Thus, the unitary-federal issue to a limited extent reflected a serious struggle for power within Congo's modern elite.[13]

Within days of independence, political instability led to a revolt of African soldiers against the officer corps of Congo's army, which was still white and hostile to independence. It resulted in violence against European civilians, panic in European quarters and the unilateral decision of the Belgian government to send metropolitan troops. This led to mutineers retaliating against whites and the declaration of Katanga's independence by Tshombe, who was actively aided by Belgian troops.[14]

Diplomatic relations with Belgium were severed and Kasavubu and Lumumba called for UN intervention. However, the United Nations sent contingents, many of them provided by African states, to prevent an escalation of the crisis into a world conflict, not to end the Katangan secession itself. At first, Lumumba failed to obtain direct military assistance from African states. As he could not obtain Western support either, he became

---

9   E. Bustin, 'The Congo', in G.M. Carter (ed), *Five African States: Responses to Diversity* (Ithaca, 1963), p 105.

10   See his speeches in J. van Lierde, *La pensée politique de Patrice Lumumba* (Brussels, 1963).

11   Bustin, 'The Congo', p 100 and Young, *Politics*, pp 388-393.

12   R. Segal, *African Profiles* (Harmondsworth, 1962), p 160 ff and Young, *Politics*, pp 481-504.

13   Bustin, 'The Congo', pp 99 and 105 and Young, *Politics*, pp 358-367 and 522-532.

14   Young, *Politics*, pp 315-318.

more and more concerned about his government's territorial survival. When some military assistance started to arrive from the Soviet Union, the lack of confidence that the West held in him turned into hostility and Congolese circles around Kasavubu became increasingly hostile to Lumumba as well.[15] This added a Cold War element to the crisis.

Militant circles, both in Congo and various African states, got the impression of a Western reconquest of the heart of Africa. After all, Belgium gave considerable support to Katanga, while the Americans criticized Lumumba's actions and for the moment acquiesced in Katanga's secession.[16] France opposed any role for the UN altogether. This was exacerbated by the nature of the Katangan coalition supporting the secession: this alliance included European settlers, large colonial corporations, white mercenaries and African leaders who could not be heard articulating much anti-Western nationalism; in short, an unholy alliance of everything evil in militant-nationalist eyes.[17] In more conservative circles, both at the inter-African level and in Congo itself, Lumumba became suspect as a result of the moral support he got from militant African states and the assistance given by the Soviet Union. However, no state awarded official recognition to Katanga. Few of them provided much support to Tshombe's regime, with the exception of Congo-Brazzaville, Madagascar and the white regimes of Southern Africa.[18]

The perception of a Cold War element contributed to the rift between Kasavubu and Lumumba and facilitated a coup d'état by Colonel Mobutu. The latter threw out the Soviets and established an alliance with Kasavubu. The fall of Lumumba, at least tacitly supported by the West and several UN officials, led to his imprisonment and the withdrawal of his followers from the capital to Stanleyville under the leadership of vice-premier Gizenga. The latter claimed to represent the legitimate government of Congo. Thus, by the end of 1960, the country had been effectively split in three or four autonomous parts.[19]

Africa's emergent state system could not cope with the bewildering pace of events. In a matter of weeks this huge country, in the very heart of the continent, had begun to disintegrate. Numerous non-African powers had started to interfere, among which were countries that were violently opposed to Africa's impending emancipation. Worse still, one of the richest regions of the continent, Katanga, seemed to have fallen prey to their greedy forces. Militant-nationalist circles everywhere were furious about what was seen, and not without justification, as a dramatic halt to Africa's march towards independence and a blatant attempt by Africa's former white suzerains to consolidate their hold on the continent's most symbolic and important region. It engendered an emotional shock wave that had serious implications for inter-African relations.

In November 1960 both Kasavubu and the Lumumbists claimed the Congolese seat at the United Nations. Militant African states, the Soviet Union and several moderate

---

15   *Ibid.*, pp 319-325 and Bustin, 'The Congo', p 123.
16   See generally S. Weismann, *American Foreign Policy in the Congo 1960-1964* (Cornell, 1974).
17   Young, *Politics*, pp 502-503.
18   I. Mayall, *Africa: the Cold War and After* (London, 1971), p 121; Bustin, 'The Congo', p 142; and C. Hoskyns, *The Congo Since Independence: January 1960 - December 1961* (London, 1965), p 343.
19   Mayall, *Africa*, pp 118-120; Hoskyns, *Congo Since Independence*, pp 200-201 and 215-216; Bustin, 'The Congo', pp 125-126 and 142; and Young, *Politics*, pp 330-331.

African countries wanted to postpone a decision on the matter until later. However, Western countries and most conservative African states, *i.e.* Francophone countries that had now arrived on the international scene, pushed through a final vote to the advantage of Kasavubu.[20] The radical African powers, as well as some of the moderate ones, were furious as many of them had sent troops to the Congo and held high stakes in the conflict's outcome. The bulk of UN contingents, which were dependent on financial and logistical support from the great powers, consisted of forces from Egypt, Ghana, Guinea and Morocco of the militants and Ethiopia, Liberia, Nigeria, Sudan and Tunisia[21] of the moderate countries. All of these had attended the second CIAS and participated in the informal group of African UN ambassadors.

However, most Francophone countries distrusted the military presence of several radical African regimes in the Congo — not just that of Ghana.[22] After all, the UN operation was seriously marred by incidents and political interference involving UN officials, members of the Congolese army, local politicians and officers and diplomats of the countries that had sent contingents. The Francophones also criticized the general foreign policy postures of the other African states, as exemplified by the CIAS and their group of UN ambassadors.[23] Their victory in the UN debate added to the frustration of the radical countries. These resented the UN line on Katanga, suspected Western complicity in the fall of Lumumba and criticized the manner in which their own troops were used. Most of them therefore increasingly inclined to the unilateral intervention that Lumumba had vainly asked for earlier. The more moderate countries, however, shared the militant critique of UN policy on Katanga but did not back the radical support for Lumumba.[24]

Thus, by the end of 1960, inter-African cleavages over the Congo started to crystallize in terms of "radical", "conservative" and "moderate". In most cases these labels also corresponded roughly, but never completely, with general ideological orientations on domestic and foreign policy as discussed in the preceding chapters. As they took shape over the Congo question, inter-African cleavages looked as follows:

radical:	Algeria, Egypt, Ghana, Guinea, Mali and Morocco[25]
moderate:	Ethiopia, Liberia, Libya, Nigeria, Togo, Somalia, Sudan and Tunisia
conservative:	Cameroon, Central African Republic, Chad, Congo-Brazzaville, Dahomey, Gabon, Ivory Coast, Madagascar, Mauritania, Niger, Senegal and Upper Volta.[26]

20   Hoskyns, *Congo Since Independence*, pp 259-266.
21   Senegal also contributed troops, as did some Asian and Western states. See Hoskyns, *Congo Since Independence*, pp 258 and 294.
22   See on Nkrumah's motives for intervening in Congo W.S. Thompson, *Ghana's Foreign Policy 1957-1966: Diplomacy, Ideology, and the New State* (Princeton, 1969), ch. 4 and K. Nkrumah, *Challenge of the Congo* (London, 1967).
23   Hoskyns, *Congo Since Independence*, pp 257-258.
24   *Ibid.*, pp 256-257.
25   Morocco's hardly militant regime adopted a radical attitude to withstand pressures of its opposition favouring the Lumumbists and to get support of the radical states for its claim over Mauritania, as demanded by another party, the Istiqlal. Wallerstein, *Politics of Unity*, p 48.
26   Hoskyns, *Congo Since Independence*, p 257.

The Brazzaville conference — December 1960

The twelve conservatives consisted exclusively of Francophone countries that were also determined to develop their own foreign policy on other issues. In December 1960 they convened in Brazzaville to hammer out common policies on the Congo and the FLN's war of independence in Algeria. They also wished to develop principles for political, diplomatic, defence, economic and technical co-operation, which led to the formation of several inter-governmental organizations. The principal ones were the "Union Africaine et Malgache" (UAM), the "Organisation Africaine et Malgache de Coopération Economique" (OAMCE) and the "Union Africaine et Malgache de Défense" (UAMD). The twelve aimed at the formation of an exclusive alliance, based on their common (*i.e.* Francophone) culture and community of interests.[27]

They emphasized respect for international frontiers, non-interference in internal affairs and the prohibition of subversive activities against another state, f.i. by aiding governments in exile. They also promised to come to each other's aid in case one of them would become the victim of aggression.[28] Where the enemy might come from was left in no doubt as in the conference's discussion of the Congo, they deplored attempts by "the rival blocs" to "re-colonize" the country, directly or through "l'intermédaire de certains Etats asiatiques et africains". This was a slimly veiled reference to the radical African powers inclining to unilateral intervention with Soviet aid. The Brazzaville meeting, which was attended by Kasavubu, Tshombe and moderate Lumumbists, only recommended a Congolese round table conference to solve the country's problems.[29] Thus, it effectively favoured doing nothing, which worked to the advantage of Tshombe and to a lesser extent conformed to the position of Kasavubu-Mobutu.[30] The Leopoldville regime therefore applauded the emergence of the Brazzaville group and welcomed its support for Kasavubu in the UN.[31]

The Brazzaville position on Algeria was rather pro-French. France resisted UN involvement, which the twelve also rejected as "facile", "illusory" and "negative". They emphasized their friendship with Paris and called for Algerian self-determination with reciprocal guarantees for both parties.[32] Finally, the group promised political support to Mauritania, whose territory was claimed by Morocco.[33]

The Casablanca conference — January 1961

The challenge to the radical powers was obvious, as the Brazzaville decisions not only rubbed salt in militant wounds over the Congo, but also adopted a tone on Algeria that was likely to irritate radical countries. Thus, the FLN's provisional government of Algeria (GPRA) had reason to be disturbed by the Brazzaville conference, as did

27   Communiqué, Brazzaville, 19 December 1960 and Déclaration sur la Politique de Coopération Africaine, Brazzaville, 15-19 December 1960.

28   Résolution sur la Conférence Economique, Brazzaville, 15-19 December 1960 and Déclaration sur la Politique ... (n. 27).

29   Communiqué: Problème Congolais, Brazzaville, 19 December 1960 and Hoskyns, *Congo Since Independence*, p 276.

30   Young, *Politics*, pp 521-522 and Hoskyns, *Congo Since Independence*, pp 275-276.

31   *Le Courrier d'Afrique* (Zaire), 21/12/60.

32   Communiqué: Problème algérien, Brazzaville, 19 December 1960.

33   Communiqué: La Mauritanie, Brazzaville, 19 December 1960.

Morocco in view of the Mauritanian issue. Brazzaville strove for a form of exclusive co-operation which was clearly directed against the radical states. This co-operation possessed a defensive and conservative tone and did not move beyond old colonial patterns of influence. Confronted with a relatively large, emergent alliance, radical states had to search for allies.

Morocco announced that it would organize a conference to discuss the Congo crisis. The Brazzaville countries were not invited because they opposed Lumumba and supported Mauritania. Ethiopia, Liberia, Nigeria, Somalia, Sudan, Togo and Tunisia declined to attend, the latter because it had recognized Mauritania. The conference was held in Casablanca in January 1961 and was attended by Egypt, Ghana, the GPRA, Guinea, Libya — which did not participate in later meetings — Mali and Morocco itself.[34] It took place in an emergency atmosphere in which the anger over the Congo clearly predominated.[35] The preceding months seemed to have given more contents to the concept of neo-colonialism, which had hitherto hardly been elaborated. Thus, the conference's resolutions sounded angry and hostile and appeared to be written in acid.

Nevertheless, disagreement surfaced over what to do. While the majority favoured a withdrawal of its UN contingents and a switch of allegiance to Gizenga's regime in Stanleyville, Nkrumah was reticent for fear of stimulating superpower intervention and losing his leverage in the crisis.[36] Thus, the radical powers issued an ultimatum without a time limit to the UN: they declared their intention to withdraw their contingents, as their sole purpose had been to help Congo's legitimate government of June 1960 — i.e. the Kasavubu-Lumumba couple — in safeguarding Congo's independence and territorial integrity. The UN was urged one last time to disarm "the lawless bands of Mobutu", release members of the legitimate government, reconvene parliament and eliminate Belgian and other foreign forces outside UN supervision. If it failed, the radical powers reserved the right to take "appropriate action". This alluded to recognition of the Gizenga regime and the provision to Stanleyville of military assistance, such as Soviet hardware for which Ghana secretly agreed to serve as a channel.[37] In fact, by the end of the month Egypt, Guinea, Morocco, Indonesia and Mali had withdrawn their forces. Nkrumah recognized Gizenga upon the announcement of Lumumba's murder (February 1961) and withdrew his contingent later in the year.[38]

Although actual support to the Gizenga regime remained limited due to its geographical inaccessibility, the implications of the Casablanca decision were not lost on others. For example, Tanganyika, which like many PAFMECSA members sided with the moderate countries, observed that the Casablanca decision might mean armed support to

---

34 Some Asian countries had also been invited. Only Ceylon attended the first meeting as observer. There are, however, conflicting reports on who were invited. *West Africa*, 7/1/61 and 14/1/61 and Wallerstein, *Politics of Unity*, p 48.

35 *West Africa*, 14/1/61.

36 See Young, *Politics*. Also Wallerstein, *Politics of Unity*, p 48; Thompson, *Ghana's Foreign Policy*, pp 152-154; and Nkrumah, *Challenge of the Congo*, ch. 9.

37 Communiqué concerning the situation in the Congo, Casablanca, 3-7 January 1961; Thompson, *Ghana's Foreign Policy*, pp 156-157.

38 This left only moderate African and some Asian powers in place. Wallerstein, *Politics of Unity*, p 48; Mayall, *Africa*, p 123; Nkrumah, *Challenge of the Congo*, p 111; and Hoskyns, *Congo Since Independence*, p 465 (+ n. 46).

Lumumba, whom many countries did not like to see to return to power anyway. It argued that the Casablanca group represented a minority that took the law into its own hands.[39] Understandably, the reaction from Leopoldville was much sharper. It accused the Casablanca powers of a new form of imperialism and racism.[40]

The tone of many of their resolutions was indeed dynamic, if not outright aggressive. As a concession to Morocco, the conference dubbed Mauritania a "puppet state" set up by France to exploit the economic wealth of this area, strengthen its domination over the Sahara and secure an outlet to the Atlantic. Mauritania was the "southern portion" of Morocco's territory, from which it had been separated. This was a typical example of "colonial intrigues". France was "encircling" African states, securing bases and increasing the number of French "satellites". The increase of "artificial states" constituted a threat to the continent's security. The Casablanca group therefore approved "any action taken by Morocco on Mauritania for the restitution of her legitimate rights".[41]

This near carte blanche for Moroccan conquest amply shows Casablanca's opportunism. Yet, the radical states did have other reasons to be angry with France. Paris had just tested another nuclear device in the Sahara, which was seen as an act of intimidation of Africa's peoples. These were asked, over their governments' heads, to prevent any further tests from taking place. All African countries were invited to reconsider their relations with France.[42] Moreover, what was seen as French stalling over Algeria came in for fierce criticism and encouraged the conference to increase the pressure for change. All governments were asked to recognize the GPRA, which the conference saw as the legitimate representative of the Algerian people, and a call went out for the immediate withdrawal of all African troops serving under French command in Algeria.[43]

These pronouncements deepened the rift between the radical and conservative states as Algeria was a subject of acute embarrassment to the latter. Considering themselves nationalists, the Brazzaville leaders could sympathize with the aspirations of the Algerian people. However, their dependence on Paris made them wary of adopting a line that might anger the French. Thus, they refused to recognize the GPRA, although it already fully participated in inter-African conferences. This created considerable obstacles to Pan-African co-operation. The Brazzaville countries also opposed the use of violence to achieve independence and, worse, many of them had citizens serving in the French army fighting the FLN. Casablanca's militant attitudes to defence and colonial issues therefore put the conservative countries on the defensive[44] and made a rapprochement difficult. For example, Guinea had already called for an end to the "scandal of African participation in a war against Africans".[45]

For the conference to succeed the radical powers needed to placate Nasser by adopting a resolution that strongly denounced Israel. However, the latter enjoyed good

39   *Tanganyika Standard*, 12/1/61.
40   *Le Courrier d'Afrique* (Zaire), 12/1/61.
41   Resolution on Mauritania, Casablanca, 3-7 January 1961.
42   Resolution on Nuclear Tests, Casablanca, 3-7 January 1961.
43   Resolution on Algeria, Casablanca, 3-7 January 1961. Also, E. Behr, *The Algerian Problem* (Harmondsworth, 1961), p 180.
44   See f.i. *Le Courrier d'Afrique* (Zaire), 12/1/61.
45   *Ethiopia Observer*, August 1960, p 292.

relations with Ghana and other sub-Saharan states.[46] The quid pro quo for Nkrumah was the adoption of the "African Charter of Casablanca". This stipulated the creation of a "Joint African High Command", involving a Ghanaian proposal to assemble the chiefs of staff of the Casablanca powers to ensure Africa's common defence. The Charter also called for an "African Consultative Assembly", which was a Moroccan suggestion involving the getting together of African parliamentarians. It was especially these announcements that gave the Casablanca group a dynamic, supra-national image.[47]

The Monrovia conference — May 1961

Before these structures are discussed, it should be noted that the successful conclusion of the Casablanca meeting did not amount to the creation of a solid bloc. The group had assembled at heads of state level for an immediate, short-term reason. Despite attempts to institutionalize its co-operation it was unable, in the next two years, to stick together. Thus, while Ghana had reason to be glad about the conference's results, Egypt only spoke vaguely about unity meaning the unity of heart and spirit to reach common objectives and not necessarily political unification. Later it observed that the participating states retained their individual identities.[48] Outside the group, Ivory Coast noted that Casablanca served diverse causes.[49]

Nevertheless, the Congolese and Algerian conflicts had created a wedge in inter-African relations that was difficult to close. In the emotionally charged atmosphere of the times, the explicit challenge by the Brazzaville alliance, accompanied by an embarrassing position on Algeria and open support for the Congolese status quo, had elicited a violent response from the radical powers. However, the latter's militant resolutions on the Congo and other issues only worsened the political climate. Thus, a spiralling effect of alliances and counter alliances had been set in motion, which was difficult to halt as everyone tried to avoid diplomatic isolation.[50]

A few months after Casablanca, another conference was held in Monrovia, of which the origins and intentions appear confused. Senegal wanted to prevent a tough UN resolution on the Congo and wished to bring the radical and conservative groups into one framework, possibly because it was itself relatively isolated within the Brazzaville group dominated by Ivory Coast.[51] The idea to bring the two blocs together was also entertained by Liberia, Togo and Nigeria. Like Ivory Coast these countries desired to counter any threat coming from Ghana, which was suspected of subversive activities and had just launched the seemingly supra-national UAS with Mali and Guinea.[52]

However, even Mali and Guinea agreed to join the planning for the Monrovia conference. The former was rather cautious over its participation in the Casablanca group.

---

46   Resolution on Palestine, Casablanca, 3-7 January 1961.
47   *West Africa*, 14/1/61. Text in L.B. Sohn (ed), *Basic Documents of African Regional Organizations*, vl. I (New York, 1971), pp 42-43.
48   *The Egyptian Gazette*, 5/1/61 and 19/6/62 and Thompson, *Ghana's Foreign Policy*, pp 154-155.
49   See interview with the chairman of the Ivorian parliament in *Fraternité* (Ivory Coast), 29/6/62.
50   See on this period Zartman, *International Relations*.
51   Mayall, *Africa*, p 129; Wallerstein, *Politics of Unity*, p 54; and Thompson, *Ghana's Foreign Policy*, p 198.
52   Wallerstein, *Politics of Unity*, p 54 and Thompson, *Ghana's Foreign Policy*, pp 198 and 203. See f.i. the guarded comment on UAS in *The Ethiopian Herald*, 9/5/61.

It also aspired to reconciliation with Ivory Coast, the country's major access route to the outside world after its break with Senegal. Guinea had its own growing problems with the Osagyefo, many of which were of a personal nature and some related to policy such as the Congo.[53] Nkrumah did not want to attend as the conference would assemble many of his rivals, was at least partially aimed against him and would probably agree to forms of co-operation not up to his standards. At the last minute, however, all Casablanca powers decided to boycott the summit. Ghanaian financial assistance to Guinea and Mali may have led them to reverse policy, while Morocco put pressure on all Casablanca states not to attend as Mauritania had been invited. Moreover, the GPRA had not been invited so as not to offend the Brazzaville twelve. This made the price for attendance by the Casablanca powers too high as GPRA was a full member of their alliance.[54]

The result was disastrous. The attendance of the Monrovia summit (May 1961) by both the conservative and moderate states[55] implied the establishment of a new, much larger alliance that set the radical powers against all other countries and therefore hardened the wedge between them. In a predictably violent reaction Nkrumah remarked: "Which view is dedicated fully to the interests of Africa, unrestrained by fear of external pressure and influence, and reflecting *the true voice of Africa?*".[56] *The Ghanaian Times* had already given some clarification of this by claiming that "the imperialists" had influence in Liberia.[57] It carried the implication that, in militant Pan-Africanist eyes, all might be Africans but some were better nationalists than others, a message that could not go down well with other state elites.[58] Nkrumah's conclusion illustrates how bad state elites could behave in the emotional and hectic atmosphere of 1960-62:

> Let the leaders of Africa take note that among the masses of Africa there is a great moral and spiritual force which will overwhelm the traitors of Africa and their colonial masters alike in an angry avalanche. As I have stated before, the handwriting is written in blood for all to see.[59]

Ghanaian anger had been fuelled by several attacks on its foreign policy, especially its support of opposition elements from other countries. The Monrovia summit had emphasized the "absolute equality" of all states "whatever may be the size of their territories, the density of their populations, or the value of their possessions". This was an answer to Nkrumah's ideas on balkanization as described in section 3.4.[60] The summit had condemned "outside subversive action by neighbouring States", asking all countries

---

53 See Wallerstein, *Politics of Unity*, p 46. Also Thompson, *Ghana's Foreign Policy*.

54 Thompson, *Ghana's Foreign Policy*, pp 198 and 202-203 and Mayall, *Africa*, pp 130 and 206 n. 17.

55 Sudan did not attend. Admittedly, like the GPRA Congo was not invited either to avoid complications. See Wallerstein, *Politics of Unity*, p 54.

56 Article in *Ghana Today*, 24/5/61. Emphasis added.

57 16/5/61.

58 A.A. Mazrui, *Towards a Pax Africana: A Study of Ideology and Ambition* (London, 1967), pp 49-50.

59 *Ghana Today*, 24/5/61 (article).

60 Resolution on the Means of Promoting Better Understanding and Co-operation Towards Achieving Unity in Africa and Malagasy, Monrovia, 8-12 May 1961. Also Thompson, *Ghana's Foreign Policy*, pp 229-232.

to refrain from helping dissident groups of other States with bases and finance.[61] Nevertheless, in a spirit of compromise the Monrovia meeting had called on all states to desist from "hasty recognition of breakaway régimes" — *i.e.* Tshombe's Katanga — and denounced "assassinations as a means to attain political power", a reference to the murder of Lumumba.[62]

The rationale of unity: the Casablanca perspective

Still, the rift with the militant bloc had now developed into a comprehensive cleavage dividing African states on numerous fundamental and minor issues. A first point of disagreement was the tendency of all groupings to see their own alliance as the beginning of a continental framework of co-operation. Thus, the UAM had launched an appeal to all states desirous of co-operating with them "sur la base des principes définis à Brazzaville".[63] The Monrovia summit had expressed confidence about the great majority of states it had assembled and hoped the Casablanca states might attend subsequent meetings. This would then lead to the creation of a continental organization.[64] The Casablanca powers, too, emphasized their "responsibilities towards the African Continent", asking all countries "to associate themselves with our common action": "Were this pilot pattern extended to include all the independent States of Africa", *the Egyptian Gazette* wrote, "the continent's problems would be largely solved".[65] Casablanca's limited membership combined with its radicalism led to accusations that it desired the leadership in Africa's inter-state relations.[66] The existence of competing alliances did not enhance the perception of security, judging from statements by participating countries that their own organization did not represent a "bloc" or "closed shop".[67]

The most fundamental point of disagreement concerned the question which objectives and interests inter-African co-operation — usually paraphrased as "unity" — should serve or against which countries that unity should be directed: in other words, *why* unity should be striven for. It is contended here that this question was in large part responsible for the rift between the respective groups and that another point of disagreement, *i.e.* on the question of *how* unity should be institutionalized, flowed in substantial part from this issue.[68]

---

61   Resolution on the Means of Promoting Better Understanding ... (n. 60).
62   Resolution on Threats to Peace and Stability in Africa and the World, Monrovia, 8-12 May 1961.
63   Déclaration de Politique Générale, Yaoundé, 25-28 March 1961.
64   Resolution on the Means of Promoting Better Understanding ... (n. 60). See also *Daily Times* (Nigeria), 9/5/61 and 12/5/61.
65   *The Egyptian Gazette*, 19/6/62. Also African Charter of Casablanca; interview with the Secretary-General of the Casablanca bloc in *l'Essor* (Mali), 26/12/62; and on a similar Ghanaian claim concerning the UAS, *The Ghanaian Times*, 3/7/61.
66   *The Ethiopian Herald*, 20/6/62 and Resolution on the Means of Promoting Better Understanding ... (n. 60).
67   *The Egyptian Gazette*, 9/1/61 and 19/6/62 and interview with the president of Gabon in *Fraternité* (Ivory Coast), 21/12/62. Admission to organizations was regulated in art. 1 UAM Charter; art. 2 OAMCE treaty; art. 15 UAMD Pact (text all three in *UAM documentation* [no author, Paris, 1963]); art. 16 Protocol of African Charter of Casablanca; art. 14 UAS Charter; and art. 35 IAMO Charter (text all three in Sohn, *Basic Documents*, vl. I).
68   This is hardly ever stated in the literature. See f.i. H.F. Strauch, *Panafrika: Kontinentale*

The Casablanca countries aimed their unity against the influence of non-African powers.[69] The preamble of their charter spoke of the liquidation of colonialism and neo-colonialism, the discouragement of foreign troops and bases in Africa and the desire to rid the continent of "political and economic interventions and pressures". The tone was forceful and dynamic and repeated in accompanying resolutions: "colonial intrigues", "forces of imperialism" and French attempts to "encircle" African states alluded to the outside world and non-African powers on the continent.[70]

This is confirmed by the individual attitudes of the countries involved. Egypt's rationalization of the need for unity, while not lacking in propagandistic qualities, pointed clearly to non-African forces: the High Command had been created with a view to the dangers of neo-colonialism, Israel and the liberation of Southern Africa.[71] In the Malian *l'Essor* the Secretary-General of the Casablanca group claimed that an end to all forms of foreign domination formed one of its "idées-forces": the fact that on their own they could not realize development, safeguard independence, offset foreign influences or handle the great powers was the fundamental reason for the realization of unity.[72]

This rationale was, indeed, at the heart of Nkrumah's visionary ideas. In *Africa Must Unite*, the need for continental unity was developed through a discussion of Africa's development problems and the dangers posed by imperialism, especially in its neo-colonial form. While Africa's economic potential was enormous, so were its development needs. The continent should therefore get rid of its role of producing raw materials and itself embark on industrial development. In order to eradicate Africa's poverty, improve infrastructure and introduce modern science and technology vast amounts of capital were necessary, as well as large expanses of land with natural resources and massive populations providing skills and consumer markets. The necessary capital could only be accumulated by employing resources on a continental scale. This called for central organization. As radical changes were needed, full economic integration rather than customs unions, formed a *sine qua non*.[73]

To Nkrumah, political direction on a continental scale was also needed to fight imperialism, which was still oppressing the peoples of Southern Africa and threatened the security of Africa's independent states. Common defence would deter any aggressor and continental non-alignment could eliminate Cold War rivalry.[74] Moreover, imperialism was exerting its influence through the more subtle policy of neo-colonialism. This concept

---

Weltmacht im Werden? Anfänge, Wachstum und Zukunft der afrikanischen Einigungsbestrebungen (Zurich, 1964). A more comprehensive approach in *Problèmes actuels de l'unité africaine: colloque d'Alger (25 mars-22 avril 1971)* (l'Université d'Alger: Algiers, 1973). Also Wallerstein, *Politics of Unity*; Legum, *Pan-Africanism*, ch. 3; and C. Chime, *Integration and Politics among African States: Limitations and Horizons of Mid-Term Theorizing* (Uppsala, 1977), ch. 9.

69   See for a rare confirmation of non-African influence as the real issue dividing Casablanca and the others, S. Singleton, 'Conflict Resolution in Africa: The Congo and the Rules of the Game', in *Pan-African Journal*, vl. 8, 1975, no. 1, p 10.

70   African Charter of Casablanca and resolutions quoted above.

71   *The Egyptian Gazette*, 28/12/60 and 9/1/61.

72   *l'Essor* (Mali), 26/12/62. See also *The Ghanaian Times*, 2/1/61; a similar argument by Morocco in *Le Courrier d'Afrique* (Zaire), 12/9/62 (article); and *Ethiopia Observer*, August 1960, p 297.

73   *Africa Must Unite* (New York, 1984 [1st ed. 1963]), ch. 17.

74   *Ibid.*, ch. 19.

involved the exercise of indirect control over Africa by Western imperialism through the offer of "semi-independence" to moderate elements in the "aristocratic class" within the confines of small, weak and unviable client states.[75]

For this, imperialists had balkanized the continent. They had encouraged divisions, fomented coups d'état, maintained defence pacts with, and military bases in, African countries and negotiated arrangements involving aid and preferential access to markets. Alluding to the association between the EC and the Francophone countries, Nkrumah referred to the latter as pawns in neo-colonial arrangements, which guaranteed Europe's prosperity and perpetuated the traditional role of Africa's economy. Thus, the wheel turned full circle as economic progress, genuine political independence, military security and liberation from colonialism could only be realized by one continental Union of African States.[76]

In the totality of Nkrumah's thinking, African peace was indivisible: against the total onslaught of neo-colonialism, the continent needed total defence, total freedom and, so, total union. While the other Casablanca powers did not go as far as the Osagyefo, their rationalizations also alluded, as shown above, to neo-colonialism[77] and balkanization. They also involved articulations of conspiracy theory, which, however, was not the exclusive province of the radicals.[78] Moreover, the consistent reference to non-African powers did not imply Casablanca's opposition to all forms of collaboration with the Western world. Nkrumah agreed that Africa still needed foreign capital through arrangements respecting African independence.[79] Egypt claimed that African unity did not amount to autarky, as co-operation with East and West remained necessary.[80]

The militants had, however, started off with strong language, earning them the reputation among moderate-conservative countries of being "demagogues". They were supposed to suffer from a lack of "realism", to concentrate too much on world political issues[81] and were criticized on the point of collaboration with the Western world. The Tanzanians said that many states wished to have good relations with Israel and that militant attacks on Western countries were detrimental to aid flows. Ivory Coast and Gabon also emphasized that aid remained necessary and that African states should therefore co-operate with outside powers, a point that had actually not been disputed.[82]

---

75   *Ibid.*, ch. 18. See on neo-colonialism further below.

76   *Ibid.* Also see K. Nkrumah, *Neo-Colonialism: The Last Stage of Imperialism* (London, 1965) and K. Nkrumah, *Axioms of Kwame Nkrumah* (London, 1967), pp 59-65.

77   See f.i. *The Egyptian Gazette*, 9/1/61 and S. Touré, *l'Afrique et la révolution* (Paris, 1967), pp 320-321.

78   See *The Egyptian Gazette*, 5/1/61; *The Ghanaian Times*, 15/5/63 and 18/5/63; *The Ethiopian Herald*, 30/3/61, 30/12/62 and 26/5/63; *Daily Times* (Nigeria), 27/5/63; statement by Modibo Keita in *l'Essor* (Mali), 29/7/63; and *Le Courrier d'Afrique* (Zaire), 29/3/61.

79   *Africa Must Unite*, pp 101-102 and 185-186.

80   Thompson, *Ghana's Foreign Policy*, p 202 and *The Egyptian Gazette*, 27/3/61.

81   *The Ethiopian Herald*, 10/5/61 and 13/5/61; *Le Courrier d'Afrique* (Zaire), 12/1/61; and communiqué of Madagascar's foreign ministry in *Nouvelles Malgaches Quotidiennes*, 11/5/63.

82   *Tanganyika Standard*, 12/1/61 and 7/4/61 and interview with the president of Gabon in *Fraternité* (Ivory Coast), 21/12/62.

The rationale of unity: the Brazzaville and Monrovia perspectives

The Brazzaville countries propounded an inward-looking conception of unity that was very defensive as regards the political status quo in Africa. It was articulated in language lacking the dynamism and flamboyance of the Casablanca powers. Their co-operation, rationalized in the term "solidarité africaine",[83] represented the co-operation of the privileged few tied "par un passé historique commun et une culture commune".[84] They wished to reinforce their solidarity, secure the friendship of France and consolidate security and development. Their co-operation covered a wide range of fields such as diplomacy, communications and a host of technical, economic and financial matters characterized by a low-key posture.[85]

Setting themselves apart, the UAM countries articulated a non-continentalist view of co-operation and decided to form their own ambassadors' group at the UN.[86] While confirming that the UAM was a part of the larger Monrovia group, they intended to preserve their own institutions as a regional group within the framework of a continental organization to be formed at a later date.[87] They said they would not commit themselves in global affairs, but it was clear they closely allied themselves with France. The UAM states therefore frequently confirmed their friendship with Paris, although they admitted that they should uphold a common UAM front in their negotiations with the EC.[88]

Thus, the Brazzaville countries might in certain circumstances aspire to common action vis-à-vis non-African powers, but their conception of unity was essentially collaborative with regard to the old patterns of influence in Africa. Decolonization and disarmament were not emphasized and economics all the more. They emphasized responsible leadership[89] and used cautious, defensive language paying homage to "la paix", "la négociation", "le dialogue", "la vérité" and international legal principles.[90] Balkanization did not figure in their vocabulary.

Originally intended to realize a rapprochement between all African states, Monrovia rarely alluded to outside (African or non-African) powers, against which its co-operation could be set in sharper relief. It did, however, call for greater African representation in the UN, a "united front to all world problems" and peaceful settlement of disputes. Its posture on decolonization, disarmament and nuclear tests was more forceful than that of the Brazzaville countries.[91]

---

83 See f.i. Déclaration sur les Problèmes Internationaux, Tananarive, 6-12 September 1961.
84 Communiqué Final, Bangui, 25-27 March 1962.
85 See f.i. the texts in *UAM documentation* (n. 67).
86 Art. 5 UAM Charter.
87 Déclaration sur les Problèmes Internationaux, Tananarive, 6-12 September 1961 and Communiqué Final, Bangui, 25-27 March 1962.
88 Communiqué Final, Bangui, 25-27 March 1962.
89 See the opinions of the chairman of the Ivorian parliament in *Fraternité* (Ivory Coast), 29/6/62 and 7/9/62.
90 A good example is the Déclaration sur les Problèmes Internationaux, Tananarive, 6-12 September 1961.
91 Resolution on Threats to Peace and Stability in Africa and the World and Resolution on Settlement of Conflicts which may Arise Between African States, both at Monrovia, 8-12 May 1961.

The institutionalization of unity: opposing views

The question of the need for unity easily flowed over into a debate on the manner in which it should be institutionalized. The Casablanca powers alluded to a supra-national conception by introducing the idea of an inter-African parliament. This, however, was never implemented. Besides the African High Command, the Casablanca group consisted of political, economic and cultural committees that were made up of the heads of state or ministers. These were to be held together by a "Liaison Office" composed of a Secretary-General and his staff. In practice, the committees were merely ministers-in-conference that met on an irregular basis. Thus, there was no doubt about Casablanca's[92] inter-governmental nature. In fact, its documents avoided words like "integration", "union" and "unification".[93]

Nkrumah, however, foresaw enormous tasks for his continental structure, so he could only advocate the formation of a fully-fledged Union of African States. This implied a limitation of national sovereignty. Yet, the individual parts of the Union would be equal and their essential sovereignty would not be infringed, as they would continue to exercise authority except in security and development. Nkrumah did not elaborate on this and his reassurances on the point of national sovereignty were unconvincing. His political union involved an "African Common Market", common currency, monetary zone, central bank, one "Defence Command for Africa" and united foreign policy and diplomatic representation. Nkrumah proposed a continental parliament, made up of a lower house as a deliberative body with representation "based on population" and a higher house with equal representation for every state.[94]

These proposals clearly went too far for all other countries, including the Casablanca ones. Besides fears of losing control of their own states and the potential abuse that could be made of a supra-national structure, their rationales of unity did not necessitate such strong measures anyway. Casablanca's alliance therefore did not really differ, in institutional respects, from the UAM or the Monrovia group.[95] However, Casablanca's flamboyant, aggressive postures and Nkrumah's unrelenting propaganda for political union and union government resulted in the unity debate focusing especially on institutional-legal elements. It had the effect of deepening, as well as exaggerating, the cleavage between the respective groups, which were principally divided over the question of the need and direction of unity. The Brazzaville countries therefore stated explicitly that "il n'y a plus lieu à l'heure actuelle de procéder à la création d'un organisme à caractère supra-national".[96] Respect for sovereignty, equality and non-interference in internal affairs should be the corner-stones for Africa's new political order.

---

92 As it never adopted a formal name of an organization, it was known as the Casablanca group or African Charter of Casablanca.

93 See African Charter of Casablanca and Protocol of the African Charter.

94 *Africa Must Unite*, ch. 21.

95 UAM structures were wide-ranging and in some technical areas ahead of Casablanca. See Protocol on Relations among UAM Organizations (text in Sohn, *Basic Documents*, vol. I, pp 353-354). Monrovia formed its own organization, the Inter-African and Malagasy Organization (IAMO), only in December 1962.

96 Preamble, OAMCE treaty.

Within the Monrovia group, too, these principles found expression. With regard to Casablanca's activities, it was claimed that political union was unwieldy and premature.[97] The unity Africa should strive for was "unity of aspirations and of action", leading to the formation of a mere advisory organization.[98] Socio-economic and technical co-operation were emphasized as more effective steps towards African unity, an attitude that seemed functionalist in conception.[99]

However, in view of limited continental economic integration and despite the logical priority given to development issues, one may wonder to what extent these views were used as an excuse to oppose continental unification or prop up an anti-militant coalition. The UAM states had themselves realized a considerable degree of political, diplomatic and defence co-operation. Nevertheless, in almost all their policy statements, both Brazzaville countries and the Monrovia group as a whole laid much more stress on economic and technical co-operation than the radical powers.[100] Still, in part it was also a matter of pace. The Monrovia powers, which spoke of inter-African rather than *Pan*-African co-operation, rejected the flamboyant Casablanca approach, that seemingly aimed at immediate results, in favour of gradual steps towards unity.[101]

Closely related to this was the question whether unity should be realized by aiming first at regional co-operation. Especially in economic matters UAM and Monrovia opted for a regional approach.[102] Nkrumah, and at least rhetorically some other Casablanca powers too, articulated a naive Pan-African view that ignored the lack of continental economic integration. They were influenced by a continentalist mystique that was grounded in the observation of the continent as a geographical "unit". If united politically and economically as well, it could form the source of considerable power.[103] This argument implied that the continent could act as a kind of leverage mechanism that would enhance the power of Africa's state elites.

However, the Casablanca view also involved the circular argument that Africa's problems could only be solved by realizing continental unity, as all those problems implicated the whole continent precisely *because* Africa formed a unit. It was a unitarist idea that failed to differentiate between regions, underestimated the multiple roles of states in foreign affairs and politicized the meaning of any incident: non-African involvement in one part of Africa, however localized, would be inflated as an attack against the whole continent. This totalitarian perspective, though understandable with regard to the Congo crisis, carried the germs of paranoia and conspiracy theory. To some extent this was

97   *Daily Times* (Nigeria), 9/5/61.
98   Resolution on the Means of Promoting Better Understanding ... (n. 60).
99   See f.i. *The Ethiopian Herald*, 21/6/60, 9/5/61 and 10/5/61; *Fraternité* (Ivory Coast), 7/9/62 (article); interview with President Tsiranana in *Nouvelles Malgaches Quotidiennes*, 20/5/63; and *Daily Times* (Nigeria), 9/5/61 and 1/7/61.
100   Resolution on the Means of Promoting Better Understanding ... (n. 60); art. 1.2 and 2.a IAMO Charter; and f.i. *UAM documentation* (n. 67).
101   Art. 3 OAMCE treaty; Résolution no. 1/62/OAMCE; and *Nouvelles Malgaches Quotidiennes*, 24/5/63 (article).
102   Résolution sur la Conférence Economique, Brazzaville, 15-19 December 1960; Résolution no. 1/62/OAMCE; Resolution on Economic and Financial Co-operation, adopted by Monrovia group, Lagos, January 1962; and *The Ethiopian Herald*, 13/5/61.
103   F.i. *Africa Must Unite*, p xi and *The Egyptian Gazette*, 24/5/63.

self-victimization, rather than a contribution to effective conscientization about Africa's problems.

It was most rigidly articulated by Nkrumah, who felt disappointed about the UAS, feared that regional groupings as the UAM represented balkanization and antagonized Nyerere in his desire for an East African federation.[104] He tried to fortify his argument by claiming that all Africans shared a deep-rooted, intrinsic one-ness, which others recognized as true but insufficient for unity.[105] Léopold Senghor of Senegal held the belief that at least sub-Saharan Africa was a cultural unity, but opposed Nkrumah's continentalism as smacking too much of autarky, favouring multiple levels of co-operation instead.[106]

Other disagreements: military and security aspects

As Casablanca's Joint African High Command aimed at the defence of the entire continent, others felt that its formation should not only concern a minority of states.[107] The radical countries presented this idea as one of their most important projects, earning them a reputation for "militarism".[108] This criticism was to some extent unfair. While the Casablanca states managed to hold at least one joint military exercise, the other radical countries were less enthusiastic about the plan than Ghana. The powers of the Command, comprising the national chiefs of staff, were limited. Moreover, the defence organ of the UAM states, UAMD, also involved structures for military co-operation.[109]

Thus, the fundamental cause for disagreement did not lie in the formation of defence communities as such, but in the perception of the enemy.[110] The African High Command was aimed at any non-African powers — including Southern Africa's racist orders — or their "neo-colonial" African clients as the Leopoldville regime. It therefore induced a very hostile reaction. The UAMD took a defensive line, extolling the principles of international law, claiming no responsibility for continental security and enabling its members to sign military agreements with third states, "whether African or not". This referred to the far-reaching military co-operation established by the defence accords between France and several Francophone countries.[111]

Predictably, the UAMD did not pay lip-service to non-alignment, while the Casablanca countries referred to it consistently. Like some Monrovia powers these

---

104 See *Africa Must Unite*. Also Thompson, *Ghana's Foreign Policy*, p 329 ff and R. Cox, *Pan-Africanism in Practice. An East African Study: PAFMECSA 1958-1964* (London, 1964), p 6.

105 See *The Ethiopian Herald*, 10/5/61.

106 Mazrui, *Pax Africana*, pp 54-55. Amadou Kebe, Conseiller of the Senegalese embassy in Ethiopia, also associated Pan-Africanism with autarky, in interview with author, Addis Ababa, 3/10/89.

107 *The Ethiopian Herald*, 20/6/62.

108 See *The Egyptian Gazette*, 9/1/61; *The Ghanaian Times*, 2/1/61; *The Ethiopian Herald*, 13/5/61; and *Le Courrier d'Afrique* (Zaire), 12/1/61.

109 Arts. 4, 5, 6 and 12 UAMD Pact and for Casablanca's High Command, Thompson, *Ghana's Foreign Policy*, pp 201 and 218-219.

110 See f.i. *Le Courrier d'Afrique* (Zaire), 29/3/61.

111 Arts. 9 and 16 UAMD Pact and for the 1960-61 defence accords between France, CAR, Congo-Br. and Chad and between France, Ivory Coast, Dahomey and Niger, Sohn, *Basic Documents*, vl. II (New York, 1972) pp 855-861 and 921-925.

actively participated in the non-aligned movement. As shown in section 2.3, however, each country gave its own practical interpretation to the concept. Still, in the militant perspective of the early 1960s this concept made the presence of foreign military bases unacceptable, as well as the defence agreements with non-African powers and France's nuclear tests in the Sahara. Nkrumah fulminated that the Francophone defence treaties had been forced upon France's neo-colonial clients, giving it control over their foreign policy and military bases that made their independence questionable.[112] Guinea called for withdrawal of all foreign military installations and Nasser said military pacts were more directed against "internal fronts of nations" than foreign aggression.[113]

France's disregard for African opinion on the point of the Sahara tests was infuriating to many states, radical and moderate. Between the end of 1959 and late 1960 alone, three nuclear blasts took place. Ghana froze French assets as Nkrumah was personally outraged.[114] Nigeria broke its diplomatic relations with Paris and Ethiopia expressed its "disappointment". The North African countries reacted more violently. Libya and Morocco denounced the tests, with the latter severing diplomatic ties with Paris. Egypt tried to belittle French power as a paper tigre by saying that nuclear weapons were "but a sorry stop-gap".[115] African anger was caused not so much by the objective threat that French atomic might constitute as by the unperturbed manner in which Paris continued its testing. This was a psychological blow that strengthened state elite awareness of impotence vis-à-vis Western powers. Thus, Tunisia remarked that "France treats Africa as a fief where she can do as she pleases".[116] The issue also contributed to inter-African cleavages. The *Daily Times* of Nigeria remarked acidly that De Gaulle was able to continue testing as Francophone Africans failed to protest as long as French Francs kept pouring in.[117]

Not surprisingly, the UAM opposed tough action against Britain and France over decolonization policy and was only prepared to back sanctions against South Africa and Portugal.[118] Monrovia countries in general adopted a stronger posture, at least rhetorically.[119] The Casablanca countries felt no inhibitions. However, as shown in section 3.4 the North and West African countries had disagreed on the question whether violence should be used to encourage decolonization. The desire to further decolonization was also subject to leadership competition, especially between Cairo, Accra and Conakry. Nevertheless, several Casablanca countries gave material and financial support to nationalist groupings.

---

112   *Africa Must Unite*, p 174.
113   *Ethiopia Observer*, August 1960, p 292 and Text of Speech delivered by President Gamal Abdel Nasser at the Conference of Non-Aligned Nations, Belgrade, p 25 (no d. or pl.).
114   Thompson, *Ghana's Foreign Policy*, pp 98-99.
115   *Ethiopia Observer*, August 1960, pp 289, 295, 297 and 300.
116   *Ibid.*, p 294.
117   *Daily Times*, 12/3/63.
118   Déclaration de Politique Générale, Yaoundé, 25-28 March 1961 and Déclaration sur les Problèmes Internationaux, Tananarive, 6-12 September 1961. See also A. Tevoedjre, *Pan-Africanism in Action: An Account of the UAM* (Harvard, 1965), pp 82-84.
119   Resolution on Threats to Peace and Stability in Africa and the World, Monrovia, 8-12/5/61 and *The Ethiopian Herald*, 5/7/61.

Other disagreements: economic aspects

More relevant to inter-African cleavages were attitudes towards *neo*-colonialism. This concept alluded to Africa's new political-economic order. It was thus related to questions of whether or not, and to what extent, state elites should resist or accommodate to the structures forced upon them by the Western world. The term itself was principally articulated by radical countries and hardly ever by any of the Brazzaville powers, as these had gone a considerable way in swallowing France's demands. What neo-colonialism entailed exactly was therefore open to debate. Apart from Nkrumah's description referred to above, the third AAPC, held in Cairo in March 1961, gave its own definition: neo-colonialism represented the survival of the colonial system through indirect and subtle domination; for this, the former colonial powers used economic, political, social, technical and military means, such as the regrouping of states; balkanization; establishment of military bases; consolidation of monetary dependence; economic infiltration by unequal investment contracts; and, if all else failed, recourse to violence. The main perpetrators of neo-colonialism were the United States, Western Europe, Israel and South Africa. Their African client regimes were deemed to be "puppet" governments.[120]

Naturally, the concept engendered considerable hostility among Africans themselves, not only between governments but also between state elites and non-governmental groups. The reference to neo-colonialism was an affront as it held that some states were in theory independent but in reality directed by the West, thus touching on the political legitimacy of state elites.

Among governments, the principal bone of contention was the association agreement with the EC. However, non-Francophone states did not necessarily hold a dialectical conception of Eur-African relations. While no state was willing to break with Europe economically, many thought that association with the EC would consolidate the traditional role of Africa's economy. A more non-aligned posture would strengthen Africa's bargaining position and result in a more advantageous relationship. The Francophone countries claimed that confrontation with Europe would only have adverse effects and that association implied the transfer of funds with which to transform Africa's economy. Ties with the EC should therefore be strengthened.[121] In the context of *inter*-African relations, the association issue led to tensions as UAM states did not favour an end to EC discriminatory treatment of Commonwealth exports.[122] Many Commonwealth states also feared the possible entry of Britain into the EC, as it might have an adverse effect on trade.[123]

However, it was the idea of European integration as such that also led to concern. After all, a stronger Europe could dominate Africa even more than it already did now.[124] Around 1962, EC motives were therefore called into question. Association was portrayed as "economic bondage", a new form of colonialism and contrary to non-alignment. As it

---

120   Resolution on Neo-Colonialism, 3rd AAPC, Cairo, 25-31/3/61.
121   Wallerstein, *Politics of Unity*, pp 138-140.
122   Recommendation No. 3/62, Libreville, 31/8-1/9 1962. Yet, see quotation of Senghor in Nkrumah, *Africa Must Unite*, pp 159-160.
123   *The Ethiopian Herald*, 19/9/62.
124   Mazrui, *Pax Africana*, pp 85-88.

consolidated economic links with Europe, it was regarded as incompatible with the establishment of an African Common Market.[125]

The creation of such a market was proposed by the economically disparate Casablanca group with typical immediacy. Yet, this did not reflect their genuine attitudes, even of Ghanaians outside Osagyefo's direct vicinity.[126] Nevertheless, the issue added to all the other disagreements. While UAM countries did not regard EC association as incompatible with closer inter-African co-operation, they claimed that an African Common Market could only be realized in a long, drawn-out process. Such a gradual approach was also propounded by the Monrovia group as a whole.[127]

4.3   Towards reconciliation 1962-1963

Developments in Algeria and the Congo
Until the beginning of 1962, it was impossible for Africa's state elites to heal the rift between them. As the management of the Algerian and Congolese crises had created a deep wedge between the militant states and the Brazzaville powers, any chance for reconciliation had to wait until some solution could be found for the two catalysts that had brought inter-African cleavages to the surface. However, by 1962, the French and the FLN were involved in complex negotiations about the granting of independence to Algeria, which culminated in a peace accord at Evian in March 1962. This agreement entailed a suspension of hostilities, the formation of a transition government and a referendum in which Algerians voted overwhelmingly for independence. This was proclaimed on 3 July 1962.[128]

The situation in the Congo had been changing as well. The balance of power between Leopoldville, Stanleyville and Katanga had been shifting continually. The Leopoldville regime, however, had better infrastructure and superior access to the outside world. After the summer of 1961, a new central government was formed, which included Lumumbists and was headed by the relatively neutral Cyril Adoula. This gave the signal for a redefinition of Congo's institutional structure and reduced the dissidence of Stanleyville, despite a second, short-lived revolt by Gizenga in the latter half of the year. Tshombe had meanwhile refused to give up a confederal formula agreed on earlier and continued to defy United Nations troops. The latter's mandate had been strengthened in February 1961 to include the use of force to remove foreign troops from Katanga. By mid-1962, Western powers were also changing course, believing that Katanga's secession would prevent a return to stability. They therefore put pressure on Tshombe to

---

125   *The Ethiopian Herald*, 19/9/62; *Ethiopia Observer*, August 1960, p 295; and *Daily Times* (Nigeria), 15/9/62 (article).
126   Thompson, *Ghana's Foreign Policy*, pp 216-218.
127   See Madagascar's foreign ministry communiqué in *Nouvelles Malgaches Quotidiennes*, 11/5/63; interview with the chairman of the Ivorian parliament in *Fraternité* (Ivory Coast), 29/6/62; Résolution No/2/62/OAMCE, Bangui, 25-27/3/62; and Resolution on Economic and Financial Co-operation, Lagos, 25-30/1/62.
128   See for details A. Horne, *A Savage War of Peace: Algeria 1954-1962* (London, 1977), part 3.

reintegrate his province. After several military setbacks, UN troops were to reoccupy Katanga and put an end to the secession in December 1962 — January 1963.[129]

Shifting alignments

The attitudes of inter-African alliances shifted with the events. When Algeria became independent, the UAM states could freely participate in conferences attended by the Algerians without risking the wrath of France. Many governments realized that an important stumbling block had thereby disappeared.[130] With regard to the Congo, the UAM states had first welcomed a confederal solution favourable to Tshombe, but by September 1962 were to endorse the UN plan for Katanga's reintegration.[131] For the Casablanca powers, the supply of military hardware to the Lumumbists had been difficult from the beginning. Support to Gizenga's second rebellion against the legitimate government of Adoula, which they had welcomed, was politically inopportune. Although by the end of 1962 Adoula had removed the Lumumbists from his cabinet, the principal militant demand was fulfilled: the end of the Katangan secession, which had been the symbol of foreign influences hostile to Africa's new political order.[132]

From early 1962 moves were therefore made towards reconciliation. But if the two major catalysts for Africa's division were about to disappear, what about the other issues on which African states had disagreed so violently? Naturally, some of the disagreements between radicals and Monrovia powers had been exaggerated through the use of strong rhetoric so typical of the times. Yet, the fundamental point of disagreement between the radical powers and the moderate-conservative countries was the issue of non-African influences on the continent. It had led to a prisoners' dilemma of mutually unco-operative postures, which entailed that the public good (Pan-African co-operation) was not produced. Hegemonic stability theory posits that one can only break out of this by the action of a hegemon.[133] However, the rapid appearance of inter-African cleavages formed *prima facie* evidence of the absence of one continental hegemon that could have prevented the formation of two opposing alliances.

Yet, while disagreement over non-African influences had by no means disappeared, by 1962 both blocs were themselves confronted with internal disagreements that weakened their solidity. In both groupings there were centrifugal forces at work that started a process of fragmentation, leading to a search for new alignments in inter-African relations. Thus, the lack of hegemonic stability also extended to the sub-continental level. For example, Ivory Coast had an influential position in the Brazzaville group, yet beyond the vicinity of its immediate neighbours its influence was more limited. This was exemplified by its competition with Senegal. Nigeria's role in the Monrovia group was

---

129   See Young, *Politics*, ch. 13 (n. 8)

130   Communiqué Final, Bangui, 25-27 March 1962; *Fraternité* (Ivory Coast), 6/7/62 (article); and *Le Courrier d'Afrique* (Zaire), 12/9/62 (article).

131   Déclaration de Politique Générale, Yaoundé, 25-28 March 1961 and Communiqué Final, Libreville, 10-13 September 1962.

132   Wallerstein, *Politics of Unity*, pp 56 and 62 (n. 2). Also K. Nkrumah, *Challenge of the Congo* (London, 1967).

133   J. Gowa, 'Rational Hegemons, Excludable Goods, and Small Groups: An Epitath for Hegemonic Stability Theory?', in *World Politics*, 1989, pp 307-324 and D. Snidal, 'The Limits of Hegemonic Stability Theory', in *International Organization*, 1985, p 581.

also very important, but to some extent attenuated in a cadre with so many actors. Inside the Casablanca group, there were several countries that competed for leadership of the alliance.

This was enhanced by the fluid nature of inter-African relations at the time. Interaction patterns were still relatively new and inexperienced state elites were testing the degree of their international influence. In the context of a more even spread of power than would exist in later decades, small-sized actors like Ghana could be tempted to compete for hegemony as well, thus blurring even further the sight on who was actually in control. In short, even at the regional level differentiation of power was too limited for would-be hegemons to coerce all alliance members into maintaining co-operative postures.[134] Their inability to preserve consensus on rules of interaction pointed to the limits of regional hegemonic ties.[135]

In addition, African states from all groupings were faced with certain common problems that made Pan-African co-operation imperative. The identification of these problems was to set in motion centripetal pressures for continental reconciliation, which hastened the fragmentation of the opposing groups.

We will first discuss the centrifugal forces that began the process of their fragmentation. This is followed by a discussion of the centripetal forces, that lay at the basis of Pan-African rapprochement, and an analysis of the manner in which the process of reconciliation was set in motion. The nature of the impending rapprochement is put in relief by a description of its consequences for non-governmental groupings.

Fragmentation

The specific form in which the radicals had come together, *i.e.* the Casablanca alliance, had, more than the other groups, been dictated by short-term considerations, especially militant dissatisfaction over the Congo. Thus, the Algerians were reported as saying that the objectives that had brought Casablanca into being had *to a certain extent* passed by.[136] This means that some of the short-term justifications for the alliance had disappeared. The radicals could not expand it to other state elites and felt rather vulnerable in their isolated minority position. They had not given up their militant stance, but most members wished to pursue their radical objectives within other frameworks. This is confirmed by the fact that, after the formation of the OAU, the cleavage between moderates-conservatives and radicals reappeared.

Moreover, Casablanca had been a disparate group from the start. Algeria was now independent and could behave more freely in inter-African affairs. Egypt was preoccupied with other matters. Even Nkrumah, who had invested most in the alliance, lost some interest in the group as his preaching fell on deaf ears. Mali needed inter-African reconciliation to break its economic isolation. Guinea, too, was moving towards a middle position, especially after its rupture with the USSR in December 1961. While Sékou Touré was not to give up his militant criticism of the UAM as such, he gambled that

---

134   See on coercion by the hegemon Snidal, 'Limits of Hegemonic Stability Theory'.

135   See on this also R. Iyob, 'Regional Hegemony: Domination and Resistance in the Horn of Africa', in *Journal of Modern African Studies*, 1993, pp 257-276.

136   Emphasis added. C.F. Gallagher, 'The Death of a Group: Members of the Casablanca Pact Fall Out', *American Universities Field Staff Reports*, North Africa Series, vol. IX (1963), no. 4, p 5.

reconciliation with the Francophones would better serve his interests than continuation of a difficult relationship with Ghana's Osagyefo. He even embarked upon negotiations with France to end the hostility between them, which was to culminate in a co-operation agreement in May 1963.[137] Morocco had always been an odd member of the alliance. After the death of Muhammad V, King Hassan II was faced with the fact that his father had allied his country with states with which it did not feel ideological affinity.[138]

Apart from Ghana's problems with Guinea, the Casablanca group was riven by numerous other tensions. The Ghanaians had started to move back to their original friendly attitude to Mauritania, which did not improve relations with Morocco. Relations between Morocco and Guinea had come under pressure by an extradition dispute and from the summer of 1962 the Moroccans developed bad relations with Egypt and Algeria. Rabat opposed Egyptian involvement in Yemen. Its ties with Algeria deteriorated sharply as the latter criticized the conservative nature of the Moroccan kingdom, regarded Mauritania as a political reality and started moving closer to Nasser. A border dispute was to lead to mounting tensions between the two Maghreb neighbours.[139] Moreover, North Africa's hostility to Israel was not shared by most sub-Saharan countries, which from the start had adopted a more friendly attitude to the Jewish state.

The Monrovia group lacked solidarity as well. Many states were upset over French nuclear tests and the question of EC association, matters that touched on relations with the Brazzaville group inside the alliance. The UAM itself was not free from internal tensions either. Relations between Ivory Coast and Senegal were cooling. A dispute between Gabon and Congo-Brazzaville strained relations in Central Africa. These had already suffered by the support that the latter had given to Tshombe's struggle with the Leopoldville regime.[140] Moreover, the UAM's Secretary-General, Albert Tevoedjre, became involved in a personal dispute with President Maga of Dahomey, leading to the former's dismissal in the spring of 1963.[141]

Finally, a coup d'état in Togo, accompanied by the murder of President Sylvanus Olympio in January 1963, was to contribute even further to the process of fragmentation, which by then was already well under way. The Ghanaians were widely suspected of involvement, as relations between Ghana and Togo had been bad because of irredentist activity on both sides of the border, mutual fears of subversion by exiled opposition elements and Nkrumah's designs on Togolese territory. Guinea freely aired its anger and used the event to distance itself from the Osagyefo even further. Nigeria, which had had close relations with Olympio, reacted violently as well and led a campaign against the

---

137   *Horoya* (Guinea), 3/8/63 and *Le Monde* (Paris), 14/5/63 and 24/5/63 (article).
138   Zartman, *International Relations*, pp 32-33 (n. 3); Thompson, *Ghana's Foreign Policy*, pp 199 and 217-220 (n. 22); and J. Woronoff, *Organizing African Unity* (Metuchen, NJ, 1970), p 76. Also Gallagher, 'Death of a Group'.
139   Gallagher, 'Death of a Group', pp 3-7.
140   Woronoff, *Organizing African Unity*, p 77; on the Congo-Br. - Gabon dispute Tevoedjre, *Pan-Africanism*, ch. 4 (n. 118); and for evidence of formerly strained relations between Leopoldville, Brazzaville and UAM two articles on the UAM Tananarive conference in *Le Courrier d'Afrique* (Zaire), 13/9/61.
141   Tevoedjre, *Pan-Africanism*, ch. 3 for a partisan account and for its observation in the governmental press, *The Ethiopian Herald*, 10/3/63; *Fraternité* (Ivory Coast), 22/3/63 (article); and *Le Courrier d'Afrique* (Zaire), 19/3/63 (article).

recognition of Grunitzky, the new Togolese leader. In this it more or less enjoyed the sympathy of Guinea, Ivory Coast, Upper Volta and Sierra Leone, while Ghana, Senegal and Dahomey quickly recognized the Grunitzky regime. Cameroon wished that the matter be left to the discretion of each government. Thus, the Togo issue cut right across Monrovia and Casablanca lines.[142]

Centripetal forces

Apart from the fragmentation of the existing alliances there were certain centripetal pressures that demanded continental co-operation. It has often been argued that, at the time, there was a strong attachment to the doctrine of African unity. Nkrumah, but others too, claimed that Africans shared a deep-rooted feeling of their one-ness as Africans. African unity was "organic", so inter-African divisions were intolerable and the ideal of unity was partly responsible for the move towards reconciliation. However, in sections 3.4 and 4.2 it was emphasized that unity in itself means nothing and that it serves as an instrument to realize certain other objectives. Emphasis on the intrinsic value of African unity may have been a psychological reaction of elite Africans to their sense of vulnerability and inferiority in interaction with the Western world.[143]

An article by Julius Nyerere published in early 1963 alludes to the fundamental reasons for a Pan-African rapprochement. The Tanganyikan president emphasized the need for Africa's leaders to act in unison: they should sort out their conflicts in private and not publicly judge each other's internal policies. These matters should be discussed with the leader of the state concerned and not with "the world at large". For the sake of Africa's *states*, unity should come. The *states* were the instrument for the continent's reunification.[144]

While Nyerere claimed that this type of unity would contribute to Africa's progress, it was essentially an elitist conception, as opposed to the populist interpretation officially held by some non-governmental groups. As has been shown, the creation of rival alliances did not contribute to the perception of elite security. All regimes were vulnerable to attack from elite sections excluded from power and could become the victim of subversion. Reconciliation could undercut aid by other governments to domestic opposition. Thus, it is noteworthy that it was the Monrovia group, originally conceived as a conference to realize reconciliation, that proposed mechanisms for the peaceful settlement of inter-African disputes.[145]

Secondly, without a rapprochement Africa's state elites could not hope to achieve some of their common, external objectives. By 1962 it was clear that the non-African world would not provide all the economic aid that African leaders desired. As of 1963,

---

142 Tevoedjre, *Pan-Africanism*, ch. 5; Woronoff, *Organizing African Unity*, p 78; Zartman, *International Relations*, p 34; Wallerstein, *Politics of Unity*, p 64; and Thompson, *Ghana's Foreign Policy*, pp 309 and 316.

143 Nkrumah, *Africa Must Unite*, p 132; Mazrui, *Pax Africana*, ch. 3; Chime, *Integration and Politics*, p 167 (n. 68); and J. Mayall, 'African Unity and the OAU: The Place of a Political Myth in African Diplomacy', in *Yearbook of World Affairs* (London), 1973, pp 110-133.

144 Emphasis added. J.K. Nyerere, 'A United States of Africa', in *Journal of Modern African Studies*, 1963, pp 1-6.

145 Resolution on Settlement of Conflicts which may Arise Between African States, Monrovia, 8-12 May 1961 and art. 28 IAMO charter.

France started reducing aid to its Brazzaville clients, while Guinea had already experienced the risk of a close relationship with the USSR. Moreover, non-African powers did not automatically accept all elite African ambitions in world affairs: at the United Nations all African states desired a greater voice for their continent, which as a result of their disunity was difficult to realize. The Monrovia group had already called for an expansion of African representation in UN organs as the Security Council and the Economic and Social Council, a call that was repeated by the UAM and by the Monrovia group itself in January 1962.[146] To the UAM such a Pan-African front was also meant to achieve greater representation at the IMF and World Bank.[147] In 1962 African states started working jointly for the Africanization of the UN Economic Commission for Africa and the CCTA, an organ for inter-African technical co-operation of colonial origin.[148]

Thus, earlier on the Monrovia group had argued in a more general way that African states should present "a united front in the future to all world problems with which Africa might be faced at the United Nations".[149] These pleas sometimes involved the argument that a united Africa might be able to exert considerable weight in global affairs. This implied the reflection that the continent, politically constructed through inter-African co-operation, could act as a leverage mechanism. This could provide states more influence than they exerted individually and enlarge Africa's power as a whole in the global order of things. It had been most explicitly articulated in the propositions of Nkrumah and, to a lesser extent, the other Casablanca states. At Casablanca's founding conference King Muhammad V had claimed that, if it would unite,

> l'Afrique cessera d'être faible, paralysée, muette; elle sera, au contraire, un continent puissant, respecté et jouissant de l'audience qui lui est due dans le monde.[150]

By 1962, this reflection was also articulated more explicitly by Monrovia countries and even taken up by Brazzaville powers. Thus, the government press in Ethiopia alluded to a future world power status for Africa.[151] Ivory Coast also hoped that a fusion of the two blocs would enable Africa to exert its weight and contribute to the world balance of power.[152] The Leopoldville regime thought that the reconciliation conference should unite "cet immense continent", on whose force, it added meaningly, it did not want to anticipate.[153]

In the context of fragmenting coalitions, these elite considerations about state security and external influence generated enough centripetal pressure to initiate the search

146 Resolution on Threats to Peace and Stability in Africa and the World, Monrovia, 8-12 May 1961; Déclaration sur les Problèmes Internationaux, Tananarive, 6-12 September 1961; and Resolution on United Nations, Lagos, 25-30 January 1962.

147 Résolution No. 19/63/OAMCE, Ouagadougou, 10-13 March 1963.

148 Wallerstein, *Politics of Unity*, p 59.

149 Resolution on Threats to Peace and Stability in Africa and the World, Monrovia, 8-12 May 1961.

150 Text of speech in *Al Istiqlal* (Morocco), 14/1/61. See also the interview with Casablanca's SG in *l'Essor* (Mali), 26/12/62.

151 *The Ethiopian Herald*, 10/5/61 and 30/12/62.

152 *Fraternité*, 7/9/62 (article by chairman of parliament).

153 *Le Courrier d'Afrique*, 16/5/63.

for Pan-African reconciliation. Whether it was sufficient to lead to a genuine continental front in world politics will be assessed in sections 4.6 and 8.3.

The process towards reconciliation

With the removal of the Algerian and Congolese problems, Guinea obtained approval from the Casablanca powers, at their Cairo meeting in June 1962, to work for reconciliation with the Monrovia countries. The UAM states, which had earlier called for a rapprochement during Monrovia meetings, repeated their desire for a reconciliation conference in September.[154] This led to a spate of diplomatic activity involving a great number of countries. President Ahidjo of Cameroon was the first UAM leader to re-establish contact with Nasser (October 1962). Senghor visited Tunisia, whose government helped to prepare the ground for a conference of Maghreb countries in February 1963 and the reconciliation conference to be held later. The Ugandans decided not to join the Casablanca group in the interest of reconciliation, while Tanganyika had always discouraged the formation of rival alliances. The Malians visited Ivory Coast in September 1962. They were to agree to a frontier treaty with Mauritania and improve relations with Senegal by an agreement on the disposition of their federation assets in February 1963.[155]

However, the crucial role was played by Guinea, Ethiopia, Ivory Coast and Nigeria. The volatility that had characterized inter-African relations during the preceding years led to meticulous and long drawn out preparations. Thus, Guinea received visits from Ivory Coast, Niger, Senegal, Togo and Mauritania. Guinean emissaries, among whom figured subsequent OAU Secretary-General Diallo Telli, had by August 1962 visited eighteen capitals in West and Central Africa. Conakry agreed to co-operate with a committee made up of seven countries to work out the details. The committee was carefully balanced in ideological and geographical respects. It included Ethiopia, Egypt, Liberia, Ivory Coast, Senegal, Congo-Brazzaville and Nigeria, but not Ghana.[156]

In fact, Nkrumah's isolation was vividly illustrated when Sékou Touré attacked the Osagyefo by saying that unity should not imply that it had to be formed around one single state or president.[157] On his part, Nkrumah still hoped that a third CIAS could yet be held in Tunis, as had been decided in 1960. This series of conferences, whose 1960 session had adopted a relatively sharp tone, was perceived to be close to the Casablanca powers. It had been regarded by them as an acceptable forum for reconciliation as they had been original participants. However, Nkrumah's hope proved in vain and his diplomatic counter-offensive (January 1963) came far too late. Nevertheless, he had not given up any of his ideas and he therefore sent emissaries to most capitals to persuade leaders not to support an Ethiopian plan for a charter, to be discussed below. On 11 May 1963 he was to publish his *Africa Must Unite*, whose anti-Francophone bias did not to endear him

154 On Casablanca, Thompson, *Ghana's Foreign Policy*, p 220 and on UAM, Communiqué Final, Libreville 10-13 September 1962.

155 Woronoff, *Organizing African Unity*, pp 76-77; Chime, *Integration and Politics*, p 172; Zartman, *International Relations*, pp 32-33; Strauch, *Panafrika*, p 147 (n. 68); and Wallerstein, *Politics of Unity*, p 61.

156 Strauch, *Panafrika*, pp 146-147 and Thompson, *Ghana's Foreign Policy*, p 307.

157 See A. Lewin, *Diallo Telli: le tragique destin d'un grand Africain* (Paris, 1990), p 128.

to his many enemies.[158]

Guinea's reconciliation offensive had started with a visit by Touré to Ethiopia. The latter had kept a relatively neutral profile even though it participated in the Monrovia group.[159] However, the Ethiopian government had begun to develop a leadership role for itself in inter-African politics. From January 1962, Haile Selassie increased his diplomatic activity. A very cautious diplomat, who preferred to wait for the right time to act and operate in the background, he presented himself as the ideal mediator between Africa's quarrelling leaders.[160] For this purpose, the Ethiopians tried to exploit the powerful symbolism that attached to their country in Pan-Africanist eyes and African diplomatic circles.[161] Moreover, Haile Selassie enjoyed seniority over all other leaders. As the man who survived the onslaught of fascist Italy he had enormous prestige among his colleagues, especially Nkrumah and Kenyatta.[162]

Haile Selassie had strong motives to become active in inter-African affairs. His state was fragile as a result of its complex ethnic make-up, disputed international frontiers and the feudal nature of the political order. This could easily become the object of radical criticism, as illustrated by a PAFMECSA call for democracy throughout the continent.[163] A more active foreign policy could enhance Ethiopia's world role and, hence, strengthen Haile Selassie's hold on power.[164]

The movement towards rapprochement can be noticed in the governmental press as of mid-1962. Diallo Telli declared that, despite different political and economic situations, a profound "communauté de vues, d'aspirations et d'idéal" should be realized through co-operation that respected each other's national institutions.[165] In June, the Ivorians were already talking of a common organization of political life. Later they referred to decolonization as one of its objectives and spoke of aspirations to African unity, instead of the concept of "solidarité africaine" as the UAM had used before.[166] Africa's states were likened to children of one family that were soon to be reunited. A comparable, conciliatory tone was adopted by the Secretary-General of the Casablanca group.[167]

Thus, by the end of the year, it had become clear that a reconciliation conference would be held in Addis Ababa in May 1963. By January, a record 31 states had accepted

158   Thompson, *Ghana's Foreign Policy*, pp 307 and 318-320.

159   F.i. *The Ethiopian Herald*, 13/5/61 and 5/7/61. Others that had kept distance to the continental divide were Tanganyika, Libya, Tunisia and Sudan. Also Wallerstein, *Politics of Unity*, p 57.

160   Wallerstein, *Politics of Unity*, p 58 and C. von Ulm-Erbach, *Aethiopiens Beitrag zur Gründung der Organisation für Afrikanische Einheit: Eine Studie zur Rezeption des Pan-afrikanismus in die afrikanische Politik und Anpassung Aethiopiens an diese Entwicklung* (Bern, 1974), pp 93-94.

161   See f.i. Ministry of Information of the Imperial Ethiopian Government: 'Second Conference of Independent African States, Addis Ababa, June 24 to 26, 1960' (Addis Ababa, n.d.), pp 2-5.

162   Ulm-Erbach, *Aethiopiens Beitrag*, p 110 and Thompson, *Ghana's Foreign Policy*, p 39.

163   Ulm-Erbach, *Aethiopiens Beitrag*, p 108. See Freedom Charter of the Peoples of East and Central Africa (text in Cox, *Pan-Africanism in Practice*, p 82 [n. 104]).

164   See for a recent analysis of this Iyob, 'Regional Hegemony'.

165   *Fraternité* (Ivory Coast), 7/9/62 (article).

166   Interview with the chairman of the Ivorian parliament in *Fraternité*, 29/6/62 and article in *ibid.*, 7/9/62.

167   *Le Courrier d'Afrique* (Zaire), 12/9/62 (article) and interview with Casablanca's Secretary-General in *l'Essor* (Mali), 26/12/62. On the use of kinship terminology, J.F. Bayart, *L'état en Afrique: la politique du ventre* (Paris, 1989), pp 220-221.

an invitation for this from Haile Selassie. It was decided that the conference would consist of a foreign ministers conference followed immediately by a summit of heads of state, as any delay between the two might increase the chance of a final hiccup.

Despite the projected summit, the Monrovia powers held their own meeting in Lagos in December 1962, where they signed a charter for an "Inter-African and Malagasy Organization" (IAMO). With most of them postponing ratification until after the Addis Ababa summit, it had the effect of strengthening their bargaining position. The IAMO charter could be used as a quid pro quo and its impending ratification could create the impression that the summit would be the last occasion at which rapprochement could be achieved.[168] While the IAMO charter emphasized the desire for reconciliation, it stipulated the formation of a strictly inter-governmental structure.[169]

Casablanca's Secretary-General also continued to make plans for the implementation of objectives that the militants had agreed on earlier.[170] Unfortunately, a few weeks before the Addis Ababa summit, the Moroccans had to call off a preparatory conference of the Casablanca powers, as several members had no interest to attend.[171] Brazzaville powers similarly tried to elaborate their co-operative framework, which now also included the Leopoldville regime. During a meeting in Ouagadougou (March 1963), the UAM tried to hammer out internal differences and prepare a common stance for the Addis summit.[172] Thus, pressure was clearly building up and states on all sides were digging in to enhance their negotiating position.

Pan-African reconciliation and non-governmental groups
The nature of the centripetal pressures meant that non-governmental groups, especially exiled opposition elements from independent African states, were to become a principal victim of the Pan-African rapprochement at hand. The militant states in particular were forced to show greater respect to the sovereignty of other countries and stop supporting subversion by radical opposition parties. An important member of the UPC of Cameroon was thus thrown out of Cairo before the visit of Ahidjo to Nasser.[173] The AAPC also became a victim of inter-African reconciliation. It was financed by independent states of the Casablanca group and thus dependent on their goodwill. As its membership had changed, with moderate nationalist parties striving for independence being replaced by opposition elements from independent states, the AAPC had become increasingly radical. It therefore elicited growing hostility from moderate and conservative countries.[174] Even Nkrumah had lost interest in the organization, as its achievements and the limits on

---

168   Ulm-Erbach, *Aethiopiens Beitrag*, pp 56-57.

169   See preamble and arts. 1-3, 9 and 11 IAMO charter.

170   *Le Courrier d'Afrique* (Zaire), 12/9/62 (article); interview with Casablanca Secretary-General in *l'Essor* (Mali), 26/12/62; and Thompson, *Ghana's Foreign Policy*, p 218.

171   Gallagher, 'Death of a Group' and Strauch, *Panafrika*, pp 107-108.

172   *Fraternité* (Ivory Coast), 22/3/63 (article); interview with the president of Gabon in *ibid.*, 21/12/62; Madagascar's foreign ministry communiqué in *Nouvelles Malgaches Quotidiennes*, 11/5/63; and Communiqué Final, Ouagadougou, 10-13 March 1963.

173   Strauch, *Panafrika*, p 147.

174   Woronoff, *Organizing African Unity*, p 52; *The Ethiopian Herald*, 10/5/61; *Tanganyika Standard*, 7/4/61; and *Le Courrier d'Afrique* (Zaire), 29/3/61.

Ghanaian influence had disappointed him.[175] By early 1962, both Mali and Guinea had decided to end their support of the AAPC, whose scheduled fourth conference in Bamako in February was called off. Significantly, in April a Pan-African youth organization was founded in Conakry, to which the Guineans invited government-approved youth groups from the UAM states, instead of any of the exiled opposition.[176]

The latter predictably criticized the impending rapprochement. "Sawaba", a militant opposition party from Niger, warned that African unity should not imply a trade union of the powerful trying to resist revolutionary change.[177] The UPC pleaded that Casablanca be kept alive and continue to assist nationalist movements struggling against colonialism and neo-colonialism. Reconciliation was a trap set by the reformist camp of Monrovia and the UAM. They were lackeys of imperialism which, at the request of the Western world, wanted to create a counter-revolutionary organization oriented to the acceptance of Africa's subordination to Western interests.[178]

4.4 The preparatory conference of foreign ministers, Addis Ababa, 15-21 May 1963

Introduction

Addis Ababa, May 1963, "Africa Hall": since its construction as the ECA headquarters in 1959, this huge, modern building in glass, marble and mosaics had received wide acclaim as an example of the new times that had arrived for the African continent. Situated on one of the hills of the Ethiopian capital, in the centre of the city opposite one of the imperial palaces, it had to stir the imagination of many elite Africans, in particular by its beautiful, stained glass windows conceived by the young Ethiopian Afewerk Tekle: symbolizing the subjugation and liberation of Africa they show an African holding a flaming torch, whose radiant, red light illuminates the skies above. A child is holding his right hand and at his left someone is looking up hopefully to the amber-coloured heavens, absorbed in prayer. In the background there are several people in different traditional garments. A knight, with the United Nations emblem on his light-blue, mediaeval armour, carries a sword and raises a mailed fist.[179]

These windows symbolized the desire of elite Africans to break with the degrading memories of the colonial past in the expectation that their continent was to enter a new epoch of freedom, prosperous growth and a just, dignified order. For the *Zeitgeist* was still marked by optimism and confidence, in spite of all the problems of preceding years. Thus, the Secretary-General of the Casablanca group claimed that in twenty years' time, Africa could reach the same level of development as Europe and enter the atomic era. The

---

175 Thompson, *Ghana's Foreign Policy*, pp 89-90.
176 Wallerstein, *Politics of Unity*, pp 58 and 61.
177 Quoted in *ibid.*, p 63.
178 From a pamphlet entitled 'Unité Africaine ou Néo-Colonialisme', quoted in a UPC book by E. M'buyinga, *Pan-Africanism or Neo-Colonialism? The Bankruptcy of the O.A.U.* (London, 1982), p 51.
179 See also the cover of this book and for some information *Le Courrier d'Afrique* (Zaire), 30/5/63 and *Le Monde* (Paris), 16/5/63 (both articles).

Courrier d'Afrique argued that in a co-operative effort, African states could try to do in one stroke what other continents had achieved after centuries and that they could take the hurdles of unification by storm.[180] In this messianic age, the historical significance of the Addis Ababa conference had therefore beforehand become established: it would be the "highest summit" the continent had ever seen, as for the first time, with only two exceptions, all of Africa's leaders would congregate, regardless of ideological persuasion.[181]

However, this did not preclude hard bargaining. On a more mundane level, many governments were jockeying for position. Before going to Addis Ababa, Egypt and Algeria were involved in close consultations. Senghor and Houphouët paid their respects to Paris. Adoula visited Nigeria, Nkrumah conferred with Dahomey and Touré popped in on Dakar, Abidjan and Lagos.[182] Of the 31 delegations[183] only Morocco was not to be represented at head of state or government level, as King Hassan opposed the participation of Mauritania. The Moroccan delegation was to adopt a low-key profile. As shown below, of all independent states, only Togo was not to participate at all, although the foreign minister of the Grunitzky regime vainly tried to gain admission.[184]

Judging from the documents, official delegates numbered more than 500. Almost sixty participants, who were members of nationalist parties in dependent territories, had observer status. It was, indeed, a massive occasion: one press report speaks of 3,000 "participants". This would include the people of the press corps, hundreds of Ethiopian workers and some non-governmental groups such as southern Sudanese separatists, who tried to win conference delegates for their cause.[185]

In fact, the continent has never witnessed anything like it since. According to the conference lists *tout* Africa was to be there, at the foreign ministers sessions or the summit following it, most notably nearly all the founding fathers of the present-day states. One could mention Ahmed Ben Bella; Amadou Ahidjo; Joseph Kasavubu; Haile Selassie; Sékou Touré; Houphouët-Boigny; William Tubman; Modibo Keita; Sir Abubakar Tafawa Balewa; Léopold Senghor; Julius Nyerere; Habib Bourguiba; Milton Obote; Gamal Abdel Nasser; and Kwame Nkrumah with many of his well-known followers, such as K. Botsio, J. Tettegah, A.K. Barden and Mrs. Padmore. Some of the observers were Oginga Odinga; Holden Roberto; Jonas Savimbi; Kenneth Kaunda; Eduardo Mondlane; Joshua Nkomo; Ndabaningi Sithole; Robert Mugabe; Amilcar Cabral;

180   Interview with Casablanca's SG in *l'Essor* (Mali), 26/12/62 and *Le Courrier d'Afrique* (Zaire), 16/5/63.

181   *Fraternité* (Ivory Coast), 19/4/63 and *Le Courrier d'Afrique* (Zaire), 16/5/63.

182   See *Fraternité* (Ivory Coast) and *Le Monde* (Paris) in April-May 1963; *West Africa*, 11/5/63; M. Dei-Anang, *The Administration of Ghana's Foreign Ministers, 1957-1965: A Personal Memoir* (London, 1975), p 45; and Strauch, *Panafrika*, pp 147-151.

183   Algeria, Burundi, Cameroon, CAR, Chad, Congo-Br., Congo-Leo., Dahomey, Ethiopia, Gabon, Ghana, Guinea, Ivory Coast, Liberia, Libya, Madagascar, Mali, Mauritania, Morocco, Niger, Nigeria, Rwanda, Senegal, Sierra Leone, Somalia, Sudan, Tanganyika, Tunisia, Uganda, UAR and Upper Volta. See List of Delegations in *Proceedings of the Summit Conference of Independent African States*, vol. 1, section 2, Addis Ababa, May 1963 (hereinafter as *Proceedings*, vl. 1, sct. 2).

184   Strauch, *Panafrika*, p 150 and *Le Monde* (Paris), 18/5/63, 21/5/63 (article) and 24/5/63 (article).

185   See List of Delegations; List of Observers in *Proceedings*, vl. 1, sct. 2; press report in *Le Courrier d'Afrique* (Zaire), 30/5/63 (article); and *Voice of Southern Sudan*, vl. 1, no. 3, 1963.

Sam Nujoma; and Oliver Tambo. The size of delegations differed, with an average of ten to fifteen. The smallest delegation, from Rwanda, numbered three and the largest delegations were from Tunisia (25), Ivory Coast (27), Ethiopia (31), Nigeria (33) and Egypt (38). However, in characteristic fashion the Osagyefo beat them all, with a retinue of 41.[186]

The agenda

The foreign minister of Ethiopia, Ketema Yifru, was elected as chairman and the Ethiopian UN ambassador, Tesfaye Gebre-Egzy, was chosen as the conference's secretary-general.[187] As a tool for the discussions, the Ethiopians had collected and distributed all the resolutions and declarations of conferences of the preceding years. They had also introduced a draft agenda stipulating discussion of an "organization of African states" with a charter and a permanent secretariat, as well as socio-economic, educational, cultural and defence co-operation, decolonization, apartheid, disarmament and regional economic groupings.

However, fourteen other countries submitted their own agenda proposals, containing specifications as well as new subjects. Thus, Ghana proposed to discuss the creation of a "Political Union of African States" and the Somali's, who had frontier conflicts with Ethiopia and Kenya, wanted to discuss territorial disputes and a machinery to settle them. Liberia had specified the discussion of an African development bank, a common market and the CCTA, as well as the elimination of inter-African groupings. Sudan proposed the creation of a liberation fund, the provision of military training facilities to liberation movements and the discussion of atomic tests and the elimination of foreign military bases. Uganda proposed the discussion of equitable African representation in international organizations. Nigeria's very large agenda proposal presented the IAMO charter as "basis for the foundation of African Unity".

Still, it was decided to use the Ethiopian draft as the working agenda, which was expanded to include the discussion of a permanent conciliation commission and "Africa and the United Nations". Delegates could submit their amendments to the conference secretariat, which faithfully added them parallel to the items on the Ethiopian agenda with which they corresponded.[188]

The Togo affair

Debate during the second session became rather acrimonious because some countries tried to have Togo admitted. It began with an incident. The Ghanaian foreign minister tried to prevent a motion unfavourable to him, but was cut short by the chairman, who gave the floor to Guinea's representative to air his views on the Togo issue. While arguing that the

---

186   See the List of Delegations and List of Observers.
187   *Proceedings of the Summit Conference of Independent African States: Verbatim Record* (hereinafter as *VR*), FM, I, 1-6. "FM" refers to foreign ministers' meetings; "SM" to heads of state meetings (of "summit"); "C" to committee meetings, all followed by number of meeting and page.
188   *VR*, FM, I, 18-28; Agenda Proposals and Amendments for the Preparatory Conference of Foreign Ministers and Agenda of the Preparatory Conference of Foreign Ministers, both in *Proceedings*, vl. 1, sct. 1.

matter be referred to the heads of state, who had already made it clear that they wanted to discuss the matter themselves, the Guinean delegate allowed himself some acid remarks on the Grunitzky government. This regime had been brought to power by a "dastardly and murderous corporal"[189] and was still under control of the military. The legitimacy of the new government was contested by the people and it was therefore an unlawful regime that could not represent the Togo nation. Guinea refused to be pressurized by news of the impending arrival of Togo's foreign minister, who would land in Addis the following day,[190] and warned that it would leave if Togo would be welcomed.[191]

The Nigerian foreign minister, Wachuku, was very angry about the attempt to invite the Togolese and introduced a barrage of arguments to thwart it. He said that the matter depended on the number of countries that had recognized the Grunitzky regime, claiming that only some six countries had done so.[192] He noted that the UAM had originally decided to deal with the matter after the Addis conference and asked whether it had changed its mind. Moreover, difficult problems should be insulated and referred to the heads of state.

Apart from its purely political implications for inter-African relations, many state elites were deeply upset by the assassination itself, which represented one of Africa's first bloody take-overs. Wachuku emphatically argued that he opposed recognition of regimes that had come to power by murder, warning that he was not to be "bulldozed into accepting the unacceptable". He reiterated Nigerian conditions for recognition, such as reintroduction of the rule of law, release of political prisoners and free elections. Wachuku dramatically emphasized that no head of state, government leader or politician was immune from assassination and that the Togo question therefore raised "the question of salvation".[193] In other words, the murder of Olympio had graphically exposed the mutual vulnerability of Africa's state elites and the dangers that all of them faced. The fierce debate therefore alluded clearly to the protective function that Pan-African reconciliation was meant to have for the collectivity of state elites. In the end, the matter of Togo's admission was left, despite Ghanaian objections, to the heads of state. These shelved the issue as well, leaving Togo unrepresented at the conference.[194]

Pan-African agreement on the rationale of unity
Progress was exceedingly slow as two days had already been lost with procedural and other matters. The representative of Congo-Brazzaville therefore pleaded with delegates to speed up the proceedings. They should be "good Africans", inspired by a spirit of conciliation. They had to aim at the establishment "of a new Africa" and not "give birth to a mouse"!

189   *VR*, FM, II, 2. An allusion to Gnassingbé Eyadéma, who was reputed to have been involved in the coup and Olympio's death. See *West Africa*, 18-24/5/92 for discussion of recent evidence.
190   *Le Monde* (Paris), 18/5/63 (article).
191   *VR*, FM, II, 1-3.
192   R. Cornevin, *Le Togo: des origines à nos jours* (Paris, 1988), p 318, speaks of fifteen states that had already recognized.
193   *VR*, FM, II, 3-7.
194   Inevitably, all countries recognized Grunitzky's regime later on and Togo was to sign the OAU Charter in July 1963. *VR*, FM, II, 7-9 and M. Wolfers, *Politics in the Organization of African Unity* (London, 1976), p 3.

In one of the two plenary committees that were formed to discuss the agenda items, various statements were made on African unity. These confirmed the new views expressed on its rationale during the preceding year, as discussed in section 4.3.

According to the Leopoldville delegate unity encompassed the entire continent and involved the desire of liberation from (neo-)colonial practices, the consolidation of independence and the will to put an end to underdevelopment. The Ghanaian representative spoke of proud, free Africans determined to assert their personality in the community of nations. Alluding to the formation of the European Community, he argued that a unified foreign and defence policy would "make a united Africa great and powerful and ... strengthen its impact on world affairs". This could only come about, however, if African unity did not mean "mere co-operation" but involved genuine political union.[195] The Algerian rationale for unity also alluded to the non-African world: the conference was being watched by Europe, colonialists and ex-colonialists. The country's delegate warned that "Africa must not be available to others, but to Africans it must be available and generously so". According to Guinea Africa should unify in order to safeguard dignity and to prove it had "a word to say in the world". Tunisia, too, alluded to "great international entities" in the rest of the world as the rationale for establishing a structure of unity.[196]

These allusions to the outside, non-African world were elaborated in a discussion about Africa's role in the United Nations. Tunisia emphasized the need of equitable representation in the UN, something that was repeated by the delegates of Liberia, Congo-Brazzaville, Gabon, Ethiopia and Sudan. The Tunisian argument that this demanded greater cohesion in African ranks was also articulated by Nigeria and Sierra Leone. Cameroon pleaded for the establishment of a "UN African Group", emphasizing the fact that African states constituted a very large group of countries. The tone in the debate was characterized by clear indignation over the unwillingness in non-African quarters to concede greater African representation. African states should withstand manipulation by the great powers. If they were "to be respected" and "to be felt", then on global matters they should stand together.[197]

The disastrous experience of their disunity in the world body and the use that non-African powers had made of it, such as in the Congo crisis, was in the minds of all the delegates. Under-representation in international organizations touched on their self-esteem as state elites that were aspiring to equal status with governments in other parts of the world. The emphasis that several delegates put on the fact that they were with so many pointed to a realization that the large number of states formed, by way of a kind of leverage mechanism, a source of great potential power, both for the individual regimes and the continent as a whole. These reflections formed an emphatic part of the discussions and could, moreover, help to smooth over inter-African cleavages.

Thus, considerations about the external role of Africa and its states interlocked with reflections on the state of inter-African relations, *i.e.* the mutual security of state elites, to form a dualist rationale for the establishment of a Pan-African organization. The external

---

195   *VR*, CI-I, 6-7 and 9-10.
196   *VR*, CI-I, 12, 22 and 31.
197   *VR*, CI-I, 34-40.

part of this rationale was itself made up of two aspects, namely the desire to increase, by way of leverage, the power of both Africa and its component states and, related to this, an aspiration to equality of status with other state elites. The concurrent statements by delegates on this carried several implications. First, while the radicals and moderate-conservatives had in the past disagreed on the gravity of non-African influences and this had now not necessarily vanished, all countries — even Ghana — could agree on the *related* need to improve the continent's role in the global order. Second, Nkrumah stood isolated not with regard to this issue, but in terms of his totalitarian interpretation of non-African influences on the continent and his concomitant prescriptions of how unity should be implemented. The other radical powers and the Monrovia countries did not have to follow this view, as seemingly not more than a minimal structure was necessary to improve the mutual security of state elites and Africa's position in world affairs. Fears about the possible manipulation of a supra-national structure by ambitious powers like Ghana and Egypt and the risk of losing control of one's state structure only enhanced these considerations.

Thus, of the militant countries Algeria opposed the immediate formation of a "union of African states" in favour of an inter-governmental structure. Mali spoke of a "most modest enterprise" and Guinea also agreed with a minimum programme "acceptable to all" based on "African realities". The latter concept served to legitimate concessions of militant goals or rhetoric, in order to secure a rapprochement with the Monrovia powers.[198] This approach conformed to the attitudes of the Brazzaville countries. To give only a few examples: Dahomey spoke of a minimal approach and Cameroon explicitly stated that "African unity cannot at present be based on anything else but on an Africa of States". Niger stressed egalitarian co-operation, mutual respect and non-interference. Monrovia powers like Nigeria and Liberia, but also countries that had kept relatively aloof from competition with the militants, such as Sudan and Tunisia, to a greater or lesser extent reiterated this minimal, pragmatic view.[199] Thus, Nkrumah's grand plans for political union were quickly buried.

Nigerian obstruction
But this is as far as agreement went. The delegations experienced great difficulty in agreeing on the procedures that should be followed in implementing their ideas on unity. Some claimed they had no mandate to commit themselves to a draft charter, while others preferred the drafting of a declaration of principle to the heads of state, which could serve as a charter preamble only. Several representatives even argued that the drawing up of a charter should be reserved for a future conference. These included the delegations of Ghana, Uganda, Sudan, Cameroon, Somalia and the Senegalese committee chairman. Thus, this attitude was held by countries, each for their own reasons, right across the Monrovia-Casablanca divide.

After much squabbling, it was decided to form two subcommittees. The second subcommittee, made up of three Monrovia members and three Casablanca states, would consider the matter of the United Nations. The first subcommittee should study the

---

198   *VR*, CI-I, 11-13, 21 and 31.
199   *VR*, CI-I, 13-22. Some of the latter had participated in PAFMECSA.

formation of an organization with a charter and secretariat and contained only three Casablanca states, *i.e.* Algeria, Ghana and Guinea. The rest consisted of Brazzaville and Monrovia countries (Cameroon, Madagascar, Nigeria) and some with relatively neutral profiles towards inter-African cleavages (Ethiopia, Tanganyika and Tunisia).[200] Its Tanganyikan chairman proposed to take an Ethiopian draft charter as the basis of discussion. This document had been prepared with the assistance of a Chilean expert on the Organization of American States. The Ethiopians hoped that an example from outside the African context could be agreed on by all the delegations and prevent a resurgence of inter-African cleavages.[201]

The objectives in the Ethiopian charter were nevertheless similar to IAMO goals and the forms of co-operation were literally copied from the IAMO charter, with an emphasis on economic issues. Institutional and legal arrangements guaranteed a strictly inter-governmental organization similar to IAMO, although the Ethiopian charter also provided for a Defence Board. Numerous provisions were (almost) literally identical to the IAMO treaty, with the exception of the preamble, which was relatively neutral in character.[202]

It therefore came as a big surprise that the Nigerian delegate, in whose country the IAMO charter had been signed, vehemently objected to the Ethiopian draft as basis for the discussion and wished to combine the IAMO and Casablanca charters instead. He said that the Ethiopian draft did not reflect the Casablanca and IAMO treaties. Other delegates argued that the Ethiopian draft had already been accepted as the basis of discussion, that the subcommittee's mandate entailed that other charters could, and had to be, taken into consideration and that the Ethiopian charter was already a compilation of the Casablanca and IAMO treaties. Nevertheless, the Nigerian delegate refused steadfast to consider using the Ethiopian charter as basis for the proceedings. The Ghanaians complicated the debate even further by trying to postpone the drafting of a charter altogether.[203]

The Guinean delegate, however, wanted to proceed with the Ethiopian draft. He emphasized that they had not come as representatives of blocs, but to build something new. The Casablanca and IAMO charters were elements of discord that should be left at home in the respective capitals, an argument that touched on the crux of the matter, namely the pride that Nigeria took in having "its" IAMO charter accepted. Cameroon accused Nigeria of "obstructionist" manoeuvres and others tried to soothe the Nigerians by observing that the charter could still be amended by the heads of state. Proceedings became noisier and the Nigerian delegate continued his opposition by resorting to petty arguments. A short recess was held but to no avail, as Nigeria wrecked discussion of the Ethiopian draft by reading an IAMO article instead. In this way two and a half hours were lost and delegates were back at square one. The Algerian representative asked for a formal vote to decide whether or not to use the Ethiopian draft as the basic document. While Ghana and Nigeria abstained, the others voted in favour.[204]

---

200 *VR*, CI-I, 25-32 and 40-42 and Report of Committee I of the Preparatory Conference of Foreign Ministers, in *Proceedings*, vl. 1, sct. 1, 2-4.
201 Thompson, *Ghana's Foreign Policy*, p 320 and Ulm-Erbach, *Aethiopiens Beitrag*, (n. 160), p 119.
202 See Ethiopia: Proposed Charter of the Organization of African States, in *Proceedings*, vl. 1, sct. 1.
203 *VR*, SC-I-I, 1-7 and 14-15.
204 *VR*, SC-I-I, 5-22.

Tanganyika tried to enforce acceptance of the vote by threatening to vacate the chair. Nigeria responded that it would not participate anymore. Algeria said it had not tried to defeat a minority with a majority vote, but to reach unanimity. However, Wachuku, Nigeria's foreign minister, remained obstinate. He admitted his sabotage of the deliberations and appealed to Ethiopia to withdraw its draft. The atmosphere turned ugly, with the Nigerian delegate telling the chairman that he didn't "want to be shut off by anybody". Yet, Ethiopia refused to comply, so the debate had reached complete stalemate. Long after midnight the chairman therefore proposed to adjourn.[205]

Breakthrough

The reconciliation conference, which had been prepared so meticulously, was in deep trouble as time was rapidly running out. Substantive discussions had not even started, while in a few days time, the heads of state were to arrive and threatened to be confronted with complete failure. Long and intensive consultations were therefore held at subcommittee level to reach a way out of the impasse. It finally resulted in an informal agreement between Nigeria and Ethiopia to accept, in principle, the Ethiopian charter as basis of discussion by the heads of state. The latter would be asked to set up "machinery" to examine it and present a report to a next foreign ministers conference. The plenary committee involved accepted this solution but decided to recommend to the summit of heads of state that the next foreign ministers conference, at which the final draft charter would be presented, be held within six months' time.[206]

Thus, while Nigeria managed to extract some dilatory measures, it failed to force its favourite charter upon the other delegates, exposing the limits of its influence in this large gathering. In fact, the crude behaviour of Nigeria's short-tempered foreign minister formed the antithesis of the subtle exercise of influence implied in the concept of hegemony, both in its application in regional international relations and the benevolent versions of hegemonic stability theory.[207] More will be said about this in section 5.6.

At last substantive discussion began on the resolutions which had been drafted by the subcommittees and would be presented, besides the draft Ethiopian charter, to the heads of state. A resolution on the United Nations was quickly carried and would later on be accepted, with minor amendment, by the heads of state as well. It reaffirmed African faith in the UN and called for equitable representation in its major organs. It asked African governments to constitute a more effective African Group with a permanent secretariat in order to secure better co-operation, yet without prejudice to participation in the Afro-Asian group.[208]

A recommendation on the Ethiopian draft charter listed the most important aspects of the dualist rationale underlying African unity, namely the strengthening of inter-African

---

205   *VR*, SC-I-I, 22-29.
206   *VR*, CI-III, 1 and 6-7.
207   Iyob, 'Regional Hegemony' (n. 135); R. Lemarchand, 'On Comparing Regional Hegemons: Libya and South Africa', in R. Lemarchand (ed), *The Green and the Black: Qadhafi's Policies in Africa* (Bloomington and Indianapolis, 1988), p 169; Snidal, 'Limits of Hegemonic Stability Theory' (n. 133); and I. Grunberg, 'Exploring the "Myth" of Hegemonic Stability', in *International Organization*, 1990, p 452.
208   *VR*, CI-III, 7-9. See final text, as adopted by the heads of state, in *Proceedings*, vl. 1, sct. 1.

understanding, co-operation and stability; safeguarding of independence against (neo-) colonial activity; enabling Africa to play a role in world politics; the speeding up of decolonization; and the realization of collective defence, modernization and development. Cameroon managed to have the following "basic principles" included:

- sovereign equality
- non-interference in internal affairs
- respect for sovereignty, territorial integrity and independence
- peaceful settlement of disputes
- condemnation of political assassination and subversion
- development of means of co-operation
- dedication to Africa's decolonization
- non-alignment to all blocs

As a mixture of moderate and militant aspirations, adoption of the recommendation did not create any serious difficulties.[209]

Economic issues

The atmosphere had by now improved considerably, with the Nigerians keeping relatively quiet. Some resolutions on education, science, culture, health and social matters were adopted without debate as they were not considered controversial. They would later on also be accepted, with minor revision, by the heads of state.[210]

Debate on economic matters was more protracted. Some sceptical remarks were made about relations with the European Community. Nigeria said it favoured an African Common Market as an alternative and hoped that barriers to inter-African trade would be removed. Congo-Leopoldville argued that African states should adopt a common policy towards the EC to avoid relations detrimental to an African Economic Community. However, even outside the Brazzaville group this met with some caution, as can be gauged from interventions by Algeria, Mali and Libya. This attitude was naturally most explicit in the case of the Brazzaville powers themselves. For example, Senegal warned against facile comparisons between the EC and the African situation. Cameroon argued that without economic unity African countries could not defend themselves against "gigantic concentrations". Still, no state could be persuaded to give up "the bird in the hand" (EC association), which wouldn't prevent the formation of a future African Common Market anyway. The Nigerien delegate was more level-headed. He read a definition of a fully-fledged economic community and observed that the establishment of a common market would be difficult. Another, unidentified but probably Francophone, speaker ridiculed some of the earlier non-committal statements as Don Quixote behaviour. EC association was not incompatible with a future African community and brought temporary advantages which could not be abandoned for a meaningless African policy.[211]

Thus, the Francophone countries were left off the hook. The final resolution on

---

209   *VR*, CI-III, 9-28. Final text in *Proceedings*, vl. 1, sct. 1.
210   *VR*, CI-III, 43-44. Final text in *Proceedings*, vl. 1, sct. 1 .
211   *VR*, CI-II, 1-23.

economic co-operation, while calling for studies of the various aspects of a common market, did not mention EC association or the idea of an African Common Market as such.[212] More in line with the new rationale underlying African unity were calls for greater control over international institutions engaged in Africa's development. Thus, a resolution was adopted calling for the CCTA's inclusion in the Pan-African organization to be established, a suggestion to be accepted by the heads of state as well.[213] Algeria also wanted to establish a "genuinely African institution" to guide economic co-operation. While this would duplicate the work of the ECA, the delegate deemed this acceptable as the latter was still technically a UN body even if its membership was African.[214] The final text of the general economic resolution, later on endorsed by the heads of state, also spoke, among others, of concern over Africa's terms of trade and the ways and means to improve them, such as through concerted negotiations in UNCTAD and a call for the restructuring of international trade.[215]

Defence and decolonization issues

A resolution on disarmament was drafted by a subcommittee in which Monrovia-Brazzaville powers (Nigeria, Cameroon, Upper Volta) predominated. Only one Casablanca state (Egypt) had been included, besides two relatively neutral countries (Ethiopia and Sudan).[216] Nevertheless, its resolution evoked some resistance among UAM states, as it stipulated that Africa be declared a denuclearized zone and nuclear tests be banned. Manufacture of nuclear weapons should be stopped and existing ones should be destroyed. Non-African bases should be removed and states should disentangle themselves from military pacts with foreign powers.[217]

Part of the background to this resolution was the fact that France, apart from its military facilities in sub-Saharan Africa, had not yet wound up its military bases in the Maghreb, where as recently as March, a nuclear test had taken place in defiance of North African protest. The issue of denuclearization was an important topic for countries actively involved in the non-aligned movement, which included most of the Casablanca states and some (Anglophone) Monrovia powers. Yet, as the USSR had just called for denuclearization of the Mediterranean, presumably in an effort to influence the Addis Ababa summit,[218] this issue could also be perceived as favouring the Eastern bloc.

Of the UAM states Senegal and Madagascar were the most emphatic in their opposition. The former only agreed to a denuclearized zone if it were connected to global denuclearization. Calling exclusively for the denuclearization of Africa would play into the hands of the Soviets and jeopardize the continent's non-alignment. Madagascar supported Senegal and backed its criticism on the issue of foreign military bases and

---

212   Text in *Proceedings*, vl. 1, sct. 1.
213   *VR*, CI-IV, 1-11. Text in *Proceedings*, vl. 1, sct. 1. See on CCTA's inclusion in the OAU C.O.C. Amate, *Inside the OAU: Pan-Africanism in Practice* (New York, 1986), pp 495-499.
214   *VR*, CI-III, 28-43.
215   See *Proceedings*, vl. 1, sct. 1.
216   Report of Committee II of the Preparatory Conference of Foreign Ministers, in *Proceedings*, vl. 1, sct. 1.
217   Text in *Proceedings*, vl. 1, sct. 1.
218   *Le Monde* (Paris), 23/5/63 (article).

pacts, as this was not within the province of the conference. The Malagasy delegate coldly observed that if "Madagascar in the full exercise of its sovereignty would appeal for foreign troops, I do not see how the Conference could interfere in a domestic affair of Madagascar".[219]

However, this resistance was not pushed too far, as the Francophones were conceded victory on the issue of EC association. The disarmament resolution would be presented to the summit of heads of state, at which reservations might be aired. In the end, the latter were to adopt a mitigated version that decided "to affirm and respect the principle" of denuclearization; "oppose", rather than "ban", nuclear tests and the manufacture of nuclear weapons; and to realize "by means of negotiation" the elimination of bases. Any reference to pacts was omitted.[220]

Naturally, the issue of decolonization, apartheid and racial discrimination proved easier to handle. Liberation movements had been invited to make suggestions on how Africa's states could contribute to decolonization. Nevertheless, there was some tension between the non-governmental groups and the state elites. Oginga Odinga from Kenya, a colony soon to become independent, was clearly irritated about his status as petitioner/observer. He said that representatives of dependent territories were only in an earlier stage of development than the state elites, which seemed to have forgotten their own past experiences. State delegates therefore tried to pacify the non-governmental participants with soothing remarks.[221]

State delegates felt that action was most urgent with regard to Portuguese territories and Southern Africa, where the settler or colonial powers resisted all progress towards African emancipation. They emphasized that, if there were several liberation movements in one country, a united front should be created. The petitioners called on African goverments to create an organ and financial fund to support liberation movements, set target dates for the independence of dependent territories and establish a corps of "volunteers" to help the liberation struggle in ways that were, however, not specified.[222]

Many of these and other demands found their way in the final resolutions drawn up by the state delegates. The resolution on decolonization spoke of the duty of African states to support dependent peoples in their struggle. Britain was warned not to transfer sovereignty to the white settlers in Southern Rhodesia. If this were to happen, African states would take "measures" against states that would recognize the white minority regime. This was a softened version of an earlier proposal which spoke of an immediate rupture in diplomatic relations with states according recognition. The resolution also warned the Pretoria regime not to annex South West Africa. The great powers were asked to stop support of colonial regimes, especially that of Portugal, which was waging "a real war of genocide". Diplomatic and consular ties between African states and Portugal and South Africa should be severed. Importation of their goods by African states should be forbidden, as well as their use of African ports, airfields and overflying facilities.

---

219   *VR*, FM, IV, 9. Also Madagascar's foreign ministry communiqué in *Nouvelles Malgaches Quotidiennes*, 11/5/63.
220   *VR*, FM, IV, 8-14 and *Le Monde* (Paris), 22/5/63 (article). Final text in *Proceedings*, vl. 1, sct. 1.
221   *VR*, CII, 2-3, 10-13 and 25-26.
222   *VR*, CII, 4-12.

Liberation movements should establish "common action fronts" to increase their effectiveness. A "Co-ordinating Committee" of nine states should be formed to harmonize assistance to nationalists in dependent territories. Assistance should consist of a "Special Fund", made up of (voluntary) financial contributions by African states.[223]

A separate resolution on apartheid and racial discrimination called on non-African states to end all relations with South Africa and referred to apartheid as a criminal policy. Racial discrimination in Africa, Europe and other parts of the world was condemned, a paragraph that also alluded to racial harassment of African students in Bulgaria. The final paragraph expressed concern about discrimination of "communities of African origin" in the United States and appreciated the measures of the American government to put an end to these "intolerable practices". These were "likely seriously to deteriorate" relations between African peoples and governments on the one hand and the American government on the other.

Cameroon and Dahomey regarded this section as excessive and demagogic. They emphasized the elitist nature of the conference, which was made up of "men conscious of their responsibilities" who should moderate their language. Yet, other delegates disagreed and the paragraph was retained. They alluded to the increase in power that the leverage mechanism, underlying their Pan-African organization, would deliver, noting that the "opponents of Kennedy" should know that 32 African states, commanding the confidence of 214 million Africans, would not tolerate their humiliation. Moreover, indignation was also fed by an elitist imagination of racial discrimination, as it was observed that once an African head of state would lose his position, he could suffer the same indignity as any Afro-American or African.[224]

Evaluation

The results of the foreign ministers' conference proved a mixed blessing. Having overcome the complications entailed by the Togo affair and Nigeria's obstruction, it had met, at the eleventh hour, with relative success. The deliberations had removed nearly all controversial topics from the agenda of the heads of state, who could therefore concentrate on the fundamental issue of how to institutionalize co-operation. The acceptance of a new rationale underlying African unity showed that the Monrovia, Casablanca and Brazzaville countries were, despite fundamental disagreements, all concerned about certain external and inter-African developments that pushed them towards some sort of co-operation. They had also agreed on joint resolutions that the heads of state were to accept, with minor revisions, as well, thereby preparing the ground for inter-African reconciliation.

On the other hand, the conference of foreign ministers had ended in an anticlimax. It had resulted in a mere recommendation to use the Ethiopian draft charter as the basis for discussion, which in the minds of the foreign ministers could only be finalized at a future conference. As it was therefore up to the heads of state to decide whether or not to push through a final agreement, the Addis Ababa conference had not yet brought the

---

223   The heads of state were to adopt the resolution in slightly amended form. Final text in *Proceedings* vl. 1, sct. 1. Also *VR*, FM, IV, 18-9.

224   *VR*, FM, IV, 1-3 and 15-18. Final text in *Proceedings*, vl. 1, sct. 1.

participants beyond the point of no return.

It is clear that Ethiopia and Guinea were going to be active in this respect, as they had put an explicit seal on the foreign ministers meeting. Based on the number of oral interventions — irrespective of length and contents — one may conclude that Algeria (32), Cameroon (42), Dahomey (33), Tunisia (thirty) and Senegal (25) played substantial roles as well. The fact that some of these were countries of relatively insignificant stature confirms the contention in the preceding section that power relations were still rather blurred. As such, the foreign ministers conference confronted an undoubtedly important country like Nigeria with the limits of its influence, even though it was by now clear that a small-sized power as Ghana could not hope to impose its will. Section 4.6 will show which countries were, as the most influential actors, responsible for hammering out a definitive accord. This will also entail an assessment of the lack of Africa's hegemonic stability and the strength of centripetal forces with which its states were confronted in relation to the nature of the Pan-African rapprochement that was finally reached.

4.5   The summit of heads of state and government, Addis Ababa, 22-25 May 1963

Public speeches

Haile Selassie was determined to reach a definitive accord. He opened the summit with a forceful speech, emphasizing that the conference could not "close without adopting a single African Charter. We cannot leave without having created a single African organisation". "If we fail in this, we will have shirked our responsibility. If we succeed, then and only then, will we have justified our presence here".[225] The heads of state all resided in the prestigious "Ghion Hotel", only 300 meters away from Africa Hall, and travelled in limousines to the conference building. Gazed at by the city crowds, they marked their distance from the populace.[226] Yet, in this way the circumstances were ideal for consultations and no one could escape the urgency of the situation. Haile Selassie and others could operate actively behind the scenes to convince everyone that the time had come for Africa to become organized at the continental level.

The agenda closely followed that of the foreign ministers conference. The first five sessions of the summit heard public speeches of all the heads of state and government.[227] While their significance should not be overrated as they were intended for the public ear, they did contain some general clues as to the direction that the summit would take.[228] Many speakers made it clear that the conference could, indeed, not close without the establishment of a Pan-African organization of some sort. So much prestige was now at stake that they could not afford the conference to fail before the eyes of the world.

Numerous heads of state, from across the radical-Monrovia divide, referred to the

---

225   Text in *Proceedings*, vl. 1, sct. 2.
226   See *Le Courrier d'Afrique* (Zaire), 30/5/63 (article).
227   Agenda Proposal of the Preparatory Conference of Foreign Ministers for the Summit Conference, in *Proceedings*, vl. 1, sct. 1; *Le Monde* (Paris), 24/5/63 (article); and Wolfers, *Politics*, p 16 (n. 194).
228   All speeches can be found in *Proceedings*, vl. 1, sct. 2.

enhanced influence that such an organization would bring. They stressed that Africa had to assert its role in world affairs and occupy the place that it deserved. Many spoke of aspirations to equality with other world powers and continents. Not only Nkrumah but others like Haile Selassie, Houphouët-Boigny, Joseph Kasavubu and Sékou Touré also referred to the increased influence that would be generated by continental co-operation. The most euphoric allusion to this was made by President Yameogo in a reference to the nuclear arms race between the superpowers. He claimed that "the first African bomb will burst in Addis Ababa; a super-atomic bomb it will be, ... beneficial for our peoples, deadly for colonialists ...; it will be the bomb of AFRICAN UNITY".

The need for inter-African reconciliation was not forgotten either. Several delegates stressed the importance of the fact that, for the first time, they had the opportunity to get to know leaders of rival groupings. Nasser had, together with Ben Bella, already conferred with Bourguiba to initiate a North African rapprochement.[229] Modiba Keita paid hommage to Léopold Senghor. Applauded by other delegates, the two men embraced to signify that they had settled their differences over the break-up of the Mali federation. The sole incident was caused by President Osman, who accused Ethiopia of having annexed Somali territory.

The only leaders to call for a form of supra-national unification were Kwame Nkrumah and Milton Obote. All others favoured a flexible, minimal structure and a gradualist conception of Pan-African co-operation. They emphasized respect for territorial integrity, sovereignty, non-interference and peaceful settlement of disputes and condemned subversion and aspirations to hegemony in inter-African relations.

All delegates spoke of the need to liberate the continent from the indignities of colonialism and apartheid. Even leaders of Brazzaville countries like Houphouët-Boigny and Fulbert Youlou articulated a rhetoric that was more militant and in line with that of the radicals and Anglophone Monrovia powers. The issue could, indeed, put the final seal on the process of reconciliation. Thus, the turning-point of the Addis Ababa conference came with an impassioned and irresistable speech by President Ben Bella of Algeria, who told the delegates that Algerian volunteers were waiting to help their oppressed brethren in Southern Africa. He emphasized that the independent states had to commit themselves to the ideal of liberation. He spoke of an African blood bank and said that everyone had to agree "to die a little" for the peoples still under colonial domination.[230]

Discussion of the charter

The summit was now in a positive, constructive mood. It was clear that finalization of an agreement would not be left for a future occasion. After all heads of state had had a chance to scrutinize a revised version of the Ethiopian draft charter, the summit proceeded, behind closed doors, with discussion of the document.

The preamble, which was adopted with little revision, differed from the original Ethiopian draft. It alluded to ideas of the various inter-African groupings and even acknowledged the contributions that Nkrumah had made to African unity. Thus, the first consideration (second paragraph) — "Convinced that it is the inalienable right of all

---

229   *West Africa*, 1/6/63 and *Le Monde* (Paris), 26-27/5/63 (article).
230   See for reactions to Ben Bella's speech *Le Monde* (Paris), 26-27/5/63 (article).

people to control their own destiny" — had been taken almost literally from a resolution that Nkrumah had drafted at the Fifth Pan-African Congress in Manchester in 1945. The fourth paragraph stressed responsibility to harness natural and human resources for the continent's advancement and could be interpreted as an acknowledgement of Monrovia and UAM ideas. The fifth paragraph seemingly alluded to Pan-Africanist ideals as it called for understanding and co-operation "in response to the aspirations of our peoples for brotherhood and solidarity, in a larger unity transcending ethnic and national differences". The seventh paragraph paid lip-service to both Casablanca and Monrovia doctrines, as it spoke of a determination to safeguard "the hard-won independence as well as the sovereignty and territorial integrity of our States, and to fight against neo-colonialism in all its forms".[231]

However, the name of the new organization led to some hard bargaining. The biggest problem was to convince President Tsiranana to drop his demand of having the word "Malagasy" or "Madagascar" included, as had been customary among the Francophones. Tsiranana argued that without their inclusion it would look as if his country was not a member of the organization. When he was pressed on this by Nyerere and others, he admitted that he did not regard himself as fully African. He doubted whether all islands surrounding the continent were really African and slily pointed to Sardinia and Corsica. Although the Malagasy felt closer to Africa than Asia, they had two ancestries and were "not quite African and not quite Asian". Sékou Touré answered that the organization to be established was a "continental union" grounded on a geographical, not a racial, basis. While this implied that "Africa" constituted, at bottom, nothing more than a geographical entity, it was clear that for many delegates this Africa at least encompassed the mainland and various islands surrounding it. They retorted that mention of Madagascar would also necessitate inclusion of Cape Verde, Zanzibar, Mauritius and other islands. Tsiranana was thus forced to give in, although it was agreed to include an article stating that the "Organization shall include the Continental African States, Madagascar and other Islands surrounding Africa".[232]

The name of the organization involved still another political problem. Nkrumah objected to the title "Organization of African States", ostensibly because the acronym (OAS) would be identical to that of the armed group of white Algerian settlers, the "Organisation de l'Armée Secrète". He therefore proposed to adopt the title "Union of African States" instead.[233] President Maga of Dahomey, who may have acted on a suggestion by Nkrumah,[234] finally came with the winning title of "Organisation de l'Unité Africaine", OUA, which he had introduced in an attempt to mollify Tsiranana's attitude.

---

231 Official text of the Charter in *Proceedings*, vl. 1, sct. 1 and Appendix E of this study.

232 *VR*, SM, VI, 4-8. See art. 1.2 OAU Charter. Which "other islands" should be part of the organization and thus formed part of "Africa" remained unclear. According to Nkrumah's *Africa Must Unite* (p xi) the following ones were part of Africa: Canaries; Cape Verde islands; Madeira; Selvagens; Arquipelago dos Bijagos; Los island; Fernando Po; Príncipe; São Tomé; Annobon; Ascension; St Helena; Tristan da Cunha; Gough; Prince Edward; Marion; Madagascar; Bassas da India; Ile Europa; Réunion; Mauritius; Rodriquez; Comoros; Seychelles; Socotra; Dahlach Chebir; Zanzibar; Pemba; Mafia.

233 *VR*, SM, VI, 6. He did not go into the problem of the Organization of American States, whose acronym also is OAS.

234 Dei-Anang, *Administration of Ghana's Foreign Relations* , p 45 (n. 182).

Its English translation was taken up by President Tubman of Liberia, who said that it should be "Organization *of* African Unity" instead of "Organization *for* African Unity".[235] His argument implied that, in the former case, the OAU represented the mere institutionalization of an existing, "organic" unity, while in the latter there would be the suggestion that the OAU would still have to realize such unity and that, without it, the continent was divided.[236]

After these ideological hurdles had been taken, discussion centred on the substantive provisions in the charter. Article 2 was adopted without debate. It listed as purposes:

- promotion of the unity and solidarity of Africa's states
- co-ordination and intensification of their co-operation
- defence of sovereignty, territorial integrity and independence
- eradication of colonialism from Africa
- promotion of international co-operation such as through the UN

In terms of language and contents it was a compromise between Monrovia and Casablanca aspirations. In order to realize these objectives, article 2.2 stipulated various forms of co-operation. These were taken from the IAMO treaty but presented in a revised order, possibly to satisfy the Casablanca powers. Thus, political and diplomatic co-operation came first, followed by:

- economic co-operation, including transport and communications
- educational and cultural co-operation
- health, sanitation and nutritional co-operation
- scientific and technical co-operation
- co-operation for defence and security

Articles 3 to 8 were also adopted with little debate. Article 3 mentioned the principles that member states should adhere to. As discussed in section 4.4, these had been introduced at the request of Cameroon and, with the exception of non-alignment and decolonization, aimed at preserving the political-territorial status quo among Africa's state elites.[237]

Article 7 listed as principal institutions an "Assembly of Heads of State and Government"; a "Council of Ministers"; a "General Secretariat"; and a "Commission of Mediation, Conciliation and Arbitration". There was some argument over the frequency of Assembly meetings, with some moderate-conservative states arguing for biennial sessions. Others objected that this would jeopardize the effectiveness of the Organization and it was therefore decided to hold annual meetings.[238]

As regards the position of the "Administrative Secretary-General", there was some

---

235   *VR*, SM, VI, 7-9.
236   Thus, in 1976 *The Ethiopian Herald* (14/1/76) criticized the habit of many who referred to the OAU as Organization *for* African Unity. These were the "enemies" of Africa who used this "peculiar nomenclature" to justify their attempts to divide the continent.
237   The final text of article 3 differed only slightly from the version by Cameroon.
238   *VR*, SM, VI, 9-16.

disagreement that cut right across radical-Monrovia lines. Sékou Touré wanted the epithet administrative dropped as superfluous. In his view, the official should execute Assembly decisions, direct the General Secretariat and co-ordinate the Organization's activities. President Tubman of Liberia also pleaded for a Secretary-General whose powers would not be too circumscribed. Yet, most leaders wanted an official whose prerogatives would not challenge their supremacy. They argued successfully for retention of the epithet administrative. Thus, Tsiranana said that the Secretary-General's role should not be political. Modibo Keita and Hubert Maga feared that this official might consider himself a "super chief of state" and argued that he should direct "the services and nothing else". Ironically, the crudest plea for a weak Secretary-General came from the Pan-Africanist Osagyefo, which was, however, in line with Nkrumah's leadership complex and frustrations over UN policy in the Congo. He proposed to call the Secretary-General "Administrative Secretary" and to leave out the word General:

> We don't want a super-something. Executive Secretary, simple. He would think he is Hammarskjold.[239]

Adoption of charter and resolutions

After adoption of the charter, the seventh, closed, session discussed the resolutions prepared by the foreign ministers. This provoked little controversy. Nkrumah proposed that the 25th of May should henceforth be celebrated as "African Liberation Day".[240] Algeria suggested that Dar es Salaam become the headquarters of the co-ordinating committee (usually known as the "Liberation Committee"), provided for in the resolution on decolonization, to harmonize assistance to liberation movements. Mali proposed Ethiopia, Algeria, Egypt, Uganda, Tanganyika, Guinea, Congo-Leopoldville, Senegal and Nigeria as its members. All these proposals were quickly accepted. The debate became more painful, however, when militant states, notably Algeria and Ghana, stressed the need for immediate contributions to the new Liberation Committee. Many delegates engaged in competitive offers of financial assistance to the embarassment of poorer countries and those for which the anti-colonial struggle formed a lower priority. The radical states made it clear, however, that the measures agreed on in the resolution were to be serious commitments from which member states could not simply withdraw.[241]

The other resolutions presented no difficulties. It was decided to entrust the formation of a provisional secretariat to Ethiopia, with its headquarters in Addis Ababa. It would be seconded by a committee of experts composed of Congo-Brazzaville, Nigeria, Niger, Uganda and Egypt. Decisions on who would become the OAU's permanent Administrative Secretary-General and where the permanent headquarters would be located, were postponed until the first session of the Assembly (July 1964).[242] After a final skirmish over the Togo issue and an announcement by a Moroccan delegate that his

---

239 *VR*, SM, VI, 19-22.
240 Originally this had been 15 April. It had been introduced to commemorate the first CIAS in Accra, April 1958.
241 *VR*, SM, VII, 4-24.
242 *VR*, SM, VII, 40-47 and text of the relevant resolution in *Proceedings*, vl. 1, sct. 1.

country reserved the right to join the OAU later,[243] the meeting was adjourned. At two o'clock in the morning of Sunday the 26th of May 1963, the heads of state convened for the solemn signing ceremony. The august assembly also included Nkrumah, who had to be persuaded by Haile Selassie to put his signature under the document establishing the OAU.[244]

4.6   Of mice and bombs: evaluations

Re-alignment of inter-African relations

At its simplest, the formation of the OAU represented a new patterning of inter-African politics. In the two preceding sections it was shown how members of different groupings sought each other's support, a complex process that regularly cut across the Casablanca-Monrovia/Brazzaville divides.

Thus, one of the results of the conference was an agreement that the OAU should be the only organization to institutionalize political co-operation at the continental level. All rival groupings, such as Casablanca, Monrovia, PAFMECSA, UAS and UAM, should be dissolved. This hardly proved a problem in the case of Casablanca and UAS, which had already disintegrated. The Monrovia coalition was also too incoherent, as well as too vast, a body to survive for long. Despite its IAMO treaty, its existence had become increasingly questionable in the wake of the shifting alignments of the preceding year. This was enhanced by the fact that some of its members, notably PAFMECSA countries from East Africa, had distanced themselves from the old cleavages.

Only the Brazzaville coalition had survived the Addis Ababa conference more or less intact, despite the complex, cross-cutting manoeuvres that some of its members had performed during its proceedings. As their relatively solid organization, the UAM, catered for political co-operation with almost continental dimensions, it could form a serious challenge to the OAU. Other OAU members, especially Guinea, therefore demanded that it should be transformed into an organization for non-political co-operation. While the Brazzaville countries agreed to do so, their political alliance was to survive these reforms.[245]

A continental regime

Yet, the OAU was more than a re-alignment of inter-African relations, as Africa now possessed something that might be called a continental regime. As more than a temporary arrangement between states, the OAU formed a new, intervening variable between the continent's actors and their behaviour: for the first time all African states had accepted, at least formally, Pan-African norms of inter-state behaviour, something that would, as

---

243   It signed the Charter on 19/9/63 subject to a reservation that it did not renounce certain territorial claims. *United Nations Treaty Series*, 1963, no. 6947, p 88.

244   *VR*, SM, VII, 48-52 and Ulm-Erbach, *Aethiopiens Beitrag*, p 128.

245   CM/Res.5 (I); *Horoya* (Guinea), 3/8/63; interview with Tsiranana *in Nouvelles Malgaches Quotidiennes*, 16/8/63; and I. Wallerstein, 'The Early Years of the OAU: The Search for Organizational Preeminence', in *International Organization*, 1966, pp 774-787.

Krasner argues, influence foreign policy calculations.[246]

In view of the sub-optimal outcomes of their earlier interaction, African states had now clustered together different aspects of co-operation. The emerging nesting pattern observed at the conference had facilitated co-operation as different issues had been linked and side-payments had been arranged to enhance the possibility for mutual concessions. That improvement of information that states have of each other is an important function of regimes showed itself in the stress laid at the summit on the significance of getting to know leaders of rival groupings. Another intended aim was the reduction of transaction costs in extra-African relations, as can be gauged from the decision to form a new Pan-African alliance in the United Nations.[247] As Krasner puts it, in this way the new regime might be used as a source of power by relatively weak states, enhancing their ability to influence the global order without necessarily altering underlying capabilities.[248]

However, this really depended on the strength and, concomitantly, the coherence and clarity of the regime. As it still existed only on paper, yet contained allusions to a world power status, the question was whether the OAU would develop into the effective voice of Africa or would remain weak and divided: in other words, was the Organization, as the Brazzaville representative had feared, a tiny mouse or could it become, as Yameogo had hoped, Africa's own atomic bomb?

From the perspective of its formation in 1963, one must incline towards the first metaphor. The Addis Ababa conference had resulted in the establishment of a strictly inter-governmental organization to be controlled by an organ made up of Africa's heads of state themselves. It was to have few organs that were not plenary in composition and enjoyed autonomous powers. As will be shown in section 5.2, the Charter carried few concrete obligations for member states. It stipulated, in a very broad and general manner, co-operation in various fields of endeavour and provided for egalitarian organs in which every state was formally equal and decisions were to be taken with ordinary or two-thirds majorities. With its strong emphasis on sovereignty, non-interference, territorial integrity and national independence, the Charter principally represented a consolidation of Africa's political status quo. With the exception of Ghana and Uganda, no country, big, small or of whatever alliance, preferred a supra-national formula to the weak regime that had now been founded.

External factors in the formation of the OAU

Why did delegates opt for the kind of structure that was established? Depending on one's perspective of Africa's international relations, there are two explanations. Looking at the continent's external ties, it should be realized that, as argued by Rothstein, regime creation is not an autonomous process unaffected by outside factors. This is especially so if its participants are relatively weak states.[249]

---

246   S.D. Krasner, 'Structural causes and regime consequences: regimes as intervening variables', and *ibid.*, 'Regimes and the limits of realism: regimes as autonomous variables', both in S.D. Krasner (ed), *International Regimes* (Ithaca and London, 1983), pp 1-21 and 355-368 respectively.

247   See H. Milner, 'International Theories of Cooperation Among Nations: Strengths and Weaknesses', in *World Politics*, 1992, pp 475-478.

248   Krasner, 'Regimes and the limits of realism'.

249   R.L. Rothstein, 'Regime-Creation by a Coalition of the Weak: Lessons from the NIEO and the

The Addis Ababa conference had aimed at a restructuring of international power relations and its hostility to some of the West's allies in Southern Africa was unmistakable. However, its resolutions on economics and disarmament were very moderate and, like other documents, betrayed an essentially collaborative global posture.[250] In view of this reformist approach and scepticism over the effectiveness of its anti-colonial programme, the Western world could not feel dissatisfied about the OAU's birth.[251] The doctrine of African unity as such did not elicit an *a priori* negative Western response, as all depended on the objectives of such unity.[252] Thus, French policy did not oppose regional regroupments, while the Americans favoured a continental structure similar to the Organization of American States on the condition that it contributed to "stability" and "development".[253]

So the kind of organization that was established hardly formed a threat to Western, long-term interests. These interests proved, in fact, instrumental in inducing the conference to adopt a moderate, collaborative profile, something that is best illustrated by the behaviour of the Brazzaville powers. Thus, after the close of the summit several Francophone leaders made a detour through Paris, where the French president was reported by Senghor as having qualified the conference as "positive" and "constructive".[254]

Still, while the results of the Addis Ababa conference were not surprising in relation to Africa's external dependence, the very fact of the OAU's formation also points to the validity of the subtler strands in dependency theory. In its original, rather crude version, the Organization's establishment would simply have been superfluous.[255] The rationale of the OAU, however, pointed clearly to dissatisfaction among Africa's state elites over certain aspects of global international relations.

Nevertheless, the intensity of centripetal pressures emanating from these reflections should not be over-estimated, as there were several concerns that underlay the external part of the Organization's rationale. The aspiration for a greater (individual and collective) world role and, related to this, equality of status with other state elites, entailed a desire to improve Africa's voice in the UN and other international organizations. It also included the pursuit of more remunerative economic relations between the continent and the rest of the world. Concern about economic power blocs as the European Community, at least among some of the OAU's membership, played a role as well. Coupled to reflections on the state of inter-African relations — the internal part of the OAU's rationale —, there

Integrated Program for Commodities', in *International Studies Quarterly*, 1984, pp 307-328.

250   See also *Daily Times* (Nigeria), 27/5/63; *Le Courrier d'Afrique* (Zaire), 11/6/63 (article); *l'Essor* (Mali), 29/7/63 (article); and *The Egyptian Gazette*, 26/5/63.

251   See for some of the congratulatory messages from several world leaders, *Proceedings*, vl. 1, sct. 2 (n. 183).

252   A similar response to the unity doctrine was given by Drs. A. Heldring, temporary chargé d'affaires of the Netherlands embassy in Ethiopia, in interview with author, Addis Ababa, 15/9/89.

253   Y. Benot, 'l'Unité africaine vue par l'impérialisme (France et U.S.A.)', in *Problèmes actuels de l'unité africaine* (n. 68), pp 457-466.

254   *Le Monde* (Paris), 29/5/63, 1/6/63 and 2-3/6/63 (all articles).

255   See on degrees of dependence T. Smith, 'Requiem or New Agenda for Third World Studies?', in *World Politics*, 1985, pp 532-561.

was thus a plurality of factors that deprived the Organization of specificity of focus. Fundamentally, this was caused by different patterns of external dependence and absence of hegemonic leadership. Resultant perceptions of common goals and enemies suffered from lack of consensus and, hence, strength. This is best illustrated by the conference's posture on the EC.

However, as Stein has remarked, a state's self-interest may still generate concern for joint gains with other actors. This can give rise to an alliance in which there is not necessarily an absence of internal disagreement but some shared interests induce the members to constrain their behaviour towards each other.[256] Moreover, as was shown in section 2.2 Ayoob has argued that contradictory behaviour with regard to short- and long-term security concerns is typical of Third World countries and is part of one and the same desire for security and influence.[257] Thus, the OAU regime might be a weak one, but it might be sufficient for realizing the common goal of, for example, a strengthened African voice in the United Nations. Yet, with regard to institutionalizing the leverage mechanism implicit in the OAU delegates did not wish to go further than establishing an African Group at the UN.

Inter-African factors in the formation of the OAU
The modest results of the Addis Ababa conference can also be explained by the relations between African states themselves. As Snidal argues, the likelihood of collective action depends on distribution of power and interests. If states are small and numerous hegemonic stability theory predicts that collective action is more difficult.[258] Regimes may mitigate this, but are themselves, in the absence of a hegemon, rather weak.

In the preceding years Africa's power relations had been rather blurred. The OAU's founding conference, however, provided greater clarity of which countries mattered in the reconciliation process. The course of its proceedings were principally influenced not by one, but by several countries. There was thus not one single hegemon, as may be gleaned from Nigeria's defeat over the issue of the IAMO charter. However, it would be an overstatement to argue that the group of influential countries amounted to, what De Vree calls, a "dominant coalition". This concept involves a group of actors that are sufficiently powerful to initiate, for example, a process of political integration, leading to a structure with an enhanced capacity to regulate political processes. They should be capable to force other actors to agree to the outcome of the integration process, while the latter must be incapable to disturb that outcome.[259] With so many actors involved and, as will be shown in following chapters, OAU inability to punish violation of its rules, the evidence points to the absence of a truly dominant coalition.

Nevertheless, at the conference some countries had mattered more than others:

---

256   A.A. Stein, *Why Nations Cooperate: Circumstance and Choice in International Relations* (Ithaca and London, 1990), ch. 7.

257   M. Ayoob, 'The Third World in the System of States: Acute Schizophrenia or Growing Pains?', in *International Studies Quarterly*, 1989, pp 67-79.

258   Snidal, 'Limits of Hegemonic Stability Theory', p 595 (n. 133).

259   J.K. de Vree, 'Politieke integratie en desintegratie', in M.P.C.M. van Schendelen (ed), *Kernthema's van de Politicologie* (Meppel and Amsterdam, 1981), pp 205-209.

- Ethiopia exerted considerable influence by preparing the summit and Haile Selassie's mediatory activities. Thus, the OAU's definitive headquarters were to be established in Addis Ababa.
- Guinea, too, proved crucial. Its active posture can be inferred from a total of 56 oral interventions.[260] It was to be rewarded with the election of a Guinean to serve as the OAU's first Administrative Secretary-General.
- Cameroon intervened orally in more than sixty situations, which may point to its attempt, as a French- and English-speaking country, to operate as a broker between different groups.
- There is evidence that Mali and Tanganyika proved important in this respect as well,[261] although their intervention rates were lower (36 and 22).
- While Ivory Coast was the most important Brazzaville power and saw its ideas on inter-African co-operation by and large accepted, at the conference it probably exerted influence from a background position as it intervened only three times.
- Judging from intervention rates Senegal (52), Nigeria (fifty), Algeria, (44) and Tunisia (42) were very active. Of these Algeria was perhaps most successful, as its militancy on colonialism was accepted by, and provided the turning-point of, the conference.

Thus, Nigeria's claim to leadership did not received unequivocal confirmation. Yet, it was the Osagyefo's country that, more than any other, was humiliated. Nkrumah's ideas on union government were completely rejected and Ghana had not even been allowed a seat on, or the headquarters of, the new Liberation Committee. Nasser had also been kept at arm's length,[262] although his preoccupations undoubtedly lay elsewhere. Minor actors that failed to exert influence were Madagacar, with its failure in the name issue; Morocco and Somalia, in the defeat of their territorial ambitions; and Togo, in its inability to gain admission.

The ideology underlying the OAU's formation
Contrary to what some authors have propounded,[263] the ideas giving rise to the OAU did not amount to Pan-Africanism as such. In interviews, no OAU official or African diplomat claimed that Pan-Africanism formed its ideological basis, even though this is contradicted in OAU propaganda material.[264] However, several ideas that make up the amorphous body of Pan-Africanism were used to articulate the motives that led to the Organization's birth.[265] Thus, the doctrine of African unity expressed the drive for

---

260 Figures in this section are totals, calculated from the foreign ministers and heads of state conference combined. 34 interventions by delegates were unidentified, while the *Verbatim Record* does not pertain to informal sessions.
261 *Le Monde* (Paris), 28/5/63 (article).
262 *VR*, CI-I, 19-20; 25; and 36 and *Le Monde* (Paris), 3/6/63 (article).
263 F.i. Thompson, *Ghana's Foreign Policy*, p 323.
264 One diplomat denied, after a question about this, that Pan-Africanism formed the ideological basis of the OAU. Interview with Amadou Kebe, Conseiller of Senegal's embassy in Ethiopia, Addis Ababa, 3/10/89. An example of OAU propaganda claiming that the Organization is the embodiment of Pan-Africanism is *OAU 10th Summit Anniversary* (Press and Information Section, General Secretariat, Addis Ababa, n.d.).
265 M.L. Ropivia ('Critique des fondements conceptuels de l'unité politique de l'Afrique', in *Cahiers de*

inter-African reconciliation and aspirations to a world role and equality of status with other state elites. Continentalist notions formed an important aspect of this, although Madagascar found it hard to swallow and the North African countries adopted it with varying degrees of enthusiasm.

Motivations were formulated in Pan-Africanist rhetoric, such as in the defence of "Mother Africa", the assertion of the "African Personality" and lip-service to the anti-colonial struggle. This may explain why in interviews OAU officials and African diplomats mentioned the struggle against Southern African regimes as the reason for the OAU's foundation.[266] However, this struggle was only one, and not the most important, consideration that gave rise to the Organization. Its dualist rationale involved two inter-locking parts. The external one could easily be justified with Pan-Africanist notions. So could the internal part (inter-African reconciliation), although here state nationalist concepts like sovereign equality, non-interference, condemnation of subversion, dispute settlement and territorial integrity proved equally important. In sections 6.1 and 7.1 it will be shown how the objectives of the struggle against colonialism and African conflict management emanated from this dualist rationale.

The OAU Charter and its accompanying resolutions formed a brilliant ideological compromise. Both militants and moderate-conservatives saw several of their aspirations reflected. There was even a wink at the Osagyefo in the name of the Organization and the allusion to the Fifth Pan-African Congress. Article 2 referred to unity, solidarity (a UAM concept), state sovereignty and the eradication of colonialism. The Casablanca states could feel satisfied with the prominence given to political and diplomatic co-operation and the mentioning of defence, non-alignment and a commitment to decolonization.[267]

Yet, the Charter bore striking resemblance to the IAMO treaty and the compromise clearly favoured the moderate-conservatives. Allusions to non-African influence and interventions on the continent, which had been so prevalent in Casablanca documents, were by and large absent. The concept of neo-colonialism did not figure in the Charter's operative sections, while the resolution on economic co-operation remained silent on EC association. Moreover, the disarmament resolution did not threaten the alliance between France and its UAM clients, as it was generally assumed that the reference to non-alignment prohibited membership of blocs operating exclusively in a Cold War context.[268] The quid pro quo obtained by the militants were the measures stipulated against the regimes in Southern Africa.

Thus, the ingenious complexity of the compromise could be interpreted at will.[269] Still, most reactions were one of jubilance, mixed with surprise.[270] It was argued that

---

l'IPAG, no. 10, June 1990, pp 93-191) overlooks this and ignores the continentalization of Pan-Africanist ideology by Nkrumah and Padmore.

266   Interviews with Ambassador Mamadou Bah, Director of the General Secretariat's Political Department, and R.S. Iskandar, Ambassador of Egypt, Addis Ababa, 18 and 27/9/89 respectively.

267   Arts. 2.2.a, 2.2.f, 3.6 and 3.7 OAU Charter.

268   Mayall, *Africa* (n. 18), p 149.

269   *The Ethiopian Herald*, 26/5/63; *l'Essor* (Mali), 3/6/63; *The Egyptian Gazette*, 30/5/63; and Address by Osagyefo the President to the National Assembly on the Occasion of the Ratification of the Charter of the Organization of African Unity, Friday, 21/6/63.

270   *Daily Times* (Nigeria), 27/5/63; *l'Essor* (Mali), 3/6/63; and *The Ethiopian Herald*, 26/5/63.

after centuries of colonialism the continent had broken with the past.[271] Africa had now moved from a mere geographical entity to a political community with its own consciousness.[272] Most countries emphasized the external considerations in the OAU's rationale,[273] although the struggle against colonialism was also stressed. This may be explained by its role in the reconciliation process, but also as a sign of increased self-confidence in Africa's capacity to affect political developments.[274] Yet, opposition groups from independent African states could find little comfort. For example, the UPC noted that the conference had limited itself to verbal condemnations of neo-colonialism.[275] Retrospectively, a spokesman would portray the OAU's foundation as amounting to balkanization and stabilization of the neo-colonial system.[276]

Caution in *Sunday News* (Tanganyika), 26/5/63; *Nouvelles Malgaches Quotidiennes*, 27/5/63 (interview); and *Le Courrier d'Afrique* (Zaire), 11/6/63 (article).

271 *The Ethiopian Herald*, 26/5/63 and *The Ghanaian Times*, 27/5/63.
272 *Fraternité* (Ivory Coast), 31/5/63 (article); *Le Courrier d'Afrique* (Zaire), 31/5/63; *The Ethiopian Herald*, 26/5/63; *Ghana Today*, 5/6/63; and *l'Essor* (Mali), 3/6/63 and 29/7/63 (article).
273 *Daily Times* (Nigeria), 27/5/63 and *Le Courrier d'Afrique* (Zaire), 9-10/6/63 (article). Also *Sunday News* (Tanganyika), 26/5/63; and *Nouvelles Malgaches Quotidiennes*, 27/5/63 (interview).
274 *Daily Times* (Nigeria), 27/5/63; *Le Courrier d'Afrique* (Zaire), 31/5/63; and *l'Essor* (Mali), 3/6/63 (poem).
275 See the pamphlet 'Le néo-colonialisme au Cameroun' quoted in Y. Benot, *Idéologies des indépendances africaines* (Paris, 1972), pp 174-176.
276 M'buyinga, *Pan-Africanism*, pp 55-57 (n. 178).

5

The internal functioning
of the OAU

5.1 Introduction

In order to understand the impact of the OAU regime on the structures of African politics, in terms of its institutions, norms and decision-making procedures, it is necessary to provide insight in the internal make-up and functioning of the Organization. As this functioning takes place within the broad confines of the OAU Charter, section 5.2 will give an analysis of this document. Section 5.3 provides a cursory outline of the OAU's structures and organizational evolution so as to situate its most important organs in their proper institutional perspective.

The structure and functioning of the General Secretariat are discussed in section 5.4. Much has already been written on its institutional aspects, but very little on the perceptions that Secretariat officials have of their role and the functioning of this organ within the OAU structure.[1] Special emphasis will therefore be put on how these functionaries experience their work and position in the Organization, based on interviews that were conducted with OAU officials for this purpose. This perspective is also in line with the centrality that the reconstruction of the Organization's ideological ground-work occupies in this study.

Similarly, the discussion of the OAU's budgetary difficulties (section 5.5) is informed by an analysis of perceptions and facts gleaned from interviews with both Secretariat officials and member state diplomats. The Organization's financial predicaments and some of the problems facing the Secretariat are put into sharper relief with the help of the concept of collective or public goods and the related free rider dilemma.

The role of the OAU's major policy organs is studied in section 5.6, in which

---

1   See f.i. A. Ba, B. Koffi and F. Sahli, *l'Organisation de l'unité africaine: de la charte d'Addis-Abéba à la convention des droits de l'homme et des peuples* (Paris, 1984). C.O.C. Amate, *Inside the OAU: Pan-Africanism in Practice* (New York, 1986) pays more attention to these aspects. The author was ambassador to Ethiopia between 1976 and 1979.

emphasis is put on the nature and structures of the process of decision-making. A general evaluation of the OAU's internal functioning is given in section 5.7.

5.2 Some legal parameters

Rights and obligations of member states
The OAU's official "Purposes" mentioned in section 4.5 are stipulated in article 2.1 of the Charter.[2] In order to realize these goals, member states are required, under article 2.2, to co-ordinate and harmonize their policy in the field of politics, diplomacy and defence, as well as in socio-economic and more technical areas. Article 2 does not establish any priority between the different purposes and fields of co-operation.

In pursuit of these purposes, the member states are required to adhere to several "Principles" listed in article 3. These principles are legally binding, as under article 6 member states "pledge themselves" to their observance. This terminology denotes the will to be bound, although the entailing duties consist of an omission of certain behaviour or are formulated in such a general way that few concrete obligations emanate from them. As mentioned in section 4.4, most of them aim at consolidating the political-territorial status quo in inter-African relations. However, the last two principles stipulate dedication to the anti-colonial struggle and affirm a policy of non-alignment. Chapter 6 analyses what dedication to the anti-colonial struggle entailed in practice. As has already been argued, the policy of non-alignment was not supposed to preclude alliances between France and its Francophone clients. Moreover, chapters 7 and 8 will show that the principle has hardly had any effect on alignments with superpowers. The extent of the principle of non-interference in internal affairs is discussed in chapter 7.

Article 4 stipulates that each "independent sovereign African State shall be entitled to become a Member of the Organization". However, the granting of membership is not automatic, as under article 28.2 admission has to be decided by a simple majority of the member states. Apart from certain procedural requirements (art. 28.2) the Charter does not formulate any other conditions for membership. Nevertheless, it goes without saying that new states must agree with the objectives and principles of the OAU, something that excluded membership of South Africa under its apartheid regime.[3] Dependent territories and liberation movements were also excluded from membership, although liberation movements recognized by the OAU were granted observer status. Under the Charter a member state cannot be expelled or suspended. A Senegalese proposal to include the possibility of expulsion, in case of non-compliance with obligations, was rejected at the founding conference.[4] Member states may, however, leave the Organization of their own

---

2   See for its text Appendix E.
3   One might say that the phrase "independent sovereign African State" implies a state controlled by Africans and so excluded South Africa. T.O. Elias, 'The Charter of the Organization of African Unity', in *American Journal of International Law*, 1965, p 247, pp 250-251. Differently Z. Cervenka, *The Unfinished Quest for Unity: Africa and the OAU* (London, 1977), p 16.
4   *Proceedings of the Summit Conference of Independent African States: Verbatim Record* (hereinafter as *VR*), SM, VI, 35. "SM" (of "summit") refers to meetings of the heads of state and "C" to committee meetings, all followed by number of meeting and page.

accord, for which certain procedures are provided under article 32 of the Charter.

Article 5 states that member states "shall enjoy equal rights and have equal duties". Although the OAU has some organs with limited membership the Charter does not grant special rights to certain countries. Yet, the provisions concerning the budget constitute an important exception to the principle of equal duties. Article 23 stipulates that the budget shall be provided by contributions from member states "in accordance with the scale of assessment of the United Nations". As this scale is partly related to unequal national incomes, this means that members contribute unequal sums to the budget.

The legally binding nature of member state contributions can be deduced from the language used in article 23. It stipulates that the budget "*shall*" be provided by member states. The word "shall" denotes, in international legal parlance, an obligation.[5] The article adds that members "agree to pay their respective contributions regularly". This must be explained as a sign of concern that contributions might not come forward on a sufficiently regular basis to ensure the continuity of the Organization, irrespective of the legal obligation to contribute as such.[6]

OAU practice confirms that the obligation to pay contributions is a legally binding one.[7] Thus, in 1979 a sanction provision was introduced, in a separate regulation, to enforce compliance. Moreover, the fact that members often fail to comply, or to comply fully or in time, with their obligations does not invalidate this conclusion. As shown in section 5.5, member states do not contest the legally binding nature of the budget or their individual dues, but argue about the height of the budget and respective contributions. The absence of Charter provisions for sanctions against defaulting states and the unwillingness which the Council of Ministers showed, until the 1990s, to enforce the 1979 sanction directive do not justify a different assessment but merely explain the practical difficulties in implementing budget regulations.

Decisions of OAU organs

An evaluation of the legal effect of OAU decisions[8] is difficult, as the Charter and various "Rules of Procedure", on which more below, are usually silent on their legal status. The lack of clarity characterizing these documents is typical of the Organization and ensures that member states have considerable freedom in developing the OAU as they see fit, without being hindered by too many express commitments.[9] As shown in chapter 4, Africa's states only wanted to agree to a weak, inter-governmental regime and merely encouraged the co-ordination and harmonization of their policies.

Nevertheless, all decisions related to the *internal* functioning of the OAU, such as interpretation and amendment of the Charter, budget contributions, admission of new members, the formation of new organs or the appointment of officials, are binding on member states. The opposite would create intolerable consequences for the functioning of

---

5   *Black's Law Dictionary* (4th ed.: St. Paul, Minnesota, 1951), pp 1541-1542.

6   At the founding conference, the article was adopted with little debate. See *VR*, SM, VI, 28.

7   F. Borella, 'Le système juridique de l'O.U.A.', in *Annuaire français de droit international*, 1971, p 241 and Ba, Koffi and Sahli, *l'Organisation de l'unité africaine*, p 19.

8   The words "decision" and "decide" will be used in a broad sense, irrespective of any legal connotations. Depending on context, they refer to binding or recommendatory decisions.

9   Cervenka, *Unfinished Quest*, p 22.

the Organization. However, in terms of the relations between OAU organs themselves, the Assembly of Heads of State and Government, as the "supreme organ" of the OAU, may review the decisions of all other organs and specialized agencies (art. 8). This implies that all decisions of the Assembly have internally binding force for the other organs but that, vice versa, decisions taken by subordinate organs can be revised by the OAU's supreme organ. Even the decisions of the Council of Ministers are not binding on the Assembly, to which it is responsible (art. 13.1 Charter). Yet, in the case of the budget, which under art. 23 is approved by the Council, a binding decision can be imposed on member states without Assembly approval.[10] Still, it must be realized that, in the Charter, legal enforcement mechanisms to force member states to respect decisions on the OAU's internal functioning are lacking.

Decisions of OAU organs that do not pertain to internal functioning have no legally binding force. This distinction between internal and external effects of decisions constitutes a fundamental feature of the Organization and severely restricts its functioning and impact on Africa's international relations. However, this does not mean that expressions of OAU policy lack all significance. As argued in section 5.6 the significance of resolutions has to be determined on a case by case basis.

OAU organs are relatively free to choose the *form* in which decisions on internal or external matters are issued. In fact, it says little or anything about their legal status. Expressions of the Assembly's will are formally called "resolution" or "decision", but neither Charter nor relevant Rules of Procedure clarify their status or the difference between the two. Worse still, where the English text of article 10 of the Charter speaks of "resolutions" the French one uses the term "décisions". Yet, in practice both Council and Assembly formulate "resolutions" to express attitudes and policies of the Organization on external issues.[11] These resolutions, adopted under arts. 10 and 14 of the Charter, are therefore not legally binding on member states, not even on those that voted in their favour.[12] Their recommendatory character is confirmed by the language in which they are formulated, with both organs "appealing to", "requesting" or "calling on" member states to act in certain ways. If Council and Assembly want to express themselves on an important topic, their utterances are sometimes called "declaration" or "statement". These are usually synonymous with resolutions and so legally not binding.[13] In contrast, Council and Assembly utterances that are called "decisions" are usually issued in cases pertaining to the internal functioning[14] of the Organization and therefore binding.[15]

Under art. 11 and 15 of the Charter respectively, the Assembly and Council have adopted their own Rules of Procedure. As they regulate the internal functioning of the

---

10   Also Amate, *Inside the OAU*, p 68. This is rather academic, as the ministers making up the Council are in their own countries subordinate to the heads of state, who compose the Assembly.

11   Resolutions rarely relate to internal topics, in which case they are binding. See f.i. CM/Res.89 (VII) or AHG/Res.152 (XXII).

12   Naturally, this also holds true for the external decisions of other subordinate organs.

13   Sometimes they pertain to the OAU's internal functioning and thus have binding force. See f.i. AHG/Decl.3 (XXIX).

14   With the exception of the "décisions" taken under the French version of art. 10 Charter, which correspond to the "resolutions" in the English text.

15   Naturally, in the case of the Council they are binding on members in so far as they have not been revoked by the Assembly. See for this below.

organs concerned, they possess binding force. The same is true of the "Functions and Regulations of the General Secretariat", the "Protocol of the Commission of Mediation, Conciliation and Arbitration", the Rules of Procedure of the various "Specialized Commissions" (on which more below) and various other internal documents to which reference will be made. Thus, not *form* but *contents* determines the legal status of the decisions, in their broadest sense, of OAU organs.

Some institutional provisions
Article 7 of the Charter lists four "principal institutions":

- the Assembly of Heads of State and Government
- the Council of Ministers
- the General Secretariat
- the Commission of Mediation, Conciliation and Arbitration

The Assembly
The Assembly and Council are the major policy organs of the Organization. As the OAU's supreme organ, the Assembly may rescind decisions of other organs, including those of the Council.[16] It may also discuss "matters of common concern to Africa" in order to co-ordinate and harmonize general OAU policy. However, this broad, deliberative power is subject "to the provisions of this Charter" (art. 8). This means that, until 1990, its deliberative function was limited by the principle of non-interference in internal affairs (art. 3.2).[17] The Assembly may also decide questions of interpretation and amendment of the Charter (arts. 27 and 33 Charter), appoint the Secretary-General and his "Assistant Secretaries(-General)" (arts. 16 and 17 Charter) and establish permanent Specialized Commissions or ad hoc committees.[18]

The Assembly is composed of the heads of state and government "or their duly accredited representatives" and must meet at least once a year. However, if requested by a member state and on approval of two-thirds of the membership, the Assembly may meet in extraordinary session (art. 9 Charter). At its ordinary session the Assembly decides by simple majority on the venue of its next meeting, which may be in Addis Ababa or elsewhere.[19] Each member state has one vote (art. 10 Charter). All decisions and resolutions must be carried by a two-thirds majority of the entire membership and not merely of those present and voting. While this provision was introduced to prevent decisions taken by a minority, in the context of absenteeism this may easily lead to a blocking of the vote.[20] Nevertheless, questions of procedure must be determined by a simple majority of the membership and whether or not a question is a procedural one is decided in similar fashion. Two-thirds of the membership constitutes the quorum for any

---

16   As was explicitly confirmed after a clash of competence in an Assembly decision of 1968. See AHG/Dec.21 (V).
17   See further section 8.1.
18   Article 20 Charter and Rule 37, Rules of Procedure.
19   Rule 6, Rules of Procedure.
20   Rule 25, Rules of Procedure and *VR*, SM, VI, 16-18. One may presume that statements and declarations have similar requirements.

meeting. (art. 10.3 and 10.4 Charter). Meetings are held in private unless otherwise decided by simple majority.

At the start of each annual session, the Assembly elects a head of state as chairman, who is seconded by eight, elected "meeting" (vice-)chairmen (Rule 9). Together they constitute the Assembly "Bureau". The chairman has ordinary, relatively modest, procedural functions. The provisional agenda of an ordinary session, which is drawn up by the Council, is very flexible, as it may include items submitted by the Assembly, member states, the Council and any "other business" (Rule 11). Ordinarily, voting takes place by the raising of hands, unless a member state requests a roll-call vote (Rule 30). Voting for elections is secret, however, and also in special circumstances as decided by simple majority (Rule 31).

The Council

Article 12 of the Charter provides for the Council of Ministers, which "shall consist of Foreign Ministers or such other Ministers as are designated by the Governments of Member States". In practice, ambassadors or other accredited officials may represent member states.[21] The Council must meet at least twice a year and if requested by a member state and approved by two-thirds of the membership, it shall meet in extraordinary session.[22] Its ordinary annual session must be held in February to consider, *inter alia*, the budget and programme of the Organization for the next fiscal year. The other session, which is mainly to prepare the Assembly meeting, is supposed to be held in August. In practice, it varies with the date of the session of the superior body, which until 1970 used to be held during the second half of the year, but since then has usually been held before the annual session of the UN General Assembly, most often in June or July.[23]

Council meetings may be held at the Headquarters in Addis Ababa, unless a member proposes to host the Council. Additional travel expenses of the Secretariat are in that case borne by the state concerned.[24] Meetings are held in private unless otherwise decided by simple majority (Rule 9). The provisional agenda of an ordinary meeting is drawn up by the Secretary-General and must comprise discussion of the Secretary-General's annual report and items proposed by the Assembly, the preceding Council session, the Specialized Commissions, member states or "other business".[25]

At the commencement of each session, the Council elects, by secret ballot and simple majority, a chairman, three vice-chairmen and a rapporteur. Their term of office usually ends six months later at the next ordinary session. Together they comprise the "Bureau" of the Council, to which they cannot be re-elected until other states have held office (Rule 11). The chairman has procedural tasks similar to his colleague in the

---

21   Amate, *Inside the OAU*, p 68.
22   Art. 12.2 Charter. In which case it is convened by the Administrative Secretary-General. See Rule 16, Rules of Procedure of the Council of Ministers.
23   See Rule 6, Rules of Procedure of the Council; AHG/Dec.49 (VII); and Amate, *Inside the OAU*, p 12.
24   Rule 8. Originally, this Rule provided that sessions would be held in Addis Ababa "or at such other places as the Council may decide by simple majority". The Rule was revised as quoted above in 1966. See CM/Dec.13 (VII).
25   Rules 14-17.

Assembly (Rule 12). Each member state has one vote (art. 14 Charter) and all resolutions are determined by a simple majority of the Council's membership.[26] Two-thirds of the membership constitutes the quorum.[27] Other provisions in the Rules of Procedure elaborate on debating and voting rules similar to those of the Assembly.

The Council is answerable to the Assembly, whose conferences it prepares. It also implements Assembly decisions and co-ordinates the forms of Pan-African co-operation listed in art. 2.2 Charter and in conformity with Assembly instructions (art. 13 Charter). Furthermore, it may establish ad hoc committees and temporary working groups as it deems necessary (Rule 36). It decides on the budget of the Organization, determines privileges and immunities of OAU officials working in member states (art. 31 Charter) and approves the internal regulations of the Specialized Commissions (art. 22 Charter).

As the Assembly normally convenes only once a year, the two sessions of the Council provide the Organization with a greater sense of continuity. Although the Council is supposed to execute Assembly decisions, it can only do so in the case of the internal functioning of the OAU. In other cases, it is really the member states themselves that execute decisions of both Council and Assembly.[28]

The General Secretariat

This organ is directed by the (Administrative) Secretary-General (SG for short). The latter official is, together with his Assistant Secretaries-General, appointed by the Assembly by secret vote and a two-thirds majority.[29] While the appointment of the SG shall not be subject to regional considerations, that of his Assistants must reflect the representation of the different regions of the continent. However, in all cases professional qualifications must be the most important criterion for election.[30] The term of office for all these functionaries is four years. While they can be re-elected, the Assembly may also fire them, on the basis of a similar voting procedure.[31]

In the Functions and Regulations cited earlier, the General Secretariat is described as the OAU's central and permanent organ. Its task is described as supervision of the implementation of Council decisions in the different areas of co-operation and is largely administrative: provision of technical and administrative services to the various organs, such as preparation of sessions; custody of their documents; drafting of an annual report; preparation of the annual programme and budget to be considered by the Council; and other, more technical, duties.[32]

Article 18 of the Charter provides for the international status of the Administrative Secretary-General and his staff. The SG is responsible to the Council for the discharge of his duties. His tasks are largely financial and administrative: he must submit reports to various organs, manages the Secretariat and executes numerous functions concerning the

---

26   And presumably decisions as well, although this is not explicated. See Rule 29.
27   Art. 14.3 Charter and Rule 18, Rules of Procedure.
28   See also E. Jouve, *l'Organisation de l'unité africaine* (Paris, 1984), p 64.
29   Arts. 16 and 17 Charter and Rules 32 and 34, Rules of Procedure of the Assembly.
30   Rules 32 and 34, Rules of Procedure of the Assembly.
31   Rules 33, 35 and 36, Rules of Procedure of the Assembly.
32   Rule 2, Functions and Regulations of the General Secretariat.

budget.[33]

    While he has no automatic right to participate in the deliberations of the OAU's organs, in practice the Secretary and his Assistants do attend their meetings.[34] The Secretary-General has no power to convene Council or Assembly on his own initiative. Under the Charter he lacks a prerogative to develop political activities such as the UN Secretary-General is allowed to do under article 99 of the UN Charter. The highest OAU official has always been allowed much less leeway by member states. Both in the Organization's original, constitutive documents and within the structural confines of Africa's inter-state relations his position is rather weak and any political role is severely circumscribed. Nevertheless, during the last three decades his actual powers have been subject to political vicissitudes. In section 5.4 it will be shown how and when Secretaries-General were able to develop a political role for themselves and how this led, during the early 1990s, to a formal upgrading of the Secretary's position.

Commissions

The Commission of Mediation, Conciliation and Arbitration is a dormant institution. It will be discussed in section 7.2. Under art. 20 Charter, the Assembly established five Specialized Commissions, composed of member state ministers. These were to institutionalize co-operation in their respective fields of specialization. Their annual budget has to be approved by the Council of Ministers. They are normal OAU organs that do not enjoy autonomy vis-à-vis the rest of the Organization.[35]

Evaluation

The Charter carries few concrete commitments for member states. Even if legal obligations are stipulated, they are very general ones and legal enforcement mechanisms are, at least in the Charter, absent. Member states can easily control the functioning of the Organization through the supremacy of the Assembly, whose review function subordinates all other organs to the will of the heads of state. In most cases, the Council of Ministers needs the approval of the Assembly, while the Secretary-General is responsible to the Council for the discharge of his duties. The legal position of the Secretary and his Assistants is much weaker than that of their counterparts at the UN. Even if there would be a conflict of interest, it is the member states that can settle the matter by way of the Assembly.[36] Organs that are not made up of member states have few autonomous powers, which are usually administrative or technical. Formulation of OAU policy is in the hands of member states, which must also execute the decisions of Council and Assembly. Charter and Rules of Procedure therefore entailed a rudimentary international organization based on relatively voluntary co-operation between member states. How the OAU evolved in practice is the subject of following sections.

---

33   See, among others, Rule 11, Functions and Regulations.

34   Rule 9, Functions and Regulations, says that this right must be governed by the Rules of Procedure of these organs. Yet, these are silent on this matter. Also Cervenka, *Unfinished Quest*, p 29.

35   See also Elias, 'The Charter', p 265.

36   The Assembly is the only organ that may amend, and give an official interpretation of, the Charter. Arts. 27 and 33 Charter.

5.3 The institutional evolution of the OAU: an overview

Through the years, the OAU has developed activities in various fields of endeavour, as a result of which the Organization has grown into a large and complex structure made up of numerous committees, agencies and commissions. While some lead a more or less dormant existence, other organs are much more active and have developed a relatively high profile within the Organization. Some organs are fully integrated in the structure of the OAU, while others maintain only a weak link with the main OAU bodies.[37]

The simplified organigram in figure 5.1 shows the situation of the early 1990s. It includes, besides the major organs discussed above, the so-called "Specialized Agencies" and observer organizations. The latter are technically not a part of the OAU family, but are independent international organizations (NGO's or inter-governmental), which have been granted observer status. They include such diverse institutions as the Union of African Journalists, the Inter-African Coffee Organization and the Commission of the Lake Chad Basin. More important are the Specialized Agencies. These are separate inter-governmental organizations, which do not necessarily involve the entire OAU membership. As independent organizations, they are autonomous vis-à-vis the OAU, yet they have a close working relationship with the latter. This has been recognized by the granting of the official status of Specialized Agency. By the early 1990s they included, for example, the Pan-African News Agency (until 1997), the Supreme Council for Sports in Africa and the Pan-African Telecommunications Union.

The OAU Specialized Commissions have experienced a more chequered existence. Originally totalling five,[38] their number rose to seven during the mid-1960s.[39] However, several Commissions frequently failed to reach the required quorum as a result of the multiplicity of conferences and overburdened member state agenda's. Several Commissions were therefore merged.[40] By the mid-1980s the Organization included an Economic and Social Commission, a Labour Commission[41] and the original Defence Commission.

Especially Commissions involved in socio-economic co-operation suffer from the fact that members prefer to pursue many of these objectives within the cadre of regional organizations. Moreover, the work of these Commissions overlaps with that of the ECA and UN Specialized Agencies. Despite the fact that countries were at first suspicious of the perceived lack of African control over ECA and the institutional rivalry it developed with the OAU, many realized that African states could benefit more by working through or with UN institutions. These are better funded and have more expertise than the OAU

---

37   Several books present competent overviews of OAU institutions. See f.i. Jouve, *l'Organisation de l'unité africaine* (n. 28); Ba, Koffi and Sahli, *l'Organisation de l'unité africaine* (n. 1); and A. Sesay, O. Ojo and O. Fasehun, *The OAU After Twenty Years* (Boulder and London, 1984).

38   Economic and Social Commission; Educational and Cultural Commission; Health, Sanitation and Nutrition Commission; Defence Commission; and Scientific, Technical and Research Commission.

39   AHG/Res.4 (I) and AHG/Res.20 (I).

40   AHG/Dec.5 (III) and AHG/Dec.6 (III).

41   See for its formation CM/Res.444 (XXV).

FIGURE 5.1

Figure 5.1   Structural Outline of the OAU

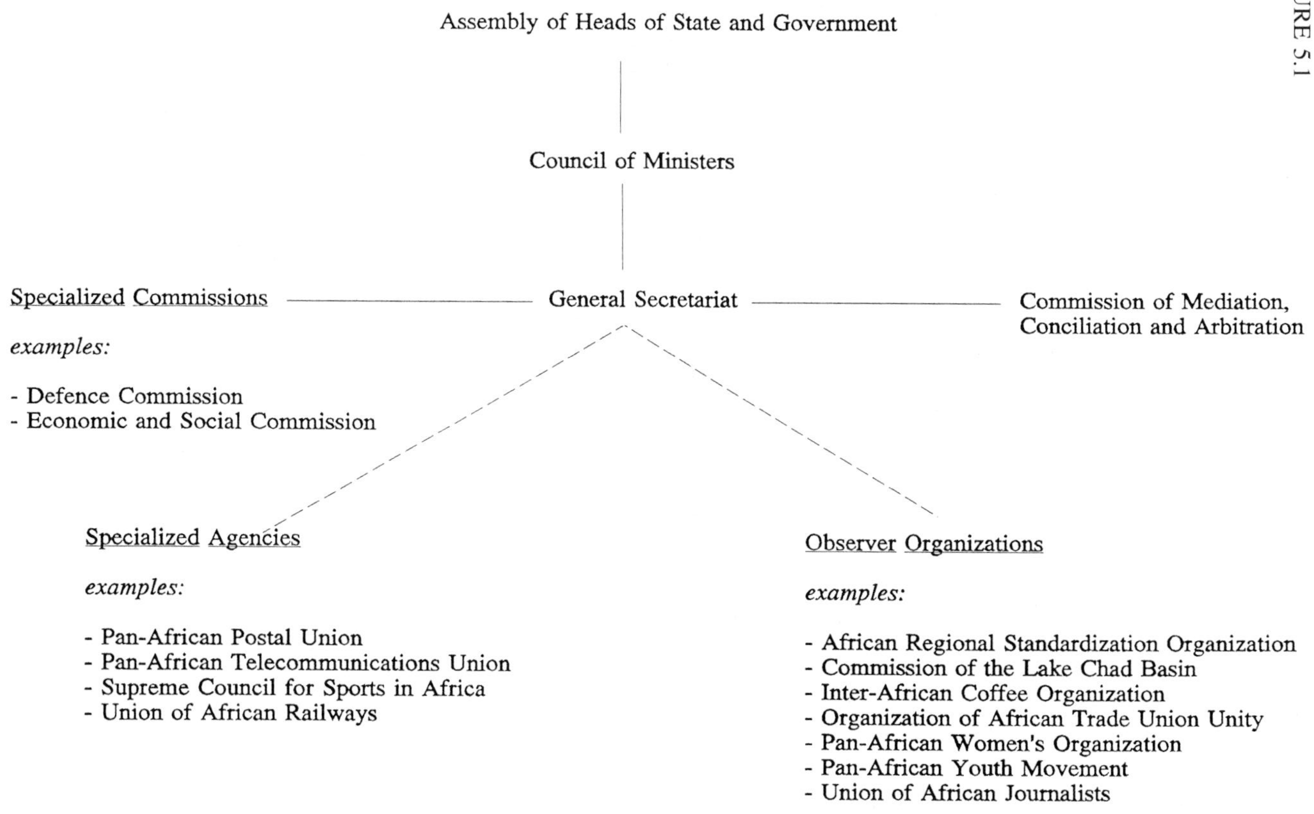

Assembly of Heads of State and Government

Council of Ministers

General Secretariat

Commission of Mediation,
Conciliation and Arbitration

Specialized Commissions

examples:

- Defence Commission
- Economic and Social Commission

Specialized Agencies

examples:

- Pan-African Postal Union
- Pan-African Telecommunications Union
- Supreme Council for Sports in Africa
- Union of African Railways

Observer Organizations

examples:

- African Regional Standardization Organization
- Commission of the Lake Chad Basin
- Inter-African Coffee Organization
- Organization of African Trade Union Unity
- Pan-African Women's Organization
- Pan-African Youth Movement
- Union of African Journalists

General Secretariat. The latter has therefore developed a working relationship with the ECA.[42] Furthermore, with encouragement of Council[43] and Assembly African ministers also pursue socio-economic objectives in ministerial conferences. These are convened for specific purposes, or function as preparatory meetings of the UN African Group and are called before sessions of UN Specialized Agencies.[44] Nevertheless, with the onset of the economic crisis during the 1980s, economic issues have become an increasingly important topic on the agenda of the Council and Assembly themselves.

The OAU General Secretariat maintains relations with so-called "regional" offices, which are OAU organs outside Addis Ababa (see figure 5.2). These were established as a result of the steady expansion of OAU activities in various fields and the desire of member states to gain a share of OAU institutions. It should be realized, however, that international organizations like the OAU are subject to contradictory trends of expansion and contraction. Thus, while in the early 1980s regional offices numbered more than fifteen,[45] after the mid-1980s some of these were closed down as a result of financial difficulties.

The more important of these offices were given the title "Executive Secretariat". Examples are the Executive Secretariat which services the African Group at the UN in New York and the Executive Secretariats for the African Groups in Brussels and Geneva. These last two are responsible for preparing Pan-African policy towards the European Union and the UN Specialized Agencies based in Europe. The former Liberation Committee in Dar es Salaam was also backed by an Executive Secretariat, while an Executive Secretariat that is now based in Cairo[46] liaises with the Arab League. Although Executive Secretariats are naturally more autonomous than subdivisions of the General Secretariat in Addis, the latter has to liaise with them on a regular basis. It must supervise them and co-ordinate their operations with that of the main Organization.

5.4   The house of Africans: the General Secretariat in perspective

Introduction
This section attempts to approach the Secretariat's functioning especially from the perspective of the human individuals involved. To this purpose, it will present a host of perceptions, gleaned from interviews, that Secretariat functionaries have of their own role and the Organization as a whole. The underlying aim is to enrich our view of the OAU as an institution that is not merely made up of structures and procedures but also of different individuals, each with their own views on the problems of inter-African politics and the

---

42   See AHG/Res.46 (II) and Agreement on Co-operation Between the Organization of African Unity and the United Nations Economic Commission for Africa, New York, 15 November 1965. Also see Amate, *Inside the OAU*, chs. 17, 18 and 20.

43   The Assembly established the so-called "third committee" of the Council of Ministers to consider issues of economic, social and cultural co-operation. See AHG/Res.46 (II).

44   Amate, *Inside the OAU*, ch. 20.

45   See f.i. the statement by Secretary-General Ide Oumarou in *Africa Research Bulletin* (Political, Social and Cultural Series; hereinafter as PSC), 1986, p 7995.

46   Letter by Mr. J.B. Thundu, Chief of Press Section, Information Division, Office of the Secretary-General, to author, 27/7/93.

166

FIGURE 5.2

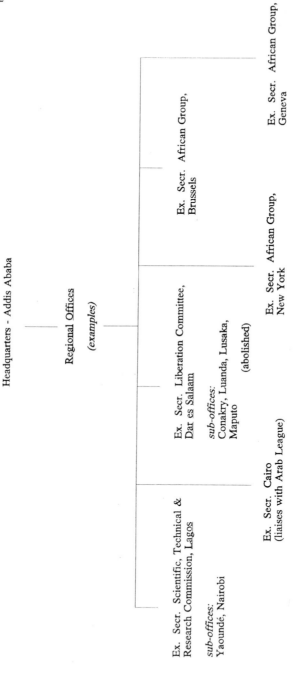

Figure 5.2 General Secretariat: Headquarters and Regional Offices

role of the OAU therein. While this section focuses on their perceptions of the Secretariat as such, following chapters present their views on the different fields of OAU co-operation with which they are concerned.

First, an outline is given of the Secretariat's structure, its principal officials and their working procedures, as well as the composition of all its personnel. Then the exact role of the Secretariat and the extent of the powers of its functionaries are discussed, followed by an analysis of their working environment. It is contended that, if one regards the Secretariat as the very heart of the public or collective good that the OAU represents, the concomitant free rider dilemma provides a good explanation of member state attitudes towards this organ. The section concludes with an outline of the political influence that the Secretary-General can exert inside the OAU structure.

Structure and principal officials

In 1964 the Assembly decided to appoint four Assistant Secretaries-General, coming from different African regions, to help the Administrative Secretary-General in his work. This decision was essentially a political one, as it was made to enable the various African regions to participate in the functioning of the Organization.[47] In order to cover the different areas of Pan-African co-operation and provide a task for the Assistant Secretaries, the first Secretary-General, Diallo Telli, divided the General Secretariat into four Departments, each of which operated under the responsibility of an Assistant Secretary. This Departmental structure remained unchanged until the late 1970s.[48]

In 1978, the Assembly decided to create the post of a fifth Assistant Secretary-General to keep pace with the OAU's expanding membership. Member states were now divided into five regions — North Africa, West Africa, Central Africa, East Africa and Southern Africa — and the Secretariat's Departmental structure was adapted to create a domain for a fifth Assistant Secretary.[49]

During the 1980s two Departments involved in social, cultural and technical co-operation were merged. The "Administration, Finance and Conferences Department" was split into two, reunited, and again divided into two separate Departments. The "Political (Affairs) Department" was left untouched by these reforms, while a plan for a "Department for Planning and Co-ordination" had, by the early 1990s, not yet been implemented.[50] The Secretariat's Departmental structure, since 1992, is presented in figure 5.3.

The Departments are themselves made up of several subdivisions, which are variously referred to as "Divisions", "Bureaux" or "Sections". For our purpose, the structure of the Political Department is most relevant and included in figure 5.3. It is

47   Amate, *Inside the OAU*, pp 88-89.

48   *OAU 10th Summit Anniversary*, (OAU Press & Information Section: Addis Ababa, 1973), pp 35 and 40; *OAU Ten Years* (Tesfa Press: no d. or pl.), p 83; and Amate, *Inside the OAU*, p 90. For the first years J.H. Polhemus, 'The Provisional Secretariat of the O.A.U., 1963-4', in *Journal of Modern African Studies*, 1974, p 292.

49   CM/Res.464 (XXVI); AHG/Res.91 (XV); and Amate, *Inside the OAU*, p 112.

50   Interview with Ambassador Brownson N. Dede, Assistant Secretary-General for Administration and Finance, Addis Ababa, 22/9/89; *The OAU in a Nutshell* (OAU Information Service: Addis Ababa, n.d., early 1990s) and letter by Mr. J.B. Thundu to author, 27/7/93 (n. 46).

concerned with general political issues, collective defence matters, refugee problems and, in the past, decolonization issues.[51] In 1992, its structure was revised by the formation of a special "Division on Conflict Management", an area which until then had been handled by the Department's "General Political Affairs, Defence and Security Division".[52]

The Departments provide information to the OAU's policy organs, prepare their decisions, supervise implementation of decisions and monitor developments in their field of competence. They are led by an Assistant Secretary-General and a "Director". The latter is appointed chiefly on merit, while the former is an official chosen by the policy organs and is therefore politically responsible. According to one Assistant Secretary his position is comparable to that of a minister in a national government, while the Director is a sort of secretary-general of a national, ministerial department. This last comparison was also made by the Director of the Political Department.[53] This official argued that he and his staff actually do all the work, with the Assistant Secretary approving or rejecting their plans.[54]

Apart from the Departments, the Secretariat has an "Office of the Secretary-General", made up of several Divisions and led by a "Chief of Cabinet" (figure 5.3).[55] This Office acts like a group of personal advisers to the SG. As such, the Chief of Cabinet and others in this Office are in principle personal appointees of the Secretary-General. The Chief of Cabinet handles the various documents that are brought to the attention of the SG and prepares summaries of them, thereby acting as a "filter" between the head of the Secretariat and subordinate staff.[56]

Consultation patterns between principal officials

Although based on limited evidence, co-ordination and communication between principal Secretariat functionaries seem to have improved as compared to the early years. Then it was customary for the SG and Directors to consult each other directly, thus side-stepping the Assistant Secretaries. Also, the latter would deal directly with the subordinates of the Director but rarely meet with the Secretary-General himself.[57]

Thus, as the Director of the Political Department himself claimed, he sees the Assistant Secretary regularly, *i.e.* every day. In the Political Department, their offices are located close to each other, though on separate floors. Conversations also take place by telephone, there being no fixed consultation procedure. The Director claimed that he does not contact the SG directly, as this must take place through the Assistant Secretary.

51   Interview with Abdillahi Ali Dualeh, Chief of the General Political Affairs Section, General Political Affairs, Defence and Security Division, Addis Ababa, 18/9/89.

52   Letters by Dr. C.J. Bakwesegha, Head of Conflict Management Division (since March 1992), to author, 7/12/92 and 14/8/95 and Brief: General Political Affairs, Defence and Security Division (n.d., c. 1989).

53   Interview with Brownson N. Dede, Addis Ababa, 22/9/89 (n. 50) and Ambassador Mamadou Bah, Director of the Political Department, Addis Ababa, 18/9/89.

54   Interview with Mamadou Bah, Addis Ababa, 18/9/89.

55   *The OAU in a Nutshell* and Amate, *Inside the OAU*, p 116.

56   Interview with Brownson N. Dede, Addis Ababa, 22/9/89.

57   See for these early years Amate, *Inside the OAU*, ch. 3.

Figure 5.3 General Secretariat: Internal Structure (situation in 1992)

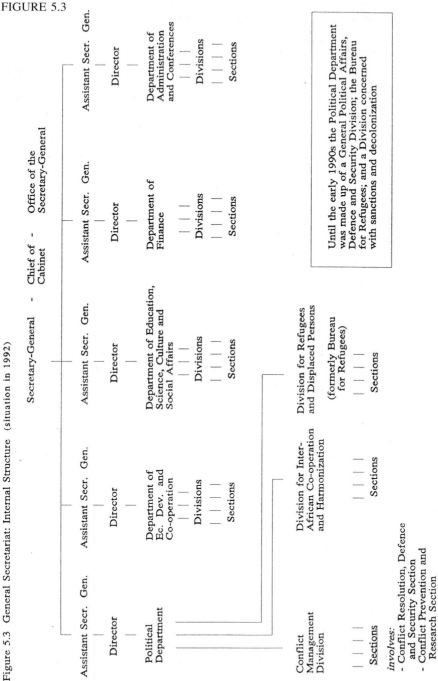

FIGURE 5.3

However, the latter may, in his absence, allow the Director to consult the chief of the Secretariat directly: "It happens", it was added.[58]

While there is little consultation between the Directors of different Departments,[59] there is consultation among the Assistant Secretaries themselves. This usually occurs on an informal basis, such as through personal contacts in the corridors and each others' offices. It may also take place by telephone, as was illustrated during an interview when the Assistant Secretary for Administration and Finance was called to the telephone by his colleague at Political Affairs.[60] Consultation procedures between Assistant Secretaries and Directors of other Departments are also informal.[61]

For general co-ordination between Assistant Secretaries and the Secretary-General, there are formal cabinet meetings. These used to be called only for important matters. However, when taking office in 1989, Secretary-General Salim planned to have cabinet meetings on a regular basis, even if no important issues are at stake. Consultations between an Assistant Secretary and the Secretary-General also take place informally, for example by telephone. This was illustrated during an interview when the Assistant Secretary for Administration and Finance was called to the telephone by the SG.[62]

If an Assistant Secretary wants an extensive conversation with his chief, he will make a formal appointment through the Chief of Cabinet. However, the Assistant Secretary for Administration and Finance emphasized that he and his colleagues take care that the Chief of Cabinet does not become an obstacle between them and the Secretary-General. In this respect the Assistant Secretary stressed that he was a chosen official and the Chief of Cabinet a personal appointee of the SG.[63] Thus, it appears that their political mandate allows Assistant Secretaries some room of manoeuvre within the personnel structure of the Secretariat.

A recurrent problem has been posed by the relations between the Secretariat and Executive Secretaries outside Addis Ababa. These used to consult directly with the Secretary-General, circumventing both Directors and Assistant Secretaries. After earlier recommendations on consultation procedures between Executive Secretaries, Assistant Secretaries and Directors[64] co-ordination appears to have improved: Executive Secretaries now report directly to the Assistant Secretary and the SG, while a copy of this is sent to the Director.[65] Nevertheless, a lower placed official admitted that the "semi-autonomous" status of Executive Secretaries sometimes causes confusion.[66]

---

58   Interview with Mamadou Bah, Addis Ababa, 18/9/89.
59   *Ibid.*
60   During an interview with Brownson N. Dede, Addis Ababa, 22/9/89.
61   *Ibid.*
62   *Ibid.*
63   *Ibid.*
64   See for this Amate, *Inside the OAU*, ch. 3.
65   Interview with Mamadou Bah, Addis Ababa, 18/9/89. This confirms a conclusion by Amate, *Inside the OAU*, p 117.
66   Interview with Abdillahi Ali Dualeh, Addis Ababa, 18/9/89. The projected Department for Planning and Co-ordination was to become responsible for co-ordination of Executive Secretariats. Interview with Brownson N. Dede, Addis Ababa, 22/9/89.

Personnel structure in perspective

The functioning of the General Secretariat has been influenced by one overriding factor, *i.e.* the tight budget on which member states force the Organization to operate. This has had a negative impact on the quality and level of the Secretariat's staffing, working conditions and the quality of its output. During the 1960s and 1970s member states were not very motivated to address the problem. A favourite tactic of the Council of Ministers was the formation of ad hoc committees to investigate and report on the Secretariat's functioning and working conditions. Subsequently, it would defer discussion of the reports or commission new ones. Between 1969-79 five major reports were produced in that way by expert committees whose recommendations were by and large ignored.[67] The 1980s hardly brought any fundamental improvement, with the OAU's financial basis becoming increasingly precarious.

Nevertheless, the total number of personnel grew steadily as a result of expansion of OAU activities in various fields of co-operation and the concomitant rise in the officially voted budget. During the first decade, the total number of staff, including the General Secretariat and regional offices, rose more than tenfold: starting with a mere eighteen functionaries in 1964, the number grew to 288 in 1972.[68] The second decade witnessed continued expansion, leading to a doubling of staff by 1981 (596).[69] During the mid-1980s budgetary constraints led to cut-backs, but by the early 1990s OAU staff totalled 600 people.[70]

Under the "Staff Rules and Regulations" of 1979,[71] OAU personnel is divided in three categories. The first group consists of political appointees, *i.e.* the SG and his Assistant Secretaries. The second group consists of the "professionals" and technical staff. The latter comprises people with specific "technical" responsibilities, such as translators and editors. The professionals are all those officials with managerial tasks, such as Chiefs of Sections, Heads of Divisions, Directors of Departments, the Inspector-General and Executive Secretaries. Standing at 52 in 1968, the professional grade involved some 150 people by the early 1990s.[72] The third group is made up of general service personnel. This includes clerical staff and auxiliaries and forms the largest group of functionaries.[73]

---

67 Contents and manner in which the Council responded to them are discussed extensively by Amate, *Inside the OAU*, ch. 3.

68 CM/412 (Part II): Report of the Administrative Secretary-General Covering the Period from June 1971 to February 1972, p 9 [hereinafter as CM/412 (Part II): Report of the SG, June 1971-Febr. 1972].

69 Jouve, *l'Organisation de l'unité africaine*, p 75 (n. 28) and Amate, *Inside the OAU*, Appendix C.

70 Interview with Mr. J.B. Thundu (n. 46; at the time he was deputy to Ibrahim Dagash, Head of Information Division, Office of the Secretary-General), Addis Ababa, 14/9/89 and *The OAU in a Nutshell*, p 3.

71 CM/896 (XXXI), Annex I and II.

72 CM/212 (Part 2): Report of the Administrative Secretary-General Covering the Period from February to September 1968, Algiers, September 1968, p 7 [hereinafter as CM/212 (Part 2): Report of the SG, Febr.-Sept. 1968]; interview with Mr. J.B. Thundu, Addis Ababa, 14/9/89; and *The OAU in a Nutshell*, p 3.

73 CM/896 (XXXI), Annex II, art. 6.

As in many inter-African organizations,[74] recruitment of staff has for long been a difficult undertaking. In the past, modest working conditions and continued expansion of OAU activities made the hiring of qualified personnel arduous. Complicating factors were formed by the proximity of the ECA, with its better terms of employment, and the unwillingness of many governments to let qualified staff serve at the OAU in view of their own shortage of educated personnel.[75] Yet, it will be shown below that, by the 1980s, the growth in graduates and poor job prospects in member states had made secondments to Addis Ababa more popular.

Recruitment must also effect an even spread in terms of national and regional origins of the staff, a vital requirement if the Secretariat wants to preserve member state support and minimize the effects of the political-institutional vacuum in which all secretariats of international organizations operate.[76] To effect balanced distribution has been difficult, especially with the rapid expansion of the OAU's membership.[77] Fortunately, from 1979, the maximum number of people of the same nationality allowed to serve with the OAU, *i.e.* ten, has been limited to the profesional grade and made conditional on recruitment possibilities. Merit is considered the prime consideration in recruitment policy, even if the principle of national and regional distribution must be taken sufficiently into account.[78]

The Secretariat does not have a fully balanced staff structure. As shown in table 5.1, the professional grade is dominated by nationals from a restricted number of countries.[79] In 1982, thirteen countries had no professionals, especially Africa's least powerful states but including Ivory Coast and Gabon.[80] Ethiopia's high score had much to do with the fact that it houses the General Secretariat. If one excludes it, Nigerians scored highest in respect of important positions. Since then their number cannot have decreased very much, as an OAU press official explained that with the collapse of oil prices many Nigerians flocked to the Ethiopian capital.[81] Thus, based on the 1982 figures, one can say that composition of the professional grade is uneven — although less than in earlier years —, favouring countries that occupy an influential position in inter-African relations.[82] Yet, powerful members as Algeria, Zaire, Morocco (until 1984),

---

74   J.F. Clark, 'Patterns of Support for International Organisations in Africa', in T.M. Shaw and K.A. Heard (eds), *The Politics of Africa: Dependence and Development* (London, 1979), pp 327-331.

75   In general governments were more willing to second staff to proximate, specialist organizations than more distant, general ones as the OAU. Clark, 'Patterns of Support', pp 329-331.

76   I.L. Claude, *Swords into Plowshares: The Problems and Progress of International Organization* (New York, 1964), pp 175-176. Also Th. Meron, *The United Nations Secretariat* (Lexington and Toronto, 1977).

77   See f.i. the SG's complaints and appeals in CM/351: Report of the Administrative Secretary-General Covering the Period from September 1970 to February 1971, Addis Ababa, February 1971, p 10 [hereinafter as CM/351: Report of the SG, Sept. 1970-Febr. 1971] and CM/412 (Part II): Report of the SG, June 1971-Febr. 1972, p 8.

78   CM/896 (XXXI), Annex II, art. 12.

79   General service staff have always been, and still are, predominantly Ethiopian.

80   Ba, Koffi and Sahli, *l'Organisation de l'unité africaine*, pp 579-580.

81   Interview with Mr. J.B. Thundu, Addis Ababa, 14/9/89.

82   In terms of inter-African classifications the picture was as follows: over-represented: Anglophone countries and East Africa; proportional representation: West Africa; under-represented: radical countries (slightly), Central Africa (slightly), North and Southern Africa (grossly) and

Egypt and Libya are under-represented, as are lesser ones like Gabon, Angola and Ivory Coast.[83] In this the OAU is not unique, however, as after thirty years in operation the UN's secretariat was also still characterized by uneven national representation.[84]

Table 5.1

Composition of professional staff by country of origin[*]

Ethiopians	17
Nigerians	10
Tanzanians	9
Cameroonians	7
Sudanese	7
Ugandans	7
Egyptians	6
Ghanaians	6
Zaireans	6

* Calculated for the year 1982. The table shows major staff contributors only.
SOURCE:
A. Ba, B. Koffi and F. Sahli, *l'Organisation de l'unité africaine: de la charte d'Addis-Abéba à la convention des droits de l'homme et des peuples* (Paris, 1984), pp 579-580.
    In 1968 and 1973 Egypt, Ethiopia and Nigeria predominated with 9 and 12 officials, 7 and 9, and 4 and 6 respectively (*sources*: CM/212 (Part 2): Report of the Administrative Secretary-General Covering the Period from February to September 1968, Algiers, September 1968, pp 6-7 and C.O.C. Amate, *Inside the OAU: Pan-Africanism in Practice* [New York, 1986], pp 576-577).

The role and prerogatives of the Secretariat

Although some documents describe implementation of decisions of the policy organs as a task of the Secretariat,[85] this only holds true for the internal consequences of such decisions. While the policy organs usually order it to formulate plans for co-operation or work out the details of decisions they have taken, it must be emphasized that Secretariat officials lack all powers to enforce OAU policy with regard to member states. Thus, they are aware that the essence of their task is to *encourage*[86] co-operation. Rule 2 of the Functions and Regulations of the General Secretariat correctly speaks of *supervision* of the implementation of OAU decisions. If these do not relate to the Organization's internal functioning, it is, as shown in section 5.2, the member states themselves that must implement them.

Secretariat work therefore entails formulation of propositions for certain lines of action to be taken by the collectivity of member states as assembled in the policy organs. To this purpose its functionaries organize or attend conferences, hold seminars or draw up activities reports, which through the Secretary-General find their way to Council and Assembly.[87] A related and important part of this work consists of monitoring events,

Francophone members. Own computation.

83   Well represented small countries are Benin, CAR, Gambia, Ghana, Mauritius, Mali, Rwanda, Senegal and Togo. Ba, Koffi and Sahli, *l'Organisation de l'unité africaine*, pp 579-580.

84   See Meron, *United Nations Secretariat*, especially p 184.

85   See Brief: General Political Affairs, Defence and Security Division, p 2.

86   Interview with Abdillahi Ali Dualeh, Addis Ababa, 18/9/89.

87   Interview with Col. Zoula Gustave Pana, Chief of the Defence and Security Section, General

engaging in research, undertaking field missions and advising the Secretary-General to react to certain developments.[88] Yet, the Secretary and his subordinates can only appeal to member states, or at best argue with them, to follow up their policy decisions, keep past promises or accept Secretariat plans.[89]

The SG's political role in the OAU structure is discussed in the last part of this section. It is important for all Secretariat officials to possess diplomatic skills to persuade members to conform to OAU policy.[90] Lacking all coercive powers, theirs is a work of waiting, following and arguing, which can be rather frustrating and demands perseverance and optimism. Not surprisingly, documents frequently contain complaints about the policy organs deferring decisions or not living up to their promises.[91] Questionnaires sent to member states to obtain comments, information and suggestions on projects or areas of co-operation are frequently left unanswered.[92] Secretariat work is sometimes also hampered by the reluctance of member states to involve officials in certain meetings or conferences.[93] The work that is demanded of Secretariat staff may also be made impossible by the refusal to grant requisite funds.[94] Even the modest task of research is hindered by the fact that the Secretariat has, according to one functionary, no library "worth the name". Financial constraints have prevented the purchase of important reference material and therefore hamper research and monitoring work. Officials are often forced to use ECA facilities at Africa Hall.[95] Under these circumstances, output by Secretariat officials may not be free from criticism, but is at times commendable. Member states' calls for a more efficient and stronger Secretariat are at best exceptional, if not half-hearted and hypocritical.[96]

Secretariat staff and their working environment
Naturally, general working conditions have a strong bearing on the way in which the Secretariat operates. While salaries have often been regarded as insufficient,[97] Council decisions on other conditions of service have frequently been exemplary of an uncaring,

---

Political Affairs, Defence and Security Division, Addis Ababa, 19/9/89.

88   Interviews with Abdillahi Ali Dualeh (n. 51) and Dr. C.J. Bakwesegha, Director of the Bureau for Refugees, Political Department, Addis Ababa, 18/9/89 and 2/10/89 respectively.

89   Interviews with Abdillahi Ali Dualeh and Col. Zoula Gustave Pana, Addis Ababa, 18/9/89 and 19/9/89 respectively.

90   Interview with Dr. C.J. Bakwesegha, Addis Ababa, 2/10/89.

91   Early examples are CM/270 (Part 1): Introduction to the Report of the Administrative Secretary-General, Covering the Period from February to August 1969, Addis Ababa, August 1969, p 22 [hereinafter as CM/270 (Part 1): Report of the SG, Febr.-Aug. 1969]; and CM/378 (Part II): Report of the Administrative Secretary-General Covering the Period from February to June 1971, pp 31-32 and 38 [hereinafter as CM/378 (Part II): Report of the SG, Febr.-June 1971].

92   See f.i. CM/Res.198 (XIII); CM/Dec.127 (XV); CM/Res.226 (XV); CM/Res.799 (XXXV); and CM/Res.1066 (XLIV)/Rev. 1.

93   Brief: General Political Affairs, Defence and Security Division, pp 3 and 6.

94   See f.i. *OAU News Bulletin*, October-November 1973, p 3.

95   Interview with Abdillahi Ali Dualeh, Addis Ababa, 18/9/89. Also Brief: General Political Affairs, Defence and Security Division, p 3.

96   See f.i. *East African Standard* (Kenya), 23/6/81 and 26/3/86 and *Daily News* (Tanzania), 5/7/74 (article).

97   For criteria determining remuneration levels CM/Dec.57 (XII).

avaricious attitude.[98] In spite of a major revision of salary scales during the late 1970s,[99] the Secretariat has still to cope with a host of problems caused by modest remuneration and limited funding. Poorly qualified personnel, administrative irregularities, limited promotion prospects, low morale, poor discipline and, as shown above, lack of sufficient equipment, are some of the bottlenecks.

While the Assistant Secretary for Administration and Finance denied that during his term of office there had been irregularities in financial administration, he said that he had studied the issue with six Norwegian auditors only the year before. He said that irregularities were not caused by fraud but inefficiency. He argued that some of the staff were intelligent but inexperienced, adding that some could not even properly draw up reports. He therefore intended to professionalize recruitment, hand out manuals on working procedures and provide training courses. The Assistant Secretary still regarded amenities insufficient, though some improvements had been made or were in the process of being realized. He hoped that with UN aid the library could be expanded and the Secretariat could improve its housing. This had been below standards when he was appointed, even such basic facilities as decent bathrooms![100]

Understaffing was still considered a problem, as was the level of remuneration. Economists, for instance, preferred working elsewhere.[101] Yet, remuneration scales have not prevented people from flocking to Addis Ababa by the grace of Africa's deteriorating economies. However, mobility was still insufficient. One official, who worked five years in his present position, claimed there was little mobility unless someone died.[102] Another seemed to air his frustration by noting that he had better qualifications than his interim superior.[103] As in the United Nations, the demand of geographical distribution in staffing composition may play a role in this, for it introduces political elements in personnel matters alongside the criterion of merit.[104] Nevertheless, lack of career prospects or instability at home may compensate for this. One Malawian, employed as a professional for seven years, preferred to continue working for the Secretariat as competition from university graduates had diminished domestic job opportunities.[105] A Mozambiquan, employed as a clerk, confirmed that it was preferable to work in Addis Ababa rather than in his own war torn country.[106] Yet, morale wasn't boosted when during the mid-1980s

---

98   For pathetic examples CM/Dec.23 (IX) and CM/Dec.138 (XVI).

99   After this the SG and Assistant Secretaries received $ 37,000 and $ 24,000 and Executive Secretaries and Directors $ 22,000 to $ 24,000 (US $). Amate, *Inside the OAU*, p 110 and Ba, Koffi and Sahli, *l'Organisation de l'unité africaine*, pp 632-637. Political appointees have special benefits as chauffeur driven cars and free housing. Conditions of service enjoyed by all include sick leave, a pension scheme, travel allowances and health insurance. Non-Ethiopians are entitled to post adjustment allowances on UN scales. CM/896 (XXXI), Annex II, arts. 19-26.

100   Interview with Brownson N. Dede, Addis Ababa, 22/9/89.

101   Some people had not had a salary increase for over ten years. Interview with Dr. J.A. Tesha, Minister/Counsellor at the Tanzanian embassy Addis Ababa, 25/9/89. Also Brief: General Political Affairs, Defence and Security Division, pp 4 and 6.

102   Interview with Abdillahi Ali Dualeh, Addis Ababa, 18/9/89 and Dr. J.A. Tesha, Addis Ababa, 25/9/89.

103   Interview with Col. Zoula Gustave Pana, Addis Ababa, 19/9/89.

104   See Meron, *United Nations Secretariat*, pp 125-128.

105   Interview with Mr. J.B. Thundu, Addis Ababa, 14/9/89.

106   Conversation with Mozambiquan clerk, Addis Ababa, 14/9/89. Such factors have also been

dozens of people were fired as a result of budgetary constraints. One diplomat admitted that these measures, mercilessly referred to as the "dead wood operation", had not been executed with much sensitivity.[107]

The Secretariat's appeal is also limited by its location. Many officials are less than enthusiastic about the dilapidated world of Addis Ababa. Like many African diplomats, they regard a secondment to Paris or London as the height of their ambition.[108] Moreover, the diplomatic corps has had to cope with problems emanating from Ethiopia's political instability, even if OAU staff enjoy diplomatic immunity vis-à-vis its government.[109] After a new regime had come to power in Addis Ababa in 1991, OAU officials started complaining about harassment in the streets. They were also confronted with obstacles in international money transactions; introduction of special identity cards violating the "General Convention on the Privileges and Immunities"; body searches upon entering Ethiopian public buildings; and seizure of luggage on one's definitive departure from the country.[110]

Yet, this should not lead to the conclusion that the Secretariat fails to appeal to non-Ethiopian diplomats, safe those that cannot get jobs elsewhere. Although admittedly based on superficial impressions, many professional staff seemed enthusiastic, even determined, about their work. Some appeared to come close to what Claude described as "idealistic dreamers", for whom the common interests of Africa seemed more than an abstract idea.[111] Moreover, the international composition of the staff was regarded as an additional incentive. Thus, when asked how he regarded his work at the OAU, a Mozambiquan clerk smiled and said cheerfully that this was "the house of Africans" and therefore an interesting place to work.[112] On top of such cosmopolitan pleasures, some Ethiopian general service staff enjoyed the fact that their position protected them against harassment by the Ethiopian regime. One functionary, employed as a clerk, took great pleasure in openly vilifying the Mengistu government and another told that, apart from a better salary, a position at the OAU absolved people from compulsory participation in district meetings of Ethiopia's ruling party.[113]

The Secretariat as a collective good

The question is, of course, why member states often adopt less than constructive attitudes towards Secretariat functionaries, their roles and working environment. As this organ

observed for the UN. Meron, *United Nations Secretariat*, p 132.

107 Interview with Dr. J.A. Tesha, Addis Ababa, 25/9/89. Still, as recently as February 1989, several people were sacked for disciplinary reasons, such as the consumption of alcohol. Interview with Mr. J.B. Thundu, Addis Ababa, 14/9/89. See the detailed disciplinary code in CM/896 (XXXI), Annex II, art. 31.

108 Interview with Brownson N. Dede, Addis Ababa, 22/9/89.

109 General Convention on the Privileges and Immunities of the Organization of African Unity, adopted by the Assembly of Heads of State and Government, Accra, 25 October 1965; Agreement between Ethiopia and the Organization of African Unity, signed at Addis Ababa, 6 July 1965; and CM/896 (XXXI), Annex II, art. 30.

110 *Jeune Afrique*, 4/6 - 10/6/92.

111 Claude, *Swords into Plowshares*, pp 9 and 183. Also Meron, *United Nations Secretariat*, p 132.

112 Conversation with Mozambiquan clerk, Addis Ababa, 14/9/89.

113 Addis Ababa, 15/9/89. Names suppressed on request.

works for all member states and no member can be prevented from enjoying the fruits of its efforts or from having some of its nationals fill Secretariat posts, it embodies much of the collective good that the OAU forms for Africa's states.[114] Many members therefore adopt a free rider attitude by profiting from its labours while paying very little, or letting others pay, for it. With this collective good already there, the absence of a constructive attitude towards the Secretariat and its resultant, limited output entail a situation in part comparable to the tragedy of the commons metaphor explained in chapter 1: while Secretariat work is not destroyed by negative member state behaviour, the latter certainly detracts from its quality.[115]

Moreover, the fact that collective goods never exist in pure form[116] and that certain aspects of the Secretariat's position detract, indeed, from its jointness, has not made its functioning any easier. Thus, despite their international civil servant status as provided in art. 18 of the Charter, Secretariat officials are often regarded by their governments as "their" representatives, rather than as Pan-African civil servants working for the greater good.[117] Already in the 1960s, the Council ruled that staff could only be appointed with the agreement of the state involved,[118] partly in order to prevent political dissidents from using the Secretariat as a base to organize opposition against national governments.[119] Conversely, sometimes functionaries have been sent to Addis Ababa as a form of political exile.[120]

Many states have taken the liberty to recall "their" OAU officials when they see fit. For example, after the fall of Mengistu's regime in Ethiopia, the Assistant Secretary-General for Political Affairs, Yilma Tadesse, was forced to resign. While for some officials it is hard to withstand their government, others have, in contravention of art. 18 Charter, sometimes deliberately sought member state intervention to satisfy personal interests.[121] Still, in the African context it is especially important to preserve ties with the home base, if only because functionaries have to return there in the future. The tragic fate of the first Secretary-General, Diallo Telli, is perhaps the most graphic illustration of this.[122] Conversely, as a matter of self-preservation it is important for the

---

114   See on collective or public goods M. Olson, *The Logic of Collective Action: Public Goods and the Theory of Groups* (Cambridge, Mass., 1965), ch. 1.

115   This question is pursued further in section 5.5 in the discussion of OAU budgetary predicaments. On the commons problem G. Hardin and J. Baden (eds), *Managing the Commons* (San Francisco and Reading, 1977).

116   See f.i. I. Grunberg, 'Exploring the "Myth" of Hegemonic Stability', in *International Organization*, 1990, pp 442-443.

117   One official denied that members intervened in Secretariat work. Interview with Mr. J.B. Thundu, Addis Ababa, 14/9/89.

118   As in many inter-African organizations. Clark, 'Patterns of Support', p 327.

119   Amate, *Inside the OAU*, p 89.

120   R.A. Fredland, 'Service at the Organization of African Unity: Gain or Loss in the Home Polity? (A Tentative Hypothesis about the Domestic Political Benefits for Senior Staff at the OAU)'; paper delivered at the International Studies Association Meeting, Los Angeles, March 19-22, 1980, p 4.

121   Amate, *Inside the OAU*, pp 104 and 125 and for Tadesse's resignation *Jeune Afrique*, 19-25/6/91.

122   After returning to Guinea Telli became minister of justice. Yet, he was purged in 1976. Because of his international stature Sékou Touré regarded him as a threat. This partly accounts for his arrest and ignominious death. See A. Lewin, *Diallo Telli: le tragique destin d'un grand Africain* (Paris, 1990), chs. 6-7.

Secretariat to recruit staff that is sufficiently loyal to the home state. These problems are, of course, not unique to the OAU, as other international secretariats also suffer from interference by member states that expect a share of their functionaries and regard them as their representatives. The United Nations is a case in point.[123]

The political role of the Secretary-General
Of all OAU functionaries, the performance of the Secretary-General is most heavily influenced by political factors. As was shown in the preceding chapter, member states did not wish another Dag Hammarskjöld challenging their supremacy. Yet, the personality of the Secretary-General, as well as Africa's changing political circumstances, may strengthen his political role. The first SG, Diallo Telli, was a dynamic figure who did not acquiesce in administrative duties. He used various devices to develop a political role, such as by attending mediation missions, holding press conferences, inserting items on the Council agenda he deemed important and using his annual reports to the Council for political *tours d'horizon* and criticism.[124] The need to establish an administrative machinery and the urgency of some goals, such as the liberation struggle, provided him some freedom of manoeuvre. Yet, after two consecutive terms Telli's militant posture became his undoing.[125]

His successors did not display the same drive or achieve similar stature. One must realize that a Secretary-General with political ambitions walks a tight-rope.[126] The Assembly may fire him, although it has never done so. If a serious conflict threatens, the Assembly can always cut the SG down to size.[127] The context of inter-African politics also entails limitations for the political influence of a Secretary-General. Inter-African cleavages and the preference given to heads of state in conflict management restrict his political role. Its evolution is also hindered by competition from the Assembly chairman, a figure that has become increasingly important and, with the supreme organ, dominates the policy-making process. Another factor limiting the Secretary's influence is the small size of his staff.[128]

Nevertheless, it was admitted during the 1970s that the SG did not merely have an administrative role. International secretariats are always politically active, as there is no

---

123   Meron, *United Nations Secretariat*, ch. 3. Also P.R. Baehr and L. Gordenker, *The United Nations in the 1990s* (London and Basingstoke, 1992), p 31.

124   F.i. CM/212 (Part 2): Report of the SG, Febr.-Sept. 1968, pp 41-63; CM/270 (Part 1): Report of the SG, Febr.-Aug. 1969, pp 20-31; CM/378 (Part II): Report of the SG, Febr.-June 1971, pp 23-40; and CM/351: Report of the SG, Sept. 1970-Febr. 1971, pp 28-41.

125   See for an example of a negative appraisal *East African Standard* (Kenya), 18/9/68 and 8/12/70.

126   See for the perception of this f.i. *Révolution Africaine* (Algeria), 18-24/5/73 (article). The most politically active SG after Telli, Edem Kodjo, found this out during the RASD debacle (see section 6.4), after which he could forget a second term. In his defence it has to be said that his first term (1978-1983) was seriously hampered by radical-moderate/conservative tensions.

127   As happened to the second SG, Nzo Ekangaki (1972-74). For the Lonrho controversy surrounding his resignation f.i. N.K. Kale, 'Crisis in African leadership: OAU's Secretary-General and the Lonrho Agreement', in *The Pan-Africanist*, no. 5, Sept. 1974, pp 12-25.

128   B.D. Meyers, 'The OAU's Administrative Secretary-General', in *International Organization*, 1976, pp 509-520 and R.O. Ogunbambi, 'The Administrative Secretary-General in the OAU System: Some Interpretative Observations', in *Nigerian Journal of International Affairs*, 1988, no. 1, pp 189-203.

sharp distinction between policy and administration.[129] Thus, in 1977 the Assembly granted the SG the explicit prerogative to investigate, albeit as an interim measure, all cases of conflict which in his opinion could endanger peace and security and to submit his findings to the Assembly chairman for further action.[130] In 1979, it was decided to drop the epithet "Administrative" from the title of Secretary-General, although this did not imply an increase in prerogatives.[131] In 1982, however, the "Charter Review Committee"[132] proposed to formulate a new provision along the lines of article 99 of the UN Charter. It stipulated that the SG might draw the attention of member states to acts of another member that could prejudice OAU objectives or constitute a menace to Africa's peace and security.[133]

While the Assembly deferred a decision on this proposal and in 1989 it was still contended by one ambassador that the SG was the "chief administrator" with the Assembly chairman bearing "political responsibility",[134] by the early 1990s the time was ripe for an upgrading of the Secretary's political role. As will be shown in chapters 7 and 8, under the forceful personality of Secretary-General Salim Ahmed Salim[135] the OAU's chief functionary has obtained the right to take diplomatic initiatives to try and prevent that conflicts get out of control. He may now call the Assembly Bureau into session to discuss political emergencies, send special envoys and fact-finding or mediation missions and take decisions necessary for the deployment of civil or military observer missions decided upon by the Bureau.[136]

5.5 Operating on arrears: the OAU and its budget

An outline of budgetary procedures
After an initial two year period in which the Organization was funded on a provisional basis,[137] the OAU slowly developed the procedures concerning the drafting, submission, approval and execution of its budget. These procedures can be found in the "Financial Rules and Regulations" of 1979, which incorporated many of the experiences that the Secretariat and the policy organs acquired during the first two decades.[138] The regular OAU budget involves two funds: a general fund made up of member states' contributions

---

129 Claude, *Swords into Plowshares*, p 189. See the observation on this by Mali's foreign minister in *l'Essor*, 8-9/7/78 (article).

130 AHG/Dec.109 (XIV).

131 Despite a plea by President Traoré of Mali. See his speech to the Assembly in *l'Essor*, 29-30/7/78. Also M. Wolfers, 'The Institutional Evolution of the OAU', in Y. El-Ayouty and I.W. Zartman (eds), *The OAU After Twenty Years* (New York, 1984), p 89.

132 Established by the Assembly in 1979 to examine the need of revising the OAU Charter. AHG/Dec.111 (XVI).

133 CAB/LEG/97/DRAFT/RAPT.RPT (III) Rev. 2, par. 34.

134 Interview with R.S. Iskandar, ambassador of Egypt, Addis Ababa, 27/9/89. In that year Egypt had the Assembly presidency.

135 See f.i. the (non-governmental) view of him in *Weekend Mail* (South Africa), 13-19/7/90 (article).

136 AHG/Decl.3 (XXIX)/Rev.1.

137 See CM/33 (III): Memorandum by the Provisional Secretary-General on Special Arrangement for Interim Financing of the Secretariat; CM/Res.46 (III); and AHG/Res.24 (I).

138 CM/896 (XXXI), Annex III.

and a working capital fund consisting of excess of revenue. The general fund is used to meet the OAU's normal obligations. The working capital fund is necessary to meet immediate obligations, unforeseen expenses and the payment of advances.[139] The regular budget also feeds a separate fund for the care of refugees and, as of 1994, a special fund for peace-keeping operations,[140] which are discussed in chapter 8.

Until the end of 1993 the Organization worked with annual budgets running from 1 June till 31 May.[141] Since February 1994, the OAU operates on biennial budgets.[142] A "Board of External Auditors", made up of financial experts representing member states, is responsible for *a posteriori* auditing of the accounts, verification of Secretariat performance and formulation of proposals to improve financial, budgetary and accounting management.[143] The Board submits its report to an "Advisory Committee on Administrative, Budgetary and Financial Matters". Besides examining the Board's report, this Committee checks on the conclusion of the preceding budget and the programme and budget for the following year as proposed by the Secretariat. Final approval of the budget is given by the Council, until 1994 at its annual session in February.[144]

In 1977 the Advisory Committee was transformed into a plenary committee with the proviso that member states serving on the Board of External Auditors were excluded from membership. The expansion of the Committee was brought on by the desire of member states to get a say in the level and composition of the budget. The result was that debates in the Committee became more and more protracted, while the Council of Ministers stopped focusing on details and used its February session to discuss general budgetary policy.[145] The Advisory Committee is composed of diplomats representing their state in Ethiopia. Its work is prepared by a sub-committee of diplomats resident in Addis Ababa and an Ethiopian representative. The sub-committee was originally established to decide on excess and unauthorized expenditure[146] and must follow and control the execution of the budget.

The structural tension point
The process of submission, discussion and final approval of the budget often entails difficult, protracted negotiations between the Advisory Committee and Secretariat officials.[147] In view of the dualist structure of international institutions[148] it is submitted here that every international organization possesses a tension point in its institutional structure, where national interests and those of the organization at large clash more easily than at any other point in the organization. Usually, it can be found in the organ concerned with the organization's finances. In the OAU one can identify relations

---

139 CM/896 (XXXI), Annex III, arts. 14-27.
140 Budget figures in this section are all in US dollars. They include regional offices and exclude the special funds.
141 CM/896 (XXXI), Annex III, art. 3.
142 See *West Africa*, 14-20/2/94.
143 CM/896 (XXXI), Annex III, art. 88 and Amate, *Inside the OAU*, ch. 4.
144 CM/896 (XXXI), Annex III, arts. 32-33, 84-86 and 90.
145 CM/896 (XXXI), Annex III, arts. 84 and 90 and Amate, *Inside the OAU*, pp 146-147.
146 CM/Dec.55 (XII).
147 An account of this frequently lamentable tale is given by Amate, *Inside the OAU*, ch. 4.
148 Claude, *Swords into Plowshares*, p 9.

between the Advisory Committee and the Secretariat as the major point of tension. Thus, in 1989 the ambassador of Egypt claimed that friction between the Committee and the Secretariat was only natural and *due to their contradictory interests*.[149]

These contradictions have manifested themselves in consistent complaints by Committee members about maladministration at the Secretariat, the process of budget submission, the manner in which contributions are assessed and allegedly excessive budgets. Secretariat officials on their part have frequently criticized budget levels as too low and complained about lack of financial expertise of Committee members, their unco-operative attitude and unwillingness to pay up arrears. We will first examine Committee and Secretariat attitudes to the issues concerning the budget and assess the contents and validity of their mutual recriminations. After this a general assessment is given of the budgetary process, followed by an explanation of member state behaviour in this respect and a discussion of the way in which the Secretariat tries to secure its financial resources and manages to operate in the face of member state arrears.

Committee attitudes to budget issues
Committee complaints about maladministration at the Secretariat have concerned issues like overexpenditure, underspending on programmes for which funds have already been allocated, irregularities in the accounting system and lack of control over regional offices.[150] To this could be added past allegations about excessive travel by Secretariat officials, excessive expenditure on cables and fuel for vehicles, unauthorized purchases of equipment, overpayment of salaries and (unauthorized) allowances and even embezzlement of funds.[151]

In the past improvements were made in the Secretariat's auditing system so as to offset some of the Committee's criticism. Thus, a "Division for Budget Control" is obliged to provide the Secretary-General with periodical reports on the execution of the budget. A special "Financial Controller", who is responsible to the SG, must supervise the regional offices. Personal and financial responsibility of the Director of the Department of Finance is regulated. The Inspectorate-General in the Office of the SG must co-ordinate and control the activities of the various controllers and examine administrative, personnel and financial management with the aim to guarantee efficient functioning and respect for regulations.[152] Yet, by 1989 some administrative irregularities still persisted, as was shown in the preceding section. Nevertheless, these irregularities appear to a considerable extent to be less important for their factual significance than for their political role in the struggle between Secretariat, Advisory Committee and Board of Auditors over the determination of the budget.[153]

---

149 Emphasis added. Interview with R.S. Iskandar (n. 134), Addis Ababa, 27/9/89.
150 F.i. Amate, *Inside the OAU*, pp 134-5; CM/Dec.136 (XVI); CM/351: Report of the SG, Sept. 1970-Febr. 1971, p 7 and CM/412 (Part II): Report of the SG, June 1971-Febr. 1972, p 3.
151 Amate, *Inside the OAU*, pp 141-142.
152 CM/896 (XXXI), Annex III, arts. 52-55, 67-71 and 96.
153 See f.i. on a very critical Auditors' Report for 1986-87, *Africa Research Bulletin* (PSC), 1988, pp 8771-8772: it involved accusations of embezzlement vehemently denied by the Secretary-General. The latter obtained a vote of Committee confidence and accused the chairman of the Board of Auditors of politicking.

Another Committee argument in the struggle over the budget pertains to the procedures followed with regard to its submission. In 1989 the Egyptian ambassador criticized the fact that the budget proposals, which involve hundreds of pages, were submitted to the Committee one day before it went into session. This meant that it had to adjourn and reconvene a few days later. He had therefore suggested that budget proposals should be submitted a couple of months earlier, in order to give national experts an opportunity to study them. The ambassadors would then discuss main budget issues and instruct financial experts of their embassies to examine the details.[154] However, by 1989 the Egyptian proposal had not yet been acted upon,[155] perhaps because it may have been prompted by a desire to effect budgets cuts, rather than greater procedural efficiency. Still, the Assistant Secretary-General for Administration and Finance argued that he was willing to propose a reform of temporal procedures so as to enable member states to take their OAU contributions into account when drawing up national estimates.[156]

The manner in which constributions are assessed has been the subject of endless argument too. Art. 23 Charter stipulates that contributions must be made "in accordance with the scale of assessment of the United Nations", which is partly related to national income. Yet, no member may be assessed an amount exceeding twenty per cent of the budget, which was later cut back to ten, while a minimum contribution was stipulated of 0,55%. Members have frequently questioned the reliability of the economic indicators used to calculate their dues. Arguments in this respect are often insincere, as many states have consistently failed to answer Secretariat questionnaires about national statistics. The result was that a new scale introduced in the late 1960s[157] remained in force until the late 1970s. During the following decade different sets of criteria were used in response to member complaints, such as GDP, per capita income, population and comparative income. Without statistical information from member states, these criteria were frequently based on figures supplied by the UN.[158]

Ironically, the outcome of these reforms had little effect on distribution of budget shares. Ever since 1965, some ten member states have been responsible for half the budget. Thus, in 1979 twelve countries represented 67.77% and by 1989 ten states paid some ten million out of a budget of twenty to 25 million dollars.[159] By the early 1980s, Nigeria and Egypt were, with the legal maximum of ten per cent, the highest paying members, although Egypt's share had by 1989 declined to c. eight per cent.[160] They were

154   Interview with R.S. Iskandar, Addis Ababa, 27/9/89.
155   *Ibid.*
156   Interview with Brownson N. Dede, Addis Ababa, 22/9/89 (n. 50).
157   See AHG/Res.41 (II); CM/Dec.34 (X); AHG/Dec.25 (V); and M. Boumba, 'l'O.U.A.: le système des contributions financières et la représentation administrative des états membres', in Ba, Koffi and Sahli, *l'Organisation de l'unité africaine*, pp 518-519.
158   See draft committee report CM/992 (XXXIII), scts. 1, 5 and 7; CM/Res.764 (XXXIII); CM/Res.903 (XXXVII); CM/Res.1066 (XLIV)/Rev.1; *West Africa*, 14/3/88; and Boumba, 'système des contributions', p 519. For the later criterion of comparative income D. Venter, 'An Evaluation of the OAU on the Eve of South Africa's Accession', in *Africa Insight*, 1994, pp 55-56.
159   Interview with Dr. J.A. Tesha, Addis Ababa, 25/9/89 (n. 101); Ba, Koffi and Sahli, *l'Organisation de l'unité africaine*, pp 576-77; and Boumba, 'système des contributions', p 521.
160   Interview with R.S. Iskandar, Addis Ababa, 27/9/89.

followed by Algeria, Libya and Morocco, whose share ranged, in 1981, from six to nine per cent.[161]

Finally, member states have regularly argued about the level of the budget and individual dues as such. In the past it was argued that savings or underspending proved that the budget was sufficient or too high. Savings and excess contributions were sometimes used to reduce future budgets or individual dues.[162] In some cases, the new budget was not accepted and the old one revoted or the Council issued a temporary authorization for expenditure on a monthly basis.[163] Decisions on expansion of activities without respective financial allocation occurred as well. Member states have often entered negotiations with the Secretariat with the sole aim of effecting a decrease in national dues, leading to quibbling over insignificant budget items.[164]

Secretariat attitudes to budget issues

Besides responding positively to some of the Committee's complaints, Secretariat officials have never hesitated to point at the failings of the policy organs themselves, including of the Advisory Committee. Despite some of the Secretariat's own internal irregularities, which only enhanced opportunities to subject it to financial blackmail,[165] its functionaries have regularly criticized the limited size of the OAU's budget. For example, in the late 1960s-early 1970s, the Secretary-General argued that the "Advisory Committee's desire to economize clearly prevailed over that of the need for effectiveness" and that in specific cases the Committee's proposals were likely to "paralyse the Organization's important sectors of activity" and were "far short of the strict minimum necessary for the normal operation of the various OAU organs".[166]

In 1989 one diplomat admitted that the OAU's budget total did, indeed, not amount to much and was equal to what his own foreign ministry could spend.[167] As is shown in table 5.2, the Organization's financial resources were, and still are, extremely modest. From the mid-1970s the budget underwent considerable expansion, which, however, was due largely to world inflation, devaluation of the dollar and a revision of salary scales of Secretariat personnel. Later on the opening of new regional offices and measures by the Ethiopian government involving new bank charges and rent increases

161 Ba, Koffi and Sahli, *l'Organisation de l'unité africaine*, pp 576-577. Six (Sudan, Ghana, Tunisia, Kenya, Ivory Coast, Ethiopia) were taxed c. three per cent, while Zaire, Tanzania and Zambia had to pay 2.35% to 2.86%. North African members had to pay over 35% of the budget, Lusophone ones four per cent, English-speaking ones some 27% and Francophones twenty. Boumba, 'système des contributions', pp 521-522. Moderate-conservative states scored over sixty per cent and radicals barely one third.
162 See f.i. CM/Dec.47 (XII); CM/Dec.102 (XIV); and CM/Dec.116 (XV); and generally Amate, *Inside the OAU*, ch. 4.
163 F.i. CM/Dec.135 (XVI) and Amate, *Inside the OAU*, pp 131-132.
164 This was also borne out in an interview with a member state diplomat, Dr. J.A. Tesha, Addis Ababa, 25/9/89. See f.i. also CM/351: Report of the SG, Sept. 1970-Febr. 1971, p 5.
165 Which occurs in many international organizations. See Claude, *Swords into Plowshares*, ch. 10.
166 CM/412 (Part II): Report of the SG, June 1971-Febr. 1972, pp 4-6. Also CM/212 (Part 2): Report of the SG, Febr.-Sept. 1968, p 8; and CM/351: Report of the SG, Sept. 1970-Febr. 1971, p 6.
167 Interview with Dr. J.A. Tesha, Addis Ababa, 25/9/89.

accounted for much of its growth.[168] From the mid-1980s the budget stagnated and

Table 5.2

Evolution of OAU budgets*

1965-66	$ 4,421,983.00
1966-67	$ 1,891,536.00
1970-71	$ 2,666,746.50
1971-72	$ 3,256,980.00
1975-76	$ 7,633,975.00
1979-80	$ 14,474,568.00
1981-82	$ 19,515,071.00
1984-85	$ 25,305,171.00
1988-89	c. $ 25,300,000.00
1992-93	$ 24,500,000.00
1993-94	$ 24,760,000.00

* Figures in US dollars. They include regional offices
  and exclude the special funds.
SOURCES:
OAU Ten Years (Tesfa Press), n.d., p 83; CM/Dec.88 (XIV); CM/Dec.142 (XVI); C.O.C. Amate, *Inside the OAU: Pan-Africanism in Practice* (New York, 1986), pp 137-138 and appendix D; *Africa Research Bulletin* (Political, Social, Cultural Series), 1988: p 8772 and 1993: p 10880; and *West Africa*, 14-20/2/94.

levelled off, in part as a result of austerity measures. Considering inflationary pressures, the gradual expansion of OAU activity and member arrears (on which more below), it meant that the OAU's financial basis deteriorated. However, as of 1994 the budget began rising again, which was caused not only by inflation but also by new responsibilities in the field of conflict management.[169]

Another point of criticism that Secretariat functionaries have frequently levelled against the Committee is the lack of financial expertise of many of its members. In the early 1970s, the Secretary-General emphasized that members of the Committee should be appointed on the basis of their experience in budgetary matters.[170] Yet, in 1989 the Egyptian ambassador admitted that neither he nor most of his colleagues were financial specialists.[171] In an interview with the Assistant Secretary-General for Administration and Finance it was claimed that certain Committee members were "incompetent" and "unmotivated".[172] The Assistant Secretary confessed losing his temper from time to time when confronted with embassy officials who were unqualified, had not read the documents or asked "stupid questions". He argued that relations with the Committee had "deteriorated" during the late 1980s, but added that they had now improved somewhat. Yet, having said that, the Assistant Secretary was called away to the telephone by "the boss" and discussed some proposal with the Secretary-General that had been sent to the

---

168   Amate, *Inside the OAU*, pp 137-138.
169   *West Africa*, 14-20/2/94.
170   CM/412 (Part II): Report of the SG, June 1971-Febr. 1972, p 7.
171   Interview with R.S. Iskandar, Addis Ababa, 27/9/89.
172   Interview with Brownson N. Dede, Addis Ababa, 22/9/89.

Committee. He told the SG that its members had "huffed and puffed" and muttered objections, and that something really ought to be done now![173]

Finally, the most serious Secretariat complaint against member states relates to the perennial problem of arrears in contributions. The issue dates back to the first years of the OAU's existence and has refused to go away ever since. Since the 1980s it has become the most serious obstacle threatening the functioning of the Organization. The Secretariat has also complained about the consistent delays in payment by members that do fulfil their quota, which constitutes an additional complication.[174] While members owed the Organization only four million dollars by 1971, total arrears had grown to sixteen million ten years later.[175] Since 1986 the figure has not been below the 35 million dollar mark, *i.e.* well over an entire annual budget.[176] As of 1981, only 24 countries. *i.e.* almost half the membership, could boast a contribution record for the period 1965-1980 that was not marred by arrears, a figure that ignored past arrears and delays in payment settled by that time. Chad, Central African Republic and Tunisia had developed arrears over every single budget.[177] During the 1980s, Libya and Sudan began defaulting seriously too.[178]

Budgetary predicaments as a free rider situation
One cannot deny the existence of some administrative irregularities, and perhaps of some procedural inefficiencies, as regards Secretariat handling of budget matters. Yet, one should guard against accepting Committee arguments at face value, as they serve principally as political ammunition in the struggle of member states to keep their financial commitments to a basic minimum. This is best seen in the haggling over national economic indicators, used to assess contributions, and member state preoccupations with effecting budget savings. Secretariat concerns about the modest budget level and member states' poor record of payment deserve a more sympathetic hearing, as do complaints about incompetence of Committee members. Secretariat allegations about unco-operative attitudes encountered in the Committee were confirmed in two interviews with member state diplomats.[179] Thus, OAU budgetary decision-making constitutes a difficult, very politicized process.

Mere reference to the dualist nature of international organizations[180] hardly provides a satisfactory explanation of member state behaviour. After all, they *do have* an interest in the OAU's functioning. Fundamentally, the OAU's predicaments are caused by the free rider dilemma confronting member states. For them the OAU represents a public or

---

173   Interview with Brownson N. Dede, Addis Ababa, 22/9/89. The telephone conversation was held in
       the presence of the author.
174   For example, arrears and delays limited the payment rate for 1989-90, 1990-91 and 1991-92 (as of
       Febr. '93) to 41%, 26% and 23% respectively. *Africa Research Bulletin* (PSC), 1993, p 10880.
175   Ba, Koffi and Sahli, *l'Organisation de l'unité africaine*, pp 574 and 583.
176   See *Africa Research Bulletin* (PSC), 1986: p 8141; 1987: p 8387; 1988: p 8771; 1990: p 9542;
       1992: p 10445; and 1993 (Economic Series; hereinafter as ES): p 11155.
177   Ba, Koffi and Sahli, *l'Organisation de l'unité africaine*, pp 582-583.
178   Interview with Brownson N. Dede, Addis Ababa, 22/9/89.
179   Interviews with Dr. J.A. Tesha and R.S. Iskandar, Addis Ababa, 25/9/89 and 27/9/89 respectively.
       The latter confirmed this implicitly when arguing about inherently contradictory interests between
       Committee and Secretariat.
180   Claude, *Swords into Plowshares*, p 9.

collective good, even if not in pure form. The jointness of its Secretariat is imperfect as a result of member state interference. Moreover, as is argued by Snidal, one can only treat a regime as a collective good if its members can choose between that particular regime or none at all. The OAU's formation therefore entailed the supply of a public good, as Pan-African co-operation had not existed on that scale before. However, with the present existence of numerous inter-African organizations governments have the opportunity to pursue their objectives in various cadres. This detracts from the OAU's character as a public good,[181] as in its purest theoretical manifestation no one can *escape* consuming such a good.[182] Still, as will be shown below, it is nearly impossible to sanction defaulting members, so that at least the OAU's "non-excludability" — a major feature of public goods — is more or less guaranteed.

Thus, one can argue that OAU budgetary predicaments amount to a free rider situation. Hegemonic stability theory posits, in its benevolent version, that one can only escape this dilemma by way of a hegemon which provides the public good while bearing the costs itself. This will occur if it has an interest in doing so, which presumes its ability to capture enough of the public good for itself so as to outweigh the costs of its provision. The hegemon's ability to do this flows from its size.[183] This, of course, forms the crux of the problem in the African context, where such size is lacking. While it is shown below that a number of countries is usually prepared to pay their contributions for the OAU to make do, this does not add up to benevolent hegemonic leadership. As more coercive hegemonic leadership is also precluded by the structures of Africa's international relations, member states can "ride" on the OAU at will.

However, in view of what was argued in section 1.3 one should not automatically attribute malevolence to member states that do not contribute (sufficient) resources to the Organization. The essence of Olson's logic of collective action, underlying the free rider dilemma, is that states are rational actors which are desirous of co-operation but are also acting rationally by trying to get things as cheaply as possible.[184] In itself this does not say anything about their degree of commitment to the OAU. Thus, the Assistant Secretary for Administration and Finance, as well as the Egyptian ambassador, played down the role of political commitment as the cause of OAU arrears. The latter emphasized that Egypt's contribution constituted a significant drain of state coffers.[185] The Assistant Secretary also emphasized the role of the economic crisis. He referred to a study that his own country, Nigeria, had once undertaken about the total level of contributions it had to pay to international organizations. It was a very significant amount of money.[186]

This would, indeed, explain why free riding increased so rapidly during the 1980s. It should also be noted that the OAU is not the only inter-African organization that is owed money, even if its arrears constitute, in view of its meagre budgets, such a serious

---

181   See D. Snidal, 'The Limits of Hegemonic Stability Theory', in *International Organization*, 1985, p 591.

182   The so-called "forced rider dilemma". B. Russet and H. Starr, *World Politics: The Menu for Choice* (New York, 1989), p 502.

183   Snidal, 'Limits of Hegemonic Stability Theory', p 589.

184   Olson, *Logic of Collective Action* (n. 114).

185   Interview with R.S. Iskandar, Addis Ababa, 27/9/89.

186   Interview with Brownson N. Dede, Addis Ababa, 22/9/89.

problem.[187] It is not a uniquely African phenomenon either. Moreover, the Assistant Secretary denied any correlation between arrears and member classification in terms of inter-African cleavages.[188] This seems to be correct as countries without debts, at least over the period 1965-79, were as diverse as Algeria, Botswana, Ivory Coast, Ghana, Burundi and Zaire.[189]

Still, while the free rider dilemma explains, *in general,* why and how the OAU is faced with a precarious financial basis, it does not explain why some members do and other members do not respect their obligations. Thus, one may argue that the degree of individual commitment does influence a member's inclination to resort to free riding. For example, the Assistant Secretary referred to poor countries like Guinea-Conakry and Swaziland which always paid their dues,[190] while observing that countries like Chad, Sudan and Libya failed to respect their obligations.[191] Such commitment may be absent as a result of resentment about specific OAU policies. For example, Libyan arrears may be linked to Qaddafi's defeat over the Tripoli summit of 1982.[192]

This, however, may be exceptional as disagreement with OAU policy does not necessarily lead to arrears. Up to 1980 Ivory Coast always respected its financial obligations,[193] even though it seriously disapproved of the Organization's posture towards Pretoria. Some countries are therefore, as a matter of policy, committed to respect the obligations they have taken on in relation to the OAU.[194] For example, Algeria, Senegal, Zimbabwe, Zambia and Tanzania have from time to time been very critical about members' arrears, while they themselves possessed a clean slate.[195] Tanzania in particular has criticized OAU arrears as a "scandal of continental proportions".[196]

Improvisation and continuity
Yet, even though it is severely hindered by meagre budgets and very serious payment problems, the OAU has found makeshift ways in order to survive and to continue

187   For example, arrears to ECOWAS amounted to $ 28 million in 1992. *Africa Research Bulletin,* 1992 (ES), p 10903.
188   Interview with Brownson N. Dede, Addis Ababa, 22/9/89.
189   As of 31/5/80. Nor could a correlation be established between arrears and regional classification or location on the scale of assessment. Statistics in Ba, Koffi and Sahli, *l'Organisation de l'unité africaine*, pp 573-574; 576-577 and 582-583.
190   See, however, for the Swazi record up to 1980, *ibid.*, p 583.
191   Interview with Brownson N. Dede, Addis Ababa, 22/9/89.
192   According to Kenya, Libya developed arrears "out of sheer pique". *East African Standard*, 26/3/86.
193   See the statistics in Ba, Koffi and Sahli, *l'Organisation de l'unité africaine*, pp 573-574; 576-577 and 582-583.
194   See for a study of member commitment to inter-African organizations Clark, 'Patterns of Support', (n. 74).
195   *I.e.* at least up to 1980. See statistics in Ba, Koffi and Sahli, *l'Organisation de l'unité africaine*, pp 582-583.
196   *Daily News* (Tanzania), 5/4/71 and 5/7/77. Yet in 1987 it called for budget cuts because of the economic crisis. *Africa Research Bulletin* (PSC), 1987, p 8387. See also *Le Soleil* (Senegal), 25/2/81 and 29/2/84 (articles); *Révolution Africaine* (Algeria), 24/5/73; *The Herald* (Zimbabwe), 10/6/83; *Zambia Daily Mail*, 26/2/71 (article); and *Cameroon Tribune*, 12/7/90 (article). Less altruistic attitudes to OAU finances in *l'Essor* (Mali), 20/3/67 (article); *Daily Times* (Nigeria), 27/7/87; *Cameroon Tribune*, 26-27/7/87 (article); and *East African Standard* (Kenya), 26/3/86.

functioning.

Thus, several steps are taken to persuade members to pay up. While the Charter does not provide enforcement measures, article 97 of the Financial Rules and Regulations of 1979 filled this gap by stipulating that a member is barred from voting if its arrears are equal to, or in access of, the contribution it owes for the last two years. However, the Assembly may allow the member state to participate if it is concluded that its defaulting is due to circumstances beyond its control.[197] In 1982, the Charter Review Committee formulated a provision permitting the Assembly to bar any member, which defaults longer than two years, from participating in meetings as such.[198]

Yet, this proposal was not accepted and during the 1980s the policy organs failed to implement article 97 of the Financial Rules and Regulations. While the Council decided in 1990 to apply the sanction and, in addition, bar any defaulter from taking the floor at meetings and putting up candidates for posts, defaulters were granted a five year reprieve before the sanction would actually take effect.[199]

Exertion of political pressure is a more worth-while strategy as the structures of inter-African relations do not permit strong measures. In budgetary matters lack of hegemonic leadership is hardly compensated by the benign effects of reciprocity. In view of the large number of defaulters, attempts to implement legal sanctions may seriously endanger political consensus. While interaction in the OAU is a sort of iterated game, its large number of actors, tied together by a low degree of interdependence, increases the opportunity of defection and diminishes the feasibility of sanctions. The upshot is a regime with a high regard for national sovereignty but weak financial norms.[200]

In the words of the Assistant Secretary for Administration and Finance, the OAU is an "organization of appeals":[201] the SG brings arrears to the attention of the policy organs[202] and writes reminders to member states.[203] He also makes dramatic statements, in which figures sometimes seem to be exaggerated for tactical purposes.[204] The Assembly chairman issues appeals in letters and during visits to heads of state. Finally, at the summit the chairman and SG present a survey of outstanding contributions. This attempt to "shame" members into paying up usually has some positive effect, with payments coming in shortly before the Assembly goes into session.[205] Enforcement of obligations is therefore mainly a matter of politicking. While being an inefficient procedure, to some extent it produces results.

---

197   See for the procedure CM/896 (XXXI), Annex III, art. 97.

198   Cases of force majeure excepted. CAB/LEG/97/DRAFT/RAPT.RPT (III) Rev. 2, par. 25.

199   *Africa Research Bulletin* (PSC), 1990, p 9749. Also CM/Res.1279 (LII) and *Cameroon Tribune*, 12/7/90 (article).

200   K.A. Oye, 'Explaining Cooperation Under Anarchy: Hypotheses and Strategies', in K.A. Oye (ed), *Cooperation Under Anarchy* (Princeton, 1986), pp 19-20.

201   Interview with Brownson N. Dede, Addis Ababa, 22/9/89.

202   See for an old example CM/412 (Part II): Report of the SG, June 1971-Febr. 1972, p 2.

203   See f.i. a letter to the government of Congo-Br., in Ba, Koffi and Sahli, in *l'Organisation de l'unité africaine*, pp 571-572.

204   Arrears often seem to have decreased with tens of millions after a few months. It is possible that a following budget is included in arrear statements to dramatize things. See *Africa Research Bulletin* (PSC), 1990: p 9542 and 1992: pp 10445 and 10600.

205   Interview with Brownson N. Dede, Addis Ababa, 22/9/89.

Moreover, even in the face of continual arrears the Organization manages to make do. According to one well informed diplomat some ten countries, responsible for a large share of the budget, always pay their dues. This amounts to some ten million dollars. As an equal amount or more is coming in as back-payments, the OAU has some twenty to 25 million at its disposal.[206] The Assistant Secretary for Administration and Finance, too, said that, while payments were "not very encouraging", members regularly catch up on some of their old arrears while new ones enter the books. "We operate on arrears", as he put it: if back-payments are not immediately needed they are put aside; that way, even if no new contributions are forthcoming the Secretariat can hold out for two years.[207] Old and new arrears therefore form an expanding and contracting pool of vital additional income. It is probably this kind of improvisation talent that was echoed in a remark by the SG in 1987 that arrears make the running of the OAU "tortuous, but not impossible".[208] Nevertheless, such a state of affairs can only continue as long as arrears do not spiral out of control. By the mid 1990s the financial regime was tightened and sanctions against defaulters began to be applied, with several countries losing out on some of their rights.[209] Yet, while this tougher stand on arrears may have improved financial discipline somewhat,[210] there are still occasions on which these rules are waived to allow members to participate in the Organization's business.[211]

5.6   The African family: the policy organs in perspective

Introduction
This section first discusses the role of the Council, after which some general aspects of the Assembly are reviewed. The relevance of alliances to decision-making is discussed in a section on regional coalitions and one on wider alliance patterns. This is followed by an analysis of the way in which individual members, especially the more powerful ones, try to influence decision-making. After that, a general outline is given of decision-making procedures and of the OAU's function as a vehicle for communication and legitimation among member states. The section concludes with a discussion of the significance of the policy organs' output, *i.e.* their resolutions.

The Council of Ministers in operation
There is some overlap in the tasks of the Assembly and the Council, as their policy-making roles cannot be clearly distinguished.[212] In practice the Council serves as a

---

206   Interview with Dr. J.A. Tesha, Addis Ababa, 25/9/89. This diplomat obviously had relatively good access to the Secretariat as he telephoned the SG in the presence of the author.
207   Interview with Brownson N. Dede, Addis Ababa, 22/9/89.
208   *African Concord*, 13/8/87, p 12. This may only be true for the General Secretariat. By 1990 some regional offices had not paid staff for months. *Africa Research Bulletin* (PSC), 1990, p 9749.
209   At the end of 1995 ten countries were said to have lost certain rights. *Africa Research Bulletin*, 1995, p 12189 and 12373 (ES) and 11874 (PSC).
210   In 1995 the threat of sanctions encouraged back-payments considerably. *Ibid.*
211   See f.i. *Africa Research Bulletin* (PSC), 1996, p 12146.
212   Amate, *Inside the OAU*, p 11. See also J. Woronoff, *Organizing African Unity* (Metuchen, NJ, 1970), pp 158-167.

liaison point and clearing-house between all subsidiary organs and the Assembly, as it considers the reports and resolutions of subsidiary organs and channels them through, amended or not, to the highest body. This provides it an important position inside the OAU's institutional structure, even if the resolutions it is supposed to draft are in practice usually formulated by the Secretariat or subsidiary organs like ad hoc committees.[213]

The Council's influence is enhanced by the laborious functioning of the Assembly. Yet, the positive effects of this for the Council are limited, as the Assembly's difficulties have not led to a strengthening of the powers of other organs. Composed of Africa's heads of state, the Assembly remains supreme and maintains all other organs in a dependent relationship.[214]

Still, the Council is the more dynamic of the two. It is much easier to convene at short notice than the Assembly, as it does not operate on the highest political level. Between 1964 and 1988, the Assembly met only three times in extraordinary session, while the Council convened more than ten times in such capacity.[215] Better equipped to act fast, the foreign ministers have tended to be, especially in the past, more forceful than their political superiors, whose heavy responsibilities give rise to greater caution. Thus, during the 1960s the Council — usually made up of men who were younger than their heads of state — sometimes adopted strongly worded resolutions that went beyond mere "preparation" of Assembly policy. It developed a role as a political trouble-shooter and was sometimes noted for its emotional conduct.[216]

Its preparatory functions with regard to Assembly summits give the Council some influence in its relation with the superior body. Moreover, the Assembly always has much shorter working sessions, with the result that it has no choice, short of deferment, but to adopt policies as formulated at the lower echelons. Thus, the Assembly usually adopts all Council resolutions *en bloc*, as it has no time to consider them one by one.[217] Furthermore, as the supreme organ often suffers from absenteeism by heads of state, the Assembly is in part composed of the same ministers that confer in the Council. The latter's policy-making task is thereby strengthened, as its ministers prepare, and in part also definitively sanction, OAU policy.[218]

Yet, the Assembly has never formally upgraded the Council's position, which means that it can always force the latter back in its subordinate role.[219] Thus in some cases, especially during the 1960s, the Assembly repudiated Council resolutions containing more radical language and decisions than the heads of state wished to condone.[220] Moreover, in the African context foreign ministers are strictly subordinate to

213   Amate, *Inside the OAU*, p 11.
214   M. Kamto, 'Les mutations institutionnelles de l'OUA', in M. Kamto, J.E. Pondi and L. Zang (eds), *l'OUA: rétrospective et perspectives africaines* (Paris, 1990), pp 18-19.
215   Not counting the special Assembly conference with the Arab League in 1977.
216   *Times of Zambia*, 17/7/78.
217   See f.i. AHG/Res.2 (I); AHG/Res.3 (I); AHG/Dec.54 (VIII); and AHG/Dec.55 (VIII). See Amate, *Inside the OAU*, p 7 ff.
218   Kamto, 'mutations institutionnelles', p 20.
219   *Ibid.*, pp 26-28.
220   Woronoff, *Organizing African Unity*, pp 164-167. See for its reaction to Council resolutions f.i. AHG/Dec.4 (III); AHG/Dec.23 (V); and AHG/Dec.27 (V). For a recent example *Le Soleil* (Senegal), 7/6/91 (articles). Resolutions that met with criticism were CM/Res.134 (X);

their heads of state. Council autonomy is therefore restricted. The result is that in practice the Council is allowed some leeway but is expected to refer controversial issues to the Assembly. Much depends therefore on the political insight of the foreign ministers.

During Council sessions, which last seven to ten days, delegates attend both the general plenary and the meetings of plenary committees, as well as of the so-called "drafting committee". While the plenary Council discusses member state disputes, UN issues and other general political topics, one plenary committee is concerned with refugee problems and, in the past, decolonization issues. Another focuses on economic and technical co-operation. The result of their deliberations is passed on to the drafting committee. This organ is limited in composition, although other members are allowed — without the right to vote — to participate in its discussions. The drafting committee formulates (new) drafts of resolutions, which the plenary Council usually adopts with little revision, either because it is pressed for time or because members feel they have been able to sufficiently influence the committee proceedings.[221]

Some general aspects of Assembly functioning
The procedures concerning an Assembly session have to cope with a host of political difficulties. The first issue is the problem of siting. While the Assembly often convenes in the Ethiopian capital, it may also meet in another place, if a simple majority of member states so desires.[222] Members frequently want to play host to the Assembly, despite the great expenses involved.[223] As it gathers together most or part of the continent's presidential leadership, a summit provides a host-leader considerable prestige and may, in difficult times, give vital inter-African support for his regime. Decisions on future venues are therefore subject to political lobbying among member states.

The reverse side of this medal is that the Assembly may be dragged into the domestic or foreign policy conflicts of the host state. Thus, in 1965 several Francophone members refused to attend the Assembly summit in the Ghanaian capital Accra to protest against the support given by Nkrumah to opposition elements from their countries.[224] In 1971 the summit's projected venue was Kampala, but in protest against the coup d'état by Idi Amin the majority decided to convene in Addis Ababa.[225] When in 1975 the Assembly session was nevertheless held in the Ugandan capital, Tanzania, Zambia and Botswana boycotted it as a consequence of Tanzania's dispute with Idi Amin and in protest against

---

CM/Res.151 (XI); and ECM/Res.13 (VI).

221   Amate, *Inside the OAU*, pp 13 and 16-20.
222   Rule 6, Rules of Procedure of the Assembly of Heads of State and Government.
223   For non-governmental criticism of this M. Mustapha, *Big Game in Africa* (no pl., 1980). See also V.B. Khapoya, 'The Politics and the Political Economy of OAU Summitry'; paper presented at the 25th Annual Meeting of the African Studies Association, Washington D.C., Nov. 4-7, 1982 and G.O. Roberts, 'The Impact of Meeting Sitings of the Organization of African Unity', in *Liberian Studies Journal*, 1980-81, pp 35-46.
224   Some of the speeches at the Council session discussing the issue in *Fraternité* (Ivory Coast), 25/6, 2/7, 9/7, 16/7 and 23/7/65. For negative reactions to the boycott *Kenya Weekly News*, 5/11/65 (article) and *The Nationalist* (Tanzania), 27/10/65.
225   Uganda disputed the legality of this decision. Rule 6 of the Assembly's Rules of Procedure stipulates that the decision on the next venue is taken by simple majority at the organ's *ordinary* (*i.e.* preceding) session. See Cervenka, *Unfinished Quest*, pp 80-81 and for negative reactions to the decision *East African Standard* (Kenya), 14/6/71 and *Fraternité* (Ivory Coast), 4/6/71.

the latter's human rights record.[226] The worst case, however, was the projected summit in Tripoli (1982). It failed to take place twice, partly because of the Western Sahara question and resentment of conservative-moderate countries over Libyan involvement in Chad. The dead-lock between those favouring Tripoli as venue and those opposed became so serious that the summit had to be postponed.[227] After that it was decided to continue holding summits in Addis Ababa, as some Francophone governments had pleaded before, in order to avoid similar problems in the future.[228] Yet, by the early 1990s the dust seemed to have settled enough for the summit to be held again in different capitals.[229]

If the Assembly convenes outside Ethiopia, the host leader is, by unwritten convention, chosen as chairman. Otherwise the presidency circulates among the heads of state. The nomination is decided before the summit, for which some lobbying takes place as this function involves considerable prestige. The eight vice-chairmen, together with the chairman forming the Assembly Bureau, are elected on the basis of the five African regions mentioned in section 5.4. In the past their function usually came to an end after the summit. In practice it was possible to reconvene the Bureau during the coming year in order to discuss a particular crisis, but until the early 1990s this was highly exceptional. Since 1993 the Bureau has acquired a semi-permanent status with the specific task to improve the management of African conflicts. With the outgoing chairman remaining a member of the Bureau, the organ must be convened, besides its annual function at the summit, twice a year at ministerial level and once a month at the level of ambassadors.[230]

While on paper the chairman has modest powers, de facto the Assembly presidency has developed into an important function. The chairman is a major OAU spokesman between Assembly sessions. He therefore provides some permanence to policy and often overshadows the SG. This development became more explicit during the 1980s and was partly due to Assembly indecision, brought on by serious inter-African conflicts.[231] It can also be seen as an Assembly attempt to reinforce its control over the Organization.[232] Thus, the chairman's role became more important after the Western Sahara crisis in 1982, which was aggravated by a serious blunder by Secretary-General Kodjo.[233]

With the strengthening of the chairman's role, the head of state occupying this position began to be seen as "the president of Africa"[234] who, instead of the SG, symbolizes the Organization.[235] The chairman's political tasks involve conflict mediation,

---

226 See *Daily News* (Tanzania), 26/7/75 (article); *Times of Zambia*, 28/7/75 and *Botswana Daily News*, 21/7/75 (article).
227 See further sections 6.4 and 8.2.
228 See f.i. Entente communiqué of June 1971 in *Fraternité* (Ivory Coast), 11/6/71. However, instability in Ethiopia itself could give rise to doubts about this solution. See *Le Soleil* (Senegal), 3/6/91 and *Notre Temps* (Ivory Coast), 24/6/92 (articles).
229 In 1991 the summit took place in Abuja, in 1992 in Dakar and in 1993 in Cairo.
230 The required quorum is two-thirds. AHG/Decl.3 (XXIX)/Rev. 1, par. 20. See further chs. 7-8 and for an overview of Assembly Bureaus up to 1981 Amate, *Inside the OAU*, pp 588-591.
231 Kamto, 'mutations institutionnelles', p 24.
232 J.E. Pondi and D.B.A. Karimou, 'L'évolution de la fonction de "président en exercice" de l'OUA', in Kamto, Pondi and Zang, *l'OUA*, p 53.
233 See section 6.4.
234 F.i. *Cameroon Tribune*, 28/7/87 (article) and *Daily Mail* (Sierra Leone), 24/6/81.
235 Pondi and Karimou, 'évolution de la fonction de "président en exercice"', p 46. Also f.i. *l'Essor* (Mali), 1-2/7/89 (article).

visiting African capitals and meeting with government leaders outside Africa. He also speaks to the UN to represent the OAU standpoint,[236] while the Assembly may order him to watch over policy implementation. On paper this is a function of the Secretariat.[237] Yet, if chairman and SG are willing to co-operate, the OAU's effectiveness may actually be enhanced. Much depends on how SG and chairman see their role. Moreover, the chairman's influence is limited by the short duration of his function. Among his peers he merely is the *primus inter pares*. Furthermore, since the late 1980s circumstances have allowed the Secretary-General a greater political role.[238]

While the Assembly is supposed to operate at the level of heads of state and must, theoretically, assemble the highest political leaders of the continent, in practice it is impossible to gather together all of Africa's top leadership. Many states often send "duly accredited representatives",[239] who may be (prime) ministers or lower rank officials. As shown in table 5.3, the rate of presidential attendance fluctuates. It may be influenced by the importance of the issues on the agenda; the presence of serious rifts in inter-state relations; the relevance attributed to the OAU as an institution to tackle Pan-African issues; or rival engagements. If presidential absence is related to attendance of other international conferences, the political implications are serious. Clark has shown that during the 1960s the OAU scored one of the lowest attendance rates of inter-African institutions, although he could not establish a clear link with high attendance rates at other conferences.[240] Yet, on the level of perception there is a relation between absenteeism at the OAU and, especially, attendance of Franco-African summits.[241] Moreover, in the African context the presence of heads of state is important.[242] It affects the Assembly's decision-making capacity, as heads of state provide more weight to policy decisions than lower rank functionaries.

A related issue affecting decision-making is the complete absence of member states. Such absence is uncommon and usually limited to one or two countries.[243] Still, in the context of inter-state conflicts member states sometimes resort to deliberate, premeditated boycotts or walk-outs. As these usually involve only a limited number of countries they do not affect the required quorum. Yet in 1982, when inter-African relations were soured by the Western Sahara and Chadian crises, a wholesale boycott

---

236   See f.i. P.F. Gonidec, *l'OUA trente ans après: l'unité africaine à l'épreuve* (Paris, 1993), p 35.

237   Rule 2, Functions and Regulations of the General Secretariat.

238   See for details Pondi and Karimou, 'évolution de la fonction de "président en exercice"', pp 45-70.

239   This is allowed under Rule 2, Rules of Procedure.

240   Clark, 'Patterns of Support', pp 332-335 and 347-351 (n. 74).

241   See f.i. the PANA article on the consequences of the Franco-African summits for the OAU in *Ehuzu* (Benin), 25/5/88.

242   As such it is widely reported in the governmental press. See f.i. *Le Courrier d'Afrique* (Zaire), 6-7/11/65; 7/11/66; and 11/9/67 (articles and attendance list); *Daily News* (Tanzania), 12/6/72 (article); *Daily Times* (Nigeria), 9/11/66; *The Standard* (Kenya), 29/7/75; and *Cameroon Tribune*, 5/6/91 (article).

243   See f.i. the list of full absentees for 1963-1983 in El-Ayouty and Zartman, *OAU After Twenty Years*, pp 369-376. (n. 131).

Table 5.3
Assembly attendance rates*

1964	29 heads of state
1966	13 heads of state and 3 prime ministers
1970	14 heads of state, 3 vice-presidents and 3 prime ministers
1972	at least 20 heads of state
1973	22 heads of state, 4 vice-presidents and 5 prime ministers
1976	10 heads of state
1978	30 heads of state and 4 prime ministers
1980	16 heads of state, 6 prime ministers and 1 vice-president
1981	34 heads of state and 6 prime ministers
1983	27 heads of state
1988	over 30 heads of state
1991	34 heads of state, 48 foreign ministers and 3 vice-ministers
1992	23 heads of state
1993	32 heads of state, 5 heads of government and 14 other

* After 1978 there was some growth in attendance, which seems unrelated to the Organization's growing membership. The biggest increase in membership took place during the 1960s and mid-1970s. It stood at 32 in 1963, 42 in 1970, 48 in 1976 and 50 in 1980.

SOURCES:
E. Jouve, *l'Organisation de l'unité africaine* (Paris, 1984), p 60; *Le Courrier d'Afrique* (Zaire), 7/11/66 (article); Y. El-Ayouty and I.W. Zartman (eds), *The OAU After Twenty Years* (New York, 1984), pp 369-376; *Daily News* (Tanzania), 12/6/72 (article); and *Africa Research Bulletin* (Political, Social, Cultural Series), 1988: p 8864; 1991: p 10152; 1992: p 10636; and 1993: p 11064.

made the realization of the quorum impossible, the first time in OAU history that this happened. The Assembly's quorum rule is a rather strict one, as it demands two-thirds of the entire OAU membership[244] and not merely of those "present and voting" once it has gone into session. Some therefore argued at the time that this procedural barrier was a millstone around the OAU's neck.[245] However, the 1982 crisis was due to unique political circumstances that combined to make the summit impossible.[246] Normally, it would be very difficult for members to assemble a sufficiently large following that would be willing to wreck the quorum, something that has not been repeated since.

Nevertheless, partial boycotts and walk-outs may turn OAU consensus, which is the preferred basis of decision-making, into a hollow concept. In itself consensus must already be distinguished, as in other international organizations, from unanimity.[247] Contrary to unanimity, which entails actual voting, consensus involves debate culminating in a more or less general agreement that is formulated by the chairman in his

---

244 Rule 14, Rules of Procedure.
245 Y. El-Ayouty, 'Future of the OAU: As Seen from its 19th Summit', in El-Ayouty and Zartman, *OAU After Twenty Years*, p 345.
246 See section 6.4.
247 H.G. Schermers, *Inleiding tot het Internationale Institutionele Recht* (Deventer, 1983), par. 382. See for more extensive treatment H.G. Schermers and N.M. Blokker, *International Institutional Law: Unity in diversity* (The Hague, London and Boston, 1995), pars. 772 and 787.

summary of the deliberations or his announcement that resolutions stand adopted. If no objections are raised, consensus has emerged.[248]

Before such consensus can materialize members will jockey for position in order to influence the debate and its resultant decisions. In a gathering of so many actors, this goes hand in hand with formation of alliances or coalitions. Apart from facilitating decision-making by reducing the number of participants, individual states may in this way, as Keohane argued, influence outcomes by influencing other states.[249] Grouping patterns therefore emerge, something that is, however, not unique to the OAU.[250] It occurs as a result of the desire to affect proceedings of an organization in such a way as to get one's ideas adopted. Grouping patterns therefore tend to follow the cleavages which characterize international relations and which involve the sharing of certain ideas by some states, as opposed to others. Moreover, the need to realize a geographically balanced composition of an organization's organs forms an additional stimulus to group patterning.[251]

In inter-African relations there is no group of states large enough to determine OAU policy. This implies that the different groupings need each other to create a basis broad enough to carry through a particular decision. Usually there is ample opportunity for such a basis to emerge as the many cleavages marking inter-African relations often cut across each other and can therefore phase each other out to create a consensus.

Decision-making and regional group patterning
Thus, the intensity of regional interaction patterns mentioned in section 2.4 has often prevented inter-African fissures from developing into continent-wide rifts that preclude Pan-African consensus and threaten the OAU's survival.[252] If regional coalitions are themselves divided this is exactly what may happen. For example, the dead-lock that ensued over the Angolan crisis was in part caused by divisions in the alliance of Frontline states. Their proximity to the conflict led Zambia and Botswana to line up with the moderate-conservative side. This decision was rather anomalous as on colonial issues they usually sided with radical states, even though they themselves were moderate and conservative governments respectively. Thus, the split in the Frontline alliance gave the Angolan crisis, in combination with other aspects, the character of a clash between radical countries on the one hand and moderate and conservative ones on the other.[253] On other occasions the Frontline alliance provided an essential basis for Pan-African consensus, such as during the struggle over Zimbabwe. Similarly, in 1969 and late 1971 a group of

---

248   See f.i. *VR*, CI-II, 14-15 (n. 4). See on the role of the chairman in this J. Kaufmann, *United Nations Decision Making* (Alphen aan den Rijn and Rockville, 1980), pp 127-129.

249   R.O. Keohane, 'The Study of Political Influence in the General Assembly', in L. Goodrich and D.A. Kay (eds), *International Organizations: Politics and Process* (Madison and London, 1973), p 149.

250   See f.i. M.J. Peterson, *The General Assembly in World Politics* (Boston, 1986).

251   L. Zang and D. Sinou, 'Dynamique des groupes au sein de l'OUA et unité africaine', in Kamto, Pondi and Zang, *l'OUA*, pp 138-146.

252   Also I.W. Zartman, 'The OAU in the African State System: Interaction and Evaluation', in El-Ayouty and Zartman, *OAU After Twenty Years*, p 40.

253   Notwithstanding a few other anomalies. See further section 6.3.

East and Central African states, organized through regular summit conferences, played an important role in upholding consensus on anti-colonial strategy.[254]

For the realization of its economic objectives the OAU relies heavily on institutions as SADC and ECOWAS.[255] The latter commands, with its sixteen members, considerable influence and even plays a constructive role in preparing consensus on political issues. For example, in 1982-83 it contributed to the realization of an agreement on staging the nineteenth Assembly summit in Addis Ababa, thus getting the OAU out of its quorum crisis.[256] Still, the active role that ECOWAS has assumed, since the early 1990s, in peace-keeping can only detract from the relevance of the Pan-African forum.[257]

Regional alliances, whether or not formalized in organizations, must be distinguished from the regional categories mentioned in chapter 1 and previous sections. The classification of members in five "groups"[258] has an institutional purpose, namely to achieve a geographically balanced composition of organs. One should think here of the Council's drafting committee, the Council and Assembly Bureaux and the Assistant Secretaries-General. These groups are wider than, and rarely coincide with, the regional alliances discussed above and do not seem to play a role in decision-making in non-institutional issue areas.

Decision-making and wider inter-African cleavages

Yet, institutional matters can be highly political, which is most obvious with regard to the choice of the Secretary-General. This cannot be arranged by way of a quiet search for consensus and thus takes place on the basis of an election involving actual voting. A successful candidate must command a two-thirds majority in the Assembly.[259] In combination with the prestige of the function this procedure tends to sharpen competition between the various groupings. None of the above-mentioned regional groups commands a two-thirds majority, not even the relatively large categories of English-speaking, Francophone and former radical, moderate and conservative states.[260] The election of a Secretary-General therefore involves a lot of lobbying and extremely laborious negotiations. Sometimes dozens of ballots are held before a candidate obtains the required number of votes.

Until the late 1980s the cleavages between radical, moderate and conservative countries played an important role in the election process. Thus, Diallo Telli owed his election and re-election to support from radical and moderate members.[261] Conversely,

---

254   See section 6.2.
255   See f.i. Plan d'Action de Lagos pour le Développement de l'Afrique and Acte Final de Lagos, Lagos, 28-29/4/80; Africa's Priority Programme for Economic Recovery 1986-1990, Addis Ababa, 18-20/7/85; and the treaty on an African Economic Community (text in *International Legal Materials*, 1991, pp 203-243).
256   Interview with Mamadou Bah (n. 53), Addis Ababa, 18/9/89. See section 6.4.
257   See further section 8.2.
258   North Africa; West Africa; Central Africa; Southern Africa; and East Africa.
259   Rule 32, Rules of Procedure of the Assembly of Heads of State and Government. The choice of an Assistant Secretary is usually arranged by prior consensus within the region he represents. Ogunbambi, 'Administrative Secretary-General' (n. 128).
260   See also Zang and Sinou, 'Dynamique des groupes', p 167.
261   See f.i. Meyers, 'OAU's Administrative Secretary-General', p 515 (n. 128).

Nzo Ekangaki's election owed much to moderate and conservative dissatisfaction with Telli's leadership.[262] With the deterioration of inter-African relations over the Western Sahara and Chad it was impossible, in 1983, to secure agreement between radicals and conservatives. The stalemate could only be broken by the introduction of a third candidate.[263]

However, the fissures between English-speaking and Francophone states, as well as North African and sub-Saharan members, cut right across the radical - moderate/conservative cleavage. While this complicated every election process, it also made final agreement possible. Thus, the ideological orientation of a candidate's home state could sometimes compensate for a linguistic group's "defeat".[264] Anglophone - Francophone competition has always exerted influence on the election process.[265] This partially accounts for the fact that on two separate occasions candidates from Cameroon acceded to the highest post of the Secretariat. Coming from a Francophone country with an English-speaking region, a Cameroonian candidate could be seen to bridge the linguistic divide. Moreover, Cameroon also has a sizeable Muslim community, something that could placate North African countries. The latter also exert influence on the election process, which was most clearly seen in their support for a Somali candidate in 1974.[266]

All these fissures also exert influence on other aspects of decision-making. The remainder of this section therefore reviews, in a general way, how these cleavages relate, or related, to OAU functioning.

Conservative Francophone regimes have always had a special, and at times not very constructive, role inside the OAU. While one should not regard them as a fully homogeneous group,[267] together they have always constituted a special minority as a result of their close ties with the West and the former colonial power and, in the past, their clear hostility to the Eastern bloc and divergent attitude to the anti-colonial struggle. In this last issue area, deviant postures by some of these states entailed the actual violation of OAU consensus, as happened during the dialogue affair.[268]

Moreover, during much of the last three decades the co-ordination of their viewpoints was facilitated by a considerable degree of institutionalization, thus reinforcing what would otherwise have been an informal coalition. In view of their divergent attitudes, coupled to their minority position and high degree of dependence on France, this could, and still can, undercut any Pan-African consensus or detract from the relevancy of the OAU by transferring issues to other fora. Thus, in 1965 Francophone countries established the "Organisation Commune Africaine et Malgache" (OCAM) out of dissatisfaction with certain OAU policies. As it was concerned with political co-operation

---

262 Wolfers, 'Institutional Evolution of the OAU', p 90 (n. 131). See for a governmental perception f.i. *Botswana Daily News*, 6/7/72 (article).
263 Wolfers, 'Institutional Evolution of the OAU', p 91.
264 See f.i. the approval expressed by Tanzania, a radical state, for the Francophone Telli in *The Nationalist*, 22/7/64.
265 See for perception of this f.i. *Times of Zambia*, 16/11/84 and *Daily Times* (Nigeria), 25/5/88 (article).
266 Meyers, 'OAU's Administrative Secretary-General', p 516. He was one vote short of winning. Amate, *Inside the OAU*, p 121.
267 See section 6.2.
268 See *ibid*.

and its membership was distributed across the continent, it was regarded as a rival to the OAU.[269]

Dissolved in 1987, OCAM's role was overtaken by the Franco-African summits, which encompass an even larger group of countries. The French denied that its aim was to replace the OAU.[270] However, a critical Senegalese diplomat claimed, in an interview in 1989, that African participation in this forum does not contribute to OAU functioning. The Franco-African summits may provide special economic benefits,[271] yet also serve as a channel for Paris to exert political pressure. In certain cases this may jeopardize OAU policy.[272] He also held that such repercussions can emanate from participation in the Commonwealth, although a Tanzanian diplomat emphasized at the time that the latter served a useful purpose with regard to OAU objectives in South Africa.[273]

The cleavages between radical, moderate and conservative countries have regularly come to the fore in decision-making. As noted in chapter 1, the ideological orientations involved did not always determine a country's line-up, with other considerations also influencing postures. Yet, following chapters show that these fissures assumed considerable importance in crises with elements of superpower alignment and, what could be presented or perceived as, a clash of global ideologies as Marxism and the political-economic values of the West.

Thus, during the early 1960s the radical-moderate/conservative divide paralysed inter-African relations in the wake of the Congo crisis. After that, a high water mark was reached during the Angolan and Western Sahara conflicts (1976 and 1982). While moderate and conservative countries were always in the majority, after the mid-1970s the position of the radical powers was strengthened by the emergence of new regimes articulating militant, Marxist-inspired postures. Without the neutralizing effect of criss-crossing group patterns the effects of these fissures could, in a conflict with the above-mentioned features, be very nefarious. This became clear during the Angolan crisis, in which the Frontline alliance was split, and the Western Sahara conflict, in which several countries in the region held contradictory positions.

In other contexts these different ideological orientations also played a role but did not paralyse decision-making. Moreover, after the mid-1980s the worsening economic crisis diminished the relevance of these cleavages. By the early 1990s, they had disappeared through the combined effects emanating from the end of the Cold War, the transition to multi-partyism and the implementation of structural adjustment

---

269   See further R.A. Fredland, 'OCAM: one scene in the drama of West African development', in D. Mazzeo (ed), *African Regional Organizations* (Cambridge, 1984), pp 103-130.

270   See the 1982 presidential statement quoted in Jouve, *l'Organisation de l'unité africaine*, pp 257-258.

271   This was also argued by Ambassador Mamadou Bah, the Director of the Political Department of the OAU's General Secretariat, in interview with author, Addis Ababa, 18/9/89.

272   Interview with Amadou Kebe, Conseiller of Senegal's embassy, Addis Ababa, 3/10/89. It is remarkable that this criticism was aired by a Senegalese diplomat, as his government clearly follows a different line. He therefore stressed this was his personal opinion. For a radical perspective *Ehuzu* (Benin), 25/5/88.

273   Interview with Dr. J.A. Tesha (n. 101). This is not unconvincing. See on congruence between OAU and Commonwealth aims D. Ingram, 'The OAU and the Commonwealth', in Y. El-Ayouty (ed), *The Organization of African Unity After Thirty Years* (Westport and London, 1994), ch. 11.

programmes.[274]

Finally, North African states have always had a special place in the OAU too. These countries, which also interact in the Arab League, possess strong ties with the Asian part of the Middle East. These links pull them to a greater or lesser extent away from, and reduce the priority attributed to, the OAU forum, thus adding to the ambivalence that has traditionally characterized their relations with sub-Saharan states. However, the North African countries have for long been divided over various political issues and have therefore not been able to operate as an alliance in the OAU or take important issues away from the Pan-African forum. Moreover, some of them have given considerable priority to international co-operation in the OAU, such as Algeria has done in the field of decolonization.[275]

Many League and OAU objectives are similar and dual membership is therefore, in principle, not inimical to OAU decision-making. Thus, during the 1970s states in both groups tried to realize broad Afro-Arab co-operation, involving economic aid to sub-Saharan states and Arab support of the struggle against white minority regimes. In return, sub-Saharan countries began backing the struggle against Israel and ended their formerly friendly relations with the Jewish state. The high water mark of Afro-Arab co-operation was the joint OAU-Arab League summit in Cairo in 1977.[276] Yet, since the late 1970s this co-operation has suffered from cleavages within the Arab world itself and certain conflicts with an Arab-African dimension, such as in Sudan and Mauritania. Arab interference in certain sub-Saharan states and the latter's fear of religious fundamentalism and disappointment about Arab aid levels added to this.[277]

Decision-making and the influence of individual members

Some member states, notably the more powerful ones, may on their own try to exert influence on the process of decision-making. There are several opportunities for this. For example, countries that have nationals serving in important Secretariat posts may be better placed in negotiations by having more information and greater access to OAU officials.[278] Furthermore, as much of OAU policy is formulated at committee level member states may exert considerable influence by gaining appointment to restricted committees. Their influence may also be enhanced by sending better qualified delegates, with sufficient mandates, than the smaller, poorer OAU members are able to do. Even if committees are

---

274   Interview with Col. Zoula Gustave Pana (n. 87), Addis Ababa, 19/9/89; P.B. Wild, 'Radicals and Moderates in the OAU: Origins of Conflicts and Bases for Coexistence', in P.A. Tharp (ed), *Regional International Organizations: Structures and Functions* (New York, Toronto and London, 1971), pp 36-50; and O. Aluko, 'Alliances within the OAU', in El-Ayouty and Zartman, *OAU After Twenty Years*, pp 74-75.

275   See f.i. Clark, 'Patterns of Support', pp 338-341.

276   See Déclaration Politique; Déclaration sur la Coopération Economique et Financière Afro-Arabe; Organisation et Procédure de la Mise en Oeuvre de la Coopération Afro-Arabe; Déclaration et Programme d'Action sur la Coopération Afro-Arabe, Cairo, 7-9/3/77.

277   B. Boutros-Ghali, 'The OAU and Afro-Arab Cooperation', in El-Ayouty, *Organization of African Unity After Thirty Years*, ch. 10. Generally, M.O. Beshir, *Terramedia: Themes in Afro-Arab Relations* (London and Khartoum, 1982).

278   One Tanzanian diplomat (Dr. J.A. Tesha, see n. 101), for example, had clearly good access to the Secretariat as he telephoned the Secretary-General in the presence of the author.

plenary this does not mean that all member states exert equal influence. As shown in section 2.4, many countries, especially the smaller ones, do not have a diplomatic representative in Ethiopia.[279] Moreover, if there are diplomatic ties this does not mean that the diplomat involved actually resides in Addis Ababa. Diplomats often represent their government in several adjacent countries at once in order to save costs. Smaller countries may also have greater difficulty in coping with the multiple obligations and tasks emanating from their membership of several international organizations, something that benefits members with larger foreign policy bureaucracies.[280]

Thus, the more powerful countries with residential ambassadors can exert greater, permanent influence on parts of the decision-making process. The country whose ambassador is the dean of Addis Ababa's African diplomatic community is in this respect particularly well placed. Amate recounts the tale of how the ambassador of Cameroon, for some time doyen of the African diplomatic corps, would actively confer with his residential colleagues, well before any formal meetings, to decide on the election of countries to committees, Bureaux and other conference functions. By the time that sessions were poised to begin, it was very hard for other countries to reverse any nominations.[281]

Because of evidential problems it is difficult to find out how the more important members manage to influence the decision-making process once meetings have begun. Verbatim records do not give information on informal meetings, consultations and lobbying behind the scenes. Yet, sometimes they do contain clues as to the manipulative efforts of certain states. This may help to understand how, in general, the more important countries exert influence on OAU decision-making.

A good example is provided by the verbatim record pertaining to an extraordinary Council meeting in February 1964. This session was convened in Dar-es-Salaam at the request of Tanganyika, which had survived an army mutiny with British military assistance. It seems that it had struck a deal with Nigeria to replace the British contingents with Nigerian troops. Apparently, it wished this decision to be seen as having been taken, or at least approved, by the OAU. The outcome of the Council session was that the OAU, indeed, endorsed Tanganyika's decision to replace British troops by "African" ones. Not surprisingly, the contingents that Tanganyika subsequently picked were Nigerian.[282]

How did the two countries manage to influence the Council in such a way that it took the desired decision? During much of the first plenary meeting the Nigerian foreign minister, Wachuku, was absent, probably in order to confer with the Tanganyikans and lobby behind the scenes to persuade other delegations to follow their strategy. This entailed the formation of a restricted committee, which was to advise the Council to take the decision mentioned above. Thus, at one point during the plenary a "consensus" emerged on the setting up of such a committee. Senegal mentioned ten specific countries,

279   See n. 193, ch. 2
280   See also H.K. Jacobson, W.M. Reisinger and T. Mathers, 'National Entanglements in International Governmental Organizations', in *American Political Science Review*, 1986, p 158.
281   Amate, *Inside the OAU*, pp 14-15. For a recent reference to the dean's role in the decision-making process M.C.D. Wembou, 'A propos du nouveau mécanisme de l'OUA sur les conflicts', in *Afrique 2000*, February 1994, p 9.
282   ECM/Res.2 (II). See further section 8.2.

among which were Tanganyika and Nigeria, and proposed their nomination as committee members. However, Liberia and Cameroon, which had not been mentioned, resented the actual naming of countries. Cameroon wanted to adjourn the meeting to allow for consultations "so that any proposal adopted [did] not appear to have been imposed by any one country or by a group of countries".[283] Moreover, Morocco demanded the right for every delegation to attend the meetings of the restricted committee without taking part in the debate. The Malinese chairman therefore said that every delegation would have such access. After some further arguing he also announced, in the absence of any explicit opposition, the nomination of the committee members. With minor revision, these were the same as those mentioned by Senegal.[284]

At that point the Nigerian foreign minister appears to have walked in. Wachuku's less than diplomatic attempt to find out how things stood drew an irritated response from Sudan, one of the committee members.[285] Still, Nigeria subsequently dominated proceedings both at the level of the committee — of which it was elected chairman upon nomination of Ethiopia and Niger — and the plenary discussions held to consider the committee findings. During the latter Uganda and Ghana still argued for another approach to the mutiny case, but at this stage it was too late. Interventions by Nigeria and Tanganyika managed to steer the plenary towards approval of the committee resolution.[286]

This episode shows two things. First, Africa's more powerful countries are able to exercise more influence on decision-making.[287] A particular aspect of this is the fact that other countries may be unable or unwilling to oppose a consensus. Consensus is a political rather than a legal concept.[288] It does not necessarily involve a unanimous accord, something that can also be observed in other international fora as the UN General Assembly.[289] As shown above, it may cover less than complete agreement, which is possible because voting does not take place. It would be much easier to hold out against dominant states if decision-making operated under the rule of unanimity. This involves voting and so would entail, at least on paper, veto power for every OAU member.[290]

However, dissent must be limited to a few members, otherwise consensus cannot be said to materialize. As consensus demands that most states support a decision, the more powerful countries are forced to make concessions and negotiate with other OAU members in order to get what they want.[291] This is exactly what the example shows. In order to appease certain delegations all member states were allowed access to the restricted committee, something that has become regular OAU practice. That Nigeria and

---

283   *Verbatim record* of the Second Extraordinary Session of the Council of Ministers, Dar-es-Salaam, February 1964 (hereinafter as *VR*, ECM2, Dar-es-Salaam, Febr. 1964), ECM/PV2, pp 64-70.

284   *VR*, ECM2, Dar-es-Salaam, Febr. 1964, ECM/PV2, pp 61-74. Members became Sudan, Tanganyika, Uganda, Kenya, Mali, Algeria, Madagascar, Nigeria, Ivory Coast, Niger, Ethiopia and Senegal.

285   *Ibid.*, pp 74-80.

286   *VR*, ECM2, Dar-es-Salaam, Febr. 1964, ECM/PV3, pp 1-50.

287   In this case Tanzania's status was greater than usual, as its domestic affairs were the actual subject matter.

288   Schermers, *Inleiding*, par. 382.

289   Peterson, *General Assembly*, pp 84-87.

290   See also Amate, *Inside the OAU*, p 21.

291   See also Peterson, *General Assembly*, p 88.

Tanganyika were forced to negotiate with other members may be inferred from the part played by Senegal in the attempt to decompose the decision-making context and, concomitantly, provide them with more influence on how things would go. Similarly, Niger and Ethiopia were instrumental in delivering Nigeria the committee presidency. The behaviour of these countries suggests that crucial consultations had taken place with the Nigerian-Tanganyikan couple.[292] Furthermore, the way in which the plenary debate proceeded, even after it had become clear in which direction the conference was supposed to go, shows that important members need considerable tact to steer the others towards approval of the desired outcome.

Thus, in OAU decision-making contexts there is no leadership by a hegemon, *i.e.* one actor more powerful than all others in terms of the ability to control the outcome of interaction.[293] Nor can one speak of a dominant coalition, as it was noted in section 4.6 that this concept involves the ability, on the part of the coalition members, to force others to an agreement. While power relations between members are certainly unequal, the asymmetry in inter-African relations is not sufficiently pronounced to allow a dictation of OAU policy by the most important countries. The situation bears some resemblance to the model of power relations of Kurczewski and Frieske: the most powerful actors are constrained to negotiate with the weaker ones to get what they want or, more generally, to mark their dominant position. This implies that weaker actors have bargaining power which forces the more powerful ones to make concessions. OAU decision-making thus resembles a context of mutual control between the more and the less powerful.[294]

A regime, such as the OAU, therefore enhances the ability of weak actors to exercise influence, even though underlying capabilities have not changed.[295] Yet, the analogy with the model of Kurczewski and Frieske, formulated with regard to a context of domestic economic power relations, should not be pushed too far. The extent to which the OAU regime, as an interactive variable,[296] alters the distribution of influence and assessment of interests is limited. If powerful actors cannot get what they want through the OAU they can try to pursue their goals in fora with more limited membership, thus evading "control" by the numerous and weak. An obvious example is Nigeria's intervention in the Liberian civil war through ECOWAS.[297] Moreover, the system of collective bargaining implicit in the OAU regime does not prevent asymmetry in the trade-off of concessions between the more and the less powerful actors.

However, our example does point to the absence, at least in the OAU cadre, of hegemonic ties in the sense of relations based on norms legitimating the dominance of the

---

292 In fact, Ethiopia became committee member upon Tanganyikan request and subsequently provided an air wing to Dar-es-Salaam. *VR*, ECM2, Dar-es-Salaam, Febr. 1964, ECM/PV2, p 62 and section 8.1.

293 A.A. Stein, *Why Nations Cooperate: Circumstances and Choice in International Relations* (Ithaca and London, 1990), p 182.

294 See J. Kurczewski and K. Frieske, 'Some Problems in the Legal Regulation of the Activities of Economic Institutions', in *Law and Society Review*, 1977, pp 489-505.

295 S.D. Krasner, 'Regimes and the limits of realism: regimes as autonomous variables', in S.D. Krasner (ed), *International Regimes* (Ithaca and London, 1983), pp 355-368.

296 *Ibid.*

297 See section 8.2.

would-be hegemon.[298] As witnessed in Cameroon's criticism of decision-making procedures, such legitimacy is disputed. Members neither believe in the intrinsic value of norms justifying dominance by a few powerful countries nor need to regard such dominance as likely. In terms of Scott's twofold distinction of the consensual basis of hegemony, there is neither consent nor acquiescence in such a state of affairs.[299] In our example the reverberations of this showed themselves in the fact that the subtle manipulation of the dominated, implicit in the concept of hegemony, was at least partially lacking in the behaviour of Wachuku.

Procedures of decision-making

It comes as no surprise, then, that OAU decision-making is a cumbersome process. The search for consensus often entails long, drawn out debate. While such consensus cannot be thwarted by the muted resistance of a few isolated delegations, any vocal opposition or protest on the part of several delegates precludes its emergence.[300] Moreover, if need be, member states can try to force a vote or insist that reservations to a resolution are recorded. Although they may be defeated in a vote their opposition will have become clear.[301]

Yet, this remains exceptional as consensus is the preferred basis of decision-making. Fundamentally, this is due to lack of hegemonic stability, which hampers execution of policy. If decisions are carried by consensus there is greater chance of implementation. The provisions for majority voting enhance the inclination to consensus as members will usually try to avoid the risk of being outvoted.[302] The desire for effectiveness of decisions entails rejection of majority voting, which in the context of hegemonic instability carries even less significance than consensus. As pointed out by Peterson, reaching majorities does not imply the possession of sufficient executive power outside an organization.[303] Outvoting is therefore usually not very constructive. In the African context, where the strong emphasis on state sovereignty has added to the intrinsic value attached to consensus, it is seen as divisive. Arguments in response to the 1982 quorum crisis to introduce simple majority voting therefore met with little favour.[304]

The laborious nature of decision-making is not just due to the consensus technique. The essence of hegemonic stability theory is that absence of leadership precludes the emergence of sufficient collective will to make optimal outcomes possible. Even if a

---

298 See on such legitimation R. Iyob, 'Regional Hegemony: Domination and Resistance in the Horn of Africa', in *Journal of Modern African Studies*, 1993, pp 257-276.

299 See J.C. Scott, *Domination and the Arts of Resistance: Hidden Transcripts* (New Haven and London, 1990), pp 70-76.

300 Amate, *Inside the OAU*, p 21.

301 See for cases of such recorded opposition f.i. CM/St.5 (XVII); CM/Res.678 (XXXI); CM/Res.732 (XXXIII); CM/Res.734 (XXXIII); CM/Res.817 (XXXV); CM/Res.1039 (XLIV)/Rev.1; CM/Res.1052 (XLIV)/Rev.1; CM/Res.1055 (XLIV)/Rev.1; CM/Res.1057 (XLIV); CM/Res.1061 (XLIV); CM/Res.1069 (XLIV)/Rev.1; AHG/Res.76 (XII); AHG/Res.77 (XII); and AHG/Res.158 (XXII).

302 Schermers, *Inleiding*, par. 382.

303 Peterson, *General Assembly*, p 82.

304 See f.i. *The Standard* (Kenya), 1/12/82 and Amate, *Inside the OAU*, p 21. For a positive view *Sunday Times of Zambia*, 28/11/82.

regime compensates for this, the absence of a hegemon may have a slackening effect on the necessary interaction.[305] Thus, members and OAU officials are aware of the related problem that the large number of actors has a retardatory effect on decision-making.[306]

Additional complications are formed by the use of four official languages[307] and, concomitantly, the time needed to translate documents. Delegates often have little time to study documents anyway, leading to postponement of debate. Poor communication between Addis Ababa and the home state also slows down decision-making. Without representation in Ethiopia delegates may only face unexpected issues once the Council has gone into session. Even if there is an embassy, this does not mean that diplomats can telegraph their government at will.[308] This is all the more serious, for in view of presidential dominance of domestic decision-making lower officials are often sent to Addis without instructions. Both speed and nature of domestic decision-making thus reverberate upon the OAU.[309]

Furthermore, the general procedures of the policy organs are far from efficient. Council and Assembly sessions are meticulously staged rituals starting with an opening address of the host state, followed by welcoming speeches of delegates representing each of the language groups. Then the outgoing chairman reads a report on his presidency, after which the new Bureaux are elected. Once in business, Council and Assembly listen to the Secretary-General reading his periodical review and the prepared speeches that member states want to make on the state of the world. Speeching ritual therefore takes up much of conference time.[310] Contrary to the UN General Assembly, where some streamlining of debate has occurred,[311] the OAU allows members more leeway in this respect. It is hard to cut short a speaker, especially if it concerns one of the towering figures of Africa's domestic political scenes, *i.e.* a head of state.[312] Debate may thus drag on, something that is articulated in member state perceptions of OAU meetings as "talking shops".[313]

Disputes can turn debate into an interminable affair, with delegates exercising the right to reply to accusations. Despite rules on decorum this can degenerate in undignified shouting matches, even in the Assembly.[314] While this usually leaks out,[315] there is a

---

305 Also Snidal, 'Limits of Hegemonic Stability Theory', p 595.
306 Interview with Brownson N. Dede, Addis Ababa, 22/9/89 (n. 50). Oye's argument of co-operation getting harder with actor increase ('Explaining Cooperation Under Anarchy', p 4 [n. 200]) is articulated in *Daily Times* (Nigeria), 6/8/75.
307 English, French, Portuguese and Arabic. *The OAU in a Nutshell* (n. 50).
308 Interview with R.S. Iskandar, Addis Ababa, 27/9/89 (n. 134). In contrast, the Egyptian embassy may telegraph to Cairo four times a day. *Ibid.*
309 Amate, *Inside the OAU*, p 19.
310 *Ibid.*, pp 4-7 and 12-20.
311 Peterson, *General Assembly*, pp 103-111.
312 Contrary to the Council Rules of Procedure (Rule 22), those of the Assembly do not have formal provisions on time limits.
313 See f.i. *The Standard* (Kenya), 26/3/86; *The Herald* (Zimbabwe), 11/7/85; and *Daily Times* (Nigeria), 13/6/72; 1/7/77; 15/7/78; and 18/7/85.
314 Amate, *Inside the OAU*, p 21.
315 See f.i. *Daily Mail* (Sierra Leone), 20/7/79 (editorial and article) and *Sudanow* (Sudan), August 1979.

strong tendency to keep quarrels *in camera*.[316] More generally, the political psychology underlying the OAU, which as previously shown has been fed by vulnerability to enemies and an inferiority complex with regard to the West, has generated an inclination to secrecy among the heads of state and a desire to treat issues as the discretionary preserve of the Assembly. This monopolistic trait has entailed a refusal to delegate to the point of taking lack of results to boot.[317] The desire for discretion may even have been partially responsible for the failure to produce transcripts of the taped recordings of sessions.[318] Secrecy and masking of discord can, of course, be observed in all contexts of international relations. Yet in the OAU it developed a particularly nefarious character, as it prevented criticism of the treatment by state elites of their own population.[319]

The cumbersome nature of decision-making has often been rationalized away by reference to perverted images of an African palaver.[320] Such rationalizations often stress that the OAU is a typically "African" organization, which finds "African" solutions to problems.[321] Usually they involve lip-service to the doctrine of African unity in an attempt to paper over differences.[322] Related to this is the use of terminology derived from kinship, whose patriarchal language has served to legitimate hierarchy in domestic contexts. Thus, one finds images of the OAU as the epitomized "African Family", which stands united in a spirit of brotherhood.[323] However, due to the variance in contexts this metaphor assumes a different meaning in the OAU. Here the African Family expresses rejection of any hierarchy and emphasizes the equality of its members. With each country ideally represented in the Assembly by its own "pater familias" all states are equal and sometimes hold each other to ransom to the point of dead-lock.

Usually such indecision concerns conflicts between member states or, more generally, issues that are deemed controversial. However, absence of hegemonic leadership and the functioning of the OAU as an instrument to protect the interests of state elites seem to have induced, at least until the late 1980s, a general lethargy. By this even the simplest of issues have at times posed problems. For example, it took until 1969 before the policy organs could concur on adoption of an OAU emblem while six years passed before they could agree on the Organization's anthem.[324]

---

316 See for an example *Sudanow* (Sudan), August 1979.

317 Desire for exclusive control even led to rejection of an aid offer by the Black Caucus of the United States Congress for construction of an OAU conference building. Interview with Dr. J.A. Tesha, Addis Ababa, 25/9/89.

318 These have become rare since the 1960s. Amate, *Inside the OAU*, pp xii-xiii fails to explain this.

319 See further section 8.1.

320 See f.i. *Fraternité* (Ivory Coast), 21/6/74 (article); *l'Essor* (Mali), 14/8/82 (article); *Le Soleil* (Senegal), 27-8/11/82 (article); and *Zambia Daily Mail*, 18/6/71.

321 See for two early examples *l'Essor* (Mali), 7/10/68 and *Fraternité* (Ivory Coast), 25/9/64 (article).

322 References to unity doctrine abound in governmental ideology. To give but one example see *The Ethiopian Herald*, 11/6/83.

323 See f.i. *Malawi News*, 24/7/64; *Info Madagascar*, 16/9/67 (article); *Sudanow* (Sudan), August 1979; *Daily News* (Tanzania), 22/7/85; and *l'Essor* (Mali), 21-22/7/90 (article).

324 CM/Dec.4 (VII); CM/Dec.27 (IX); CM/Dec.42 (XI)-A; CM/Dec.64 (XII); CM/Dec.74 (XIII); AHG/Dec.38 (VI); and CM/Res.1054 (XLIV).

The OAU as vehicle of communication and legitimation

Decision-making is therefore often characterized by time pressure, overloaded agenda's, bloc acceptance of resolutions and deferment.[325] However, this appraisal should not lead to a blanket negative conclusion about the OAU's role in inter-African politics, for the following chapters will show that, despite the hurdles of the decision-making process, the policy organs do formulate Pan-African policies and take decisions to act on them.

Moreover, the OAU is not only a body of action, but especially one for the exchange of ideas.[326] Like every international organization it provides a forum whose purposes lie in the realm of education and communication. In their desire to further national interests states want to estimate the balance of power in inter-state relations, identify the prime issues of foreign affairs, test reactions of other governments to their foreign policy, seek to gain as much support for their standpoints as possible and assess the objectives of other countries.[327] Speeching ritual, for example, is one of its manifestations.

Member state perceptions of the OAU show in this respect clear awareness of its role as a vehicle of communication.[328] In view of the limited patterns of bilateral interaction and, more generally, underdeveloped communication facilities, the opportunities of intercourse of multilateral cadres are very important. The OAU offers one of the rare possibilities for states, located in different regions, to establish contact with each other. Such communication takes place through debates and participation in coalitions to influence OAU decision-making.[329] More widely, it also occurs by the use of sessions as a facility to lobby, to seek or offer mediation services and to establish informal contacts behind the scenes or during joint travel to Addis Ababa.[330] By OAU membership countries can therefore improve their information base and reduce the costs of engaging in interaction.

In the course of this a process of socialization takes place, in the sense that governments get to know each other, try to get approval for their policies and adjust their behaviour in search for a modus vivendi.[331] Especially weaker states can use the OAU to exert greater influence than they could without its existence. They can confront stronger powers with a debate of certain issues or develop a specific foreign policy role, such as that of mediator. Assessment of influence and interests is, in general, altered by the infusion of inter-African politics with the norms and principles that are the essence of the OAU regime.[332]

---

325 See for deferments f.i. CM/Dec.8 (VII); CM/Dec.12 (VII); CM/Dec.42 (XI)-F; CM/Dec.68 (XIII); CM/Dec.109 (XIV); CM/Dec.151 (XVI); AHG/Dec.113 (XVI); but also AHG/Dec.1 (XXVIII).

326 See W.S. Thompson and R. Bissell, 'Legitimacy and Authority in the OAU', in *African Studies Review*, 1972, p 28.

327 Claude, *Swords into Plowshares*, p 308 (n. 76).

328 See f.i. *Sunday News* (Tanzania), 28/11/82; *The Standard* (Kenya), 16/7/79; *Le Renouveau* (Tunisia), 25/5/88 (article); *Ehuzu* (Benin), 25/8/88 (article); and *El Moudjahid* (Algeria), 31/7-1/8/87.

329 See on this in the UN Peterson, *General Assembly*, p 246.

330 See for an example *Jornal de Angola*, 8/1/76 (article), which reports on six foreign ministers flying together to Addis Ababa.

331 See generally, Peterson, *General Assembly*, p 242 ff.

332 Generally Krasner, 'Regimes and the limits of realism'.

Yet, the effects of socialization must not be overstated. Large countries can strike deals outside the OAU and members can in general take recourse to rival fora. In a context of external dependence, lack of hegemonic stability and limited interdependence absence of continent-wide understanding on a specific issue is to some extent something with which members can live. That the OAU exists, above all, for Africa's leaders to *talk* is in itself evidence of the importance of words in inter-African interaction. Due to the limited ability to influence each other by other means governments also take recourse to such "symbolic politics".[333] This also implies that there are limits on the degree of criticism to which members can be (effectively) subjected in the cadre of the OAU.

Collective (de-)legitimation of member state behaviour is an important aspect of an organization's communication role. It involves the dispensing of politically significant approval (*i.e.* "legitimacy") or disapproval of the claims, policies and actions of states during an organization's sessions by way of debate, resolutions or informal means.[334] As it is important to states to gain support for their policies, they are easily forced to defend and debate them in the framework of international organizations. This is also true for the OAU. Thus, at the Assembly summit of 1979 Tanzania had to make considerable effort to defend its invasion of Uganda to topple the regime of Idi Amin.[335]

By handing out political (dis-)approval of member state actions the OAU can exert considerable influence on inter-African politics. Thus, it dealt a blow to the position of Biafra by immediately condemning all forms of secession. Acquisition of OAU membership is an important form of legitimation for new states. During the early 1970s the Organization restricted the pursuit of dialogue with South Africa by explicitly delegitimating it. In 1977-78 it weakened Somalia's position over the Ogaden by reiterating the principle of respect for colonial frontiers. Morocco's withdrawal from the OAU (1984) was perhaps in the long run unavoidable as its annexation of the Western Sahara flouted the norms of territorial integrity and self-determination.[336]

As indicated above, however, there are limits to this normative influence. The Organization's (de-)legitimating role is closely tied up with the legitimacy *of* the OAU itself. This may in its turn be limited by its effectiveness in the respective issue areas and, related to this, the existence of rival fora.[337] More generally, Popitz argues that authority is a relation between actors with specific characteristics that occurs only in a specific context. In that context those who acknowledge another's authority, *i.e.* are "authority-dependent", ascribe specific attributes to that actor. Outside that context such authority-dependence may not exist, as authority does not flow from the existence of attributes as such.[338] Thus, when the towering figures of the domestic political scenes assemble in the egalitarian African Family the degrees of authority-dependence are sharply reduced. This means that the extent to which the OAU can, as a collectivity, delegitimize the behaviour of one of its members is limited. Until 1990 the non-intervention principle forced it to

---

333   The phrase is from Peterson, *General Assembly*, pp 183-194.
334   See I.L. Claude, *The Changing United Nations* (New York, 1967), ch. 4.
335   See section 8.2.
336   See sections 7.2, 6.2, 6.4 and 8.1.
337   Thompson and Bissell, 'Legitimacy and Authority'.
338   H. Popitz, *Phänomene der Macht: Autorität-Herrschaft-Gewalt-Technik* (Tübingen, 1986), pp 11-14 and 25-26.

manoeuvre very cautiously when faced with domestic conflicts, while explicit condemnation of governments in resolutions was impossible.[339]

Moreover, most OAU norms, *i.e.* the criteria of legitimacy it can provide, in part serve to legitimate the position of state elites as against their peoples, rather than each other. Furthermore, in many contexts there are several principles at work instead of one. One may hold that sovereignty, as inherited upon decolonization, is the dominant criterion of legitimacy in inter-African relations. Other principles stemming from this are territorial integrity, respect for frontiers, non-interference, sovereign equality, prohibition of subversion and secession, but also dedication to the anti-colonial struggle. In practice, these norms may conflict, be contested or elicit contradictory interpretations. This detracts from the regime's cohesion and, hence, its (de-)legitimating influence.[340]

Thus, delegitimation of Biafra was weakened by four members that accorded it recognition because of other concerns. If conflicting principles are held by large groupings, OAU influence on a problem is greatly reduced. For example, management of the Western Sahara crisis could have been more effective if the criterion of membership admission and elements of alignment with non-African powers — as interpreted differently by radical and moderate-conservative countries — had not appeared besides the norms of self-determination and territorial integrity.[341] One can argue that, in general, such cleavages have centred on opposing (interpretations of) principles of legitimacy, which at times have seriously jeopardized the policy organs' functioning.

The output of the policy organs

Resolutions are of considerable importance. First, they are instruments with which the OAU can express approval or, albeit implicitly, disapproval for member state policies. Second, they can serve as vehicles by which its norms are reaffirmed. If carried by broad consensus they can have considerable political weight. More generally, they can be seen as the transcription of the specific balance of power reached by members in a particular issue area. Resolutions can thus inform not only on the viewpoints of Africa's states but, if subjected to the careful interpretation as discussed in chapter 1, also on the cleavages and disagreements between them.[342] In all these cases their formulation as such represents the "solution" to a problem, the outcome of a particular interaction or the discharge of tensions. Real implementation does not (have to) follow.[343]

As this function of resolutions is usually not understood, they and the body producing them sometimes elicit negative perceptions with regard to utility.[344] Moreover, in other cases they involve a decision to realize a concrete policy. Here, failure to move to implementation does constitute a problem. It must be noted that the normative value of, and hence respect for, resolutions can sometimes be marred by bloc acceptance, outvoting

---

339   See section 8.1. Also *Daily Times* (Nigeria), 25/4/80.
340   Thompson and Bissell, 'Legitimacy and Authority', p 27.
341   See sections 8.1 and 6.4.
342   Gonidec, *l'OUA trente ans après*, p 20.
343   See the SG's citation in Amate, *Inside the OAU*, p 10. This function is overlooked by Claude, *Swords into Plowshares*, p 314.
344   *Ehuzu* (Benin), 25/5/88, (article); and *Daily Times* (Nigeria), 1/7/77; 15/7/78; 19/11/84; and 18/7/85. Differently *Times of Zambia*, 25/5/73 and 22/7/79.

of minorities or the inability of some to resist "consensus". In such a case it involves acquiescence in, rather than support for, a resolution. The following chapters will show that, in general, lack of hegemonic enforcement has led to a poor record of implementation.

Finally, resolutions may have the escapist function to rationalize away awareness of impotence. Those on the anti-colonial struggle are sometimes a perfect example. In general the enormous multiplication of resolutions during the last three decades, both in number and subjects, betrays a longing for a continent empowered by modern industrial development and high levels of prosperity. Reading these documents, especially those on economic objectives,[345] is almost a surrealist experience as they constitute a blue-print for a post-colonial Africa that never came.[346] One can explain this by reference to the lack of continental leadership and resultant insufficiency in the co-ordination of collective will, which is amplified by patterns of external dependence that impinge on OAU functioning. Yet, some of these resolutions merely involve non-committal posturing. In some cases their interpretation must therefore relate to the domestic position of the state elites that compose the OAU.

5.7 Evaluations

The OAU Charter established a rudimentary inter-governmental structure without legal enforcement mechanisms and with few concrete commitments for member states. It also stipulated control of the Organization by the member states by way of the Assembly. Practice has shown that it is extremely difficult to revise the Charter. However, it has been possible to introduce minor reforms by way of separate decisions that circumvent the OAU's constitutive document. This provides to some extent for the OAU's flexibility and, hence, its survival.[347] Moreover, as shown in section 5.3 the Organization has grown into a large, complex structure with several specialized organs that may possess some sort of autonomy vis-à-vis the main body.

Nevertheless, the OAU's institutional evolution has left the supremacy of the Assembly unimpaired. Inefficiency in task allocation therefore remains. Institutional capacity is low, something that restricts constructive roles in conflict management and other issue areas. Although the Secretary-General has now obtained a greater political role, he must still exercise his duties in conflict management under the authority of the Assembly Bureau and in consultation with its chairman.[348] More generally, while in many cases one can contend that the identity of an international organization resides in its secretariat,[349] in the case of the OAU this is only partly so. Member states exert

---

345   See f.i. CM/Res.112 (IX); CM/Res.113 (IX); CM/Res.132 (IX); CM/Res.315 (XXI); CM/Res.440 (XXV); and CM/Res.1042 (XLIV).

346   See for a likeness to the ambitious programmes of mercantilism T. Callaghy, 'Politics and Vision in Africa: The Interplay of Domination, Equality and Liberty', in P. Chabal (ed), *Political Domination in Africa: Reflections on the Limits of Power* (Cambridge, 1986), p 35.

347   Kamto, 'mutations institutionnelles', p 43 (n. 214).

348   AHG/Decl.3 (XXIX)/Rev.1, par. 22.

349   Claude, *Swords into Plowshares*, p 174.

considerable influence even in areas that should be the natural preserve of the Secretariat. Work in the Secretariat is thus hindered by a sense of marginalization, both in terms of its institutional position in the OAU and the organ's geographical location. Still, the difficult working conditions lead to improvisation on the part of Secretariat functionaries in order to fulfil their arduous task of monitoring, policy preparation, persuasion, appealing and arguing with member states.

Makeshift responses also guarantee continuity in the vital area of budgeting. Yet, such improvisation can probably only continue as long as arrears do not get out of hand. By the mid 1990s the financial regime was therefore tightened somewhat. Moreover, in such a context long-term planning becomes hazardous, something that prevents reinforcement of OAU institutions and roles. The same can be said of budget levels as such, even if most of the budget is necessary for meeting administrative expenses and the payment of salaries.

However, it is the structural impediments of inter-African relations that constitute the most important bottleneck in internal functioning. This is graphically illustrated by the cumbersome decision-making of the policy organs, which not only ensures the exclusive control exercised by the Assembly, and thus the individual member states, but also entails inefficiency and indecision. How the Organization functions under these circumstances in specific policy areas is the subject of the following chapters.

6

The OAU and the
struggle against colonialism

6.1 Introductory observations

In November 1984, the twentieth session of the OAU Assembly witnessed the definitive admission of the Western Sahara as a full — albeit phantom — member state of the Organization of African Unity. It led to the angry withdrawal of Morocco, the first time in the history of the OAU that a state renounced its membership. While all eyes were set on this drama, the Assembly issued, almost imperceptibly, a declaration on Southern Africa which provided one of the most explicit presentations of the rationale behind the Organization's goal to liberate the continent from colonialism. As was shown in chapter 4, one of the two major reasons for the OAU's formation was the aspiration of state elites to a greater role of Africa and its component states in world affairs and the related desire to equality of status with other continents. However, if Africa and its state elites were ever to reach similar status and power for their continent, they would have to rid it from the very symbol of their past humiliation — colonialism. The continued existence of colonies or white minority regimes could only detract from the power that the continent, united by inter-African co-operation, could generate and constituted an affront to the dignity of African state elites. Moreover, white rule also formed a genuine threat to the security of the independent African states in Southern Africa.

Thus, the 1984 declaration stated that as long as minority rule in Southern Africa persisted, the continent could not assert its "rightful place in the world system of international relations". Africa's enemies would divide and paralyse the continent and, with their bridgehead in Southern Africa, oppose "Africa's declared intention to participate in world affairs on the basis of equality". The struggle against white minority rule therefore concerned the whole of Africa and would have to end with the complete elimination of apartheid and colonialism. That these political systems rested in large part on the denial of universally accepted values of racial equality could only provide additional, moral force to the OAU's argument. Thus, the 1984 declaration held that Africa's struggle against colonialism and apartheid stemmed from its determination to assert the dignity of all people: if the dignity of one man was denied because he was black, the dignity of all black peoples was in jeopardy.[1]

This is not to say that the moral side of the OAU's decolonization objective represented mere hypocrisy. While it could strengthen the realization of state elites' self-interest, section 6.2 shows in its analysis of the dialogue affair that one must not discount the sincerity of the indignation that elite Africans felt about white supremacy in Southern Africa. It is submitted, however, that the struggle against colonialism and apartheid stemmed, first and foremost, from the desire to improve Africa's global power position, rather than *directly* from moral indignation about colonial and white minority regimes as such. It is important to emphasize this, for it has often been wrongly contended that, once these regimes would disappear, the OAU would wither away as it would have lost its fundamental objective and, thus, its relevance. Defeat of its principal enemies would deprive it from cohesion.[2] These contentions are based on incorrect assessments of the Organization's ideological groundwork. This ideology implies that the OAU's existence depends, ultimately, on the structural inequalities between Africa and the Northern hemisphere. This also meant that, even when the OAU's contribution to the struggle against white minority rule became increasingly irrelevant, it could not alter or revoke its political position but had to resign itself to persistent ritual condemnation of colonialism and apartheid.

There has never been any disagreement in the OAU about what exactly constitutes "colonialism". In its perspective this term does not refer to the configuration of political-economic power relations inside member states themselves. These could be regarded at best as forms of *neo*-colonialism. However, as shown in chapter 4 this concept can engender a lot of controversy and so does not figure in the operative sections of the Charter. Section 8.1 will show that the struggles of groups fighting to overthrow the governments of member states or to achieve autonomy or secession have never been seen as an exercise of self-determination. This exercise can, in principle, only take place once, namely at the date of decolonization. Moreover, it must involve the entire population, as a collectivity, of a state or colony. With the structure of colonial partition determining the socio-geographical cadre of self-determination, its exercise cannot be restricted to particular ethnic groups.

Thus, in the OAU colonialism referred only to European colonies or white minority governments on the African continent.[3] The Charter stipulated, as shown in section 5.2, a

---

1   AHG/Decl.1 (XX), paragraphs 4-21.
2   See f.i. W. Mangwende, 'The OAU: An Analysis of the Function, Problems and Prospects of the Organization of African Unity', in *Zambezia*, 1984/85, no. 12, p 37. This view was often expressed by the apartheid's ruling party organ. See f.i. *Die Burger*, 24/7/79 and figure 6.1 in this study.
3   See for the complication of Morocco's rule over Western Sahara section 6.4. It was never explicated whether South Africa was seen as a form of colonialism. The Charter, which was the legal basis for action against the Pretoria regime, does not mention apartheid. Support to the struggle of black South Africans could thus only be based on art. 2.1.d ("eradicate all forms of colonialism") and art. 3.6 ("absolute dedication to ... emancipation of the African territories ... still dependent"). Yet, OAU resolutions always distinguished between "colonialism" and "apartheid". In 1975 the Council considered rejection of South Africa's status as an independent state, as requested

legally binding duty for member states to display "absolute dedication" in realizing the decolonization of these territories. This chapter will show what this dedication actually involved. OAU strategy vis-à-vis white minority regimes consisted of two forms of activity. First, it involved diplomatic action, both in Africa and the United Nations. Its objective was principally to impose sanctions on, and to isolate, the target regimes. The efforts that were made to implement this objective are analysed in section 6.2. Second, OAU strategy entailed financial and material support to liberation movements fighting white supremacist governments, which is discussed in section 6.3. It should be realized that most African states consider self-determination, in terms of the interpretation described above, as dominant over all other norms of international law, including the prohibition, under article 2.4 of the UN Charter, of the use or threat of force in international relations. In this perspective principles like the non-intervention norm, peaceful settlement of disputes and prohibition of subversion could not obstruct, or take precedence over, assistance of African states to liberation movements fighting colonial or white minority regimes.[4]

Section 6.4 provides a mirror image to the OAU's stand on colonialism and apartheid by outlining its reaction to expansionist aspirations on the part of member states themselves. A general evaluation of the OAU's role in the struggle against colonialism and the meaning of its anti-colonial stance is given in section 6.5.

6.2 Between shifts and ambiguities:
OAU diplomacy on Southern Africa

International context
What made the regimes targeted by the OAU so special, both in the eyes of many Africans and the world generally, was the fact that they involved governments which were solidly grounded, and sought their legitimation, in contentions of white racial superiority or outmoded structures of classical colonialism. They could not but form an affront to the sense of human dignity among Africans. In the context of Africa's general transition to political independence and the ostensible demise, since World War II, of ideologies of racial inequality, these regimes constituted a painful anachronism.

---

by a PAC memorandum which saw it as a "perpetuation of colonialism". A commission of legal experts was to study South Africa's legal status, but the matter was shelved. Par. 20, Lusaka Manifesto (see below) had, after all, already recognized South Africa as "an independent, sovereign State". While the OAU was prepared to see it as a "product of colonial conquest", it confronted it essentially for its racist form of government, which violated its concept of self-determination. See CM/Res.435 (XXV); CM/Res.500 (XXVII); CM/Res.428 (XXV) and pars. 8, 22 and 23 of Dar es Salaam declaration discussed below.

4 P.B. Engo, 'Peaceful Co-existence and Friendly Relations among States: The African Contribution to the Progressive Development of Principles of International Law', in Y. El-Ayouty and H.C. Brooks (eds), *Africa and International Organization* (The Hague, 1974), p 40 ff and B. Andemicael, *The OAU and the UN: Relations between the Organization of African Unity and the United Nations* (New York and London, 1976), p 106. See for these and other arguments also M. Pomerance, *Self-Determination in Law and Practice: The New Doctrine in the United Nations* (The Hague, Boston and London, 1982).

214

Figure 6.1 A South African Perception of the OAU's Rationale

"Broers, broers, vergeet julle so gou dat ons nou al van Amerika moet leer dat die beste saambindende krag 'n anti-Suid-Afrikaanse standpunt is!?"

The contents of the caption runs: "Brothers, brothers, do you forget so quickly that now we already have to learn from America that the best uniting force is an anti-South African standpoint!?"

Source: *Die Burger* (South Africa), 6 July 1977

Racial bonds and its own historical role in Africa meant that the Western world was, from a moral perspective, considerably implicated in their protracted existence. Worse still, the West was extremely reticent in forcing these regimes to give up their monopoly of power and introduce government elected by way of non-racial universal suffrage. For a long time Western countries continued to collaborate with these regimes for economic gain, both openly and in covert ways, despite ritual condemnations and lip service to the principles of democracy and racial equality.[5] While by the 1960s African countries constituted a sizeable force in the UN, the problem was that the General Assembly could only *recommend* action against colonial and white minority regimes. Binding enforcement measures could only be issued by the Security Council, where Western countries could prevent such decisions with their veto power.

The story of UN action against apartheid and colonialism has been told in great detail elsewhere.[6] Suffice it to say that Rhodesia was the only country that was confronted with comprehensive economic sanctions. While these probably helped in weakening the Rhodesian regime,[7] they were systematically busted by South Africa, Portugal and Western multinationals.[8] Portugal was supported throughout its remaining years in Africa by various NATO countries.[9] Furthermore, it took until the late 1970s for South Africa to be faced with a binding arms embargo. Admittedly, boycott measures against the apartheid regime were taken relatively early on in the symbolic fields of sports and culture. However, selective economic sanctions were imposed, by the EC and individual Western countries, rather belatedly (*i.e.* during the 1980s) and with considerable reticence.[10]

Outline of OAU sanctions policy

There was thus ample justification for independent African action. OAU diplomatic activity consisted mainly of attempts to increase the isolation of the white minority regimes. This and the next section provide a general outline of the evolution, during the last three decades, of OAU boycott measures and the policy consequences of sanction violations. Following sections analyse, from a roughly chronological perspective, the vicissitudes of the OAU's policy consensus, its implementation and its significance to developments in Southern Africa.

At the Organization's founding conference, it had been decided to break off diplomatic and consular relations with Portugal and South Africa; to prohibit imports from

---

5   See for such ties with South Africa during the 1960s and early 1970s R. First, J. Steele and C. Gurney, *The South African Connection: Western Investment in Apartheid* (Harmondsworth, 1973).
6   See f.i. Andemicael, *OAU and the UN*, ch. IV.
7   See for arguments on this W. Minter and E. Schmidt, 'When Sanctions Worked: The Case of Rhodesia Reexamined', in *African Affairs*, 1988, pp 207-237, but also N. Chandhoke, *The Politics of U.N. Sanctions* (New Delhi, c. 1981).
8   See f.i. H.R. Strack, *Sanctions: The Case of Rhodesia* (Syracuse, 1978); M. Baily, *Shell and BP in South Africa* (London, 1978); and H.P.B. Moshi, 'Multinational Corporations and Sanctions in Southern Africa', in *Utafiti*, 1979, pp 183-194.
9   See f.i. W. Minter, *Portuguese Africa and the West* (Harmondsworth, 1972).
10 See f.i. H. Weiland, 'Wirtschaftssanktionen gegen Südafrika: a never ending story', in *Internationales Afrikaforum*, 1986, pp 83-88 and R.C. Riddell, 'New Sanctions Against South Africa', in *Development Policy Review*, 1988, pp 243-267.

these countries; close ports and airfields to South African and Portuguese planes and shipping; and forbid their aircraft overflying African states.[11] A resolution of the Council of Ministers of 1964 widened this, in the case of South Africa, to include "any other means of communication" and the use of "any other facilities" in African states.[12] The omission in the 1963 resolution of a prohibition on exports was probably an oversight, for the resolution also spoke of the relevance of instituting an *effective* boycott against Portugal and South Africa. Thus, a Council resolution on Portugal of 1966 emphasized a boycott of *all trade* with Portugal, while in 1964 the Assembly stressed the implementation in all its aspects of the decision "to boycott Portugal". A similar Council resolution of 1964 spoke of an end to the supply of minerals and other raw materials to South Africa and later resolutions spoke of the severance of "commercial and other ties" with the South Africans.[13]

While OAU boycott policy therefore had, in editorial respects, less than perfect origins, for member states its meaning was quite clear. In 1964, the policy organs decided on the formation of machinery within the Secretariat to co-ordinate sanctions against South Africa and Portugal; ensure implementation of all resolutions concerning these countries; harmonize co-operation with non-African states in order to realize an effective boycott; collect and disseminate information about trade practices; and promote the campaign for international economic sanctions.[14] This "Bureau of Sanctions", later renamed the "Sanctions Section", was part of the Division responsible for decolonization issues inside the Political Department. However, as the Secretariat lacks powers to enforce policy, unrelated to internal functioning, the Sanctions Section had to limit itself to research work and reporting on South Africa's international trade relations and the effect of measures against Rhodesia, South Africa and Portugal.[15] The related "Decolonization Section" had to monitor, in a more general way, the development of the liberation struggle; liaise with liberation movements and the OAU Liberation Committee; and consult with the African Group at the UN and its Specialized Agencies.[16]

Yet, in 1978 the Council of Ministers spoke of the need to strengthen the Sanctions Section and called on the Secretary-General to establish an appropriate reporting system to enable members to report on their compliance with the measures. It also decided to form a "Standing Committee on Sanctions", which should monitor sanctions issues, co-operate with similar organs in other international organizations and report to the policy organs.[17]

That there was, apparently, a need for stricter monitoring of sanctions suggests that

---

11 Resolution on decolonization, paragraphs 8-9, in *Proceedings of the Summit Conference of Independent African States* (hereinafter as *Proceedings*), vl. 1, sct. 1.
12 CM/Res.13 (II).
13 CM/Res.83 (VII); AHG/Res.9 (I); CM/Res.31 (III); and CM/Res.142 (X). Separate sanctions on Namibia and Rhodesia were hardly issued. As South Africa occupied Namibia and this territory was a UN responsibility, action on it took place through OAU sanctions against Pretoria and in the context of the UN. Since UDI, most OAU pressure for sanctions against Rhodesia also took place via the world body. See, however, also CM/Res.347 (XXIII).
14 CM/Res.31 (III); CM/Res.34 (III); AHG/Res.6 (I) and AHG/Res.9 (I).
15 See *OAU 10th Summit Anniversary* (OAU Press and Information Section: Addis Ababa, 1973), p 34.
16 *Ibid*. See on the Liberation Committee section 6.3.
17 CM/Res.634 (XXXI) and CM/Res.623 (XXXI).

all was not well. The boycott measures involved resolutions on an external topic and were, as argued in section 5.2, therefore legally not binding or enforceable. They merely represented policy statements with considerable political significance. Moreover, binding economic enforcement measures cannot be taken without authorization of the UN Security Council.[18] Although most countries agreed with OAU strategy, cutting economic links with the white minority regimes was very hard for those Southern African countries bordering the white controlled states. As a result of long and complex historical developments,[19] these countries had become deeply dependent on the white south in terms of import and export patterns and labour migration. However, even states situated farther away and not dependent on trade with the white minority regimes conformed, in the judgement of Cervenka,[20] only gradually with the boycott stipulations. Thus, seven years after the OAU had come into existence, its Secretary-General had to confess that the sanction measures had "hardly been carried out in practice".[21] The only course of action open to the policy organs was, however, the exertion of political pressure on those members that had not complied with sanctions. Time and time again, therefore, Council and Assembly passed resolutions which contained paragraphs appealing to member states, that had not yet done so, to conform to OAU policy.[22]

Notwithstanding the limited effect of their resolutions, the policy organs decided to widen the measures to include an oil boycott against South Africa and a refusal to let ships, aeroplanes or other means of communication, regardless of nationality, use member state ports, airfields, roads and railways or overfly African territory, if they came from, or were en route to, South Africa or the Portuguese colonies.[23] Plans were made for an African aeronautical conference to study the problem of non-African airlines stepping into the gap left by African carriers and using African airports for transit and stop-over purposes.[24] However, by 1980 this meeting had not yet materialized due to indifference and opposition by some members.[25] During the following decade the OAU's boycott stipulations were reported to be regularly violated.[26] In non-governmental circles the OAU's record was in this respect deemed "disgraceful".[27]

---

18   See art. 53.1 UN Charter.
19   See f.i. R. Palmer and N. Parsons (eds), *The Roots of Rural Poverty in Central and Southern Africa* (Berkeley and Los Angeles, 1977).
20   Z. Cervenka, *The Unfinished Quest for Unity: Africa and the OAU* (London, 1977), p 113.
21   ECM/2 (VII), Parts 1-2: Report of the Administrative Secretary-General to the 7th Extraordinary Session of the Council of Ministers and the Third Ordinary Session of the OAU Defence Commission held in Lagos on 9 December 1970, pp 6 and 14 (hereinafter as ECM/2 (VII), Parts 1-2: Report of the SG to the Extraordinary Session of the Council of Ministers, Lagos, 9/12/70).
22   See CM/Res.31 (III); CM/Res.34 (III); CM/Res.48 (IV); CM/Res.49 (IV); CM/Res.76 (VI); CM/Res.102 (IX); CM/Res.268 (XIX); CM/Res.490 (XXVII); CM/Res.734 (XXXIII); CM/Res.817 (XXXV); CM/Res.855 (XXXVII); CM/Res.1056 (XLIV); AHG/Res.6 (I); and AHG/Res.9 (I).
23   See CM/Res.13 (II); CM/Res.272 (XIX); and CM/Res.817 (XXXV).
24   CM/Res.473 (XXVII).
25   CM/Res.734 (XXXIII) and CM/Res.816 (XXXV).
26   See *Africa Research Bulletin* (Political, Social and Cultural Series; hereinafter as PSC), 1987, p 8556 and 1988, p 8863.
27   E. M'buyinga, *Pan-Africanism or Neo-Colonialism? The Bankruptcy of the O.A.U.* (London, 1982), p 198.

As the continued existence of white minority regimes could, as shown in the preceding section, only detract from the international influence and status of the continent and its component states, as well as constitute an explicit affront to elite African conceptions of dignity, this poor record of implementation needs to be explained.

First, if there is one area where external factors impinge on the functioning of a regime of relatively weak actors it is economics.[28] The patterns of African dependence on the Western world, whose economic penetration of the continent was particularly pervasive in the regions where white minority rule was established, made compliance with norms prescribing a rupture of those ties extremely difficult. Even if countries were not dependent on trade with the white south, the general fragility of African economies made norms calling on governments to forgo economic benefits rather problematic. While the OAU's specific notion of gain that would accrue from compliance — *i.e.* enhanced influence and status for the continent and its states as a result of an end to white minority rule — formed a genuine aspiration, it was not sufficiently elaborated, as well as too distant, to warrant abandonment of short-term economic interests. The crisis of the 1980s only amplified this.

Second, those countries that, as shown below, were later to provide some sort of leadership in the execution of OAU policy were themselves highly dependent on economic interaction with the white south. They were thus the principal transgressor of the sanction norms. This did not persuade others to comply and, so, the prohibition on economic ties was hardly internalized in foreign policy calculations. If it had been, this could have altered the balance of pay-offs emanating from defection and compliance.[29] The OAU's diminishing relevance as policymaker and executive in decolonization issues after the mid-1970s, on which more below, did in this respect not provide any countervailing influence.

Finally, inclinations to take a free ride on collective efforts to bring down white minority regimes by economic means were facilitated by the structural features of inter-African relations. OAU sanctions policy meant checking boycott measures of over fourty or fifty countries and watching the numerous trading patterns on the continent. This constituted a very demanding task for the Organization's weak Secretariat, especially if such trading contacts, such as in the case of South Africa, took place in more or less covert ways. More generally, the potentially high number of actors involved in the OAU's sanctions regime implied relatively high levels of anonimity for its participants and, thus, high costs of verification of defection from, or compliance with, the sanction norms. As argued by Oye, if the number of actors goes up information costs increase and the feasibility to punish defectors diminishes. This militates against the realization of a

---

28   See also R.L. Rothstein, 'Regime-Creation by a Coalition of the Weak: Lessons from the NIEO and the Integrated Program for Commodities', in *International Studies Quarterly*, 1984, pp 307-328.

29   K.A. Oye 'Explaining Cooperation Under Anarchy: Hypotheses and Strategies', in K.A. Oye (ed), *Cooperation Under Anarchy* (Princeton, 1986), p 11.

common interest.[30] The result is a low degree of reciprocity between actors in a given issue area, which makes violation of norms cheap as the risk of retaliation is minimal.

Policy consequences of sanction violations

Naturally, this state of affairs weakened the OAU's negotiating position vis-à-vis Western countries. Yet, in view of the rationale behind its decolonization policy and Southern Africa's deteriorating security situation during the 1980s, the Organization could not but continue pressing for sanctions. As far as South Africa was concerned, the OAU's call for a worldwide economic boycott was only logical and imperative. Many Western countries had intensive dealings with South Africa and trade with the Western world was of the utmost importance to the South African economy, much more so than trade with African countries.

Thus, Western countries were usually sharply condemned, with their names explicitly mentioned, for their reluctance to cut economic links with South Africa, Rhodesia and Portugal.[31] It was pointed out that countries collaborating with the white regimes in the economic-military sphere encouraged them to persist in their policies and were therefore responsible for an aggravation of the situation and the repression of the African majority.[32] They were thus endangering international peace and security and thereby violating the UN Charter.[33]

Western multinationals came in for a lot of criticism too. In 1980 the Council of Ministers claimed that multinationals were susceptible to being integrated into apartheid's military programme. Any supposedly constructive role played by them would therefore be offset by the valuable support they meant for the government apparatus. Any action short of total corporate withdrawal, such as the formulation of investment codes, would be inadequate.[34] During the 1970s, the Council had already called for retaliatory measures such as blacklisting of companies and the imposition of punitive tariffs on the exports of countries that invested in South Africa.[35] Naturally, the chance that its own members would implement these measures was slim, considering their reluctance to respect the ordinary, general sanctions against the minority regimes. Some conservative member states from time to time listed their explicit disapproval of such militant resolutions.[36]

Throughout the last three decades, Western arms sales to South Africa were vehemently criticized. So were all forms of scientific and, especially, nuclear co-operation.[37] NATO countries were regularly condemned for their military assistance to

---

30 Contrary to Oye, ('Explaining Cooperation Under Anarchy', p 19), we assume that *identification* of this interest as such was not at issue.

31 See f.i. CM/Res.48 (IV); CM/Res.102 (X); CM/Res.209 (XIV); CM/Res.234 (XV); CM/Res.242/rev.1 (XVII); CM/Res.268 (XIX); CM/Res.299 (XXI); CM/Res.623 (XXXI); CM/Res.821 (XXXV); and CM/Res. 1052 (XLIV)/Rev.1.

32 CM/Res.86 (VII); CM/Res.102 (X); and CM/Res.235 (XV).

33 CM/Res.272 (XIX).

34 CM/St.15 (XXXV).

35 CM/Res.348 (XXIII) and CM/Res.734 (XXXIII).

36 See for reservations by a few conservative members to certain resolutions containing sanctions measures CM/Res.734 (XXXIII); CM/Res.817 (XXXV); CM/Res.855 (XXXVII); and CM/Res.1039 (XLIV)/Rev.1.

37 CM/Res.102 (IX); CM/Res.209 (XIV); CM/Res.232 (XIV); CM/Res.299 (XXI); CM/Res.485

Portugal, which enabled it to continue its war against liberation movements fighting for independence.[38] During the 1970s and 1980s attempts were made to involve OPEC in boycotts of the white minority regimes[39] and the OAU became actively involved in publicity campaigns with the objective to vilify apartheid and keep the Pretoria regime under pressure.[40] As shown above, however, most Western countries refused to cut, or severe completely, their economic links with South Africa in view of their economic and strategic interests.

Thus, the repercussions of the OAU's own sanctions record were, with regard to its extra-African posture, rather limited because of the obstinacy of the white supremacists and their intensive ties with the Western world. However, the consequences of the OAU's sanctions record were far more serious for the Organization's *internal* consensus. From the outset it had been clear that several countries bordering the white minority regimes would find it extremely difficult, if not impossible, to implement the sanctions regulations. Moreover, while some were quite willing to work towards execution of OAU strategy, others were rather hesitant or even opposed to it. Botswana, for example, was quite adamant about the OAU's confrontation policy, arguing that it could neither cut its links with South Africa and Rhodesia nor afford to harbour guerrillas of liberation movements in view of its economic, geographical and military vulnerability. It claimed the right to formulate its policies independently of the OAU, such as by banning guerrillas from its territory.[41]

Indeed, one of the problems with OAU policy was that it implied not only that everyone agreed with the means with which it sought to eradicate colonial and white minority rule in Southern Africa, but also that all members were in a similar economic, geographical and military position as regards the target regimes. Yet, the former British so-called "High Commission" territories (Botswana, Lesotho and Swaziland) were tied, neck and foot, to the South African economy, even formally by way of their participation in the "Southern African Customs Union".[42] In contrast, the real so-called Frontline states[43] agreed with the main line of OAU policy and were willing to make economic and

(XXVII); CM/Res.490 (XXVII); CM/Res.624 (XXXI); CM/Res.821 (XXXV); and CM/Res.1052 (XLIV)/Rev.1.

38 CM/Res.151 (XI); CM/Res.155 (XI); CM/Res.209 (XIV); CM/Res.234 (XV); CM/Res.235 (XV); CM/Res.241/Rev.1 (XVII); CM/Res.242/Rev.1 (XVII); CM/Res.268 (XIX); CM/Res.270 (XIX); CM/Res.272 (XIX); CM/Res.350 (XXIII); ECM/Res.17 (VII); ECM/Res.18 (VII); and CM/St.3 (XIV).

39 CM/Res.623 (XXXI); CM/Res.634 (XXXI); CM/Res.731 (XXXIII); CM/Res.817 (XXXV); and CM/Res.865 (XXXVII).

40 See f.i. the Paris Declaration on Sanctions against South Africa, 27 May 1981 (text in *Africa Contemporary Record*, 1981-82, C30-35); CM/Res.304 (XXI) (on the 1973 Oslo conference); CM/Res.490 (XXVII); CM/Res.734 (XXXIII); and CM/Res.864 (XXXVII).

41 See f.i. *Botswana Daily News*, 11/11/66; 18/9/67; and 20/9/68 (articles).

42 See G.R. Haworth, 'The Southern African Customs Union: A Legal and Political Analysis', in Institute of Foreign and Comparative Law, Un. of South Africa: *Alternative Structures for Southern African Interaction* (Pretoria, 1982), pp 5-17.

43 Apart from Botswana they were Tanzania, Zambia and, since the mid 1970s, Angola and Mozambique. After 1980, they were joined by Zimbabwe and in 1990 by Namibia.

military sacrifices by closing their borders to trade and bearing the brunt of assistance to liberation movements and consequent white counterattacks.[44]

Yet, even in their case, it was obvious that not all economic dealings could be discarded. It took some time, however, before the OAU openly acknowledged that not all members were in identical geographical and economic circumstances and could be expected to conform fully to the sanctions requirements. It began to emphasize the need to grant assistance to the Frontline members and the former High Commission territories and to this purpose established the so-called "Committee of Nineteen on Assistance to the Frontline States".[45] It also publicly conceded, in 1979, that "some" independent states in Southern Africa, as well as Cape Verde, were obliged to maintain "some" economic relations with the South African regime "by virtue of historical and geographical circumstances".[46]

At the beginning of the 1980s, the OAU decided to investigate the effects of sanctions on Southern African economies and to examine the possibilities of co-operation among these countries. A report of 1981 outlined the most serious forms of dependence on South Africa, which constituted the principal enemy. It suggested concrete measures to reduce such dependence and, thus, offset the negative effects of sanctions compliance.[47] In a way, this line of action was a more constructive approach in the struggle against apartheid than the simplistic call for sanctions compliance during the first two decades. It also implied strong encouragement of the "Southern African Development Co-ordination Conference", an organization formed by the various Southern African states in 1979-80 with the aim to reduce their dependence on Pretoria.[48] Unfortunately, by the late 1980s this had not yet led to any fundamental changes in dependence patterns, let alone to an increased capacity to enforce sanctions. The principal reasons for this were the economic crisis, drought and, especially, the onslaughts of South Africa's armed forces and its proxies, which resulted in a disastrous deterioration in humanitarian and security conditions.[49]

---

44 See f.i. *Daily News* (Tanzania), 14/6/72. However, with aiding guerrilla's not only Botswana, but also Zimbabwe refused to serve as a base from which attacks could be launched. See f.i. *The Herald* (Zimbabwe), 4/7/80.

45 CM/Res.349 (XXIII); CM/Res.786 (XXXV); CM/Res.817 (XXXV); CM/Res.855 (XXXVII); CM/Res.864 (XXXVII); and AHG/Dec.112 (XVI).

46 CM/Res.734 (XXXIII).

47 PL/SA/39 (IV) 59.81 Rev.1: Consideration of All Aspects of Sanctions Against South Africa. Report Submitted by the Organization of African Unity to the International Conference on Sanctions Against South Africa, Paris, 20-27 May 1981.

48 See f.i. A. Tostensen, *Dependence and Collective Self-Reliance in Southern Africa: The Case of the Southern African Development Co-ordination Conference (SADCC)* (Uppsala, 1982).

49 For OAU concern with this BR/27/ICRSSA/50.87: International Conference on the Plight of Refugees and Displaced Persons in Southern Africa; BR/COM/XV/92: Aide-Mémoire: International Conference on the Plight of Refugees, Returnees and Displaced Persons in Southern Africa; and SARRED/88/L.1/Rev.II: Oslo Declaration and Plan of Action on the Plight of Refugees, Returnees and Displaced Persons in Southern Africa (SARRED). On South Africa's total war strategy and wider context f.i. Ph. Johnson and D. Martin (eds), *Destructive Engagement: Southern Africa at War* (Harare, 1986) and Th. Ohlson, 'Strategic Confrontation versus Economic Survival in Southern Africa', in F.M. Deng and I.W. Zartman (eds), *Conflict Resolution in Africa* (Washington, 1991), pp 219 ff.

Policy consensus under pressure 1965-1969

However, during the last three decades this dependence of Southern African countries never had serious consequences for the OAU's internal consensus, for it was obvious that they could be excused on the grounds of *force majeure*. In contrast, during the second half of the 1960s the divergent attitudes of certain countries to OAU strategy did, indeed, put Pan-African consensus at risk. Because by then this strategy had not yet delivered much concrete, its basic presumption that white minority regimes had to be softened up with economic, diplomatic and military means, before negotiations could persuade them to give in, came under increasing pressure.

In a review of the struggle in Southern Africa the Secretary-General observed, in 1968, that the white minority regimes were reinforcing their economic and military position, were receiving help from their Western allies and still dwarfed independent Africa with their technical and military superiority. South Africa had turned itself into a police state. Portugal had increased its war budget by ten per cent and with well over 100,000 soldiers in its colonies was retaliating against independent African states. In fact, the military situation was deteriorating.[50] Moreover, the case that Ethiopia and Liberia had brought before the International Court of Justice over South Africa's violation of its Namibian mandate had been lost in 1966, when the Court dismissed it on procedural grounds. The fact that the proceedings had been collectively financed by OAU members transformed the Court's decision into a defeat of OAU policy.[51]

In the case of Rhodesia, the OAU had suffered a painful defeat when in 1965 the white minority unilaterally declared its independence from Britain while retaining its monopoly on power. With this act of defiance it ignored repeated and sharp warnings by the OAU to Britain to prevent such action from taking place.[52] When it did, African states, especially the militant ones, were furious. The Council of Ministers issued strongly worded statements, in which it alluded to a possible use of force to assist Rhodesia's black majority.[53] However, it was clear that there were deep divisions over strategy. As a military response would be difficult if not impossible, the only realistic option, apart from sanctions, was an attempt to force Britain to restore order in Rhodesia. An ultimatum stipulating that, if the British did not crush the rebellion by 15 December 1965 OAU member states would severe their diplomatic ties with the United Kingdom,[54] could somewhat satisfy the anger of the radical states and curtail inter-African divisions.

However, it soon became clear that the Council had gone too far. Many heads of state were not prepared to cut their links with Britain. For example, Nigeria claimed that a rupture with Whitehall was unrealistic, as was the suggestion to use force. Black Rhodesians should be assisted, but a military struggle was first and foremost their own responsibility.[55] In the eyes of many, especially moderate, members like Kenya and

---

50   CM/212 (Part 2): Report of the Administrative Secretary-General Covering the Period from February to September 1968, Algiers, September 1968, pp 41-54.

51   See Resolution on decolonization, paragraph 5; CM/Res.58 (IV); CM/Res.71 (V); CM/Res.81 (VII); and AHG/Res.39 (II).

52   F.i. CM/Res.14 (II); CM/Res.33 (III); CM/Res.62 (V).

53   ECM/Res.13 (VI); ECM/Res.14 (VI); and ECM/Res.15 (VI).

54   ECM/Res.13 (VI).

55   *Daily Times* (Nigeria), 20/10/65 and 11/12/65. Similarly, *East African Standard* (Kenya), 6/12/65.

Zambia, a decision on breaking diplomatic ties could only be taken by the Assembly.[56] Thus, the Council ultimatum did not enjoy broad consensus. With important countries like Nigeria, and even a Frontline member like Zambia, opposed to it, there was no group of actors strong enough to guarantee its implementation. In the end only nine, predominantly radical, members executed the ultimatum and severed their ties with Britain.[57] The Assembly later only "took note" of the Council resolution.[58]

The affair showed that the divisions between moderate-conservative members on the one hand and radical ones on the other were still in existence, even if they had been papered over at the OAU's founding conference. Moreover, several conservative countries like Malawi and certain Francophone states had their own distinct position on anti-colonial strategy, which they now began to argue for openly. They held that the Rhodesian debacle had exposed the ineffectiveness of OAU strategy and that the time had therefore come to change course. Shortly after the Rhodesian issue, Malawi crossed the thin line between retaining, out of dire need, links with minority regimes and downright collaboration. While it depended considerably on its existing links with the white south, its president, Hastings Banda, decided to *expand* and *consolidate* these ties and enter into diplomatic relations with Pretoria. Malawi claimed that this did not imply full agreement with South Africa's policies. It emphasized that OAU members should be "realistic" in facing their development needs and in accepting that South Africa was there to stay. It also argued that with regard to trade it was merely doing what others did in secret.[59]

Other OAU members reacted angrily, especially Zambia and Tanzania, which already had various disputes with the Malawian leader. Zambia tried to have Malawi expelled from the OAU. Although some moderate member states expressed understanding for Malawi's position,[60] the country had clearly overstepped the limits of collective acquiescence in violations of OAU policy. Banda's openness about trading, and his decision to establish diplomatic ties, with South Africa called into question elite African conceptions of honour and dignity and so touched on part of the rationale underlying the OAU's decolonization objective. Thus, one Nigerian comment wondered how Banda, who was likened to Hitler, could enjoy respect and dignity if the blacks in South Africa could not?[61]

However, what was at issue was not the fact that Malawi had trade links with South Africa, but that, apart from its deliberate decision to expand them, it was *open* about it. Many governments realized that economic links could sometimes not be discarded. Yet, in

---

56   See f.i. *East African Standard* (Kenya), 6/12/65 and *Fraternité* (Ivory Coast), 10/12/65 (article). For a legal point of view confirming this position T.O. Elias, 'The Legality of the O.A.U. Council of Ministers' Resolution on Rhodesia in December 1965', in *The Nigerian Law Journal*, 1969, pp 1-12.

57   These were: Egypt, Algeria, Mauritania, Guinea, Mali, Ghana, Sudan, Tanzania and Congo-Brazzaville. See the list in Y. El-Ayouty and I.W. Zartman (eds), *The OAU After Twenty Years* (New York, 1984), p 377.

58   AHG/Dec.4 (III). See for non-governmental criticism of this affair M'buyinga, *Pan-Africanism*, p 221.

59   J. Woronoff, *Organizing African Unity* (Metuchen, NJ, 1970), p 309 and *Malawi News*, 6/10/67 and 22/8/69.

60   Cervenka, *Unfinished Quest*, p 113.

61   *Daily Times* (Nigeria), 12/9/67.

such cases discretion should be exercised,[62] so that Africa's "dignity" could be upheld. In view of the ambiguity of this argument it must be noted that hegemonic stability theory holds that international systems dominated by one powerful actor can lead to a strong regime whose norms are clear.[63] In our case one may argue that, conversely, a regime that does not enjoy hegemonic leadership and faces powerful external factors impinging on its functioning, will generate norms that are highly ambiguous.[64]

While Malawi's actions contributed towards the growing controversy over anti-colonial strategy, the divergent attitudes of certain Francophone countries were, as will be shown below, potentially more damaging. In an attempt to preserve consensus several East and Central African governments approved a document in 1969, which was later adopted by the OAU Assembly.[65] This "Lusaka Manifesto" formed one of the most important and detailed statements of OAU strategy on Southern Africa. In a calm, dignified manner it explained why the white minority regimes constituted an affront to the dignity of Africans, without pretending that independent Africa's own record of socio-political organization was unblemished. The Manifesto pointed to the institutionalization of the doctrine of racial inequality, which made the white minority regimes, indeed, unique in the present day world. It claimed that Africa's confrontation with the minority regimes did not represent a form of African expansionism, as it did not desire revision of boundaries but establishment of African majority rule in these territories. Reversion of the racialist order was explicitly rejected in favour of a political system in which everyone, regardless of colour, could live on the basis of the doctrines of human equality and dignity.

The Manifesto emphasized that African states preferred negotiations rather than force as a way to settle the conflicts in Southern Africa. It even proposed a flexible approach to timetables and transitional arrangements, once the minority regimes had accepted the principles of human equality and self-determination. However, if they would continue to oppose change African states had no choice but to persevere in their support of the armed struggle in the various colonies, as well as the total isolation of South Africa.

Although this exposé of strategy was fully in line with the policies that the OAU had followed since its formation,[66] particularly in its combination of peaceful and violent tactics, the Manifesto was misinterpreted in the Western world as the rejection of the armed struggle. Indeed, several conservative African regimes articulated a similar interpretation as Western governments and observed, quite rightly, that the Manifesto's

---

62   See *Kenya Weekly News*, 11/10/68, no. 2226 and J. Mayall, 'African Unity and the OAU: The Place of a Political Myth in African Diplomacy', in *Yearbook of World Affairs* (London), 1973, p 126.

63   R.O. Keohane, 'The Theory of Hegemonic Stability and Changes in International Economic Regimes 1967-77', in O.R. Holsti, R.M. Siverson and A.L. George (eds), *Change in the International System* (Boulder, 1980), p 132. See also P. van Ham, 'The lack of a Big Bully: Hegemonic stability theory and regimes in the study of international relations', in *Acta Politica*, 1992, p 36.

64   Rothstein, 'Regime-Creation' and D. Snidal, 'The Limits of Hegemonic Stability Theory', in *International Organization*, 1985, p 595.

65   Manifesto on Southern Africa, Conference of East and Central African States, Lusaka, 16 April 1969. Adopted by the Assembly in AHG/Dec.36 (VI).

66   As noted f.i. in *Zambia Daily Mail*, 18/4/69.

language was markedly more moderate and conciliatory than the OAU had sounded before.[67]

The dialogue affair

The upshot of the Lusaka Manifesto was, therefore, that it did not achieve its intention of ending the growing controversy on strategy. Worse still, South Africa's prime minister, John Vorster, was making overtures to African states to establish diplomatic and economic relations.[68] Several countries, such as Ivory Coast, Madagascar, Mauritius and Lesotho, appeared to be interested.

In view of these developments the growing debate on strategy began to focus on the OAU's posture towards Pretoria. The protagonists of change were led by Ivory Coast. They now argued for negotiations between African states and South Africa, "dialogue" for short, as the armed struggle and sanctions had, in their eyes, failed. African states did not have the economic-military power to confront the apartheid regime. A dialogue with South Africa could, on the other hand, encourage a peaceful settlement between whites and blacks and bring an end to apartheid.[69] The Ivorians claimed that they desired, like everyone else, the complete decolonization of the African continent, but that armed struggle and "bellicose verbalism" would merely endanger the peace while not bringing a solution to the apartheid problem any closer.[70] In actual fact, however, it was Houphouët-Boigny's hostility to communism and the Eastern bloc, and his fear of a threat to the stability of his and allied African governments, that formed the basis of this attitude.

However, several radical member states, as well as some moderate ones, were firmly opposed to a change in OAU policy. The Nigerian government — which after the end of the civil war began to adopt a more forceful and self-conscious foreign policy posture — conferred with the leaders of Ethiopia and Kenya and emphasized that dialogue with South Africa could only take place on the basis of human equality and dignity, as demanded by the Lusaka Manifesto.[71] The Secretary-General and the Liberation Committee were opposed to the Ivorian alternative as well.[72]

In 1971 the opponents to dialogue decided to force a show-down by putting the proposal for dialogue not only on the agenda of the Assembly, but also, despite Ivorian objections, on that of the Council. They also managed to have the debate held in public to force the protagonists to come into the open with, what was seen as, a conciliatory posture towards the apartheid regime. In spite of objections by dialogue supporters, it

---

67 See f.i. *Info Madagascar,* 27/9/69; *Fraternité* (Ivory Coast), 18/6/71 (editorial and article); and Mayall, 'African Unity and the OAU'.

68 On South African ideas on co-operation with its neighbours J. Barber, *South Africa's Foreign Policy 1945-1970* (London, 1973), chs. 16-17 and, later, J. van der Meulen, *Zuid Afrika als Regionaal Machtscentrum* (The Hague, 1986), ch. 1.

69 *Info Madagascar*, 16/1/71; 6/3/71; and 14/8/71 (articles) and Cervenka, *Unfinished Quest*, p 117.

70 See *Fraternité*, 26/2/71 and 18/6/71 (article) and the statement of the Ivorian leader in *Jeune Afrique*, 17/11/70.

71 Cervenka, *Unfinished Quest*, pp 117-118. Also *East African Standard* (Kenya), 22/6/71.

72 This may be inferred from statements made by the SG in CM/270 (Part 1): Report of the Administrative Secretary-General Covering the Period from February to August 1969, Addis Ababa, August 1969 (hereinafter as: CM/270 (Part 1): Report of the SG, Feb.-Aug. 1969), pp 24-26. See on Liberation Committee section 6.3.

was decided to use a Tanzanian document rejecting dialogue as the basis of discussions. The result was that Houphouët-Boigny declined to come and let his foreign minister face the wrath of the majority of member states.[73]

The Council session that preceded the Assembly summit got off to a bad start by the angry walkout of the Ivorian and Gabonese delegations. They were followed by the representatives of Upper Volta, Dahomey and Togo, which did not really disagree with the Tanzanian document but wanted to show their solidarity with their fellow member of the Entente.[74] The result was that almost all speeches at the session condemned the dialogue proposal. The tone of the discussions was one of anger and fierce indignation, fed by, among others, injured race pride.

Part of the objections of the opponents rested on the vagueness of the concept of dialogue as articulated by its supporters. Dialogue in its proper sense should mean that the parties engaged in negotiations recognized each other as equals, were willing to understand each other and were intent on working towards equitable solutions.[75] It was emphasized that the only purpose of Vorster's offer of dialogue was to force a diplomatic breakthrough in Africa, split African ranks and counter the negative effects of the OAU's isolation policy. Thus, dialogue as understood by Pretoria aimed at restoring South Africa's international respectability without having to give up the apartheid system.[76]

In a more fundamental vein, the Malian representative observed that negotiations only made sense if both parties were roughly equal in strength.[77] Under the present circumstances, negotiations would imply abandonment of the liberation struggle, result in a dialogue between "the rider and the horse" and lead to a consolidation of the status quo. Most delegates therefore noted that dialogue could only take place on the basis of the Lusaka Manifesto, which South Africa had rejected.[78]

Almost all representatives added that there should first be a genuine dialogue between Pretoria and its black citizens, rather than between South Africa and its external African neighbours. Many aired a fundamental objection to the idea of African states engaging in negotiations with Pretoria on behalf, and about the lot, of black South Africans. Only the black majority's representatives of the ANC and PAC were entitled to a real dialogue with Pretoria. As long as the whites were not prepared to engage in this, the OAU had no choice but to continue supporting the armed struggle.[79] Several delegates noted that the dual strategy of negotiations and armed force had been misinterpreted. They

---

73   *Daily Times* (Nigeria), 21/6/71 and *Fraternité* (Ivory Coast), 18/6/71 and 25/6/71 (articles).

74   Cervenka, *Unfinished Quest*, p 118.

75   See speeches by delegates of Somalia; Sierra Leone; Liberia; Burundi; Mali; Kenya; Guinea; and Senegal in the verbatim record called *The Principles of the OAU Charter, the Lusaka Manifesto, Dialogue and Future Strategy* (OAU General Secretariat: Addis Ababa, 1971), pp 20, 23, 49, 65, 75, 80 and 119. All material is taken from this verbatim report.

76   Speeches by Nigeria, Tanzania, Somalia, Sierra Leone, Sudan, Liberia, Cameroon, Libya, Gambia, Kenya, Tunisia, Botswana and Zambia: pp 12, 17-8, 21, 23-25, 43, 49, 53, 56, 68-9, 80, 103, 107 and 133-4.

77   See his speech, p 75.

78   Speeches by Nigeria, Tanzania, Sierra Leone, Liberia, Botswana, Senegal and Guinea, pp 13, 17, 24, 51-2, 107, 113 and 123. See also CM/Res.209 (XIV).

79   Speeches by Algeria, Nigeria, Tanzania, Sierra Leone, Sudan, Libya, Mauritania, Kenya, Egypt, Tunisia, Botswana, Senegal, Morocco and Guinea: pp 11, 13, 15, 17, 22, 31-2, 45, 56-7, 62, 78, 81, 93, 103, 106, 111, 116 and 124.

correctly observed that the Lusaka document spoke of a *preference* to negotiations and had added that, if the minority regimes were not interested in genuine talks, violent struggle should continue.[80]

Another *faux pas* by the protagonists of dialogue concerned the manner in which it had been launched. Instead of presenting his proposal first to the OAU, which was the only institution entitled to decide on Pan-African strategy, Houphouët had introduced his initiative at a highly publicized international press conference. In terms of OAU psychology, which as shown in section 5.6 is characterized by a monopolistic, discretionary disposition of the Assembly, this was a clear mistake. Delegates strongly resented the opportunities given to the Western media, arguing that the proposal had been "planted from outside Africa".[81] It was therefore regarded as a "Trojan horse trick" and an "insult" to their continent.[82] In short, the way in which it was presented implicated a collective inferiority complex, as it easily led to an inference that extra-African forces could impinge on something that in the self-esteem of state elites was regarded as the preserve of their OAU.

Naturally, the violent tone of the debate may be explained as an attempt to shout down dissenting voices. Yet, the anger of delegates was also prompted by a sense of wounded dignity. However ambiguous the OAU's record on sanctions had already become by then, Africa's collective inability to coerce the racist regimes into submission did not diminish indignation about the racialist order itself. Many emphasized that in South Africa blacks were treated as sub-humans who were forced to be the hewers of wood and the drawers of water for other races.[83] The pretence of racial superiority was regarded as an affront to the dignity of all Africans.[84] That such emotional statements amounted to more than lip service to Pan-Africanist solidarity is shown by the awareness of several delegates that, under the South African system, their own social status would not have counted for much. In fact, this elite African imagination of what apartheid amounted to provided sincerity to their anger. Thus, the Zambian foreign minister sharply observed that

> it makes very little difference whether an African is a Foreign Minister of a respectable independent African State. He is a nigger Foreign Minister ...
> It does not matter what the African is or what position he occupies, he is still a nigger.[85]

Other delegates added that, at worst, diplomatic ties with Pretoria would turn permanently stationed African diplomats into envoys of apartheid and, at best, force upon them a pampered life in splendid isolation. They would be nothing more than "honorary whites".[86] This cynicism had seemingly been confirmed by a statement of President

---

80   See f.i. par. 12 of the Lusaka Manifesto. See speeches by Mali, Ghana, Botswana and Zambia: pp 76, 99, 106 and 131.

81   Speeches by Nigeria and SWAPO: pp 14 and 144.

82   Speeches by Nigeria, Mali and Guinea: pp 14, 75 and 119.

83   Speeches by Tanzania, Liberia, Ghana, Tunisia and Guinea: pp 15, 51, 94, 104 and 120.

84   Speeches by Somalia, Burundi and Cameroon's speech in the Assembly: pp 19, 63 and 155.

85   Speech by Zambian delegate: p 130. In a less crude manner the Lusaka Manifesto, par. 21, had already noted this as well.

86   See speeches by Sudan, Ethiopia and Gambia: pp 43, 60 and 68, and *The Standard* (Tanzania),

Tsiranana of Madagascar six months earlier. In a reference to the usefulness of human contact between the Malagasy people and white South African tourists and students, as a means to convince South Africa's whites to give up apartheid, this staunch supporter of dialogue had remarked:

> désirons-nous montrer aux Blancs d'Afrique du Sud que le Noir est l'égal du Blanc, *que le Noir peut être civilisé*, et que le Blanc peut s'entendre avec lui au nom de la fraternité humaine et de l'égalité.[87]

In this respect, the opponents of dialogue criticized the mystifying nature of some of the arguments that its supporters had used.[88] The proponents also stood accused of dividing the continent, which, if it were to occupy its rightful place in international affairs, should inspire respect and act in unison.[89]

All in all, this was enough for several delegates to ridicule the proposal and even, in the case of the Guinean delegate, to accuse its advocates of "high treason".[90] The whole exercise was not so much a debate,[91] as a collective warning of what was politically the bottom line in acceptable behaviour in inter-African relations.[92] In this respect the proceedings stood out for the ridicule, laughter and regular applause for opponents' speeches and, more generally, the public nature of the debates.[93]

Yet, it should be realized that these condemnations rested principally on the contention that the proponents of dialogue Ivorian style were not really motivated by a desire to find a genuine solution to the problems of Southern Africa. After all, Zambia, which sided with the opponents of dialogue, had secretly been engaged in talks with the South African government since 1968 in a bid to realize a peaceful end to white minority rule in Rhodesia.[94]

If the debate never gave the protagonists of dialogue a fair hearing, it is also true that some had already walked out at the start, thus clearing the way to their opponents. Shying away from a lucid presentation, its supporters limited themselves to a muted defence. Lesotho and Swaziland articulated a sympathetic viewpoint in which their fear of a racial holocaust engulfing Southern Africa predominated. Malawi's speech was almost completely incoherent.[95] More to the point, the written message of Houphouët and the speeches of Madagascar could not explain why dialogue with Vorster's regime would be

---

21/6/71.

87   *Info Madagascar*, 16/1/71 (article). Emphasis added.

88   Speeches by Tanzania, Botswana and Guinea: pp 16, 106 and 118.

89   Cameroon's speech at the Assembly: p 155; *Zambia Daily Mail*, 21/6/71; and *l'Essor* (Mali), 5/7/71 (article).

90   See the Guinean speech, p 122.

91   See for its perception as "Africa's great debate" *Daily Times* (Nigeria), 21/6/71.

92   *Info Madagascar*, 14/8/71 (article) later spoke of an OAU "diktat". See also Mayall, 'African Unity and the OAU', p 126.

93   Zambia asked for the full verbatim record to be circulated in view of its importance. Some delegates objected to the public nature of the debate and the refusal not to concede to the Ivorian request to discuss the matter only in the Assembly. Speeches by Zambia, Liberia, Ghana: pp 47, 95, 129.

94   D. Martin and Ph. Johnson, *The Struggle for Zimbabwe: The Chimurenga War* (London and Boston, 1981), p 132 ff.

95   Speeches by Malawi, Lesotho and Swaziland: pp 70-73, 82-90, 114-115 and 170-174.

a more effective means to eradicate apartheid than the OAU's present strategy. Mystifying pronouncements about "peace" and "moderation" could not dispel the impression that these countries were less interested in a genuine alternative than in improving their economic prospects, through profitable contacts with the white south, and in consolidating their regime against, what was perceived as, the encroachment by international communism.[96]

In the end, 27 countries in the Council and 28 in the Assembly voted for a declaration on the question of dialogue, which reiterated that the Lusaka Manifesto was the only basis for a solution of the problems of apartheid and colonialism. It also emphasized that no member should on its own engage in any action that would undermine the obligations of the Charter. Any attempt to tackle the problems of colonialism and apartheid should be undertaken in the framework of the OAU and in consultation with the liberation movements. Dialogue that did not solely aim at achieving the legitimate rights of black South Africans was rejected, while it was noted that a meaningful dialogue should first commence between Pretoria and black South Africans themselves.[97]

In the Council only Lesotho, Madagascar, Malawi and Swaziland voted against the delaration. Upper Volta and Dahomey, which had walked out at the start of the session, were registered as "not voting" and "abstaining" respectively. While Niger also abstained, seven countries were registered as absent.[98] In the Assembly six countries voted against: besides Lesotho, Madagascar and Malawi they were Gabon, Ivory Coast and Mauritius. While the Central African Republic and Uganda were registered as absent, five countries abstained: Dahomey, Niger, Swaziland, Togo and Upper Volta.[99]

Notwithstanding the debate's outcome Ivory Coast, as well as Madagascar until the coup d'état of 1972, persisted in dialogue with Pretoria.[100] While this led to their isolation in the OAU, it also signified collective inability to enforce policy. Even with most members opposed to dialogue it was hard to punish offenders, particularly if it concerned relatively influential actors that were to some extent shielded from retaliatory action by their dependence on, or close collaboration with, extra-African powers as France. If it wasn't inability, but unwillingness or, rather, inadequate co-ordination of collective resolution, that stood in the way of enforcement, absence of continental hegemonic leadership still provides a persuasive explanation for this state of affairs.

Naturally, the failure to retaliate might be explained as disinterest by other states, as it was only a few that continued to violate policy. None of these belonged to the group of influential Southern African states which, as shown in the next section, exerted

---

96   See written Ivorian message and the Malagasy speeches: pp 33-39 and 157-169 and for emphasis on economic co-operation with South Africa, *Info Madagascar*, 23/1/71, 6/3/71, 27/3/71, 3/4/71, 24/4/71, 21/8/71, 27/11/71 and 4/12/71 (all articles).

97   See CM/St.5 (XVII) and on a South African government reaction *Die Burger*, 28/6/71.

98   Ivory Coast, Gabon, Togo, CAR, Zaire, Mauritius and Uganda. Some were absent for other reasons. M. Wolfers, *Politics in the Organization of African Unity* (London, 1976), pp 38-45 and the list of the roll-call vote in the verbatim report, p 5.

99   See the list of the roll-call in *ibid*.: p 6. Togo, Mauritius and Dahomey were not against the declaration as such, but objected to certain procedures or a certain paragraph. See their speeches in *ibid*.: pp 176-177 and 179.

100   See f.i. *Fraternité* (Ivory Coast), 25/2/72 (editorial and article) and *Info Madagascar*, 14/8/71 (article). For non-governmental criticism M'buyinga, *Pan-Africanism*, pp 142-144.

considerable influence on the OAU's liberation strategy. Moreover, one should not overestimate the significance of these deviations, as dialogue in the above-mentioned form never popped again in such a free and easy way. Several countries got involved, during the 1970s and 1980s, in various more or less overt economic dealings with South Africa. Yet, most shied away from engaging in open, high profile diplomacy with Pretoria. This would have meant transgression of — what had been confirmed as — an unambiguous norm. Its internalization in foreign policy altered the balance in pay-offs between defection and compliance in favour of the latter: future retaliation by way of a debate in OAU fora was always possible, which in view of the ferocity of the dialogue dispute was not an enticing prospect.[101]

Finally, while dialogue had brought into the open certain cleavages in inter-African relations,[102] in this context they should not be overrated. The gravity of the defection by some small Southern African states and the maverick leadership of Malawi was limited by their restricted influence on OAU strategy. The conservative Francophones, united in OCAM, were split by the issue. Several OCAM members had come out against dialogue, while even fellow Entente members like Upper Volta, Dahomey, Niger and Togo dragged their feet rather than toe the Ivorian line.

The Council session in Dar es Salaam, April 1975
In the years after dialogue OAU summits laid much more stress on the armed struggle as a result of important advances made by liberation movements in certain territories, notably Guinea-Bissau and Mozambique.[103] Following the militant "Mogadiscio Declaration" of October 1971,[104] the Assembly session in Rabat (1972) was dominated by a radical and forceful spirit in which concrete decisions were taken to enhance the effectiveness of the armed struggle.[105] However, after independence of the Portuguese territories (1974-1976), attention shifted to the problem of Rhodesia. The armed struggle there was still in its infancy and was going to prove very hard. Contrary to Portugal, the white minority regime in Salisbury did not have to transport troops from overseas and was a modern Western government commanding a well equipped fighting machine. With the powerful backing of Pretoria, the Rhodesian regime posed a considerable threat to the security of the Frontline states. As the preceding decade had shown, these had not even been able to

---

101   Oye, 'Explaining Cooperation Under Anarchy', p 11 ff. Also H. Bull, *The Anarchical Society: A Study of Order in World Politics* (London, 1977), p 67.

102   See f.i. *Révolution Africaine* (Algeria), 11-17/6/71 (article); *l'Essor* (Mali), 5/7/71 (article); and *Daily Mail* (Sierra Leone), 24/6/71.

103   T.H. Henriksen, *Revolution and Counterrevolution: Mozambique's War of Independence, 1964-1974* (Westport and London, 1983) and B. Davidson, *No Fist is Big Enough to Hide the Sky: The Liberation Struggle of Guiné and Cape Verde. Aspects of an African Revolution* (London, 1981).

104   See St/2/ECAS/VII: Mogadiscio Declaration, adopted by the 7th Summit Conference of East and Central African States, Mogadiscio, 18-20 October 1971, esp. paragraph 13 (publ. by OAU General Secretariat, Addis Ababa),

105   CM/Res.267 (XIX) - CM/Res.272 (XIX). Yet, decisions on military support to Frontline states were never implemented. Cervenka, *Unfinished Quest*, p 57 and on the so-called "spirit of Rabat" *Révolution Africaine* (Algeria), 16-22/6/72 (article); *Daily Mail* (Sierra Leone), 17/6/72; *l'Essor* (Mali), 24-5/6/72 (article); *Daily News* (Tanzania), 13/6/72 and 14/6/72 (articles); *Info Madagascar*, 24/6/72 (article); and *Botswana Daily News*, 23/6/72 (article).

prevent and defend themselves against punitive raids by the Portuguese.[106] Moreover, as events in Angola had shown[107] divisions within the liberation movement of one territory could easily lead to foreign, even superpower, intervention, thus increasing the likelihood of escalation and East-West confrontation.

The major Frontline states of Tanzania, Botswana, Mozambique and, especially, Zambia were therefore intent on exploring the possibilities of peaceful change in Rhodesia. After the dialogue affair this constituted a rather ironical, although not really contradictory, change in tactics. Vorster's government was willing to talk as well. With the coming to power of Marxist regimes in Mozambique (1975) and Angola (1976), the battle line had moved towards South Africa's sphere of influence. This threatened its military security and put at risk economic interests such as its eastern transport links. A negotiated settlement in Rhodesia would preclude a military defeat of its white minority and allow Pretoria to scale down its assistance. However, these considerations were part of a wider policy perspective in which Pretoria, once again, aimed at consolidating the status quo by inducing its African neighbours to relieve international pressure and co-operate with the South African regime. This time the proposal was christened "détente".[108]

Talks ensued between South Africa and Zambia, which was backed by Tanzania. They were followed by negotiations at Victoria Falls between the Rhodesian government and its freed African nationalist opponents. However, these diplomatic skirmishes — and with it détente — quickly collapsed as South Africa was not prepared to force African majority rule down white Rhodesian throats. The full details of these developments have been dealt with elsewhere.[109] What is important here is that this diplomatic opening by the Frontline states, presented only by Vorster as "détente", rapidly generated controversy in the OAU, as many saw détente as a resurrection of dialogue.

Especially radical regimes outside the Southern African region such as Guinea and Algeria, but also Kenya, were suspicious of the attempt to find a peaceful solution to the Rhodesian problem. As they were situated far away from the scenes of battle, they could afford to be militant, as well as rigid, as regards implementation of OAU objectives. Algeria decided to call for an extraordinary session of the Council of Ministers, which was convened in Dar es Salaam. Algiers resented the fact that certain heads of state were again talking about "dialogue", a statement that might refer to a response from Ivory Coast, which argued that current developments vindicated its opinions.[110]

It is clear, however, that the Frontline states had no intention of reaching a rapprochement with Pretoria over apartheid. They only wished to update strategy

---

106 A notorious example was the attack on Guinea-Conakry from neighbouring Portuguese Guinea (Nov. 1970), which triggered off an emotional session of the Council to rally, if only morally, to the support of Sékou Touré's government. See ECM/2 (VII), Parts 1-2: Report of the SG to the Extraordinary Session of the Council of Ministers, Lagos, 9/12/70.

107 W.J. Foltz and J. Widner, 'The OAU and Southern African Liberation', in El-Ayouty and Zartman, *OAU After Twenty Years*, pp 254-255. See on Angola section 6.3.

108 Van der Meulen, *Zuid Afrika*, ch. 1 and C. Legum, *Vorster's Gamble for Africa: How the Search for Peace Failed* (London, 1976), part 2.

109 Martin and Johnson, *Struggle for Zimbabwe*, chs. 8-10 and S.J. Stedman, *Peacemaking in Civil War: International Mediation in Zimbabwe, 1974-1980* (Boulder and London, 1991), ch. 2.

110 *Révolution Africaine* (Algeria), 11-17/4/75 and Legum, *Vorster's Gamble*, pp 14-19.

concerning Rhodesia. The Tanzanians warned against "ultra-radicalism" in the OAU and called for "correct strategy and tactics". As far as South Africa itself was concerned, OAU isolation policy should continue. Speaking to the Council, the Zambian foreign minister argued that their initiative only represented a change in tactics, saying that the sole objective was the eradication of colonialism and apartheid. He denied that Zambia was involved in dialogue with Pretoria (presumably over apartheid itself), although he acknowledged that Vorster had so far co-operated as regards the Rhodesian issue.[111] In the end the Frontline ministers managed to persuade their peers to condone the initiative, which was sanctioned in the "Dar es Salaam Declaration on Southern Africa".[112]

The declaration observed that with the collapse of the Portuguese empire and the increased importance of the Rhodesian question a re-examination of strategy was necessary. While strategy and tactics might change from time to time, the OAU's objective remained unchanged and non-negotiable. In this respect the declaration was, in fact, unequivocal: "Africans cannot, and will never, acquiesce in the perpetuations [sic] of colonial and/or racist oppression in their continent. That is why any talk of détente with the apartheid regime is such nonsense that it should be treated with the contempt it deserves". It added that there was nothing "for free Africa to talk to the leaders of the apartheid regime in connection with their policies in South Africa".[113] The OAU would not be fooled by propaganda or cosmetic reforms. The system itself must be dismantled.

The declaration obtained the approval of the radical members as it reaffirmed the dual strategy of peaceful change and — if this failed — violent struggle, and carefully distinguished between negotiations with Pretoria over its own system of government on the one hand and peaceful change in Rhodesia and Namibia on the other. It observed that the different territories made it necessary to adopt different tactics.[114] If majority rule in Rhodesia could be won by negotiations the OAU should do everything possible to guarantee their success, a statement that sanctioned the diplomatic activities of the Frontline states. However, they should work in close consultation with the nationalists. If the latter concluded that negotiations had failed, the OAU should continue to assist the armed struggle.[115]

This qualification implied that it was the nationalists in a dependent territory that should negotiate with the enemy and that the OAU and Frontline states could neither strike a deal over their heads nor force them to accept its outcome.[116] Nevertheless, political practice was more intractable than the ideological purity of OAU dictates might suggest. For example, Zambia's policies deviated from time to time considerably from the line taken by the liberation movements of Rhodesia and Namibia. At one time it even contemplated the possibility of giving up the armed struggle, in which case it walked the

---

111   *Daily News* (Tanzania), 9/4/75 (editorial and speech by Zambia's foreign minister) and 10/4/75.
112   ECM/St.15 (IX), reaffirmed in CM/Res.428 (XXV), par. 1. See *The Standard* (Kenya), 9/4/75.
      Also *Daily Mail* (Sierra Leone), 11/4/75, which emphasized the need for a time limit to the talks
      with Vorster and Smith and continuation of the armed struggle.
113   ECM/St.15 (IX), par. 10 and 24.
114   This had already been sanctioned in the Lusaka Manifesto, par. 12 ff.
115   ECM/St. 15 (IX), par. 15.
116   Significantly, this was emphasized by the Algerian government. See *Révolution Africaine*, 11-
      17/4/75 (article).

thin line between implementing and violating OAU resolutions.[117] The Frontline states in general were to show, during the 1970s and 1980s, that they were at times prepared to force the liberation movements to submit to certain procedures or to swallow an unpleasant compromise.[118]

The Frontline alliance as OAU executive

With its official approval of the Frontline initiative the OAU remained, formally, the supreme institution regarding decolonization policy. More than anything else, however, the outcome of Dar es Salaam marked the decline of the direct relevance of the OAU as the policymaking body and, especially, the executive, of decolonization strategy in Southern Africa.[119] It had to cede this role to the emerging Frontline alliance.

Although the functioning of the Frontline alliance has been analysed elsewhere,[120] it is important to give a rough outline of its role in relation to the OAU. First, an analysis is given of how it functioned as executive of the OAU and why it could perform this role. After that, the nature of this leadership will be assessed. As an informal alliance of states situated close to the line of battle it was able, especially in the struggle for Zimbabwe,[121] to contribute at vital stages towards Pan-African decision making. Moreover, it could operate in a flexible manner and react more swiftly to developments than the OAU. It could also preserve a larger measure of secrecy, necessary for diplomatic-military initiatives, than could be guaranteed in the Pan-African organization. As it provided the various liberation movements with base camps, training facilities, arms and financial backing, it could, when necessary, coerce them in accepting a certain political or diplomatic procedure or a more accommodating posture in peace negotiations.[122]

In this respect it was sufficiently small and enjoyed adequate co-ordination to act as the OAU's executive. While its role in advancing Pan-African consensus had also been observed in the formulation, by a group of East and Central African states, of the Lusaka Manifesto (1969) and the Mogadiscio Declaration (1971), the Frontline alliance was, in fact, to prove instrumental in the actual *implementation* of the OAU's objective. Its functioning formed a good illustration of Oye's game theoretical contention that regional decomposition of issues, so as to reduce the number of actors, is one way of realizing co-operation in a context with numerous states.[123]

---

117   See Martin and Johnson, *Struggle for Zimbabwe*.

118   See f.i. Foltz and Widner, 'OAU and Southern African Liberation', p 262 and Martin and Johnson, *Struggle for Zimbabwe*.

119   Also Cervenka, *Unfinished Quest*, p 132.

120   See f.i. M.A. El-Khawas, 'Southern Africa: A Challenge to the OAU', in *Africa Today*, 1977, no. 3, pp 36-41; R. Jaster, 'A Regional Security Role for Africa's Frontline States', in R. Jaster (ed), *Southern Africa: Regional Security Problems and Prospects* (Aldershot, 1985), pp 89-106; and A. Sesay, 'The Roles of the Frontline States in Southern Africa', in O. Aluko and T.M. Shaw (eds), *Southern Africa in the 1980s* (London, 1985), ch. 2.

121   Foltz and Widner, 'OAU and Southern African Liberation' and Martin and Johnson, *Struggle for Zimbabwe*.

122   Interview with David Busiku Mainza, First Secretary at the Zambian embassy, Addis Ababa, 28/9/89 and Foltz and Widner, 'OAU and Southern African Liberation', pp 255-256.

123   Oye, 'Explaining Cooperation Under Anarchy', p 21.

The moral justification for this development was not hard to find. The Frontline states suffered considerably under the retaliatory actions of the white minority regimes. During the 1980s, the deterioration in Southern Africa's security put their very survival and territorial integrity at risk.[124] As such, the OAU could do little more than show understanding for, rather than condemn, Mozambique's decision to sign the "Nkomati Accord" with South Africa (1984). This non-aggression treaty implied, among others, the forced removal of ANC guerrillas from Mozambique in exchange for a South African promise to end its attacks, directly and by way of proxy, on Mozambiquan territory.[125]

Yet, one of the reasons for the successful functioning of the Frontline alliance was that its members sought the political backing of the OAU. The Council session in Dar es Salaam showed that the activities of the Frontline states could trigger a critical response from other OAU members, especially the radical ones. As there was always the possibility that they could be called to account, interaction in the OAU did not approach a single-play but, as Oye would argue, an iterated game situation. Thus, reciprocity in continental interaction was not completely absent. With the shadow of the future hanging over them, the Frontline states could be encouraged also to co-operate through the framework of the OAU.[126]

However, another explanation, besides the structural features of inter-African relations, is that their objectives did not fundamentally differ from those of the OAU as a whole anyway. Working within the cadre of OAU policy lines, the Frontline states deliberately involved the Liberation Committee[127] and tried to mobilize OAU diplomatic support for certain outcomes. For example, when the Frontline countries had recognized the "Patriotic Front" (PF) as Zimbabwe's sole liberation movement, they asked for, and got, its exclusive recognition from the Assembly summit in Libreville.[128] Moreover, they closely co-operated with the Nigerian government, which clearly aspired to a leadership role in inter-African relations. Lagos therefore actively supported the Frontline states and sought to back up their position with the means that its oil resources provided.[129] Thus, in an interview in 1989 a Zambian diplomat claimed that the Frontline alliance merely tried to "enhance " the OAU and did not work "on its own". While Frontline reports on Southern Africa considerably influenced its policy decisions, they did not preclude contributions by other member states.[130]

---

124   See Johnson and Martin, *Destructive Engagement* and Ohlson, 'Strategic Confrontation' (see n. 49).

125   Mozambique's action was basically justified by a reference to *force majeure*. See *Africa Research Bulletin* (PSC), 1984, pp 7164 and 7431. Also *Le Soleil* (Senegal), 3-4/3/84 (article). On South Africa's violation of the accord D. Martin and Ph. Johnson, 'Mozambique: To Nkomati and Beyond', in Johnson and Martin, *Destructive Engagement*, pp 1-41.

126   Oye, 'Explaining Cooperation Under Anarchy', p 3.

127   See on the Committee section 6.3.

128   AHG/Res.84 (XIV).

129   Foltz and Widner, 'OAU and Southern African Liberation', pp 254-260. Also f.i. O. Arikpo, 'Nigeria and the OAU', in *Nigerian Journal of International Affairs*, 1975, no. 1, pp 1-11 and O. Aluko, 'Nigeria, Namibia and Southern Africa', in Aluko and Shaw, *Southern Africa*, ch. 3.

130   Interview with David Mainza, Addis Ababa, 28/9/89, in response to the deliberately suggestive question whether the alliance had not taken over the OAU's role.

Having shown why and how the Frontline alliance emerged and acted as the OAU's executive, an important question to be asked is how its leadership must be characterized. One may contend that Frontline leadership represented one of the rare instances of benevolent hegemony by a coalition. This coalition was made up of the right actors as they commanded sufficient political-military influence to work effectively towards realization of black majority rule.[131] They were prepared to provide the collective good of decolonization while bearing a disproportionate share of its costs. Following the arguments of hegemonic stability theory, however, their interest in doing so would at least have been influenced by the expectation that they could seize enough of this good in the form of friendly ties with a future neighbouring African regime.[132] Provided the Frontline states operated in a subtle manner their leadership was afforded some legitimacy by other member states. However, this consensual aspect probably constituted acquiescence, rather than genuine consent,[133] in their domination of OAU Southern Africa policy. Thus, some members resented the fact that they pressed the OAU in giving the PF exclusive recognition. Moreover, it was never easy for the Frontline states to force their client guerrilla's to work together.[134] Yet, one may argue that this acquiescence was sufficient to constitute a form of benevolent hegemony as hegemonic rule allows for varying degrees of legitimacy.[135] The Frontline alliance did certainly not amount to a dominant coalition: while it was able to implement the liberation objective, it could not enforce member state compliance with sanctions or the financial commitments to the Liberation Committee.[136]

The OAU institutionalized the emergence of its Frontline executive by establishing, in 1986, the "Ad Hoc Standing Committee of Heads of State and Government on the Question of Southern Africa", which had to monitor all developments in the area. It was composed of the current and outgoing Assembly chairmen, the chairmen of liberation movements, the heads of state of Nigeria and the Frontline countries, as well as four radical member states, namely Algeria, Ethiopia, Cape Verde and Congo-Brazzaville.[137]

The successful outcome of the struggle in Rhodesia, which became independent as Zimbabwe under a black majority government (1980), legitimized the domination of policy by the Frontline states. The course of this struggle has been recounted elsewhere. Suffice it to say that it was the activities of nationalist guerrilla's, which began in earnest only after 1972, that were decisive in bringing down the white minority regime. The war of the Patriotic Front, whose ZANU component was the most powerful force, was waged in close collaboration with the Frontline states, most notably Mozambique. The military, economic and diplomatic efforts of the Frontline states were therefore the secondary cause — although closely related to the first one — that contributed towards the demise of the

131   Foltz and Widner, 'OAU and Southern African Liberation'.
132   Snidal, 'Limits of Hegemonic Stability Theory', pp 581 and 589.
133   On this distinction J.C. Scott, *Domination and the Arts of Resistance: Hidden Transcripts* (New Haven and London, 1990).
134   See *Africa Research Bulletin* (PSC), 1977, pp 4310 and 4487 and Martin and Johnson, *Struggle for Zimbabwe*.
135   See W.L. Adamson, *Hegemony and Revolution: A Study of Antonio Gramsi's Political and Cultural Theory* (Berkeley, Los Angeles and London, 1980), ch. 6.
136   See also section 6.3.
137   AHG/Dec.1 (XXII).

Rhodesian regime. OAU diplomacy needs to be seen as a background factor.[138]

The OAU hardly played any role in the run-up to the peace accord in Namibia, although the basis on which the conflict was settled generally conformed to the position that the Organization had held all along.[139] Namibia always was a UN responsibility. Its accession to independence under the nationalist government of SWAPO (1990) was the result of a complex of factors, such as South African military setbacks in Angola, a worsening economic and political situation in Namibia and South Africa itself, continuing pressures of the Frontline states and Western governments, as well as the end of the Cold War.[140] The OAU's diplomatic role was nearly fully irrelevant with regard to developments that brought an end, in April 1994, to the apartheid regime in South Africa. However, the success of the Frontline alliance was also less obvious with regard to developments in Namibia and South Africa than it had been in the struggle for Zimbabwe.

OAU recognition policy

While OAU diplomacy was only of secondary importance in the struggle for African majority rule, the Frontline states were instrumental in using to the full one of its most important weapons, *i.e.* its policy of recognition. If, in the eyes of the Pan-African organization, a territory had been liberated from colonialism or white minority rule and had acceded to independence under a genuinely African majority-led government, the country would be admitted as an "independent sovereign African state"[141] to the OAU. The granting of OAU membership acted in this way as a definitive conclusion that decolonization had taken place and that its new government was, in terms of inter-African relations, politically legitimate. This would open the door to global interaction, including UN membership. This procedure was of special significance when the outcome of the struggle was still muddy or unclear, *i.e.* where there was suspicion that a government was still controlled by the white minority or there were rival contenders for governmental status.[142]

Thus, the Organization refused to grant recognition to the "internal settlements" in Rhodesia and Namibia, which white Rhodesians and South Africa introduced in the late 1970s in an attempt to forestall a governmental take-over by SWAPO and the PF. In the Rhodesian case, for example, this internal settlement involved the establishment, after elections by universal suffrage, of an African-dominated cabinet, which did not really end minority rule as effective power remained in white hands.[143] In a slightly different vein,

---

138 See f.i. Martin and Johnson, *Struggle For Zimbabwe* and Stedman, *Peacemaking in Civil War*, ch. 5.

139 As aptly observed by G.W. Shepherd, 'The OAU and African Collective Security in the Post Cold War Era: An Editorial', in *Africa Today*, 1988, nos. 3 & 4, pp 3-6.

140 See for more detailed treatment B. Wood, 'Preventing the Vacuum: Determinants of the Namibia Settlement', in *Journal of Southern African Studies*, 1991, pp 742-769. See for Namibia's admission to the OAU also *The Namibian*, 6/7/90 (article).

141 Arts. 4 and 28 Charter.

142 See on the merely declaratory effect of the recognition of *states* under international law, f.i. I. Brownlie, *Principles of Public International Law* (Oxford, 1979), ch. V.

143 In Rhodesia it concerned the settlement scheme of 1978-79 and in Namibia the Turnhalle constitutional agreement. See R.J. Alperin, 'The Distribution of Power and the (June, 1979) Zimbabwe Rhodesia Constitution', in *Journal of Southern African Affairs*, 1980, pp 41-54 and on

the OAU refused to recognize South Africa's homelands or bantustans, some of which supposedly acceded to independence. While it was obvious that white South Africans were fully in control of this "independence", the OAU rejected it on the basis of the principle of territorial integrity as enunciated in art. 3.3 of the Charter.[144] In this way, the OAU managed to do serious harm to the policies of white minority regimes, especially because it could, via the UN African Group, thwart any attempt to gain international recognition. It was also made clear to all OAU members themselves not to violate consensus on this point.[145] The significance of this background role cannot be gainsaid.

Admittedly, OAU procedures of recognition of governments are, as in international politics generally, relatively vague. In the case of the Southern African territories, there were no explicit guidelines for deciding what exactly constitutes "African majority rule". Yet, it is obvious that the main criteria were, at the date of admission to OAU membership, universal suffrage and control by the resultant African-dominated regime of the government apparatus. Thus, suggestions by some members to admit South Africa in 1992 came to naught, as events at the time showed that whites still kept hold of power.[146]

Naturally, such criteria are subject to political interpretation. For example, most members, including the Frontline states, had an important stake in corroborating the outcome of South Africa's first genuinely general elections.[147] This can be gleaned from the fact that by November 1993 nearly thirty states had already established, at varying levels of formality, diplomatic ties with Pretoria.[148] Nevertheless, in terms of OAU objectives the final admission of South Africa under the interim administration headed by Nelson Mandela[149] formed the logical conclusion to its Southern Africa strategy.

Evaluation

As this section was concerned with the OAU's diplomatic action, its contribution to Africa's decolonization is to some extent understated. Part of this contribution was made through its encouragement of guerrilla activities, which is discussed in the next section. Still, it is clear that the impact of OAU diplomacy on developments in Southern Africa was limited. This was due in part to its inability to make sanctions effective. As the context in which it operated was characterized by a great number of actors, absence of one dominant hegemon and patterns of external dependence strongly impinging on it, implementation of policy was structurally impeded. Thus, when the struggle against white minority regimes became harder, it was rendered increasingly irrelevant.

Turnhalle *Africa Contemporary Record*, 1976-77, B767-70; 1977-78, B843-4; and 1978-79, B826-7. On their rejection by the OAU CM/Res.679 (XXXI); CM/Res.680 (XXXI); CM/Res.719 (XXXIII); CM/Res.720 (XXXIII); and CM/Res.788 (XXXV).

144 See CM/Res.492 (XXVII) and CM/Res.854 (XXXVII).

145 See CM/Res.492 (XXVII).

146 See *Le Soleil* (Senegal), 6/6/91, 7/6/91 and 30/6/92 and *Weekly Mail* (South Africa), 3-9/7/92 (all articles).

147 April 1994.

148 *Jeune Afrique*, 25/11-1/12/93. For ANC criticism *Le Soleil* (Senegal), 27/6-28/6/92 (article). Recognition of governments is a prerogative of individual members. Admission to the OAU is a collective act. See art. 28 Charter and section 6.4.

149 South Africa was admitted as the OAU's 53rd member state on 23/5/94. *Africa Research Bulletin* (PSC), 1994, p 11426.

For its diplomacy to be effective it needed a smaller group of actors, which it found in the Frontline alliance. Although the OAU did not have much choice but to accept its executive role, it responded to this development with flexibility and pragmatism. Moreover, in spite of economic interaction with the white south and some violations of its anti-dialogue stance, it managed to uphold a high degree of diplomatic isolation of the white minority regimes. This taboo on normal, open interaction was reinforced by one of its most powerful weapons, namely its policy of recognition.

6.3 "No alternative but the use of force":[150] the OAU and the armed struggle

Outline of the Liberation Committee
The Liberation Committee always articulated a more militant, activist posture with regard to the struggle against colonialism and apartheid than the policy organs. During the OAU's founding conference it was already clear to many states, notably the radical ones, that angry words and sanctions would not be enough to break the obstinacy of the white supremacists. This contention was confirmed, at least in militant eyes, by the limited results of the diplomatic struggle during the OAU's first decade. It was also implicitly articulated by the Secretary-General himself.[151]

The Liberation Committee, which was finally abolished at a meeting in Arusha on 15 August 1994,[152] found its origins in the resolution on decolonization adopted in Addis Ababa in 1963.[153] Officially known as the "Co-ordinating Committee for the Liberation of Africa", it had its headquarters in Dar-es-Salaam. Its aim was to harmonize the assistance given by African states to liberation movements and to manage the "Special Fund" set up for that purpose. The armed struggle in Southern Africa formed its major preoccupation. Yet, it was also involved, by way of financial assistance, mediation efforts and negotiations, in the more peaceful struggles for independence, such as in the High Commission territories and Djibouti.[154] As an organ of limited composition, it only had nine members at the start. However, it steadily expanded so that by the 1980s membership had risen to 21.[155] Membership was not only determined by the requirement of equitable geographical representation, but also by the proximity of the member state to dependent territories, its material means and its experience in combat. Member state delegations to Committee sessions had to comprise at least one military officer.[156]

By the early 1980s the Liberation Committee possessed two standing, plenary

---

150   *OAU Military Bulletin: A Periodical Review of the Military Activities of African Nationalist Movements*, issue no. 1, June 1970, p 4 (Ex. Secr., Liberation Committee: Dar-es-Salaam).
151   CM/270 (Part 1): Report of the SG, Feb.-Aug. 1969, p 24.
152   See *Africa Research Bulletin* (PSC), 1994, p 11535.
153   See n. 11
154   See Amate, *Inside the OAU*, ch. 10 and Ph. Oberlé and P. Hugot, *Histoire de Djibouti: des origines à la république* (Paris and Dakar, 1985), pp 272-280.
155   They were: Algeria, Angola, Cameroon, Congo-Br., Egypt, Ethiopia, Ghana, Guinea, Guinea-Bissau, Liberia, Libya, Mauritania, Morocco, Mozambique, Nigeria, Uganda, Senegal, Somalia, Tanzania, Zaire and Zambia. See art. 1 Rules of Procedure of the Liberation Committee.
156   See f.i. *Révolution Africaine* (Algeria), 18-24/5/73 (article) and art. 4.2 Rules of Procedure.

committees, made up of member states. The "Standing Committee on Political Affairs, Information and Defence" had to collect and publicize information on the armed struggle, "demoralize the enemy" with propaganda[157] and recommend on matters of general policy and requests for material assistance submitted by liberation movements. The "Standing Committee on Administration and Finance" had to authorize disbursement of financial and material aid as proposed by the Executive Secretary.[158]

This functionary headed the Liberation Committee's Executive Secretariat, which had regional offices located closer to the areas of combat. One was housed until 1974 in Conakry and another in Lusaka, which was opened in 1971. Later on, regional offices were established in Luanda (1978) and Maputo (1977), but by the early 1990s all had been closed down.[159] As a rule, the Executive Secretary was nominated by the Tanzanian government. He was seconded by two Assistant Executive Secretaries elected by the Committee, on a rotation basis, from among Africa's regions. Executive Secretary's tasks involved preparation of meetings; co-ordination of activities of Standing Committees and liberations movements; co-ordination of implementation of the Liberation Committee's decisions with the Secretary-General and member states; and drafting of reports to the Council of Ministers.[160]

The Liberation Committee in the OAU

The position of the Liberation Committee within the OAU's structure at first led to tensions with the General Secretariat in Addis Ababa. As shown below, the organ achieved some autonomy vis-à-vis the rest of the OAU. However, the independent line that was taken by the Executive Secretary sometimes put the Secretary-General in Addis in an awkward position. This led to attempts by the latter to establish control over activities in Dar es Salaam. During the second half of the 1960s the SG managed to establish administrative supervision over the Executive Secretariat by taking control of its organizational expenses and personnel issues.[161] Yet, some rivalry remained, as during the 1970s the SG made an attempt to limit the Executive Secretariat's autonomy even further. This led to angry exchanges with the Tanzanians, who managed to protect the Executive Secretary's institutional autonomy from further encroachments.[162]

In matters of *policy* the Liberation Committee was accountable to Council and Assembly.[163] However, it managed to retain some freedom of action with regard to these organs as well. Never actually failing to meet, it adopted an active, forceful posture. It often took concrete action to encourage the armed struggle, in spite of its small budget, the less than constructive attitude of members in the policy organs, the disunity among liberation movements and the power of white minority regimes. As in the case of the

---

157   See f.i. the *OAU Military Bulletin* quoted in note 150.
158   Art. 34 Rules of Procedure.
159   Letter by J.B. Thundu, Chief of Press Section, General Secretariat, Addis Ababa, to author, 27 July 1993. Also CM/Res.256 (XVII); CM/Dec.100 (XIV); Amate, *Inside the OAU*, p 234; and Cervenka, *Unfinished Quest*, p 51.
160   Arts. 3, 5, 6 and 7-9 Functions and Regulations of the Executive Secretariat.
161   See AHG/Res.7 (I); *Africa Research Bulletin* (PSC), 1966, p 652; Amate, *Inside the OAU*, pp 222-231; and Functions and Regulations of the Executive Secretariat, arts. 1, 11 and 12.
162   See *Daily News* (Tanzania), 22/5/73 (article) and 28/5/73.
163   See arts. 3.3 and 3.6, Rules of Procedure.

Frontline alliance it bore out the game theoretical contention that a context of fewer actors is more conducive to co-operation. Policy co-ordination becomes easier and less costly in terms of the efforts that actors must make to negotiate a transaction and gather necessary information.[164] This means that such a group of actors can also move more swiftly.

While its structural context goes some way to explain how the Committee could function differently from the OAU as a whole, it was its geographical location, the nature of its mandate and the involvement of particular members that explain *why* it adopted an activist posture and achieved some autonomy vis-à-vis the policy organs. With its headquarters in Tanzania the Committee was both closer to the area of combat and some distance away from the intrigues in Addis. Its activism was enhanced by the determination of its Executive Secretaries, some of whom were military officers.[165] The Committee's relative autonomy was justified with a reference to the need for secrecy, so as not to leak information to the enemy or endanger its functioning. The close interest that the Frontline states, notably Tanzania, and many radical members took in Committee proceedings provided some protection against interference by the plenary organs.[166]

Thus, by the early 1980s four Frontline states[167] were members of the Committee. Radical members were, as a category, also proportionally better represented in the Liberation Committee than in the policy organs. Until 1965 at least four out of nine members were former Casablanca participants or, in the case of Tanzania, articulated radical ideas on foreign policy.[168] By the 1980s the Committee's 21 members included nine radicals, besides Nigeria and Zambia, two countries with strong views on decolonization.[169]

Nevertheless, while the Committee enjoyed some autonomy vis-à-vis the generality of member states, both its structural position and policy choices led to difficulties with OAU members. Its structural problems are discussed in the remainder of this section, while those on policy are analysed in subsequent sections. The problems concerning its structural position were in essence part of a free rider dilemma. Southern Africa's liberation would contribute, it was hoped, to an objective shared by *all* members, *i.e.* a reinforcement of international status and influence. Yet, whatever contribution other members would care to make, it was obvious that the Frontline states and a few radical countries would continue to make great efforts to eradicate colonialism anyway. The liberation effort thus formed a public good as its institutionalized pursuit was guaranteed, whether or not other members paid, or paid less, for its realization.

---

164   See Oye, 'Explaining Cooperation Under Anarchy', pp 19-22.
165   A Tanzanian perception of this functionary in *Daily News*, 28/5/73.
166   Amate, *Inside the OAU*, 282 and Cervenka, *Unfinished Quest*, pp 62-3. See for its perception as an activist body also *The Standard* (Tanzania), 20/8/69 and 30/8/69.
167   Zambia, Tanzania, Mozambique and Angola.
168   See resolution on decolonization, par. 11.
169   See *Révolution Africaine* (Algeria), 18-24/5/73 (article) and Rules of Procedure, art. 1.

This hardly encouraged members situated far from the battle-field to take on financial burdens *in addition to* the collective diplomacy discussed in the previous section. As shown below, the Special Fund continually suffered from huge arrears in payments. In Olson's perspective these members were, while desirous of the liberation objective as such, merely acting rationally by contributing less[170] in a context of structural impediments that stood in the way of adequate co-ordination of political will to achieve optimal results. Many member states tried to justify their free rider behaviour by criticizing the Committee's financial and administrative record. The Tanzanians condemned these and other criticisms as "camouflage evasions of responsibilities".[171] This qualification seemed to be partially validated by the fact that, after financial and administrative reforms, accusations about irregularities disappeared but arrears in contributions did not.[172]

Still, the free rider dilemma does not entirely explain these problems, as the Liberation Committee did not constitute a genuinely public good. Because many OAU members were barred from (full) participation in its functioning — even though they had to contribute towards its funds — and the Committee shrouded its operations in secrecy, it lacked one of public goods' major criteria, *i.e.* non-excludability. However, in the context of egalitarianism that characterizes interaction in the OAU this deficiency only strengthened free rider behaviour. It also led to efforts to limit the Committee's exclusiveness. Thus, in response to distrust and resentment of member states, Committee membership was progressively expanded. In 1967 it was decided to allow every country that was not a Committee member to attend as observer.[173]

Naturally, this did not contribute towards the organ's resolution, as did a decision to distribute reports to all OAU members. Free circulation of documents implied that sensitive information could fall into the hands of target regimes — assuming these had difficulty in finding out about Committee secrets in the first place. The policy organs allowed the Committee to "reserve the right ... not to circulate documents to those Member States who [had] diplomatic relations with Portugal and the regimes of Pretoria and Salisbury".[174] However, this hardly decreased their distribution. The Committee therefore tried to withhold certain documentation from observers, even the Secretary-General himself, and reserved the right to hold closed sessions — presumably without the presence of non-members. Yet, by 1976 copies of documents were distributed to all observers.[175]

The Committee and liberation movements
Committee policy was characterized by a strong preference for the more active and radically inclined liberation movements. This sometimes led to tensions with the more

---

170   See M. Olson, *The Logic of Collective Action: Public Goods and the Theory of Groups* (Cambridge, Mass., 1965).
171   *Daily News*, 25/5/73 (article).
172   Amate, *Inside the OAU*, p 236.
173   Cervenka, *Unfinished Quest*, p 46. See also art. 4.3 Rules of Procedure on observer status of OAU members.
174   CM/Res.175 (XII).
175   See art. 4 Rules of Procedure and Amate, *Inside the OAU*, pp 231 and 234.

moderate and conservative member states. Thus, the Committee principally backed the PAIGC in Guinea-Bissau, FRELIMO in Mozambique, SWAPO in Namibia and the South African ANC and PAC, to the detriment of less active groupings.[176] During the 1970s, the OAU organ strongly supported the more active guerrilla forces in Rhodesia. While the policy organs failed to reach a consensus on whether or not to support POLISARIO, the Committee gave it its whole-hearted (political) backing, despite protests from its Moroccan and Mauritanian members. It also supported the PLO in its struggle against Israel.[177] Even in the case of Angola the Committee took a radical line: here it had initially backed the FNLA of Holden Roberto. FNLA activity against the Portuguese, however, diminished with the years.[178] The Committee therefore later threw its weight behind the more active MPLA. Although it recommended the withdrawal of the OAU's premature recognition of the FNLA's government-in-exile (the "GRAE"), the policy organs found it hard to take a firm stand because of the support that the FNLA received from Zaire.[179]

Most of the liberation movements supported by the Committee possessed a radical posture in terms of nationalist ideology, ideas on socio-economic organization and international alignments. Several of them, such as the MPLA, PAIGC and FRELIMO, articulated a version of Marxist ideology. However, if there was more than one grouping claiming to be the nucleus of a country's liberation movement, the differences between them had also much to do with other features. For example, guerrilla movements could be distinguished by the social background of their leadership and their principal ethnic or regional following. Frequently, their conflicts involved cut-throat competition for state power and the clashing of dominant personalities.[180] Yet, at the level of inter-African politics their international alignments and ideas on nationalism and socio-economic organization were of special relevance. These were of influence, although only partially, on the decision of neighbouring states which grouping to assist. They were also partly related to patterns of extra-African support and the backing by other OAU members.

Despite Committee support for certain liberation movements, there were some conflicts of interests between these recipients of aid on the one hand and the Liberation Committee, and the OAU generally, on the other. The mere transformation of nationalist movements into state elites had created new interests and perceptions and new forms of behaviour and linkages that set them, as a whole, apart from groupings that had yet to attain similar status.[181] This became quickly apparent through the difference in prerogatives in OAU cadres. The rights of liberation movements were, at least during the first decade, poorly regulated. Thus, at the Assembly session in Rabat (1972) Amilcar

---

176   Woronoff, *Organizing African Unity*, ch. 4 (n. 59).

177   *Africa Research Bulletin* (PSC), 1976, pp 3888 and 4047 and AHG/Res.75 (XII) and AHG/Res.81 (XIII).

178   J.P. Cosse and J. Sanchez, *Angola: le prix de la liberté* (Paris, 1976), pp 56-59. For circumstances of this decision J. Marcum, *The Angolan Revolution*, vl. 2: *Exile Politics and Guerrilla Warfare 1962-1976* (Cambridge, Mass., 1978), pp 93-99.

179   See f.i. CM/Res.255/Rev.1 (XVII) and Amate, *Inside the OAU*, pp 247-248.

180   A survey in R. Gibson, *African Liberation Movements: Contemporary Struggles Against White Minority Rule* (London, 1972).

181   D.E. Apter and J.S. Coleman, 'Pan-Africanism or Nationalism in Africa', in American Society of African Culture (ed), *Pan-Africanism Reconsidered* (Berkeley and Los Angeles, 1962), p 103 ff.

Cabral of the PAIGC said that, although liberation movements did not pretend to be equal to the heads of state, they were entitled to their respect. He demanded that no one should take decisions in their place.[182]

At first, liberation movements could only present petitions to the Committee, but were not allowed to participate in its sessions. It took until 1972 before they could attend as observers, although at first they did not gain access to all documentation.[183] Moreover, the Liberation Committee wished to exert financial control over the way in which movements spent its grants, something the latter were unwilling or unable to concede. Secrecy was not the greatest Committee virtue and the amounts of money involved were not very large anyway.[184] Guerrilla leaders and supporting states sometimes also clashed over tactics and strategy. Member states, especially during the difficult 1960s, could express dissatisfaction with the lack of progress and military activity that some, like FNLA or ZAPU, exhibited.[185] They also criticized the disunity in their ranks. After all,

> One thing money can't do is to buy the will of a people. The Organisation of African Unity can spend millions on the Liberation Movements but can achieve very little if the people in the countries seeking liberation do not show the will to fight. Another point is that the continued division in most of the Liberation Movements will not help the struggles. It is therefore important that the people so dominated should show to the OAU and the world at large that they are prepared to make the necessary sacrifices in human lives and hardships ... .[186]

This uncharitable critique was a bit unfair and one-sided, for as shown below OAU grants never reached the millions it alluded to. Thus, appeals were often made for an increase in assistance. For example, in 1973 the PAIGC noted that the Committee had "regrettably" not yet been able to satisfy its needs.[187] Moreover, the bureaucratic intricacies of OAU decision-making sharply conflicted with the acute needs of liberation movements. Early on they already pleaded that "speed", rather than "delays" and "red tape", should characterize OAU efforts.[188]

Assistance of the Liberation Committee

The circumstances under which the Committee executed its mandate were therefore extremely difficult. It was under constant pressure from different quarters to change course, persist in policies, cut aid or increase it. Even though the administrative costs of the Executive Secretariat were in 1969 transferred to the General Secretariat,[189] the most

---

182   See Cabral's speech in *l'Opinion* (Morocco), 17/6/72.
183   See CM/Res.271 (XIX); art. 4.4 Rules of Procedure; *Daily News* (Tanzania), 17/6/72 (article); Amate, *Inside the OAU*, pp 232-234; and Wolfers, *Politics*, p 187 (n. 98).
184   Amate, *Inside the OAU*, pp 291-292.
185   See f.i. the Committee's criticism of ZAPU in Martin and Johnson, *Struggle for Zimbabwe*, p 223 (n. 94) and of FNLA in *Africa Research Bulletin* (PSC), 1968, p 971.
186   *Daily News* (Sierra Leone), 17/6/72.
187   See interviews with PAIGC and FNLA officials in *l'Essor* (Mali), 16-17/6/73.
188   Statement by the Liberation Movements to the Assembly of Heads of State and Government of the Organisation for [*sic*] African Unity, held in Algiers, September 1968, p 11.
189   Amate, *Inside the OAU*, p 236.

serious bottleneck constituted the Committee's finances.[190] Initially, the Special Fund stood at a mere 700,000 pound sterling. By 1973, it had only risen to some 1.4 million pounds or 3.3 million US dollars. It remained stagnant at that level until well into the 1980s and decreased to some 3.1 million dollars for the financial year 1987-1988.[191] Its purchasing power steadily diminished as a result of inflationary pressures, although its relative size increased somewhat, as the number of liberation movements supported by the OAU sharply dropped after 1975-1980.

Official figures, however, do not take account of arrears. In 1970, these totalled some two million dollars. By 1978 they had risen to twelve million and they still stood at 11.9 million in 1987.[192] Almost all countries were at one time or another in arrears, whether they were full members of the Committee or not. Only some members, such as Algeria, Tanzania and Zambia, usually paid up in full or contributed more than their share. By 1988, just thirteen OAU members had no arrears or had (temporarily) contributed more than their official dues. These included several radical countries, three Frontline states and Nigeria.[193] Thus, the Committee's functioning depended on the political will of a minority of states.[194] Yet, as the Frontline alliance this group did not constitute a dominant coalition, as it lacked sufficient leverage to make others pay. Its slice of the Committee budget was not big enough to refer to the group's contributions as a form of benevolent hegemony either.[195]

However, the Committee's financial contributions to the armed struggle were dwarfed by the value of direct assistance of African states. They were equally insignificant when compared to the military hardware and humanitarian assistance of the Eastern bloc and a few Western countries respectively. In the years 1967 to 1969, for instance, the largest Committee grant (all in US$) was given to FRELIMO and totalled 264,000 The PAIGC was promised 216,000 the Angolan organizations 180,000 and the Zimbabwean ones 30,000 Yet, the amounts that were actually paid out were much lower or very slow in coming.[196] By contrast, Swedish humanitarian aid to the movements in Mozambique, Angola and Guinea-Bissau amounted to some three million US dollars in

---

190   Voluntary at first, the Assembly decided in 1964 to make contributions for the coming year compulsory. See AHG/Res.7 (I). Thereafter it was unclear whether they were obligatory, though arguments used to make members pay suggest this. See Amate, *Inside the OAU*, pp 239-40 and CM/1492 (XLVIII): Report of the 50th Ordinary Session of the OAU Co-ordinating Committee for the Liberation of Africa to the 48th Ordinary Session of the Council of Ministers, 19-24 May 1988 (excerpts in *Africa Contemporary Record*, 1988-89, C25-C33; hereinafter as CM/1492 (XLVIII): Report of the 50th Session of the Liberation Committee, 1988).

191   Amate, *Inside the OAU*, pp 221 and 235 and CM/1492 (XLVIII): Report of the 50th Session of the Liberation Committee, 1988).

192   All US $. *Africa Research Bulletin* (PSC), 1970, p 1692; Amate, *Inside the OAU*, p 238-239; and the list in CM/1492 (XLVIII): Report of the 50th Session of the Liberation Committee, 1988.

193   See the statistics in F. Ansprenger, *Die Befreiungspolitik der Organisation für Afrikanische Einheit (OAU) 1963 bis 1975* (Grünewald, 1975), pp 217-221 and CM/1492 (XLVIII): Report of the 50th Session of the Liberation Committee, 1988.

194   Cervenka, *Unfinished Quest*, p 63; Amate, *Inside the OAU*, pp 239-240; and CM/1492 (XLVIII): Report of the 50th Session of the Liberation Committee, 1988.

195   Those that had paid, or paid more, at the 1988 datum represented some 35% of the total. See CM/1492 (XLVIII): Report of the 50th Session of the Liberation Committee, 1988.

196   El-Khawas, 'Southern Africa', p 30 (n. 120) and E.J. Kisanga, 'The Organization of African Unity (OAU) and the Liberation Struggle in Southern Africa', in *Taamuli*, 1977, no. 2, p 39.

the period 1971-1973, *i.e.* nearly an entire annual Committee budget.[197] According to American (rather speculative) sources, the value of Soviet arms shipments to the MPLA (1960-1974) was around 27 million pound sterling.[198] It was estimated on the basis of SIPRI figures that, during the struggle for independence, thirty to fourty per cent of military resources given[199] to movements in the Lusophone territories came from the Soviet bloc.[200]

The value of direct African aid to liberation movements, though of crucial import, is more difficult to estimate. Apart from some North African arms shipments, most of this aid consisted of the provision by Frontline states of training facilities, base camps, sanctuaries for refugees, access to combat zones and assistance in procurement of hardware from non-African sources.[201] The costs of this to the Frontline countries were enormous. By 1976 the costs of the Rhodesian sanctions to the economy of Zambia totalled well over 400 million pound sterling.[202] The damage inflicted by South Africa's total war strategy against Mozambique, in retaliation of its support for the South African ANC and the guerrilla war in Zimbabwe, seemed beyond comprehension. Its RENAMO proxies murdered thousands of people and inflicted untold suffering through the abduction, maiming and starvation of civilians. Apart from the destruction of the country's infrastructure, the deliberate disruption of Mozambique's trade flows totalled, by 1983, some four billion US dollars.[203]

Yet, the assistance of the Liberation Committee was not without significance. Part of its value lay in its multilateral character, which in theory made dependence on, and direct influence of, a donor country more difficult. These aid flows were also less likely to lead to a backlash than direct assistance from extra-African powers.[204] Moreover, aid and recognition by the OAU had the effect of legitimizing the armed struggle and the bilateral assistance from donor countries in and outside Africa. They also gave liberation movements access to international diplomatic channels such as the UN. Thus, all liberation movements wished to apply for OAU support, however insignificant its financial grants were.[205]

In this respect, it should be noted that the Liberation Committee embarked, during the 1970s, on various international goodwill missions to ask non-African donors for assistance. This resulted in numerous donations, financial and material, to its clients.[206] It also attempted to raise funds from private sources in member states, which resulted in the

---

197 Henriksen, *Revolution and Counterrevolution*, p 192 (n. 103).

198 C. Legum and T. Hodges, *After Angola: The War over Southern Africa* (London, 1976), p 19.

199 The argument here concerns total aid levels irrespective of the conditions attached.

200 Henriksen, *Revolution and Counterrevolution*, p 268 n. 91.

201 P.M. Whitaker, 'Arms and the Nationalists', in *Africa Report*, May 1970, pp 12-13.

202 Martin and Johnson, *Struggle for Zimbabwe*, pp 132 and 286.

203 Martin and Johnson, 'To Nkomati and Beyond', (n. 125), pp 29-31.

204 Foltz and Widner, 'OAU and Southern African Liberation', p 263 (n. 107) and f.i. Whitaker, 'Arms and the Nationalists', p 14.

205 See Amate, *Inside the OAU*, p 283 and the example of the FNLA's attendance of the Assembly summit in 1973 in *l'Essor* (Mali), 16-17/5/73.

206 See the Committee's 'Accra Declaration on the New Strategy for the Liberation of Africa', 8-13 January 1973, par. 21-24 (text in Ansprenger, *Befreiungspolitik*, pp 209-213) and for the results of these missions Amate, *Inside the OAU*, pp 297-298.

donation of small amounts of money. As minute and pathetic as these gestures might seem,[207] the powerful symbolism involved enhanced the legitimacy of the armed struggle.

Aid and recognition criteria

Technically, if a liberation movement was recognized by the OAU, it was entitled to observer status in some of the Organization's organs, as well as financial and material assistance by the Liberation Committee.[208] However, no African state was powerful enough to force its criteria or choice of clients on Council and Assembly. OAU recognition policy was therefore chaotic and, as in international relations generally, heavily influenced by expediency. Recognition policy varied, its criteria were hazy and its consequences were uncertain: the Committee, which usually moved more swiftly, sometimes granted assistance to movements not formally recognized by the policy organs, while it withheld aid from some with official OAU status. As numerous organizations at one time or another enjoyed varying degrees of recognition or support, it is impossible to mention them all. The most important ones, however, were FRELIMO, PAIGC, MPLA, FNLA, SWAPO, ANC, PAC, ZANU and ZAPU.[209]

In principle, the OAU did not favour governments-in-exile, which were sometimes established by liberation movements to strengthen their diplomatic position. While Africa's state elites may have wished to distinguish themselves from non-governmental groups, recognition of governments-in-exile could also erode the value attributed to state sovereignty. This and the status of state elites depended, in the final analysis, on the efficacy of control that governments exerted over their population, even if this fell short of the *étatiste* dominion established in other parts of the world. So in the case of liberation movements it was actual guerrilla operations and popular support that were the *sine qua non* for success. Pan-African diplomatic backing was of secondary importance and was only useful if these conditions were fulfilled. Thus, the Liberation Committee held the practical view that the OAU should strive for governments that were formed by "the people" inside the dependent territory. This presumably referred to movements that actually enjoyed support on the ground and were engaged in guerrilla activity.[210]

The risk that inhered in recognition of governments-in-exile was that, if it did not correspond (anymore) with the actual situation on the ground, as happened in the case of the FNLA, it not only did not help, but could also have negative consequences for the struggle and the OAU. It might, in the words of the Council, "lead some liberation movements to complacency" and diminish "their dynamism and vigor".[211] As recognition entailed the right to participation in, or even admission to, the OAU and this might be difficult to reverse if these "governments" did not achieve independence or lost power to a rival grouping, their defeat would pose an institutional problem for the OAU itself. As shown in the next section, the difficulty to remove the FNLA's status was to pale into insignificance when compared to the problems the OAU encountered later over the

207 For example, in 1965 the National Union of Tanganyikan Workers donated 2,000 pounds sterling. *Africa Research Bulletin* (PSC), 1965, p 267.
208 See Cervenka, *Unfinished Quest*, p 47.
209 See Wolfers, *Politics*, pp 188-189.
210 *Africa Research Bulletin* (PSC), 1968, p 971.
211 CM/Res.136 (X). Also *Daily News* (Tanzania), 25/5/73 (article).

Western Sahara. There was only one other case in which the OAU did not abide by its principle. Thus, in November 1973 it admitted the PAIGC's government of Guinea-Bissau. This did not create problems as the PAIGC was already firmly in control of the territory.[212]

The biggest problem was what to do if there was more than one group in the same territory claiming to be engaged in the armed struggle. In such cases, the Liberation Committee often sent fact-finding missions to ascertain which movement enjoyed most support and was most active in guerrilla operations. The symbolism of these visits was powerful. It underlined the lack of control exerted by colonial regimes, which in practice always involved one of the Portuguese territories. As these visits were sanctioned by an international organization, they could counter allegations that the activities of liberation movements and African states amounted to "terrorism" and "subversion".[213]

Nevertheless, the Committee experienced enormous difficulties in mediating and choosing between rival claimants, especially in Angola and Rhodesia. A radical posture could not be a formal criterion for support, even if a majority in the Committee favoured the more militant organizations. At first, the Committee decided to call on rival groups to unite in common action fronts, as the OAU's founding conference had done.[214] To this effect, it undertook numerous mediation efforts to end the conflicts between rival movements. If they failed to unite, the Committee threatened to support only one.[215] As this approach had no tangible effect on the rivalry between different groups, the Committee decided in 1966 to accord priority, though not exclusive preference, to organizations engaged in combat against the colonial regime; organizations that established common action fronts; or those whose struggle had been effective for some time or whose victory could positively influence the struggle in adjacent territories.[216]

At least on paper this hardly amounted to any priorities at all. The problem was that the Committee lacked the leverage to force rival groupings to work together. As the stakes were extemely high, namely future state power, liberation movements refused to submit to the leadership of rival groups or merge in one permanent structure. The Committee's meagre aid flows could hardly entice them, especially as most organizations received bilateral assistance from neighbouring countries. These granted support to their favourite group, among others to obtain influence with the government of the future independent state. Thus, the pay-off that could emanate from defection from Committee strategy by directly backing one's client, was infinitely higher than the rewards of compliance.[217] The effectiveness of Committee operations was in this respect limited by the interests and diplomatic manoeuvring of its members. Neighbouring countries would frequently protest against Committee decisions unfavourable to their client. This could lead to a reversal of

---

212   See f.i. Daily News (Tanzania), 21/5/73 (article). Also Ansprenger, *Befreiungspolitik*, pp 60-63.
213   See f.i. CM/Res.51 (IV) and CM/Res.154 (XI) and for a visit to Angola in July 1969, *Zambia Daily Mail*, 15/7/69 (article).
214   See Resolution on decolonization, par. 10 (n. 11).
215   Amate, *Inside the OAU*, p 284.
216   Woronoff, *Organizing African Unity*, p 314.
217   See on this Oye, 'Explaining Cooperation Under Anarchy'. See f.i. for close relations between FNLA and Mobutu's regime, involving family ties, Cosse and Sanchez, *Angola*, pp 56-59 and for close political relations between FRELIMO and Tanzania, W.J. Schneidman, 'FRELIMO's Foreign Policy and the Process of Liberation', in *Africa Today*, 1978, no. 1, p 58.

the decision or the disbursement of token aid.[218]

Even if it became clear that organizations, such as the FNLA, were more active in fighting other groups than the colonial government,[219] the effects of a factual analysis confirming this were restricted by the influence that patron states could exert in the Committee or the policy organs. Thus, in some cases during the 1960s the Committee was lured into accepting wishful presentations about client groups as "facts".[220] Under those circumstances, it was extremely hard to withhold support from less effective groups, at least in a formal sense. The policy organs often adopted a less than helpful attitude. They called over and over again on rival groups to form a common front, yet had conceded at the start that decisions on aid grants should take the interests of neighbouring states into account.[221]

However, for the Committee factual military developments were, in the long run, decisive. When, for example, it became obvious that the MPLA was the only movement fighting the Portuguese, Committee aid was increased.[222] In 1973 it decided to earmark the larger part of its resources for the struggle in the Lusophone colonies. It was influenced in this by improved military prospects, notably in Guinea-Bissau and Mozambique, as well as the decision of the Assembly (1972) to increase Special Fund contributions by fifty per cent. It also resolved only to grant recognition and assistance to common front organizations which were "politically and militarily united" and which could provide evidence of effective operations.[223]

In the latter half of the 1970s, the Committee also threw its weight behind the Patriotic Front of Zimbabwe, which represented a temporary merger of ZANU and ZAPU. In this case the Committee benefited from the fact that the Frontline states co-ordinated their policies much better than neighbouring countries had done over Angola. Though conceding leadership to the alliance, Committee aid could be more effective. Between 1977 and 1979 it made financial grants to the PF ranging from half a million to 700,000 US dollars annually. During the last stages of the Zimbabwean war, 500,000 dollars was allocated for the airlifting of guerrilla's from base camps in Tanzania.[224]

---

218   Ansprenger, *Befreiungspolitik*, ch. 4.
219   See Marcum, *The Angolan Revolution*; B. Davidson, *In the Eye of the Storm: Angola's People* (Harmondsworth, 1975); and Cosse and Sanchez, *Angola*.
220   See A. Margarido, 'l'OUA et les territoires sous domination portugaise', in *Revue française d'études politiques africaines*, 1967, no. 22, pp 89-91.
221   See f.i. ECM/Res.10 (V); CM/Res.49 (IV); CM/Res.51 (IV); CM/Res.66 (V); CM/Res.67 (V); CM/Res.96 (VIII); CM/Res.101 (IX); CM/Res.103 (IX); CM/Res.108 (IX); CM/Res.135 (X); CM/Res.137 (X); CM/Res.153 (XI); CM/Res.154 (XI); CM/Res.206 (XIII); CM/Res.210 (XIV); CM/Res.236 (XV); CM/Res.259 (XVIII); CM/Res.299 (XXI); CM/Res.350 (XXIII); and Ansprenger, *Befreiungspolitik*, p 42.
222   Amate, *Inside the OAU*, p 243 ff.
223   Accra Declaration on the New Strategy for the Liberation of Africa, par. 15-16. For a list of disbursed funds Ansprenger, *Befreiungspolitik*, p 72.
224   Amate, *Inside the OAU*, ch. 10 and Cervenka, *Unfinished Quest*, pp 61-62.

The Liberation Committee: an assessment

The Liberation Committee provided more concreteness and sincerity to the OAU's anti-colonial objectives. Various countries, including relatively poor and small ones far away from the battle-field, *did* provide the Committee with financial resources, however limited. In view of the continent's poverty this remains worthy of note.[225] While its significance lay principally in the realm of symbolism, it was a very powerful one. Committee aid also carried certain practical advantages, such as enhanced legitimacy and improved access to foreign arms supplies and international diplomatic channels.

The Committee managed to maintain an autonomous role vis-à-vis the rest of the Organization. It used its political space with great energy, articulating an activist conception of OAU ideals. Its structural context formed, in this respect, a typical example of actor reduction tactics as formulated in game theory.[226]

Its activist posture to some extent explains perceptions of the OAU by radical member states — many of which accorded high priority to the Committee's operation — as an organization involved in a heroic struggle for the freedom of Africa's peoples. Such perception manifested itself most clearly in graphical form, such as in an Algerian presentation of the OAU as an automatic weapon (see figure 6.2). Yet, direct intervention by member states never was a credible option, even if some militants argued for this. They simply lacked the military clout. Moreover, liberation movements themselves were opposed to it.[227] Intervention by foreign armies would increase dependence on outside forces. The role in the armed struggle of the Committee itself was also of secondary importance. In contrast, the activities of liberation movements and the states situated on the frontline were crucial.

The functioning of the Liberation Committee was seriously hampered by parsimonious resources, unco-operative attitudes of member states and disunity between rival liberation movements. In essence, its financial difficulties and the problems with member states were exemplary of free rider behaviour that was greatly facilitated by the structural impediments of inter-African relations. Just as the Frontline alliance was able, in the Zimbabwean war, to implement the liberation objective but unable to force compliance with sanctions, the Committee's autonomy did not imply sufficient power to make the generality of OAU members adopt a more co-operative attitude. The Committee and its supporters did not constitute a dominant coalition.

However, its difficulties with liberation movements also show that there was no question of benevolent hegemony either. Bilateral assistance from those states that were relatively close to the line of battle (especially Tanzania, Zaire, Congo, Zambia), point to the absence of consent or acquiescence in a Committee monopoly over aid flows. The lack of unity among these states meant insufficient leverage for the Committee over

---

225 See f.i. for a list of actual contributions to the Special Fund (1964-73) Ansprenger, *Befreiungspolitik*, pp 217-221.

226 Oye, 'Explaining Cooperation Under Anarchy', pp 19-22.

227 See f.i. *The Ethiopian Herald*, 6/7/77; *Africa Research Bulletin* (PSC), 1973, p 3007; Ben Bella's speech to the OAU's founding conference in *Proceedings*, vl. 1, sct. 2 (n. 11); and L.T. Kapungu, 'The OAU's Support for the Liberation of Southern Africa', in Y. El-Ayouty (ed), *The Organization of African Unity After Ten Years: Comparative Perspectives* (New York, 1976), pp 144-146.

250

Figure 6.2   The OAU and the Anti-Colonial Struggle: An Algerian Perception

Source: *Révolution Africaine* (Algeria), 18-24 May 1973

liberation movements. As shown in the preceding section, it was only when the Frontline alliance got into operation during the war over Zimbabwe that an effective form of leadership was generated. In this new configuration the Committee played an appendant role. Thus, while it enjoyed some autonomy vis-à-vis the generality of OAU members, it did not — and in fact never had — such freedom of action with regard to the states on the frontline. For example, its Executive Secretariat was not allowed to purchase arms and ammunition itself, but had to leave this to the governments that hosted guerrilla armies.[228]

The Angolan crisis 1975-1976

If the significance of the Liberation Committee to the armed struggle was rather limited, the remainder of this section will show how OAU influence could be practically reduced to nill by the introduction of superpower intervention. The crisis that engulfed Angola in 1975 in this respect graphically illustrated the risks that inhered in the armed struggle as a strategy for decolonization.

Angola is a huge country endowed with many natural resources such as oil, coffee and diamonds. As it was Portugal's most important colony, some 50,000 to 60,000 troops were sent to contain the onslaught of nationalist guerrilla's.[229] Due to its strategic position in the southern Atlantic, Angola was also very important to the Western world, as well as an attractive arena for the Eastern bloc to compete for influence. The forces that had been fighting, or purported to confront, the Portuguese were deeply divided along regional and ethnic lines and the social make-up of their leadership. They also had different international linkages, a fact that provided maximum opportunity for foreign interference. Despite many efforts by the OAU, all initiatives to create a common political-military front had come to naught. Thus, after the coup d'état in Lisbon (1974), which had brought to power a new government intent on winding up its colonies, the Portuguese signed separate cease-fire accords with the FNLA, MPLA and the emerging UNITA.[230]

These forces became quickly involved in armed clashes. The prospect of divided Africans negotiating with Portugal over the handover of power was deeply worrying to many African governments. However, the MPLA rejected attempts in the OAU to contribute towards a united and peaceful transition to independence as interference in Angola's internal affairs. The other two questioned the OAU's impartiality because they had been shunned by the Liberation Committee for a long time.[231] Yet, on the initiative of the latter, President Kenyatta of Kenya managed to persuade the three organizations to negotiate collectively with the Portuguese. This culminated in the "Alvor Agreement" of January 1975, which stipulated 11 November of that year as the date of independence and called for elections to be held not later than October. Arrangements were to be devised for the integration of the guerrilla armies. In the meantime the country would be ruled by a transitional government, headed by a Portuguese High Commissioner and composed of

228   Amate, *Inside the OAU*, pp 293-4 and Cervenka, *Unfinished Quest*, p 199 n. 1.
229   On Portuguese Angola G.J. Bender, *Angola Under the Portuguese: The Myth and the Reality* (Berkeley and Los Angeles, 1980).
230   *Africa Research Bulletin* (PSC), 1974, pp 3273 and 3402.
231   *Ibid.*, 1975, p 3684.

MPLA, FNLA and UNITA as "sole and legitimate representatives of the Angolan people".[232]

However, fighting only increased. The Portuguese told an OAU-UN fact-finding mission in April 1975 that Lisbon intended to withdraw by 11 November no matter what. At the time the MPLA was already receiving Soviet arms shipments via Congo and, directly, through Luanda. The Americans, and to a lesser extent communist China, were giving money to the FNLA and sending arms through Zaire.[233] The fact-finding mission could only recommend the formation of a government of national unity. A warning by the Liberation Committee against foreign interference and an appeal for national unity led to another accord negotiated by Kenyatta, which was shot to pieces on the eve of the Assembly session in Kampala (July).[234]

The summit elected President Idi Amin of Uganda as chairman. Amin became actively involved in mediation efforts, especially as he and President Mobutu of Zaire, the man behind him, regarded realization of a government of national unity as being favourable to the FNLA-UNITA side.[235] At the time UNITA was still an insignificant military force. The FNLA commanded a substantial regular army in Zaire, but had a narrow political basis as its support was limited to the north of the country and Bakongo refugees across the border. The MPLA, in contrast, possessed a well trained guerrilla army, with a decade of combat experience. With Soviet arms shipments it was growing in strength day by day.[236]

The Kampala summit asked Amin to form a "Fact-Finding Commission of Enquiry and Conciliation" and requested the OAU Defence Commission to study the need for an "OAU Peace Force".[237] The fact-finding mission failed to convince the warring sides to lay down their arms. Amin then took the extraordinary step of calling a meeting of the Bureau of the Assembly, the first time in OAU history that this was done.[238] However, this meeting could only send the commission back to Angola and issue another appeal for national unity.[239] Hostilities had meanwhile developed into a full-scale war as a result of increasing international intervention. A shock wave went through governmental circles when it was learnt that the OAU's arch-enemy, Pretoria, had invaded southern Angola. Intent on helping the UNITA-FNLA side, South African troops had started entering the country during the summer and early autumn. They were to grow to between 1,000 and 2,000 men and involved regular forces and mercenaries. The military success that the

---

232 Text in *Africa Research Bulletin* (PSC), 1975, pp 3501-3502.
233 See f.i. Legum and Hodges, *After Angola*, part 2; M. Wolfers and J. Bergeral, *Angola in the Frontline* (London, 1983), chs. 2-4; and A.J. Klinghoffer, *The Angolan War: A Study in Soviet Policy in the Third World* (Boulder, 1980), ch. 2. Also E. Harsh and T. Thomas, *Angola: The Hidden History of Washington's War* (New York, 1976).
234 *Africa Research Bulletin* (PSC), 1975, p 3705 and Amate, *Inside the OAU*, p 252.
235 Legum and Hodges, *After Angola*, pp 28-29.
236 *Ibid.*, pp 49 ff.
237 AHG/Res.72 (XII). See also CM/Res.424 (XXV).
238 *Fraternité* (Ivory Coast), 16/1/76 (article). He was advised in this by the fact-finding commission. Legum and Hodges, *After Angola*, p 80. Also Amate, *Inside the OAU*, p 253. In 1975 the eight vice-chairmen were Guinea-Bissau, Mozambique, Comoros, Niger, Cape Verde, São Tomé, Upper Volta, Sudan. Amate, *Inside the OAU*, Appendix J.
239 Amate, *Inside the OAU*, p 253 and Cervenka, *Unfinished Quest*, pp 142-143.

MPLA had by then achieved were seriously jeopardized, the more so as US arms shipments to the FNLA and UNITA were becoming larger by the day. However, South Africa's invasion gave the Soviet bloc an ideal excuse to increase its assistance to the MPLA. Early November Cuban troops began landing, in massive numbers, to come to its rescue. Growing to over 10,000 men and equipped with Soviet arms, the Cubans were to halt the South African advance by the beginning of 1976.[240]

UNITA and the FNLA agreed to form a coalition government between the two of them. The MPLA, however, rejected the call of the Assembly Bureau, issued on 1 November, for a government of national unity as it was gaining the upper hand.[241] A few days later, Amin convened a meeting of the OAU Defence Commission. It condemned South Africa's invasion and expressed concern over arms supplies to the warring movements. It decided to form an advisory military committee — made up of Egypt, Guinea, Kenya, Uganda, Nigeria and Libya — to assess the need for a peace-keeping force and of a mission to help the government of national unity to build up its administration and army.[242] However, this decision only concealed the irrelevance of OAU strategy, as there was no national government to be assisted. It also masked collective reticence to send a peace-keeping force. The need for one was quite obvious, yet in the context of full-scale hostilities hardly proved an enticing prospect for the Organization's members.

On Angola's independence day (11 November 1975) the leader of the MPLA, Agostinho Neto, was sworn in as President. With various, mainly radical, member states according him recognition and many others calling for a government of national unity, Amin acted on a suggestion of several members to convene an extraordinary session of the Assembly, the first one in the organ's history. In part this reflected serious concern over the escalation of hostilities and the massive scale of superpower interference, as well as anger over South Africa's invasion.[243]

The summit was held in Addis Ababa from 10 to 13 January 1976. As the MPLA had by then by and large defeated the FNLA and was pushing the South Africans back with the help of Cuban troops, it did not bother to participate. In contrast, Savimbi and Holden Roberto attended the summit as observers.[244] However, it was already apparent before the summit that the OAU's membership was split right down the middle over the Angolan issue.[245] On the moderate-conservative side, the Zambians, who seemed to favour Savimbi's UNITA,[246] admitted that South Africa's invasion was "detestable". Yet, they pressed for condemnation of all foreign intervention, stressing Soviet involvement in

240 Legum and Hodges, *After Angola*, pp 55-58 and Wolfers and Bergerol, *Angola in the Frontline*, chs. 3-4.
241 Legum and Hodges, *After Angola*, pp 20-21 and 36 and Wolfers and Bergerol, *Angola in the Frontline*, chs. 2-3.
242 Z. Cervenka and C. Legum, 'The Organization of African Unity', in *Africa Contemporary Record*, 1975-76, A72.
243 *The Ethiopian Herald*, 9/1/76; *l'Essor* (Mali), 10-11/1/76; and *Togo Presse*, 7/1/76 and 9/1/76 (articles).
244 *Togo Presse*, 12/1/76 (article) and *Africa Research Bulletin* (PSC), 1976, pp 3883-3884.
245 This reconstruction of member state postures is, with the exception of that of Ivory Coast, not based on Assembly documents but governmental comment before, during and after the summit.
246 The Zambian position was rather complex. See Legum and Hodges, *After Angola*, pp 33-35.

particular.[247] The emphasis on the role of foreign powers was to some extent hypocritical as even countries like Zaire, which actively co-operated in American and Chinese arms shipments to the FNLA, expressed itself in this vein. It was clear, however, that Zaire was, like Ivory Coast, principally concerned about the presence of Cubans and Soviets on Angolan territory, where they had almost annihilated their FNLA client. According to Kinshasa "imperialism" also existed on the left.[248]

The Sierra Leoneans presented a plan for a round table conference of the warring movements to decide Angola's future. The OAU should call for a cease-fire and countries that had influence with any of the Angolan groups should try to convince them of the need for reconciliation. The objective should still be a government of national unity. This was also argued by Botswana, which qualified recognition of the MPLA's government as premature.[249] Togo observed in this respect that, because the OAU had never withdrawn its recognition of the three movements, it could not recognize one particular group now. President Senghor of Senegal emphasized that such recognition would amount to a violation of the Charter. In his speech to the Assembly meeting, the Ivorian foreign minister spoke of "pseudo-governments" which were illegal and whose recognition would add to the confusion. All three movements had been "fighters for freedom", he said, and were entitled to Africa's admiration. Both Togo and Senegal considered that the OAU should organize a plebiscite in which the Angolan people could express itself.[250] It was clear, however, that these Francophone countries did not favour the Marxist-oriented MPLA. Even thirteen years later, the Counseiller of the Senegalese embassy in Addis Ababa maintained that the MPLA had staged a coup d'état. He contended, quite wrongly, that at the time the MPLA controlled the smallest portion of Angolan territory whereas UNITA held the largest part of the country.[251]

In the end, 22 members sponsored a draft resolution condemning all international intervention and calling for cessation of arms supplies, withdrawal of all foreign troops, termination of hostilities, freezing of military positions and formation of a government of national unity.[252] The sponsors were mostly conservative (Francophone and other) member states, but also involved various moderate powers. Two members of the Frontline alliance, Zambia and Botswana, lined up with this group.[253]

With regard to South Africa, the Ivorian foreign minister told the Assembly that the Angolan crisis had nothing to do with the problem of apartheid. In an apologetic vein he argued that Pretoria's intervention should not make Africa lose sight of the real issue; if Angolans would have solved their problems without the help of foreign powers —

247   *Times of Zambia*, 13/1/76 and 28/7/75.
248   Interview with Zairean envoy in *Daily Mail* (Sierra Leone), 8/1/76; speech of Ivorian foreign minister to the Assembly [text in *Fraternité*, 16/1/76]; and *Togo Presse*, 6/1/76 and 19/1/76.
249   *Daily Mail* (Sierra Leone), 10/1/76 and 15/1/76 and *Daily News* (Botswana), 16/1/76 and 20/1/76 (all articles).
250   *Fraternité* (Ivory Coast), 16/1/76 and *Togo Presse*, 7/1/76, 9/1/76 and 12/1/76 (articles).
251   Interview with Amadou Kebe, Conseiller of the Senegalese embassy, Addis Ababa, 3/10/89.
252   Cervenka and Legum, 'Organization of African Unity', A72-A73.
253   The 22 were: Botswana, Cameroon, CAR, Ivory Coast, Egypt, Gabon, Gambia, Upper Volta, Kenya, Liberia, Lesotho, Malawi, Morocco, Mauritania, Rwanda, Togo, Senegal, Sierra Leone, Swaziland, Tunisia, Zaire and Zambia. El-Ayouty and Zartman, *OAU After Twenty Years*, Annex 5 (n. 57).

USSR, USA, China and Cuba — the South Africans would not have invaded the country.[254]

Yet, the role of Pretoria was precisely the point on which radical and moderate-conservative states disagreed. Even some moderate member states sided, in this respect, with the more radically oriented regimes. The Kenyans, who supported the moderate draft resolution, admitted that FNLA and UNITA were "no longer viewed credibly by a majority of the O.A.U. member States, and the more so after their flirtation with the South Africans".[255] Nigeria had initially backed UNITA, then wavered, and opted for the MPLA when South Africa's intervention became apparent.[256] Any reservations about the massive Cuban and Soviet involvement were quickly cast aside when the level of South African interference became clear. From the perspective of inter-African perceptions Jonas Savimbi therefore made a mistake when he accepted South African support while not being sure he was going to beat the MPLA. The fact that South African troops had penetrated hundreds of kilometres into Angola enraged several states and caused concern over the prospects for liberation of Namibia.[257]

Radical governments considered that the role of the Soviet bloc was different anyway, as it had always helped Africa in its struggle against colonialism and apartheid. They were therefore ready to measure the intervention of the superpowers by different standards. In the words of the Malians, one could not put the USSR and Cuba on a par with South Africa because the former respected the self-determination of peoples while Pretoria's policies formed a challenge to African freedom and dignity. The moderates had implicitly defended South Africa, which according to the Malian foreign minister was "scandalous".[258]

Tanzania and Algeria stressed that UNITA and FNLA were not genuine liberation movements but imperialist traitors who wanted to sell their land and people. The MPLA was the only force willing to resist the machinations of imperialism, which intended to recolonize the continent. Militant fury was also directed at the United States for its support to, what were seen as, South Africa's proxies. A circular letter of the American president to African heads of state, asking for condemnation of all foreign interference, was in this respect a rather clumsy move, also because it aroused the collective inferiority complex.[259] Thus, the Nigerians called on the US to stop "insulting" Africa.[260]

A draft resolution sponsored by the militants condemned South Africa and its collaborators and appealed to all countries and the OAU to give aid to the MPLA. This implied a call for its recognition as the government of Angola.[261] Nevertheless, while radical ranks had been swelled by the advent of Marxist-inspired regimes such as Madagascar, Ethiopia, Mozambique and the other smaller Lusophone states, they still

---

254   *Fraternité* (Ivory Coast), 16/1/76.
255   *The Standard* (Kenya), 13/1/76.
256   See, however, for the complexity of the Nigerian position Legum and Hodges, *After Angola*, p 35.
257   Cervenka, *Unfinished Quest*, pp 144-145 and *l'Essor* (Mali), 17-18/1/76 (article).
258   *l'Essor* (Mali), 17-18/1/76 (article).
259   *Révolution Africaine* (Algeria), 9-15/1/76; *Daily News* (Tanzania), 13/1/76; and Cervenka and Legum, 'Organization of African Unity', A74.
260   *Daily Times* (Nigeria), 9/1/76. Also Legum and Hodges, *After Angola*, pp 30-31.
261   Cervenka and Legum, 'Organization of African Unity', A73.

consituted a minority. Yet, they managed to get exactly the same number of countries (22) to support their draft. Moderate powers like Nigeria lined up besides them, as did more conservative members like Chad and Niger.[262] Ethiopia abstained, because as host it did not want to aggravate the situation although it was to recognize the MPLA government quickly afterwards. However, this was compensated for by Uganda. While following the moderate-conservative line, it also abstained. It preferred to adopt, as Assembly chairman, a neutral attitude.[263] Contrary to Zambia and Botswana, the other Frontline states (Tanzania and Mozambique) sided with the militant group.

Thus, total dead-lock ensued. After more than two days of debate, delegates were exhausted. A proposal by Amin to let six "wise men", three each of the militant and moderate-conservative side, sort out the problem was rejected in favour of a neutral communiqué. The text merely observed that the Assembly had considered the Angolan issue and had asked its Bureau to continue following developments.[264] The Cubans and the MPLA subsequently forced the issue on the battle-field. After defeat of the FNLA, UNITA and their foreign backers, it was inevitable that the MPLA's government was recognized by OAU members, although in some cases rather belatedly. It was admitted to the OAU barely a month after the summit.[265]

The OAU and the armed struggle: evaluation
The Angolan crisis showed the logic behind the Liberation Committee's terms of reference, *i.e.* the provision of *co-ordination* to the activities of liberation movements and African states. It also confirmed the rationality of the internal part of the OAU's ideological ground-work: the desire to protect the mutual security of state elites entails a necessity to keep inter-African discord in bounds and, thus, discourage extra-African intervention. Full-scale superpower interference not only nearly ruined Angola's accession to independence, but also increased tensions and divisions between member states and reduced their collective influence. The Angolan events thus formed a worst-case scenario involving a double failure in terms of OAU objectives. While interference by superpowers also went against the external part of the OAU's rationale — enhancing Africa's global status and influence —, short-term calculations made many leaders unwilling to stop it, irrespective of their ability to do so. This contradictory behaviour is a good example of Ayoob's dualist concept of Third World security concerns.[266]

---

262   The twenty-two were: Algeria, Guinea, Ghana, Mali, Benin, Congo-Br., Libya, Tanzania, Mozambique, Guinea-Bissau, Cape Verde, São Tomé & Príncipe, Somalia, Madagascar, as well as Nigeria, Mauritius, Burundi, Equatorial Guinea and Comoros, Chad, Niger and Sudan. *Ibid.*

263   *Africa Research Bulletin* (PSC), 1976, p 3884; *The Ethiopian Herald*, 10/1/76, 1/11/76, 13/1/76, 16/1/76; *l'Essor* (Mali), 17-18/1/76 (article); and *Togo Presse*, 7/1/76 and 9/1/76 (articles).

264   Final Communiqué, Extraordinary Session of the Assembly of Heads of State and Government, Addis Ababa, 10-12 January 1976. Though having roughly equal representation the militants' view was, incidentally, predominant in the Bureau, as noted in *Fraternité* (Ivory Coast), 16/1/76.

265   *l'Essor* (Mali), 6-7/3/76 (article). In March '76 it was admitted to the Liberation Committee. *Jornal de Angola*, 6/3/76.

266   M. Ayoob, 'The Third World in the System of States: Acute Schizophrenia or Growing Pains?', in *International Studies Quarterly*, 1989, pp 67-79.

It could happen because the lack of continental hegemonic leadership made it impossible to impose one Pan-African strategy. Angola's neighbours were deeply divided and therefore unable to provide leadership. This was made worse by penetration of extra-African forces, which afforded members greater immunity against efforts to implement a collective policy. The OAU partly failed to realize a negotiated settlement because few members really pursued a peaceful solution as their main objective. The radical states only wanted to see an MPLA-led government and were greatly satisfied with its military victory. Many moderate-conservative regimes considered resistance to Soviet influence their main priority and therefore desired an FNLA or UNITA-led government or, at best, a coalition composed of all sides. To this purpose, they were prepared to manipulate the OAU's institutional and procedural potential. Mediation efforts that were undertaken under its auspices were therefore to some extent a façade behind which members held fundamentally divergent opinions. In the end, it was the MPLA that emerged victorious. The OAU stood, as an institution, as the biggest loser.

The Angolan crisis involved major questions of superpower alignments and could be seen as a clash between Marxism and Western ideological values. In combination with the divisions between neighbouring countries this turned the conflict into a crippling struggle between radical and moderate/conservative states, notwithstanding some anomalies in line-up mentioned above. Partly because the radicals had by now improved their numerical strength it was impossible to reach a way out of the impasse. The Angolan conflict did therefore not contribute to the quality of overall relations between radicals and moderate-conservatives. The militants were clearly annoyed by the result of the summit. It was stressed that the others had not behaved like "genuine Africans" or represented imperialist interests and had their foreign policy decided in Western capitals and Pretoria.[267] Guinea even proposed the formation of a separate organization for radical states.

Angola aside, divisions between states on the frontline in general limited the effectiveness of the OAU's contributions to armed struggle. Part of these divisions were caused by rivalry between liberation movements, especially in Angola and to a lesser extent Zimbabwe. In this respect Lemarchand has argued that splits between client factions constrain policy choices of patrons. More generally, the patron-client link is a two-way relationship involving reciprocal manipulation. It generates conflict and co-operation and holds uncertainties that may set the patron on a course with unanticipated outcomes.[268] Angola was a typical example. Constraints on patrons also showed themselves in the struggle for Zimbabwe. As mentioned in section 6.2 the Frontline states managed to co-ordinate their policy towards liberation movements, but sometimes found it difficult to make them act in unison. All this calls into question the element of power in the concept of hegemony as applied in more limited, regional contexts. In any case, the fact that in the Angolan crisis competition for regional hegemony between patrons escalated and backfired, encouraged regional states to work in unison when the struggle

---

267 *The Ethiopian Herald*, 16/1/76; *l'Essor* (Mali), 24-25/1/76 and 6-7/3/76 (articles); *Révolution Africaine* (Algeria), 16-22/1/76; and *Jornal de Angola*, 13/1/76 and 14/1/76.

268 See on this also R. Lemarchand, 'On Comparing Regional Hegemons: Libya and South Africa', in R. Lemarchand (ed), *The Green and the Black: Qadhafi's Policies in Africa* (Bloomington and Indianapolis, 1988), p 176.

for Zimbabwe began in earnest.[269]

6.4 Greed and a touch of megalomania: the OAU and the Western Sahara crisis

Historical background

An important test for the OAU's sincerity regarding colonialism came with Morocco's occupation of the Western Sahara. While the OAU stance on colonialism referred, in practice, to European or white minority rule, Rabat's actions violated the principle of self-determination, not only because the local population was not consulted, but also because such self-determination should, in the OAU perspective, take place through the geographical cadre of colonial partition. The concept of territorial integrity is therefore closely bound up with the OAU's anti-colonial principles.

In 1975 Spain decided to abandon the Western Sahara and hand it over to Morocco and Mauritania, which divided it between themselves. Morocco's appetite had been wetted by the territory's huge deposits of phosphates. It had already sent thousands of its citizens to the territory on a so-called "Green March" to consolidate its claims. According to Rabat, the Western Sahara had been part of the Moroccan kingdom before the advent of colonialism and should return to the Sharifian fold as its "recuperated Saharan provinces". For the Moroccan regime it formed an ideal instrument with which to rally its citizens behind the throne of their dictatorial monarch,[270] whose domestic position was far from comfortable. His irredentist claims rested on historically spurious grounds. It was true that the area had since time immemorial had regular contacts with the Moroccan kingdom but these had never amounted to permanent suzerainty that far south.[271] Moreover, this argument could not counter the OAU's principles of self-determination and territorial integrity. The latter had been elaborated in a specific policy to respect colonial frontiers as inherited upon decolonization.[272]

Rabat's designs also clashed with the aspirations of POLISARIO. This local liberation movement was founded in 1973 and enjoyed the support of the Liberation Committee in its aim to evict the Spaniards and proclaim the Western Sahara as an independent state. It had the solid backing of Algeria, which had no claim to the territory but hoped that its independence might guarantee Algerian influence and check Moroccan expansionism. POLISARIO formed an effective guerrilla force that organized spectacular raids against Morocco and Mauritania. The latter's security was so much jeopardized, that the Mauritanian government was forced to sign a peace treaty with POLISARIO and leave the territory (1979). Its withdrawal, however, led the Moroccans to occupy the whole of the Western Sahara. While POLISARIO was given Soviet arms by Algeria and Libya,

---

269 Foltz and Widner, 'OAU and Southern African Liberation', p 254.
270 This also worked. See the position taken on the Western Sahara by the opposition paper *l'Opinion*, 14, 15 and 16/11/84 (editorials and articles). This was also noted by other countries. See f.i. *Le Soleil* (Senegal), 13/11/84 (article).
271 See f.i. J.F.A. Ajayi and M. Crowder (eds), *History of West Africa*, 2 vols. (vl. 1: New York, 1977; vl. 2: London, 1974).
272 AHG/Res.16 (II). See further section 7.2.

Rabat enjoyed substantial financial and military assistance of several Western powers. These attributed considerable strategic importance to North-West Africa and thus did not favour POLISARIO, which articulated a militant nationalist, Marxist-oriented ideology.[273] However, the effectiveness of POLISARIO's struggle sharply decreased when Morocco proceeded to erect, from 1980 onwards, huge sand walls along the eastern and southern borders of the territory. Stuffed with modern radar equipment, this defence system diminished the possibilities for POLISARIO's landrover-borne attacks.[274]

The Western Sahara before the OAU 1979-1984

All along, however, the OAU had stressed that a referendum should be organized in which the indigenous Sahraouis could express themselves; the principle of self-determination was paramount.[275] As the issue was treated as one of decolonization, the OAU accused Morocco, albeit only implicitly, of behaving as a colonial power. Practically all member states opposed its action. The militant states in particular were deeply offended and criticized its expansionist drives in more straightforward language. For example, Zimbabwe regarded Morocco's claim as "immoral" and grounded in "greed and a touch of megalomania".[276] It was not only emphasized that its actions formed a violation of the sanctity of frontiers but also that it constituted colonialism pure and simple: Sahraouis were no Moroccans. It was made quite explicit that in its "territorial aggrandizement" Rabat was in violation of some of the most fundamental values in inter-African politics.[277]

In 1979 the OAU therefore called for preparation of a referendum in which the Sahraouis could choose between independence or integration with Morocco. Various ad hoc committees were formed to implement the OAU's strategy. The referendum should be organized by an implementation committee together with an impartial administration and a UN peace-keeping force. It was to be held in the "Western Sahara" as delimited on maps deposited at the United Nations. All Sahraouis listed in the Spanish census of 1974 and eighteen years or above would be eligible to vote, whether living in the Western Sahara or in Algerian refugee camps. This would exclude the tens of thousands of Moroccan immigrants that Rabat had sent to the territory.[278]

The Moroccan government, however, had manoeuvred itself into a position from which it could not withdraw without serious domestic repercussions. It therefore refused to give in and employed various delaying tactics in its encounters with the OAU. Thus, during the Assembly summit in Nairobi (1981) King Hassan personally pledged to accept

---

273 An extensive analysis in V. Thompson and R. Adloff, *The Western Saharans: Background to Conflict* (London and Totowa, NJ, 1980).

274 See for some information T. Hodges, 'Western Sahara: Edging to the brink of a regional conflagration', in *Africa Contemporary Record*, 1984-85, A84-85.

275 CM/Res.272 (XIX); CM/Res.301 (XXI); CM/Res.334 (XXIII); and AHG/Res.92 (XV).

276 *The Herald* (Zimbabwe), 24/6/81.

277 See f.i. *Révolution Africaine* (Algeria), 11-17/7/80; *Sunday News* (Tanzania), 6/7/80; *Daily News* (Tanzania), 14/11/84; *Times of Zambia*, 9/7/80; *The Ghanaian Times*, 24/6/81; and *Madagascar Renouveau*, no. 8, 1978 (text of Assembly speech).

278 AHG/Dec.114 (XVI); AHG/103 (XVIII) B; and the decision of the implementation committee (text in *Africa Contemporary Record*, 1981-82, C36-38).

the plan for a plebiscite and to fully co-operate with the ad hoc organs[279] without any genuine intention to submit the territory's future to a referendum. On the contrary, Morocco continued working towards a fait-accompli. POLISARIO's diplomatic position was nevertheless improving as its Arab Sahraoui Democratic Republic (RASD) was recognized by more and more member states. By 1981 26 of the Organization's fifty members had granted it recognition.[280]

In February 1982 Secretary-General Edem Kodjo decided to admit RASD as a formal member to the OAU by having it seated at the Council session taking place at the time. By this act the issue became an institutional problem for the OAU itself and the Pan-African forum was plunged into the most serious crisis in its history. Kodjo took this step partly because several radical states, as well as most Southern African ones, pressed him to admit RASD as a means to break Moroccan resistance to Western Sahara's independence.[281] It is also possible that Kodjo's ambition for a second term in office encouraged him to listen to majority opinion on the desirability of RASD's admission.[282] His decision nevertheless transgressed OAU doctrine, which as shown in the previous section tied the concept of state sovereignty to efficacy of control. It also violated the OAU's own plans on the Western Sahara, which held that a referendum should decide who should rule over the Sahraouis. The fact, however, that many countries suspected Morocco of employing dilatory tactics[283] played a role in the decision to admit RASD.

A serious conflict ensued between supporters and opponents of admission, which partly centred on interpretation of the OAU Charter. Thus, its article 28 says that if a candidate wants to join, it notifies the Secretary-General, who communicates this to all members. Admission is then decided by a simple majority of member states. Kodjo claimed that it was therefore in his competence to admit RASD, even without informing the chairman of the Assembly. The latter, President Moi of Kenya, was against RASD's admission and claimed that it was up to the Assembly to decide the matter. This argument seems incorrect as article 28 does not mention this institution but only speaks of the member states. However, while it is true that more than half the membership had recognized RASD, it should be realized that there is a distinction between recognition, which is a prerogative of individual states, and admission to the OAU, which is a collective act and not automatic. Moreover, the first section of article 28 speaks of "any independent sovereign African State" as potential candidate, a qualification that RASD hardly fulfilled. Article 27 stipulates that any question which arises over interpretation must be decided by a two-thirds majority of the Assembly, which RASD did not yet command. Members that opposed admission therefore spoke of a violation of the Charter, a "legal hold-up" by Kodjo and a "dangerous precedent".[284]

---

279   AHG/Res.103 (XVIII).

280   *Sunday News* (Tanzania), 28/6/81.

281   See for states calling for RASD's admission f.i. *Révolution Africaine* (Algeria), 26/6-2/7/81; *Sunday News* (Tanzania), 28/6/81; and *Dikgang Tsa Gompieno* (Botswana), 5/3/82.

282   *Le Soleil* (Senegal), 2/3/82 (article) and *Africa Research Bulletin* (PSC), 1982, p 6357.

283   See f.i. *Botswana Daily News*, 3/7/81.

284   *Le Soleil* (Senegal), 24/6/81, 27-28/2/82, 1/3/82, 2/3/82 and 3/2/82 (articles); *Dikgang Tsa Gompieno* (Botswana), 10/3/82 (article); *The Standard* (Kenya), 27/11/82; and *Zaïre-Afrique*, 1982, pp 195-196. Legal analysis in M. Kamto, 'Le retrait du Maroc de l'OUA', in M. Kamto, J.E. Pondi and L. Zang (eds), *l'OUA: rétrospective et perspectives africaines* (Paris, 1990), ch. 3.

There were also serious political considerations involved. While most opponents to RASD's admission were in principle in favour of the exercise of self-determination by the Sahraoui people, this did not automatically imply support for the militant nationalists of POLISARIO. Moreover, the fact that Tripoli had been chosen as venue of that year's summit and Colonel Qaddafi would become Assembly chairman complicated matters by tying the conflict to the Chadian crisis and the role played by Libya. In combination with this conflict and its external linkages the Western Sahara issue was politicized even further, developing into a struggle between moderate-conservative and radical member states. Many moderate-conservative members suspected Libya of subversive activities against West African states and opposed its intervention in the Chadian civil war. The United States openly encouraged their challenge of the Tripoli venue and Qaddafi's presidency, while Saudi Arabia also opposed the radical Libyan leader and could woe African states with prospects of financial aid.[285] Moreover, the French resisted Libyan penetration of Chad and also gave strong support to the Moroccan regime.

Moderate-conservative members thus had several reasons to adopt an anti-radical, *i.e.* anti-RASD, line.[286] 1982 saw many accusations that they were following the orders of outside powers,[287] which was not surprising in view of open American pressure to change the venue of the summit. This underlined that extra-African forces could impinge on matters that were considered as the preserve of the OAU and so inflamed passions further. Thus, there was some mention of forming separate organizations for moderate-conservative and militant states.[288]

Many moderate-conservative members decided to boycott the OAU's sessions as long as RASD would be seated, although cleavages did not run entirely along the radical-moderate/conservative divide. For example, Somalia, which usually lined up with the radicals, joined the anti-RASD camp, while various moderate-conservative countries did not. The fact, however, that the countries closest to the conflict were deeply divided meant that there was no solid leadership to get the OAU out of its institutional predicament[289] and that, once again, the radical-moderate/conservative divide led to an impasse. A compromise backed by the General Secretariat and Nigeria to have RASD seated at the Council but not the Assembly, was rejected. Thus, the summit, projected originally for August 1982, failed to take place for lack of the required quorum.[290] Even

285   Z. Cervenka and C. Legum, 'The OAU in 1982: A Severe Setback for African Unity', in *Africa Contemporary Record*, 1982-83, A43-48.

286   See *Le Soleil* (Senegal), 27-28/2/82 and 1/3/82 (articles).

287   *Dikgang Tsa Gompieno* (Botswana), 6/8/82; *Le Soleil* (Senegal), 4/8/82 and 27-28/11/82 (articles); *The Standard* (Kenya), 27/11/82; *The Ghanaian Times*, 10/8/82; *Daily News* (Sierra Leone), 26/11/82 and 1/12/82 (articles); *Jamahiriya Review* (Libya), December 1982; and *l'Essor* (Mali), 14-15/8/82 (article).

288   As noted by *Daily News* (Sierra Leone), 6/8/82 and *Révolution Africaine* (Algeria), 3-9/12/82 (article).

289   For irritation, as articulated by Morocco's allies Zaire and Guinea, with North African countries for introducing the issue to the OAU, *Le Soleil* (Senegal), 12/11/84 and 3/8/82 (articles).

290   *Le Soleil* (Senegal), 4/8/82 and 3/8/82 and *l'Essor* (Mali), 14-15/8/82 (all articles). The quorum was 34 members. Those that did not come or participate in the informal preparatory meeting were: Cameroon, CAR, Comoros, Djibouti, Eq. Guinea, Gabon, Gambia, Guinea, Ivory Coast, Liberia, Morocco, Niger, Senegal, Somalia, Sudan, Tunisia, Upper Volta, Zaire, UAR, Uganda, Sierra Leone. J. Damis, 'The OAU and Western Sahara', in El-Ayouty and Zartman, *OAU After Twenty*

in view of the absence of hegemonic leadership this defection from co-operation — *i.e.* the earlier decision on the choice of chairman and venue —, was exceptional as it carried the risk of iteration and probably the demise of the OAU. Explanations of this crisis must therefore take patterns of external dependence into account.[291]

Because of Libya's involvement in Chad a second attempt to stage the summit failed as well, although RASD had "voluntarily" decided not to attend. Several countries began looking for ways to break the dead-lock. Combined efforts of the members of ECOWAS and a committee of countries that had gone to Tripoli before, as well as diplomatic activities by individual countries like Kenya, Senegal and Nigeria, finally led to an agreement to hold the summit in Addis Ababa in June 1983. While no preconditions had been set, it could only get under way after RASD had been persuaded not to attend.[292] The Assembly managed to hammer out a compromise "à l'Africaine"[293] which, ironically, constituted a big diplomatic step forward for POLISARIO. A resolution for the first time named POLISARIO and Morocco as parties to the conflict and called on them to negotiate a cease-fire. This should lead to a referendum, to be held in December. King Hassan was reminded of his past pledges and the "Sahrawi leaders" were thanked that they had withdrawn so that the Assembly could meet.[294]

By the end of 1983, however, no progress had been made as Morocco refused to negotiate directly with POLISARIO. The referendum dead-line passed and Morocco's position in the OAU became increasingly untenable. One of Hassan's allies, Sékou Touré of Guinea, died in 1984. Early that year, even Mauritania recognized RASD, as did the new militant regime of Thomas Sankara in Upper Volta (Burkina Faso). By the end of 1984 those favouring RASD's admission numbered 29, while opponents had dropped to 21. Just before the Assembly was scheduled to meet (November 1984) Nigeria followed suit. Its decision to recognize RASD had a positive effect on those that still had hesitations.[295] With RASD determined to take its seat, it was decided to admit it as a full and formal member to the OAU. Only Zaire protested by temporarily suspending participation in OAU fora. However, Morocco declared that it renounced membership altogether, accompanied by a spiteful farewell message from its monarch.[296]

Yet, the change of heart on the part of RASD's opponents had been of Rabat's own making. Its flouting of basic OAU principles such as territorial integrity, the sanctity of frontiers and self-determination had been accompanied by broken promises and an obstinate refusal to work towards a compromise. In the end, Morocco had left RASD's opponents no arguments with which to resist Western Sahara's admission. Many were fed up with Rabat's intransigence and threats that it would leave if RASD were admitted.

Years, pp 280-281.

291 Generally Rothstein, 'Regime Creation' (n. 28) and on tit-for-tat tactics Oye, 'Explaining Cooperation Under Anarchy', pp 14-16.

292 For negotiations on its preparations *Le Soleil* (Senegal), June 1983 and 'O.A.U. '83: Nigeria's Role' (Dep. of Inf.: Lagos, n.d.).

293 As hoped beforehand by *Le Soleil* (Senegal), 6/6/83 (article).

294 AHG/Res.104 (XIX).

295 *Le Soleil* (Senegal), 27/2/84, 5/3/84 and 12/11/84 and *Révolution Africaine* (Algeria), 16-22/11/84 (all articles).

296 At one point Hassan's address runs: "il ne nous reste plus qu'à vous souhaiter bonne route avec votre nouveau partenaire". Text in *l'Opinion* (Morocco), 14/11/84.

Members of both groups accused Morocco of "diplomatic blackmail".[297] RASD's admission implied, however, that the OAU's role in finding a solution to the conflict had effectively come to an end. As the armed struggle was no practical option anymore, attempts at a settlement would have to be made through the UN.[298]

Conclusion

Several mistakes were made which in the final analysis did not further POLISARIO's cause. It would have been better to strengthen recognition of POLISARIO as a liberation movement and grant it assistance rather than admitting its "state" to the OAU. Radical members had in this respect badly manipulated OAU procedures, just as the moderate-conservatives had done over Angola. Some of the latter stood accused of boycotting the OAU to the point of destruction. As in Angola, divisions between the states most involved precluded the emergence of leadership to execute an unequivocal strategy. As in Angola, external interference transformed this lack of leadership and, thus, insufficient co-ordination of collective will, into paralysis.

RASD's admission led to the withdrawal of a state that really existed in exchange for one that only functioned on paper. Yet, by 1984 there seemed no other way out of the impasse as there are no legal possibilities for expulsion of a member state that violates the OAU's principles and any attempt to this effect might have split its membership.[299] Moreover, the Western Sahara showed that, in the end, the OAU was serious about its anti-colonial stance. This also marked the difference between Morocco and other members. In its search for influence it went further than other countries, even to the point of transgressing another fundamental principle of Africa's post-colonial order, *i.e.* the norm of territorial integrity. This forced it to leave the OAU.

6.5 Evaluation and afterthoughts

The context of Africa's international relations meant that the OAU's anti-colonial programme was seriously impeded by the absence of continental hegemonic leadership and the patterns of external dependence. The OAU's role in the struggle against colonialism shows that more effective co-operation could only be achieved by the game theoretical strategy of actor reduction. It also shows that precisely when the states closest to the theatre of operation were divided, the OAU's goal could not successfully be pursued. In conjunction with extra-African interference this could lead to complete paralysis.

Only the Frontline alliance managed, in the struggle for Zimbabwe, to provide effective leadership representing a form of benevolent hegemony by a coalition. As in the Angolan conflict, however, these regional states suffered from constraints inherent in patron-client interaction and the consequences of inter-client rifts. The aspect of effective

---

297 *Le Soleil* (Senegal), 12, 13 and 16/11/84 (articles); *Révolution Africaine* (Algeria), 3-9/12/82 and 16-22/11/84 (articles); and *The Ghanaian Times*, 24/6/81. Also *Daily Times* (Nigeria), 19/11/84.

298 Interview with Ambassador Mamadou Bah, Director of the Political Department, General Secretariat, Addis Ababa, 18/9/89.

299 *Le Soleil* (Senegal), 13/11/84 and 16/11/84 (articles).

influence in the concept of regional hegemony is called into question by this and is explored further in chapter 9. The OAU lacked hegemonic leadership, let alone leadership by a dominant coalition, in all other dimensions of the struggle, such as sanctions, the functioning of the Liberation Committee and, more particularly, the Angolan and Western Sahara crises. In this context its institutional-procedural potential could be used for other purposes than they were ostensibly meant.

Thus, the OAU's sanctions record was ambivalent and the rules on contacts with the white south ambiguous. Violations of these policy aspects were advantageous to colonial and white minority regimes, whose survival went against part of the OAU's general ideological ground-work, *i.e.* its aspiration to enhance Africa's global influence. While these violations therefore also transgressed the Organization's general ideology, the gain of enlarged global influence accruing from compliance was too distant to induce members to forgo short-term interests. As with member state willingness to accept non-African support in the Angolan and Western Saharan crises, this behaviour was in essence part of Ayoob's dualist dilemma in Third World security concerns.[300]

Yet, the dialogue debate points to the sincerity of the OAU's anti-colonial objective in the sense that it stemmed, secondarily, from an elite African imagination of what white minority rule amounted to. Thus, the OAU managed to uphold a high degree of diplomatic isolation of the white minority regimes, by which it managed to do considerable harm. On the whole, however, the direct impact of OAU diplomacy was limited and rendered increasingly irrelevant when the struggle against white minority rule became harder. Still, through its relative autonomy vis-à-vis the generality of the membership the Liberation Committee did make some practical and concrete contributions to the struggle and underlined the seriousness of the OAU's anti-colonial vocation. The obstinacy of Portugal and white minority regimes made this dual strategy of peaceful and violent pressure imperative, even if Angola's decolonization exposed the dangers involved. Finally, the course of events in the Western Sahara points to the importance the OAU attributed to the norms of self-determination and territorial integrity. This meant that, despite complicating factors, it would never condone Morocco's annexation.

In view of the above it is logical that the role of the OAU was marked by an awareness of impotence. The Organization continued drafting long and angry resolutions even when its direct influence over developments had largely become irrelevant. In many policy statements, the OAU could do no more than appeal, recount events and express indignation. Its verbal capabilities seemed in this respect inversely proportional to its lack of influence: references to "unholy alliances" of white minority regimes, the "hateful doctrine of apartheid", "surrogate bandits of the Pretoria regime" and "barbarous aggression" were no exception. Statements about South Africa's government as "a full-fledged fascist power bent on perpetuating the ruthless domination of the indigenous people" and "an entrenched system of national oppression ... and fascist terror perpetrated against the black majority" stood out as the more remarkable of qualifications.[301]

---

300   Ayoob, 'Third World in the System of States' (n. 266).
301   See f.i. CM/Res.151 (XI); CM/Res.206 (XIII); CM/Res.241/Rev.1 (XVII); CM/Res.428 (XXV); CM/Res.821 (XXXV); ECM/Res.17 (VII); and AHG/Dec.2 (XXII). US "constructive engagement" policy on Namibia-Angola was even dubbed a hostile act against the OAU itself. See AHG/Decl.1 (XXII). In such cases conservative, often Francophone, members sometimes expressed reservations

In this respect, it comes as no surprise that editorial comment on the OAU in the organ of South Africa's ruling "National Party" did not involve violent tirades. Usually it adopted a mildly condescending attitude, which sometimes turned into contempt. It would focus on the political, economic and social problems of OAU members, their violations of sanctions and the absence of OAU criticism of this. Its tone only showed disappointment or anger when the OAU managed to do harm to South Africa's position, such as in its recognition policy, dialogue and renewed calls for sanctions. Yet, it almost seems as if the National Party sensed part of the OAU's fundamental rationale. At one point it accused African leaders of an "oordrewe gevoel van eiewaarde" and "natuurlike strewe tot grootdoenery", which were related to Africa's mistaken impression that it could play an important role in international politics.[302]

The OAU's verbal abuse thus barely concealed its impotence. Nevertheless, at least it prevented the disappearance of the issue from the international agenda and exposed, in modern parlance, its political correctness.

---

or abstained.

302 The quotations in Afrikaans mean "exaggerated feeling of self-esteem" and "natural aspiration to displaying one's importance". See *Die Burger* (South Africa), 4/8/75. Also *ibid.*, 28/6/71; 5/7/77; 6/7/77; 21/7/78; 24/7/79; 7/7/80; 29/7/86; 1/8/86; and 3/8/87.

The OAU and the management
of Africa's political order (I)

7.1 The world's village idiot:
the OAU's rationale of dispute settlement

Independence brought in its wake numerous patterns of competitive interaction between state elites, which regularly led them into conflict with one another. Conflict or dispute is defined here as the incompatibility of goals or the violent expression of such incompatibility.[1] The last three decades have shown that such conflict could involve various issues, such as personal animosity between leaders, subversive support for each other's domestic opposition and border or territorial disputes. While they rarely involved large claims over neighbouring territory, border conflict could result from disagreement about the location or demarcation of frontiers or from tension relating to cross-border traffic. Problems of living conditions in the border region entailed uncertainty for state elites about the extent of control over their population and could engender suspicions about the aims of neighbouring leaders.[2]

As mentioned in section 2.4, conflicts about the location of frontiers as such have been relatively infrequent. Domestic instability became a far more important source of inter-state disputes, as social and ethnic strife could easily spill over into neighbouring territory through flows of refugees and lead to clandestine support to domestic factions by neighbouring regimes. As a result of a general intensification of domestic and inter-state conflicts, the massive rise in armaments, increasing superpower rivalry and the worsening economic crisis the continent suffered, from the mid-1970s onwards, a progressive deterioration in security, bringing untold misery to millions of people.[3]

---

1   See for this I.W. Zartman, 'Conflict Reduction: Prevention, Management, and Resolution', in F.M. Deng and I.W. Zartman (eds), *Conflict Resolution in Africa* (Washington, 1991), ch. 11.

2   Zartman, 'Conflict Reduction'.

3   See R.W. Copson, 'Peace in Africa? The Influence of Regional and International Change', in Deng and Zartman, *Conflict Resolution in Africa*, pp 19-41.

Naturally, it may be contended that, from a theoretical point of view, conflict is inevitable as it is inherent in the existence of numerous actors and their choices. It stems from the incompatibility of their goals and actions and the need to test each other's commitment to these objectives. To a limited extent, then, conflict, whether violent or not, is functional.[4] This is true both for domestic society and international relations, whether in Africa or elsewhere.

However, if conflict becomes extended, escalates or becomes more expensive as a result of technological developments, it can also become dysfunctional[5] or even "destructive" for all parties concerned. "Destructive" conflict means that it becomes detached from its original causes and that parties pursue maximalist options. Such a zero-sum situation tends to perpetuate and escalate the conflict. Important elements that may contribute towards this are an anarchical context impeding rational decision-making; internal conflicts inside the parties themselves; cognitive rigidity with regard to alternatives; and various forms of misperception.[6]

While the inevitable and instrumental features of at least some disputes make prevention, and frequently even resolution, a theoretical exercise, one may argue that it should be possible to *manage* conflict. Such management may involve the reduction of the means with which the parties pursue their dispute.[7] It may also involve its transformation by the introduction or reinforcement of the consonant interests in the relations of the parties and the restriction or redefinition of the contentious issue so as to circumvent core values on which compromise is impossible.[8] As "settlement" of conflicts usually involves such management and only much less frequently their resolution, both these terms will be used interchangeably.

The disputing parties themselves may or may not feel the need for management or resolution of the conflict. However, they may be unable to find a way out as a result, for example, of their failure to recognize alternative options; suspicions of, or misperceptions about, the other party's intentions; a breakdown in communication; or an overcommitment to victory. It is here that "mediation", as a form of third-party intervention for the purpose of abating or resolving the conflict through negotiations, comes in. Such mediation differs from international legal arbitration and judicial settlement[9] in the sensethat mediation carries no advance commitment of the parties to accept its outcome. This study assumes, after Touval and Zartman, that mediation is a political process between mediator and disputants, which are tied in a triangular relationship in which power political

---

4   See f.i. R. Väyrynen, 'To Settle or Transform? Perspectives on the Resolution of National and International Conflicts', in R. Väyrynen (ed), *New Directions in Conflict Theory: Conflict Resolution and Conflict Transformation* (London and New Delhi, 1991), ch. 1.
5   Zartman, 'Conflict Reduction', pp 299-301.
6   M. Deutsch, 'Subjective Features of Conflict Resolution: Psychological, Social and Cultural Influences', in Väyrynen, *New Directions in Conflict Theory*, pp 37-50 and M. Deutsch, *The Resolution of Conflict* (New Haven and London, 1973), p 351.
7   Zartman, 'Conflict Reduction', p 300.
8   Väyrynen, 'To Settle or Transform?', p 5; Deutsch, 'Subjective Features', p 38; and I.W. Zartman and S. Touval, 'Conclusion: Mediation in Theory and Practice', in S. Touval and I.W. Zartman (eds), *International Mediation in Theory and Practice* (Boulder and London, 1985), p 267.
9   See for these concepts M. Akehurst, *A Modern Introduction to International Law* (London, 1980), pp 226-227.

considerations inform the behaviour of both the parties *and* the mediator. The mediator intervenes not so much for altruistic reasons as for realizing his self-interest. This intervention may occur because his interests are threatened by the conflict or because the mediator wishes to extend his influence with one or both parties or prevent a rival power from enhancing its influence by intervening. Thus, the mediator also has a stake in the terms of the settlement and is likely to press for an outcome that enhances his influence.[10] This will be pursued further in the next section.

On a wider level, international organizations have their own interest in the settlement of disputes. The internal part of the OAU's ideological ground-work points to an interest, held by the collectivity of Africa's state elites, in the protection of their mutual security. In chapter 4 it was shown how this concern, fed by an awareness of vulnerability to domestic and external enemies, dictated a need for inter-African reconciliation. Any discord should therefore be kept in bounds and, thus, extra-African intervention, particularly by the great powers, should be discouraged. The disunity of the early 1960s had shown how easy it was for those powers to interfere in African affairs and how this could deepen African divisions and make co-operation impossible. It intensified conflicts and could contribute to the consolidation of rival inter-African coalitions. Furthermore, by strengthening divisions such interference could weaken African influence in world politics and thus jeopardize the external part of the OAU's rationale, namely the aspiration to increase the global influence of Africa and its component states and, related to this, the desire to equality of status with state elites of other continents.

Section 8.2 will in this respect show how the Assembly summit in Libreville (1977) was unable to affect developments in the Shaba crisis, which was characterized by extra-African intervention, disagreement among member states about the role of non-African powers and, in the background, East-West rivalry. Some members were conniving in this interference as during Angola's accession to independence, whose after-effects (*i.e.* a massive Cuban presence) were to some extent mixed up with the Shaba events. Having been unable to prevent extra-African intervention, come up with an unambiguous stance and so affect developments, the Libreville summit adopted a highly contradictory resolution that only underlined the ludicrous image that the crisis imparted to the OAU. In a lamentation over the summit, the *Times of Zambia* complained about member state complicity in non-African interference and criticized the machinations of the superpowers. It also chided member state rivalry in the Western Sahara and the Horn, where the OAU was equally unable to make a change. In an implicit reference to the self-esteem of state elites that was at stake here, it argued that African conflicts and their causes — which it held were sometimes as absurd as cattle-theft — made the continent "look like the village idiot of the world".[11]

In other words, extra-African intervention touched on the internal and external part of the OAU's ideology. It put inter-state relations in jeopardy and would detract from Africa's collective influence and call in question the equality of status of its state elites. The metaphor of the world's village idiot therefore constitutes a succinct presentation of

---

10   S. Touval and I.W. Zartman, 'Introduction: Mediation in Theory', in Touval and Zartman, *International Mediation*, pp 7-9.

11   *Times of Zambia*, 6/7/77.

the rationale underlying OAU conflict management, as emanating from its general ideology: keeping discord in bounds and discouraging extra-African intervention. More specifically, it alludes to how elite African embarrassment about the continent's global image affects the OAU's posture and strategy towards managing African conflicts.

During the last three decades African state elites shared a deep-seated fear of non-African intervention in the political affairs of their continent, especially by that of the superpowers.[12] Their desire for some sort of autonomy in this respect set the African context apart from other regional arena's of international relations, although not from the Third World as a whole. However, these considerations operated mainly at the collective level of the OAU and were, as noted by the *Times of Zambia*, not necessarily (always) entertained by individual states. These could hold different opinions about the various non-African powers. Moreover, concern about external interference would usually not take precedence over shorter-term security predicaments and, thus, the need for extra-African support.[13]

This and the following chapter will be concerned with the ways in which the OAU has sought to manage, in the widest sense, Africa's political order. They should therefore be seen in conjunction. The present chapter will, by focusing exclusively on inter-state disputes, provide a general outline of the various ways, mechanisms and strategies with which the Organization is active in the field of conflict management. Many of these mechanisms, procedures and approaches are also utilized, and provide an essential basis for insight, in the management of domestic conflicts. They are elaborated further in the next chapter in so far as they have been adapted or specially introduced to suit the settlement of such internal conflicts.

Chapter 8 deals with the more specific aspects of the management of Africa's political order and is therefore of a composite nature. The first section discusses domestic conflicts; section 8.2 analyses the military dimensions of managing the continental order; section 8.3 concentrates on the external aspects of its management; and section 8.4 provides a general evaluation of the Organization's role in structuring Africa's politics.

Section 8.1 will show that until 1990 the OAU was, in dealing with domestic conflicts, faced with a difficult legal position. The principle of non-interference in internal affairs of member states seriously constricted its role in the mediation of domestic conflicts. Yet, this section also argues that the OAU at times *did* intervene, in various ways, in such conflicts if they were marked by substantial non-African involvement or otherwise had important repercussions for inter-African relations. This approach was in line with the general rationale of conflict management as decribed above and should, among others, be seen as a logical expression of concerns in the Cold War era. Thus, section 8.1 ends by arguing that, after 1990, the OAU's rationale of conflict management began shifting towards a more activist and humanitarian approach. This approach entailed that inter-state conflicts were not the only subject of concern anymore. Domestic conflicts, whether or not marked by extra-African interference, could also become the subject of

---

12   Also W.J. Foltz, 'The Organization of African Unity and the Resolution of Africa's Conflicts', in Deng and Zartman, *Conflict Resolution in Africa*, pp 355-356.

13   See M. Ayoob, 'The Third World in the System of States: Acute Schizophrenia or Growing Pains?', in *International Studies Quarterly*, 1989, pp 67-79.

OAU scrutiny, as well as wider aspects of domestic political developments. However, it will be concluded, in the final section, that these shifts in the rationale underlying conflict management have not (yet) led to a significant transformation in the general ideological ground-work of the Organization: fears of extra-African intervention have naturally diminished, yet this has not given rise to a general ideology that differs from the one analysed above.

In its discussion of the military dimensions to conflict management section 8.2 will focus on peace-keeping in inter-state contexts as well as on military interventions in domestic conflicts. In the course of this various ideas on some sort of Pan-African security structure are also discussed and contrasted with the actual reliance on bilateral security arrangements.

It was shown above that the OAU's rationale in the management of Africa's political order has also been part and parcel of the objective to enhance the continent's influence in world politics. Thus, in extra-African fora as the UN the OAU's African Group tries to influence decision-making on all issues that are important to Africa. Control of African agenda's outside the continent is naturally also important in the more narrow field of conflicts, as this pertains directly to issues like extra-African intervention and Africa's ability to settle its own disputes.[14] However, section 8.3 will, in a wider sense, analyse the ways in which the OAU has sought to activate the leverage mechanism, implicit in its Pan-African cadre, to strengthen the continent's global influence. We will focus particularly on the perceptions concerning this mechanism and, more generally, the views held on the potential power that the continent could generate and its repercussions for the state of inter-African politics.

7.2 Not peace, not war: the OAU and the management of inter-African conflicts

Introduction

As conflict may encompass any layer of issues that are articulated in only one particular fashion, the problem of what constitutes the "merits" of a case is relatively intractable. A typology of conflicts is therefore eschewed. Still, in the context of this study a deeper understanding of the nature of African conflicts is crucial, as this pertains directly to the OAU's ability to mediate successfully in disputes. A cursory assessment of the contentious issues will therefore be integrated in the analysis, both in this chapter and the next.[15] In the course of this section not all conflicts with which the OAU has concerned itself can be mentioned, let alone studied in greater detail. However, an overview of the OAU's mediation of disputes is given in table 7.1. The main text will regularly mention various conflicts, drawn from this survey, as examples to illustrate a certain argument. Only one conflict will be presented as a case study, namely the territorial dispute between

---

14   Foltz, 'Organization of African Unity', pp 357-358.
15   See also R.O. Matthews, 'Interstate Conflicts in Africa: A Review', in *International Organization*, 1970, pp 337-344 and Z. Cervenka, *The Unfinished Quest for Unity: Africa and the OAU* (London, 1977), pp 68-69.

Somalia on the one hand and Ethiopia and Kenya on the other. Justification of this choice is given in the relevant section.

The analysis in this section begins with a discussion of the theoretical dimensions of mediating in conflicts. This is followed by discussion of the OAU's institutional and procedural strategies in, and of the relevance of its normative provisions to, the management of disputes. The case study, a general evaluation of OAU effectiveness in managing inter-state disputes and a survey of reform proposals conclude this section.

Conflict mediation in theoretical perspective

As was mentioned in the previous section, it is assumed that elements of power politics are crucial to the mediation process. Both the mediator and the parties have their own specific interests and the mediation context is therefore not devoid of tension. As the mediator will principally intervene in pursuit of his own interests, he is rarely hired by the parties but usually acts on his own initiative. His acceptance by the parties is not un-conditional. His role is often not clear from the start, as it is determined by all the actors concerned in a negotiated, evolutionary process.[16]

In principle, the mediator has a stake in a settlement and the parties have an interest in victory. That the mediator will only act if this is propitious to his interests is also true for mediation by an international organization as the OAU. While in theory its mediatory facilities are permanently available, it is itself made up of states, which are also its most important mediators with their own interests. Parties may wish mediation not merely for peace but for several other reasons too. They may think that a mediated outcome will be better guaranteed than one resulting from bilateral negotiations. They may use mediation as a dilatory tactic or seek it because the compromise involves a face-saving formula. Mediation may be desired because it is hoped that it will enhance the legitimacy of one's position. A party may also seek mediation merely to persuade the other party of its point of view, to convey a message or to improve its general relations with the mediating state.[17]

Parties will sometimes try to change the triangular relationship into a dyadic one between themselves and the mediator against the other party. Thus, while parties seek mediation because they think it will work in their favour, intervention by a third actor entails unpredictable outcomes. It also involves risks for the mediator. He may fail in his mediation or in the process damage his relations with the parties.[18]

From this power political approach it follows that strict neutrality on the part of the mediator is not necessary. A slight bias towards a party provides him some influence over that disputant. Naturally, the mediator must not be too careless with regard to his perceived (im-)partiality, although he does have some latitude in this respect. In general, parties will not attribute full credibility to the mediator but interpret his action in terms of his assumed motives. Acceptance of his mediation is based on considerations of the

---

16   See Zartman and Touval, 'Conclusion', p 263; Touval and Zartman, 'Introduction' (n. 8 and 10); and Th. Princen, *Intermediaries in International Conflict* (Princeton, 1992), pp 219-220.

17   Touval and Zartman, 'Introduction'; Zartman and Touval, 'Conclusion'; and Princen, *Intermediaries*, ch. 1.

18   Princen, *Intermediaries*, ch. 10 and Zartman and Touval, 'Conclusion', p 253.

consequences of acceptance or rejection on the actual, ultimate settlement and on their ties with the potential mediator.[19]

For the mediator leverage over the parties is the crucial element. The main source of his leverage is stalemate between the disputants. Such stalemate may lead to a mediated settlement if there is no chance to realize a decisive victory; the stalemate is mutually hurting; there is a way out by way of a mutually agreeable, mediated formula; and all these conditions are also perceived by the parties.[20] In order to keep them in stalemate, maintenance of balance between the disputants in the triangular relationship is important. This may induce the mediator to side temporarily with the weaker party to make sure that no one prevails.[21]

However, there can be different types of stalemate, which carry different opportunities for a mediated settlement. A simple stalemate, resulting from exhausted resources, is most amenable to settlement. A repeated stalemate occurs when parties cannot escalate the conflict, but from time to time try to break out of the simple stalemate by reviving the dispute. The so-called compound stalemate results when disputants replenish their resources and escalate the conflict until a new limit is reached. Yet, because of the costs involved it increases pressures for victory, something that is called entrapment or overcommitment. Finally, a grinding stalemate arises when a conflict drags on, gradually intensifies and occasionally escalates. Naturally, the last three types of stalemate produce fewer opportunities for a mediator, as the parties have learned to live with it and expect relief through escalation.[22]

Assuming there is a workable stalemate, the mediator can do several things. While international law distinguishes several forms of intervention by third actors[23], these are usually unhelpful analytical constructs. They are hard to prove empirically as the internal dynamics of mediation are often shrouded in secrecy, perhaps even more so in the case of the OAU.[24] Moreover, different mediation techniques may be used simultaneously. Generally, a mediator can, first of all, repair communication between the parties by transmitting messages. He may hold one party's concessions in temporary reserve so as to avoid a hardening in position of the other party. The exchange of concessions through the mediator also works as a face-saving device. Second, the mediator can formulate proposals of his own, which redefine the issue or provide a formula for a settlement. Parties may be so bogged down that they fail to see alternatives through cognitive rigidity, distrust and misperceptions.[25] Such proposals need a quick follow-up, as they may remove the painful aspects of the stalemate and thus, paradoxically, remove the pressure for a settlement.[26]

---

19   Touval and Zartman, 'Introduction' and Zartman and Touval, 'Conclusion'.
20   Zartman, 'Conflict Reduction' (n. 1).
21   Touval and Zartman, 'Introduction'.
22   Zartman, 'Conflict Reduction', pp 306-311.
23   Such as "good offices", "mediation", "inquiry", "conciliation", "arbitration", "judicial settlement". See Akehurst, *Modern Introduction*, pp 221-226.
24   Zartman, 'Conflict Reduction', pp 313-314 and Foltz, 'Organization of African Unity', pp 356-357.
25   See also Deutsch, 'Subjective Features' (n. 6).
26   Zartman, 'Conflict Reduction' and Touval and Zartman, 'Introduction', pp 11-12.

The persuasive powers that the mediator requires in this respect are, in general, his most important assets. The personal qualities and the rank of the mediator come into play here. Being an intermediary as such may also provide for subtle forms of influence, as it may provide focus to, and change the tone of, discussions and impose standards of inter-action.[27] However, the influence emanating from the intermediary nature of mediation is hard to prove empirically. In any case, its outcome depends primarily on the balance of power. While mediation is rarely decisive in ending a conflict, the mediator may be able to tip an actual balance in favour of settling sooner than later.[28]

Naturally, besides acting as communicator and formulator the mediator can take on a more active role. Yet, this manipulative aspect is less important than persuasion of the parties that stalemate is intolerable and that there is a good alternative. Manipulation involves the application of sticks and carrots. Sticks are the shifting of weight to one party, threats of a worse outcome or the termination of mediation efforts. An example of carrots is the hand-out of side-payments, *i.e.* rewards in areas unrelated to the conflict. In principle, the stronger the ties between mediator and parties, the more effective the application of sticks will be. However, the mediator must be careful in applying negative incentives in order not to cause parties' withdrawal from negotiations. Moreover, threats of his own withdrawal can be self-defeating. Manipulation, then, is a delicate matter and the leverage it implies can be elusive.[29]

Institutional and procedural provisions

Under its Charter the OAU was provided with its own mediatory institution. However, this "Commission of Mediation, Conciliation and Arbitration" (CMCA), which was made up of 21 legal experts acting in their professional capacity,[30] was never seized with any dispute as member states preferred to settle their conflicts through other channels.[31] While the principle of settling inter-state disputes peacefully (art. 3.4 Charter) is legally binding for OAU members, they are not obliged to do so through the CMCA, nor even within the Organization as such.[32] This was also confirmed in an interview with a Senegalese diplomat.[33] Even if there were a legal obligation in this respect, the absence of hegemonic leadership would make it impossible to force the CMCA upon member states and guarantee their compliance with its verdicts. From time to time efforts were made to

---

27   See on this especially Princen, *Intermediaries*.

28   Zartman and Touval, 'Conclusion' and Princen, *Intermediaries*, ch. 1.

29   Zartman and Touval, 'Conclusion' and Touval and Zartman, 'Introduction'.

30   Arts. 7 and 19 Charter; draft protocol of Committee 1, Sub-Committee 2 of Council of Ministers, Dakar, 7 August 1963; CM.36 (III): The Work of the Committee of Experts on the Draft Protocol of Mediation, Conciliation and Arbitration (Council, Cairo, July 1964); CM/Res.25 (II); CM/Res.42 (III); definitive Protocol published by Press & Information Division, General Secretariat (Addis Ababa, 1982).

31   Also J.H. Polhemus, 'The Birth and Irrelevance of the Commission of Mediation, Conciliation, and Arbitration of the Organization of African Unity', in *Nigerian Journal of International Affairs*, 1977, nos. 1-2, pp 1-20.

32   See art. 19 Charter and art. 13.2 of the CMCA Protocol (n. 30). Also T.O. Elias, 'The Commission of Mediation, Conciliation and Arbitration of the Organization of African Unity', in *British Yearbook of International Law*, 1964, p 343.

33   Interview with Amadou Kebe, Conseiller of the Senegalese embassy, Addis Ababa, 3/10/89.

reactivate it and change its working procedures and composition.[34] Yet, even when the Assembly was, at the end of the 1970s, overwhelmed by conflicts and decided to commission another reform — leading to the proposal to transform the legal experts into member state representatives[35] — the CMCA remained dormant.

From time to time some members expressed dissatisfaction with this state of affairs,[36] but there were clear reasons why member states preferred other ways to settle conflicts. In 1989 the Director of the Political Department of the General Secretariat contended that members consider the CMCA as too independent and "above" the states.[37] In other words, it can hardly stand in *between* disputants and command some confidence through an intermediary position and a mediator's own self-interest. Its formal, written procedures hinder the normal operation of power political considerations that induce a disputant to seek or accept a mediator in the hope that the latter's intervention will advance a party's interests or produce an acceptable settlement that will stick. The CMCA's neutrality and lack of leverage do it no good.[38] With its elaborate, unwieldy procedures it is also seen as unable to respond swiftly,[39] provide the necessary freedom of manoeuvre and avoid the setting of precedents.[40]

Yet this does not mean that the OAU has no role in conflict management. First of all, officials of the General Secretariat have a duty to monitor conflicts and draw up reports to the Secretary-General. They also recommend to him whether or not to launch a mediation initiative. This work entails research, travel and participation in ad hoc committees to be discussed below.[41]

As Secretariat officials have few autonomous powers their work is naturally of a subordinate nature and limited to advice and persuasion. As will be shown later, however, by the early 1990s Secretary-General Salim began to argue for a new and stronger role in conflict management. This led to the introduction of a more ambitious system of dispute settlement. It entailed, among others, a reinforcement of the Secretariat by the formation of a Division on Conflict Management within the Political Department (March 1992). This Division has the duty to monitor situations and gather and analyse information. Experts on political and military affairs are to be recruited in order to co-ordinate efforts aimed at establishing cease-fires and liaise between the Secretariat and mediation missions or observer operations in the field.[42] This new set-up must enable the Secretary-General to

---

34   See CM/Dec.7 (VII); CM/Res.100 (IX); CM/Dec.107 (XIV); CM/Dec.123 (XV); CM/Res.240 (XVI); CM/Res.628 (XXI); AHG/Dec.3 (III); AHG/Dec.33 (V); AHG/Dec.40 (VI); AHG/Dec.43 (VII); AHG/Dec.44 (VII); and AHG/Dec.60 (VIII).

35   See AHG/Dec.109 (XIV) and the report of the committee of legal experts on amendments of the Protocol CM/977 (XXXIII), Annex III.

36   *Times of Zambia*, 6/7/77 and *Daily Times* (Nigeria), 9/7/77.

37   Interview with Ambassador Mamadou Bah, Director of the Political Department, General Secretariat, Addis Ababa, 18/9/89.

38   Zartman and Touval, 'Conclusion' and Princen, *Intermediaries*.

39   *Daily Times* (Nigeria), 9/7/77 and AHG/Dec.109 (XIV).

40   Foltz, 'Organization of African Unity', pp 356-357. Also B. Boutros-Ghali, *l'Organisation de l'unité africaine* (Paris, 1969).

41   Interviews with Abdillahi Ali Dualeh, Chief of the General Political Affairs Section, General Political Affairs, Defence and Security Division and Mamadou Bah, Addis Ababa, 18/9/89 and Brief: General Political Affairs, Defence and Security Division (no date, c. 1989), p 1.

42   M.C.D. Wembou, 'A propos du nouveau mécanisme de l'OUA sur les conflits', in *Afrique 2000,*

establish, in collaboration with the Bureau of the Assembly, "an early warning system" with which to prevent and manage conflicts. The monitoring work of the Secretariat is the first phase in such a process,[43] although its reinforcement is in part a function of its past underdevelopment. The other aspects of this new system of conflict management are analysed further below, as well as in the following chapter.

Before 1993 the OAU's general policy organs were also concerned with the settlement of disputes. Their role was, in fact, of central importance and still is, even if the position of the Secretary-General has now been upgraded. The Council's competence can in this respect be inferred from art. 13 of the CMCA Protocol, which obliges the Commission to transfer a case to the Council if a disputant refuses to submit to its jurisdiction. This implies that the Council is entitled to discuss and mediate in inter-state disputes. It can base its involvement also on its preparation of Assembly summits, its flexible agenda and its power to establish ad hoc committees[44] with which to form groups of mediators. The Assembly can justify its involvement by reference to art. 8 Charter, which entitles it to discuss "matters of common concern to Africa".[45] As argued earlier, however, these provisions do not oblige the member states themselves to settle through these or other OAU organs.[46]

Nevertheless, Council and Assembly sessions as such can offer a convenient forum to settle conflicts. Regimes as the OAU may provide disputants with vital information about each other's intentions.[47] Such restoration of communication is, as shown above, a crucial step towards settlement. Council and Assembly sessions can, more specifically, be used to seek mediation or for unilateral initiatives by third actors.

Such mediation can take place through multilateral discussion, as illustrated in the dispute between Senegal and Mauritania in 1989.[48] In special circumstances an extraordinary session may even be called. While this is, as shown in section 5.6, very difficult in the case of the Assembly, the Council has been called into extraordinary session on several occasions. Especially during the 1960s such sessions had to deal with conflicts such as, for example, between Algeria and Morocco and civil strife in Congo(-Leo.).[49] As such plenary mediation takes place at the highest or second highest level of Africa's leadership and involves a large number of states, disputants may experience considerable pressure to settle.[50] Discussions may result in resolutions calling on disputants to reach a settlement.

February 1994, pp 10-11.

43   CM/1710 (LVI) Rev. 1: Report of the Secretary-General on Conflicts in Africa: Prospects for an OAU Mechanism for Conflict Prevention and Resolution (June 1992) [hereinafter as CM/1710 (LVI) Rev.1: Report of the SG on Conflicts in Africa (June 1992)], p 1-4 and letter by Dr. C.J. Bakwesegha, Head of Conflict Management Division (since March 1992), to author, 7/12/92.

44   Rules 15 and 36, Rules of Procedures, Council of Ministers.

45   See also Rules 11 and 37, Rules of Procedure, Assembly.

46   Also Ph. Kunig, *Das völkerrechtliche Nichteinmischungsprinzip: Zur Praxis der Organisation der afrikanischen Einheit (OAU) und des afrikanischen Staatenverkehrs* (Baden-Baden, 1981), pp 150-155.

47   H. Milner, 'International Theories of Cooperation among Nations: Strengths and Weaknesses', in *World Politics*, 1992, pp 476-478.

48   Interview with Amadou Kebe, Conseiller of the Senegalese embassy, Addis Ababa, 3/10/89.

49   See ECM/Res.1 (I); ECM/Res.5 (III); and ECM/Res.7 (IV).

50   Foltz, 'Organization of African Unity', p 357.

However, care is usually taken not to condemn any particular party.[51] There is some rationality in this, as the absence of hegemonic leadership and the OAU's large number of participants would make it hard to follow up collective denunciation with more concrete steps. Moreover, discussion in the plenary organs may not be an effective way to settle a conflict. Proceedings may be used to embarrass the other party and do not allow bargaining under the protection of face-saving formula's. Thus, mediation in a fully multilateral context is, in a more general way, not a very successful strategy.[52]

Yet, Council and Assembly have more on offer than plenary proceedings. They provide a great array of diplomatic facilities, principal among which is the opportunity for behind the scenes negotiations and mediation initiatives. Most summits have been marked by attempts to mediate in conflicts that were not part of the formal agenda and some have witnessed a temporary or permanent reconciliation of disputants.[53] International organizations, and particularly the OAU, operate on the basis of the principle of flexibility:[54] in the OAU it is seen as more important that a conflict is settled within the Organization's framework or that it is settled at all than that settlement is effected *by* the Pan-African institution.[55] For example, mediation efforts by a head of state who is also Assembly chairman are regarded as forms of OAU mediation.[56]

Selection of a mediator or group of mediators takes place on an ad hoc basis. This may amount to no more than a unilateral initiative on the part of the intervening state(s). As argued in the previous section, this must be explained by reference to the divergent interests underlying the complex of power political links between disputants and mediator. Formal appointment by the OAU to a special mediation committee will, in view of this, involve some politicking between disputants and third actors.[57] In case of a unilateral initiative, its success will usually be sanctioned and thus given added legitimacy by the OAU's policy organs. For instance, in 1978 the Assembly formally legitimized the result of a collective mediation initiative by the presidents of Liberia, Togo and Gambia in the conflicts between Guinea and Ivory Coast and Guinea and Senegal.[58]

Because of the concentration of domestic presidential power it is logical that disputants usually prefer a fellow head of state as mediator. The influential position that such a mediator occupies at home and his related prestige in inter-African relations increase the likelihood that a settlement will stick or can entice a disputant to accept mediation in the hope that this will further other power political objectives. Diplomats are

---

51　F.i. CM/Res.16 (II); CM/Res.17 (II); CM/Res.1069 (XLIV)/Rev.1; ECM/Res.4 (II); AHG/Res.19 (I); AHG/Res.94 (XV); and AHG/Res.158 (XXII).

52　Zartman, 'Conflict Reduction' and A. Sesay, O. Ojo and O. Fasehun, *The OAU After Twenty Years* (Boulder and London, 1984), pp 36-37.

53　See f.i. on the Rabat summit and the end of the Algero-Moroccan border conflict *Révolution Africaine* (Algeria), 16-22/6/72 (article) and *l'Opinion* (Morocco), 7/6/72 (article and text joint communiqué).

54　See also A. LeRoy Bennett, *International Organizations: Principles and Issues* (5th ed., Englewood Cliffs, 1991), p 102.

55　Foltz, 'Organization of African Unity', pp 356 and 365.

56　As was also borne out in an interview with Mamadou Bah, Addis Ababa, 18/9/89.

57　Zartman and Touval, 'Conclusion', p 263 and Touval and Zartman, 'Introduction'.

58　AHG/Res.88 (XV).

of secondary importance.[59] For example, Haile Selassie enjoyed considerable prestige among his peers for his work in inter-African relations. He was therefore frequently called upon, or acted on his own initiative, to mediate, whether or not in co-operation with other leaders.[60] Other heads of state are also regularly involved in mediation efforts. Often the Assembly will request a leader to mediate, give him formal encouragement or express its gratitude about his efforts afterwards.[61] Because the leader who is current Assembly chairman commands, as shown in section 5.6, substantial prestige, such a head of state is also seen as an important potential mediator.[62] Besides the power political considerations underlying mediation by heads of state, the significance of prestige attributed to them also illustrates the importance of persuasion in the mediating context.[63]

The Secretary-General has rarely been asked as mediator. Until the early 1990s he lacked formal political prerogatives. Even now his potential leverage over disputants is restricted by the Organization's limited resources. Not being a fellow head of state he lacks the clout and the kind of self-interest — other than the stake that the OAU has in the curtailment of conflicts as such — that provide the power political calculations on which disputants agree to mediation.[64]

If the policy organs, before 1993, decided to appoint a committee of several mediators care was taken to achieve balanced composition, notwithstanding the politicking that could be involved. Criteria for selection could, and still can, be the Assembly presidency and the proximity of a state to the area of conflict.[65] As shown in section 2.4, patterns of inter-African influence are more significant at the regional level. Mediators from the region therefore often perform better,[66] as they will usually have more leverage. Yet, even in the regional context influence is not unlimited. This restricts the application of sticks and carrots, although these are anyway less important than the mediator's persuasive abilities.[67]

Mediation committees may therefore include various countries, including states from in and outside the region and/or countries that are relatively influential in inter-African relations such as, for example, Algeria, Nigeria, Zaire and Ethiopia.[68] This variety in

59   See Zartman, 'Conflict Reduction', p 311.
60   Overview of his mediation efforts in Cervenka, *Unfinished Quest*, pp 67-68 and T. Maluwa, 'The Peaceful Settlement of Disputes Among African States, 1963-1983: Some Conceptual Issues and Practical Trends', in *International and Comparative Law Quarterly*, 1989, pp 318-319. Tributes to Selassie in AHG/Res.54 (V); *Zambia Daily Mail*, 18/6/71; and *The Standard* (Tanzania), 2/9/70.
61   F.i. ECM/Res.5 (III); ECM/Res.7 (IV); AHG/Res.54 (V); AHG/Res.88 (XV); AHG/Res.93 (XV); AHG/Res.94 (XV); AHG/Res.151 (XXII); AHG/Res.158 (XXII); AHG/Dec.13 (IV); AHG/Dec.18 (IV); and AHG/St.1 (IV).
62   See f.i. AHG/Res.93 (XV); AHG/Res.94 (XV); AHG/Res.143 (XXI); *Cameroon Tribune*, 26-27/7/87 and 28/7/87 (articles); *Daily Mail* (Sierra Leone), 24/6/81; and *The Standard* (Tanzania), 2/9/70.
63   Zartman and Touval, 'Conclusion' and Princen, *Intermediaries*.
64   Also B.D. Meyers, 'The OAU's Administrative Secretary-General', in *International Organization*, 1976, p 516.
65   See Sesay, Ojo and Fasehun, *OAU After Twenty Years*, p 37.
66   See Zartman, 'Conflict Reduction'.
67   Zartman and Touval, 'Conclusion'.
68   See also M. Wolfers, 'The Organization of African Unity as Mediator', in Touval and Zartman, *International Mediation* (n. 8), pp 191-192.

selection patterns can be illustrated with a few examples. The ad hoc commission that was to hammer out a definitive settlement of the Algero-Moroccan border war included Ethiopia, a country with considerable prestige; Mali, a regional state; as well as conservative and militant member states, both English-speaking and Francophone.[69] The consultative mission that conferred with Nigeria over the secession of Biafra included two presidents of neighbouring countries: President Diori of Niger, who favoured the federal cause, and President Ahidjo of Cameroon, who was known for his sympathy with the secessionists.[70] However, no regional powers were included in the committee mediating in the Sudan-Ethiopia dispute during the late 1970s, possibly because of the tense relations characterizing the Horn of Africa. It did include the country occupying the Assembly presidency (Gabon) and states with various ideological affiliations from different regions.[71] Finally, the six-nation committee that mediated in the Mauritanian-Senegalese dispute of 1989-1991 included three regional states, namely Niger, Nigeria and Togo.[72]

Normative provisions

Multilateral institutions also contribute to conflict management indirectly by introducing norms by which states must abide in their mutual interaction. Thus, in the course of its existence the OAU has introduced several norms with which it tries to manage Africa's political order. The totality of institutional and normative provisions represents the OAU's strategy to conflict management. In order to fully comprehend the role that the OAU plays in this issue area, some of these normative provisions must therefore be analysed. As not all of them can be studied here, some general remarks will first be made on the significance of OAU norms to Africa's political order, followed by a discussion of three norms that have been singled out for more detailed examination. These have been selected for their centrality in conflict management and as illustrative of the varying degrees in effectiveness of such norms. Other norms will be discussed in the course of section 8.1.

The OAU's norms must be distinguished from its decision-making procedures and rules: as standards of behaviour in terms of rights and obligations they form the defining characteristics of the OAU regime. Infusing state behaviour with these norms the OAU constitutes an interactive variable in inter-African politics, as they alter patterns of influence and the assessment of state interests.[73] Thus, section 5.6 showed that states use

---

69   They were Ivory Coast, Nigeria, Tanganyika, Sudan and Senegal. ECM/Res.1 (I).

70   AHG/Res.51 (V). The others were Zaire, which held the Assembly chairmanship, Ghana, Liberia, whose leader was the senior statesman President Tubman, and, again, Ethiopia. Also Z. Cervenka, 'The OAU and the Nigerian Civil War', in Y. El-Ayouty (ed), *The Organization of African Unity After Ten Years: Comparative Perspectives* (New York, 1976), p 156.

71   Algeria, Nigeria, Senegal, Sierra Leone, Togo, Cameroon, Zaire and Zambia. Later on, Tanzania's president was involved in the mediation effort as well. See AHG/Dec.107 (XIV) and AHG/Res.93 (XV). Also C.O.C. Amate, *Inside the OAU: Pan-Africanism in Practice* (New York, 1986), pp 445-451.

72   *Africa Research Bulletin* (Political, Social, Cultural Series; hereinafter as PSC), 1989, pp 9370 and 9402 and text of Assembly resolution in *Le Soleil* (Senegal), 12/7/90.

73   S.D. Krasner, 'Structural causes and regime consequences: regimes as intervening variables', and *ibid.*, 'Regimes and the limits of realism: regimes as autonomous variables', both in S.D. Krasner (ed), *International Regimes* (Ithaca and London, 1983), pp 1-21 and 355-368 respectively.

sessions of the policy organs to seek legitimation of their own, and delegitimation of their adversaries', arguments in terms of the norms of the OAU regime.

The norms that play a role in this process are rarely cast in legally binding sets of rules such as international treaties. Most are issued as resolutions, declarations and statements and are legally neither binding nor enforceable, as they are not related to the OAU's internal functioning. Yet, as they are adopted at the level of Africa's highest leadership and are usually carried on the basis of consensus, they do possess considerable political weight. With sessions of the policy organs as a recurrent feature of inter-African politics, states defecting from these norms risk retaliation in the future.[74]

However, while these norms encourage a certain approach in conflict management[75] they do not settle concrete disputes. Their influence is also restricted by the limits of the OAU's legitimating role as such. As observed in section 5.6, this role is circumscribed by the effectiveness and, hence, legitimacy of the OAU itself; the simultaneous relevance of conflicting norms; and the limits that the egalitarian nature of interaction in the policy organs imposes on the extent to which one can delegitimize state behaviour. Moreover, some norms are more effective than others. While most are from time to time tested, in some cases violation does not provoke effective retaliation. The absence of hegemonic leadership comes into play here. Especially since the mid-1970s, some norms have come under increasing pressure. As changes in norms point to conflict in the underlying structures of the political process,[76] these developments may form a signal of fundamental shifts in some aspects of the continental order.[77]

Nevertheless, until now most of the OAU's norms have been fairly rigid. In general, the norms and principles of a regime are very durable. Its decision-making procedures and rules change more easily, but this merely signifies a change within the regime itself. Naturally, a change in the configuration of power underlying an international regime does not immediately lead to a transformation of its norms, *i.e.* of the regime itself. Yet, the durability of many OAU norms seems more pronounced than what regime theorists would allow for in terms of the lags in the dynamics of regime transmutation.[78] This durability thus points to the solidity, rather than the inconstancy, of the underlying structures of the continental order. Moreover, most OAU norms possess explicit clarity. As hegemonic stability theory relates unambiguous norms to a strong regime dominated by a powerful actor,[79] the clarity of norms that the weak OAU regime has produced can only be explained in terms of the considerable interest that these norms hold for the totality of Africa's state elites. We will return to the question of the durability of the inter-African political order in the following chapter.

---

74 See generally K.A. Oye, 'Explaining Cooperation Under Anarchy: Hypotheses and Strategies', in K.A. Oye (ed), *Cooperation Under Anarchy* (Princeton, 1986), pp 1-24.

75 Zartman, 'Conflict Reduction', p 316.

76 S.D. Krasner, *Structural Conflict: The Third World against Global Liberalism* (Berkeley, Los Angeles and London, 1985), ch. 1.

77 See also R.I. Onwuka and T.M. Shaw (eds), *Africa in World Politics: Into the 1990s* (Basingstoke and London, 1989).

78 Krasner, 'Structural causes and regime consequences' and 'Regimes and the limits of realism'.

79 R.O. Keohane, 'The Theory of Hegemonic Stability and Changes in International Economic Regimes, 1967-77', in O.R. Holsti, R.M. Siverson and A.L. George (eds), *Change in the International System* (Boulder, 1980), p 132.

African solutions to African problems

In terms of the rationale in OAU dispute settlement, the most important norm is the prescription that member states must first try to settle their conflicts in an African cadre. The basis for this norm lies in art. 52 UN Charter, which holds that members of regional organizations should first make every effort to settle local disputes through such institutions. The Security Council must also encourage the utilization of regional arrangements, although it reserves the right to consider disputes and is the only institution to authorize or delegate enforcement action.[80]

The OAU therefore has a competence of *initial*, not exclusive, concern with inter-African conflicts. In practice, the UN has backed the OAU claim by refusing to consider such disputes and encouraging settlement through the OAU. In the past this policy was related to the unwillingness or inability of the superpowers to settle these disputes in the Security Council; the relative lack of strategic importance attributed to these conflicts, especially during the OAU's first decade; and the discouragement by the African Group of attempts to use the UN for settlement.[81]

Thus, the OAU and its member states have claimed, and at several instances reaffirmed, this competence of initial concern in resolutions, the wording of which might vary but whose basic idea remained the same.[82] For instance, in its discussion of the Algero-Moroccan border war of 1963 the Council emphasized "the imperative need of settling all differences between African States ... within a strictly African framework".[83] The need for this was later reaffirmed on numerous occasions,[84] including such recent events as the OAU's thirtieth anniversary celebrations in May 1993.[85]

However, as this competence of initial concern seeks to establish an allocation of responsibilities between the OAU and the UN, it does not prevent recourse to other inter-African organizations. Moreover, it does not extend to development issues, the humanitarian aspects of African refugee problems and the struggle against colonialism. In all these cases the OAU has been eager to solicit support by the UN. At times the OAU also asked the Security Council to discuss certain African conflicts, although it tried to restrict deliberations to, and the UN was prepared to focus on, the extra-African aspects involved.[86] As far as purely inter-state disputes are concerned, the Organization and its African Group in New York have been by and large successful in discouraging member

---

80   See arts. 34, 35, 52 and 53 UN Charter.
81   B. Andemicael, *The OAU and the UN: Relations between the Organization of African Unity and the United Nations* (New York and London, 1976), pp 91-97.
82   For treatment of this Andemicael, *OAU and the UN*, p 91 ff.
83   ECM/Res.1 (I). Also *Sudan News*, October 1964 (article).
84   ECM/Res.3 (III); ECM/Res.5 (III); ECM/Res.7 (IV); AHG/Res.58 (VI); AHG/Res.16 (I); CM/Res.794 (XXXV); and AHG/Res.106 (XIX).
85   OAU at 30: Reflections on the Past and Prospects for the Future: Address by the Secretary-General, H.E. Dr. Salim Ahmed Salim on the occasion of the 30th Aniversary of the Organization of African Unity, Africa Hall, Addis Ababa, May 25, 1993, p 25-6.
86   See for examples Foltz, 'Organization of African Unity', p 355 and Cervenka, *Unfinished Quest*, p 66.

states to refer to UN fora.[87] Yet, with the subsidence of the Cold War inhibitions to take conflicts to the UN may diminish.[88]

Moreover, even if the OAU's competence of initial concern is upheld, this does not imply that it is itself able to achieve satisfactory settlement of conflicts. From the mid-1970s many conflicts, both inter-African and domestic, intensified. Part of this was caused by, as was shown in section 2.4, increasing rivalry between the superpowers and massive growth in armaments. These developments made it very difficult for the OAU to keep conflicts in bound. Predictably, enthusiasm of individual member states regarding involvement by the OAU declined in the face of its impotence.[89] This encouraged embattled governments to seek unilateral intervention by foreign, even non-African, powers or refer to other inter-African institutions, such as ECOWAS.

The latter trend is, admittedly, less serious, as it still dissuades extra-African involvement. However, many of the most serious crises have been domestic conflicts, in which any competence of initial OAU concern was for long complicated by a different legal position. In several of these cases, such as the civil war in southern Sudan and the war in Eritrea, the OAU preferred not to act rather than bring the issues before the United Nations. Reticence to take African conflicts to the UN could therefore limit the chances of effective conflict management.[90] A total collapse of domestic security, such as in Somalia during the early 1990s, could then lead to UN involvement and unilateral extra-African intervention anyway. The repercussions to the OAU of extra-African or UN intervention and recourse to other inter-African institutions are discussed in the next chapter.

The sanctity of colonial boundaries
In the first year of its existence the OAU issued the prescription of *uti possidetis, i.e.* the norm originally formulated in Latin American state practice to respect the boundaries that the new states inherited from the colonial powers.[91] During its first summit the Assembly was confronted with a serious territorial conflict between Somalia on the one hand and Ethiopia and Kenya on the other. Somalia articulated irredentist aspirations to have all Somali people in the Ethiopian Ogaden and the Kenyan "Northern Frontier District" included in the Somali state. In an attempt to nip territorial conflicts in the bud, the Assembly adopted a resolution which emphasized in the preamble that the borders of African states formed, "on the day of their independence", a "tangible reality". The operative sections reaffirmed the "strict respect" by all member states for art. 3.3 of the Charter (respect for territorial integrity) and declared "that all Member States pledge them-selves to respect the borders existing on their achievement of national independence".[92]

---

87   *Ibid.* Rarely have disputes been referred to the International Court of Justice, such as the Burkina Faso - Mali border dispute. See Maluwa, 'Peaceful Settlement of Disputes'.
88   For example, early 1994 Cameroon vainly tried to bring a territorial dispute with Nigeria before the Security Council. *Africa Research Bulletin* (PSC), 1994, p 11353.
89   Maluwa, 'Peaceful Settlement', p 317.
90   B. Andemicael and D. Nicol, 'The OAU: Primacy in Seeking African Solutions within the UN Charter', in Y. El-Ayouty and I.W. Zartman (eds), *The OAU After Twenty Years* (New York, 1984), pp 101-119.
91   I. Brownlie, *Principles of Public International Law* (Oxford, 1979), pp 137-138.
92   AHG/Res.16 (I).

Although this norm can be deduced from the respect for territorial integrity, the resolution made it more explicit by focusing on the borders themselves. In the light of its preamble and the context in which the resolution was formulated it is clear that the last paragraph refers to frontiers as inherited upon *decolonization* and not the borders of states as existing in a distant, pre-colonial past.

However, the resolution does not solve disagreements over the exact location of colonial frontiers, a problem that may be compounded by absence of demarcation.[93] The Council of Ministers recognized this in 1986 by expressing its wish that all sources of tension pertaining to inter-state frontiers be removed. It acknowledged the existence of border problems, reaffirmed that they should be settled by peaceful means on the basis of the Assembly resolution of 1964 and encouraged member states to negotiate the demarcation of common borders by the erection of beacons.[94] Still, by this explicit stand and its regular reiteration[95] the OAU cannot actually resolve a conflict in those cases where the norm of *uti possidetis* is itself contested. In such cases most of its leverage is eliminated, as its persuasive powers depend on the ability to formulate a good alternative to stalemate. If conflict transformation, in terms of a redefinition of the contentious issue or emphasis of consonant aspects in disputants' ties, is impossible, such formulation is limited to repeating past statements.[96]

Naturally, rigid adherence to *uti possidetis* hardly contributes to an alleviation of the problems of peoples living in frontier regions. The high degree of arbitrariness of inter-state boundaries can be deduced from the fact that in many cases they cut across ethnic and even family ties. Although boundaries are far more permeable than regulations suggest Africa's strict border regimes hinder communication, especially in the case of nomadic communities.[97] As such, the OAU's norm on frontiers has become, in a more general way, a symbol of the Organization's inclination to protect the interests of state elites to the detriment of the people at large.[98]

Yet, among elite Africans criticism of colonial frontiers may be related not so much to the difficulties they cause to frontier communities, as to their significance as markers of Africa's encounter with European imperialism. Like the concepts of balkanization and organic unity discussed in sections 3.4 and 4.3, such criticism betrays a sense of vulnerability and inferiority to the Western world.[99]

However, even if representatives of state elites, such as Diallo Telli before he became Secretary-General, sometimes acknowledged the arbitrariness of colonial

---

93 An overview of border and territorial disputes since decolonization in S. Touval, *The Boundary Politics of Independent Africa* (Cambridge, Mass., 1972), pp 279-290 and one on frontier demarcation in I. Brownlie, *African Boundaries: A Legal and Diplomatic Encyclopaedia* (London, 1979).

94 CM/Res.1069 (XLIV)/Rev.1. Reservation by Somalia.

95 See f.i. AHG/Res.158 (XXII) (reservation by Libya) and AHG/Res.167 (XXIII).

96 Deutsch, 'Subjective Features', p 38 (n. 6) and Väyrynen, 'To Settle or Transform?', p 5 (n. 4).

97 See especially A.I. Asiwaju (ed), *Partitioned Africans: Ethnic Relations across Africa's International Boundaries 1884-1984* (London and Lagos, 1985).

98 E. M'buyinga, *Pan-Africanism or Neo-Colonialism: The Bankruptcy of the O.A.U.* (London, 1982), pp 186 and 199-202. Also *Cameroon Tribune*, 9/8/86 (article).

99 See f.i. *Horoya* (Guinea), 19-20/7/64 (article) and M'buyinga, *Pan-Africanism*, p 199.

frontiers,[100] most countries have emphasized, at various points in time, the need to maintain them.[101] In view of their defining function for the state, the desire to control the population and the need to prevent destabilization of inter-African relations this carries its own logic. Moreover, rigid border regimes are not inherent in *uti possidetis* as such but a consequence of the difficult relations between state elites and the social forces that are denied access to the state. Any proposal to tackle such problems by revising borders touches the surface of the issue and risks creating more serious problems than it solves. With regard to frontier communities themselves one may nevertheless argue that the negative proscription of *uti possidetis* should be accompanied by a constructive form of inter-state frontier management.[102]

While *uti possidetis* is, despite opposition from Morocco and Somalia, widely accepted among state elites,[103] this does not mean that the norm is never challenged by governments themselves. Territorial claims lie dormant as long as the structures of inter-African relations remain by and large the same. Depending on circumstance they may be resurrected. For example, in 1976-77 Togo revived territorial claims against Ghana in an effort to bring all Ewe-speaking peoples in its fold. Predictably, it got a negative response from both Ghana and other countries.[104] Only voluntary border revisions, such as between Senegal and Gambia,[105] do not arouse criticism. While going against the letter of the Assembly resolution of 1964, such revisions do not jeopardize the inter-African order.

Thus, there can be no doubt that *uti possidetis* has contributed to the stability of inter-African relations. While the low incidence of border conflicts is also due to the desire of governments not to upset their domestic ethnic balance and the limited capabilities of their armed forces, broad consensus on the norm has added to the barriers erected against attempts to change the status quo. Any state attempting to revise frontiers would face a hostile reaction during future OAU sessions. Worse still, it could be confronted with counter-claims. As argued in game theory, the pay-off of violation would thus diminish in the calculations by that state about the future. Moreover, because of its importance one can argue that the norm has been internalized in foreign policy objectives: being considered valuable in itself, the benefit of violation is reduced even further.[106]

---

100 See his remarks in *Horoya* (Guinea), 19-20/7/64 (article).
101 See f.i. *The Standard* (Kenya), 24/7/78; *l'Essor* (Mali), 8-9/7/78 (article); *Daily Times* (Nigeria), 25/4/80; *Le Soleil* (Senegal), 24/6/81 (article); and *Révolution Africaine* (Algeria), 20/5/88 (article).
102 A.I. Asiwaju, 'The Global Perspective and Border Management Policy Options', in Asiwaju, *Partitioned Africans*, pp 245-248.
103 See for a Moroccan, intellectual critique of this A. El-Ouali, '"L'uti possidetis" ou le non-sens du "principe de base" de l'OUA pour le règlement des différends territoriaux', in *Le Mois en Afrique*, 1984-85, nos. 227-228, pp 3-19.
104 *Togo Presse*, 20/1/76 (article) and 21/1/76 and *Daily Mail* (Sierra Leone), 19/2/77 (article). Background in *Africa Contemporary Record*, 1976-77, B583.
105 See *Africa Contemporary Record*, 1976-77, B570.
106 Oye, 'Explaining Cooperation Under Anarchy', p 11 and H. Bull, *The Anarchical Society: A Study of Order in World Politics* (London, 1977), p 67.

The prohibition of subversion

While prohibition of subversion is a logical corollary of the principle of territorial integrity, it was explicitly included in art. 3.5 of the OAU Charter. However, there is no norm that was and is violated so frequently as the anti-subversion norm. For most states conventional warfare is usually not a viable option due to the limited capabilities of their armies. In contrast, subversion in the form of armed support to foreign nationals is cheap and easy. It is also much harder to prove. The rewards of violation therefore become higher as such empirical hurdles make diplomatic retaliation more difficult than in the case of a conventional invasion.[107]

However, under Nkrumah the government of Ghana did not escape retribution for the assistance it provided to opposition groups in various West African states. This took the form of provision of asylum, financial aid, military training and diplomatic support.[108] Matters came to a head after an unsuccessful invasion of Niger in the autumn of 1964 by guerrilla's of Sawaba and an abortive attempt on the life of Niger's head of state (April 1965). Several Francophone governments threatened to boycott the Assembly summit that was to be held in Accra, although they had probably never intended to go to the summit in the first place so as to damage Nkrumah's regime.[109]

Nigeria requested an extraordinary session of the Council of Ministers to discuss the allegations against the Assembly's host. Besides accusations by Niger about Ghana's complicity in Sawaba's activities, the Ivorian delegate accused the Ghanaians of encouraging separatist aspirations of the Sanwi people living in their common border region. The delegate of Upper Volta gave an extensive analysis of various border incidents that had occurred between his country and Ghana.[110]

The conference ended with a resolution that gave a clue as to how governments actually defined the concept of subversion. For African regimes this covered a wide range of activities. Thus, the resolution called on Ghana to expel all persons deemed undesirable by other member states and forbid the formation of political groups whose aims were to oppose fellow OAU members.[111] The Assembly session that followed on this asked members not to create dissension within or among member states by fomenting or aggravating racial, religious, linguistic, ethnic or other differences and to combat all activities of this kind.[112] It also asked members to encourage the voluntary return of refugees, adding that the safety of political refugees from dependent territories should be guaranteed. This implied that political activities of refugees from member states should be disallowed.[113] Moreover, the Assembly also called on members not to conduct press or

---

107 Oye, 'Explaining Cooperation Under Anarchy'.

108 See W.S. Thompson, *Ghana's Foreign Policy 1957-1966: Diplomacy, Ideology, and the New State* (Princeton, 1969).

109 See f.i. Houphouët's speech at the OCAM summit in *Fraternité* (Ivory Coast), 28/5/65.

110 Text of speeches in *Fraternité* (Ivory Coast), 25/6/65; 23/7/65; and 2/7, 9/7 and 16/7/65 respectively.

111 ECM/Res.9 (V). Eight Francophone states nevertheless boycotted the Assembly session in the end, arguing that Ghana had not fully implemented the Council resolution. See f.i. the text of an Entente communiqué in *Fraternité* (Ivory Coast), 22/10/65.

112 AHG/Res.27 (II).

113 *Ibid*. See further section 8.1.

radio campaigns against each other,[114] which in times of crisis often lead to slanging matches that add to existing tensions.[115] OAU guidelines on this were applied in a successful effort to settle a dispute between Guinea and Senegal in the early 1970s, when a mediation committee recommended the cessation of all hostile propaganda through the media.[116]

However, without hegemonic leadership the OAU can often do little more than appeal not to resort to subversion, whether of the military or more harmless sort. Its impotence is especially marked if member states are fighting for regional dominance, as in the Horn of Africa during the 1970s and 1980s.[117]

The effectiveness of norms
The three norms discussed above show that, with the lack of hegemonic leadership, effectiveness depends considerably on the interest they embody for Africa's state elites. This corresponds with a contention of regime theory, which holds that one of the most important factors in the creation of regimes is the self-interest of states.[118] Such self-interest contributes towards a regime with norms that influence state behaviour in order to avoid sub-optimal outcomes. This is especially clear in the case of *uti possidetis*. As an interactive variable, the OAU regime infuses behaviour with a norm whose broad support alters calculations of state interests. In this respect the only two countries questioning the norm, Morocco and Somalia, find themselves isolated.

Effectiveness of the norm stipulating OAU competence of initial concern is, in relation to the UN, buttressed by the ability to thwart access to the world body. In other respects it suffers from limits on the OAU's ability in conflict management and, concomitantly, intervention of extra-African factors and the presence of other inter-African institutions.

Ineffectiveness is most pronounced in the case of the anti-subversion norm. Absence of a hegemon and the large number of actors are particularly nefarious here. Anonimity of the state violating it is more assured than in the case of *uti possidetis*. Retaliation becomes more difficult and pay-offs of violation, as compared to compliance, are higher.[119] Moreover, regimes matter little in issue areas characterized by zero-sum conditions like security.[120] Members have a strong stake in reserving subversion as potential foreign policy weapon and the OAU can do little more than appeal to them not to use it. Yet, conflict situations are rarely fully zero-sum. Only in disputes escalating to high levels of violence may such conditions occur, which are then still a matter of

---

114   AHG/Res.27 (II).
115   For an example *Fraternité* (Ivory Coast), 25/6/65 (text of speech of the president of Upper Volta aimed at Sékou Touré).
116   See CM/Res.253 (XVII) and for the text of the recommendation *Africa Contemporary Record*, 1972-73, C111-112.
117   See f.i. AHG/105 (XVIII): Report of the Good-Offices Commission on the Ethiopia-Somali Dispute, Lagos, 18-20 August 1980.
118   D.R. Young, 'Regime dynamics: the rise and fall of international regimes', in Krasner, *International Regimes*, pp 93-113.
119   Oye, 'Explaining Cooperation Under Anarchy', p 16 ff.
120   R. Jervis, 'Security regimes', in Krasner, *International Regimes*, pp 173-194.

perception.[121] It is therefore not surprising that no state has challenged the anti-subversion norm as such — as this is not in their interest — and that it sometimes contributes positively to the management of conflicts.

Disputed territory: Somalia vs Ethiopia and Kenya
This conflict was selected as case study because the OAU's mediation efforts involved, over the years, different strategies showing the range and limitations of its efforts in conflict management. Analysis is limited to the years 1963 - c. 1980, as OAU involvement was most explicit during this period.[122]

Contrary to other regions of the continent, large parts of the Horn of Africa are settled by one single people, the Somali's. Their cultural cohesion is based on a shared language, a strong adherence to Islam and a nomadic way of life, at least for the majority of people. While socio-political organization is grounded in sub-clans, clans and larger confederations and these institutions have drawn important cleavages within the Somali people, the degree of their cultural homogeneity is remarkable, at least if compared to other parts of Africa. A strong predilection for a nomadic way of life ensured not only that, through the centuries, Somali groups expanded and peopled large parts of the Horn, but also that they developed a difficult relationship with the modern nation-state: introduced with the advent of colonialism, this institution formed an exotic intrusion in Somali political culture, among others because it grounded state sovereignty and jurisdiction in the concept of territoriality.

This notion implied maintenance of territorial frontiers and thus clashed with the very essence of nomadic life, *i.e.* freedom of movement. Colonial rule led to the distribution of Somali people over five different territories — Djibouti, the Ethiopian Ogaden, British Somaliland, Italian Somalia and Kenya's Northern Frontier District (NFD) — and the imposition of frontiers separating nomads from certain wells and pastoral grounds. Both before and after independence this situation provided sufficient cause to various Somali groups to resist the efforts of the governments of Ethiopia and Kenya — but at times also of Somalia proper — to impose control over their lives and movement.

The government of independent Somalia, which was formed in 1960 with the merger of British Somaliland and Italian Somalia, had its own interests in encouraging Somali nationalism, which was widespread and strongly felt among many of its citizens. In the NFD and Ogaden this sentiment was articulated in secessionist movements calling for "return" to one Somali republic. This irredentist aim corresponded with the narrower interest of the Somali government to consolidate its control, as monopolized by certain socio-economic groups and clans, over the Somali people. The irredentist goal was formally inscribed in the constitution. Finally, another factor adding to the geo-political

---

121   M. Nicholson, 'Negotiation, Agreement and Conflict Resolution: The Role of Rational Approaches and their Criticism', in Väyrynen, *New Directions in Conflict Theory*, pp 61-63 (n. 4).

122   See for the following f.i. I.M. Lewis, *A Modern History of Somalia: Nation and State in the Horn of Africa* (London and New York, 1980); J. Markakis, *National and Class Conflict in the Horn of Africa* (Cambridge, 1987); S.S. Samatar, 'The Somali Dilemma: Nation in search of a state', in Asiwaju, *Partitioned Africans*, pp 155-193; and I.M. Lewis (ed), *Nationalism and Self-Determination in the Horn of Africa* (London, 1983).

problems of the region was the exact course of the borders between Ethiopia and Italian Somalia. As a result of the scramble for territory by Britain, Italy and Ethiopia at the end of the nineteenth century these were ill-defined, let alone demarcated.

During the early 1960s Somali guerrilla's, supported by the Somali government, raided targets inside the NFD and Ogaden. Early 1964 this escalated into clashes between the regular armies of Somalia and Ethiopia. Somalia preferred to have the matter discussed by the Security Council, as it did not expect the OAU, with its commitment to territorial integrity, to be very sympathetic. However, African delegations at the UN opposed this and the UN Secretary-General referred the dispute to the OAU.[123]

Ethiopia did, indeed, prefer the OAU to handle the matter. It asked for an extraordinary session of the Council of Ministers, whereupon Somalia called for OAU mediation as well. Ethiopia and Kenya wished to concentrate on the territorial ambitions of Somalia, as this could isolate their adversary in inter-African politics. Conversely, Somalia desired to focus on a cease-fire and creation of a demilitarized zone. Its irredentism made its diplomatic position very weak and the Ethiopian army was, at the time, much stronger than its own armed forces. A demilitarized zone could, moreover, strengthen the impression that the international status of the Ogaden and NFD was in doubt.[124]

Thus, the Ethiopian delegate gave a detailed exposé of his country's dispute with Somalia and recounted the numerous border incidents of the preceding years. He accused the Somali government of fomenting tension with hostile propaganda. He also claimed that Mogadishu had not only instigated guerrilla attacks but had also sent regular troops, disguised as nomads, into Ethiopian territory.[125] The Somali delegate claimed that Ethiopia had organized land and air attacks deep inside Somalia in an attempt to widen the conflict. The OAU should call for a cease-fire and appoint observers for its supervision. While circumventing the wider territorial issue, the Somali representative observed that the Ogaden guerrilla's were no bandits but people in revolt against an oppressive government. He also complained about Ethiopia's "unnecessary polemics" and accused it of speaking from a position of strength.[126] The Kenyan representative also focused on Somalia's expansionist designs and gave an account of past negotiations that Britain, Kenya and Somalia had engaged in. He also set out the growth in attacks on the NFD and Mogadishu's propaganda war for its "return" to Somalia.[127] The Somali delegate accused Kenya of ignoring the wishes of the NFD's population, which had expressed the desire to join the Somali republic. He appealed for a referendum and the territory's "reunion" with Somalia if a majority expressed itself accordingly.[128]

The Council of Ministers refused to go into the merits of the disputes and concentrated on de-fusing tension. It ignored the appeal for a demilitarized zone and

123 Touval, *Boundary Politics*, p 216 (n. 93).

124 *Verbatim Record* of the Second Extraordinary Session of the Council of Ministers, Dar es Salaam, February 1964 (hereinafter as *VR*, ECM2, Dar es Salaam, Febr. 1964), ECM/PV.4, p 2 ff and ECM/PV.5, p 20. Also Touval, *Boundary Politics*, p 218.

125 *VR*, ECM2, Dar es Salaam, Febr. 1964, ECM/PV.3, pp 51-81.

126 *VR*, ECM2, Dar es Salaam, Febr. 1964, ECM/PV.4, pp 2-23.

127 *VR*, ECM2, Dar es Salaam, Febr. 1964, ECM/PV.5, pp 13-21.

128 *Ibid.*, pp 21-25.

neutral observers and did not debate Somalia's territorial ambitions. It called on Ethiopia and Somalia to order an immediate cease-fire, refrain from all hostile action, stop all propaganda and commence negotiations for a settlement. African states with embassies in both countries were asked to assist in the implementation of the cease-fire. The resolution on the Somali-Kenyan conflict merely called for a peaceful settlement and an end to propaganda campaigns.[129]

At the Council's ordinary session at the end of February, Mogadishu repeated its call for the NFD's unification with Somalia. However, Kenya argued that the "principle of self-determination ... cannot be applied to free people living in an independent sovereign country".[130] This alluded to the way in which the OAU interpreted the concepts of colonialism and self-determination. The preceding chapter showed that, in this view, the configuration of power inside member states could not be equated with colonialism, as Somalia would later do with regard to Ethiopia's position in the Ogaden.[131] Similarly, movements struggling for autonomy or secession could not be considered as exercising the right to self-determination. This is discussed further in section 8.1.

This time the Council explicitly called on the parties to respect each other's territorial integrity. In the resolution on the Ethiopian-Somali conflict it merely spoke of a "border dispute", something that could be interpreted as more favourable to the Ethiopian-Kenyan side.[132]

After a precarious truce had, indeed, been effected, Ethiopia and Somalia engaged in negotiations in Khartoum. With mediation by the Sudanese government the meeting ended with a communiqué stipulating that, in pursuance of the OAU resolutions, military forces should be withdrawn from either side of the border; a bilateral commission should be appointed to supervise this and hostile propaganda should cease.[133] As Somalia was absent from the Assembly summit in Cairo due to a domestic political crisis, the disputes and negotiations that should follow up the truce could not be discussed. Instead, the Assembly introduced the norm of *uti possidetis*,[134] which underlined the lack of sympathy that Somalia encountered in the OAU.

Amidst minor skirmishes, Ethiopia and Somalia failed to engage in substantive bilateral talks the following year. There was no room for manoeuvre between Mogadishu's desire to discuss the status of the Ogaden and Ethiopia's insistence on recognition of its frontiers. Nevertheless, with the aid of the Ghanaian government the two sides met in the course of the Assembly summit in Accra and hammered out a formal agreement on the definition of hostile propaganda to complement the Khartoum communiqué.[135] At the summit, President Nyerere of Tanzania was asked by Somalia to

---

129   ECM/Res.3 (II) and ECM/Res.4 (II).
130   Extracts *Verbatim Record* in W.S. Thompson and I.W. Zartman, 'The Development of Norms in the African System', in El-Ayouty, *Organization of African Unity After Ten Years*, pp 31-33.
131   *Africa Research Bulletin* (PSC), 1977, pp 4525-4526 and J. Mayall, 'Self-Determination and the OAU', in Lewis, *Nationalism and Self-Determination*, pp 77-92.
132   CM/Res.16 (II) and CM/Res.17 (II).
133   Text in C. Hoskyns, *Case Studies in African Diplomacy*, no. II: *The Ethiopia-Somalia-Kenya Dispute 1960-67* (Dar es Salaam, Nairobi and Addis Ababa, 1969), pp 65-66.
134   AHG/Res.16 (I).
135   Text in Hoskyns, *Ethiopia-Somalia-Kenya Dispute*, pp 71-72.

mediate in its dispute with Kenya.[136] Mogadishu desired to somehow normalize its relations with Nairobi so as to reduce the pressure it was under from its two adversaries. The proposals it tabled were rejected, however, as Kenya still suspected territorial claims behind them.[137] The result was that relations between Ethiopia and Kenya on the one hand and Somalia on the other deteriorated again in 1966.

Yet, in the course of the Assembly summit in Kinshasa (1967), the three countries finally managed to start a process of normalization. Somalia asked President Kaunda of Zambia to mediate in the dispute with Kenya,[138] which led to adoption of a declaration in which both countries expressed respect for each other's territorial integrity in the spirit of art. 3.3 of the OAU's Charter. They also undertook to resolve remaining differences peacefully, to refrain from conducting hostile propaganda and maintain peace and security in the border region. The declaration was welcomed and endorsed by the OAU Assembly.[139] Both sides reaffirmed it in negotiations that began in Arusha two months later with the mediation of President Kaunda. This meeting led to agreement on normalizing diplomatic and economic ties, suspension of emergency regulations and the formation of a trilateral working committee to review implementation of the accords. A memorandum also spoke of a willingness to settle "major and minor differences".[140]

As far as the Ethiopia-Somalia dispute was concerned, both sides met shortly after the Kinshasa summit in Addis Ababa, where an accord was reached on minor issues that eased the tension between them. They also came to an agreement on the convening of regular meetings of regional administrators to discuss co-operation on matters affecting both sides of the border.[141]

The accord with Ethiopia did not contain an explicit retraction of Somali claims over the Ogaden. The agreement with Kenya did not entail such a retraction either. Mogadishu later contended that it had already agreed to the principle of territorial integrity by signing the OAU Charter, so its mention in the Kenyan accord did not amount to a concession. Its explanation of the accords cited paragraphs that supposedly gave Mogadishu a say in the affairs of the Ogaden and NFD.[142]

Thus, after 1973 the Ogaden dispute flared up again. Somalia revived its claim and the OAU responded by forming an eight-member "Good Offices Committee". This organ should only reduce tensions, as the OAU's commitment to the territorial status quo did not give it much room for manoeuvre.[143] Nevertheless, the conflict escalated completely in 1977. Regular Somali troops, whose capabilities had been built up with Soviet help, invaded the Ogaden. Ethiopia had been considerably weakened after the overthrow of the Emperor in 1974. In order to halt the Somali advance it called for, and received, massive assistance from the Soviet bloc, which changed sides in the course of the conflict.

---

136 Touval, *Boundary Politics*, p 223.
137 *Africa Research Bulletin* (PSC), 1965, p 426.
138 Touval, *Boundary Politics*, p 242.
139 AHG/St.1 (IV).
140 Text in Hoskyns, *Ethiopia-Somalia-Kenya Dispute*, pp 82-83.
141 *Africa Research Bulletin* (PSC), 1967, p 859.
142 Touval, *Boundary Politics*, pp 233-235.
143 *Africa Research Bulletin* (PSC), 1973, pp 2845-46 and 2849-51.

The Assembly chairman, President Bongo of Gabon, tried to have the Good Offices Committee discuss the invasion during its session in Libreville (August 1977). Somalia, however, walked out as the Committee refused to invite delegates of the (Ogadeni) "Western Somali Liberation Front". The Committee subsequently adopted a recommendation emphasizing the norm of *uti possidetis* and appealed to both sides to cease hostilities.[144] Conversely, in 1978, an OAU peace plan stipulating a demilitarized zone and a cease-fire was opposed by Ethiopia. With the aid of the Eastern bloc Addis Ababa hoped to defeat the Somali's on the battle-field, which it actually did in the following year.[145] In 1980 the Good Offices Committee again reaffirmed the norm of *uti possidetis* and in 1981 it went so far as to state explicitly that the Ogaden was part of Ethiopia.[146] Somalia had thus been dealt a military and diplomatic blow, something that was to weaken its government considerably during the following decade.[147]

Mediation in the Horn 1963-1981: evaluation
One can say that from 1964 to 1973 there was a stalemate between disputants, but one with a repetitive character: the parties were not able to escalate the conflict but periodically tried to break the stalemate by reviving the issue. However, by the late 1970s both Ethiopia and Somalia had built up their fighting capabilities and could therefore pursue the conflict on a higher level of intensity. This resulted in a typical compound stalemate, as a new limit was reached beyond which disputants could not go. Yet, their behaviour in 1977 and 1978 also betrayed signs of entrapment. Both sides rejected OAU mediation, as massive investment in the conflict encouraged expectations that they would be able to force the issue on the battlefield. Pressures to achieve victory instead of a settlement thus increased.[148]

A remarkable feature of the conflict was that, at least until 1973, the disputants themselves regularly sought mediation by third actors. According to the power political approach to mediation this rarely happens as the mediator usually intervenes in pursuit of his own interests and such intervention may entail unpredictable outcomes for the parties. Yet, this approach also predicts that parties may seek mediation for motives other than settlement.[149] This is confirmed by our case study. In 1964 Ethiopia and Kenya brought the issue before the OAU because they wanted to isolate their adversary, while Somalia hoped that OAU intervention would enhance the disputed character of the NFD and Ogaden.

However, after 1965 all three countries, but especially Somalia, increasingly felt the effects of stalemate. The conflict had led to a closure of borders, an end to trade and a deterioration in living conditions for the nomadic population. Moreover, Somalia was

---

144   *Ibid.*, 1977, pp 4525-4526.
145   AHG/Res.90 (XV) and S.O. Agbi, *The Organization of African Unity and African Diplomacy, 1963-1979* (Ibadan, 1986), pp 33-36. See also C. Legum and B. Lee, *The Horn of Africa in Continuing Crisis* (New York and London, 1979).
146   AHG/105 (XVII): Report of the Good-Offices Commission on the Ethiopian-Somali Dispute, Lagos, 18-20 August 1980 and *Africa Research Bulletin* (PSC), 1981, p 6070.
147   See f.i. I.M. Lewis, 'The Ogaden and the Fragility of Somali Segmentary Nationalism', in *African Affairs*, 1989, pp 573-579.
148   See on this Zartman, 'Conflict Reduction', pp 306-311.
149   See Zartman and Touval, 'Conclusion', pp 253 and 263 (n. 8).

starting to feel the financial burden of expansion of its armed forces, while Ethiopia and Kenya had to cope with rising costs of security operations.[150] In other words, the stale-mate was hurting everyone and no one could hope to score a decisive victory. After careful preparations, they managed to find a way out with an acceptable, if temporary, formula. The compound stalemate of the late 1970s, however, left little room for this, as both parties had overcommitted themselves.

Most of the formulas that were hammered out focused on reducing the conflict level by calling for cease-fires. The core values of disputants were usually avoided. In this area mediators had little leverage as there was no room for acceptable alternatives. Thus, the extraordinary Council session of February 1964, the Khartoum meeting and the formula's agreed on in the course of the Accra and Kinshasa summits sought, among others, to end hostile propaganda campaigns. The Addis Ababa accord of 1967 also focused on minor side-issues that could ease tension. Such redefinition or restriction of the contentious issue is a typical example of conflict transformation strategies.[151]

While the OAU's normative provisions encourage a certain approach to conflict management and indirectly influence it by their function in the legitimation process, their role is severely reduced if they are themselves part of the contentious issue. Moreover, the case study shows that in those circumstances the OAU's leverage is marginal, as it is by definition against the party violating its norms. The 1964 Council appeal for respect of territorial integrity, the introduction of *uti possidetis* and its confirmation by the Good Offices Committee (1978 and 1980) were unhelpful in settling the conflict as they negated Somalia's core value. That the Somali violation of *uti possidetis* did not lead to condemna-tion illustrates the limits of collective delegitimation in the OAU.

Among the OAU's mediatory facilities, one must emphasize the usefulness of Assembly summits as instruments to repair communication. On two occasions (Accra and Kinshasa) these provided opportunities for behind the scenes negotiations and the search for mediators. The principle of flexibility mentioned previously found expression in the multiple use of individual mediators, whether or not (self-)appointed during summits; the Assembly chairman; ad hoc committees; and Council discussions. Mediation by the plenary Council occurred only during the early stages, possible because open discussion does not involve a face-saving device with which to entice disputants to make concessions.

The case also points to the importance of the cognitive dimension. Kenya's rejection of initial Somali proposals was a missed opportunity caused by the former's distrust. The role of the mediator becomes crucial here.[152] The trust he enjoys because of his perceived bias is important in reaching a settlement: it was Kaunda who managed to bring Kenya and Somalia together rather than Nyerere, whose ties with Kenya were under strain.[153] However, it seems that by 1967 it was the balance of forces between disputants that was decisive, with the mediator merely tipping the balance in favour of settlement.

---

150 See Touval, *Boundary Politics*, pp 236-237.
151 Deutsch, 'Subjective Features', p 38.
152 See Princen, *Intermediaries*, pp 224-226.
153 Touval, *Boundary Politics*, pp 240-241. In the power political perspective to mediation calculations of the consequences of acceptance or rejection of settlement for Kenyan-Tanzanian ties could have played a role. See Zartman and Touval, 'Conclusion'.

The record of mediation in inter-state disputes

Our case study showed a clear preoccupation with management, rather than resolution, of conflict. This goes for the OAU's record in inter-state disputes in general and is, of course, in line with its rationale in dispute settlement. Such management involves forms of conflict transformation, as observed in the case study, but above all methods to reduce conflict levels. Thus, if hostilities break out the first thing the OAU will do is to say "stop" and effect a cease-fire. The result is "not peace, not war", while subsequently the factor time becomes important.[154] In other words, the OAU has studiously manipulated the temporal dimension to cool tempers down. Its objective was, according to one diplomat, to reduce conflicts so as to enable member states to co-operate in other issue areas.[155]

The reasons for this minimal strategy can also be traced to the structures of Africa's international relations. The restricted opportunity for the exertion of influence in inter-African politics means that mediators act principally as communicators rather than manipulators. Resources for side-payments and credible threats are too limited.[156] The absence of hegemonic leadership precludes a forceful OAU posture vis-à-vis disputants, especially if it concerns relatively powerful countries fighting for regional hegemony. The risk of unilateral extra-African interference reduces the OAU's potential impact even further while paradoxically adding to its necessity. Naturally, in such contexts the arguments about the positive contributions of regimes intercede.[157] However, as has been argued previously, contexts as Africa's international relations make for weak regimes,[158] something that is especially felt in issue areas where zero-sum conditions occur more frequently.[159]

In qualitative terms one can judge the Organization's mediation record on the basis of the "clarity" of the settlement effected, its "political realism" and its "permanence".[160] The OAU scores rather well as regards political realism. Yet, one may doubt its relevance in some of the more violent conflicts. For example, passions ran very high in the Mauritanian-Senegalese dispute of 1989-1991 as a result of gruesome ethnic clashes. This made OAU attempts to reduce tension ineffective, while one of its proposals to "resolve" the ethnic question looked rather unrealistic.[161] The clarity of settlements may not always be great either. For instance, the settlement effected in the dispute between Equatorial Guinea and Gabon in 1972 did not mention one of the bones of contention, *i.e.* the

154 Interview with Mamadou Bah, Addis Ababa, 18/9/89.

155 Interview with R.S. Iskandar, ambassador of Egypt, Addis Ababa, 27/9/89. Also *Sunday News* (Tanzania), 28/11/82.

156 Also Zartman, 'Conflict Reduction', p 313.

157 See f.i. Young, 'Regime dynamics' (n. 118).

158 D. Snidal, 'The Limits of Hegemonic Stability Theory', in *International Organization*, 1985, p 595 and R. L. Rothstein, 'Regime-Creation by a Coalition of the Weak: Lessons from the NIEO and the Integrated Program for Commodities', in *International Studies Quarterly*, 1984, pp 307-328.

159 Jervis, 'Security regimes' (n. 120).

160 I.L. Claude, *Swords into Plowshares: The Problems and Progress of International Organization* (New York, 1964), pp 215-216.

161 *Africa Research Bulletin* (PSC), 1989, pp 9370 and 9402. See further below.

extension by Gabon of its territorial sea.[162] The permanence of settlements may at times also be limited. With conflict reduction instead of resolution there is a chance of recurrence. This happened, for example, with the Mali-Burkina Faso border dispute. An initially successful mediation effort by President Eyadéma of Togo (1974-75) was followed by the eruption of violent skirmishes.[163]

A quantitative assessment provides additional insight in the OAU's record. A list of its mediation efforts is given in table 7.1. It reveals that in the period 1963-1983 eighteen out of 28 inter-state disputes were settled — i.e. abated or, sometimes, resolved — by or in the framework of the OAU. Looking more closely at the first two decades, Haas concluded that the OAU had an aggregate success of only twenty per cent. This was average as compared to other organizations.[164]

However, this figure was depressed by the inclusion of disputes from the more intractable category of domestic conflicts. In the years 1963 to 1965, again according to Haas, the OAU's score reached seventeen per cent. It grew to 22% in the period 1966-1970 and thirty per cent for 1971-1975. Because of the general intensification of (internal and inter-state) conflicts, growth in armaments and increasing superpower rivalry the figure dropped to ten per cent in the period 1976-1981.[165] Resultant compound stalemates are less amenable to settlement.

The analysis by Haas does not go beyond 1983. The survey in table 7.1 shows, however, that in the period 1983-1993 mediation by or in the OAU cadre led, in four out of thirteen conflicts, to forms of settlement as described above. Yet, this figure is also rather depressed as it includes, and is dominated by, domestic conflicts. With regard to purely inter-state disputes two out of five conflicts were settled.

The OAU's moderate achievements were partially reflected in the opinions expressed by member states. From time to time they articulated mildly positive assessments of its record. Yet, over the years comments also observed the decline in its effectiveness. Many put increased emphasis on the need to enhance mediation capabilities. The deterioration in security during the 1970s and 1980s, although not so much related to inter-state as to domestic disputes, exposed the OAU's growing irrelevance in the overall management of the continental order.[166]

---

162   A.O. Chukwura, 'The Organization of African Unity and African Territorial and Boundary Problems 1963-1973', in *Nigerian Journal of International Studies*, 1975, no. 1, p 78.

163   G.K.A. Ofosu-Amaah, 'Regional Enforcement of International Obligations: Africa', in *Zeitschrift für ausländisches öffentliches Recht und Völkerrecht*, 1987, p 88.

164   E.B. Haas, 'Regime decay: conflict management and international organizations, 1945-1981', in *International Organization*, 1983, p 198. The Council of Europe scored eighteen per cent, the Arab League fifteen, the UN 23% and the OAS 34%. See for the criteria employed by Haas table 7.1.

165   Haas, 'Regime decay', p 214. This decline could also be observed for most of the other organizations mentioned.

166   F.i. *Times of Zambia*, 6/7/77; 28/6/81 and 14/6/83; *The Ghanaian Times*, 24/6/81; *Ehuzu* (Benin), 25/8/88 (article); *Le Renouveau* (Tunisia), 25/5/88 (article); and *Daily Times* (Nigeria), 9/7/77 and 25/5/88 (editorial and article).

Table 7.1

OAU mediation record in inter-state and domestic conflicts 1963-1993*

Year	Parties	Outcome
1963	Algeria vs Morocco	success
1964	Ethiopia/Kenya vs Somalia	success
1964	Congo-Leo. (internal and vs Congo-Br. and Burundi)	failure
1965	- Ghana vs Ivory Coast, Upper Volta and Niger	success
	- Somalia vs Kenya	failure
1966	- Guinea vs Ghana	success
	- Rwanda vs Burundi	success
1967	- Ethiopia/Kenya vs Somalia	success
	- Rwanda vs Congo-Leo.	success
1967-1970	Nigerian civil war	failure
1971	Guinea vs Senegal	success
1972	- Tanzania vs Uganda	success
	- Equatorial Guinea vs Gabon	success
1973	Ethiopia vs Somalia	failure
1974-1975	Mali vs Upper Volta	success
1976	Kenya vs Uganda	failure
1977	- Zaire (Shaba crisis)	failure
	- Angola vs Zaire	failure
	- Tanzania vs Uganda	failure
	- Ethiopia vs Sudan	success
	- Chad vs Libya	failure
1977-1978	- Ethiopia vs Somalia	failure
1978	- Zaire (Shaba crisis)	failure
	- Angola vs Zaire	success
	- Burundi vs Rwanda	success
	- Guinea vs Ivory Coast	success
	- Guinea vs Senegal	success
1978-1979	Tanzania vs Uganda	failure
1979	Benin vs Gabon	success
1979-1982	Chadian civil war	failure
1980	Libya vs Tunisia	success
1983-1984	Chadian civil war and Chad vs Libya	failure
1985-1986	Burkina Faso vs Mali	failure
1986	Chadian civil war	failure
1986-1987	Togo vs Ghana/Burkina Faso	failure
1987-1988	Chad vs Libya	success
1989-1991	Mauritania vs Senegal	success
1990	Sudanese civil war	failure
1991-	Somali civil war	failure
1992-1993	Rwandan civil war	success**
1993	- Burundian civil war	failure
	- civil strife in Congo-Br.	success***
	- Angolan civil war	failure
	- Liberian civil war	failure

*   Mediation activities to which this table refers involved various efforts and specific objectives; the concept of "success" points to reduction of conflict and in some cases the actual resolution of conflicts, whether on a temporary or permanent basis. (Haas ('Regime decay', p 198) employs a more complex set of criteria, namely a combination of assessed capabilities in handling different dimensions of a conflict, such as isolating it, abating it for a period up to three years and putting an end to hostilities. Mediation efforts were realized by and/or in the cadre of the OAU. In certain cases they were accompanied by, or took place in co-operation with, efforts by other third parties. Two or more inter-state conflicts mentioned together, or an inter-state and domestic conflict grouped together, were counted as one. This table excludes conflicts between liberation movements or conflicts which, in the OAU perspective, were treated in the context of its decolonization objective.

**   This concerned the power-sharing agreement between the FPR and the Habyarimana regime, which preceded the UN operation and the collapse of the Arusha accords in the spring of 1994.

***   This concerned the Libreville agreement.

SOURCES: T. Maluwa, 'The Peaceful Settlement of Disputes Among African States, 1963-1983: Some Conceptual Issues and Practical Trends', in *International and Comparative Law Quarterly*, 1989, pp 318-320; Y. El-Ayouty I.W. and Zartman (eds), *The OAU After Twenty Years* (New York, 1984), pp 379-383; and *Africa Research Bulletin* (Political, Social, Cultural Series).

The OAU and inter-state conflicts: reforms

Since the late 1970s various reform proposals have been launched in order to increase the effectiveness of the OAU in the management of conflicts. One of the first attempts at institutional reform was the acceptance of a Nigerian proposal in 1977 to establish a more or less permanent "Ad Hoc Committee" for the settlement of inter-state disputes. It was composed of the Central African Republic, Gabon, Gambia, Madagascar, Togo, Tunisia, Zaire and Zambia, with Nigeria as chairman. The chairman of the Assembly would be allowed to appoint three other member states whose participation would be deemed useful, *i.e.* countries from the affected region. The Committee's rationale was based on the consideration that, as the frequency of inter-state disputes was threatening inter-African co-operation and the CMCA could not operate spontaneously, a standing committee was needed that would be able to convene at short notice.[167]

The formation of the Committee was a logical step. While conflict resolution in multilateral cadres is, in any case, more time-consuming than trilateral mediation,[168] the decentralized, ad hoc nature of OAU mediation further detracts from its promptitude. Opportunities for and initiatives of third party intervention partly depend on sessions of the policy organs. Their frequency is low. The convening of extraordinary sessions depends on member state majorities and is particularly hard in the case of the Assembly. The importance of mediators of presidential rank, as opposed to diplomats or the OAU Secretary-General, also diminishes reactive capacity. Presidential intervention is heavily dependent on the political will of the head of state concerned, his agenda and the resources required for such things as travel expenses. Lack of a swift response or follow-up is in part also caused by the OAU's methods of conflict management, such as the resort to dilatory tactics. Its rationality cannot, in view of the OAU's limited leverage, be gainsaid. Yet, it can lead to disastrous results when the lives of millions of people are at stake, as in conflicts with a strong domestic component. The built-in slowness of OAU functioning also means that its mediatory capacity is easily overwhelmed by the simultaneous eruption of several conflicts or the pace and scale of events, as in the Ogaden war of 1977-1979.

While presidential rank contributes to the persuasive power of OAU mediators, the inherent individual approach is most effective in disputes which are in essence personal rows between leaders. Its conflict reductive potential is insufficient in high intensity disputes such as the 1977-79 Ogaden crisis or conflicts marked by large-scale human suffering or, more generally, an emotionally charged atmosphere. For instance, the Mauritanian-Senegalese conflict of 1989-1991 led to a flurry of diplomatic activity by several leaders, including two successive Assembly chairmen, the OAU's Secretary-General, the chairman of ECOWAS and personalities of other inter-African organizations. Yet, it took a long time before the two sides could be persuaded to tone down their conflict behaviour.[169]

This also touches on another disadvantage of ad hoc mediation, *i.e.* co-ordination difficulties. While the policy organs can contribute towards co-ordination by the

---

167   AHG/Dec.109 (XIV) and *Daily Times* (Nigeria), 9/7/77. See also Amate, *Inside the OAU*, p 164.

168   J. Dedring, 'Multilateral Aspects of Conflict Resolution', in Väyrynen, *New Directions in Conflict Theory*, pp 170-171 (n. 4).

169   *Africa Research Bulletin* (PSC), 1989, pp 9273-9275, 9306, 9402 and 9478-9479 and 1990, p 9542.

establishment of a committee of mediators, they cannot do much in between sessions. If multiple attempts at mediation, in and outside the OAU, are made more or less simultaneously, problems of co-ordination increase. The Senegalese-Mauritanian dispute is an obvious example. As was argued above, maintenance of a balanced triangular relationship is important for the preservation of stalemate, which is the key to leverage over disputants. With the appearance of more third actors, such leverage may diminish or even be cancelled out as parties can turn to different mediators in the search for a better outcome.[170] However, this problem does not only occur with mediation by ad hoc designated mediators, but is inherent in mutilateral frameworks generally. Thus, one can argue that multilateral mediation is appropriate in multilateral conflicts, but less so in bilateral disputes.[171]

In protracted conflict as the Somali-Kenyan/Ethiopian dispute ad hoc mediation also faces problems of continuity. The succession of Assembly chairmen or mediators generally demands the transmission and accumulation of knowledge, in the absence of which any follow-up becomes difficult and the pressure for settlement may decrease.[172] However, with the limited leverage that mediators usually have it may be necessary to enlarge, rather than decrease the number of member states that are involved in mediation. Furthermore, while presidential mediation has its constraints, it has been noted that the effectiveness of ad hoc committees is often limited by a tendency to send lower rank officials to substitute their head of state.[173]

Anyway, the 1977 semi-permanent Ad Hoc Committee was regarded as a stop-gap measure to be lifted after a reform of the CMCA. In default of this and with an easing of inter-African tensions the Committee remained inactive.[174] In view of the various bottlenecks noted above, however, new proposals continued to be made to improve the OAU's capacities in conflict management. Between 1978 and 1980 Sudan, Liberia and Sierra Leone, as well as the OAU's Secretary-General, sought support for the establishment of a Security Council.[175] A Sierra Leonean plan proposed a "Political and Security Council" along UN lines, composed of fifteen states from the five regions of the continent. According to President Stevens, it should have an "appropriate mandate" to identify "trouble spots" and "effect a rapid response" to situations that might threaten peace and security. It was necessary to cut "through bureaucratic obstacles", as "speed [was] very often of the essence and such a body should be able to meet at a moment's notice, given the exigency of the situation".[176]

---

170   Touval and Zartman, 'Introduction', p 16 (n. 10).
171   Dedring, 'Multilateral Aspects', p 173.
172   Zartman, 'Conflict Reduction'.
173   See Amate, *Inside the OAU*, p 164; Foltz, 'Organization of African Unity', p 357; and Andemicael and Nicol, 'OAU: Primacy in Seeking African Solutions', p 115.
174   Col. Gustave Zoula [*sic*], 'Perspectives de renforcement des organisations régionales en matière de stabilité et de sécurité: le cas de l'Organisation de l'unité africaine (OUA)', in *Cahiers de l'IPAG*, no. 10, June 1990, p 80.
175   See *Daily Mail* (Sierra Leone), 18/7/79 and 9/8/79 (articles) and Andemicael and Nicol, 'OAU: Primacy in Seeking African Solutions', pp 115-116.
176   *Ibid.* and speech of President Stevens to Council of Ministers, Freetown, June 1980 (text in *Daily Mail* [Sierra Leone], 19/6/80).

The plan formed a good example of the game theoretical strategy of actor reduction so as to realize co-operation in a context with many states.[177] However, the idea never found favour with the majority of members, principally because it involved permanent membership for a limited number of them.[178] These would probably be the more important states, for the Council would otherwise be ineffective. Its introduction would have gone against the strongly egalitarian disposition which characterizes interaction in the OAU. At a deeper level, there was little chance, in the absence of hegemonic leadership, that sufficient political will could have been generated to have the proposals accepted. Moreover, the plan itself negated the structural features of inter-African relations, as, once again, without one hegemon — or more appropriately, hegemony by a coalition or a dominant coalition — the plan lacked the proper context. Even the proposal to determine membership by way of annual election, as suggested by the General Secretariat and two eminent OAU experts, did not evoke a positive response.[179]

However, by the late 1980s - early 1990s, Africa's security situation had deteriorated to such an extent that new reforms were considered to improve the OAU's effectiveness. This time they stood a better chance of acceptance, as the domestic and international position of African governments was undergoing significant change. Many governments were confronted with the emergence of multi-party politics and calls for democratization. During the 1980s their international position had already been weakening as a result of Africa's progressive economic marginalization. This was made worse now by the end of the Cold War, which meant the withdrawal of vital superpower support, and demands by Western donors for politico-economic reform.

In 1990 the Assembly adopted a "Declaration on the Political and Socio-Economic Situation in Africa and the Fundamental Changes Taking Place in the World", which considered all these developments. It announced the OAU's commitment to begin working towards the settlement of "*all* the conflicts on the continent".[180] This implied the arrogation of domestic conflicts to the Organization's area of competence and the restriction of the norm of non-interference in internal affairs. This is discussed further in section 8.1. Having asked the Secretary-General to contribute to implementation of the declaration, Salim formulated important proposals for the reform of OAU conflict management. Their rationale involved the desire to establish a comprehensive, more responsive and permanent mechanism and avoid some of the improvised measures employed in the past.[181] When these proposals were presented to the Assembly summit in Dakar in 1992, they gave rise to extensive debate and controversy, especially as regards the issue of domestic conflicts.[182] While accepting Salim's proposals in principle, the

---

177 Oye, 'Explaining Cooperation Under Anarchy', p 21.
178 CM/1710 (LVI) Rev.1: Report of the SG on Conflicts in Africa (June 1992) (n. 43). Governmental reactions to such a Council in *The Standard* (Kenya), 16/7/79; *Times of Zambia*, 22/7/79; and the Charter Review Committee discussions in CAB/LEG/97/DRAFT/RAPT.RPT (III) Rev. 2, par. 26.6.
179 CM/Res.958 (XLI). Also Andemicael and Nicol, 'OAU: Primacy in Seeking African Solutions', pp 116-117 and for its resuscitation Gustave Zoula, 'Perspectives de renforcement des organisations régionales', pp 87-88.
180 AHG/Decl.1 (XXVI), par. 11. Emphasis added.
181 CM/1710 (LVI) Rev.1: Report of the SG on Conflicts in Africa (June 1992).
182 *Le Soleil* (Senegal), 27/6-28/6 and 29/6/92 (articles).

Assembly called for a further study by the Secretary-General in co-operation with the Bureau of the Assembly; submission by member states of their views; and recommendations by the Council in the light of the Secretariat's study and member state comments.[183]

Consultations between the Secretary-General and member states[184] culminated in revised proposals which were definitively adopted by the Assembly summit in Cairo in June 1993.[185] In the process some of the more far-reaching aspects of Salim's reform plans were rejected or toned down. This will become only fully apparent in the discussion in sections 8.1 and 8.2 of the domestic conflict and military dimensions of the reform proposals. Here it must suffice to observe that the mechanism that was finally approved was not as comprehensive as Salim had wished. His 1992 proposals aimed at the establishment of a comprehensive system of peace-keeping and -making. This would be part of a whole process of prevention, management and resolution, involving political, judicial and military dimensions.[186]

However, the decision taken in Cairo did not focus on judicial dimensions,[187] while military activity in the context of conflict management was, as shown in section 8.2, deliberately circumscribed. Moreover, although the new system has been given the comprehensive title of "Mechanism for Conflict Prevention, Management and Resolution",[188] its major goal is to prevent or stop hostilities with a view to facilitate a subsequent settlement. Such emphasis on prevention and containment is justified with the argument that it can avoid the necessity of difficult and expensive military operations.[189] In other words the system focuses, as in the past,[190] on the reduction of conflict levels and the prevention of worst case scenario's. However, it will be shown in section 8.1 that, despite these restricted objectives, the rationale behind the OAU's activation has actually widened.

The novelty of the new mechanism lies principally in the improvement of reactive capacity, something that Salim's proposals deliberately aimed at and was approved by the Assembly.[191] Increase in promptitude is to be effected by improved co-operation between two OAU organs, the Secretariat headed by the Secretary-General and the Bureau of the Assembly.[192] The least controversial aspect of this involved the upgrading of the political role to be played by the Secretary-General and his staff. As was already observed in section 5.4, the chief OAU official has been given a broad right of diplomatic initiative: aided by the Secretariat's improved monitoring work discussed at the beginning of this section, he may intervene in conflicts by undertaking or sending mediation and fact-

---

183   AHG/Dec.1 (XXVIII).
184   Wembou, 'A propos du nouveau mécanisme', p 7 (n. 42).
185   AHG/Decl.3 (XXIX)/Rev.1.
186   CM/1710 (LVI) Rev.1: Report of the SG on Conflicts in Africa (June 1992), pp 1-4.
187   Such as a Border Commission, the Court of Justice of the OAU's African Economic Community and an Interim Arbitral Tribunal. *Ibid.*, pp 8-10.
188   AHG/Decl.3 (XXIX)/Rev.1, par. 13.
189   AHG/Decl.3 (XXIX)/Rev.1, par. 15.
190   Foltz, 'Organization of African Unity', p 358.
191   AHG/Decl.3 (XXIX)/Rev.1, par. 12 and CM/1710 (LVI) Rev.1: Report of the SG on Conflicts in Africa (June 1992), pp 1-4.
192   CM/1710 (LVI) Rev.1: Report of the SG on Conflicts in Africa (June 1992), p 3.

finding missions or dispatching special envoys. In practice the Secretary-General has already used his new prerogatives, such as by sending a special OAU envoy to Burundi in November 1993.[193] Still, he must exercise his new political role under the authority of the central organ of the new mechanism and in consultation with the Assembly chairman.[194]

The central organ of the mechanism is the Bureau of the Assembly, whose decisions must be executed by the Secretary-General.[195] A concrete example of this would be the decisions that he must take for the deployment and supervision of civil and military observer missions that have been decided by the Bureau and are discussed further in sections 8.1 and 8.2.[196] In his 1992 proposals Salim suggested that the decisions of the Bureau should be binding and enforceable vis-à-vis member states.[197] However, this was rejected. While decisions relating to internal functioning, such as the formation of a mediation committee, can be assumed to be binding, as far as their external effect is concerned the Bureau needs the consent of the disputants.[198] This is pursued further in chapter 8. The mechanism's constitutive instrument also stipulates in this respect that the Bureau, which must report on its activities to the Assembly, must generally decide its recommendations on the basis of consensus and with respect for the Assembly's Rules of Procedure.[199]

As central organ the Bureau has political responsibility and overall supervision. It lays down the guidelines for the operation of the mechanism. As the Secretary-General has, besides executive tasks as regards Bureau decisions, his own political prerogatives, Bureau and Secretary-General must co-operate closely. Preferably they should be in constant consultation with each other.[200] The essence of the mechanism is that the Secretary-General takes an initiative, which sets the whole process in motion. Then he informs the Bureau of its results and the Bureau may be convened. The role of the Secretary-General provides the necessary speedy response to conflicts. The Bureau gives vital political backing and guidance to his efforts and decides on its more far-reaching aspects, like deployment of observer missions.[201] While much of this needs to be tested and evolve in practice, close co-operation between the two is essential for the mechanism's success.

As far as purely inter-state disputes are concerned, Salim has suggested that the Bureau must accord disputants the right to be heard and, if need be, appoint ad hoc committees whose membership must remain fixed for the duration of the conflict. The organ can also mandate the Assembly chairman or individual heads of state to engage in mediation efforts. Although this copies established practice, the Bureau's involvement

---

193   *Africa Research Bulletin* (PSC), 1993, p 11232. The visit of a Secretariat mission to Cameroon to mediate in a territorial dispute with Nigeria is another example. *Ibid.*, 1994, p 11392.
194   AHG/Decl.3 (XXIX)/Rev.1, par. 22.
195   *Ibid.*, par. 17.
196   Wembou, 'A propos du nouveau mécanisme', p 10.
197   CM/1710 (LVI) Rev.1: Report of the SG on Conflicts in Africa (June 1992), p 13.
198   AHG/Decl.3 (XXIX)/Rev.1, par. 14.
199   AHG/Decl.3 (XXIX)/Rev.1, par. 20.
200   CM/1710 (LVI) Rev.1: Report of the SG on Conflicts in Africa (June 1992), p 17 and AHG/Decl.3 (XXIX)/Rev.1, pars. 18 and 22.
201   CM/1710 (LVI) Rev.1: Report of the SG on Conflicts in Africa (June 1992), pp 3-4, 13 and 15.

should provide these procedures with more co-ordination.[202] The mechanism's functioning with regard to domestic conflict management and military operations is discussed in sections 8.1 and 8.2.

A major reason in giving the Bureau a stronger role in dispute settlement was the consideration that the organ already existed and that its reinforcement would avoid unnecessary proliferation of institutions. The Bureau, which was activated in the past on an incidental basis such as in the Angolan crisis, has institutional links with all major OAU organs. Contrary to the CMCA, it is not unwieldy and relatively easy to convene at short notice: while it has a quorum of two-thirds, with its ten or eleven members this requirement is not difficult to fulfil, especially as compared to Council and Assembly sessions.[203] As shown in section 5.6, the Bureau's new membership involves, besides the Assembly chairman and his eight vice-chairmen, the outgoing president, who remains a member for one year. Moreover, the future Assembly chairman is, if he is already known, also member of the Bureau. These measures have been taken to enhance the continuity of mediation. As the Bureau's membership is elected on the basis of the five African regions and rotates annually, all states are given a chance to serve on it. While this assures the game theoretical prescription of actor reduction it also guarantees a broad political basis, in contrast to a Security Council with a few permanent members.[204]

In its new, semi-permanent form the Bureau may be convened by the Assembly chairman, the Secretary-General or any member state. Ordinarily, it meets once a month at the level of ambassadors, twice a year at ministerial level and once at the level of heads of state. Its agenda is drawn up by the Secretary-General in consultation with the Assembly chairman.[205] Like the new role played by the Secretary-General, the Bureau's reform appears to be more than a paper revision. Thus, an attempted coup in Burundi in October 1993 triggered an immediate response from the Bureau, which met at ambassadorial level in Addis Ababa on the same day. In September and October it also decided on its financial modalities[206] — which are discussed in section 8.2 — and organizational procedures. In November 1993 the Bureau met for the first time at ministerial level.[207]

The whole mechanism first needs to be thoroughly tested before one can pass definitive judgement. Moreover, several aspects relate to domestic conflict management and military operations, which are analysed in the next chapter. However, a preliminary assessment makes clear that at least one bottleneck, *i.e.* minimal reactive capacity, seems to have been addressed with some success. The whole mechanism should also be capable of improving the co-ordination and continuity of mediation efforts. The involvement of several member states and the inclusion of presidential mediation may have a positive effect on leverage.

Yet, the old minimal tactics are still by and large intact. Apart from the non-binding nature of its mediation initiatives, the OAU still employs a conflict reductive strategy.

---

202 *Ibid.*, p 8.
203 *Ibid.*, p 6 and Wembou, 'A propos du nouveau mécanisme', p 8.
204 CM/1710 (LVI) Rev.1: Report of the SG on Conflicts in Africa (June 1992), p 6 and AHG/Decl.3 (XXIX)/Rev.1, par. 18.
205 See AHG/Decl.3 (XXIX)/Rev.1, pars. 19-21.
206 Wembou, 'A propos du nouveau mécanisme', pp 12-14.
207 *West Africa*, 29/11-5/12/93.

Changes in its political environment have, indeed, induced a remarkable reform. However, any fundamental revision of the OAU's role in conflict management is hindered by the structural impediments of inter-African relations, *i.e.* absence of continental hegemonic leadership and, more generally, the limits on exertion of influence in inter-African interaction. Even after the present reforms the OAU's reductive capabilities are insufficient in high intensity conflict. This is pursued further in chapter 8. One can draw one other, related, conclusion. Most, though not all, of the OAU's norms have not been revised or discarded, nor its minimal strategy to conflict management. Viewed from Krasner's[208] contention that changes in norms signify structural conflict, this points to the relative permanence of the underlying, though conflictual, structures of (inter-)African politics. This is made more explicit in section 8.4.

---

208   See Krasner, *Structural Conflict* (n. 76).

8

The OAU and the management
of Africa's political order (II)

8.1 Is this the way you feed your children, OAU?:
the Pan-African forum and internal conflicts

Introduction

This section analyses the position of the OAU towards domestic or internal disputes
— *i.e.* conflicts taking place inside member states — and its role in the management of
such conflicts. First, we discuss the extent of the norm of non-intervention in internal
affairs. It is argued that under specific circumstances the OAU responded to domestic
conflicts, something that is illustrated with an analysis of its role in the management of a
new crisis in the Congo and its mediation in the Nigerian civil war. This is followed by a
discussion of the OAU's posture towards separatist movements and the negative image
that it has, in a more general way, among non-governmental groupings. The OAU's
policies to refugee problems and human rights issues are also analysed. A discussion of
its changing role in domestic conflict management after 1990 concludes this section.

The non-interference norm

The OAU has never claimed competence of initial concern with domestic conflicts. The
manner in which African states have for long interpreted the non-interference norm (art.
3.2 OAU Charter) stands in sharp contrast to the more restricted interpretation given to it
in United Nations practice. In general international law, the reserved domain of "domestic
jurisdiction" (internal affairs) concerns those areas where a state's jurisdiction is not
bound by international law. The evolution of international law therefore determines and
limits the extent of a state's internal affairs and its right to oppose international concern by
reference to that concept. Moreover, in general international law "interference" or
"intervention" refers to an intrusion without a state's consent in its domestic jurisdiction
and involving an activity amounting to a denial of its independence. Discussion of, or the
adoption of resolutions concerning, a state's internal affairs does not constitute

interference.[1]

However, the OAU's member states did not intend to create a mere copy of United Nations practice or general international legal principles. One must therefore look at the OAU's own practice to determine the extent of its non-interference norm.[2] On the basis of this practice Kunig concluded, in 1981, that the Organization was not only not entitled to mediate in internal conflicts, but could not even *discuss* such events or pass resolutions on them against the will of the member state concerned.[3] This contention was borne out in an interview with the Director of the Political Department of the General Secretariat.[4] In an interview with a Senegalese diplomat it was said that discussion constituted interference, as "debate led to a conclusion".[5] It was not until 1990 that the OAU was given the formal prerogative to concern itself with internal conflicts.

Yet it is not our intention to reconstruct legal convictions of OAU members on the non-intervention norm.[6] Moreover, the OAU *did* at times get involved in domestic conflict management, notwithstanding the prohibition of art. 3.2 Charter. Thus, it is more fruitful to show under what circumstances, why and how far it decided to ignore or respond to internal conflicts.[7] Generally, the historical record shows that conflicts that were marked by (the risk of) substantial non-African involvement or otherwise carried important inter-African implications could trigger some reaction. Conversely, conflicts in which these features were by and large absent, failed to elicit a response.

A second Congo crisis

In 1964 many African leaders were outraged when Moise Tshombe became Congo's new prime minister. To many radical regimes Tshombe represented the very symbol of neo-colonialism as a result of the murder of Lumumba — in which he was implicated — and his attempt, with Western assistance, to realize Katanga's independence. His appointment was brought about by the outbreak of a rebellion in Kwilu. This revolt led to the proclamation of a government in Stanleyville by the "Comité Nationale de Libération" (CNL), an organization made up of people with Lumumbist origins who were opposed to the legitimate government in Leopoldville.

It is only the inter-African implications of the revolt that concern us here.[8] As far as

---

1   I. Brownlie, *Principles of Public International Law* (Oxford, 1979), pp 291-295.

2   B. Akinyemi, 'The Organization of African Unity and the Concept of Non-Interference in Internal Affairs of Member-States', in *British Yearbook of International Law*, 1972-73, pp 396-397.

3   Ph. Kunig, *Das völkerrechtliche Nichteinmischungsprinzip: Zur Praxis der Organisation der afrikanischen Einheit (OAU) und des afrikanischen Staatenverkehrs* (Baden-Baden, 1981), pp 165-171. A different, debatable assessment in Akinyemi, 'Organization of African Unity and the Concept of Non-Interference', and O. Okongwu, 'The O.A.U. Charter and the Principle of Domestic Jurisdiction in Intra-African Affairs', in *Indian Journal of International Law*, 1973, pp 589-593.

4   Interview with Ambassador Mamadou Bah, Director of the Political Department, Addis Ababa, 18/9/89.

5   Interview with Amadou Kebe, Conseiller of the Senegalese embassy, Addis Ababa, 3/10/89.

6   This has already been done by others. Especially Kunig, *völkerrechtliche Nichteinmischungsprinzip*.

7   In the rest of this chapter the terms "intervention" and "interference", as well as their verbal derivatives, are used in a wider sense, separate from their strictly legal connotations.

8   See further L. Martens, *1958-1966: 10 jaar revolutie in Kongo: De strijd van Patrice Lumumba en*

Congo's neighbours were concerned, the CNL received the backing of Congo-Brazzaville and Burundi. In view of their militant postures CNL leaders also sought support from the Eastern bloc, from which they received limited aid, and from radical African states generally. These had all along questioned the legitimacy of Tshombe's government and were to send military assistance as well. Tshombe's regime, however, called in massive aid from the United States and Belgium and relied on the services of white mercenaries from Southern Africa to quell the revolt.[9]

The combination of external (non-)African intervention, white mercenaries and, especially, the controversial figure of Tshombe brought to the fore the old cleavage between radical and moderate-conservative member states. The former were openly hostile to Tshombe and expressed sympathy with the CNL. The latter inclined towards the Leopoldville regime. As the revolt had developed clear inter-African ramifications, member states felt no objection to a discussion of the crisis at an extra-ordinary session of the Council (September 1964).[10] While Tshombe scored a victory by his admission to the meeting and the Council decision not to invite the Stanleyville representatives,[11] he got a hostile reception from radical states.[12] He said he was willing to dispense with the services of white mercenaries if African states were prepared to send troops to restore public order. He opposed Ghanaian and Algerian proposals for a round table conference between the central government and the Stanleyville group, as this would have implied equality of status for the CNL.[13] Yet, the deployment of African troops was resisted by radical, as well as some moderate, member states, which feared that they would have to fight Tshombe's domestic enemies.[14]

In the end the Council condemned foreign intervention and the use of mercenaries as a threat to Africa's peace and security and a danger to Southern Africa's struggle for liberation. It appealed to Tshombe to stop mercenary recruitment. It also established an ad hoc commission of ten countries, presided over by President Kenyatta of Kenya. The commission was charged to mediate between Leopoldville and neighbouring states supporting the CNL, as well as to help the central government in achieving national reconciliation with its domestic enemies.[15] This last section was strongly resented by Tshombe's regime.[16] However, the OAU really overreached itself when the ad hoc

Pierre Mulele (Berchem, 1988).

9   C. Young, *Politics in the Congo: Decolonization and Independence* (Princeton, 1965), pp 583-601 and S.O. Agbi, *The Organization of African Unity and African Diplomacy, 1963-1979* (Ibadan, 1986), ch. 4.

10   F.i. the Ivorian opinion in *Fraternité*, 25/9/64 (article).

11   Egypt had refused him entry to the Cairo summit in July '64. *Le Courrier d'Afrique* (Zaire), 11/9/64; *Nouvelles Malgaches Quotidiennes*, 11/9/64; and Z. Cervenka, *The Unfinished Quest for Unity: Africa and the OAU* (London, 1977), p 85.

12   For some negative reactions to Tshombe and his policies f.i. *l'Essor* (Mali), 14/9/64 and *Horoya* (Guinea), 13-14/9/64 (articles). See for a Leopoldville evaluation of its friends and enemies in the OAU *Le Courrier d'Afrique* (Zaire), 12-13/9/64 (article).

13   *Le Courrier d'Afrique* (Zaire), 12-13/9/64 (article) and 14/9/64 (extract of Tshombe's speech) and *Ghana Today*, 9/9/64 (article).

14   *Fraternité* (Ivory Coast), 25/9/64 and *Le Courrier d'Afrique* (Zaire), 10/9/64 (articles); and Agbi, *Organization of African Unity*, pp 43-44.

15   ECM/Res.5 (III).

16   *Le Courrier d'Afrique* (Zaire), 10/9/64 and 11/9/64 (articles).

commission invited Stanleyville representatives to its first session and decided to send a delegation to Washington to plead with the US administration to stop armed support to the Leopoldville regime. Although this initiative was cold-shouldered by Washington, it was condemned by Tshombe as a violation of the non-intervention norm. This judgement was supported by the conservative member states, which stressed that the OAU was not allowed to help anyone but the legitimate government of Congo.[17]

It was clear that the non-intervention norm had, indeed, been violated. The result was that Tshombe abruptly ended his co-operation with the commission. This meant that, while it continued its work, it could not fulfil its goals. Later in 1965, when the revolt had been quelled, the Congo was taken off the agenda.[18]

As such, the OAU had committed a tactical blunder. It did not have sufficient power to force Congo's government to reach a rapprochement with its opponents. The broad interpretation given to the non-intervention norm reflected, at a deeper level, the complete lack of continental hegemonic leadership. Transgressing this norm did not imply that the problem of limited leverage inherent in the absence of hegemonic leadership had been solved. In view of the hostility that Tshombe encountered in the OAU, the persuasive powers of its mediators were negligible. The Washington initiative was an example of the application of sticks backfiring on the third party.[19]

Moreover, as argued before extra-African factors tend to weaken the clout of the continental regime.[20] The level of non-African intervention — in part called for by certain member states themselves — only enhanced inter-African divisions and, so, the weakness of African states as a collectivity. Congo was one of Africa's potentially influential actors. With massive Western backing its government did not find it hard to withstand pressures of the OAU regime. One special incident that occurred in the course of the crisis, namely the dropping of Belgian paratroopers on Stanleyville, is discussed in section 8.2.

The Nigerian civil war
The crisis in the Congo also showed that mediation in an internal conflict is hindered by an implied suggestion that the government cannot handle its own affairs.[21] Mediation between the regime and its domestic enemies puts the state's sovereignty at stake by creating or suggesting a sort of parity between disputants, which is essential for the

17   *Ibid.*, 21/9, 25/9, 28/9 and 30/9/64 (editorials and articles); a radical view in the Malian delegate's speech and his exchange with Tshombe at the March '65 Council session (text in *l'Essor* [Mali], 15/3/65); and OAU press release on Washington visit in C. Hoskyns, *Case Studies in African Diplomacy*, no. I: *The Organization of African Unity and the Congo Crisis, 1964-65* (Dar es Salaam, Nairobi and Addis Ababa, 1969), p 27.

18   *l'Essor* (Mali), 15/3/65 (delegate's speech); *Le Courrier d'Afrique* (Zaire), 29/1/65 and 26/2/65 (article); *Kenya Weekly News*, no. 2036, 19/2/65 (article); and R.C. Pradhan, 'OAU and the Congo Crisis', in *Africa Quarterly*, 1965, vol. V, pp 40-41.

19   See also S. Touval and I.W. Zartman (eds), *International Mediation in Theory and Practice* (Boulder and London, 1985).

20   R.L. Rothstein, 'Regime-Creation by a Coalition of the Weak: Lessons from the NIEO and the Integrated Program for Commodities', in *International Studies Quarterly*, 1984, pp 307-328.

21   I.W. Zartman, 'Conflict Reduction: Prevention, Management, and Resolution', in F.M. Deng and I.W. Zartman (eds), *Conflict Resolution in Africa* (Washington, 1991), p 311.

success of mediation efforts but is resisted by the government in question.[22] In the Nigerian civil war, however, the OAU showed that it was capable of manoeuvring cautiously. The objective of this and the following section is to show only[23] why and how far the Organization intervened in this domestic crisis and, secondly, what its implications were for the principle of self-determination.

As the Nigerian federal authorities, led by General Gowon, made it clear that they regarded the war as a strictly internal affair and would not condone interference, not even by way of discussion, it was hard for the Organization to concern itself with the conflict. However, hostilities rapidly developed international dimensions as both sides received assistance from abroad. Eastern bloc countries, Egypt and especially Britain supplied the federal government with arms and ammunition. Biafra obtained French, South African and Portuguese support. The Biafrans deliberately tried to internationalize the conflict in order to strengthen their case, such as by making representations to the OAU summit in Kinshasa (1967).[24] Moreover, the outcome of the fighting was for some time uncertain. This confronted African states with the question of how to react to the conflict. Such a response was to become even more acute as widely publicized reports came in about the plight of the population. It was said that civilians had fallen victim to widespread starvation as the consequence of a federal blockade and military operations.

This context provided impetus to, and some room for manoeuvre for, the OAU which the federal government found difficult to oppose. Thus, the Kinshasa summit decided to discuss the conflict. It did move cautiously, however. It dubbed the declaration of independence of Nigeria's Eastern Region as Biafra as "secession". With the events in Katanga during the early 1960s in mind, it condemned secession in any member state. The war was recognized as an internal affair, which should "primarily" be solved by "Nigerians themselves". The OAU also emphasized its confidence in, and offered its "services" to, the federal government. A six nation "consultative" mission was formed to assure the Gowon regime of the OAU's desire for Nigeria's territorial integrity, unity and peace.[25]

This confirmed the Organization's support for the federal cause and was later criticized as having encouraged Gowon to quench the revolt in blood.[26] The wording of the relevant resolution, however, actually gave the OAU a potential, if implicit, say in the future settlement of the conflict. Still, the consultative mission that was led by Haile Selassie had not been given a mandate to mediate. It conferred with Gowon and could only express agreement with the federal demand of a renunciation of the secession as a

---

22   F.M. Deng and I.W. Zartman, 'Introduction', in Deng and Zartman, *Conflict Resolution in Africa*, p 8.

23   See on the causes, evolution and international implications of the war generally A.H.M. Kirk-Greene, *Crisis and Conflict in Nigeria: A Documentary Sourcebook 1966-1970*, 2 vls. (London, 1971); J.J. Stremlau, *The International Politics of the Nigerian Civil War 1967-1970* (Princeton, 1977); and Z. Cervenka, 'The OAU and the Nigerian Civil War', in Y. El-Ayouty (ed), *The Organization of African Unity After Ten Years: Comparative Perspectives* (New York, 1976), pp 152-173.

24   Stremlau, *International Politics*, ch. 4 ; Cervenka, *Unfinished Quest*, pp 97-98; and Agbi, *Organization of African Unity*, p 60.

25   AHG/Res.51 (IV). See for the relevancy of the Katanga experience *l'Essor* (Mali), 7/10/68.

26   See *Le Courrier d'Afrique* (Zaire), 14-15/9/68 (article).

condition for a cease-fire.[27] The Biafran leaders had demanded an immediate, unconditional cease-fire and now rejected mediation by the OAU because of its stand. It was left to the Commonwealth to mediate in the conflict, but subsequent talks in Kampala also broke down over the cease-fire conditions.[28]

Yet, with growing publicity on Biafra's humanitarian plight and allegations that federal forces were guilty of "genocide", an OAU response became more acute. Haile Selassie therefore tried and managed to assemble both sides for talks in Niamey. Arrangements were discussed for relief aid and Gowon agreed to a visit of international observers, including some of the OAU, to verify the genocide allegations.[29] Trilateral talks on a permanent settlement ensued, but ended in failure as both sides stuck to their original positions. However, what is significant here is that the course of events had forced Nigeria to allow a more substantive role for the OAU. This development was essentially due to the inter-African implications of the conflict, which, in combination with the slow progress of federal forces, created some sort of temporary stalemate.

The inter-African implications became more explicit in 1968 when four member states — Ivory Coast, Gabon, Zambia and Tanzania — granted official recognition to Biafra. This went against the OAU's stand on secession. Tanzanian and Zambian motives seem to have been mainly humanitarian.[30] Those of Ivory Coast and Gabon also emphasized humanitarian considerations, but their close ties with France may have played their part. Moreover, Ivory Coast was engaged in competition with Nigeria for influence in the West African region.[31] Yet, the vast majority of member states rejected recognition of Biafra. They accused the four recognizing states of violating the OAU Charter and emphasized the dangerous precedent recognition would set. Many also pointed to non-African involvement on the side of the Biafrans. The support that their new state, which controlled Nigeria's oil reserves, obtained from France, Portugal and South Africa made their case politically suspect. It gave rise to accusations of an imperialist conspiracy aimed at balkanizing the continent and reconquering its resources.[32]

At the 1968 summit the four states that had recognized Biafra pleaded for a less partisan approach and a resolution that would call for an immediate, unconditional cease-fire. As this would have jeopardized the OAU's stand on secession and probably have led to a sharp reaction by Nigeria's federal government, a majority of members rejected this proposal. However, Gowon's regime was making some progress with its

---

27   See the communiqué in *Report of the O.A.U. Consultative Mission to Nigeria* (Nigerian National Press: Apapa, n.d.), 11-12.

28   Cervenka, 'OAU and Nigerian Civil War', pp 157-159.

29   *Ibid.*, pp 159-160. OAU observers later refuted these accusations. See Nigeria: International Observers Team Reports: Final Report of the first phase from October 5 to December 10 by the Organization of African Unity observers in Nigeria (1968). Also Cervenka, 'OAU and Nigerian Civil War', p 172 n. 6.

30   *The Standard* (Tanzania), 18/9/67 and 17/9/68 and *Zambia Daily Mail*, 8/4/69, 1/9/69 (article) and 9/9/69.

31   Gabon was a close ally of Houphouët-Boigny. See Stremlau, *International Politics*, pp 127-141.

32   F.i. *East African Standard* (Kenya), 18/9/68 and 10/9/69; *l'Essor* (Mali), 16/9/68 (article) and 7/10/68; *Le Courrier d'Afrique* (Zaire), 12/9/69 (article); and *Info Madagascar*, 27/4/68 and 5-11/9/68 (articles). Some, like Tunisia and Zaire, later proposed Nigerian unity on the basis of Biafran autonomy. *Le Courrier d'Afrique* (Zaire), 5/9/69 and *Info Madagascar*, 27/9/69 (articles).

military campaign and therefore aired reassuring remarks on minority rights and a general amnesty. It adopted a more pliable attitude that enabled the OAU to adopt a stronger resolution than the year before. While it called on the "secessionist leaders" to co-operate with the federal government to restore Nigeria's unity, it also appealed for a "cessation of hostilities". It recommended the declaration of an amnesty and co-operation with the OAU to ensure the safety of all Nigerians. In an implicit condemnation of the four countries that had recognized Biafra it called on all member states to refrain from any action detrimental to Nigeria's peace, unity and territorial integrity.[33]

Yet, at the time the resolution actually meant that Gowon's government should be left free to realize Biafra's defeat on the battle-field. This logic was partly inspired by the latter's intransigence. The breakout of military stalemate by federal forces left the OAU no leverage for genuine mediation. Thus, another meeting of Haile Selassie's consultative committee, which was held in a bid to effect a peaceful solution (April 1969), was a futile exercise.[34] While the 1969 summit called for a peaceful settlement and appealed to "the two parties" to suspend hostilities and open negotiations in order to preserve Nigeria's unity, the road was by then open for a final assault by federal forces: in January 1970, Biafra had been crushed.[35]

However, what is at issue is not that the secession was ended by force or that there was no question, in the last stages of the conflict, of genuine OAU mediation and parity between the disputants. It goes without saying that the lack of hegemonic leadership in inter-African relations makes itself most felt against the continent's more influential countries such as Nigeria. The forceful attitude of its government left the OAU little room for substantive mediation, particularly towards the end of the conflict. Its leverage was also constricted by the fact that one of its core values, the protection of the territorial integrity of member states, formed the bone of contention. This precluded the formulation of an acceptable alternative to stalemate,[36] while dealing a blow to the position of Biafra.

What is important in the context of this section is that, in the course of the conflict, the OAU managed to arrogate a more emphatic role for itself than what the federal government had at first been willing to accept. Discussion of the conflict in the Assembly led to assurances of support to the Gowon regime, followed by trilateral talks on humanitarian issues and the sending of observers, and then by substantive negotiations. While federal consent naturally proved essential in this,[37] in serious conflicts such consensual element may smack of acquiescence by force of circumstance.[38] Moreover, if a domestic crisis leads to a total break-down of order, the room for manoeuvre is much greater. This is shown in the OAU's handling of the Chadian civil war, as discussed in

---

33   The four voted against the resolution. Botswana and Rwanda abstained. See AHG/Res.54 (V); *Daily Times* (Nigeria), 20/9/68; and Agbi, *Organization of African Unity*, pp 65-71.

34   *Africa Research Bulletin* (Political, Social, Cultural Series; hereinafter as PSC), 1969, pp 1382-1383.

35   AHG/Res.58 (VI). The four recognizing states and Sierra Leone abstained. See *Zambia Daily Mail*, 10/9/69 (article).

36   See on this Zartman, 'Conflict Reduction'.

37   So from a legal perspective OAU action did not amount to intervention in internal affairs. Brownlie, *Principles*, p 294.

38   On this J.C. Scott, *Domination and the Arts of Resistance: Hidden Transcripts* (New Haven and London, 1990), pp 70-76.

section 8.2. Yet Chad aside, the Congolese and Nigerian conflicts were followed by a sharp decline in OAU concern with domestic crises. As shown at the end of this section, this picked up again after the early 1990s.

Secession

Like *uti possidetis*, the OAU's negative norm on secession is an off-shoot of the principle of territorial integrity. The ability of a separatist movement to confront the OAU with a fait-accompli is thus crucial to Pan-African acceptance of secession. In this respect it has previously been noted that African state practice has developed a restricted interpretation of the principle of self-determination.

Space does not allow an analysis of the numerous complexities surrounding the principle. Even in its universal context, however, it can be easily observed that it is not without its ambiguities. First, it is not clear which group of people is actually entitled to exercise self-determination: does the principle also refer to ethnic groups within larger political entities or is it limited to larger groupings that make up the entire population of a state or territorially well defined colony? Is it possible to exercise it several times or is there some "critical date", such as that of accession to independence, at which it must be exercised?[39]

Yet, with regard to the African context the OAU has discarded all ambiguity. In its view any meaningful exercise is in principle limited to the date of decolonization, even though one may contend that after this a people has the right to shape its destiny *within* the established state. As shown by the Somali, Katangan and Nigerian cases the principle is strictly subordinated to the territorial integrity of states. Ethnic self-determination is therefore rejected as "secession". Although the concept of "people" is not defined in the OAU's human rights charter,[40] it obviously refers to the entire population, as a collectivity, of a state or colony. The Western Sahara and Somali experiences reaffirmed that it is the structure as imposed by colonial partition that determines the socio-geographical framework of self-determination.[41] Mergers of such structures, such as of the two Somali colonies in 1960, may be accepted but must take place voluntarily.

Military, political and diplomatic capabilities are therefore decisive for any secessionist movement. Eritrea's struggle could be justified by the history of its incorporation in Ethiopia, which was characterized by a rather ambiguous exercise in self-determination.[42] Yet, it was only after the EPLF had defeated the Ethiopian army and Ethiopia's new leadership had agreed to its independence that Eritrea was recognized by

---

39   See for further details C. Young, 'Self-Determination, Territorial Integrity, and the African State System', in Deng and Zartman, *Conflict Resolution in Africa*, pp 320-346; M. Pomerance, *Self-Determination in Law and Practice: The New Doctrine in the United Nations* (The Hague, Boston and London, 1982); L.C. Buchheit, *Secession: The Legitimacy of Self-Determination* (New Haven and London, 1978); and B. Neuberger, *National Self-Determination in Post-colonial Africa* (Boulder, 1986), ch. 3.

40   See arts. 19-24 African Charter of Human and Peoples' Rights (Division of Press & Information, General Secretariat: Addis Ababa, no date).

41   Young, 'Self-Determination, Territorial Integrity', p 342.

42   See C. Young, 'Comparative Claims to Political Sovereignty: Biafra, Katanga, Eritrea', in D. Rothchild and V.A. Olorunsola (eds), *State versus Ethnic Claims: African Policy Dilemmas* (Boulder, 1983), pp 212-215.

other states and admitted to the OAU (1993).[43] However, the declaration of independence by the northern part of Somalia, which took place in the wake of the collapse of the Somali state in 1991, did not elicit a positive response. The context in which it occurred made the claim provisional at best. The Somali power vacuum generated insufficient pressure to demand Pan-African recognition.

The considerations on which the rejection of secession is based are, of course, quite rational. In view of the heterogeneous composition of African states any rash and voluntary acceptance of a secessionist claim could set in train a chain-reaction.[44] Attempts to realize separatist objectives usually involve guerrilla warfare, resistance by the central government, the search for allies and, thus, an increased likelihood of regional spreading and non-African intervention. Secession may therefore increase instability, strengthen inter-African divisions and diminish Africa's global weight. However, in the context of the OAU's relatively underdeveloped human rights policy its posture on secession may also encourage, rather than diminish, domestic instability. The negative, sterile character of the anti-secession stance has a parallel in the absence of a plea, in the *uti possidetis* norm, for constructive border management.

In specific cases there may be additional considerations to reject and ignore separatist aspirations. For instance, the struggle of "AnyaAnya" in southern Sudan could easily be ignored as support by neighbouring countries was very limited, non-African involvement non-existent and the risk of spreading marginal. With regard to the plight of the Eritrean people, Africa's leadership observed a deafening silence. Factors that played a part in this were Haile Selassie's influential position in inter-African politics, the fact that his regime housed the OAU headquarters and the UN's orginal backing of Eritrea's (federal) inclusion in Ethiopia.[45] Yet even when, during the 1980s, the SPLA's struggle in Sudan and that of the EPLF in Eritrea had reached levels that could not be ignored, a major member state like Nigeria uncharitably referred to these developments as a "separatist scourge".[46]

The image of the OAU among non-governmental groups
It can be argued that, in a more general way, the rejection of secessionist claims has been typical of the OAU's exclusive articulation of state elite interests. From the perspective of the millions of people victimized in one of the many domestic conflicts that ravaged the continent since 1960, its disregard of the well-being of the mass of Africa's peoples can only be judged as callous. While awareness of their own vulnerability frequently led state elites to articulate conspiracy theories vis-à-vis non-African forces, the OAU ended up as their own elitist plot aimed at the mass of the unprivileged and powerless. Its silence on many internal conflicts, indifference towards ethnic strife and violence and disregard of persecution and human rights violations were at the root of the negative image that non-governmental groups in Africa developed of the OAU. This stigma is one of the most

43   *Africa Research Bulletin* (PSC),1993, pp 10995-10997 and 11064.
44   Yet on this O.S. Kamanu, 'Secession and the Right of Self-Determination: an OAU Dilemma', in *Journal of Modern African Studies*, 1974, pp 366-369.
45   See f.i. *Togo Presse*, 9/4/77, which discussed an OAU communiqué denying that it had taken a stand on the conflict.
46   *Daily Times* (Nigeria), 20/7/85. Also *Le Soleil* (Senegal), 10/7/90 (article).

damning images that any international organization enjoys.

The southern Sudanese, in particular, have been known for their criticism. During the 1960s, their political groupings complained about the disregard the OAU showed for their case. They observed that the OAU had been founded on the denial of popular aspirations and dignity.[47] Its emphasis on territorial integrity and non-interference functioned as instruments for governments with which to cover up tragedies such as taking place in southern Sudan. In response to their international isolation that the OAU helped to keep in place, the southern separatists chided that no "human organisation [could] be expected to give a ... state an absolute right to murder innocent people".[48] One southern politician condemned African leaders for deliberately ignoring domestic conflicts and argued in a memorandum to the OAU Secretary-General that states lacking internal harmony hardly contributed to stability in inter-African relations.[49]

Nevertheless, appeals by southern Sudanese groups for self-determination, an OAU-sponsored referendum, an OAU police force and other mediatory initiatives[50] were to no avail.[51] In an attempt to explain their failure to break the silence of the OAU, one accusation touched on its elitist nature. A memorandum to the Kinshasa summit in 1967 included a poem, which narrated the sad tale of violence and destruction in the south and observed:

> But most of all I lament
> Because we the Negroes of the Southern Sudan are abandoned
> By all the people who call themselves our "brothers",
> By the black people of Africa,
>
> They come together in the O.A.U.
> In the O.C.A.M., for discussions.
>
> They come together at Dakar to celebrate Negritude,
> Why do they not come together
> To rescue us?
>
> Perhaps because we are weak and poor.[52]

This perception of the OAU's socially exclusive basis gave rise to two inter-related images which became a regular feature in non-governmental ideology. One is the idea that the OAU, as a tool created by Western imperialism, is a neo-colonialist cadre in which petty bourgeoisies co-operate to repress popular aspirations, paralyse revolutionary regi-

---

47   *Voice of Southern Sudan*, vol. 3, no. 1, May 1965, pp 2-3.

48   The Southern Front Memorandum to O.A.U. on Afro-Arab Conflict in the Sudan, Accra, October, 1965, pp 1-2.

49   See the memorandum of SANU leader William Deng to the OAU Secretary-General (text in *The Vigilant* [Sudan], 10/11/66).

50   The Southern Front Memorandum to O.A.U. on Afro-Arab Conflict in the Sudan, Accra, October, 1965, pp 2 and 7-10.

51   See for the rejection of the plea for self-determination by Sudan's regime during a press conference in Addis Ababa, *The Vigilant* (Sudan), 13/11/66.

52   "A Lament by a Southern Sudanese Girl", by Regina Akuany, taken from ALF Memorandum to O.A.U. Summit Conference, Kinshasa, September 11, 1967 (text in *Voice of Southern Sudan*, supplement, no. 4, News Series, April 1969, p 3).

mes and prevent the liberation of the masses.[53] According to one Sierra Leonean diatribe fulminating against the Freetown summit of 1980, the OAU was guilty of exploitative, neo-colonial morality. Instead of dedicating itself to the causes of the people, it had formulated a set of norms with which to protect state elites and oppress the masses.[54] In a more facile vein, these critiques singled out the non-intervention norm for special attention. This norm was deemed "reactionary hypocrisy". It was also argued that the OAU's emphasis on Southern Africa could not divert attention from its failure to manage Africa's conflicts.[55]

Closely related to the idea of a neo-colonialist structure is the metaphor of a trade union of the powerful. Non-governmental tracts contain numerous qualifications of the OAU as a trade union of heads of state.[56] As was shown in the last part of section 4.3, it had already been coined on the eve of the OAU's formation. One of the crudest versions of this image is that of a "cartel" of "OAU gangsterism" whose character should fill everyone with horror.[57] If this seems extreme, it should be realized that the trade union metaphor even penetrated governmental ideology. In 1970 la Semaine of Congo-Brazzaville published an article, which asked whether the OAU was a trade union of heads of state or an organization at the service of Africa's peoples. It concluded that the institution was not yet "une affaire des masses".[58] In a more forthright argument the Nigerian Daily Times, commenting on the Assembly summits of 1978 and 1979, questioned the validity of official conspiracy theories and observed that many problems were not caused by external forces but by state elites themselves. In this context the OAU had almost developed into a "mutual admiration club for African leaders", which focused more on perpetuating their monopoly of power than solving Africa's problems.[59]

Even some of Africa's top leadership, like Thomas Sankara, began articulating the trade union metaphor during the 1980s, issuing appeals for an organization that worked for "the people" rather than the heads of state.[60] In 1993 Eritrea used its admission to castigate members over the OAU's failures in this respect.[61] The idea of a popular Pan-African institution had by then gained some adherence in non-governmental critiques.[62] As one Senegalese opposition journal had it, what was needed was a new kind of "peoples OAU" open to popular representation.[63]

In an interview one diplomat qualified the trade union metaphor as a "little excessive" and "unfair". He retorted that the OAU is no more than the member states

---

53   E. M'buyinga, *Pan-Africanism or Neo-Colonialism? The Bankruptcy of the O.A.U.* (London, 1982), pp 9-10, 56, 148, 216 and 221.

54   M. Mustapha, *Big Game in Africa* (n. pl., 1980), pp 5-6 and 52.

55   M'buyinga, *Pan-Africanism*, pp 4, 9, 58, 182-183, 202-204 and 214 and Mustapha, *Big Game in Africa*, p 23.

56   M'buyinga, *Pan-Africanism*, pp 11, 162, 183, 194, 210 and 226.

57   Mustapha, *Big Game in Africa*, pp 7 and 26.

58   *La Semaine* (Congo-Br.), no. 932, 23/8/70.

59   *Daily Times* (Nigeria), 15/7/78 and 24/7/79.

60   See f.i. the remark by Thomas Sankara, quoted in P. Englebert, *La révolution burkinabè* (Paris, 1986), p 199.

61   *Le Soleil* (Senegal), 29-30/6/93 (article).

62   See f.i. M'buyinga, *Pan-Africanism*, pp 6 and 214.

63   From a 1978 article in *Ande Sopi*, quoted in M'buyinga, *Pan-Africanism*, p 212. Also *Le Soleil* (Senegal), 29/6/92 (article).

watching over their sovereignty.[64] It is true that, to some extent, all inter-governmental organizations suffer from an image problem, as they usually operate without direct popular backing. The lack of political allegiance and the underdeveloped sense of an international "community" make it hard to create a favourable image.[65]

Yet, the huge gulf separating Africa's state elites from the unprivileged and the many violent conflicts marking the post-colonial era make the OAU's stigma a special case in point. One must realize, of course, that these views are themselves elitist in the sense that the non-governmental groups articulating them are sections in the modern elite that are denied access to state power and privilege. One may argue that the modernist ideologies at the basis of the OAU, as well as of its critiques, all form relatively incomprehensible abstractions for the mass of Africa's peoples. As shown in the introduction of section 3.4, there is a parallel here with Pan-Africanism. Thus, as was argued in a more general way in section 2.3, the gulf between state and civil society confines public opinion on the OAU to sections in the modern elite. Yet this doesn't negate its value. The views analysed here point to the one-sided role of the OAU in Africa's socio-political order, something that became particularly explicit in its policy on refugees and human rights. It directed the way for some of the serious re-thinking that would be undertaken, after the late 1980s, inside the Organization itself.

Refugee policy

The OAU's defence of state elite interests does not mean that the plight of individual Africans did not come to the attention of the policy organs. By the mid-1960s internal conflicts had already created massive flows of refugees who poured across international boundaries and therefore quickly made their way to the OAU agenda. Some remarks must be made on the manner in which the Organization approached refugee issues, as it exposes its limited relevance to the well-being of individual Africans.

The OAU's approach became apparent at the first session of its "Commission on Refugees" in 1964, an organ that is discussed below. Its deliberations showed that domestic instability, coupled to the permeability of inter-state frontiers, gave rise to tensions between governments which suspected each other of condoning or encouraging subversive activities of refugees.[66] While some discussed the importance of financial aid by UNHCR and the need to have other states share the burden of refugees,[67] several delegates emphasized the security risk, that refugees posed to their own government, rather than the humanitarian issues involved.[68] Some states stressed the need to let the OAU undertake fact-finding missions. Many others, however, warned that an examination of the causes of refugee problems should not become an excuse to "meddle" in internal affairs.

---

64   Interview with Amadou Kebe, Addis Ababa, 3/10/89 (n. 5).

65   See on this I.L. Claude, *Swords into Plowshares: The Problems and Progress of International Organization* (New York, 1964), pp 4, 176 and 404.

66   See f.i. the statements of Cameroon, Uganda and Sudan, in Commission on the Problem of Refugees in Africa, 4 sessions, Addis Ababa, 1-5 June 1964 [hereinafter as Refugee Commission, June '64].

67   Statements by Burundi and Nigeria, Refugee Commission, June '64.

68   Statements by Rwanda and Sudan, Refugee Commission, June '64.

As the Sudanese delegate put it, the Commission was no "juridical tribunal".[69]

Thus, the proper management of inter-state relations, rather than alleviation of the plight of refugees, was the prime concern of the OAU. This was confirmed by the "OAU Convention Governing the Specific Aspects of Refugee Problems in Africa" of 1969.[70] This treaty nevertheless expresses humanitarian concerns by imposing an obligation on the collectivity of member states to grant asylum and stipulating the norm of "non-refoulement". This norm involves the prohibition against expulsion of refugees to a territory where they are threatened in a way as set out in the Convention.[71] The UN definition of refugees is deliberately widened to include persons not individually persecuted but compelled by "events seriously disturbing public order" to leave their country (arts. 1.1 and 1.2).[72] This reflects classical African practice of individuals who flee, as part of mass migrations, scenes of disturbance or group persecution.[73]

However, the Convention is also concerned about subversion by refugees themselves, who might be recruited by guerrilla movements or in another way retaliate against their government. It therefore stipulates that refugees must abstain from any subversive activity against member states. The latter must prohibit armed attacks and other actions likely to cause tension, such as press and radio campaigns. To this purpose, countries of asylum are obliged to settle refugees "at a reasonable distance" from the frontier of their country of origin. When, indeed, it was later noticed that member states allowed refugees to settle very close to the frontier, the Commission on Refugees reiterated the need to observe "reasonable distance".[74]

With regard to the humanitarian side of refugee problems, member states realized that they needed massive help from the UN and NGO's. This reflection was only strengthened by the sharp rise in the number of refugees during the 1970s and 1980s. Thus, the OAU developed close co-operation with UNHCR.[75] The Organization's own resources are far too limited to alleviate the misery of refugees in any significant way.

Naturally, one can try to explain this as part of a free rider dilemma, as with the OAU's low budget levels generally. Hegemonic stability theory links this dilemma to the structural features of international relations. As noted in earlier chapters, the essence of Olson's logic of collective action is not malevolence on the part of individual actors, which act rationally by trying to get by as cheaply as possible.[76] Applying this argument

---

69   See recommendations and statements by Uganda, Rwanda, Cameroon, Sudan, Nigeria and Ethiopia, Refugee Commission, June '64.

70   This came into effect in 1974. By 1989 only thirteen members had not yet ratified the Convention. See CAB/LEG/24.3 for a list.

71   See articles 1, 2 and 5 Convention.

72   This excludes internally displaced people. See also *African Refugees: Newsletter published by the Organization of African Unity* [hereinafter as *African Refugees*], no. 7, June 1985, p 8.

73   A legal analysis in R.M. D'sa, 'The African Refugee Problem: Relevant International Conventions and Recent Activities of the Organization of African Unity', in *Netherlands International Law Review*, 1984, pp 378-97.

74   Art. 2.6 and 3 Convention and BR/10/COM/XV/16.89: Activity Report of the OAU Commission of Fifteen on Refugees to the 50th Ordinary Session of the OAU Council of Ministers, [hereinafter as BR/10/COM/XV/16.89: Activity Report, Commission of Refugees, 1989], p 12.

75   Interview with Dr. C.J. Bakwesegha, Director of OAU Bureau for Refugees, General Secretariat, Addis Ababa, 2/10/89.

76   M. Olson, *The Logic of Collective Action: Public Goods and the Theory of Groups* (Cambridge,

to inter-African politics, one could argue that the OAU's members desire co-operation, but fail because the structural obstacles of their international relations prevent generation of sufficient co-ordinated will to achieve optimal outcome.

However, it has already been argued that systemic influences do not always fully explain state behaviour. Policy choices and calculations on the part of states also play a role of their own,[77] something that brings us to the state and sub-state level of analysis. Thus, it was observed in chapters 5 and 6 that some states are simply committed to paying their dues to the OAU and that aspects of its anti-colonial policy, such as the stand on dialogue, relate to the peculiar character of African state elites. Similarly, one may argue that lack of sufficient collective resources for the care of refugees is, apart from member states' own underdevelopment, tied to the socially one-sided role of the OAU.

Until the mid 1980s, OAU activities for refugees were mainly financed from UN and NGO funds. However, as outside organizations were reluctant to contribute to the OAU's operational budget, the Council of Ministers established the Organization's own refugee fund (1985). It consisted of one, and later two, per cent of the OAU budget, thus amounting to some one million dollars, including external donations.[78] The Organization cannot therefore improve the lot of refugees in a more than a marginal way, such as by funding income-generating projects and an extremely modest scholarship programme.[79] Apart from this, humanitarian concern finds expression in information activities[80] and appeals to member states to improve the legal status of refugees and grant scholarships. The OAU's attempts to resettle refugees and find employment opportunities therefore depend heavily on member state co-operation. Usually, appeals for UN and NGO action constitute the best thing it can do.

Clearly, humanitarian concern has, at least up to the late 1980s, been a side-issue. While the "Bureau for Refugees", which is part of the Political Department, has always been preoccupied with humanitarian relief,[81] the Commission on Refugees mentioned earlier must focus on the political context. As the OAU's principal organ in refugee matters, it examines all refugee problems, recommends to the Council on their solution and studies ways of providing for refugees.[82] The Commission is made up of fifteen member states from the five African regions, usually their ambassadors in Addis Ababa.[83]

Mass., 1965), ch. 1.

77   A.A. Stein, *Why Nations Cooperate: Circumstances and Choice in International Relations* (Ithaca and London, 1990), p 184.

78   *African Refugees*, no. 6, 1985, no. 8, 1986 and no. 10, 1987 and interview with Dr. C.J. Bakwesegha, Addis Ababa, 2/10/89.

79   For example, in 1989 36 refugees (!) benefited from declining sums of money. See *African Refugees*, no. 8, 1986 and BR/10/COM/XV/16.89: Activity Report, Commission of Refugees, 1989.

80   See f.i. the brochures *Africa and its Refugees: Africa Refugee Day June 20 1975* (publ. by OAU Bureau for Refugees, no pl., 1975) and *20 Questions et Réponses à l'Usage du Réfugié Africain* (*ibid.*, Addis Ababa, 1982).

81   Since 1992 the Bureau is called "Division for Refugees and Displaced Persons". See for its history CM/Res.244 (XVII); CM/Res.329 (XXII); CM/Res.346 (XXIII); CM/Res.774 (XXXIV); CM/Res.915 (XXXVIII); and C.O.C. Amate, *Inside the OAU: Pan-Africanism in Practice* (New York, 1986), ch. 16.

82   Art. 4, Rules of Procedure and *20 Questions et Réponses*, p 11.

83   They are: Algeria, Libya, Senegal, Mali, Niger, Nigeria, Sudan, Uganda, Tanzania, Angola, Zaire, Cameroon, Zambia, Zimbabwe and Swaziland. Art. 1 Rules of Procedure; *20 Questions et*

The basic idea is that the OAU should not duplicate UNHCR, which concentrates on the humanitarian dimension and is politically neutral. The Commission must smooth the political context: to this purpose it sends fact-finding missions to member states[84] and contacts them or exerts pressure to enable UNHCR to fulfil its mission.[85]

However, the clearest way in which the OAU's political focus could have been expressed was closed for years, namely by tackling root causes of refugee flows. The Organization never failed to point at the reasons behind the mass of refugees from colonial or white minority territories. Yet its members forced it to be silent on the causes of similar flows from African states. The dramatic growth of refugees, leading to a continental total of five million during the 1980s,[86] could therefore only be met with verbal concern[87] or fund-raising conferences.[88] Non-governmental critiques qualified this human misery as degrading for "Africa's shared human values".[89] In diplomatic circles it took until the 1980s before colonialism as explanation of refugee problems[90] began to give way to pleas to discuss human rights violations inside member states. However, at the time these appeals were made principally by officials of the Secretariat.[91]

Human rights

The management of refugee flows thus became part of the wider issue of human rights violations. Until the late 1970s, the OAU chose to ignore it, as it concerned domestic events that rarely developed inter-African implications. For example, the murder of at least 80,000 to 100,000 Hutu people in Burundi in 1972 was simply dismissed by the then Secretary-General as "an internal affair". President Bokassa's participation in the murder of prisoners in the Central African Republic (1972) did not evoke any official response. Even the murder in 1978 of the OAU's first Secretary-General, Diallo Telli, met with silence. And so did the horrendous "Red Terror" campaign in Addis Ababa (1977-78), which took place on the very door-step of the Secretariat.[92] All this led to damning criticism of the Organization in non-governmental circles. Its silence on human rights, combined with the high profile of its summits, triggered violent tirades:

> Yes, the summit of the insurmountable guilt, fascism, thivery [sic], deception, half-truths, publicity stunts, lack of sympathy for the plight of the hungry

Réponses, p 12; African Refugees, no. 10, 1987.

84   See f.i. BR/10/COM/XV/16.89: Activity Report, Commission of Refugees, 1989, pp 6-7 and African Refugees, no. 7, 1985.

85   Interview with Dr. C.J. Bakwesegha, Addis Ababa, 2/10/89.

86   See BR/10/COM/XV/16.89: Activity Report, Commission of Refugees, 1989, pp 5 and 8.

87   F.i. CM/Res.489 (XXVII); CM/Res.621 (XXXI); CM/Res.622 (XXXI); CM/Res.727 (XXXIII); and CM/Res.774 (XXXIV).

88   See f.i. African Refugees, nos. 3 and 7, 1983 and 1985 and SARRED/88/L.1/Rev.II: Oslo Declaration and Plan of Action on the Plight of Refugees, Returnees and Displaced Persons in Southern Africa (SARRED).

89   See African Refugees, no. 2, 1983.

90   Interview with Drs. A. Heldring, temporary chargé d'affaires, Netherlands embassy, Addis Ababa, 15/9/89. See f.i. the OAU's brochure Africa and its Refugees, pp 8-10 (n. 80).

91   Interview with Dr. C.J. Bakwesegha, Addis Ababa, 2/10/89 and African Refugees, nos. 6, 1985 and 10, 1987. For a similar member state appeal BR/10/COM/XV/16.89: Activity Report, Commission of Refugees, 1989, p 33 and Daily News (Tanzania), 19/7/79.

92   Kunig, völkerrechtliche Nichteinmischungsprinzip, pp 180-8.

masses ... IS THIS THE WAY YOU FEED YOUR CHILDREN, OAU? IS THIS
THE PRICE OF THE CORONATION?
Is it too late for the Secretary General of the OAU to table a motion calling for
the freezing of Bokassa's ill gotten bank balance? Are not the victims of
Bokassa Africans? ... OAU justice must also be seen to be enjoyed by the
African people whose taxes are maintaining the secretariat; justice and
clemency must not be restricted to OAU chairpersons and OAU dignitaries
...[93]

Declining domestic stability and the concomitant rise in human rights violations led at
least some governments to show greater sensitivity towards this one-sided approach of
the OAU. It was especially the butchery of the Amin regime that led to calls for a critical
response. In 1975 Tanzania and Botswana accused the OAU, which held its summit in
Uganda that year, of a "conspiracy of silence" with respect to human rights violations.
They called on the Organization to speak out and observed that its hypocrisy had caused it
serious damage.[94] Two years later, the situation in Uganda caused Sierra Leone to make a
similar appeal.[95]

Uganda's war with Tanzania and Amin's subsequent downfall (1979), coupled to
publicity on repression in Equatorial Guinea and massacres of school children by the
Bokassa regime, finally brought matters to a head. Countries like Tanzania, Nigeria and
Ghana began arguing that the non-intervention norm was abused by dictators who
demanded Africa's collective silence over their human rights record so as to retain their
hold on power. According to Tanzania, the credibility of the OAU's stand on colonialism
and apartheid was jeopardized by the double standards inherent in its behaviour.[96] In
reference to the excesses of Bokassa governmental opinion in Sierra Leone observed:

It makes a mockery of the OAU's principles if the organisation cannot
unanimously condemn an African leader even when there is ample evidence
that he is guilty of child-massacre.[97]

These countries, which included Zambia and Liberia, therefore called for revision of the
OAU Charter to make provision for human rights.[98] While encouragement from outside
Africa was important, it was developments in inter-African relations that proved
instrumental in stimulating this change. It had not only been shown that Amin's regime
was cruel, but also that it endangered regional stability. As shown in section 8.2, its
attempt to annex Tanzanian territory and Nyerere's subsequent decision to invade Uganda
and overthrow the volatile dictator led to an acrimonious debate at the Assembly summit
in Monrovia (1979). Some accused Tanzania of violating the norms of territorial integrity
and non-interference. Partly in order to neutralize human rights issues as a source of

---

93   Mustapha, *Big Game in Africa*, pp 16 and 19. Emphasis in original.
94   *Daily News* (Tanzania), 26/7/75 and *Botswana Daily News*, 21/7/75 and 30/7/75.
95   *Daily Mail* (Sierra Leone), 19/2/77.
96   *Daily News* (Tanzania), 19/7/79; *The Ghanaian Times*, 21/7/79; and *Daily Times* (Nigeria),
      24/7/79.
97   *Daily Mail* (Sierra Leone), 21/7/79.
98   *Ibid.*, 21/7/79 and 9/8/79 (article); *Times of Zambia*, 19/7/79; *Daily News* (Tanzania), 19/7/79;
      and *Daily Times* (Nigeria), 24/7/79.

inter-state tensions,[99] the summit ordered the drafting of the OAU's own human rights instrument.[100]

An "African Charter on Human and Peoples' Rights" was signed at the Nairobi summit in 1981 and came into force five years later.[101] Here it must suffice to note that, from the perspective of human rights protection, the treaty contains numerous flaws.[102] While human rights violations are dealt with by an independent commission of jurists, these lack judicial powers. They can only make recommendations on which the Assembly has the final word.[103] Thus, it is clear that, during the rapid drafting process, government delegates exerted pressure to protect their supremacy in the OAU's cadres and human rights measures. The absence of hegemonic leadership coupled to the social position of Africa's state elites can serve as explanation for this outcome.

Moreover, in interviews in 1989 it became clear that the non-intervention norm in the OAU Charter prevented discussion of human rights violations in Council and Assembly. Some states held the dubious opinion that, since such matters had been entrusted to the commission of jurists, these could not be treated in the policy organs where the non-intervention norm held sway.[104] Others therefore vainly argued for amalgamation of the human rights instrument with the OAU Charter. Human rights violations would then infringe the OAU Charter and states would be unable to hide behind the latter's non-interference norm.[105] However, by the early 1990s these suggestions were overtaken by the decision to give the OAU a greater role in the management of disputes.

The OAU's shifting role in domestic conflict and transition

In terms of the rationale of OAU conflict management, there was a cold logic in the disregard of domestic conflicts that did not entail substantial extra-African involvement or other important repercussions for inter-African relations. The same is true for the attitude to separatist movements, the relative neglect of the humanitarian dimension of refugee problems and the disregard of human rights. In so far as these issues did not develop significant implications for inter-African politics they were met by, what one might term, a culture of silence.

However, in the last part of section 7.2 it was shown that the way in which the OAU attempts to manage conflict underwent important reform in 1993. While since the late 1970s the effectiveness of OAU conflict management came under growing pressure one might argue that, by the late 1980s, its underlying rationale began to backfire. It was

---

99   See *Africa Research Bulletin* (PSC), 1979, pp 5329-30.

100 AHG/Dec.115 (XVI).

101 By the early 1990s, only a few countries had not yet ratified. See the list in G.J. Naldi, *Documents of the Organization of African Unity* (London and New York, 1992), pp 245-246.

102 Legal analyses of the Charter abound. See f.i. *The African Charter on Human and Peoples' Rights: Development, Context, Significance; Papers of a Symposium of the African Law Association held in Maastricht in 1987* (Marburg, 1991).

103 See arts. 47-59 African Charter on Human and Peoples' Rights (Division of Press & Information, General Secretariat: Addis Ababa, no date).

104 Interview with Amadou Kebe, Addis Ababa, 3/10/89.

105 Interview with Dr. J.A. Tesha, Minister/Counsellor of the Tanzanian embassy, Addis Ababa, 25/9/89 and Charter Review Committee discussions in CAB/LEG/97/DRAFT/RAPT.RPT (III) Rev. 2, pars. 24 and 26.4.

especially worsening security situations of domestic contexts, such as the civil wars in Liberia, Sudan, Ethiopia, Rwanda and Mozambique, that began increasingly to interfere with the proper management of Africa's continental order. Their disregard helped very little. In addition, there were significant changes in Africa's external environment and domestic pressures emanating from the transitions to multi-party political systems.

The result was that in 1990 the Assembly formally arrogated domestic conflicts to its area of competence, thus restricting the interpretation of the non-intervention norm and setting in motion a process of shifting in the rationale of OAU conflict management. Yet, it must be realized that in this process contradictory views and pressures were and are at work. While it is shown below that this has led to a remarkable change in the OAU's approach to internal conflicts and its own activation, this outcome may be provisional. The changing role of the OAU in this field and, more generally, Africa's socio-political order, therefore awaits further evaluation.

Thus, the 1993 reforms did not give the Organization a blanket right of intervention in internal conflicts. In his 1992 reform proposals the Secretary-General admitted that the entry point for intervention was not clear-cut. However, he argued for a right to intervene in situations involving a total break-down of law and order, attendant human suffering and regional spreading. Liberia was cited as an example. In such a case, intervention could be justified on humanitarian grounds and the need to restore order. Yet, even in conflicts that had not yet reached that stage some sort of pre-emptive intervention should be allowed.[106] Senegal went still further by suggesting that the non-intervention norm be withdrawn from the Charter altogether.[107]

Predictably, these proposals caused a lot of controversy and were opposed by several countries, especially Sudan and Rwanda.[108] The result was that the reforms introduced in 1993 did not give the OAU a general right of intervention and that, in any case, an intervention must be decided by the central organ of the new mechanism, namely the Assembly Bureau. Furthermore, the regulations governing its operation still include norms like respect for the sovereignty of member states and non-interference in internal affairs.[109] These were unanimously adopted at the 1993 summit. As was observed in section 7.2, the Bureau therefore still needs the consent of disputants. Nevertheless, the 1993 summit *did* agree, despite opposition from Sudan and Eritrea, that in contexts marked by severe human suffering as well as the collapse of the state the OAU has the right to intervene.[110] This is pursued further in the next section.

---

106   CM/1710 (LVI) Rev. 1: Report of the Secretary-General on Conflicts in Africa: Prospects for an OAU Mechanism for Conflict Prevention and Resolution (June 1992) [hereinafter as CM/1710 (LVI) Rev.1: Report of the SG on Conflicts in Africa (June 1992)]), p 12. Intervention in case of total domestic chaos had already been pleaded in 1991 by Uganda. M.J. den Hartog, 'De Organisatie van Afrikaanse Eenheid (OAE): Een Organisatie voor Collectieve Veiligheid?', in *Proceedings: La problématique de sécurité en Afrique sub-saharienne* (Centre d'études de défense [Belgium]: no pl., 1995), pp 79-80.

107   *Jeune Afrique*, 9-15/7/92. Senegal, besides Nigeria, played an active part in launching the proposals. See f.i. *Le Soleil*, 2/7/93 (articles) and *Jeune Afrique*, 2-8/7/92.

108   *Africa Research Bulletin* (PSC), 1992, p 10636 and *Le Soleil* (Senegal), 27/6-28/6 and 29/6/92 (articles).

109   AHG/Decl.3 (XXIX)/Rev.1, par. 14.

110   M.C.D. Wembou, 'A propos du nouveau mécanisme de l'OUA sur les conflits', in *Afrique 2000*,

Political developments confirm that the non-intervention norm is, indeed, interpreted in a more restricted fashion than ever before. Apart from situations characterized by a complete break-down of security the OAU claims, in a more general way, a role in the management of domestic conflict. This has been accepted by member states. Thus, internal developments are subject of discussion in the OAU's organs and lead to the adoption of resolutions, which may even contain denunciations of events or actions of governments. For example, the coup attempt in Burundi in October 1993 drew a sharp response of the Assembly Bureau. It vigorously condemned it and demanded that its perpetrators put an end to it and allow a return to democratic government and the restoration of the rule of law.[111]

This was unprecedented, for until then the OAU could not question the legitimacy of member state governments and the way they come to power. This was essentially due to the non-interference norm. The OAU always had to accept those who represented the group holding governmental power, even if this amounted to no more than control of the capital. While protests were sometimes made about coups which, as a result of special circumstances, had some significance for inter-African politics, such criticism was a matter of individual states. For the OAU as a whole, acceptance of a regime was in the end unavoidable as an acknowledgement of a fait-accompli.

Even if this is still the case now, the response to the Burundi coup points to greater room for Pan-African delegitimation of state behaviour. Besides such deliberative and verbal forms of concern with domestic developments, the Organization may, and actually does, engage in concrete mediation activities. Having sent a fact-finding mission and special envoy to Burundi, the OAU became subsequently involved in the country's peace negotiations. It became also actively involved, in 1992-93, in negotiations to find a peace agreement in the Rwandan civil war.[112]

Still wider aspects of internal developments can become subject of OAU scrutiny. Since the late 1980s, domestic opposition parties and embattled governments themselves have frequently asked the OAU to help in the monitoring of national constitutional conferences or elections.[113] That such missions can only take place with the agreement of the member state concerned, so as not to violate the non-intervention norm, does not negate the fact that such issues have become a part of the OAU's area of competence.

Apart from such civilian observer missions the OAU engages in military observation exercises as well. Here it must be noted that the military activity undertaken in such contexts is extremely modest in character, scope and duration. Both this and the relevant financial dimension, which are discussed in section 8.2, therefore constitute a serious bottleneck for a more wide-ranging role in domestic disputes. As was noted in section 7.2, the mechanism introduced in 1993 was not as comprehensive as the

---

February 1994, p 8. Kenya also had reservations. Yet in the end the declaration on the mechanism was passed unanimously. *Africa Research Bulletin* (PSC), 1993, p 11066.

111   Quoted in Wembou, 'A propos du nouveau mécanisme', pp 13-14.

112   It also contributed to mediation in the internal crises of Congo and Angola in 1993. Wembou, 'A propos du nouveau mécanisme', p 14; *Africa Research Bulletin* (PSC), 1992, pp 10691 and 10763; 1993, pp 10867, 11028, 11108-11109, 11208 and 11231-4; and *Le Soleil* (Senegal), 29-30/6/93 (Assembly speech).

113   Also interview with Salim in *Africa Report*, May-June 1992.

Secretary-General had wished. The desire to avoid extensive military operations was based on sober realism about their complexity and cost.[114] Emphasis was put on prevention and conflict reductive tactics at an early stage in order to avoid such operations and, in the process, preserve the OAU's credibility.[115]

Yet, the rationale behind the Organization's activation in conflict has, notwithstanding these limited objectives, actually broadened. Inter-state disputes aside, the OAU may concern itself with internal disputes *whether or not* they are marked by extra-African involvement. Humanitarian concerns may be a sufficient ground for activation, as witnessed by the OAU's mediation efforts in the Rwandan and Burundian conflicts. Regional spreading, such as in Liberia, may be another. This shift to more humanitarian concerns and an activist approach is not only a logical result of the end of the Cold War, but also of Africa's own worsening security contexts and changes in domestic political relations. This means that, apart from constrictions that structural obstacles of international relations continue to impose on Pan-African conflict management, the future of the OAU's role is tied up with the vicissitudes of Africa's domestic socio-political developments.

One can therefore observe contradictory shifts and trends. More influential countries as Nigeria, Algeria, Egypt, South Africa and Zaire could provide some sort of hegemonic leadership in the transition process of the OAU and its member states. However, events in most of those countries should caution against optimistic forecasts. Without consolidation of more open and broad based systems of government, Pan-African delegitimation of state behaviour is more difficult. Thus, when the Assembly arrogated domestic conflicts to its competence it expressed interest in a "permitting political environment" to guarantee human rights and the rule of law, but added that member states retained the right to determine, "in all sovereignty", their own system of democracy.[116] As shown by the Burundi case, however, a coup d'état may transgress the limits of collective acquiescence. Yet, whether this is also true for military take-overs in more influential countries is doubtful. In such cases the lack of hegemonic leadership makes retaliation difficult. In contrast, the Secretary-General argued in 1993 that, in whatever way member states would structure their political system, the essence should be "participatory democracy", *i.e.* the guaranteed exercise of democratic rights and accountable government operating on the rule of law, rather than the whims and patronage of the powerful. Universal elements of democracy, as social systems geared to promoting equality, an independent judiciary and a free and objective press, should also apply to Africa.[117]

The humanitarian arguments that form part of the Secretary-General's reflections

---

114 AHG/Decl.3 (XXIX)/Rev.1, par. 15.

115 Wembou, 'A propos du nouveau mécanisme', p 8.

116 AHG/Decl.1 (XXVI). See also *Le Soleil* (Senegal), 9/7/90 and 10/7/90; *l'Essor* (Mali), 21-22/7/90; and *Cameroon Tribune*, 13/7/90, which includes the Ugandan viewpoint (all articles).

117 OAU at 30: Reflections on the Past and Prospects for the Future: Address by the Secretary-General, H.E. Dr. Salim Ahmed Salim on the occasion of the 30th Aniversary of the Organization of African Unity, Africa Hall, Addis Ababa, May 25, 1993 (hereinafter as Address by the Secretary-General, May 1993), pp 20-21. For member state lip-service to democracy f.i. *Le Soleil* (Senegal), 10/7/90 (article) and 30/6/92 (Assembly speech).

extend, indeed, much further than a role in dispute settlement as such. Salim's views echo many of the critiques that non-governmental groups have levelled against the one-sided role of the OAU in Africa's socio-political order. In effect, acceptance of his ideas would entail a fundamental change in the general ideology of the OAU, in the sense of an institution that would go beyond the narrow interests of state elites. In 1993 the Secretary-General argued that the OAU should get a role in the "management of change" inside member states, which should lead to the realization of a "permitting political environment". Such environment should unleash the creativity of Africa's peoples and empower them so as to give them a say in their government. It should foster tolerance and lead to a new link of genuine partnership between government and people. In this transition the OAU should contribute to such a spirit of tolerance. It should not remain aloof to acute suffering, such as human rights violations and the misery caused to refugees, but resort to constructive action.[118] Symbolically, the silence that has been preserved over the fate of Diallo Telli was also put to an end by a plea to honour the memory and contributions of the OAU's first Secretary-General.[119]

8.2 Grandiloquent notions: the military dimensions of the continental order

Introduction

This section analyses the military aspects, in the widest sense, of the OAU's attempt to manage Africa's political order. This military dimension is studied both in reference to inter-state disputes and domestic conflicts. First, we discuss the inclination to take recourse to bilateral security arrangements. This became clear during events in Tanganyika and the Congo in 1964 and confirmed signals observed at the OAU's founding conference. Then we analyse its negative repercussions for inter-African relations, as became apparent, for example, through the use of mercenaries and the Shaba crises and Ugandan-Tanzanian war of the late 1970s. This is followed by an outline of the debate on Pan-African security. In the course of this the various obstacles to such a strategy are reviewed. The next two sections analyse the OAU's intervention in Chad, which interceded in this debate. The last section studies the military aspects of the 1993 reforms, which are contrasted with the UN's Somali operation and the ECOMOG intervention in Liberia.

Preference for bilateral security arrangements

The Charter provides for co-operation between member states in the area of defence and security. To this purpose, it established a plenary Defence Commission composed of member state ministers.[120] However, when the OAU began functioning the inclination of governments to rely on the military assistance of individual allies, rather than some Pan-African arrangement, became rapidly apparent.

---

118 Salim has been seen visiting refugee camps for people displaced in the Senegal-Mauritania conflict. See *Africa Research Bulletin* (PSC), 1989, pp 9478-9479.
119 Address by the Secretary-General, May 1993.
120 Arts. 2.2.f and 20.4 Charter.

Thus, in January 1964, units of the Tanganyikan army rebelled against their government, a mutiny that spread to Kenya and Uganda. All three countries called in British troops to disarm the rebels. After this had been accomplished, Tanganyika requested a meeting of the OAU Council of Ministers to replace its British contingent with African troops.[121] Deliberations showed that, while military assistance by an individual African country was considered politically more acceptable than that of a non-African state,[122] members had the right to appeal to an outside power to come to their aid. This confirmed the claim that the Malagasy delegate had made to that effect during the OAU's founding conference. At the extraordinary Council session most delegates were at pains to emphasize that Tanganyika had the right to call in British troops and replace them with African ones. The OAU should only note that it had done so. Ghanaian and Ugandan arguments to find a permanent, Pan-African solution for the security predicaments of member states were rejected as inopportune.[123] What happened was that the OAU was merely expected to rubber-stamp a deal that Tanganyika and Nigeria had struck behind the scenes to replace British troops with Nigerian ones. After some manipulation the Council endorsed Tanganyika's decision, "proposed" that British troops be replaced by African ones and said that Dar es Salaam should have the right to approach the state(s) of its choice. The troops should be under Tanganyikan control and costs and operations should be dealt with by Tanganyika and the state(s) concerned.[124]

Yet, this does not mean that a government could do as it pleased without ever evoking negative reactions. In the preceding section it was shown that Tshombe's use of white mercenaries to crush the CNL revolt engendered a lot of controversy. Moreover, in the course of this he conceded to a dropping of Belgian paratroopers on Stanleyville (November 1964) to rescue hundreds of Europeans who had been taken hostage by his opponents. The landing was organized with the logistical support of the British and Americans and coincided with the mercenary onslaught on the city. It caught the OAU completely off guard. Only the day before the American ambassador to Kenya had been negotiating with CNL leaders under the auspices of President Kenyatta, the chairman of the OAU mediation commission.[125] While most European hostages were saved, the population of Stanleyville was left to the mercy of the Congolese army and the mercenaries. Thousands of people were massacred.[126]

Many member states, both radical and moderate, were furious. In Kenya KANU followers were involved in riots near the American embassy. President Kenyatta said he was "shocked" and "appalled", as further negotiations on the hostage issue had been planned and his warnings against intervention had not been heeded. Dahomey, which

---

121   *Verbatim Record* of the Second Extraordinary Session of the Council of Ministers, Dar es Salaam, February 1964 (hereinafter as *VR*, ECM2, Dar es Salaam, Febr. 1964), ECM/PV1/Annex A, pp 1-6.

122   Also W.J. Foltz, 'The Organization of African Unity and the Resolution of Africa's Conflicts', in Deng and Zartman, *Conflict Resolution in Africa* (n. 21), ch. 13.

123   *VR*, ECM2, Dar es Salaam, Febr. 1964, ECM/PV2 and ECM/PV3.

124   *Ibid.*; ECM/Res.2 (II); and *Africa Research Bulletin* (PSC), 1964, p 21. Ethiopia provided an air wing to Tanganyika. See *External Affairs Bulletin Tanzania: An Official Record of Foreign Policy of the United Republic of Tanzania*, vl. 1, no. 2, July 1965, p 25.

125   Pradhan, 'OAU and the Congo Crisis', p 37 and Amate, *Inside the OAU*, p 435. (ns. 18 and 81).

126   Cervenka, *Unfinished Quest*, p 91 (n. 11).

belonged to the conservative group, questioned the humanitarian justification given by the Americans. Ethiopia criticized the events as evidence of continued racism, imperialism and colonialism in the Congo.[127] The OAU ad hoc commission accused Belgium, the United States and Britain of aggression and called for an immediate end to foreign intervention and withdrawal of the mercenaries.[128] Militant countries reacted more bitterly. Nkrumah spoke of a "flagrant act of aggression" and observed that Africa could be "terrorised into submission". Algeria also questioned the humanitarian nature of the intervention.[129] Mali was particularly scathing. It qualified the operation as an "unprecedented challenge to African dignity" and spoke of a reconquest by neo-colonial imperialism, which did not differ from "Hitlerism". In an angry exchange with Tshombe during the Council session in March 1965, its delegate questioned whether he had had any control over the operation and asked him how African states could remain indifferent to the presence of Western transport planes and paratroopers, which, he said, threatened the security of neighbouring countries.[130]

These violent reactions were prompted by several factors. First, the OAU's official mediator had been publicly snubbed. Second, despite the bad plight of European hostages and the murder of some sixty[131] of them during and after the dropping, many countries perceived an element of racism. While most Europeans were rescued, the Western powers remained indifferent to the fate of the African population. The humanitarian argument did therefore not seem convincing, especially as the dropping improved the strategic position of Tshombe's army and the mercenaries, leading to the high rate of African casualties. This perception was strengthened by the involvement of mercenaries from Southern Africa and the racist way in which these men and Western press reports portrayed the rebels against the regime in Leopoldville.[132] Indignation was also fuelled by the collective realization of the West's ability to strike deep in the heart of Africa with complete impunity. This can be gauged from references to the blows dealt to African dignity. However, some radical states also had other, more self-centred motives to condemn the operation, as they had sided with the rebels.

Tshombe's freedom of action and that of his Western allies was increased by the fact that member states had become deeply divided. Nigeria and several Francophone countries, such as Ivory Coast, Senegal and Madagascar, argued that it was Tshombe's legal prerogative to call in assistance from any quarter he liked. Although some of these states, like Ivory Coast and the Central African Republic, "deplored" what had happened, such remarks underlined merely that they did not want to distance themselves too much from the many countries that fiercely objected to the dropping. They were not meant to have political consequences. Thus, an extraordinary Council session in December 1964

127   *Africa Research Bulletin* (PSC), 1964, pp 183-184.
128   Amate, *Inside the OAU*, pp 435-436.
129   *Ghana Today*, 2/12/64; *Révolution Africaine* (Algeria), 6/3/65; and *Africa Research Bulletin* (PSC), 1964, p 183.
130   *l'Essor* (Mali), 7/12/64; 14/12/64 (article); 8/3/65 (editorial and article); and 15/3/65 (delegate's speech).
131   See *Africa Research Bulletin* (PSC), 1964 (Nov.-Dec.) and 1965 (Jan.-May). This figure is also given by Cervenka, *Unfinished Quest*, p 90.
132   Cervenka, *Unfinished Quest*, pp 89-91.

adopted a resolution that carried a muted reaction to the dropping, which was qualified as a "grave" situation and "disapproved" of as "disturbing" to Africa's peace and security.[133] The refusal by the Security Council to condemn the operation only underlined the OAU's contribution to the worsening of the crisis. As shown in section 8.1, it had turned down Tshombe's request for troops to quell the rebellion. Its mediation effort had led to a violation of the non-intervention norm and had ended in failure.

While the Tanganyikan mutiny thus confirmed the right to take recourse to bilateral security arrangements, Stanleyville pointed to the dialectics of their context. Collective awareness of vulnerability to, and related condemnation of, non-African interference went hand in hand with impotence to prevent it and complicity of member states in, and their defence of the right to call for, such intervention. In fact, the reactions to Stanleyville formed the perfect articulation of the dualist character of the security obsessions of state elites. As was explained by by Ayoob for the generality of Third World countries,[134] there might be collective fears of non-African interference because of its nefarious effect on inter-African politics and Africa's global influence, but the immediacy of security predicaments took precedence over mitigation of long-term global inequalities. Lack of hegemonic leadership made introduction of Pan-African security schemes difficult, especially as non-African powers were prepared to intervene of their own accord. Nowhere was the weakness of the OAU regime so obvious as when such external factors imposed themselves.[135]

Consequences of bilateral security arrangements
However, reliance on bilateral security could entail considerable risks. The use of mercenaries, for example, could not only generate inter-African tension, but also backfire on the regime that employed them. Thus, in 1967 the soldiers of fortune that had helped Tshombe to regain control of Stanleyville rebelled, together with Katangese units of the Congolese army, against the government of General Mobutu. While the OAU rallied to his support, it also had to mediate between the Rwandan government and the Congo. The two countries became embroiled in an argument about evacuation of the mercenaries. After their revolt had aborted they had fled to, and been interned in, Rwanda. In the end an OAU mediation commission had to propose an accord on their evacuation from Africa on the condition that their governments prevent their return to the continent.[136] This excluded extradition to the Congo to stand trial, as the Rwandan government, probably because of Belgian pressure,[137] was opposed to this.

Thus, apart from touching on racial sensitivities[138] the use of (usually white)

---

133 ECM/Res.7 (IV); *Africa Research Bulletin* (PSC), 1964, pp 184 and 201; *Nouvelles Malgaches Quotidiennes*, 30/11/64, 3/12/64 and 17/2/65; and Agbi, *Organization of African Unity*, p 50 (n. 9).

134 M. Ayoob, 'The Third World in the System of States: Acute Schizophrenia or Growing Pains?', in *International Studies Quarterly*, 1989, pp 67-79.

135 Generally Rothstein, 'Regime-Creation' (n. 20).

136 AHG/Res.49 (IV); AHG/Dec.14 (IV); and CM/212 (Part 2): Report of the Administrative Secretary-General Covering the Period from February to September 1968, Algiers, Sept. 1968, pp 60-61.

137 See on this *Africa Research Bulletin* (PSC), 1967, p 932 and 1968, p 945.

138 See f.i. *l'Essor* (Mali), 14/9/64 (article). Also AHG/Res.49 (IV); AHG/Dec.14 (IV); and CM/St.6

mercenaries could seriously jeopardize state security and become a source of inter-state tension. The OAU therefore regularly called upon members not to invite mercenaries, allow them to train and recruit or let them enter or pass en route to another country. It also asked them to extradite mercenaries to victim states. In 1977 these suggestions were transformed into a legally binding treaty.[139] Yet in the absence of hegemonic leadership the price that regimes, threatened in their survival, had to pay for defecting from these OAU norms was very low, not to mention for opposition groups that wished to challenge their government. The result was that by the late 1970s the mercenary factor began increasingly to contribute to the growth of the continent's security problems. Especially small states, like the Comoros, Benin and São Tomé and Príncipe, were vulnerable in this respect.[140]

Two invasions by opposition elements of the Zairean province of Shaba (formerly Katanga) in March 1977 and May 1978 widened the mercenary issue to extra-African intervention in general. On both occasions Angola and its Cuban and East European allies, which were still present in massive numbers after Angola had acceded to independence, were accused of complicity. Conversely, Angola blamed Zaire for encouraging FNLA and mercenary aggression. It denied Zaire's accusations and its complicity was, in fact, never substantiated beyond its probable awareness of impending trouble and the use by Shaba's invaders of East European arms.[141]

Radical countries were unwilling to rally to Zaire's support, as they were suspicious of the alliance between Mobutu and Western powers. For Mobutu, then, recourse to bilateral help was crucial. The first invasion, in 1977, was halted by Moroccan troops, which were flown in by French planes. With French instructors and some Sudanese and Egyptian aid, they chased the invaders, popularly known as Katangese gendarmes, across the Angolan border. It received the blessing of the Assembly summit in Libreville, which adopted a Senegalese-sponsored resolution on non-African interference in member states. While Zaire's accusations were based on flimsy evidence, the resolution was inspired by growing fears of Soviet and Cuban influence on the continent. However, it failed to name the powers accused by Zaire, as this would have led to strong protests by Angola and other radical members. Moreover, most states did not disapprove of the Eastern bloc's role in Ethiopia, where it helped to withstand the Somali invasion of the Ogaden.[142]

These different security dilemma's led to a generalized call to "all extra-African powers, particularly the big ones" not to interfere in African states. This text could be interpreted by radical and moderate-conservative members as alluding to either Western or

---

(XVII).

139   See ECM/Res.17 (VII); CM/Dec.158 (XVII); CM/St.6 (XVII); CM/Res.497 (XXVII); Convention on Mercenarism, Libreville, 3/7/77.

140   See f.i. *Jeune Afrique*, 12-25/8/93. OAU responses to events in these countries in CM/Res.633 (XXXI) and CM/Res. 639 (XXXI).

141   See for Mobutu's accusations during the first invasion f.i. *Togo Presse*, 26/4/77 (article) and for Angola's reaction its foreign minister's speech at the Libreville summit (text in *Jornal de Angola*, 12/7/77). East Germans may, however, have been involved in training the Shaba invaders. *Africa Contemporary Record*, 1976-77, B445-448 and B526 ff and 1977-78, B589-594.

142   *Jornal de Angola*, 10/7/77 (article) and Z. Cervenka, 'OAU's Year of Disunity', in *Africa Contemporary Record*, 1977-8, A62-63.

Eastern bloc countries.[143] In a highly contradictory vein, the resolution called on members not to take recourse to foreign intervention to settle their inter-state disputes, without prejudice, however, to "their right to conclude defence agreements of their choice intended especially to forestall outside aggressions". Yet, reaffirming OAU adherence to non-alignment, members were also asked to abrogate commitments militating against that policy, liquidate foreign military bases and stay out of conflicts emanating from without the continent![144]

Notwithstanding its Byzantine qualities this pronouncement could not prevent that the Shaba crisis exposed the OAU's impotence. The unwillingness of many to come to the aid of a regime that did not share their ideological persuasions and international alignments only encouraged recourse to (partially) non-African assistance. The Libreville response was to meet fears of extra-African interference with passivity and collective awareness of its dangers with varying degrees of individual connivance. Apart from being unable to prevent it, the OAU could not explicitly condemn specific instances of such intervention either, as it had sanctioned the bilateral approach to security.

Thus, instead of concretely affecting developments it fathered the world's village idiot, to whom a Zambian editorialist gave metaphorical birth in the wake of the summit.[145] The OAU cut a ridiculous figure especially as Shaba did not stand on its own. At about the same time it looked on helplessly as escalation of the Somali-Ethiopian dispute in the Ogaden, brought on by superpower competition, could only be halted with Soviet-Cuban intervention. One year later, during the second invasion of Shaba both Katangese gendarmes and the Zairean army went on the rampage and French legionnaires and Belgian paratroopers were air-dropped to rescue Europeans, killing hundreds of gendarmes and chasing the rest across the border.[146] In the same year the outbreak of the Ugandan-Tanzanian war exposed the ultimate consequences of the absence of a Pan-African approach to security.

Amin had invaded Tanzanian territory, ostensibly as retaliation for subversion by Ugandan exiles. He announced the annexation of the occupied region, but in the ensuing war the Tanzanian army chased the Ugandans across the border. Instead of halting at the frontier, it invaded and occupied Uganda, thus putting an end to Amin's tyranny. In the course of the war, OAU mediation efforts failed completely, as Tanzania made a cease-fire conditional on OAU condemnation of Amin's invasion. The Assembly chairman, President Numeiry of Sudan, objected to this because, he said, this would jeopardize the mediation effort. In the end, the OAU's mediation committee blamed Tanzania for the impasse.[147]

The events led to an acrimonious debate at the Monrovia summit (1979). Some Arab countries that had supported Amin condemned Tanzania. For example, Sudan warned against the precedent the counter-invasion could set. While Tanzania should have stopped at the border, it had "blatantly" intervened in another country's internal affairs

143 See f.i. *Sudanow* (Sudan), August 1977 and *Jornal de Angola*, 7/7/77 (article).
144 AHG/Res.85 (XIV).
145 *Times of Zambia*, 6/7/77.
146 *Africa Contemporary Record*, 1977-78, B589-594.
147 P.G. Okoth, 'The O.A.U. and the Uganda-Tanzania War', paper presented to the 27th Annual Meeting of the African Studies Association, Los Angeles, 25-28 October 1984, p 6 ff.

and thereby violated the Charter.[148] Moreover, it bore responsibility for harbouring Ugandan exiles, whose subversion had triggered the conflict. Nigeria also condemned the Tanzanian invasion for its precedent, arguing that "the weaker and smaller nations of Africa [would] have to look over their shoulders at their powerful neighbours". Yet Nyerere refused to react to Nigeria's criticism, as it needed its support to the Frontline alliance. Moreover, Lagos had reacted principally because of domestic, Muslim pressure. It had initially supported the Tanzanian move to counter Libyan influence in Uganda.[149] Thus, the Nigerian *Daily Times* reacted rather cautiously, stressing the need to set non-interference against human rights principles.[150]

Similarly, while Kenya did not favour a new Ugandan government allied to Tanzania,[151] it reacted rather negatively to criticism of Amin's fall as a result of the Tanzanian invasion. Ignoring Tanzania's role, newspaper comment emphasized that Amin should never have become head of state and that the OAU had also kept silent on the invasion of the Ogaden and Libya's occupation of northern Chad.[152] The Frontline states and others like Algeria, Ghana, Mali and Sierra Leone came out openly in favour of Tanzania, arguing that it had acted in self-defence and that it had toppled a repressive and inhuman regime.[153] Faced with these divisions, members could only agree that in future the OAU would condemn both aggression and "counter-aggression".[154]

The debate on Pan-African security 1963-1989
Naturally, this left the problems created by the lack of a collective security strategy unresolved. At bottom, its absence was caused by lack of hegemonic leadership and different patterns of external dependence. However, from the perspective of regime theory it has to be realized that regimes are less relevant in zero-sum conditions anyway.[155] One may, of course, argue that not all conflict situations are fully zero-sum.[156] States are not solely concerned with achieving relative gains, *i.e.* benefits that are greater than those of other states.[157] Concern with relative gains makes co-operation hard to achieve. Although section 2.3 showed that African states confirm

---

148 See f.i. *Sudanow* (Sudan), August 1979 and *Daily Mail* (Sierra Leone), 10/7/79 (both articles).

149 Z. Cervenka and C. Legum, 'The Organization of African Unity in 1979', in *Africa Contemporary Record*, 1979-80, A61-63.

150 *Daily Times* (Nigeria), 24/7/79.

151 *Africa Research Bulletin* (PSC), 1979, pp 5339-40.

152 *The Standard* (Kenya), 10/7/79. Yet, it is clear that the Kenyan government disapproved of the temporary Tanzanian occupation of Uganda as such. Also *Africa Research Bulletin* (PSC), 1979, p 5339. In this case newspaper comment may therefore not be fully equated with governmental opinion.

153 See f.i. *Daily Mail* (Sierra Leone), 9/7/79 and 18/7/79; *l'Essor* (Mali), 28-29/7/79 (article); *Révolution Africaine* (Algeria), 13-19/7/79 (article); *The Ghanaian Times*, 21/7/79; and *Times of Zambia*, 19/7/79.

154 Cervenka and Legum, 'Organization of African Unity in 1979', A62.

155 R. Jervis, 'Security regimes', in S.D. Krasner (ed), *International Regimes* (Ithaca and London, 1983), pp 173-94.

156 M. Nicholson, 'Negotiation, Agreement and Conflict Resolution: The Role of Rational Approaches and their Criticism', in R. Väyrynen (ed), *New Directions in Conflict Theory: Conflict Resolution and Conflict Transformation* (London and New Delhi, 1991), pp 61-63.

157 S.D. Krasner, 'Regimes and the limits of realism: regimes as autonomous variables', in Krasner, *International Regimes*, pp 355-368.

Grieco's contention[158] that individual survival is the prime policy goal, this does not amount to a preoccupation with such relative gains.

While co-operation in security is therefore not impossible, in this issue area a regime as the OAU may nevertheless be less coherent than in other fields.[159] This showed itself in its approval of the bilateral security approach, which contravened its rationale of conflict management. This contradiction was reflected in the political sensitivity generated by recourse to superpowers, mercenaries or South Africa, which was always greater than if such help was sought from another African state or the former colonial power.

However, it became quickly apparent that non-African intervention easily damaged collective African interests. The first Shaba crisis and the Libreville response showed, perhaps better than other incidents, that it increased inter-African tensions, detracted from collective influence over events and injured elite self-esteem. Awareness of these collective interests was at the root of the frequent suggestions, ever since 1963, to formulate a Pan-African security scheme. This debate was regularly fuelled by incidents such as UDI (1965), the Portuguese attack on Conakry (1970), the Israeli raid on Entebbe (1976) and South Africa's assault on the Frontline states. Yet, the realization of vulnerability to extra-African powers emanating from these events in part also mystified discussions, as it directed attention solely to enemies in the non-African world.[160]

Thus, during the first session of the OAU Defence Commission (1963) Nkrumah presented a grand solution to Africa's security predicaments. His representative pleaded, no less, for a "Union Joint Services Supreme Military Command Headquarters" that would organize continental defence. It would involve, among others, departments catering for planning, training, operations, weapons & equipment development, logistical support, intelligence and communications. The Supreme Headquarters would exercise authority over four "Regional Headquarters." These would organize the various countries, with their national headquarters, under their command and pursue the same functions regionally.

The Supreme Headquarters would have the disposal of a "Union Joint Services Strategic Reserve Force", to which countries would contribute a batallion or brigade. It would be composed of three major elements: a naval force equipped with submarines, transport and aircraft carriers; an army with jungle, desert, parachute and commando divisions; and an air force consisting of a strategic transport command, a ground support tactical command, a strike air command, a fighter command and a bomber command. The Force would be deployed by a (politico-military) "Union Defence Council", which would nominate commanders and issue policy directives. The Force would deal with threats by foreign powers anywhere in Africa and take care of the liberation of the dependent territories. To this purpose, it would aim at standardization of equipment, organization

---

158   See f.i. J.M. Grieco, 'Anarchy and the Limits of Cooperation: A Realist Critique of the Newest Liberal Institutionalism', in *International Organization*, 1988, pp 485-507.

159   On the coherence of regimes E.B. Haas, 'Regime decay: conflict management and international organizations, 1945-1981', in *International Organization*, 1983, p 217 ff.

160   See f.i. *Le Courrier d'Afrique* (Zaire), 6/12/65; *Daily Mail* (Sierra Leone), 9/12 and 12/12/70; *l'Essor* (Mali), 30/11/70 (article); *Daily Times* (Nigeria), 14/6/72; *Times of Zambia*, 5/7/76; *Jornal de Angola*, 10/7/79 (article); *The Ghanaian Times*, 10/7/80; and *The Herald* (Zimbabwe), 26/7/86.

and training. Planning would involve the strategic siting of bases, installations and depots and establishment of communications networks.[161]

But for reality it would have been a formidable military machine. The arguments raised against it provide some insight in the range of obstacles that a collective strategy would face. Naturally, financial requirements were said to be a serious hurdle, making Nkrumah's proposals wholly unrealistic. It was also argued that there was no consensus on the potential enemy. Delegates observed that aggression could come from member states themselves, with some adding coldly that Africa was not at war with any of the world's power blocs. Fearing that a collective structure might be used against themselves, they argued that it was first necessary to define a common defence policy.[162]

It was also objected that the proposal would severely restrict sovereignty and entail a loss of control over one's own army. Most delegates did not share Nkrumah's unitary conception of Africa. With hostilities in one region not threatening the whole continent, peace was not indivisible. Thus, it is noteworthy that some emphasized that the concept of collective security, for which the indivisibility of peace is essential, was not mentioned in the Charter.[163] Moreover, standardization issues formed, in view of different external sources of supply, a serious obstacle to formation of a Pan-African army. A legal hurdle in the way of Nkrumah's grand vision was the fact that, in case of enforcement action, it needed approval of the Security Council.[164] Ghana's call for abrogation of military pacts with foreign powers and elimination of foreign bases did not find favour either.[165] Even Nigeria's modest proposals for a central military council, which would have the disposal of individual contingents remaining under national control, did not elicit a positive response.[166]

Most of these objections were, fundamentally, tied to the combined effects of different patterns of external dependence and lack of hegemonic leadership. These structural features made it extremely difficult to create, and enforce compliance with, the financial, logistical and other conditions of a collective defence strategy. They also stood

---

161 See the minutes of the Defence Commission, First Session, October 1963 [hereinafter as DEF.1/29 October 1963], DEF.1/Memo./3; DEF.1/Memo.3/Add.1; DEF.1/Memo.3/Add.2; DEF.1/Memo.3/Add.4; and DEF.1/Memo. 3/Add.5.

162 DEF.1/29 October 1963: DEF.1/Plen./SR./3, p 10; DEF.1/COM.II/SR.1, pp 3-7, 9 and 14; DEF.1/COM.II/SR.2, pp 3, 5, 7 and 9; and DEF.1/Memo./1, p 3; and DEF.1/Memo./2, pp 1-3.

163 DEF.1/29 October 1963: DEF.1/COM.II/SR.1, pp 5 and 13; DEF.1/COM.II/SR.2, pp 5, 8 and 10; and DEF.1/COM.II/Report 1, p 2.

164 DEF.1/29 October 1963: DEF.1/COMM.II/SR.1, pp 3, 10 and 14; DEF.1/COM.II/SR.2, pp 3, 5 and 7; DEF.1/GEN.INF./1, p 7; and DEF.1/Memo./1, p 3.

165 DEF.1/Memo.3/Add.3. Yet, appeals for disarmament and denuclearization were often to be made by OAU organs, as part of the problematical concept of non-alignment. They were to remain a dead letter. See CM/Res.3 (I); CM/Res.12 (II); CM/Res.28 (II); CM/Res.38 (III); CM/Res.718 (XXXIII); CM/Res.790 (XXXV); AHG/Res.11 (I); AHG/Res.126 (XX); AHG/Res.138 (XXI); AHG/Res.154 (XXII); AHG/Res.164 (XXIII); CM.3 (III): Draft Convention for the Denuclearization of the Continent of Africa; and the Febr. '64 Council debate (extract *Verbatim Record* in W.S. Thompson and I.W. Zartman, 'The Development of Norms in the African System', in El-Ayouty, *Organization of African Unity After Ten Years*, pp 7-24 [n. 23], pp 36-46). The Assembly definitively shelved Nkrumah's plans for continental union government in 1965. CM/Res.35 (III); AHG/Res.10 (I); AHG/Res.28 (II); and the 1964 summit debate (extract *Verbatim Record* in Thompson and Zartman, 'Development of Norms', pp 7-24).

166 DEF.1/29 October 1963: DEF.1/MEMO/4.

in the way of a uniform enemy perception, which hindered the very formulation of such strategy. In contrast, member states often had good bilateral accords with non-African powers providing a solid security guarantee. It meant that the indivisibility of peace could be easily rejected.

Yet, if leadership by a hegemon would have been possible, it does not follow that this indivisibility would be guaranteed. While it was shown in chapter 1 that there is considerable confusion over just how powerful a state must be to qualify as hegemon, it must involve a state that is much more powerful than all others in order to uphold the theory's argument. Thus, in a context with a hegemon it is possible to force all actors to comply with collective decisions but impossible to take action against the hegemonic leader himself. In the benevolent version of the theory this dilemma is resolved by the contention that the result — provision of the public good — is beneficial to all. Even its coercive version predicts that all actors are better off than if they would be without hegemonic leadership.[167]

However, Snidal has shown that such benefits and their distribution are hard to prove empirically.[168] There is also a dubious normative side to the theory in the sense that leadership by one particular hegemon would be good for all.[169] In the egalitarian context of OAU decision-making the legitimacy of hegemony, by any state, is rejected and the exceptional position it would render found unacceptable. An advantage of a multilateral regime as the OAU is that it provides, especially to the smaller states, some protection against the potential risks of the (albeit limited) assymetry in inter-African relations. Moreover, conferment of special status, like that of the permanent members of the UN Security Council, would go against the collective security doctrine: its essence is that it provides security against aggression for all states, by the action of all states, against *all* states that might want to commit such aggression.[170]

In the context of the actual features of Africa's international relations and the consequent absence of consensus on enemy perceptions, Nkrumah's emphasis on non-African powers did not counter the realization that threats to security could also come from and occur within African states themselves, with or without non-African intervention. This awareness explains the concern about abuse of a collective structure and the restriction of sovereignty and loss of control over one's army.

The need for a clear definition of collective defence was made more acute by the fact that security threats do not usually emanate from conventional warfare. They often occur in the murky context of subversion, which runs counter to the moral clarity that the collective security doctrine imputes to the concept of aggression.[171] Moreover, subversion often links inter-state conflicts to domestic ones and domestic instability generally forms the most important threat to inter-African security. If the collective security doctrine, which is solely concerned with inter-state conflict, would have to assure the military

---

167   D. Snidal, 'The Limits of Hegemonic Stability Theory', in *International Organization*, 1985, pp 579-614.

168   *Ibid.*

169   Namely that by the United States. See on this I. Grunberg, 'Exploring the "Myth" of Hegemonic Stability', in *International Organization*, 1990, pp 431-477.

170   I.L. Claude, *Power and International Relations* (New York, 1966), p 110.

171   *Ibid.*, ch. 4.

dimensions of Africa's political order, this would involve a radical transformation of its contents. In any case, the risks of becoming embroiled in domestic conflicts hardly encouraged the prospects of acceptance of a collective defence structure.

Nevertheless, while there were numerous, fundamental obstacles standing in the way of a Pan-African security strategy, the problems created by its absence caused the debate on its introduction to flare up again. However, the hurdles put in its way for long prevented any decision from being taken. In terms of OAU institutions this process worked as follows. The sessions of the Defence Commission usually assembled only those countries that expressed more than average interest in the issue. Having limited powers itself, the Commission could only make proposals to the Council of Ministers, which, with most members represented at its sessions, would subsequently reject them.

Thus, two years after its first session the Defence Commission recommended the creation of an "African Defence Organization". Although Council and Assembly approved this, no action was taken. Yet, spurred on by the Portuguese attack on Conakry (1970), the Commission's next sessions proposed the formation of a "Committee of Defence Experts" inside the General Secretariat to co-ordinate the national units of a future defence force. It should consist of a "Defence Advisor" with a small military staff. "Regional Defence Units", composed of a few states, would be put at the OAU's disposal during emergencies.[172] The Council referred the proposal to an ad hoc committee that hammered out a detailed report on a regional defence system. It met, however, with the same fate as earlier proposals. With member states declining to send in comments it was obvious that there was no sufficient (co-ordination of) political will to establish a defence structure.[173] Some expressed strong or cautious support, but the majority could not be convinced. In the words of the Kenyans, the idea of an African High Command was "absurd" and "unrealistic". The OAU had better focus on practical matters instead of concerning itself with "grandiloquent notions"![174] In 1975 a renewed recommendation to set up an office of a Defence Advisor inside the Secretariat was rejected by the Council as premature.[175]

However, the Shaba invasions forced members to take some sort of action. While Shaba's inter-African repercussions made it more explicit than ever that bilateral security arrangements generated serious collective disadvantages, its aftermath introduced an additional element. When in 1978 Zaire's Western saviours had been replaced by contingents from Morocco and some Francophone countries, the West launched its own proposal for Africa's collective defence. This "Inter-African Security Force" was to be manned by Africans and intervene in the continent's trouble spots with Western support.

Although the proposal was backed by some Francophone countries, on the whole it evoked a bitter response, both from radical and moderate member states. At the Khartoum summit (1978) President Ratsiraka of Madagascar condemned it as an instrument to perpetuate Western domination. He contended that, contrary to the West, communist

172   Background Paper on the Meetings of the OAU Defence Commission from 1963 to 1986 (hereinafter as: Background Paper DEF COM 1963-1986), pp 1-3.
173   *Ibid.*, pp 3-6.
174   *East African Standard* (Kenya), 22/5/73. More positively *Times of Zambia*, 26/5/73; *Daily Times* (Nigeria), 14/6/72; and *Daily Mail* (Sierra Leone), 30/5/73 (article). Cautious comment in *l'Essor* (Mali), 24-5/6/72 (article).
175   Background Paper DEF COM 1963-1986, pp 6-7 and CM/Res.426 (XXV).

countries did not form a menace for Africa's independence.[176] Although this view was only shared by fellow Marxist-inspired regimes,[177] other militant governments, as well as moderate ones, were also convinced that the security force was aimed at defending Western interests. Libya dubbed it a colonial project and Algeria considered it a dangerous proposition. President Stevens of Sierra Leone spoke of an "ostensibly" African force controlled by others. Fear of Western influence was also reiterated in the speeches of Nigeria and Tanzania, as well as more conservative Botswana.[178] It was also argued that a Western-backed defence force would merely deepen inter-African divisions. It could even lead to the formation of a Pan-African army by the Eastern bloc. In this respect the Angolans observed that the proposal might well lead to destruction of the OAU itself.[179] Even Ivory Coast, one of the countries in favour of the force,[180] bitterly admitted that the idea had only strengthened inter-African cleavages.[181]

Apart from these concrete fears, the proposal was also a serious psychological mistake. Notwithstanding the lack of action by member states, the issue of Pan-African defence was considered, by the majority of countries, as the natural preserve of the OAU. The Western take-over of one of the Organization's own potential projects thus clashed with the discretionary, monopolistic disposition that characterizes the OAU cadre.[182] Moreover, it rubbed salt in the wounds that the Shaba invasions had inflicted in terms of the image of helplessness imparted to the collectivity of member states. Thus, governments of all persuasions condemned the proposal as an insult, a sign of Western arrogance or, amidst some soul-searching on their own culpability, a source of shame.[183] In his speech to the Assembly President Khama of Botswana observed

> Africans have been taken for granted for much too long and it is time we told the outside world that our continent has long come of age and its peoples should be left alone to manage *or mismanage* their own affairs.[184]

The OAU's official response was therefore predictably negative and ambiguous. It

---

176 Text of speech in *Madagascar Renouveau*, no. 8, 1978, pp 15-23.

177 Z. Cervenka and C. Legum, 'The Organization of African Unity in 1978: The Challenge of Foreign Intervention', in *Africa Contemporary Record*, 1978-79, A33-35 and *Sudanow* (Sudan), June 1978.

178 *Révolution Africaine* (Algeria), 19-25/7/78; Stevens' speech in *Daily Mail* (Sierra Leone), 24/7/78; Botswanan speech in *Botswana Daily News*, 26/7/78; extracts Tanzanian and Nigerian speeches in Cervenka and Legum, 'Organization of African Unity in 1978', A33-6; and Libyan view in *Madagascar Renouveau*, no. 7, 1978, p 39.

179 *Botswana Daily News*, 21/7/78 (article) and 26/6/78 (speech) and Angolan view in *Madagascar Renouveau*, no. 7, 1978, p 39.

180 These numbered some ten member states. See Cervenka and Legum, 'Organization of African Unity in 1978', A34.

181 *Fraternité* (Ivory Coast), 21/7/78. Also Tanzania's view in Cervenka and Legum, 'Organization of African Unity in 1978', A34.

182 See Mali's and Botswana's Assembly speeches in *l'Essor* (Mali), 29-30/7/78 and *Botswana Daily News*, 26/7/78. Also *The Standard* (Kenya), 24/7/78; *Times of Zambia*, 17/7/78; and *Daily News* (Tanzania), 19/7/78.

183 See *Botswana Daily News*, 26/7/78 (Presidential speech); *The Ethiopian Herald*, 16/7/78; Cervenka and Legum, 'Organization of African Unity in 1978', A33-5; and *Sudanow* (Sudan), June 1978.

184 Text in *Botswana Daily News*, 26/7/78. Emphasis added.

expressed awareness of the dangers that regular foreign interference now posed to the "very existence of the OAU" and of the need to neutralize this threat. It also issued the usual condemnation of foreign bases and pacts with foreign powers as encouraging such intervention. It emphasized that a Pan-African scheme should only be realized through the OAU and merely decided that the Defence Commission consider the desirability of an OAU-sponsored defence force.[185]

Nevertheless, the Western proposal had created some momentum. In 1979 the Assembly accepted "the principle of the creation of an OAU defence force", adding that study should be made of its financial and legal implications.[186] In 1980 a "Defence and Security Section" was created inside the General Secretariat to develop plans for a military advisor office and help in the formulation of a Pan-African defence structure.[187] At its session in August 1981, the Defence Commission drew up a draft convention for an "African Defence Force", in which the term African High Command was avoided so as not to associate it with Nkrumah's utopian schemes.[188] In 1986 its name was changed into "African Defence Organ"[189] and the convention was rewritten as a protocol to be attached to the OAU Charter.

In its 1989 version, the draft protocol stipulates as objectives the defence of member states against acts of aggression as defined in UN General Assembly resolution 3314 (XXIX); the liberation of Africa "from foreign domination"; and provision of peace-keeping/observer forces in case of conflicts between member states. In cases of extra-African aggression, "all necessary support to strengthen the military defence capability" would be extended to the member state concerned. However, deployment of the Defence Force, on which more below, could only take place with prior approval of the member in question. Domestic conflicts are not mentioned.[190]

A "Defence Council", made up of ten heads of state and elected by the Assembly on a regional basis for two years, should determine the existence of threats or breaches to the peace or acts of aggression and recommend to the Assembly on measures to be taken. Member states would be legally bound to execute its decisions. However, protocol commitments would not prejudice other defence agreements. Until the Assembly would decide, the Defence Council should take necessary provisional measures, albeit with deference for the right of individual self-defence and the supremacy of the Security Council as enunciated in arts. 24 and 51 UN Charter.[191] The Defence Council would be advised by a "Committee of Chiefs of Staff", consisting of ten high ranking military officers elected by the Assembly from among member state nationals for two or three years.[192] The Secretary-General would draw the attention of the Defence Council to

---

185   CM/Res.635 (XXXI) and CM/Res.641 (XXXI).
186   AHG/Dec.113 (XVI).
187   Interview with Colonel Zoula Gustave Pana, Chief of Defence and Security Section, General Political Affairs, Defence and Security Division, Addis Ababa, 19/9/89.
188   Interview with Col. Zoula Gustave Pana, Addis Ababa, 19/9/89 and Background Paper DEF COM 1963-1986. Text in CM/1546 (L): Council of Ministers, Fiftieth Ordinary Session, 17-21 July 1989, Addis Ababa, Ethiopia, Annex II (hereinafter as CM/1546 (L), Annex II).
189   Interview with Col. Zoula Gustave Pana, Addis Ababa, 19/9/89 and CM/1546 (L), Annex I.
190   CM/1546 (L), Annex II, arts. II, X and XI.
191   *Ibid.*, arts. IV and XII.
192   *Ibid.*, art. V.

situations demanding action.[193] To this purpose, an "Office of the Military Advisor", directly responsible to the Secretary-General, would collate intelligence reports on potential military interventions by the OAU.[194]

All member states would undertake to make available to the OAU, on the basis of special agreements, "armed forces, assistance, and facilities including rights of passage". The accords should, among others, govern numbers and types of forces. The Defence Force so established should support members in case of aggression by a "third party"; give military assistance to liberation movements; provide peace-keeping or observer forces; and co-operate with the UN.[195] It would be headed by a "Force Commander", to be appointed by the Defence Council on the advice of the Secretary-General for the duration of the operation.[196] The Commander would be responsible, through the SG, to the Defence Council for operational control and administration of the Defence Force.[197]

Admittedly, the proposal was not without its flaws. First, the fact that the protocol kept silent about domestic conflicts was unfortunate as these form a significant source of threats to Africa's political order. This omission was not surprising in view of the extensive interpretation that was still given at the time to the non-intervention norm. Consequently, the OAU did not have any *official* role in domestic conflict management, let alone with regard to its military dimensions. Inter-state disputes were therefore the prime focus of the protocol. However, its provision that, in case of contradictions, the protocol would not take precedence over other defence agreements, left the dilemma's of the bilateral security approach unresolved. Moreover, in cases of non-African aggression it did not entail a guarantee that member states would automatically deploy troops to rescue a member coming under attack.

Finally, it would not be easy to meet the scheme's financial costs, notwithstanding an argument by the responsible Secretariat official, in an interview in 1989, that its costs would be lower than what member states spent individually.[198] Both he and the Defence Commission stressed that the Defence Council and Committee of Chiefs of Staff would not be functioning on a permanent basis and that the Defence Force would only be activated in an emergency. The Secretariat functionary also argued that salaries of the troops would be paid by member states. Only the logistical costs would be borne by the OAU,[199] for which a special fund could be created.[200] Yet, the Defence Commission had to concede that the total costs of an operation would be considerable. In 1989, for example, it estimated that a force comprising some 6,000 men, to be deployed in a UN type operation as in Lebanon, would need a budget of over 140 million dollars.[201]

---

193   *Ibid.*, art. VI (2).
194   See for details *ibid.*, art. VII.
195   *Ibid.*, art. VIII.
196   See *ibid.*, arts. IV (7), V (3), VIII (b.5) and IX.
197   *Ibid.*, art. VIII (b.5). He must consult the SG's representative on the political aspects of the operation. See D. Bangoura, 'Le rôle juridique, politique et militaire de l'O.U.A. en matière de défense', in *Cahiers de l'IPAG*, no. 10, June 1990, p 35.
198   Interview with Col. Zoula Gustave Pana, Addis Ababa, 19/9/89.
199   CM/1546 (L), Annex I, pp 4-5 and interview with Col. Zoula Gustave Pana, Addis Ababa, 19/9/89.
200   CM/1546 (L), Annex I, p 5.
201   CM/1546 (L), Annex I, p 5 and Annex V.

Nevertheless, after two decades of hesitation the whole idea had been provided with firmer and more realistic foundations. The proposal was now accompanied by budget estimates and some of the legal aspects had been sorted out. If implemented, the Defence Force itself would be embedded in an elaborate system of institutional control, the absence of which had previously been used to argue against it. In the words of the Secretariat official involved, the OAU now disposed of "toute la panoplie de moyens d'intervention".[202]

To Chad and back 1980-1982

However, after 1980 any inclination to introduce a Pan-African strategy rapidly vanished in the Chadian quagmire. Space does not allow a detailed exposition of this civil war,[203] yet it is necessary to present the main elements of OAU involvement. It was in the course of the Chadian conflict that the Organization fielded the first peace-keeping force in its history.

Although FROLINAT guerrilla's from northern Chad had, by the late 1970s, taken control of the capital N'Djamena, they were split in numerous factions. Two main ones were led by Hissène Habré and his arch-rival Goukouni Weddeye. With the complete collapse of public order, Nigeria began mediating between the warring factions. Negotiations, attended by the major Chadian groups, neighbouring countries and an OAU representative, led to deployment of a Nigerian peace-keeping force to monitor a demilitarized zone around the capital. While the Nigerians were supposed to implement the accord but not to use force, the Chadian factions neither understood nor respected their neutrality. With erratic fighting continuing, the heavy-handed Nigerians were frequently harassed and, after barely one year, forced to evacuate (February 1980).[204]

However, a new peace accord had meanwhile been worked out in Lagos, which entailed the formation of a (second) "Transitional National Union Government", usually referred to by its French acronym GUNT. It was headed by Goukouni as President and Habré as Minister of Defence and was to stay in place for eighteen months in expectation of elections. In order to implement a new cease-fire, an OAU-led monitoring commission was to supervise another peace-keeping force. As Nigeria now shied away from committing itself on its own, this OAU force was to be composed of several countries.[205] The Lagos accord was ratified by the Council of Ministers[206] and it was decided that the force would be composed of non-border countries. Those involved were Congo, Benin

---

202　Col. Gustave Zoula [*sic*], 'Perspectives de renforcement des organisations régionales en matière de stabilité et de sécurité: le cas de l'Organisation de l'unité africaine (OUA)', in *Cahiers de l'IPAG*, no. 10, June 1990, p 83.

203　See R. Buijtenhuijs, *Le Frolinat et les révoltes populaires du Tchad, 1965-1976* (The Hague, Paris and New York, 1978).

204　D. Pittman, 'The OAU and Chad', in Y. El-Ayouty and I.W. Zartman (eds), *The OAU After Twenty Years* (New York, 1984), p 303 and H. Wiseman, 'The OAU: Peacekeeping and Conflict Resolution', in *ibid.*, pp 131-2. For this period also R. Buijtenhuijs, *Le Frolinat et les guerres civiles du Tchad (1970-1984): la révolution introuvable* (Paris and Leiden, 1987).

205　*Africa Research Bulletin* (PSC), 1979, pp 5374-5375. Also AHG/Res.? (XIX) entitled "On the OAU Mission to Chad".

206　CM/Res.769 (XXXIV).

and Guinea[207] and were asked not only to supervise the cease-fire, but also to disarm the population, restore order and help in establishing integrated armed forces. Unfortunately, the Congolese contingent, flown in with Algerian support, was confined to barracks as heavy fighting erupted between Habré and other GUNT forces. It was flown out again by the French in the course of 1980. Nigeria, which competed with France for influence in the area, refused to fly in the Guineans before French troops, still stationed in Chad, had left. Due to financial constraints the other troops never arrived either.[208]

In trying to retain influence in Chad, the French were playing a complicated game. They first backed President Goukouni but at certain points in time also aided the side of Hissène Habré. They were not merely trying to limit Nigerian influence, but especially that of Libya. Tripoli had occupied Chad's northern border zone.[209] It had expansionist designs in the whole sub-Saharan region and had for long intervened in the Chadian conflict by playing off one faction against another. In view of Chad's strategic location and the close relationship between Libya and the Soviet Union, the United States also opposed Libyan designs, although it is doubtful that the Russians backed Qaddafi's Chadian ambitions.[210]

In expectation of the abortive OAU force, French troops had left Chad in the course of 1980. By the end of the year, however, Libyan troops pushed south to strengthen Goukouni's position vis-à-vis Habré. With the latter driven out of N'Djamena, Libya and Goukouni's government announced a merger of their two countries (January 1981). Threatening to upset the geo-political balance of the region, this move deeply disturbed neighbouring countries. Egypt and Sudan, with the encouragement of the United States, began helping Habré in an effort to cut Goukouni, and thus Qaddafi, down to size.[211] However, Niger and Nigeria still opted for a political solution. With growing inter-nationalization diplomatic manoeuvres in the OAU intensified and deployment of a new peace-keeping force became increasingly urgent.

Yet, the Organization experienced serious difficulties in finding the necessary resources. Member states had been asked to contribute $ 50,000 each for Chad's rehabilitation, but only some twelve countries had come forward with an amount that totalled half a million dollars. With over half of it given to the GUNT the rest was spent on purchasing OAU uniforms.[212] At the Freetown summit (1980) the OAU had reiterated its support to the Lagos accord and the GUNT, while expressing concern about

---

207   *Africa Research Bulletin* (PSC), 1979, p 5411. Togo was added to the list only later. Pittman, 'OAU and Chad', p 310.

208   Pittman, 'OAU and Chad', p 309 and Wiseman, 'OAU: Peacekeeping and Conflict Resolution', p 132.

209   Mediation in this territorial dispute is not discussed. See AHG/Dec.108 (XIV); AHG/Res.94 (XV); AHG/Res.106 (XIX); AHG/Res.158 (XXII); AHG/Res.167 (XXIII); and AHG/Res.174 (XXIV). French policy in Buijtenhuijs, *Le Frolinat et les guerres civiles*, pp 112-122 and chs. IV-V. See for French assistance to Habré *ibid.*, pp 220-221.

210   *Africa Research Bulletin* (PSC), 1981, pp 6177 and 6249.

211   Wiseman, 'OAU: Peacekeeping and Conflict Resolution', pp 132-133 and Z. Cervenka and C. Legum, 'The Organization of African Unity in 1981: A Crucial Testing Time for Peacekeeping', in *Africa Contemporary Record*, 1981-82, A85. Also Buijtenhuijs, *Le Frolinat et les guerres civiles*, pp 108-112, 161, 203 and 219-220.

212   Amate, *Inside the OAU*, pp 457-458. All figures in this section in US dollars.

interference by African and non-African powers. A standing committee, with Nigeria as chairman, had been appointed to persuade the Chadian leaders to implement the accord. The OAU had repeated its call for a peace-keeping force of neutral African countries and asked members in a position to provide contingents "at their own expenses ... it being understood that logistic and operational costs be met from voluntary contributions". If after two months the OAU would have failed to raise the necessary funds, the Security Council would be asked to help out.[213]

The UN was reticent to finance the operation. Nevertheless, with growing pressure on Goukouni and Tripoli to revoke the merger and evacuate Libyan troops, the Nairobi summit (1981) reaffirmed previous resolutions on the peace-keeping force. It was added that its composition would be subject to approval by Goukouni's GUNT. With cost estimated at more than 160 million dollars for the first year and few voluntary contributions forthcoming, members were expected to seek bilateral aid. Countries supplying contingents were to maintain their troops at their own expense during the first month, after which the OAU was supposed to take over. France, the United States and Britain agreed to provide some financial and material support, not through the OAU but directly to the countries sending contingents. However, after some time it became clear that the grants were grossly insufficient.[214] Worse still, several states had agreed to contribute troops but only three actually sent detachments, namely Nigeria, Zaire and Senegal. Goukouni rejected Togolese troops as Lomé had urged him to negotiate with Habré. Other countries, such as Benin and Guinea, failed to send contingents because of financial and logistical constraints.[215]

Counting on French and OAU support, Goukouni gave in to pressure and asked Libya, in October 1981, to withdraw its forces. Qaddafi retaliated by pulling back his troops so quickly that a power vacuum was created which the OAU had difficulty to fill. Habré used this for his offensive. Caught off guard by the Libyan manoeuvre, Zairean detachments began arriving in Chad in November, followed by the Senegalese. Although they had French logistical support, they lacked essential equipment. Nigeria was therefore forced to hurry in several batallions and take care of communications, food and the medical supplies of the entire force. Initially set at 10,000 men, it was limited to 5,000 of which by January 1982 some 3,000 had taken up position.[216]

The OAU's mandate further compounded problems. The 1981 Assembly resolution said its "Peace Force" should "ensure the defence and security of the country whilst awaiting the integration of government forces".[217] Before the Force went in, its Nigerian Commander asked the OAU standing committee on Chad what this entailed. He said he could use force against anyone challenging the authority of Goukouni's GUNT or merely try and separate the warring factions. He was only told that the Force was not allowed to

---

213   CM/Res.794 (XXXV) and AHG/Res.101 (XVII).

214   AHG/Res.102 (XVIII); *Africa Research Bulletin* (PSC), 1981, p 6276; and Cervenka and Legum, 'Organization of African Unity in 1981', A86.

215   *Africa Research Bulletin* (PSC), 1981, p 6275 and Pittman, 'OAU and Chad', pp 314-315.

216   *Africa Research Bulletin* (PSC), 1981, pp 6249-51 and 6274-76. Different account of build-up in Buijtenhuijs, *Le Frolinat et les guerres civiles*, p 207. Qaddafi had several reasons to withdraw, such as his ambition to gain the venue of the 1982 summit. *Ibid.*, pp 198-204.

217   AHG/Res.102 (XVIII).

kill Chadians, an answer that inclined towards the second scenario. However, the Secretary-General, to whom the Force Commander was directly responsible,[218] signed a "status of force agreement" with Goukouni stipulating that the Force should back the GUNT.[219] Yet, the SG's personal representative in Chad defined the Force's role as keeping fighting factions apart and other statements made it clear that it would not take sides or help the GUNT. The countries that had sent contingents stressed they did not want to fight and it was said that the Force would only respond if fired upon.[220]

The Commander was also confronted with the fact that he had hardly any authority over the non-Nigerian contingents. Being to some extent financially independent of the OAU, these sometimes refused to move to specific zones when ordered. They would submit orders for approval to their own governments, which frequently gave their own instructions, altered the size of contingents without OAU authorization and even tried to issue orders to the Commander on matters pertaining to the entire Force.[221] In short, the Peace Force lacked co-ordinated political control.

The Force was at first able to guarantee some sort of order.[222] It tried to stop Habré's advance by stationing troops around N'Djamena and other cities.[223] However, the contingents were hampered by lack of transportation. As their numbers were smaller than what had been expected, they were unable to protect all operational zones from Habré's infiltration. Habré began scoring one success after another. Goukouni accused the Force of tying his hands and refusing to help him against his rival. Confronted with this volatile situation the French may have decided to change sides and intervene with the countries that had contributed troops to the Force to manoeuvre in ways that would benefit Habré's position.[224] Several states, most of them like Zaire and Senegal of conservative persuasion, came out increasingly in favour of Habré's faction. This was partly caused by Goukouni's obstinate opposition to a political solution.[225]

By February 1982, it was clear that the Peace Force was neither capable nor willing to defend the GUNT if it came under attack. Realizing the OAU threatened to become stuck in an operation that greatly exceeded its resources, member states wanted to get out. In a spectacular volte-face the standing committee on Chad decided to change course. It called for a cease-fire and negotiations in which Habré should be included. It also announced the Force's withdrawal by June 1982. Its Commander was now made responsible to the Assembly chairman, President Moi of Kenya.[226] In May Nigeria began

---

218 *Africa Research Bulletin* (PSC), 1981, p 6250.
219 Amate, *Inside the OAU*, pp 181-182.
220 *Africa Research Bulletin* (PSC), 1981, pp 6251 and 6275 and Cervenka and Legum, 'Organization of African Unity in 1981', A86.
221 Amate, *Inside the OAU*, pp 184-185.
222 Wiseman, 'OAU: Peacekeeping and Conflict Resolution', pp 134-135.
223 *Ibid.* and *Africa Research Bulletin* (PSC), 1982, pp 6302-3.
224 The United States may have been particularly active in this regard. See Amate, *Inside the OAU*, p 185 and *Africa Research Bulletin* (PSC), 1982, p 6337.
225 These included Togo, Guinea, Kenya, Morocco and, to a lesser extent, Ivory Coast and Cameroon. See Pittman, 'OAU and Chad', p 317 and *Africa Research Bulletin* (PSC), 1982, p 6302.
226 *Africa Research Bulletin* (PSC), 1982, pp 6335-36 and Amate, *Inside the OAU*, p 186. The legality of the Committee's action was confused by a conflict of prerogatives between SG and Assembly chairman. Also Buijtenhuijs, *Le Frolinat et les guerres civiles*, p 211.

pulling out troops. Zairean forces, acting on their own initiative, allowed anti-GUNT forces to occupy the Lake area. After this, Habré's troops issued an ultimatum to OAU contingents in eastern Chad to leave the area. The region was abandoned and Habré's army finally marched into N'Djamena on 7 June with the Peace Force standing by. Its remainder was withdrawn on the orders of the Assembly chairman.[227]

The Chadian adventure: assessment

With its rationale of conflict management geared to preventing radical alterations to the inter-African order, OAU manoeuvres were a success. They had led to Libyan withdrawal from most of Chad. However, as a peace-keeping mission they were a dismal failure. Several factors can be advanced to explain this. First, the conflict was not amenable to mediation. After re-armament violence escalated to a higher level of intensity and the conflict reached the stage of compound stalemate. As is often the case with such stalemate, it led to entrapment of the parties. Having invested massively, they felt considerable pressure to achieve all-out victory.[228] The war had become destructive in the sense that it was detached from its original causes and all sides pursued, as in a true zero-sum game, maximalist options:[229] nothing less than total defeat of the enemy.[230] The Peace Force's role and neutrality were therefore not respected.

The numerous factions also made it difficult to find a focus for mediation efforts. With Habré much stronger than the ramshackle GUNT coalition, any proposed compromise merely delayed a show-down.[231] The external linkages of the Chadian crisis necessitated conflict management both at the regional and domestic level. As these were intricately tied, such management should have taken place simultaneously, even though this would have increased the challenge of OAU mediation.[232]

Foreign powers were distrusted as mediator because they pursued their own interests. Western countries played contradictory roles by providing some aid to the OAU Force and backing one of the principal faction leaders. Rapid Libyan withdrawal from Chad, Egyptian and Sudanese support to Habré and interference by member states in the execution of the Force's mandate contributed towards failure. Contrary to Pittman's contention[233] rivalry between radical and moderate-conservative countries does not seem to have played a significant role. Militant members like Angola and Algeria did support the Force's deployment.[234] Reticence was probably not due to non-African support to the operation but the volatile situation in Chad itself.[235] Another reason for the failure of

227 Pittman, 'OAU and Chad', p 318.
228 Zartman, 'Conflict Reduction', pp 306-311 (n. 21).
229 M. Deutsch, 'Subjective Features of Conflict Resolution: Psychological, Social and Cultural Influences', in Väyrynen, *New Directions in Conflict Theory* (n. 156), pp 37-50.
230 See f.i. for the mutual hatred between Habré and Goukouni *Africa Research Bulletin* (PSC), 1982, p 6302.
231 Pittman, 'OAU and Chad', pp 318-320.
232 Time sequence in general is raised in S.J. Stedman, 'Conflict and Conflict Resolution in Africa: A Conceptual Framework', in Deng and Zartman, *Conflict Resolution in Africa* (n. 21), p 381.
233 Pittman, 'OAU and Chad', pp 314-315.
234 See f.i. *Jornal de Angola*, 21/11/81 (article) and *Africa Research Bulletin* (PSC), 1981, p 6252.
235 Both conservatives and radicals had doubts about it. *Africa Research Bulletin* (PSC), 1981, pp 6176-6177.

radical countries to send contingents were financial and logistical difficulties. It was only later in the year that the cleavage between militants and moderate-conservatives regained in relevance with the Western Sahara problem and the seating of rival delegations of Habré and Goukouni at the projected Tripoli summit.[236]

Other contributory factors were organizational, logistical and financial capabilities. Few member states had the ability to air-lift troops quickly in massive numbers over large distances. It therefore took too long before the Force was in place. Transporting troops is an expensive part of any military operation and the total amount required for the Force was way beyond OAU capabilities.[237]

An OAU-sponsored peace-keeping seminar later also emphasized the importance of a clear mandate.[238] This had been unnecessarily ambiguous. Naturally, in view of its non-intervention norm the OAU could only operate with the permission of the government in question. This is the essence of peace-keeping operations, which only involve, whether in an inter-state or domestic context, consent-based activity.[239] Thus, without the promise to come to the aid of the GUNT it would have been hard to persuade Goukouni to receive the Force. However, without consent of the other factions its deployment had little use. Goukouni should therefore not have been promised more than what the Force could have made good. Moreover, in a context involving a complete collapse of public order the need for consent of the formal government loses some of its intrinsic meaning. Thus, even in the case of the OAU such situations allow for more manoeuvrability and military intervention may cross the line of consent-based activity. It showed itself in the OAU's blatant betrayal of Goukouni in 1982.

The above-mentioned seminar also stressed the need for firm institutional control. The Chadian situation of separate command of contingents and member state interference should have been avoided. This was tackled later by the draft protocol for an African Defence Organ discussed in the previous section. In an analysis of UN peace-keeping, it was said that impartiality and co-operation with disputants were crucial.[240] These aspects were lacking in the Chadian case. The OAU's betrayal could in this respect only detract from the confidence it commands as mediator.[241] Yet the evidence shows the OAU was lured into Chad because of the Libyan invasion and not because it had made a thorough

---

236   See for this Y. El-Ayouty, 'Future of the OAU: As Seen from its 19th Summit', in El-Ayouty and Zartman, *OAU After Twenty Years*, pp 327-339 and f.i. the reactions to the second failure to stage the summit in the Tripoli Declaration of Heads of State and Government, 26 Nov. 1982, paragraph 3; *Sunday News* (Tanzania), 28/11/82; *Daily Mail* (Sierra Leone), 24/11/82; and the documents section of *Africa Contemporary Record*, 1982-83.

237   See for the Assembly's gratitude to those members that had participated in the Force and later renounced their right to a refund of expenses AHG/Res.159 (XXII). Also AHG/Res.145 (XXI).

238   DEF/4 (IX): Report of the Secretary-General on the Seminar on Peace-Keeping Operations (OAU Defence Commission, Ninth Ordinary Session, 27-30 May, 1986, Harare, Zimbabwe), Annex, p 3.

239   See f.i. P.H. Kooijmans, *Internationaal Publiekrecht in Vogelvlucht* (Groningen, 1991), p 155 and their qualification by the UN Assistant Secretary-General for Field Operations in DEF/4 (IX): Report of the Secretary-General on the Seminar on Peace-Keeping Operations, Annex, p 3.

240   DEF/4 (IX): Report of the Secretary-General on the Seminar on Peace-Keeping Operations, Annex, p 4 ff.

241   See the remark by a Chadian ex-minister in M. N'Gangbet, *Peut-on encore sauver le Tchad?* (Paris, 1984), p 57.

analysis of the nature of the conflict or given much thought to the role it could play once it was there.

Finally, the seminar also noted the structural constraints in peace-keeping, *i.e.* the absence of leadership.[242] The Chadian conflict was a struggle for regional dominance between Nigeria, Libya, France and, to a lesser extent, Sudan, Egypt and Algeria. Nigeria failed to impose its will on the Chadian factions. It then passed the buck to the OAU in the expectation that it would not itself end up in the frontline.[243] When it did, it became clear that a continental cadre as the OAU to some extent attenuates the influence of its more powerful members. Lagos was unable to make others pay and failed to give direction to the operation. This can in part be tied to the role played by Egypt, Sudan and, to a lesser extent, the United States and France. As argued in chapter 1, superpower support may be a vital source of influence for a regional hegemon. Although it was also contended that regional hegemony allows for varying degrees of control, Nigerian action did not amount to effective influence. It also threw doubt on the willingness to commit itself, something that some theorists consider essential.[244]

Libya, too, did not achieve its goals as it suffered from lack of legitimacy. This is also essential to the concept of hegemony, whether the consensual element involved is consent or mere acquiescence. Moreover, as was already observed in the last section of section 6.3, patron-client dialectics may constrain the hegemon's influence. The vicissitudes in Libya's position confirm this.[245] Thus, in terms of effective influence, legitimacy and commitment the Chadian crisis pointed to the dubious nature of claims to the status of regional hegemon. Only the United States and France were able to use a subtle combination of financial, diplomatic and military means to realize their objectives.

Into the 1990s: new initiatives and strategies

After the early 1980s, interest in a collective defence strategy diminished sharply, in part because of the Chadian hangover. A decision on the draft defence protocol was deferred from one session to the next.[246] However, in the new situation of the early 1990s the debate on Pan-African peace-keeping started afresh, culminating in the 1993 reforms. Their main institutional features were discussed in the last part of section 7.2. It was shown that the OAU's reactive capacity has improved through the reinforcement of the Secretariat's monitoring capacity, the granting of mediatory initiative to the Secretary-General and his co-operation with the semi-permanent Assembly Bureau. The new mechanism also provides more co-ordination and continuity to mediation efforts. Yet, the minimal strategy of conflict reduction and prevention of worst case scenarios is still intact.

---

242 DEF/4 (IX): Report of the Secretary-General on the Seminar on Peace-Keeping Operations, Annex, p 7.

243 *Africa Research Bulletin* (PSC), 1981, p 6276.

244 See Ch. Kindleberger, *The World in Depression, 1929-1939* (Berkeley and Los Angeles, 1974), ch. 14.

245 R. Lemarchand, 'On Comparing Regional Hegemons: Libya and South Africa', in R. Lemarchand (ed), *The Green and the Black: Qadhafi's Policies in Africa* (Bloomington and Indianapolis, 1988), p 176.

246 DEF/RPT (X): Report of the Tenth Ordinary Session of the OAU Defence Commission, Tripoli, Libya, 28-31 March 1989.

The last part of section 8.1 concluded, however, that the rationale behind OAU activation has actually widened to include mobilization on the grounds of humanitarian concerns, intensification or spreading, irrespective of non-African involvement. It led to domestic conflicts and developments becoming a formal part of the OAU's area of competence. Thus, contrary to the draft defence protocol of the 1980s, the new mechanism also pays attention to military activity in domestic contexts.

However, it was also mentioned that such activity is to be very modest in nature. In his 1992 proposals the Secretary-General had pleaded for a "Military Advisory Committee", made up of the military advisers of the Bureau's members. Together with the Defence Commission it would form the military arm of the mechanism and advise on military operations. The Defence Commission would recommend on standardization of training and harmonization of member state contingents for an inter-African peace-keeping force.[247] Yet, as noted in section 7.2 the mechanism introduced in 1993 emphasizes prevention and containment so as to avoid expensive peace-keeping. To that end its constitutive document only allows deployment of military observation missions of restricted scope and duration. They are to prevent or stop hostilities to facilitate mediation. If conflicts deteriorate to such an extent that more wide-ranging intervention is considered necessary, the document orders the OAU to take recourse to the UN for financial, logistical and military assistance.[248] Thus, the far-reaching provisions of the 1980s defence protocol or Salim's 1992 proposals were not included.

As with the other aspects of the new mechanism, however, the military dimension of the 1993 reforms is more than a paper revision. The sequence in deploying military observers involves, first, monitoring work by Secretariat officials, who may include military experts; mediation efforts by the Secretary-General; the convening of the Assembly Bureau, which decides on deployment; and its execution and supervision by the Secretariat. The new system received its first test with the deployment in 1992-1993 of a "Neutral Military Observer Group" (NMOG) in Rwanda. With contingents from Tunisia, Senegal, Congo and Zimbabwe it totalled only some 130 soldiers. They were flown in with the help of the UN and Western countries.[249] Intended only as the preparatory stage for a more large-scale intervention these troops had to help maintain a cease-fire and demilitarized zone between the Habyarimana government and the FPR.[250] A more massive military operation with which the OAU became concerned was the dispatch of some 2,000 Ugandan and Tanzanian troops to Liberia after requests to that effect at the Cairo summit (1993).[251]

---

247 CM/1710 (LVI) Rev.1: Report of the SG on Conflicts in Africa (June 1992) (n. 106), pp 11 and 17.

248 AHG/Decl.3 (XXIX)/Rev.1, pars. 15-16 and 25.

249 Wembou, 'A propos du nouveau mécanisme' (n. 110), p 20. Also *Le Soleil* (Senegal), 29-30/6/93 (Assembly speech).

250 The exercise took place before the 1994 catastrophe. Salim wished to let the OAU undertake the larger-scale intervention planned for a later stage to implement the Arusha accord. Yet due to French pressure the UN insisted to undertake the operation itself and refused to assist an OAU force. H. Adelman and A. Suhrke, *Early Warning and Conflict Management* (Steering Committee of the Joint Evaluation of Emergency Assistance to Rwanda: Odense, 1996), pp 27-28.

251 *Africa Confidential*, 4-11-94. An OAU military observer mission (OMIB) was sent to Burundi in 1994. *Africa Research Bulletin* (PSC), 1994, p 11476.

The financial requirements of the mechanism's military undertakings are, of course, one of the major obstacles to more large-scale interventions. In his 1992 proposals the Secretary-General asked for a special fund to be fed by an annual contribution of one million dollars from the OAU's regular budget. He also pleaded for accepting voluntary contributions from the UN, other institutions and individual states, both from Africa and outside.[252] Some members also argued for additional binding contributions for member states for each peace-keeping operation. With regard to contributions from non-African countries, however, some member states feared that such resources would influence the mechanism and entail unacceptable non-African interference.[253]

Thus, the 1993 reforms introduced a special fund for conflict management and peace-keeping that would be fed by the OAU's regular budget and voluntary contributions from member states. It may also be supplemented by voluntary contributions from other international organizations, in particular the UN. With regard to contributions by non-African states a compromise was reached in the sense that the Secretary-General may accept such grants subject to permission by the Assembly Bureau.[254] In November 1993 the Bureau decided that five per cent of the regular OAU budget would be allocated to the fund provided this amount would not be lower than one million dollars. Until the end of 1993 the fund was to receive an immediate allocation of $ 500,000.[255]

The OAU's financial clout is therefore extremely limited. This means that its new peace-keeping activities depend heavily on external contributions. NMOG and other activities taking place at the time were financed by an allocation of the OAU of some one and a half million dollars and grants totalling half a million from the United States, Nigeria, Belgium, Namibia and Lesotho.[256] The dispatch of troops to Liberia was mainly financed by an American contribution to a UN fund for that country.[257]

As was the case with its earlier interventions it is certain that the OAU needed the consent of disputants, at least for the NMOG operation.[258] The meaning of the 1993 summit consensus, mentioned in section 8.1, that the OAU nevertheless has the right to intervene in situations marked by the collapse of the state, is not clear. One might contend that, in the Liberian context, this would allow it to intervene even against the will of the parties. As in the Chadian case its potential manoeuvrability would be enlarged by the absence of genuine governmental power structures. However, the mechanism's constitutive instrument only speaks of military observer missions, which are a form of peace-keeping and thus require consent. Moreover, for enforcement action it would need authorization by the Security Council. It is true that the instrument orders the OAU, in case a conflict degenerates to the point of necessitating collective international intervention, to seek the assistance or services of the UN. While it emphasizes an OAU role in peace-keeping it also mentions that the OAU is prepared to work with the UN in

252   CM/1710 (LVI) Rev.1: Report of the SG on Conflicts in Africa (June 1992), pp 18-19.
253   Wembou, 'A propos du nouveau mécanisme', p 11 and *Jeune Afrique*, 8-14/7/93.
254   AHG/Decl.3 (XXIX)/Rev.1, par. 23.
255   As noted in section 5.5 to this purpose new budgeting rules were introduced in 1994, entailing operation of biennial budgets. *West Africa*, 29/11-5/12/93 and 14-20/2/94.
256   Wembou, 'A propos du nouveau mécanisme', pp 19-20.
257   *Africa Confidential*, 4/11/94.
258   *Africa Research Bulletin* (PSC), 1992: pp 10691 and 10763 and 1993: pp 10867 and 11207.

matters of peace-making.[259] Yet its concrete meaning in terms of the OAU's own enforcement capacity is restricted by the Organization's limited financial, logistical and military capabilities and is thus dependent on UN resources.

One can therefore draw the following conclusions. The 1993 reforms have solved some of the bottlenecks in the military dimensions of OAU conflict management, though not all. After the disastrous failure in Chad the Organization is now embarking on new, cautious peace-keeping operations. They are embedded in a new system which provides firm institutional control and shows greater realism by also focusing on domestic contexts. Some of the financial and logistical problems are tackled by closer co-operation with the UN and greater readiness to use extra-African assistance. The UN, for its part, has formally expressed its desire for a greater role in the maintenance of peace and security for regional organizations.[260] However, the OAU's readiness to take recourse to the UN bears the risk of dependence. As the latter is overburdened with peace-keeping responsibilities and does not necessarily support OAU initiatives in all cases,[261] the limits of the OAU's peace-keeping capabilities may come in sight sooner than expected.

The new mechanism has not resolved the problems inherent in the bilateral security approach either. With regard to enemy perceptions one may nevertheless observe that in the post-Cold War era the fear of extra-African intervention has diminished somewhat, thus allowing a more constructive use of non-African resources for the maintenance of the continental order. This is in line with the shifts in the rationale of conflict management towards a more activist and humanitarian approach. Still, as was shown above such fears have not completely vanished.[262]

From the perspective of the past the OAU's increased activity in peace-keeping is remarkable. Yet, its relevance in African peace-keeping is severely restricted by its limited capabilities. It points to the fact that the structural constraints of inter-African relations have not been sufficiently tackled. While one cannot deny the OAU's realism in embarking on limited forms of military interventions, it also means that the Organization is wholly unprepared for high intensity conflicts. Thus, other institutions are still needed to handle such crises. It makes the new rationale of OAU conflict management, with its concern for humanitarian issues, rather vulnerable. For example, when during the early 1990s the civil war in Somalia became more and more violent and pressures for some Western or UN response were growing, the OAU kept a painfully low profile.[263]

It is very hard to alleviate these structural difficulties. In essence two scenarios can be followed, each with its advantages and handicaps: military intervention by African contingents operating in UN cadres and decomposition of the context in which intervention takes place. The post-Cold War era has, until now, allowed greater activity

---

259   AHG/Decl.3 (XXIX)/Rev.1, par. 25.

260   B. Boutros-Ghali, *An Agenda For Peace. Preventive Diplomacy, Peacemaking and Peace-keeping: Report of the Secretary-General pursuant to the statement adopted by the Summit Meeting of the Security Council on 31 January 1992* (New York, 1992), ch. VII.

261   As happened with regard to its Rwanda initiative. See n. 250.

262   Thus in the wake of the 1994 Rwanda genocide a French proposal for a French-sponsored inter-African peace-keeping force was rejected by a majority of states. It was feared it would consolidate French/Western influence. *Africa Research Bulletin* (PSC), 1994, pp 11639-11640.

263   See f.i. the interview with the Secretary-General in *West Africa*, 28/12/92-10/1/93.

on the part of the United Nations,[264] as well as of inter-African organizations of more limited membership than the OAU. Although beyond the scope of this study two examples of this must be cited.

The first intervention of the United Nations in Somalia (UNOSOM I; 1992-1993) showed that African states are more quickly prepared to participate in international operations if they are undertaken in the framework, or with the assistance, of the UN. With the United States providing leadership, the relatively quick dispatch of more than 3,500 African troops to participate in UNOSOM I[265] vindicates the central contention in hegemonic stability theory. The prisoners' dilemma, in which states adopt unco-operative postures and the public good is not forthcoming, can only be solved by a hegemon providing the public good itself or enticing others to contribute. Only then is adequate co-ordination of collective will generated.[266] In UNOSOM I American leadership guaranteed reimbursement and logistical assistance. It also provided more direction to the operation than the OAU was able to give in Chad.[267]

However, it is doubtful whether African states attribute legitimacy to American hegemony. Their participation in UNOSOM might also be related, apart from American pressure, to concern about Western influence. Amongst elite Africans the CNN stage-managed landing of American marines on the beach of Mogadishu was in this respect seen as a humiliating blow.[268] The ability of the UN to deploy massive numbers of troops in a short space of time, or at least more quickly than the OAU, contrasts sharply with the latter's capabilities. Yet the vicissitudes of UNOSOM also point to the limited relevance of peace-keeping operations as instruments to solve complex domestic conflict. The power of international organizations appears to be over-estimated.[269]

The second scenario by which continental peace-keeping can be improved is by the game theoretical strategy of actor reduction. Oye's argument that this may encourage co-operation[270] was already confirmed in our discussion of the Frontline alliance. The new role of the Assembly Bureau is another example, as is the new tendency to allocate security issues to inter-African organizations active in one of the continent's regions, such as Southern[271] and West Africa.

---

264   See f.i. B. Andemicael, 'OAU-UN Relations in a Changing World', in Y. El-Ayouty (ed), *The Organization of African Unity After Thirty Years* (Westport and London, 1994), pp 119-138.

265   Sent by six countries (Botswana, Morocco, Tunisia, Egypt, Zambia, Zimbabwe) as of 17/1/93. *Africa Research Bulletin* (PSC), 1993, p 10870.

266   Snidal, 'Limits of Hegemonic Stability Theory', pp 580-1 ff.

267   See further S. Baynham, 'Somalia: "Operation Restore Hope"', in *Africa Insight*, 1993, pp 17-23; P.J. Schraeder, 'U.S. Intervention in the Horn of Africa Amidst the End of the Cold War' and M. Michaelson, 'Somalia: The Painful Road to Reconciliation', both in *Africa Today*, 1993, no. 2, pp 7-27 and 53-73; and D. Volman, 'Africa and the New World Order', in *Journal of Modern African Studies*, 1993, pp 1-30.

268   See African letters to the editor on this in *West Africa*, 28/12/92-10/1/93.

269   But in Somalia also the United States commitment to genuinely intervene. See J. Clark, 'Debacle in Somalia' and M. Michaels, 'Retreat from Africa', both in *Foreign Affairs*, 1992-93, pp 118-120 and 107-108 respectively.

270   K.A. Oye, 'Explaining Cooperation Under Anarchy: Hypotheses and Strategies', in K.A. Oye (ed), *Cooperation Under Anarchy* (Princeton, 1986), pp 20-22.

271   In 1994 it was decided to give SADC also a task in regional security. *Africa Research Bulletin* (PSC), 1994, p 11535.

However, Nigeria's intervention in the Liberian civil war in the framework of ECOWAS underlines the limits of this strategy. That Lagos did not embark on the operation through the OAU has much to do with the fact that its influence is more effective in a smaller forum like ECOWAS. In this West African framework it was better able to steer the operation as it saw fit.[272]

Yet the difficulties of the intervention force — the "ECOWAS Cease-fire Monitoring Group" (ECOMOG)[273] — show that collective operations in regional cadres are very susceptible to struggles for dominance between the states of the region. The course of the intervention and the related regional power struggle marked, more than anything else, the limits of influence of these countries. Nigeria initially intervened to assist former President Samuel Doe and managed to keep the major Liberian faction, the NPFL of Charles Taylor, under pressure. Because the latter enjoyed the support of Libya, Burkina Faso and Ivory Coast Lagos failed to eliminate Taylor from the scene. ECOMOG's operation developed into an outright enforcement campaign, in which it jeopardized its neutrality[274] to the point of necessitating the dispatch by the OAU of contingents, that were attached to ECOMOG, and deployment of some UN military observers. The hegemonic ambitions of Nigeria could never have evolved that far and the related military intervention have degenerated to the extent it did, had it taken place in the framework of the OAU.

8.3   In a world where it is dangerous to be on your own: the OAU and the global role of Africa

Introduction

As was argued in previous chapters the external part of the OAU's general ideology involves the aspiration to greater global influence for Africa and its component states and, related to this, the desire for equality of status with state elites of other continents. In sections 6.1 and 7.1 it was shown that the struggle against colonialism and in part also the management of Africa's conflicts, were (and are) rooted in this fundamental endeavour. The continued existence of colonial and white minority regimes and serious conflicts on the continent would only detract from its global influence. Conversely, Africa's collective, external power has been seen as having a direct bearing on its ability to manage the continental order.

This section therefore analyses the external dimension of that management. First, we discuss the perceptions of African state elites on the continent's position in world

---

272   On Nigeria's role f.i. M.A. Vogt, 'Nigeria's Participation in the ECOWAS Monitoring Group - ECOMOG', in *Nigerian Journal of International Affairs*, 1991, no. 1, pp 101-121.

273   By 1993 some 16,000 men of whom 10,000 Nigerians, the rest made up of Guinean, Ghanaian, Sierra Leonian, Malinese and Gambian troops and, at some time, Senegalese ones. E. Conteh-Morgan, 'ECOWAS: Peace-making or meddling in Liberia?', in *Africa Insight*, 1993, p 38 and *Africa Confidential*, 4/11/94.

274   Conteh-Morgan, 'ECOWAS', pp 36-41; the articles in *Issue: A Journal of Opinion*, 1993, nos. 1/2, pp 70-91; and Y. Gershoni, 'From ECOWAS to ECOMOG: The Liberian Crisis and the Struggle for Political Hegemony in West Africa', in *Liberian Studies Journal*, 1993, pp 21-43.

affairs and the roles attributed to the OAU in enhancing that position. The next section shows how the Organization actually does, in practice, generate greater influence for African states collectively and individually. The last two sections discuss, from the perspective of state elite perception, political practice and international relations theory, how the creation of such influence could be improved so as to ensure a greater role for Africa in world affairs and, thus, a more prosperous and stable continental order.

Perceptions of Africa's potential and impotence
In sections 2.2 and 2.3 it was contended that, from a psychological point of view, the experience among state elites of deprivation is at the basis of the above-mentioned desire for greater global influence and status. As argued by Laswell deprivation may entail a drive to compensate distress by way of seeking power or, if deprivation is overwhelming, by withdrawal from social interaction.[275] It was submitted that such withdrawal may take the form of refuge in escapist constructs of reality.

The deprivation of African state elites ensues from a sense of vulnerability to domestic enemies as well as external ones, both African and non-African. With regard to the Western world one can also observe an inferiority complex that has fed on two major factors.

One is the issue of racial discrimination. After independence this did not completely disappear, but continued to influence the attitude of state elites towards issues of international politics. This can be gleaned, for example, from the controversy surrounding the dialogue affair and the Stanleyville crisis. In the context of their interaction with the non-African world suspicion of racial prejudice was never far below the surface. One should not, indeed, deny its logic, even in international contexts of later years. Thus, it showed itself in an incident in 1993 involving an American senator with international negotiating experience, who made derogatory remarks about African leaders attending GATT talks in Geneva.[276]

The other major factor informing this inferiority complex is the realization among state elites of the enormous discrepancy in power between Africa and the West. It is tied to the sense of vulnerability to external enemies and constitutes a more important source of deprivation than the racial factor. Governments of every inter-African grouping and practically without exception articulated, during the whole period under study, their awareness of the imbalance in the global configurations of power. References to the strong influence exerted by Western powers in Africa abound, as do perceptions, before 1990, of competition by the Eastern bloc in specific regions and conflicts. These references alternate with inarticulate allusions to "enemies of the OAU", its "ill wishers" and "prophets of doom", which in turn give way to explicit versions of conspiracy theory. All these utterances point to an acute realization of weakness.[277]

Inter-African co-operation in the fora of the OAU was meant to correct this imbalance in global configurations. Organizing Africa's weak states was, quite apart from the psychological anxieties generated by this state of affairs, a matter of real politik that

---

275   H.D. Laswell, *Power and Personality* (New York, 1948), ch. 3.
276   *ASA News*, January/March 1994.
277   See for examples the sources cited in this section.

would, for example, also be prescribed by the arguments of regime theory.[278]

However, here we are concerned with state elite perceptions on the degree of influence that could be exerted when banding together. These seem to have been shared by member states of every inter-African grouping. There is at least no clear picture of differences in attitude with regard to Africa's potential, collective influence, as articulated by radical, moderate-conservative, English-speaking or Francophone countries or member states of a particular region. This confirms the findings of section 4.4 about the goal of enhancing Africa's global power being shared, as a lowest common denominator, by the various inter-African alliances. Moreover, most of these perceptions have been found during every decade of the OAU's functioning. Evidence on them often relates, though not always, to periods of OAU anniversaries (1973, 1983, 1988 and 1993) or times of severe inter-African tension, such as 1982.

First, many countries have often expressed the idea that they should wield collective power *externally*, namely vis-à-vis other continents or in the United Nations and other fora. Thus, with the OAU they could tell "the rest of the world" of Africa's problems. More specifically, the OAU has always been viewed as an instrument to co-ordinate Africa's stance in the UN, its Security Council and Specialized Agencies, in UNCTAD and the North-South Dialogue. It has also been seen as a vehicle to conduct collective negotiations with the European Community.[279]

Perceptions point to the idea that, collectively, the power of African countries is increased. This is done by way of co-operation between member states, which acts as a leverage mechanism augmenting influence. The major source of this mechanism is the great number of states. When, for instance, Zimbabwe joined the OAU in 1980 it was stressed that, as membership had risen "to the impressive figure of FIFTY", the Organization would exercise more influence in the world by virtue of its numerical strength.[280] Related to this is the more inarticulate notion that OAU membership (nearly) covers the whole of Africa and by this provides the Organization special, if unquantified, significance. Thus, various countries have stressed, at one time or another, that the OAU encompasses an entire continent, something other continents have not achieved.[281] The OAU is therefore "unique" and "irreplacable".[282] This notion is bound up with the strong sense, already observed in chapters 3 and 4, of the continent as a recognizable geographical unit. This vague idea[283] is articulated at different points in time,[284] while it is regularly submitted that the OAU is the voice or institutional expression of this continental

278   Krasner, 'Regimes and the limits of realism', pp 355-368 (n. 157).

279   *Le Courrier d'Afrique* (Zaire), 12/9/67 (article); *Daily News* (Tanzania), 25/5/73 (article); *Daily Mail* (Sierra Leone), 25/5/73 (article) and 6/8/82; *Daily Times* (Nigeria), 18/7/85 and 25/5/88 (editorial and article); and *Révolution Africaine* (Algeria), 20/5/88 (article).

280   *Daily Mail* (Sierra Leone), 23/6/80. Emphasis in original. Also *ibid.*, 4/9/70, 30/4/80 and 1/7/80 (article).

281   *Daily News* (Tanzania), 21/6/72 (article); *Fraternité* (Ivory Coast), 1/6/73; and *Le Niger*, 4/6/73 (both Assembly speeches).

282   *Le Soleil* (Senegal), 26/11/82 and 13/6/83 (articles).

283   Also seen as "mystique" See A.A. Mazrui, *Towards a Pax Africana: A Study of Ideology and Ambition* (London, 1967), p 118.

284   *l'Essor* (Mali), 11/11/63; *Daily News* (Tanzania), 21/6/72 (article); *Daily Mail* (Sierra Leone), 25/5/73 and 19/6/80 (text Assembly speech); and *Sudanow* (Sudan), February 1984.

identity.[285]

Views on how far the leverage mechanism could enhance Africa's influence have varied from moderately optimistic to escapist. However, before these are analysed it must be emphasized that the total picture of perceptions of the increase in power and Africa's actual global position is rather contradictory. It is shown below that, besides notions of Africa's potential, member states have lamented over continental impotence. Moreover, as time progressed ideas about the need for African unity vis-à-vis the rest of the world began to sound more and more defensive.

With regard to the leverage attributed to OAU co-operation member states have expressed, at its simplest, an idea about its external effect. Thus, if Africa would act in unison it could bring pressure to bear on international issues or even become a "great force", whose "weight" others would have to take into account in the UN and other fora.[286] In earlier years some of these perceptions involved hopeful notions about the future and progress. They contained arguments that the OAU was a power "in the making", that it could become a powerful instrument against a hostile global order and that the continent's role in the world was "growing".[287] Other views went one step further and announced that the OAU actually *was* a "strong" and "effective" cadre, which was capable to speak to the world and formed a "considerable political force" or a "formidable force to reckon with". These perceptions occurred in later years as well.[288]

The fully escapist assessments of how far the OAU enhances power have also been articulated by member states of different groupings. They do not seem to be restricted to any period, although evidence slightly favours the Organization's second decade. They can often be tied to inter-African tension[289] or general malaise.[290] Thus, reality gave sufficient reason for recourse to these escapist evaluations. In 1971 Sierra Leonean comment had it that the OAU constituted Africa's "deadliest weapon" against foreign powers. These therefore tried to eliminate it as they saw it as "a great threat to their supremacy and the means whereby Africa [could] itself become a big power".[291] Even comments of some of the more important member states sometimes expressed the idea that Africa was so powerful, that it instilled fear among non-African countries. It was most graphically argued with respect to the Organization's fifteenth anniversary by a publication in Madagascar, which depicted the OAU as a muscular, black Rambo startling a group of white, dollar-loaded businessmen (see figure 8.1). During the 1980s other

---

285 See esp. *Daily Mail* (Sierra Leone), 1/7/80 (article in the form of a letter to "Mother Africa"). Also *Botswana Daily News*, 26/7/78 (Assembly speech); *Cameroon Tribune*, 28/7/87 (article); *Daily Times* (Nigeria), 9/7/77 and 25/5/88 (article); and the interview with the OAU's SG in *Africa Report*, May-June 1992.

286 *Le Courrier d'Afrique* (Zaire), 12/9/67 (article); *Zambia Daily Mail*, 21/6/71; *Jornal de Angola*, 22/7/78 (text discussion opinion poll); and *Révolution Africaine* (Algeria), 3-9/12/82 (article).

287 See f.i. *l'Essor* (Mali), 1/9/69 and *Horoya* (Guinea), 25/5/73. Also *East African Standard* (Kenya), 24/7/78.

288 See f.i. *Daily Mail* (Sierra Leone), 25/5/73 (editorial and article), 1/7/80 (article) and 23/6/80; *l'Essor* (Mali), 1-2/6/74; and *Révolution Africaine* (Algeria), 9-15/3/77 (article). Also *Le Soleil* (Senegal), 4-5/6/83 and 13/6/83 (articles).

289 Such as 1971 (dialogue affair); 1978 (extra-African intervention); and 1983 (aftermath Western Sahara-Chadian crises).

290 As an Algerian assessment during the economic crisis of the 1980s. See n. 292.

291 *Daily Mail* (Sierra Leone), 21/6/71 (article).

comments spoke of "fears" and "quavers" among Africa's foes and the "danger" the OAU formed to imperialism.[292]

That such escapist perceptions were not merely propagandistic excess of individual countries showed itself in some of the less practical causes the OAU embraced. For example, in the anti-colonial euphoria of the 1972 summit the Council of Ministers adopted a resolution expressing support for the people of the Atlantic Ocean island of St. Helena in its apparent struggle for independence from Britain.[293] One might also argue that the decision in 1991-1992 to set up a committee to prepare a case against the West for financial reparations for centuries of Atlantic slave trade and colonial occupation had an unrealistic ring around it,[294] however justified it would be on moral-historical grounds.

Perceptions show that the leverage mechanism has not only been seen to deliver more power. It was also meant to enhance the respect in the rest of the world for the African continent. In this area its role has been important in soothing some of the anxieties of state elites. Thus, in 1965 a Malian comment argued that the OAU should serve as a "ring of dignity".[295] Later it was frequently stressed that, thanks to the OAU, Africa was a respected partner in world affairs.[296] Inability to solve serious conflicts, such as the Chadian and Western Sahara crises, could give rise to concern about the continent's image, quite apart from the conflicts themselves.[297] Fear of becoming the global laughing-stock, especially in the West,[298] underlined the importance of the OAU mandate to eliminate the village idiot or, if this was impossible, hide him from view: Africa should never lose its image of a respected continent[299] and if it overcame a difficult crisis this was seen as a source of pride for "every African".[300]

As mentioned above, it was at times admitted that all was not well with the quest for greater influence. Intermingled with allusions to Africa's "exceptionally rich" and "immense" potential in human and natural resources[301] were sorry confessions of the OAU's impotence and, more generally, the failure to let the continent take off towards a state of prosperous development and strong global influence. It was lamented that Africa "should really have become a force to reckon with in the comity of nations"[302] or that the OAU had never shown its worth.[303]

---

292   See *Daily Mail* (Sierra Leone), 30/4/80; *The Ethiopian Herald*, 11/6/83; and *Révolution Africaine* (Algeria), 20/5/88 (article).

293   CM/Res.272 (XIX).

294   See *Le Soleil* (Senegal), 3/6/91 (article).

295   *l'Essor* (Mali), 20/12/65. See in a similar vein *Jornal de Angola*, 25/5/88 (article).

296   *Daily Mail* (Sierra Leone), 25/5/73 (article) and 30/4/80; *Révolution Africaine* (Algeria), 3-9/12/82; and *Le Soleil*, 4-5/6/83 (text of an appeal to solve the 1982 quorum crisis).

297   *Le Soleil* (Senegal), 7/6/83 (article) and *The Herald* (Zimbabwe), 27/11/82.

298   See f.i. *Le Soleil* (Senegal), 16/11/84 (article).

299   *Sudanow* (Sudan), June 1978; *The Ghanaian Times*, 1/7/80; and *Le Soleil* (Senegal), 1-2/3/86.

300   *Le Soleil* (Senegal), 16/11/84.

301   See f.i. *Fraternité* (Ivory Coast), 1/6/73; *Le Niger*, 4/6/73; *l'Essor* (Mali), 29-30/7/78 (all Assembly speeches); *Révolution Africaine* (Algeria), 16-22/6/72; 9-15/5/80; and 3-9/12/82 (all articles); *East African Standard* (Kenya), 14/6/65; *Cameroon Tribune*, 25/5/88; and *Le Soleil* (Senegal), 29/6/92 (article).

302   *Daily Times* (Nigeria), 21/5/73.

303   *Botswana Daily News*, 26/7/78 (Assembly speech). Also *Révolution Africaine* (Algeria), 3-9/12/82 and *Daily Times* (Nigeria), 25/5/88.

Figure 8.1   The OAU and Africa's potential: A view from Madagascar

Source: *Madagascar Renouveau*, 1978, no. 8, p 69

The most superficial explanation that was given for this referred to conflicts among member states, which weakened the influence of the continent. Continentalist notions were, indeed, regularly contradicted, especially by radical member states during the 1970s. These emphasized, for instance, a division into "two Africa's". On the one hand there were "neo-colonial" or "reactionary" states and on the other "African", "progressive" forces which formed a genuine anti-imperialist front.[304] Yet, in 1982 Algeria argued that separate international organizations for radical and moderate-conservative countries should, above all, be avoided for it would prevent realization of Africa's political potential.[305] Later on other comment stressed the futility of Franco-African summits where continental solutions were needed for Africa's problems.[306]

This skipped the question, discussed in the next paragraphs, whether the degree of inter-African co-operation as foreseen in the OAU was sufficient to generate greater influence. It also left intact the idea of the leverage mechanism as such serving as the source of increased power. In the same vein various member states began to argue, during the 1970s and 1980s, that the broader cadre represented by Afro-Arab co-operation could provide the desired degree of influence. Thus, some sub-Saharan comments presented Afro-Arab co-operation in almost millenarian fashion. Africans and Arabs would form a "new world power".[307] The face of the world would change soon as the political and potentially economic weight of Africa, added to the financial weight of the Arab world, could "overthrow all the facts of geopolitics" and open up "the most exaltant perspectives".[308]

These hopes were to be quickly disappointed. This section concludes with some observations on how the objectives, to which the leverage mechanism was expected to contribute, came to be articulated in increasingly defensive terms.

From the beginning it was the OAU's mere survival, rather than its subversion of the global balance of power, that was emphasized as one of its merits. Positive evaluation of this meagre gain was fed by awareness of the continent's many difficulties and its weakness vis-à-vis extra-African forces.[309] Identification of the OAU with Africa itself may have encouraged this judgement. Furthermore, as Africa would have to go a long way before it would catch up with the rest of the world the goals for which increased collective influence would be used were necessarily couched in terms such as "combat" against white minority regimes, "reinforcement of ranks" against extra-African

---

304 *Daily News* (Tanzania), 25/5/73; *Jornal de Angola*, 14/1/76 and 20/7/78 (both articles); *Révolution Africaine* (Algeria), 16-22/1/76 (article); and *Madagascar Renouveau*, nos. 11-12, Jan. 1980.

305 *Révolution Africaine* (Algeria), 3-9/12/82 (article).

306 *Ehuzu* (Benin), 25/5/88 (article). See for a warning against the danger of OCAM for the struggle against (neo-)colonialism f.i. *Révolution Africaine* (Algeria), 6/3/65.

307 *Daily Mail* (Sierra Leone), 23/7/75.

308 *l'Essor* (Mali), 19-20/7/77 (article). More sober views in *Révolution Africaine* (Algeria), 1-7/8/75 (Assembly speech) and *Sudanow* (Sudan), April 1977. See also Déclaration Politique; Déclaration sur la Coopération Economique et Financière Afro-Arabe; Organisation et Procédure de la Mise en Oeuvre de la Coopération Afro-Arabe; Déclaration et Programme d'Action sur la Coopération Afro-Arabe, Cairo, 7-9/3/77.

309 See f.i. *Daily News* (Tanzania), 25/5/73; *Info-Madagascar*, 4/8/73 (article); *Daily Mail* (Sierra Leone), 25/5/73 and 1/7/80 (article); *Inside Kenya Today*, June 1973; *Révolution Africaine* (Algeria), 3-9/12/82 (article) and 27/5/88.

intervention or "attacking" underdevelopment.[310] From the early 1980s the OAU, and the collective influence it stood for, were seen in relation to preventing the continent's "sinking into a new status of colonial dependency".[311] Concern over deteriorating terms of trade was met, as always, by emphasizing the need for unity.[312] By 1993 this economic theme had become familiar. The OAU had to help combat Africa's debt crisis and marginalization by encouraging it to adopt a policy of self-reliance. It was necessary to restore the continent "back into the mainstream of world affairs" and let it retake the strategic importance it had during the Cold War era. This should be done on its own strength: rather than being "reactive standers-by", the OAU and its new conflict management mechanism should give "leadership back to Africa".[313]

Thus, throughout the last three decades the Organization was perceived as an instrument for the "survival" and "salvation" of the continent.[314] Such qualifications of the use for its leverage mechanism also allude to the insecurity of state elites with regard to their position in the global order, as well as the OAU's role in allaying such apprehension. Perhaps this psychological function was articulated most explicitly during the conflict over the Western Sahara. Faced with the failure to stage the 1982 summit African states feared the OAU's demise. One Senegalese comment expressed the hope that it would survive this crisis. It argued that members were simply condemned to listen to each other if they didn't want to become voiceless countries in "a world where it [was] dangerous to be on your own".[315]

The leverage mechanism in action

Notions of how far the leverage mechanism increased Africa's power, as well as of how exactly such power would be used, remained relatively inarticulate, as the continent was continually pushed on the defensive and any significant increase in greater global influence appeared to recede further and further into a distant future. Moreover, the perceptions analysed above did not clarify how the leverage mechanism ingrained in OAU co-operation precisely generated more power.

However, from the OAU's inception the idea of the leverage mechanism received concrete manifestation in caucus groups made up of the diplomatic representatives of member states. These African Groups, which were formed in New York, Brussels and Geneva, began to co-ordinate member state policy vis-à-vis the UN and the European Community. As others have already written on their functioning, only their general procedure is sketched, with emphasis on the Group in New York.

---

310 *l'Essor* (Mali), 16/9/68 (Assembly speech); *Révolution Africaine* (Algeria), 2-8/3/77 (article) and 19-25/7/85; *Sudanow* (Sudan), June 1978; *The Herald* (Zimbabwe), 27/11/82; and *Times of Zambia*, 14/6/83.

311 *Daily Mail* (Sierra Leone), 19/6/80 (text Assembly speech).

312 *Le Soleil* (Senegal), 20-21/7/85 (Assembly speech) and *Daily News* (Tanzania), 22/7/85. For an early example CM/St.12 (XXI).

313 Address by the Secretary-General, May 1993 (n. 117); *l'Essor* (Mali), 15/7/90; *Cameroon Tribune*, 11/7/90 and 3/6/91; and *Le Soleil* (Senegal), 29/6-30/6/93 (all articles).

314 *l'Essor* (Mali), 21/11/66 (article); *Le Niger*, 28/5/73; *East African Standard* (Kenya), 24/7/78; *Daily Mail* (Sierra Leone), 1/7/80 (article); *Cameroon Tribune*, 25/5/88; and *Le Soleil* (Senegal), 25-26/7/87 (interview with Congo's president) and 30/6/92 (article).

315 *Le Soleil* (Senegal), 3/8/82 (article).

The African Group in New York tries to obtain benefits for member states and inter-African projects and seeks to ensure that "the African views" are "unitedly and effectively" presented at the world body.[316] Its delegates must have national instructions that are flexible enough for the realization of such united action.[317] The Group holds monthly meetings and additional ones if its chairman, whose tenure rotates monthly among member states, considers it necessary. When countries want to raise an issue at the UN that needs the support of others they usually ask for such a meeting. The Group also has an important role in discouraging member states, involved in a dispute with each other, to take recourse to the UN. During the General Assembly's annual conference the Group meets on a daily basis. Its meetings are serviced by an Executive Secretariat which acts as a channel of communication with the General Secretariat in Addis Ababa and keeps the OAU informed of UN developments. Contrary to other UN geographical groups the African Group has the advantage that a collective stand is often defined in advance in resolutions of the OAU's policy organs. These serve as the basis for draft resolutions to be presented to the UN. In the course of this the Group appoints certain delegates as its spokesmen and targets non-African delegations to be lobbied for support. If the issue is of concern to other Third World countries it is brought before the Group of 77 before its presentation to the UN as a whole.[318]

With more than fifty member states the African Group exerts considerable influence in the Group of 77 and thus, through the sheer force of numbers, in the UN as a whole. This is seen in the policies and attitudes of the General Assembly. Its posture on issues as decolonization and the whole gamut of African development problems has often reflected African positions.

One area to which the Group gives priority is representation in international organizations. As shown in section 4.4, underrepresentation in the UN, especially its Security Council, touched on elite self-esteem. It has therefore always been the target of tenacious collective action.[319] If member states wish to nominate nationals for certain posts they must address a request to the Group. Its committee on candidatures sorts out applications on the basis of rotation and equitable representation of the five African regions. Candidates are then formally nominated by the Group to the UN or its Specialized Agencies. Although nominations are sometimes hotly contested, rivalry is usually kept inside the Group.[320]

Most studies conclude that the Group operates quite effectively.[321] This explains why in interviews in 1989 it was stressed with pride that the Group was "very efficient"

316 CM/Res.121 (IX).

317 F.i. CM/Res.54 (IV); CM/Res.233 (XV); and CM/Res.273 (XIX).

318 Amate, *Inside the OAU*, pp 190-198 (n. 81).

319 See for OAU statements on this f.i. CM/Res.1 (I); CM/Res.56 (IV); CM/Res.233 (XV); and AHG/Res.33 (II).

320 Amate, *Inside the OAU*, p 200 and M. Hyppolite-Manigat, 'Le groupe de l'Organisation de l'unité africaine à l'ONU', in *Revue française d'études politique africaines*, 1974, no. 104, pp 73-81. On co-ordinated nominations of candidates f.i. CM/Res.69 (V); CM/Res.95 (VIII); CM/Res.106 (IX); CM/Res.436 (XXV); CM/Res.733 (XXXIII); CM/Res.762 (XXXIII); CM/Res.783 (XXXV); CM/Res.1053 (XLIV); and AHG/Res. 169 (XXIII).

321 See f.i. Amate, *Inside the OAU* and Hyppolite-Manigat, 'Le groupe de l'Organisation de l'unité africaine'.

and "very successful".[322] Among its most concrete achievements have been the realization of greater African representation in the Security Council and ECOSOC and the growth of African seats on the governing bodies of UN Specialized Agencies.[323] In this respect it must be borne in mind that increased Security Council representation also served a more concrete purpose than elite self-esteem. Its African members are expected to represent the collective African interest and not merely that of their own government.[324] The reason for the successful functioning of the African Group lies, fundamentally, in the immediate need to collectively confront an external environment so as to extract concessions from it for goals that are shared by all member states. Moreover, for many countries interaction with the non-African world is hindered by limited resources and expertise. The African Groups furnish such resources and allow countries to participate in global politics against lower costs. As is argued in regime theory, this enables weak states to exert influence.[325] The idea of the leverage mechanism as such is therefore correct, as the Groups generate more influence for African states individually and collectively than they could have achieved by themselves.

Nevertheless, the creation of influence by caucusing is subject to limitations. In one interview it was argued that member states sometimes fall out with the rest of the Group for fear of antagonizing non-African powers like France and the United States.[326] This is an explicit confirmation of Rothstein's argument about external factors impinging on regimes of weak states.[327] One may, of course, argue that this can also be explained by the lack of hegemonic leadership. In any case, in the context of the continent's relatively even distribution of power claims to special status by the Group's more influential members only disrupt consensus, rather than generate sufficient collective will. This was witnessed in 1978 when Nigeria managed to get itself elected to the Security Council. In the process it antagonized the rest of the African Group, which stood by another, collectively nominated candidate.[328]

Even if the Group manages to preserve consensus and its leverage mechanism ensures that, in the soothing words of one Council resolution, "Africa can win still greater victories",[329] the degree of collective influence generated has been insufficient to halt the continent's marginalization in world affairs. Conference politics does not alter the global balance of power. It may prey upon its edges and affect the calculations of powerful countries, but contrary to Krasner's contention the OAU regime has not changed underlying capabilities.[330]

---

322   Interviews with Mamadou Bah, Addis Ababa, 18/9/89 (n. 4) and R.S. Iskandar, ambassador of Egypt, Addis Ababa, 27/9/89.

323   See Amate, *Inside the OAU*, pp 199-200.

324   Hyppolite-Manigat, 'Le groupe de l'Organisation de l'unité africaine', pp 78-79.

325   Krasner, 'Regimes and the limits of realism'.

326   Interview with Amadou Kebe, Addis Ababa, 3/10/89 (n. 5).

327   Rothstein, 'Regime-Creation' (n. 20).

328   See for this incident Amate, *Inside the OAU*, pp 200-202.

329   CM/Res.477 (XXVII).

330   Krasner, 'Regimes and the limits of realism'. Also K. Mathews, 'The African Group at the UN as an Instrument of African Diplomacy', in *Nigerian Journal of International Affairs*, 1988, no. 1, pp 252-254.

The alternative of integration: perceptions and practice

Thus, if the idea underlying the leverage mechanism is correct one may argue that it needs more far-reaching forms of institutionalization to harvest any significant increase in influence. Perceptions of the OAU show that state elites have been aware of this at least since the early 1970s. Some have stressed that improvement of Africa's legal position in the UN is not enough, as domination of the Security Council by certain non-African countries is a reflection of economic and military power outside the world body. Only if Africa would become economically stronger would inequalities in the UN be minimized.[331] The need for economic integration, both regionally and through the OAU, has therefore been regularly attested. It was said that the issues of African unity were "essentially economic" and that, in order to become "viable", the OAU should be restructured and engage in economic co-operation.[332] Some implicitly argued that this would reinforce the operation of the leverage mechanism, thus strengthening Africa's weight in the global order.[333]

However, such statements require careful interpretation. For example, in 1973 the president of Ivory Coast pleaded for various frameworks of continental economic co-operation so that Africa would exercise its "real" weight on the world scene. Voting resolutions would change nothing.[334] Yet, Ivory Coast also developed close economic ties with the West and was, certainly at that stage, prepared to work through established structures of international exchange, something that made economic integration in the West African region very difficult.[335] Thus, on closer inspection its comments speak of economic integration as an *ultimate* objective or lay stress on the more limited goal of caucusing in international economic negotiations.[336]

State elite perceptions of the OAU often noted the gap between formal profession of the goal of economic integration and the lack of concrete steps necessary to further that objective. Some explained this by emphasizing the importance of political will.[337] One may, indeed, argue that the absence of hegemonic leadership is at the bottom of this, especially as powerful external factors would make the generation of sufficient collective will in this issue area extremely difficult.[338] Thus, it has been shown that economic integration in the context of external dependence is hard to achieve, as in such situations it is difficult to avoid pursuance of contradictory policies.[339] Integration is, in general, hard to realize in the context of recession, while uneven distribution of its gains creates its own

---

331   *Daily Times* (Nigeria), 20/7/85. Also *ibid.*, 1/7/77.

332   See f.i. *Révolution Africaine* (Algeria), 18-24/5/73 and 9-15/3/77; *l'Essor* (Mali), 9-10/6/73; *Daily News* (Tanzania), 25/5/73; and *Daily Mail* (Sierra Leone), 1/7/80 (all articles).

333   *Le Courrier d'Afrique* (Zaire), 12/9/67 (article) and *Botswana Daily News*, 23/6/72 (extracts Assembly speech).

334   *Fraternité*, 1/6/73 (Assembly speech) and 14/6/74.

335   See generally D.C. Bach, 'The Politics of West African Economic Co-operation: CEAO and ECOWAS', in *Journal of Modern African Studies*, 1983, pp 605-623.

336   *Fraternité*, 1/6/73 (Assembly speech) and 11/5/73 (article).

337   See f.i. *Botswana Daily News*, 10/12/76 (article) and *Le Soleil* (Senegal), 19/11/84 (Assembly speech) and 18/7/85 (article).

338   Generally Rothstein, 'Regime-Creation'.

339   See on perception of such incompatibilities f.i. *Révolution Africaine* (Algeria), 9-15/3/77 and 9-15/5/80 (articles).

problems.[340]

However, there is more at stake than the structural constraints of international relations. The feelings of elite deprivation discussed above are principally articulated, as Ayoob notes for Third World countries generally,[341] at the collective level and do not take precedence over shorter-term concerns. While it is clear that all countries support the creation of greater collective power, one cannot assume consensus on its distribution in political and economic influence for individual member states. In the present this means that it is hard to convince them to sacrifice a portion of their actual power — in the sense of a restriction of state sovereignty — necessary for the leverage mechanism to generate a more significant increase in collective influence. This is reinforced by the fact that the increases in power prophesied continually recede into a distant future and that the notions on them have always been rather inarticulate. The result is that, contrary to their rhetoric, member states have not genuinely aimed at uplifting the continent and all of its peoples. Rather, they contented themselves for long with the smaller fruits of caucusing, which delivered Africa's state elites concrete influence in conference politics and soothed their personal anxieties.

The whole issue of the OAU's external collective influence is thus related to the domestic role of state elites. In this respect there appeared, during the 1980s, some frank comments in governmental publications on the reasons behind the OAU's failure to realize continental integration. One view observed that the cross-border activities of the people at large contrasted sharply with Africa's leadership, which clung to the preservation of frontiers and pursued short-term economic policies marked by egoism and xenophobia.[342] Another comment stressed that Africa's salvation would not come if the OAU's role would remain limited to that of trade union of the powerful. One needed to involve Africa's peoples in the steps towards economic integration, on the basis of a popular kind of Pan-Africanism.[343] In this respect it was stressed that among the reasons for the lack of progress were the absence of domestic pressure groups and the embryonic state of the media. Governments therefore gave priority to the problems of the day, rather than long-term objectives.[344]

Nevertheless, in the deteriorating conditions of the 1980s and 1990s it became increasingly clear to member states that co-operation had to be strengthened to stem the downward slide in the international economic order. In an interview in 1989 one diplomat argued that, as the OAU lacked the powers to do this, one had to establish an African Common Market, equipped with sufficient prerogatives.[345] This idea had already been pleaded by Nkrumah but was rejected at the time as premature. Yet, faced with a worsening crisis the OAU adopted major policy documents on collective self-reliance

---

340   See K. van Walraven, 'Some Aspects of Regional Economic Integration in Africa', in *Hague Yearbook of International Law*, 1991, pp 106-126 and for non-governmental perception of these difficulties f.i. *Téré* (Ivory Coast), 15-22/7/91 (article).

341   Ayoob, 'Third World in the System of States' (n. 134), p 72.

342   *Cameroon Tribune*, 9/8/86 (article). Also *ibid.*, 31/5/91 and the non-governmental *Téré* (Ivory Coast), 15-22/7/91 (both articles).

343   *Le Soleil* (Senegal), 25/7/86 (article).

344   *Cameroon Tribune*, 8/8/86 (article).

345   Interview with Amadou Kebe, Addis Ababa, 3/10/89.

(1980), recovery (1985) and debt resettlement (1987).[346] These could not, however, prevent further deterioration and were left unimplemented due to inaction of member states and an unco-operative Western response.[347]

The answer to the failures of the 1980s were sought, yet again, within the paradigm of unity.[348] Thus, in 1991 member states signed a treaty for a fully-fledged "African Economic Community" (AEC). Working through regional organizations as ECOWAS and SADC the AEC should be established in six stages not exceeding a total period of 34 years. It would involve full economic and monetary union. Being an integral part of the OAU it would be composed of the same organs, in addition to a "Court of Justice" with full legal powers; various "Technical Committees" and a "Pan-African Parliament".[349] The aim of such a parliament would be to fully involve the peoples of Africa in the drive towards continental integration.[350]

The alternative of integration: theoretical perspective
It remains to be seen whether the project will come to fruition. In view of the above its success would ultimately depend, among others, on a thorough restructuring of domestic socio-political configurations.[351] That there is, nevertheless, unrelenting logic in these OAU efforts is also supported by one particular strand in international relations theory. This is a school of thought that seeks a reform of the global order — which is seen as unjust to the Third World — on the basis of regional (or continental) integration.

An exponent of this argument is Kothari, who clearly articulated the idea of the leverage mechanism. He has argued that, if Third World countries combine their political and economic forces, they can bridge the gap in (political, military, technical) power between North and South. This combination of forces should realize autonomy and self-respect. With such autonomy Third World countries would have the capability to demand transformations in the international economic order. This autonomy requires the establishment of economic unions between countries on the basis of complementarity of resources and geographical contiguity. While being aware of their hurdles, Kothari has argued that this could be realized by way of regional federations. These should be marked by internal decentralization, instruments for dispute settlement and popular participation. Federal units (countries) should not be able to dominate each other, while global institutions in various issue areas should limit the risk of domination by one federation of

---

346 Plan d'Action de Lagos pour le Développement Economique de l'Afrique and Acte Final de Lagos, Lagos, 28-29/4/80; Africa's Priority Programme for Economic Recovery 1986-1990, Addis Ababa, 18-20/7/85; and the African Common Position on Africa's External Debt Crisis, Addis Ababa, December 1987.

347 Interview with Dr. J.A. Tesha, Addis Ababa, 25/9/89 (n. 105) and Address by the Secretary-General, May 1993, p 11 ff.

348 See *Le Soleil* (Senegal), 20-21/7/85 (Assembly speech) and 5/6/91 (interview with President Diouf); *Daily News* (Tanzania), 22/7/85; *Jornal de Angola*, 22/7/89 (article); *l'Essor* (Mali), 15/7/90 (article); and Address by the Secretary-General, May 1993, pp 14-17.

349 Text in *International Legal Materials*, 1991, pp 203-243.

350 Article 14.1, AEC Treaty. This idea was especially pleaded by Senegal. See *Le Soleil*, 4/6/91 (article).

351 As realized in Address by the Secretary-General, May 1993, p 19. An optimistic comment in *Cameroon Tribune*, 4/6/91, portrayed the project as the "anti-chambre" of a United States of Africa. A sober non-governmental comment in *Téré* (Ivory Coast), 15-22/7/91 (article).

another. This danger should be principally tackled by aiming at the formation, in the entire world, of some twenty to 25 federal structures that would be comparable in size, population, resources and productive potential.[352]

Thus, instead of mere caucusing in international diplomacy, the leverage mechanism would demand the formation of structures marked by a considerable degree of integration and a qualitatively high standard of internal political, social and economic relations. At least on the level of consciousness one sometimes finds similar arguments among OAU member states, that much more is, indeed, needed. For example, in 1986 Senegal argued that unity was no "invisible power", but had to be constructed, reconstructed and consolidated. It demanded discipline. Member states had to abide by OAU decisions and resolve inter-state conflicts by negotiation and dialogue.[353]

On the basis of Kothari's argument one might contend that the OAU provides the wrong geographical scale for integration. Yet other scholars, such as Guernier, have pleaded, especially on the basis of politico-economic arguments, for the establishment of a structure encompassing at least the sub-Saharan countries.[354]

Whatever the merits of that strategy, the emphasis that the AEC project puts on the importance of regional economic organizations as SADC and ECOWAS shows that this OAU initiative is not based on some naive continentalist sentiment. It takes into account that Africa is not an integrated unit, economically or otherwise, and links up with some of the African (academic and political) thinking that was spurred on by the crisis of the late 1980s and early 1990s. This thinking continues to build on the kind of integration theory as propagated by Kothari and Guernier in earlier days. For example, one scholar has argued that the continent needs "political remapping" if Africa's role in world politics is to change. This remapping should involve transformation of African states, as they suffer from lack of legitimacy. Only then would they be able to contribute positively to the life of ordinary Africans. Remapping should also involve delinking from the international economic system. This would not amount to autarky but a development approach aimed at revising Africa's role in the world economy. Its regional economic organizations could serve as catalysts for federations. The AEC project should rest on these regional organizations, but also on a "continental political project". Africa would, after all, remain a part of world politics.[355]

In this respect the author argues for a "realist" Pan-Africanism. Others, like former Secretary-General Edem Kodjo, have argued in a similar vein.[356] In the context of Africa's deteriorating political and economic conditions this modernist ideology enjoys increased popularity in non-governmental circles. For example, the Seventh Pan-African Congress, bringing together over 500 people in Uganda, discussed various issues that also figure on OAU agenda's, such as IMF structural adjustment policies, debt, aids and

---

352   See R. Kothari, *Footsteps into the Future: Diagnosis of the Present World and a Design for an Alternative* (New York, 1974).

353   *Le Soleil* (Senegal), 29/7/86 (Assembly speech).

354   See M. Guernier, *Tiers-Monde: trois quarts du monde* (Paris, 1980), pp 98-103.

355   T. Lumumba-Kasongo, *Political Re-Mapping of Africa: Transnational Ideology and the Re-Definition of Africa in World Politics* (Lanham, New York and London, 1994), chs. 7-8.

356   E. Kodjo, *... et demain l'Afrique* (Paris, 1985), ch. 12.

democratization.[357]

However, in whatever way Africa and the OAU seek to solidify and improve the continental order and increase collective influence, a fundamental problem is that the obstacles are intricately linked. As with the management of conflicts significant improvements in the continent's external influence and the OAU's role therein are simultaneously hindered by the structural impediments of international relations and the vicissitudes in domestic socio-political configurations. These factors reinforce each other. Nevertheless, with regard to the external dimension of Africa's political and socio-economic problems most solutions, whether governmental or non-governmental, are in practice sought within the paradigm of unity. We will return to these observations in the epilogue.

8.4 Evaluations

As with the struggle against colonialism and white minority regimes, OAU efforts to manage the various dimensions of the continental order have been constricted by the structural impediments of Africa's international relations. Lack of hegemonic leadership and intruding extra-African factors have restricted opportunities for the exertion of influence in (inter-)African politics. This has always precluded a forceful OAU posture vis-à-vis disputants and has made for a minimal strategy in conflict management.

While the OAU has had a moderate record in the settlement of inter-state disputes, during the last two decades this came under increasing pressure. In the changing context of the late 1980s and early 1990s important reforms were introduced to enhance the Organization's effectiveness. As can be gleaned from the improved status of the Assembly Bureau, these reforms amount to a game theoretical strategy of actor reduction. The novelty of the new mechanism lies in the improvement of reactive capacity and in greater co-ordination and continuity of mediation efforts. However, the approach to conflicts has not become more comprehensive, as the mechanism emphasizes prevention and early containment so as to avoid difficult and expensive military interventions. With the OAU's limited resources avoidance of responsibilities that it might not be able to handle shows some political wisdom.

The OAU's disregard, until 1990, of domestic conflicts that were not marked by substantial extra-African involvement or did not carry implications for inter-African politics, was founded on callous logic. Yet by the late 1980s this approach, with its related culture of silence on the predicament of the mass of Africa's peoples, began increasingly to backfire on state elite interests. Disregard of domestic security contexts helped little, as such crises tended to deteriorate and refused to go away. Confronted with a weakening position as a result of the economic crisis, aid conditionality, withdrawal of superpower support and the emergence of multi-party politics member states had to take some action to prevent further deterioration of the continental order.

Thus, the OAU formally arrogated domestic conflicts to its area of competence

---

357   3-8 April 1994. See 7th Pan-African Congress: One Struggle, Many Fronts! (Int. Prep. Committee: Kampala, n.d.). Also *New African*, June 1994 and *West Africa*, 18-24/4/94 and 25/4-1/5/94.

(1990), setting in motion a process of shifting in the rationale underlying its conflict management. While the old minimal strategy remained intact, the rationale behind the Organization's activation broadened. From now on the OAU could concern itself with internal conflicts whether or not these were marked by extra-African involvement or other inter-African repercussions. Humanitarian concerns, intensification and regional spreading may be sufficient grounds for activation. Moreover, wider aspects of internal developments, such as monitoring of constitutional conferences and elections, have also become part of the OAU's area of competence. This shift is not only a logical result of the end of the Cold War, but also of Africa's own worsening security situations and changes in domestic political configurations. The future of the OAU's role is therefore dependent on the vicissitudes in internal developments, as well as the structures of Africa's international relations. One can thus still observe contradictory shifts and trends.

In the course of these reforms the OAU has also embarked on cautious peace-keeping activities. Their relevance is severely limited by constraints in financial and logistical resources and, fundamentally, the lack of hegemonic leadership. OAU peace-keeping therefore still needs extra-African support. Nevertheless, in comparison to its debacle in Chad the new activities in peace-keeping are embedded in a cadre of firm institutional control. However, while its increased peace-keeping activity is, from the perspective of the past, remarkable, OAU capabilities are still insufficient in high intensity conflict.

In essence two scenarios can be followed to alleviate the OAU's constraints, each with its own advantages and disadvantages. First, mediation and peace-keeping in regional cadres can help in the management of the continental order. In general, mediation efforts by regional states is often more effective as they have more leverage over disputants. However, if such states are fighting for regional dominance collective impotence becomes especially marked. This could be observed in various conflicts, such as the Ethiopian-Somali war over the Ogaden and the Chadian crisis. There are parallels here with the Western Sahara and Angolan cases discussed in chapter 6. Moreover, while peace-keeping through regional inter-African organizations may be more effective than in the OAU, it is also very susceptible to regional power struggles. ECOMOG's intervention in Liberia is a case in point. Like the Chadian case, Liberia shows that the influence of Africa's more powerful states must not be overrated. Part of this is caused by the constraints inherent in patron-client dialectics. The aspect of effective influence in regional hegemony is called into question by this. Moreover, in these cases the legitimacy of would-be hegemons was usually deficient. They also point to the lack of precision of the aspect of legitimacy in the concept of regional hegemony itself.

The second scenario that can be pursued to alleviate OAU constraints is intervention in UN cadres. While it is easier to mobilize the requisite political, financial and logistical resources, the vicissitudes of UNOSOM in Somalia show the limited relevance of peace-keeping as an instrument to solve complex domestic conflict. Not all types of conflict are amenable to mediation, let alone military solutions. The Chadian case makes clear that destructive conflicts, as coined by Deutsch, are such a category.

As with dispute settlement and peace-keeping, the external dimension to managing the continental order is also hindered by the structural constraints of international relations and domestic socio-political configurations.

Nevertheless, some OAU norms have been subject to revision, signifying a change of the OAU regime itself. The restriction of the non-intervention norm is a case in point. Revised recognition policy, as witnessed in the condemnation of the 1993 Burundi coup, is another. While fear of extra-African intervention has become less relevant in OAU activation, humanitarian concerns have become more important. Acceptance of Salim's ideas on the OAU's potential role in the domestic political order would, indeed, represent a radical change towards a regime that would cater for the interests of the mass of African peoples. Finally, the OAU also seems to incline more and more towards implementing a policy of economic integration.

However, with regard to integration the signs are uncertain. Moreover, many other norms are still intact, even if they are under pressure. *Uti possidetis* is still rigidly adhered to. This is also the case with the prohibition of secession, notwithstanding the exception of Eritrea. With its minimal approach to conflicts and limited protection of popular interests in the area of human rights and refugees, the OAU's elitist character still stands out. The norm on the OAU's competence of initial concern with African conflict has come under pressure as a result of the end of the Cold War and the need for peace-keepers from the UN and other inter-African organizations. However, the debate on the financial aspects of the new conflict management mechanism shows that fear of extra-African intrusion has not completely disappeared. Moreover, while such fear has diminished, dismay over Africa's marginalization in world affairs has to some extent taken its place.

Both the internal and external parts of the OAU's general ideology may therefore be in a process of shifting, but this has not yet led to a substantially different ideological basis. In its present form it depends on the absence of continental leadership in inter-African relations, persistence of structural inequalities between Africa and the Northern hemisphere and, in domestic contexts, the durability of the old socio-political order. The fact that most OAU norms, principles and approaches have not yet undergone significant change points to the constancy of the underlying, though conflictual, structures of (inter-)African politics. It is true that some of the features of Africa's political economies are subject to profound change since the end of the Cold War,[358] or rather, that such change is deepening the effects of developments already visible since the late 1970s. Yet while marginalization and free market policies have brought forth new patterns of economic activities, opportunities and interest groups, Africa's state elites appear to have remarkable staying power. Barring the collapse of the Somali and Liberian states, the geo-political features of the continental order are therefore still essentially intact.

---

358   See esp. S. Ellis, 'Africa after the Cold War: New Patterns of Government and Politics', in
      Development and Change, 1996, pp 1-28.

Conclusions

9

9.1 Introduction

The purpose of this study was to find out how the Organization of African Unity functions, in an objective sense, in African politics. In this special emphasis was put on how this is perceived by member states and Secretariat functionaries (in terms of ideological dimensions attributed to the OAU) and African non-governmental circles. In attempting to answer this central research question we also hoped to point out the explanatory value of certain theories of politics. Thus, several conclusions may now be drawn. Those on theoretical perspectives are mainly presented in section 9.2. This is followed by an assessment of the OAU with regard to the four major queries or issue areas treated in this study: its formation in 1963; its internal functioning; and its performance in the anti-colonial struggle and functioning in (inter-)African politics. Section 9.4 provides an appraisal of the OAU's ideology and related aspects. The epilogue following these conclusions presents some reflections on the need for, and possibilities of, a restructuring of Africa's politico-economic order.

9.2 Theories of politics

OAU functioning and hegemonic stability theory
While the contention of hegemonic stability theory, that co-operation *as such* cannot not emerge without the presence of one very powerful state, has been shown to be incorrect, the preceding chapters show that the absence of such a state does, indeed, account for many of the difficulties the OAU faces in realizing effective forms of co-operation. In this regard hegemonic stability theory is, with its emphasis on the relative anarchy of international politics, the importance of power in determining patterns of interaction and the problem of co-ordination of state behaviour, an attractive model for explaining the performance of an international organization. Its explanatory value is particularly relevant

as its arguments pertain to various dimensions of an organization's functioning and the different areas of co-operation with which it is concerned.

Thus, section 4.6 showed that the results of the OAU's founding conference were modest in the sense of producing a relatively weak form of Pan-African co-operation. This was closely bound up with the blurred configuration of power, which, at the time, was specially pronounced. No country could therefore dominate the conference and guarantee more forceful results.

Chapter 5 showed how the lack of a hegemon enables member states to adopt destructive postures vis-à-vis the roles, functioning and working conditions of Secretariat officials; how its absence entails considerable freedom of action for members, leading to consistently low budget votes and an overall difficult process of collecting dues; and how the lack of continental leadership has led to decision-making being marked by laborious, inefficient procedures, indecision and deferment.

In chapter 6 it was shown that the violation of OAU sanctions by member states was at least facilitated by lack of hegemonic control. As the theory argues that strong organizations with clear rules are dependent on the presence of a hegemonic leader it can, conversely, also explain the ambiguity of norms — such as the one condemning contact with white minority regimes if it occurred in normal, open fashion — by reference to the absence of such hegemony. Similarly, with the pursuit of the collective OAU goal of armed liberation being guaranteed by a few states, the generally sloppy record of payment to the Special Fund was tied to the lack of continental leadership and, thus, free riding vis-à-vis obligations coming on top of the requirements of sanctions and collective diplomacy aimed at isolating the target regimes.

Chapter 7 showed that the lack of hegemonic leadership and, more generally, the restricted opportunities for the exertion of influence in inter-African politics preclude forceful postures in conflict mediation and dictate a minimal strategy aiming at persuasion and containment. The deleterious effects of the lack of such leadership are amplified, as illustrated in section 8.2, when dispute settlement involves the more demanding military aspects of conflict management. Thus, it seriously hampered the introduction of a Pan-African security scheme, left the OAU Peace Force in Chad with insufficient resources and direction and restricted the scope of peace-keeping activities undertaken in the context of the institutional reforms of the early 1990s.

Any objection that, as this study applied hegemonic stability theory *a contrario*, it produced no direct evidence for its validity, may be countered by reference to UNOSOM I. While being far from a successful exercise in conflict management, UNOSOM was characterized by the willingness of African states to dispatch thousands of troops in a relatively short space of time. The direction of the operation was at least less ambiguous than that of the OAU Force in Chad and enjoyed proper logistical and financial arrangements. American and UN leadership proved essential here.

As section 5.6 showed, the ingredients for the exercise of Pan-African hegemony are missing. In the OAU there is no state powerful enough to force or persuade all others to conform. Even the more influential members are forced to negotiate with the weaker ones, which successfully reject the legitimacy of claims to the status of continental hegemon on their part.

Thus, in all above-mentioned areas one can argue that the OAU was not so much hampered by lack of individual political will but by its inability, through lack of leadership, to sufficiently co-ordinate the willingness of the collectivity of states. In this respect it must be borne in mind that states are never faced with one, but with multiple, different objectives and that, without such leadership to influence their choices, the rational inclination to get by as cheaply as possible may easily prevail. By emphasizing the problems of co-ordination of individual will — rather than stressing the absence of such willingness — and therefore pointing to inability to realize effective co-operation, hegemonic stability theory in principle provides a cause for the absence of such co-operation.

However, at times its application seems to point more to *how* such co-operation fails to materialize than to *why*: that the absence of hegemonic leadership makes its realization difficult is then seen as sufficient explanation. In view of the limited degree of interdependence characterizing inter-African relations, one may indeed argue that co-operation is never self-evident and that the existence of structural impediments as such therefore often constitutes adequate explanation. One must, however, be careful not to blur the semantic distinction between why and how. Thus, in certain situations of OAU functioning lack of hegemonic leadership provides no convincing explanation, as it leads to different forms of behaviour among member states. For example, section 5.5 showed that the overall difficulties in OAU budgeting are tied to the free rider dilemma, but that individual records of payment are also influenced by the degree of a government's commitment to respect its obligations to the OAU. Apparently other explanations are needed as well.

Regional hegemony and the OAU: struggles and concept
The preceding chapters show that if certain states were competing for the status of hegemon of their region the effectiveness of the OAU would be sharply reduced. Their rivalry would diminish its leverage in crisis situations and could, in combination with extra-African forces, paralyse decision-making. The negative effects of such regional divisions were most severe in the Angolan crisis; the conflict over the Western Sahara; and the civil war in Chad. Yet to a greater or lesser extent they also played a role in the Shaba crisis; the war over the Ogaden; and, before the 1970s, in the Liberation Committee's policies towards guerrilla movements.

While their competition hampered the OAU's effectiveness, the claim of individual countries to the status of regional hegemon was, nevertheless, usually deficient. Thus, the leaders of the alliances that preceded the OAU's birth suffered restrictions on influence that ultimately helped to destroy those coalitions. In later days Southern African countries faced constraints on influence in the Angolan crisis and, to a lesser extent, the struggle for Zimbabwe. Chad confronted Nigeria and Libya with the limits of power. Even in the Liberian civil war Nigerian intervention exposed the restrictions on influence of regional powers, rather than their ability to direct the course of events. Thus, not only on a continental level but also regionally did the OAU frequently lack effective leadership. This underlines its difficulties in realizing effective co-operation and reinforces the contention of hegemonic stability theory.

Looking at the nature of the constraints on the influence of all these would-be hegemons some light is shed on the inadequacy of the concept of regional hegemony itself. In view of the above the element of power in regional hegemony appears to be rather imprecise. First, Nigeria's intervention in Chad showed that willingness to use national capabilities to maximize a country's interests is an essential condition for the successful exercise of influence. The same may be argued in terms of hegemonic stability theory.

Second, the element of influence in regional hegemony does not account for one particular phenomenon that restricts its effective exercise, namely the constraints that emanate from inter-client rifts and those that are inherent in patron-client interaction. In chapter 6 it was shown that divisions between liberation movements also involved rivalry between their patron states, which constricted the effective influence of those countries. This was the case in Angola and to a lesser extent the struggle for Zimbabwe. These cases, as well as Libya's experience in Chad, confirm Lemarchand's contention that patron-client ties are not a one way affair. They involve reciprocal manipulation and even conflictual dimensions,[1] which entail restrictions on the influence of the would-be hegemon. The concept of regional hegemony should account for this, especially in the African context where violent inter-state conflict usually takes the form of subversive support for domestic opposition groups.

Third, the more robust capabilities that must be at the source of regional hegemony — such as military might, a solid socio-economic base and support of non-African powers — are sometimes underplayed to the detriment of the more subtle sources of influence, such as a good diplomatic network[2] and the hegemon's enjoyment of legitimacy. With regard to the latter, preceding chapters showed that both in the cadre of the OAU and in regional contexts other states reject claims to such legitimacy on the part of the would-be hegemon. In cases where it is not rejected Scott's insights on the concept of legitimacy[3] would suggest that such countries at best manage to win acquiesence in their policies, rather than genuine consent. This was the case, for example, with domination by the Frontline alliance over OAU policy vis-à-vis Zimbabwe. Even if one argues, along Gramscian lines, that hegemony allows for uneven degrees of legitimacy, this weakens the effective influence of the hegemon.[4] The element of legitimacy in the regional hegemony concept therefore also needs further refinement.

---

1   R. Lemarchand, 'On Comparing Regional Hegemons: Libya and South Africa', in R. Lemarchand (ed), *The Green and the Black: Qadhafi's Policies in Africa* (Bloomington and Indianapolis, 1988), p 176. See also M. Ougaard, 'Dimensions of Hegemony', in *Conflict and Cooperation*, 1988, pp 203-204.

2   See especially R. Iyob, 'Regional Hegemony: Domination and Resistance in the Horn of Africa', in *Journal of Modern African Studies*, 1993, pp 257-276.

3   J.C. Scott, *Domination and the Arts of Resistance: Hidden Transcripts* (New Haven and London, 1990), pp 70-76.

4   W.L. Adamson, *Hegemony and Revolution: A Study of Antonio Gramsci's Political and Cultural Theory* (Berkeley, Los Angeles and London, 1980), ch. 6. Ougaard, 'Dimensions of Hegemony', p 204, solves this point by arguing that hegemony contains, besides congruent interests, conflicting patterns of a secondary nature.

External dependence, dependency theory and the OAU

If one wishes to look for explanations of OAU functioning, that are not adequately tackled by hegemonic stability theory, in the area of external dependence one may object that answers are again sought in the structures of Africa's international relations and, thus, to some extent in terms of how, rather than why, co-operation is achieved or not. In this respect it has been observed that it is not always easy to measure precisely the effect of dependence on, and how this exactly relates to, the actions or inaction of the elites in the world's periphery.[5]

However, this study shows clearly that, overall, African dependence tends to reinforce the effects of the absence of hegemonic leadership. This enhances the cogency of hegemonic stability theory. In several cases there is evidence, direct or circumstantial, for relating specific examples of the OAU's performance to the patterns of external dependence. To mention only the most obvious ones, one can think here of the contacts between Francophone leaders and De Gaulle immediately following upon the OAU's formation and the moderate approach to disarmament and economic co-operation decided at the Addis Ababa summit; the Stanleyville crisis of 1964; Belgian pressure and the 1967 evacuation of white mercenaries from Rwanda; the complications the Franco-African summits pose to OAU decision-making; non-compliance with OAU sanctions policy, especially by Southern African countries; and extra-African intervention in Angola, Shaba, the Western Sahara and Chad and the nature of the OAU's response to those crises.

Thus, while patterns of dependence may not explain all intricacies of purely inter-African interaction the above-mentioned examples point to the relevance of dependence — if not of dependency theory as such — in some very specific issues of internal OAU decision-making. Yet, some aspects of the OAU's performance show that Africa's state elites have a limited freedom of manoeuvre, as the subtler version of dependency theory would argue. The successful functioning of the Organization as an instrument with which to enhance the collective and individual influence of African states is an obvious example of this. It also points to the ambivalence of their state elites vis-à-vis the global order, something that involves the psychological dimension of dependence discussed in section 9.4. However, at least as far as the OAU is concerned the central contention of dependency theory is upheld, as the OAU's leverage mechanism and economic co-operation do not involve dissociation from the world economy and have not led to a lessening of dependence.

The OAU and the (sub-)state level of analysis

Struggles for regional hegemony and patterns of external dependence reinforce the effects of absence of leadership and, so, the central contention of hegemonic stability theory.

However, this still leaves the fact that the absence of leadership sometimes leads to different forms of behaviour among OAU member states. Thus, this study showed that some states are, as a matter of policy, committed to paying their dues to the OAU, while others apparently lack such a stance. It was also shown that some states were much more

---

5   See also S.M. Smith, 'Economic Dependence and Economic Empiricism in Black Africa', in *Journal of Modern African Studies*, 1977, pp 116-118.

determined in assisting the armed struggle in Southern Africa than others. Moreover, the contents of OAU co-operation as such cannot, in principle, be explained in terms of international relations. Hegemonic stability theory does not say anything about the substance of an organization's policies once leadership has secured sufficient collective will to act. The same is implied in the limited room of manoeuvre that the subtle version of dependency theory allows to peripheral elites.

One may, of course, argue that the contents of certain policies and the form in which they are implemented are at least affected by the structures of international relations. For example, the collective aspiration to greater influence in global politics is directly related to, and brought about by, the discrepancy in the balance of power between Africa and the West. Its logic cannot be understood without reference to the facts of international politics. Yet, these had to be perceived and processed by state elites before they could give rise to Pan-African policy. Moreover, preceding chapters showed that the precarious domestic position of state elites was part of the source of their deprivation and search for greater security and influence.

In many cases the contents of OAU policies and postures is therefore affected or determined by the particular features of African governments and their place in the domestic configurations of power. Thus, the course of the debate on dialogue was strongly affected by the historical background and character of Africa's state elites. The Organization's meagre resources for the care of refugees were related not so much to difficulties in co-ordinating the collective will of member states as to the socially one-sided role that the OAU played in regard to the continent's domestic political orders. Its past culture of silence vis-à-vis human rights violations, its disregard of the plight of the southern Sudanese and Eritreans and, more generally, its neglect of any domestic developments that did not involve substantial non-African interference or inter-African implications were similarly grounded in the peculiarities of domestic political configurations and the nature of African state elites. Even the OAU's peace-keeping effort in Chad, while seriously affected by the impediments of Africa's international relations, only got under way when it developed repercussions for the regional balance of power. The misery the war caused to the Chadian people as such did not form the reason for intervention.

Thus, international relations theories as those on hegemonic stability and dependency do not provide *comprehensive* models for understanding an international organization's functioning. This makes it imperative to adopt an eclectic approach as long as there are no theories that can satisfactorily explain all the facets of such an institution. Moreover, the above also necessitates the involvement of other levels of analysis as such.

First, there are the interaction patterns between states. Preceding chapters noted that Stein has argued that international relations do not wholly determine the choices of states. These also depend on the calculations by governments, which are affected both by what other states do and their own (original) objectives. As shown above the latter are in part determined by factors that belong to the domestic political context. The basis of calculations, that leads to an actual policy choice, is therefore a variable in its own right, separate from the structures of international relations.[6] This involves the state and sub-state level of analysis.

With regard to the calculations of governments Stein contends that there is often no clear sight on the costs and benefits of policy choices. Governments therefore often face multiple alternatives, each of which may form a rational option within the constrictions of available information. This may, for example, generate contradictions between short-term and long-term interests, with the way in which states assess their priority on the basis of their perception of security. States whose survival is guaranteed can afford to think in the long-term.[7]

This argument explains the vicissitudes, *over time*, in some of the collectively held OAU policies. It provides added force to the dualist dilemma that Ayoob sees in the security concerns of Third World countries.[8] As was shown in preceding chapters this dualism explains some of the contradictory behaviour of countries that collectively feared and sought to discourage extra-African intervention in continental affairs and desired an end to white minority regimes, but individually would, if necessary, invite non-African backing in conflicts or violate OAU sanctions against South Africa. This in turn explains the innately dialectical nature of some of the OAU responses to particular events, like its reactions to the Stanleyville dropping (1964) and the stand of the Libreville summit on the Shaba crisis (1977).

The above shows not only that domestic politics needs to be integrated in theories of international co-operation[9] but also that, more generally, the very distinction between international and domestic politics must be called in question. In the African context this distinction is even more artificial than elsewhere. Because of the external origins of the post-colonial state, its difficult relations with civil society and the porous nature of state frontiers the line between domestic and international is blurred. Despite governmental emphasis on state sovereignty and strict formal border regimes patterns of interaction regularly cut across frontiers. Instability emanating from the dialectical ties between state and civil society easily spills over state boundaries. While flows of refugees, subversive support to opposition groups of other states and aspirations to regional hegemony, with its related patron-client ties, transgress the distinction between domestic and international politics, they also restrict — as the controversial character of the post-colonial state itself — the salience of these concepts. Any model of international relations in Africa therefore needs to take these fundamental features of "domestic" politics into account.

Game theoretical perspectives and co-operation in the OAU
This study confirms the contention that measures to reduce the number of actors can improve the effectiveness of co-operation. Such reduction makes situations more transparent and diminishes anonimity and therefore the possibilities of free riding. It

---

6   A.A. Stein, *Why Nations Cooperate: Circumstances and Choice in International Relations* (Ithaca and London, 1990).

7   *Ibid.*

8   M. Ayoob, 'The Third World in the System of States: Acute Schizophrenia or Growing Pains?', in *International Studies Quarterly*, 1989, pp 67-79.

9   As argued by H. Milner, 'International Theories of Cooperation Among Nations: Strengths and Weaknesses', in *World Politics*, 1992, pp 488-495.

improves reciprocity between actors and, hence, the likelihood of their compliance with policy.[10] Thus, in certain cases the OAU delegated tasks to, or allowed them to be executed by, a few member states in order to realize one of its Pan-African policies. The principal examples are the role of the Frontline alliance in fulfilling the OAU's goal to end white minority rule; the reliance on ECOWAS to intervene in the Liberian civil war; and the establishment of a semi-permanent Assembly Bureau to enable the OAU to take swifter action in conflict management. In all these cases decision-making was or is more effective than when it occurs in the OAU's general policy organs.

However, there are also other ways to create conditions for the realization of OAU goals. Improving reciprocity of interaction between states may also be achieved by way of future sessions of the general policy organs. As they make it possible to put pressure on members, they serve as a threat of potential retaliation against those that do not comply with policy. Examples are the pressure exerted on members to pay their dues before summit conferences and the fierce debate on dialogue, which made any open, high profile diplomatic contact with Pretoria an unattractive prospect. Pressure towards compliance may be even stronger when the norms in question are internalized by the member states, *i.e.* considered as valuable in themselves.[11] Examples of this in the OAU were and are the stand on dialogue and the norm of *uti possidetis*.

Yet, in the OAU actor reduction tactics are a more effective means to improve the possibilities for co-operation than reliance on sessions of the policy organs. These are rather infrequent. Moreover, interdependence in general is underdeveloped and legal sanctions are non-existent or cannot (readily) be applied. This precludes a forceful posture towards members, as do the opportunities for delegitimizing state behaviour. These were, for long, extremely limited. Furthermore, some OAU postures are rather ambiguous, such as the criticism of trade links with South Africa in so far as these were unnecessarily expanded or engaged in openly. Violation of other norms is sometimes hard to prove, as shown in the empirical difficulties surrounding the enforcement of the anti-subversion norm. This also limits possibilities for delegitimating state behaviour. Threatening retaliation in case of widespread violations, as with regard to budget payments and sanctions against South Africa, may anyway be counter-productive. It can invite the collapse of co-operation altogether.

The OAU in terms of regime theory

At the beginning of this section it was noted that hegemonic stability theory is incorrect when it argues that, without a leader, co-operation cannot emerge *at all*. Regime theory explains this by observing that the influence of an international regime can compensate the lack of hegemonic leadership and still make co-operation possible. In so far as the OAU provides for forms of Pan-African co-operation in the context of a complete absence of continental leadership it confirms this contention of regime theory. There are two dimensions to this.

---

10   K.A. Oye, 'Explaining Cooperation Under Anarchy: Hypotheses and Strategies', in K.A. Oye (ed), *Cooperation Under Anarchy* (Princeton, 1986), pp 20-22.

11   *Ibid.*, pp 11 and 16-17.

First, the OAU provides for inter-African co-operation on a continental scale. Because of the limited patterns of bilateral interaction its sessions represent a rare possibility for countries located in different regions to get in touch with each other. Co-operation through the OAU thus delivers information and reduces the costs that states have to make to engage in interaction. Moreover, it was shown that through the OAU the smaller states can exercise influence in inter-African politics, as the more powerful actors are forced to negotiate with the weaker ones to get approval of certain policies. The numerous smaller actors have bargaining power with which to extricate concessions or even prevent the stronger ones from realizing certain goals.

Thus, in the Chadian crisis the egalitarian features implicit in the Pan-African cadre restricted Nigeria's ambitions much more than West African states could when Lagos intervened in Liberia. A regime like the OAU therefore enhances or circumscribes the ability of states to exercise actual influence. It is its norms and principles and its ability to legitimize or condemn state behaviour in terms of these collective values that are crucial here. For example, delegitimation of secession dealt a blow to Biafra's diplomatic position; pursuit of dialogue was restricted by its collective denunciation; and the Somali position over the Ogaden was weakened by the OAU's reiteration of *uti possidetis*. Member states therefore always manoeuvre in a bid to obtain approval of their policies or disapproval of those of other governments. Naturally, this does not alter underlying capabilities of states. The OAU's powers of denunciation are limited. Moreover, the more powerful countries can circumvent control by the numerous and weak by taking recourse to other fora, as Nigeria did with regard to Liberia. They may even leave an organization altogether, as Morocco did with regard to the OAU over the Western Sahara crisis. Such options, however, may not always be practical.

In any case, the above confirms Krasner's contention that regimes do affect the behaviour of states and the patterns of actual influence. It contradicts, however, his argument that regimes may also alter the underlying capabilities of power.[12] This is also the case with the extra-African dimension of co-operation provided by the OAU. As the structures of Africa's international relations would nevertheless be different if the OAU would not exist, the Organization does, indeed, constitute a regime. While some of its norms may not always be very effective and are ignored or transgressed by member states we do not share the contention of Haas that the failure to punish violations of a regime's norms is a sign of its non-existence.[13] Yet, it is obvious that the OAU regime is a weak one, especially in issue areas marked by (perceived) zero-sum conditions. In such cases, however, regimes in general tend to matter less than in other fields.[14] The overall weakness of the OAU regime also confirms the more general observations of Snidal and Rothstein that in state systems characterized by lack of hegemonic leadership, large

---

12   S.D. Krasner, 'Regimes and the limits of realism: regimes as autonomous variables', in S.D. Krasner (ed), *International Regimes* (London and Ithaca, 1983), pp 355-368.

13   E.B. Haas, 'Regime decay: conflict management and international organizations, 1945-1981', in *International Organization*, 1983, p 198.

14   See R. Jervis, 'Security regimes', in Krasner, *International Regimes*, pp 173-194 and for an equally sombre view J.J. Mearsheimer, 'The False Promise of International Institutions', in *International Security*, 1994/95, vol. 19, no. 3, pp 5-49.

numbers of small actors and intruding external forces resultant regimes are rather feeble.[15] Thus, regime theory does not subvert the key arguments of hegemonic stability theory and dependency theory.

9.3 The functioning of the OAU

Assessment in metaphor

Chapter 1 noted that metaphor is the key to understanding ideology. Thus, this study showed that the discourse in which Africans construct the OAU is often metaphorical. In this section OAU performance is evaluated as much as possible in terms of the central metaphors that figured in the titles of preceding chapter sections and around which the arguments of this study were constructed. The reasons are threefold. First, these metaphors reflect the OAU's functioning in a very lucid way and, second, relate to an aspect specially emphasized, namely the perceptions of this functioning in terms of roles and aims attributed to the OAU. In this way the link between objective performance and the ideological dimensions evaluated in the next section becomes more explicit. Finally, it will show that the different format in which Africans often describe (political) reality can be fruitfully combined with the more abstract forms of argument common in Western analytical traditions.[16]

The establishment of the OAU

At the close of its founding conference it was clear that, while the new continental regime was more than a temporary re-alignment of inter-state coalitions, no atomic blast had perturbed the political skies of inter-African relations or the world order. Yameogo's nuclear device had given off a squeak, as the Addis Ababa conference had resulted in a strictly inter-governmental organization with few autonomous powers and a strong emphasis on the sovereignty of the member states. Nevertheless, if a mouse had caused the Brazzaville delegate at the foreign ministers' conference some apprehension, it did squeak audibly. While not an atomic bomb it could, like all inter-governmental organizations, gnaw at the edges of the configurations of power.

Thus, the political fall-out of the OAU's birth was soon picked up in other parts of the world, as its member states became noticeably more vociferous and demanding on the point of action against colonial and white minority regimes.[17] With the help of their African Group they also began pressing for greater African representation in global fora. Moreover, the OAU's formation led to the abolition of competing organizations that catered for political co-operation on a Pan-African scale, although the survival of alliance

---

15   D. Snidal, 'The Limits of Hegemonic Stability Theory', in *International Organization*, 1985, p 595 and R.L. Rothstein, 'Regime-Creation by a Coalition of the Weak: Lessons from the NIEO and the Integrated Program for Commodities', in *International Studies Quarterly*, 1984, pp 307-328.

16   See on the cognitive role of metaphors in international relations generally K.L. Shimko, 'Metaphors and Foreign Policy Decision Making', in *Political Psychology*, 1994, pp 655-671.

17   See f.i. *Le Monde* (Paris), 23-24/6/63.

structures among Francophone states showed the limits of the OAU's supremacy and, hence, of its clout in African politics.

The establishment of the OAU was the result of a combination of forces, that to a greater or lesser extent had fragmented the Casablanca and Monrovia/Brazzaville alliances, and of centripetal pressures emanating from a collective awareness of certain common interests that made Pan-African co-operation imperative. The distinction in views underlying the alliances preceding the OAU, as well as the nature of the compromise reached with its foundation, are evaluated in the next section. Here it may be observed that the approach that the Addis Ababa conference adopted towards the global order and Africa's role therein was rather moderate. This was caused by powerful extra-African forces, that affected the attitudes and constricted the options of African state elites, and by the plural composition of these forces and patterns, which deprived the OAU of specificity of focus and, thus, strength. The countries that played a central role in the conference exerted considerable influence on its outcome but together were not powerful enough, as a dominant or hegemonic coalition, to guarantee more forceful results.

Nkrumah cannot be credited with the OAU's formation, at least not directly. His supra-national formula for union government never stood a chance of acceptance. In fact, the whole conference was a humiliation for the Osagyefo, as he had resisted its convocation and had tried to prevent any concrete outcome other than his grand vision. The proceedings were clearly marked by his isolation and limited influence in inter-African politics. The countries that dominated the conference and exercised the greatest influence on its outcome were Ethiopia, Guinea, Cameroon, Algeria and, to a lesser extent, Senegal, Tunisia, Mali, Tanganyika and Dahomey. Even Nigeria, whose role was equivocal, could be more satisfied with the OAU than Nkrumah.

Yet, one may contend that through the sheer noise he had made in preceding years he had given the question of Africa's unity such a sense of urgency that it survived the rifts in inter-African relations and even Ghana's own loss of leadership. Ironically, his actions also made it imperative to construct an institution that would preclude such claims to Pan-African hegemony. In this sense, Nkrumah's influence on the OAU's foundation is unmistakable.

Internal functioning

As was alluded to in the previous section, the modest outcome of the Addis Ababa conference was also reflected in the OAU's institutional make-up. It possesses a highly egalitarian structure which precludes conferment of privilege to certain members only. Organs of limited composition are therefore few and often have to allow access to all member states, if only in observer capacity. Moreover, in practice the distinction between observer and full membership is not always self-evident. The powers of organs not made up of member state representatives are usually limited to administrative and technical areas. It is the individual members, rather than the Secretariat, that must implement OAU policy. While the Organization has grown into a large structure with numerous agencies and committees, this evolution has left the control of member states over the OAU unimpaired. Their dominance is reflected in the dearth of concrete obligations they face, with only decisions on internal functioning being legally binding and provisions for sanctions lacking or not enforceable. Member states exercise their control of the OAU through the supremacy of the Assembly and, more generally, the dominant position of the general policy organs.

Thus, the house of Africans stands in an outlying locality. Its occupants are forced to limit themselves to formulating, launching and elaborating ideas that are decided and acted on elsewhere in the Organization or outside it. While they also observe and follow events unfolding in other parts of the continent and occasionally travel to the spots where these occur, they can only try to affect such developments and the decisions taken by others with appeals, pleas and arguments. So Secretariat staff need perseverance and optimism, but also improvising skills, as the house is generally poorly maintained.

As compared to other international organizations the occupants are modestly rewarded and have to perform their duties with insufficient funds, few and moderately trained hands and in a house with limited facilities. It has no good library, so the residents often borrow other people's books. With little professional mobility residents are often forced to stay in the quarters to which they were originally assigned. Moreover, those that pay for the house often interfere with the way it is run by the occupants. Member states do not always respect the international status of Secretariat officials. The latter are regularly criticized for their household routines and individual occupants are sometimes evicted.

The house's peripheral location also extends to the spatial dimension. Addis Ababa is sometimes dubbed Africa's diplomatic capital[18] but this may be an exclusively member state perception. As the lights of Paris and London are a greater attraction for elite Africans than the derelict world of the Ethiopian capital, the sense of marginalization surrounding the house's occupants is both political and geographical. Yet poor economic circumstances outside the house, in Ethiopia and elsewhere, provide it some power of attraction. In a more positive way, its cosmopolitanism appeals to the residents. With many of its occupants determined about their work, Claude's idealistic dreamers appear to have some spokesmen in the house of Africans.[19]

Their perceptions of the Secretariat's political importance may have become positively affected by the fact that, since the early 1990s, the house has undergone some renovation and reinforcement. Its task in monitoring conflicts received new impetus with the formation of a Division on Conflict Management. Reforms to tackle some of the financial problems of peace-keeping went hand in hand with a greater role for the Secretariat in OAU fact-finding and mediation efforts and the formal conferment to the Secretary-General of a broad right of diplomatic initiative. Again, an assessment of this can only be preliminary. The vicissitudes of budgeting will be crucial in determining whether the house can be lifted up and moved to a more central position in the OAU's structure. Moreover, even the upgrading of the role of the Secretary-General has left the Assembly's supremacy, through its Bureau, unimpaired, at least in a formal sense.

---

18   See f.i. *Dikgang Tsa Gompieno* (Botswana), 8/6/83 (article).
19   I.L. Claude, *Swords into Plowshares: The Problems and Progress of International Organization* (New York, 1964), pp 9 and 183.

It would therefore be an overstatement to argue, along the lines of Claude's view of international secretariats,[20] that the OAU's identity resides in the house of Africans. The embodiment of the Organization is the African Family itself. Its behaviour mirrors many of the fundamental features of (inter-)African politics. Thus, equality of all the kinsfolk is the Family's dominant value when it gathers to discuss lineage affairs. There being no official head of the Family, all brothers are equal. Although this perverts actual kinship conditions at the sub-state level, it means that all member states must be involved when decisions have to be made. No brother may be excluded — usually not even from organs of limited composition, like committees made up of a few member state delegates who prepare policy on aspects coming up for discussion in Council and Assembly.

Naturally, not all brothers exert equal influence. The ones continually present in the Family compound are better placed to affect events. Thus, countries with residential ambassadors in Addis Ababa are able to exercise considerable influence in the preparatory stages of OAU summits. Those brothers that are stronger, have louder voices and are better educated have an obvious advantage over their less endowed kin. As Nigeria showed by its intervention in Liberia, they can even be tempted to take matters out of the Family's purview and go it alone. Moreover, once the Family reaches a decision, its consensus may actually involve muted dissent on the part of some member states.

Nevertheless, its gatherings strongly espouse the values of egalitarianism. Leadership by any one brother is unlikely and its virtue is disputed, perhaps much more than in other, including non-African, contexts. This also means that it is hard to call Family members behaving badly to order. Beyond the collective compound every brother is a patriarch in his own right. Once assembled in the Family gathering they cannot recognize each other as their superior, something that illustrates Popitz's views on the context-dependent nature of authority.[21] Moreover, Family values for long served to protect brotherly interests alone, which implicitly legitimated the maltreatment of those not considered as kin. This was very clear before the early 1990s when the Family often assumed the workings of a trade union of the powerful. The result was that the suffering inflicted by state elites on the unprivileged masses of Africa's domestic political orders met with the OAU's culture of silence.

Since then brothers are confronted with new values outside the Family compound, such as democracy, multi-partyism and the rule of law. In part emanating from the house of Africans, some of these values trickle into the Family gathering, so that there is more room for calling brothers to account. Restriction of the non-intervention norm, humanitarian concerns as justification for mediating domestic crises and denunciation of the 1993 Burundi coup show that brotherly criticism can be targeted against Family members more than used to be the case.

Family membership entails that all those who are not kin are excluded from its decision-making. Brothers are generally rather vulnerable to enemies from Africa's domestic political order and its external (African and non-African) environment. They also suffer a sense of inferiority vis-à-vis the world's more powerful lineages. Thus, the

---

20   *Ibid.*, p 174.
21   H. Popitz, *Phänomene der Macht: Autorität-Herrschaft-Gewalt-Technik* (Tübingen, 1986), pp 11-14 and 25-26.

Assembly's discretionary, monopolistic disposition must uphold the pretence of Family autonomy and shield the collectivity of state elites from criticism by African non-governmental circles and the peering eyes of the West. Family rows being the worst kind of fights, sessions of Council and Assembly are held *in camera* and disputes between member states preferably kept inside. Above all, the village idiot must remain hidden from view inside the Family compound.

Without any single leader Family affairs are cumbersome. Speeching ritual detracts from Council and Assembly resolution, although it must be admitted that Family gatherings also have purely social functions — apart from deciding on action. Discussions easily become interminable, especially when matters involve brotherly disputes or are, more generally, considered controversial. Decision-making is often marked by indecision, deferment and, in view of the Assembly's monopolistic disposition, overloaded agenda's and inefficient task allocation.

Restricted possibilities of delegation entail low institutional capacity and hamper institutional development. Such evolution is also hindered by low budgetary levels and the practice of operating on arrears. This impairs long-term planning. The makeshift way in which back-payments are used depends on a constructive minority of countries that ensure continuity by always paying their dues. Since budgetary improvisation can only continue as long as arrears do not get out of control, the financial regime was tightened by the mid 1990s. Institutional flexibility is in this respect provided by the tendency to introduce reforms by separate decisions that circumvent the Charter, which is virtually unchangeable.

In the preceding section it was concluded that the most important condition under which the OAU is capable of realizing its objectives is by limiting the number of member states in the process of decision-making. The above shows, however, that it is quite difficult to forbid brothers entering the Family compound. In this respect the new semi-permanent Assembly Bureau, with its rotating restricted membership, constitutes a significant innovation that not only improves the OAU's resolution but also points to a shift in its underlying institutional culture. The tougher financial regime points in the same direction.

Barring actor reduction tactics decision-making depends heavily on the benign effects of criss-crossing alliance patterns. The significance of the various cleavages in inter-African relations were to this purpose evaluated in the fourth and fifth parts of section 5.6. Suffice it to say here that consensus in regional groupings is usually of great importance for realizing Pan-African postures. Divisions in such coalitions weaken the OAU's resolve. During the Cold War era such discord between close relatives could, in combination with non-African powers intruding in the compound, cripple Family life. The break-up of its gatherings as a result of brothers who leave the compound *en masse* is, however, never very likely, as this represents a social event with heavy repercussions of the ancestors or, in our case, for the state of inter-African relations.[22] The next section will in this respect evaluate the significance of the quorum crisis of 1982. In any case, the

---

22   See in this respect for references to the OAU's "founding fathers" and the "spirit of 1963" *The Ghanaian Times*, 21/7/79 and *The Herald* (Zimbabwe), 27/11/82.

disappearance of the cleavages between radical and moderate-conservative member states may have a positive effect on the Organization's resolution.

Finally, South Africa's accession to membership may also provide the OAU with more dynamism. Yet its effect should not be over-estimated. While a powerful regional actor, in the African Family it takes its place among the other influential brothers. Together they can considerably affect OAU decision-making but are not powerful enough to dictate continental policy. The result is that they are still constrained to negotiate with the Family's numerous Benjamins.

The anti-colonial struggle

The OAU's efforts to free the continent from colonial and white minority rule entailed two forms of activity. One of these was diplomatic action with the objective to isolate target regimes and keep them under pressure with the help of sanctions. However, the OAU's impact on the regimes in Southern Africa was rather limited, principally because of its inability to make sanctions effective. External economic dependence made it hard for member states to forgo benefits from trade with the white south. This was especially true for the Frontline states themselves, whose transgression of OAU sanctions policy did not form a stimulus for other members to comply with its requirements. In this context the complete absence of a continental leader, as well as the large number of actors, made it hard to make sanctions stick.

Although this weakened Africa's negotiating position vis-à-vis the West the Organization could do nothing but continue to press for international sanctions. Southern Africa's deteriorating security and the intensive economic links between South Africa and the Western world made this imperative. Moreover, member state violation of OAU sanctions could be excused in case of *force majeure*. Pan-African consensus was only violated when countries, such as Malawi, engaged in trade with target regimes *openly* or deliberately tried to expand these economic links. Nevertheless, the essential ambiguity of this stand and the general ineffectiveness of sanctions meant that, once the struggle against white minority regimes became harder, the influence of OAU diplomacy became increasingly irrelevant.

Yet there was one other form in which OAU diplomatic action could affect developments in Southern Africa, even in a decisive way. This was by the policy of diplomatic isolation, in which the weapon of recognition played a crucial role. The international fate of South Africa's bantustans and the internal settlements in Rhodesia and Namibia bears witness of this. The refusal to corroborate these entities and agreements meant the denial of legitimacy in terms of inter-African politics and, thus, access to licensed interaction with other states in and outside Africa. The OAU's African Groups could in this respect help extend the efficacy of the Organization's taboos to global fora.

It had significance, however, as a background factor. Political and military pressures by nationalist movements and neighbouring states were far more important. Moreover, the OAU's diplomatic role was less obvious in the struggle to free Namibia — which always was a responsibility of the United Nations — than during the run-up to independent Zimbabwe. With regard to the elimination of apartheid in South Africa it was almost completely irrelevant. However, the role of the Frontline alliance itself was also greater in Zimbabwe than in Namibia and South Africa. This group provided the OAU's anti-colonial stance with some teeth. In the struggle for Zimbabwe its leadership constituted a form of benevolent hegemony by a coalition. In a more general way the OAU and the Frontline alliance adopted a constructive and co-operative posture towards each other over the latter's assumption of executive duties in OAU decolonization policy.

It cannot be gainsaid that the anti-colonial objective was more important for some states than for others. Yet explaining the poor sanctions record simply in terms of hypocrisy or the absence of political will misses important points. These are the structural difficulties to co-ordinate individual member state will and the sincerity of indignation over white minority rule that lay partly at the basis of the OAU's anti-colonial stance. Thus, the dialogue debate made clear that members of Africa's state elites rejected being "nigger foreign ministers" as implied in the survival of white minority rule. Indignation over this was in part responsible for the high degree of diplomatic isolation that the OAU managed to uphold with regard to white minority regimes. Moreover, the stand on the Western Sahara confirmed the OAU's anti-colonial rectitude, as this issue involved, in the Zimbabwean view, greed and megalomania on the part of one of its own member states.

The essence of the OAU's anti-colonial diplomacy, as expounded in the Lusaka Manifesto, was the willingness to negotiate with white minority regimes *if* these were prepared to accept the principles of equality and self-determination. However, if they were not to be moved by words there was, in terms of the Liberation Committee's own documentation, no alternative but the use of force. As the Malian delegate aptly observed in the debate over dialogue, negotiations made no sense unless the parties were equal in strength. This involved an unrelenting logic that is sometimes overlooked, especially in Western arguments on the importance of non-violent conduct of foreign affairs.[23]

Thus, OAU activity against colonial rule involved, besides diplomatic action, assistance to the struggle of recognized liberation movements. Yet, this did not entail a little dying and blood-letting: contrary to Ben Bella's plea at the OAU's founding conference, direct military intervention was considered impossible and undesirable. The activism of the Liberation Committee was therefore the only way in which the Organization could contribute more concretely to the anti-colonial struggle.

It is, of course, easy to belittle its concrete effects on guerrilla struggles, especially as compared to the direct aid provided by non-African powers. Yet in view of the absence of continental leadership and the gross imbalance in African and non-African military capabilities, this was inevitable and, in a sense, also not that important. Non-African aid, though not without its risks, was easily available and at least brought realization of anti-colonial goals closer. The small financial contributions which for decades came from Africa's numerous states, even from the poor, small and distant ones, were significant for their symbolism, notwithstanding the mundane practicalities involved in making members live up to these commitments. They underlined Pan-African consensus on the

---

23   As argued by M.G. Hermann, Ch.W. Kegley and G.A. Raymond ('The Decay of the Nonintervention Norm'; paper prepared for the Second Pan-European Conference on International Relations, Paris, 13-16/9/95, p 15) Western democratic governments emphasize co-operative over confrontational exchanges in foreign policy.

unacceptability of colonial and white minority rule and legitimized the cause of, and the provision of bilateral aid to, liberation movements. Committee recognition and assistance also improved their access to international diplomatic channels.

Moreover, some countries were, indeed, prepared to die a little in this struggle. The enormous material and human sacrifices of the Frontline states gave concrete form to anti-colonial militancy. This they shared with other countries, especially several radical member states. It explains the perception in figure 6.2 of the OAU as the incarnation of an intimidating machine-gun put to use in heroic battle.

Nevertheless, Committee effectiveness was constricted by the financial and institutional difficulties generated by the absence in this issue area of solid leadership and resultant free riding. In order to cope with these — essentially structural — problems the Committee insulated itself to a certain extent from the generality of the membership, albeit at the price of dependence on the Frontline states. These could neither force the other countries to adopt more constructive postures to the Committee, nor overcome the debilitating effects of disunity among liberation movements and themselves. In this respect the struggle for Zimbabwe was, to a degree, an exception.

The Angolan crisis of 1975-76 showed the importance of multilateral co-ordination in the armed struggle and the risks that inhered in the use of force. The catastrophe was a double failure in terms of OAU objectives: it nearly ruined Angolan accession to independence, reduced collective African influence and increased inter-African tensions. The crisis was the result of divisions among Angola's neighbours coupled to intervention by the superpowers. The states of the region could therefore not provide the necessary leadership to realize a Pan-African strategy. With extra-African interference these divisions assumed the dimensions of a continent-wide rift between moderate-conservative and radical member states. By the time of the extraordinary OAU summit few members really pursued a peaceful solution to the crisis. Radical members desired to see the MPLA sanction its impending military victory by admission to the OAU. Moderate-conservative states manipulated OAU procedures to realize a government of FNLA or UNITA, or at best of all three sides, rather than as an effort to mediate a peaceful settlement as such. Although total dead-lock ensued, at least they delayed MPLA admission. However, this was of little use as the MPLA's military victory could not be undone by diplomatic moves.

Similarly, radical pressure to admit RASD hardly brought Western Sahara's independence closer, as by 1982 POLISARIO's military struggle fared badly. As in Angola, diplomatic victories at the OAU did not deliver control on the ground, so provision of aid to POLISARIO would have been better. The radical move violated OAU doctrine on recognition of governments-in-exile and contradicted OAU policy on the Sahara itself. Worse still, RASD admission turned the issue into the most serious institutional crisis the OAU had ever faced.

Yet, radical action was rational in so far as it was meant to put pressure on Morocco, which was only buying time and working towards a fait-accompli. Its greed and megalomania flouted not only the principle of self-determination but also that of territorial integrity and, thus, the rejection of hegemony so characteristic of inter-African politics. It is therefore highly unlikely that the OAU would ever have condoned the

Moroccan annexation. While regional divisions together with external intervention resulted in its paralysis and its role came effectively to an end with RASD's admission, it was inevitable that Morocco had to leave the OAU.

Its withdrawal and refusal, to this day, to bow to the wishes of OAU policy underlined the relativity of the Organization to the management of inter-African relations: it did apparently not entail a degree of isolation in continental politics so as to necessitate a change in the Moroccan stand. Yet it cannot be argued that its withdrawal and Zaire's temporary suspension of participation signified the "death" of the OAU regime. This would only be the case if Morocco's action would have been followed by other major states.[24] The 1982 quorum crisis was due to unique circumstances. Even with the absence of continental leadership it cannot be explained without reference to the pressure exerted by non-African powers. After all, the boycott could have backfired on moderate-conservative members themselves in the sense of destroying the OAU altogether. While it is doubtful whether the OAU could have survived unscathed more than two failures to stage the summit, subsequent developments exposed its resilience. This was rooted in its role in African politics as expressed in its general ideology. Although the Western Saharan issue and Moroccan withdrawal were serious in terms of the OAU's anti-colonial stance and cohesion, they were not important enough to destroy the Organization and hinder the pursuit of its fundamental objective, as contained in its underlying dualist rationale.[25] For the same reason the end of apartheid did not signify the end of the OAU. More on this is said in the next section.

Finally, if the OAU's contribution to the anti-colonial struggle was often less than what some hoped for, its posturing served to soothe Pan-African awareness of impotence vis-à-vis target regimes. It also kept the issue on the international agenda. On the whole, OAU activity constituted a powerful reminder of the unacceptability of colonial and white minority rule. Recollection of such regimes may now refer to a distant past. Yet this should not make one forget the fierce brutality with which they resisted change or their exceptional status as institutionalized forms of white racist thought. Nor should it make one lose sight of the moral and historical implications of their protracted survival in the post-1945 era — particularly for the Western world. Contentions that the history of the Second World War signified the official demise of Western ideologies of racial inequality are in this respect firmly invalidated by Southern Africa's long struggle for black majority rule.

The OAU's *document humain* of anti-colonial policy, the Lusaka Manifesto, conceded that this does not gainsay the facts of political oppression in its own member states. However, the reverse argument is equally valid, even if such oppression and OAU connivance complicated the anti-colonial struggle from a tactical point of view. The OAU-sponsored debate on whether the West should pay reparations for centuries of slaving and colonialism points in this respect at the painful recollections Africans often have of the history of their relations with Europe.[26] It also alludes to the topicality of the

---

24   See also Haas, 'Regime decay', p 217.

25   See f.i. *Le Soleil* (Senegal), 3/12/82 and 4-5/6/83 (text appeals) and *Dikgang Tsa Gompieno* (Botswana), 8/6/83 (article).

26   See for example also *Jornal de Angola*, 25/5/88 (article).

structural inequalities involved. Nevertheless, while the anti-colonial struggle did not bring economic independence, we would argue that, in Nkrumah's words,[27] the political kingdom still constitutes the first precondition for tackling these issues.

The management of Africa's political order

For the OAU it has always been important to try and get rid of the village idiot or, if this was impossible, hide him from view or limit the potential embarrassment he could cause. If inter-African discord was not kept in bounds and non-African interference was allowed to grow unchecked the mutual security of state elites would be put at stake and the quest for greater global influence be jeopardized. The resultant impotence of the OAU vis-à-vis crisis situations and the connivance of individual member states in extra-African intervention would impart an image of helplessness to, or cast ridicule upon, the collectivity of state elites. Instead of furthering the cause of equality of status with state elites elsewhere, such a course of events would injure elite self-esteem.

Yet, containing the village idiot has never been easy as Family affairs are cumbersome and entail a lack of collective clout. Absence of hegemonic leadership and different patterns of extra-African dependence restrict opportunities for the exertion of influence. This precludes a forceful OAU posture to disputants and makes for a minimalist strategy in conflict management. Instead of acting as manipulators, mediators must rely on their persuasive powers. As resources for side-payments or credible threats are insufficient third parties can usually only act as communicators. OAU mediation in the Horn points in this respect to the utility of Assembly summits.

During its first two decades the OAU had a moderate record in the settlement of inter-state disputes. In line with OAU ideology and the strictures of international relations its involvement usually resulted in neither peace nor war. Conflicts were reduced rather than resolved. Because of the individual approach inherent in its presidential form of mediation such reductive efforts were usually most successful in personal rows between leaders. However, the decentralized, ad hoc nature of mediation detracted from its promptitude and suffered from problems of co-ordination and continuity. As it was partly dependent on presidential agenda's and the frequency of OAU sessions, reactive capacity was low, the more so as mediation was marked by dilatory tactics to reduce conflict levels by letting time cool tempers down. This could lead to disastrous results in high intensity conflicts, like the Mauritanian-Senegalese dispute of 1989-1991.

Built-in slowness also meant that the OAU could be easily overwhelmed by the pace and scale of conflicts. This was clearly shown in our case study of OAU mediation in the territorial conflicts in the Horn. In 1977 Somalia could break the stalemate with extra-African assistance, as could Ethiopia during 1978-1979. Without such stalemate the OAU had little leverage, which according to the power political approach to mediation is the key to success. In this case leverage was already limited because the bone of contention involved a norm of the OAU, which meant the Organization disagreed by definition with one of the disputants.

Many norms for the management of the continental order stand out for their clarity. With the lack of hegemonic leadership this clarity, as well as the effectiveness of these

---

27   See f.i. *Africa Must Unite* (New York, 1984 [1st ed. 1963]), p 50.

norms, depends largely on their congruence with the self-interest of Africa's state elites. *Uti possidetis* is in this respect an example of a norm whose effectiveness has contributed to the management of the continental order. Other norms, such as anti-subversion and the one on OAU competence of initial concern with conflicts, have been less effective or not effective at all. The norm on competence of initial concern has been relatively effective with regard to inter-state disputes, but much less so with regard to domestic conflicts. This was caused by the OAU's legal position and at a deeper level its rationale of conflict management, as well as its limited ability to manage internal disputes and resultant intervention by rival organizations or extra-African forces. Ineffectiveness has been most pronounced in the case of the anti-subversion norm. This has much to do with the zero-sum character of the issue area in combination with the lack of continental leadership, the large number of actors and the relative anonimity in which the norm can be violated.

From the mid-1970s the village idiot was increasingly exposed to the glare of outside attention. OAU impotence in managing conflicts became more and more obvious, although this was primarily due to worsening domestic security contexts. Yet, the reforms to which this gave rise by the early 1990s left the minimalist approach to conflicts intact. It is still not comprehensive, as the focus is on reduction and early containment. Although this makes sense in view of the strictures inherent in inter-African relations, the new situation involves a certain built-in tension as the rationale behind OAU activation has actually broadened. More on this is said below. Preservation of the minimalist approach also means that, notwithstanding the improvement in reactive capacity, OAU capabilities are still grossly insufficient in high intensity conflicts.[28]

The new mechanism entails improved co-ordination and continuity of ad hoc mediation and requires close co-operation between the Assembly Bureau and the Secretary-General. Apart from reinforcing the monitoring work of the Secretariat the reforms have given the Secretary-General himself a more explicit political role. This brings his position more in line with the situation in other international organizations, such as the United Nations. These reforms and the resultant increase in OAU activity can in this respect be partially related to global trends of the post-Cold War era. With the end to superpower interference and Africa's growing (politico-military and economic) marginalization the OAU's room of manoeuvre has increased somewhat, even if the lack of hegemonic leadership restricts the scope of autonomy. In the past the support by the superpowers to African states and their role in fuelling conflicts made any attempt at reform futile.

During much of the last three decades the OAU fed some of its children very badly or not at all. Yet, while the non-intervention norm constricted its role in domestic contexts, the Organization *did* intervene in internal conflicts if these were marked by substantial non-African involvement or posed other inter-African implications. Non-African presence in conflicts was considered particularly serious if it involved the superpowers, white settler regimes or their mercenary representatives. Thus, despite the

---

28   As is the case in the OSCE. See for a recent evaluation f.i. P.W. Gorissen and H.G. Scheltema, 'CVSE, conflictpreventie en crisisbeheersing: Een tussenstand', in *Militaire Spectator*, 1994, no. 4, pp 171-177.

non-intervention norm the OAU intervened in the Congolese and Chadian crises. Even in the Nigerian civil war it managed to arrogate a role to itself that the federal authorities had at first not being willing to accept.

However, in other cases it did not act. The OAU has always refused to feed those children that wish to run away. Self-determination has to take place in the territorial cadre of the (post-)colonial state, so secession cannot be accepted. In view of the risks of precedents and the potentially destabilizing effects for inter-African relations the prohibition on secession is, indeed, quite rational. Yet, as with its stand on colonial frontiers the OAU's approach to separatist movements has always been negative: it would simply issue a prohibition, coldly refuse to listen to anyone with secessionist aspirations and hope the phenomenon would go away. The children of southern Sudan and Eritrea never accepted this and in the latter case finally forced themselves upon the OAU.

In the process the Organization assumed the guise of a trade union of the powerful. Thus, the numerous children without abode were always poorly fed. As the OAU was worried about the disruption refugees could cause to union interests its approach to them was mainly affected by concerns over possible subversive actitivies on their part, rather than the conditions in which they had to live. Even those children trampled upon and maltreated by union members did not receive a sympathetic ear. Human rights and their violations were simply aspects of the internal affairs of member states. Even the OAU's human rights charter did not constitute a significant departure from this.

Nevertheless, during the 1980s and early 1990s children's voices grew louder and many union members became weaker. The OAU was therefore finally forced to take notice of all of Africa's progeny. In 1990 it formally arrogated domestic conflicts and developments to its area of competence. It may now concern itself with internal conflicts irrespective of the fact whether they are marked by substantial extra-African involvement or other inter-African repercussions. Intensification of a conflict, its regional spreading or humanitarian concerns now constitute sufficient grounds or excuse for activation. More broadly, the OAU may focus its attention on non-violent internal developments, such as processes of political transition.

However, it has not been given a blanket right of intervention. In situations characterized by state collapse and massive human suffering the OAU has the right to intervene, but the meaning of this is not clear and in any case limited by its modest military capabilities. The policy organs may discuss internal developments, issue resolutions on them and even condemn member states. Yet for more intrusive forms of action, such as deployment of military or civilian observers and mediation efforts generally, it requires the consent of the disputants. Moreover, it may be doubted whether more powerful governments can be reprimanded so easily as were the Burundi military in 1993.

Still, the OAU's concern with domestic conflicts and wider developments as such, as well as its increased mediatory activities in this area, constitute a remarkable break with the past. Its broader concern with conflicts, however, is not congruent with its minimalist approach when actually handling them. How this is to be resolved is uncertain and depends both on the structures of Africa's international relations and the vicissitudes of domestic socio-political configurations. Trends are therefore contradictory.

Thus, the Secretary-General himself is clearly desirous that the OAU feed all its children better. With his views on democratization and the potential role of the OAU in processes towards more tolerant, equal and less conflictual relations between governments and peoples, the trade union of the powerful might lose some of its social exclusivism. This depends, however, wholly on developments in the member states themselves. Yet, even if the OAU does not get rid of the stain of elitism, the village idiot can probably roam about more freely. This is implicated in the decline of extra-African interest in the continent's affairs and the growing frankness with which the OAU has begun to face crises that in the past would have been ignored: the changing circumstances have simply forced it to become more active and somewhat reduced fears of non-African intrusions; this has diminished the negative role of elite embarrassment about Africa's global image in the management of the continental order.

However, the grandiloquent notions so feared by the Kenyans have never been allowed to improve that management. Its military dimensions were from the start handled by way of bilateral security arrangements. The right to do so was confirmed by the OAU's posture on the Tanganyika mutiny and contravened its original rationale of conflict management. With different patterns of external dependence and in the absence of hegemonic leadership security calculations would differ between member states and over time, giving rise to multiple security arrangements and contradictions between short-term and long-term security concerns. The resultant absence of uniform enemy perceptions meant that plans for a Pan-African arrangement were hindered by fears of its manipulation and of the restriction of the weapon so crucial for state elites in their domestic arenas, *i.e.* the control of state sovereignty.

Thus, as shown by the Stanleyville and Shaba crises, management of the military dimensions of the continental order took place in a fundamentally dialectical context. Collective awareness of vulnerability to, and related fears of, non-African interference went hand in hand with impotence to prevent it and complicity of member states in such intervention. Short-term security threats meant that they were not prepared to rescind the right to rely on bilateral (non-African) aid. The result would be highly contradictory OAU postures, as the one of the Libreville summit on extra-African interference in continental politics. Such events exposed the village idiot to the full glare of negative attention and underlined the dangers of bilateral arrangements to the general security of state elites. The Stanleyville and Shaba crises were in this respect no exception, as shown by the Ogaden crisis, the Ugandan-Tanzanian war and, more generally, the problems entailed by the resort to mercenaries.

While the right to use bilateral arrangements as such was not disputed, their negative repercussions could therefore engender a lot of controversy. This was especially the case if it did not involve help by another African state or the former colonial power, but recourse to South African aid, superpower backing or (white) mercenaries. Such interventions — whether on behalf of or against member states — thus provided a stimulus to a debate on Pan-African security, even if they directed attention exclusively to enemies from the non-African world. Yet this debate also had, apart from the contents of the arguments involved, a psychological function in the sense of helping state elites to come to terms with the deprivation ensuing from the vulnerability and inferiority they experienced vis-à-vis the West. More on this is said in the next section.

Thus, no one took Nkrumah's grandiloquent notions seriously. Their introduction was hindered by the above-mentioned objections against, and factors relevant to, Pan-African security schemes. To this one could add the financial and logistical difficulties involved. Western pressures after the second Shaba crisis spurred the OAU on to take concrete steps. But formulation of a collective defence strategy with proper institutional controls, a defence force and fulfilment of the legal, budgetary and procedural conditions grinded to a halt in the aftermath of the Chadian civil war.

Apart from the desire to seek Libyan withdrawal OAU manoeuvres in Chad were, as a peace-keeping mission, a spectacular failure. This was caused by several factors. The destructive nature of the conflict led to full escalation, as the warring parties had become committed to maximizing their gains. Without respect for the role and neutrality of the Peace Force the peace-keeping operation could not succeed. Moreover, the OAU's posture to the disputants was weakened by the absence of hegemonic leadership. This lack was felt both at the continental level and regionally and was amplified by extra-African interference. The operation therefore lacked direction and firm logistical-financial back-up.

In the context of the post-Cold War era new OAU efforts at peace-keeping have taken some of the Chadian lessons into account. The Organization's military role has now been formally extended to include domestic conflicts and is grounded in a system of firm institutional control. Yet the military aspects of the new mechanism are still far from grandiloquent, as they only allow military observer missions of limited scope and duration. For more far-reaching forms of intervention and long-term operations the OAU remains dependent on assistance by the UN, both in terms of legal powers and financial, logistical and military resources. As fears of extra-African intrusion have diminished somewhat there is greater readiness to make constructive use of extra-African resources generally.

However, such dependence constitutes the OAU's main bottleneck in conflict management. Its activities are therefore restricted in relevance and susceptible to failure. Thus, the low profile vis-à-vis the collapse of Somalia violated its new and broader rationale of activation. Moreover, reliance on other countries and organizations still carries risks for (inter-)African stability. It should in this respect be realized that the new mechanism does not end the bilateral approach to security. It may therefore still entail potentially negative repercussions for the continental order,[29] even if these have become smaller in view of declining extra-African interest. Delegation of peace-keeping duties to regional organizations may provide for more forceful collective action, yet ECOMOG has shown that such activities are susceptible to regional power struggles. UN operations may also be more effective than those of the OAU as they benefit from stronger leadership and greater resources. However, the world body is itself overburdened with

---

29   The French role in the 1994 crisis which engulfed Rwanda and seriously jeopardized regional relations is a good example. See f.i. 'Question à l'actualité. Rwanda: la responsabilité de la France', in *Politique africaine*, June 1994, pp 2-6.

peace-keeping duties[30] and may not always be willing to support OAU initiatives. The problem is that, even with the OAU's greater room of manoeuvre, it is hard to tackle the structural absence of continental leadership. Grandiloquent solutions to Africa's many conflicts and security problems are therefore as far away as ever, whether with or without extra-African support.

In this respect it must be borne in mind that fears of extra-African intrusions have not completely disappeared. Thus, the realization of state elites that they live in a world where it is dangerous to be on your own continues to inform attitudes to the global environment. Their concern over non-African interference has now to some extent been replaced by alarm about continental marginalization. However, their inferiority complex and vulnerability to enemies have, from the OAU's very inception, stimulated a desire to enhance the global influence of the continent and its states and claim equality of status with state elites elsewhere. This last aspect has had a clear psychological role in soothing elite anxieties.

To these purposes state elites have always articulated the argument that Pan-African co-operation presents levering possibilities by virtue of their numerical strength in global cadres and, more vaguely, the fact that the OAU forms the representation of an entire continent. Views on how far African influence can thereby be enhanced have tended to vary from moderately optimistic to escapist. The Madagascan muscle man depicted in figure 8.1 is the clearest articulation of the latter. Yet inevitably, the objectives to which his impressive brawn was expected to work were, with the years, expressed in increasingly defensive terms. The war against white minority rule was seen to give way to more hopeless combat against deteriorating terms of trade and galloping debts; a battle for the continent's very survival; and a struggle to end its passive role in global developments.

From the start the levering possibilities of Pan-African co-operation manifested themselves in African caucus groups at other organizations. As a result of their immediate confrontation with a non-African environment, which is not necessarily willing to concede on the goals shared by Africa's state elites, these groups tend to operate relatively effectively. This has had positive results for OAU conflict management in the sense of keeping inter-state conflicts away from non-African fora; for African objectives on representation in international organizations; and for UN postures on decolonization and development issues. Thus, these caucus groups do indeed generate more influence for African states collectively and individually than if state elites would face the world on their own.

However, this has been insufficient to halt the continent's marginalization in world affairs, as conference politics affects the configuration of power but does not alter underlying capabilities. For long there have therefore been arguments on more far-reaching forms of institutionalizing the OAU's potential leverage so as to reap greater influence. Yet, genuine politico-economic integration failed to materialize as a result of the lack of hegemonic leadership, contradictory dependence patterns and the fact that sovereignty constitutes a vital resource for state elites in their struggles to retain

---

30   Also B. Boutros-Ghali, *An Agenda for Peace 1995* (2nd ed.: with the new supplement and related UN documents, New York, 1995).

dominance in the domestic configuration of power. Thus, contrary to rhetoric they contented themselves with concrete influence in conference politics and the soothing reassurance of caucus groups that they were not on their own in this dangerous world.

Whether the OAU will ever move beyond catering for such limited political and psychological needs is not sure. With the continuous deterioration of Africa's economies, the weakening position of state elites vis-à-vis domestic forces and declining non-African interest, the Organization recently launched the far-reaching project of a future continental economic community. Such a goal, however, also depends on a restructuring of domestic configurations of power. Thus, while some OAU norms, attitudes and postures have since the late 1980s undergone significant revision, others are still intact and rigidly adhered to, something that points to the constancy of the continental order.

9.4   Some ideological perspectives

The accepted views of the OAU's ideological ground-work are clearly in need of refinement. First, contrary to contemporary observations it was found that the differences of opinion between the Casablanca and Monrovia/Brazzaville alliances did not centre on the form that African unity should take, *i.e.* on arguments for or against supra-national or inter-governmental co-operation. The real bone of contention was the issue of non-African influences and presence on the continent, against which the Casablanca powers adopted a more critical attitude than the other two coalitions. While the radical group aimed its unity against such non-African forces, the moderate-conservative group pleaded more inward-looking conceptions of co-operation.

The debate on the direction and need for unity flowed over into arguments on the form it should take. Yet, these only served to sharpen disagreement on the more fundamental issue of the rationale of unity as such. Thus, the Casablanca group actually adopted a form of inter-governmental co-operation very similar to that of the Brazzaville and Monrovia powers. This was despite Nkrumah's supra-national aspirations, which must be seen in relation to his more extreme interpretation of the necessity of unity. Similarly, the differences between radicals and moderate-conservatives on military co-operation centred on enemy perceptions rather than institutional arrangements.

Arguments on economic co-operation were related not to any discord between radicals and moderate-conservatives about the prematurity of integration, but to disagreement between Francophone and other countries on the risks of association with the EC and the effects of its trade preferences on Commonwealth economies. The dispute on gradual versus instant steps towards unity was more a matter of foreign policy styles. Yet Casablanca's flamboyance was partly caused by the dangers it attributed to non-African influences. This was also true for its opposition to regional, as opposed to continental, forms of co-operation. The debate on regionalism, however, was primarily fuelled by Nkrumah's totalitarian view of the necessity of unity.

In their 1963 compromise the opposing coalitions found each other in a dualist rationale. Their co-operation should improve the mutual security of Africa's state elites in the context of their inter-state relations, as well as increase the external influence of the continent and its component states and guarantee equality of status for their state elites. Disagreement on the gravity of non-African influences had not necessarily vanished, yet all could agree on this *related* set of objectives.

This was even true for Nkrumah, who stood isolated essentially because of his absolutist interpretation of non-African influences and concomitant institutional prescriptions. Thus, his indirect influence on the OAU's formation showed itself in the name of the Organization and the preamble of its Charter. However, the drive for unity did not depend exclusively on the Osagyefo. Practically all states shared the ideal of some sort of unity as it had instrumental logic, *i.e.* served to further certain concrete objectives. Contemporary ideas on African unity being nature-given or organic may be related to elite perceptions of vulnerability with regard to Africa's external environment.

Contrary to popular belief the struggle against Southern Africa's white regimes did not form the primary reason for the OAU's establishment. Rather, its anti-colonial stance emanated indirectly from the fundamental endeavour, as ingrained in the external part of its dualist rationale, to enhance Africa's global influence and realize equality of status with state elites of other continents. The survival of colonial and white minority regimes could only detract from Africa's collective weight and injure elite self-esteem. Thus, the OAU's existence is not jeopardized by fulfilment of its anti-colonial aims, but depends on the persistence of the structural inequalities between Africa and the Northern hemisphere. This also shows that the frequent predictions of the OAU's impending demise are unwarranted.[31]

That the endeavour to enhance the global influence of the continent and its states always remained relatively inarticulate and its realization receded into the distant future meant that there was a weak spot in OAU anti-colonial ideology. The elusive nature of the fundamental collective gain that would accrue from an end to colonial rule hardly encouraged member states to respect OAU sanctions policy. However, the affront that white minority rule formed to the status of African state elites provided, at a secondary level, a certain urgency to the OAU's anti-colonial mandate. In fact, one can argue that its formation and functioning constituted the logical end to the continent's political decolonization. In view of the process of Africa's political transition begun in the late 1950s the OAU's establishment was, in a way, inevitable as this transition necessitated a search for a restructuring of international power relations.

Like its ideas on economic co-operation and disarmament, however, the Organization's posture on colonialism was essentially reformist, despite the support to the armed struggle it involved. As shown by the 1975 Alvor Agreement which should have led Angola to independence and the attitude to Britain's responsibility in ending the Rhodesian rebellion[32] the OAU aimed at constitutional, or at least orderly, transfers of power. Moreover, its stance on colonialism referred almost exclusively to *European* supremacy. Self-determination was narrowly conceived as limited to the date of independence and through the territorial cadres inherited from the colonial powers. Repression in member states could never be seen as forms of colonialism. As the

---

31   See f.i. for an early example of such predictions one made thirty years ago by D. Austin and R. Nagel, 'The Organization of African Unity', in *The World Today*, 1966, p 529.

32   See f.i. ECM/Res.11 (V).

Zimbabwean metaphor of greed and megalomania implies, Morocco owed the OAU's wrath over the Western Sahara as much to its territorial expansionism as to its violation of the principle of self-determination.

The emphasis in recent years on humanitarian concerns in conflict management could therefore provide more social balance to OAU ideology. Especially those aspects of it that relate to the settlement of disputes have for long been callously geared to the needs and anxieties of state elites. The rationality of the neglect of popular interests that this involved was only falsified by the late 1980s when the narrow focus on the inter-African level of politics, in a bid to protect state elite interests, began to backfire. However, the built-in tension between the OAU's broadened rationale of activation and minimalist approach when handling disputes makes its new ideology of conflict management less coherent than when it dictated disregard of domestic developments. The old contradiction between the political aspects of this ideology and its military dimensions legitimating the bilateral approach to security has similarly not been resolved. Disagreement on, as well as temporal changes in, enemy perceptions are part of this.

The resolution of this contradiction may have been brought closer by the decline in fears over extra-African interference. Yet there are limits to this. The desire to halt Africa's downward slide in the global hierarchy and even increase its external influence remains an essential part of the Organization's dualist ideology. By definition this implicates the continent's relations with extra-African powers, in particular from the Western world, into the jigsaw puzzle the OAU faces in trying to manage Africa's political order. This is true quite apart from what kind of policies are pursued by Western countries. Hence, any coherent OAU ideology necessitates a perspective that does not uncritically herald African-Western interaction as the solution to the continent's predicaments. On the contrary, it should *problematize* those Eur-African relations. This point is taken up in the epilogue.

Any contradictions in the OAU's ideological ground-work point to disagreement among member states about its role in Africa's political configurations. However, despite some of its contradictory and incoherent aspects it must be noted that, in recent years, OAU ideology has not yet evolved into something that differs fundamentally from what it was three decades ago. Nevertheless, it is at present subject to an interesting process of shifting, especially with regard to conflict management. In order to map these changes with more precision more research ought to be undertaken on member state perceptions as articulated during the first half of the 1990s. Views on the OAU's role in domestic conflict management, its potential role in democratization and its competence to delegitimate member state behaviour would be particularly important subjects for research. The extent to which concerns over extra-African intrusions have diminished should be studied in greater detail, as this pertains directly to the possibilities of non-African contributions to the continent's security.

Although an effort has been made to analyse the OAU's ideological dimensions as precisely as possible, this study cannot claim to be a comprehensive reconstruction of its ideological ground-work. For this other issue areas, like economic co-operation, should be investigated as well.[33]

On the basis of this study one may conclude that the relationship between the OAU and the ideology of Pan-Africanism is more complex than is usually realized. One can neither say that the Organization's ideology is Pan-Africanist nor that Pan-Africanist discourse has nothing to do with it. The essence of its ideology is made up of a combination of concepts of state nationalism and Pan-Africanist doctrines.

The OAU's task to protect state elites against their African enemies has been articulated through state nationalist concepts as sovereignty, territorial integrity and non-interference. Their systematic abuse in the struggle between state elites and the mass of the unprivileged has made them into the most contested part of the Organization's ideology. Another problem of the doctrinal link with state nationalism is that the recent inroads made by domestic and non-African forces into the position of the African state have by definition called into question the OAU's rationale, so much so that ideas not part of the kind of state nationalism described in chapter 3 are being put forward in its search for a new role in Africa's political configurations. The emphasis by the Secretary-General on the OAU's contribution to peaceful change in member states and more permitting environments characterized by respect for human rights is pertinent here.

Pan-Africanist notions are specially relevant to the external part of OAU ideology. Aspirations to equality with other state elites and greater global influence are usually articulated in Pan-Africanist ideas like the concept of dignity, the doctrine of African unity and the related emphasis on a continental identity. Political crises could induce some to contradict these ideas, while Africa's deteriorating global position put them under increasing pressure. Yet this did not lead to the abandonment of the unity of Africa as the central paradigm, nor of the use of Pan-Africanism for rhetorical[34] purpose.

It is necessary to refine one particular assumption entertained at the outset of this study, namely that Pan-Africanism forms one of the OAU's useful assets. This is not always the case, especially as far as the inter-African context is concerned. Thus it was shown that, because of its Pan-African membership, the Organization is held by Africans as emblematizing the continent and as forming its key institutional expression. In this sense it enjoys more political prestige, or rather conspicuity, than individual states or any other organization.[35] The result is that the OAU is often judged on the basis of many of the negative developments of the post-colonial era. These are then squarely blamed on the Organization and its performance is found wanting. For example, in one member state's perception of the mid 1980s the continent's economic problems were noted and it was

---

33   An overview in L. Zang, 'L'action économique de l'OUA depuis 1963', in M. Kamto, J.E. Pondi and L. Zang (eds), *l'OUA: rétrospective et perspectives africaines* (Paris, 1990), ch. 7.

34   See f.i. OAU at 30: Reflections on the Past and Prospects for the Future: Address by the Secretary-General, H.E. Dr. Salim Ahmed Salim on the occasion of the 30th Aniversary of the Organization of African Unity, Africa Hall, Addis Ababa, May 25, 1993, p 30; *Jornal de Angola*, 25/5/88 (article); and *Le Soleil* (Senegal), 29-30/6/93 (Assembly speech).

35   See also D. Venter, 'An Evaluation of the OAU on the Eve of South Africa's Accession', in *Africa Insight*, 1994, p 50. Whether this is translated in concrete commitment to it by member states is a more complex matter. See f.i. J.F. Clark, 'Patterns of Support for International Organisations in Africa', in T.M. Shaw and K.A. Heard (eds), *The Politics of Africa: Dependence and Development* (London, 1979), pp 327-331.

simply stated that the OAU should unfold a strategy with which to get Africa out of its predicament![36] In another view it was held that hunger, starvation, illiteracy, malnutrition, lack of drinkable water and inadequate health care showed that the Organization had betrayed Africa's hopes.[37]

The point is not so much that the OAU is the object of facile denunciations. Nor that it is unreasonable of Africans to expect from an organization with such limited powers to deliver them all the fruits of prosperity and put an end to the miseries and afflictions they are made to suffer. Rather, the variant criteria on which their assessments are based, while not a part of the OAU's ideological core, are definitely linked to its political and institutional symbolization of the continent. As the epitome of Africa itself the OAU thus assembles all the continent's ambiguities and contradictions, as well as the hopes and frustrations of its people. It is therefore inevitable that the Organization is often mocked or scorned, while it finds it hard to overcome images of impotence, helplessness and lethargy. The fact that, by the same token, some of the rarer positive developments are at times attributed to the OAU[38] confirms this argument.

The equation between Africa and the OAU thus entails, besides some limited advantages, a heavy moral burden. That the image of the OAU will always remain a contested one is shown very clearly in non-governmental perceptions. Partly because of the OAU's actual postures and partly because of its continental symbolism these images tend to be among the most negative of all international organizations, possibly in the order of the public relations problems of the International Monetary Fund.[39]

Our analysis of the OAU's ideological dimensions provides some insight into African political thought, as articulated by state elites, on international politics. The central notions that make up this body of ideas are the paradigm of the unity of Africa, combined to the recognition that the continent is tied through contradictory patterns to external actors; the notion that co-operation with such actors, such as international organizations, NGO's and individual states, should continue — whether or not by force of circumstance and despite the inequalities involved and the emphasis on self-reliance; the pivotal role of the state and its sovereignty in the continental order, however precarious this may have become; the idea that *l'union fait la force* with regard to African participation in global cadres; and, more generally, the importance of *power* in international relations.

Thus, it was shown that awareness of the enormous discrepancy in power between Africa and the West is a central element in the latent inferiority complex of African state elites, much more so than the racial factor in their encounters with the non-African world. This represents an important nuance to Appiah's contention that, in order to understand the psychology of post-colonial Africa, one must not exaggerate the inferiority complex that educated Africans experience(d) as a result of racial discrimination during the colonial

---

36   *The Herald* (Zimbabwe), 11/7/85.

37   *Daily Times* (Nigeria), 25/5/88 (article)

38   See f.i. *Daily Mail* (Sierra Leone), 1/7/80 (article); *Révolution Africaine* (Algeria), 3-9/12/82; *Daily Times* (Nigeria), 25/5/88; and *Cameroon Tribune*, 25/5/88, which credit it with Southern Africa's decolonization.

39   For example, the *Weekend Mail* (South Africa), 13-19/7/90 has likened the IMF to an emperor having no clothes on.

period.[40] This inferiority complex is, as far as those elite Africans engaging in the conduct of foreign affairs are concerned, principally fed by an acute realization of the imbalance in the global configurations of power. It should therefore not be underestimated. Moreover, the racial factor should not be completely discounted either. This is shown clearly in the dialogue affair and, to a lesser extent, the collective reactions to the Stanleyville crisis, the use of white mercenaries and South Africa's backing to UNITA in 1975.

The mental complexes underlying OAU ideology are therefore crucial to an understanding of the Organization's role and functioning. Sometimes this is overlooked or ignored by Western policy-makers, with the result that their initiatives on African issues may backfire. The openness with which they try to influence OAU decision-making or launch proposals to reinforce the Organization's role in peace-keeping violates the pretence of its discretionary power over African affairs or rubs salt in the wounds inflicted by images of collective African impotence. The US circular letter on Angola to African heads of state in 1976; public American pressure to change the venue of the Tripoli summit in 1982; and the Western proposal in 1978 for an inter-African security force are cases in point.

All this reveals a political psychology that graphically illustrates the ambiguities of dependence. The mental postures of African state elites on the global status quo are marked by a high degree of ambivalence. The sources used for this study show that most African regimes, of whatever persuasion, grouping or region, share in feelings of external weakness and insecurity; in resentment of the damage this may cause to elite self-esteem; and in dismay over Africa's increasing marginalization, up to the point that it leads to escapist posturing. It was shown that this is even true for many of the Francophone regimes, notwithstanding their usually warm ties with France and the economic stakes that lead them to defend the unequal ties with the former metropole — of their own accord and by force of circumstance.[41]

The idiosyncracies of African state elite attitudes to the international order and the role of the OAU therein warrant the conclusion that views on international politics are strongly affected by the politico-cultural background of its observers or, rather, are heavily context-dependent. Realization of this fact may be as crucial for our understanding of the practice of international politics as any theories of international relations that purport to provide abstracted and universally applicable explanations of political behaviour. Dependency theory should in this respect pay more attention to the psychological dimensions of the dependency complex. Insight in the mental postures of the modern elites at the periphery of the global order can explain some aspects of organizations as the OAU better than is possible in terms of a mechanical link with the

---

40   K.A. Appiah, *In My Father's House: Africa in the Philosophy of Culture* (New York and Oxford, 1992), pp 6-7, but also his ch. 3.

41   Some argue that the 1994 devaluation of the CFA Franc may herald a gradual loss of French influence over these countries and thus the beginning of a mental decolonization of the latter's leadership. See *Jeune Afrique*, 20-26/1/94 and G. Martin, 'Continuity and Change in Franco-African Relations', in *Journal of Modern African Studies*, 1995, pp 1-20.

economic manifestations of dependence. Inclusion of these psychological dimensions could therefore enhance the explanatory force of dependency theory.[42]

Finally, a few words are in order on the concept of ideology as such and the sources that are at one's disposal for its analysis in the African context. This study shows that ideology continues to be relevant, both as a means to articulate particular individual or group interests in a specific social context and as a central concept with which to gain insight in politics. Ideology is often referred to rather negatively in Western (post-Cold War) contexts. Yet implicit in this is the assumption that only comprehensive, structured and closed systems of thought, such as Marxism, amount to ideology while more incoherent, implicit and concrete sets of ideas — like many politico-economic notions dominant in the West — do not.[43] From the perspective of the less demanding conditions set for the concept of ideology in this study one must conclude that this is not the case and that ideology figures in every socio-historical context. With the aid of a subtle form of, what is called, contextual reading the concept of ideology therefore helps to elucidate crucial aspects of the political process, such as the objectives of its actors.

African newspapers are an underrated source in analyses of African political thought. Even governmental papers filled with the most barren propaganda include comments that, with careful interpretation, often yield interesting insights. Thus, the complaint of one author during the 1960s, that African political theory was still in the age of the pamphlet,[44] may still be true but hardly relevant.[45] Even in its cruder manifestations such pamphlets contain important elements of political reasoning. The metaphorical forms in which Africans often argue their case, as well as some of their graphical presentations of ideological argument, constitute powerful examples of this.

This is in no way meant to belittle African political thought. A study of ideological argument in the West could also reap more or less vulgarized forms of ideology — apart from the fact that Africa can boast various examples of well argued and intellectually refined treatises. Names as Cabral and Fanon are pertinent.[46] We would also argue that the views analysed in this study are, despite some contradictory points, too enduring and consistent to warrant Clapham's old iconoclastic contention that the ideas of African leaders do not amount to structured political thought, as they would be too incoherent and context-dependent.[47]

This conclusion is not gainsaid by the fact that the OAU itself is especially important, though never wholly successful, in *soothing* anxieties — besides or rather

---

42   While J. Galtung mentions the psychological dimension in his 'A Structural Theory of Imperialism' (in *Journal of Peace Research*, 1971, p 87 ff) he does not analyse its significance in his five types of imperialism, including the cultural one.

43   D. McLellan, *Ideology* (2nd. ed.: Buckingham, 1995), ch. 5.

44   H. Glickman, 'Dilemmas of Political Theory in an African Context: the Ideology of Julius Nyerere', in J. Butler and A.A. Castagno (eds), *Boston University Papers on Africa: Transition in African Politics* (New York, Washington and London, 1967), p 196.

45   As argued also by J.A. Langley, *Ideologies of Liberation in Black Africa 1856-1970: Documents on modern African political thought from colonial times to the present* (London, 1979).

46   See f.i. A. Cabral, *Unity and Struggle: Speeches and Writings* (Heinemann African Writers Series: London, 1980) and F. Fanon, *Pour la révolution africaine* (Paris, 1964).

47   C. Clapham, 'The Context of African Political Thought' in *Journal of Modern African Studies*, 1970, pp 1-13.

than giving expression to articulate ideas about the global order of things. However, this role implies that the OAU as such only contributes in a limited way to the conscientization of Africans about their predicaments.

Epilogue:
Africa and unity

The continental order created by way of the OAU will hardly elicit many positive reactions, especially outside the exclusive circles of African leadership. While it had to diminish the vulnerability of state elites, enhance their influence and soothe their self-indulgent anxieties, this continental order has represented violence and persecution to the unprivileged and become increasingly peripheral to global developments. Thus, in terms of its marginalization, economic decline, unequal and violent political configurations and African perceptions of this the African continent amounts to more than a geographical entity. In spite of its manifold differences and contradictions it can therefore be argued that "Africa" does, indeed, exist in a politico-economic sense, if not in a very positive way.[1]

Moreover, the durability of this Africa is remarkable. While it can be argued that in the Cold War era African states enjoyed a certain measure of influence as a result of their manipulation of superpower competition, the benefits of this were in the long-term elusive as such rivalry intensified conflicts, deepened divisions and weakened collective influence in global fora. Playing off superpowers against each other amounted to victimization, of others and in the long run of everyone. Yet because of its progressive economic — and now also strategic — marginalization, the end of the Cold War did not enhance the continent's collective influence either.[2] The demise of the Eastern bloc, the rise of multi-partyism and the disappearance of the radical-moderate/conservative divide expanded the OAU's room of manoeuvre. Yet as previously noted, this only led to a limited increase in activity because Africa's predicaments are the result of an intricate complex of absent continental leadership, excruciating degrees of economic dependence and domestic orders whose socio-political basis is often very narrow.

---

1   See for philosophical treatment of this V.Y. Mudimbe, *The Invention of Africa: Gnosis, Philosophy, and the Order of Knowledge* (Bloomington and Indianapolis, 1988); L. Nauta, 'Afrika bestaat niet', in *Nieuw Wereldtijdschrift*, 1985, no. 1, pp 71-80; and K.A. Appiah, *In My Father's House: Africa in the Philosophy of Culture* (New York and Oxford, 1992).

2   Also B. Ndiaye, 'A Vision of Shared Responsibilities', in A. Adedeji (ed), *Africa within the World: Beyond Dispossession and Dependence* (London and Atlantic Highlands, NJ, 1993), pp 121-122.

The fact that the shoe pinches at different points creates a vicious circle of post-colonial decline that is extremely difficult to break. This is a reality that is usually forgotten in Western prescriptions on African politico-economic reform, which can often be dubbed as facile or even simplistic. If one contemplates on possible roads ahead one might, nevertheless, conclude that the first opportunity for Africans to halt the decline would probably present itself at the domestic end of their afflictions, as tackling the continent's international relations would mean direct confrontation with even more powerful obstacles and interests. In view of the numerous domestic conflicts, the challenge to the privileged position of state elites and the latter's determination to hold on to the asset of state sovereignty it is obvious that the relationship between state and society is in need of fundamental reform. As argued by the OAU's Secretary-General, African states need a much higher degree of popular participation in the political system.[3] The mass of Africa's peoples has become considerably alienated from the structures of the post-colonial state, whose political legitimacy is therefore often grossly deficient. With Davidson we would plead that it is only possible to remedy this by way of very thorough political reform from the bottom upwards — thus starting with the local government level[4] rather than the top down approach of the Western-sponsored transition to multi-partyism.

Nevertheless, Davidson's reckoning with the post-colonial state ought not to be followed too far. Despite all the recent critiques of the African state there do not seem to be many practical alternatives to its reinforcement by way of enhanced legitimacy. With the destruction, albeit partial, of pre-colonial structures and patterns the existence of viable, as well as spatially extensive, polities is essential if Africans are to conquer a greater social and economic space for themselves. Flourishing economies demand political structures that provide for infrastructure, a reliable administrative cadre and a stable political environment.[5] They are also needed to prevent potential abuse of African power vacuums by external actors, such as drug cartels, arms dealers and mercenaries.[6]

Davidson's critique understates in this respect the significance of the discrepancies in the continent's external relations of power. Recent Africanist debate on democratization has similarly suffered from analysing Africa's processes of transition quite detached from their international dimensions.[7] Africa is, however, not an isolated continent. Without arguing that developments are mechanically determined by external factors it must be

---

3   See OAU at 30: Reflections on the Past and Prospects for the Future: Address by the Secretary-General, H.E. Dr. Salim Ahmed Salim on the occasion of the 30th Aniversary of the Organization of African Unity, Africa Hall, Addis Ababa, May 25, 1993 (hereinafter as Address by the Secretary-General, May 1993).

4   B. Davidson, *The Black Man's Burden: Africa and the Curse of the Nation-State* (London, 1992), pp 290-322.

5   Also W. Kühne, 'Looking South After the End of the Cold War', in I.W. Zartman (ed), *Europe and Africa: The New Phase* (Boulder and London, 1993), p 18. To the OAU's SG the state is also axiomatic. Address by the Secretary-General, May 1993, pp 2-3.

6   See f.i. on recent mercenary activity *New African*, November 1995 and for a different angle to the external context S. Ellis, 'Africa after the Cold War: New Patterns of Government and Politics', in *Development and Change*, 1996, pp 19-20.

7   See on this also R. Buijtenhuijs and E. Rijnierse, *Democratization in Sub-Saharan Africa (1989-1992): An Overview of the Literature* (Leiden, 1993), pp 88-89.

realized that there is continuous interaction between African and non-African actors. This involves two-way traffic, which in view of the unbalanced configuration of power is much more intensive as far as extra-African influence on Africa is concerned. Thus, if a transition to less conflictual domestic orders is to stand a chance it is vital that Africans are assured of external political backing and access to Western markets.

Yet it is by no means certain that Western support for political reform is truly forthcoming and if it is, whether it is sufficient. Fundamental restructuring of state-society relationships, especially along the lines described above, may not necessarily elicit Western support or be considered as in a Western actor's interests. The continuous assistance that the continent's dominant external power, France, provides to despotic regimes such as in Cameroon, Togo and, formerly, Zaire reveals that Western actors do not by definition travel the road of reform. British attitudes to countries like Kenya and Malawi for long betrayed similar features. Professed commitment to African democratization should thus be set against concrete examples of bilateral interaction patterns and policies in specific issue areas, such as arms sales.[8]

One may also doubt non-African willingness to engage in genuine reform of Eur-African economic relations. Continuation of established patterns of co-operation and the prolonged refusal, at least until 1996, to engage in significant debt resettlement[9] do not point in that direction. European Union arrangements have not encouraged African competitiveness and do not focus on importation of higher value added African products. With the structural constraints of African economies and global GATT-induced tariff cuts, this leaves African producers ill-prepared for foreign competition. Trade liberalization reduces the value of preferential access to the European market, which is becoming a harsher environment due to integration and competition from other regions. Increased raw materials exports hardly compensate for this because of low and unstable prices, while future aid levels are likely to come under pressure.[10] Moreover, the demands that Western governments can make — especially because of the debt crisis — on the issue of Africa's political and economic governance seem to go hand in hand with decreasing interest in African economies. This undercuts the effects of reform, while such demands may to some extent function as justification for Western withdrawal and consolidate Africa's traditional economic roles — in their effect if not in intent.[11]

It must be realized, however, that Africa's external relations involve various groups of actors, African as well as non-African, whose interests are either congruent or patterned dialectically. Questions of politico-economic reform therefore tend to arouse resistance as well as support. In a similar vein, Western actors differentiate between African countries when assessing their stakes on the continent. Some of these are targeted

---

8   See also G. Martin, 'Continuity and Change in Franco-African Relations', in *Journal of Modern African Studies*, 1995, pp 14-18 and for the British case M. Robinson, 'Will Political Conditionality Work?', in *IDS Bulletin*, 1993, no. 1, pp 58-66.

9   See also S. George, 'Uses and Abuses of African Debt', in Adedeji, *Africa within the World*, p 62 and *Africa Confidential*, 18/10/96.

10   See J. Ravenhill, 'When Weakness Is Strength: The Lomé IV Negotiations'; C. Cosgrove, 'The Impact of 1992 on EC-ACP Trade and Investment'; and R.C. Riddell, 'Aid Performance and Prospects', all in Zartman, *Europe and Africa*, chs. 5, 6 and 9.

11   See also George, 'Uses and Abuses of African Debt', pp 68-70.

for aid and assistance more than others and will probably never be abandoned. One could think here of countries which in chapter 2 were called semi-peripheral. These are likely to enjoy continuous external support while the really peripheral states may become exposed to increasing levels of impoverishment and external disinterest.[12]

Many of the more fortunate countries will undoubtedly continue to give priority to policies based on their own endowments and external alliances[13] and be encouraged by extra-African actors to do so. Yet the semi-peripheral countries are especially vulnerable to fluctuations in international commodity prices and many of them have equally suffered socio-economic decay. The limits on the influence of Africa's so-called hegemons similarly underlines the questionable nature of semi-peripheral status.[14]

Thus, while African countries do not sink *collectively* into oblivion it is clear that almost all of them have to a greater or lesser extent suffered from the forces of decline and marginalization. With the grossly unequal terms of trade that mark Africa's international economic links it is very difficult to find an evolutionary way out of this. Revision of terms of trade could only take place through development of output with much higher added value. This being extremely difficult within the present structures of the international economic order such re-definition requires — besides viable states pursuing cleverly devised economic policies[15] — a substantial increase in external influence. Since African countries, whether peripheral or semi-peripheral, are unlikely to generate such influence and improve their economic standing on their own, Africans are correct in searching for solutions within the unity paradigm. Indeed, it must be realized that, for all the crudeness of his arguments, Nkrumah *was* right when he kept dinning in the centrality of the power issue. By banding together African countries could at least partially rectify the imbalance in politico-economic influence between themselves and external forces, something that would make it possible to tackle some of the structural problems of Africa's international economic relations. Trade restrictions and subsidies in the economic power blocs of the Northern hemisphere, as well as debt relief, would be obvious issues.[16]

So Africa *should* unite. This remains the supreme paradox of a context marked by non-existent integration, absent continental leadership and so many cleavages and contradictions. Yet it is an inference in line with the insights of scholars as Kothari, Guernier and, indirectly, dependency theorists.[17] A strategy of continental integration would only become superfluous if sufficient numbers of semi-peripheral countries would achieve a definitive breakthrough on the path of development — *i.e.* structural economic change — in the process drag along several of their neighbours and thus break up Africa as the unity of the deprived.

---

12   See also T.M. Shaw, 'Africa in the New World Order: Marginal and/or Central?', in Adedeji, *Africa within the World*, p 86.

13   See f.i. Ravenhill, 'When Weakness Is Strength', p 48 and *Le Soleil* (Senegal), 4/6/91 (article).

14   See for a theoretical argument on the limited influence of semi-peripheral economies T. Smith, 'Requiem or New Agenda for Third World Studies?', in *World Politics*, 1985, pp 532-561.

15   On the importance of the state in development also R. Wade, 'East Asia's Economic Success: Conflicting Perspectives, Partial Insights, Shaky Evidence', in *World Politics*, 1992, pp 270-320.

16   Also Kühne, 'Looking South', p 24.

17   See also Adedeji, *Africa within the World*.

Short of this, Pan-African integration remains a relevant strategy. Perhaps fundamental reform of domestic orders might in this respect result in more broadly based governments that would not just cling to shrinking privileges as sovereignty, aid and preferential treatment of raw materials. Such governments could be more constructive towards issues of state power and economic integration. Working through regional organizations such integration could expand consumer markets, which usually are too small due to low population levels. Other obvious but difficult targets would be diversification of mono-cultural production to lessen vulnerability to extra-African price-setting; expansion of food production through financial stimuli to farmers; and improvement of manufacturing potential so as to move away from low valued commodity exports. Development of industries supporting agricultural production could be a first step.[18]

Yet while integration would also increase external influence it represents no easy solution. It could only get off the ground if the complementarity of economies is enhanced, something that necessitates diversification. Integration by tariff reduction is hard, as tariffs generate part of government incomes and their reduction can lead to shifts in trade flows. Integration can therefore sharpen regional differences in prosperity, especially if it leaves extra-African trading patterns unimpaired. Thus, genuine inter-African integration demands extrication from multiple ties of dependence on outside powers — which brings one back to part of the original problem.[19]

Maybe continued marginalization could provide encouragement. It has in this respect been argued that the devaluation of the CFA Franc, with the decline of French influence this may lead to, could spur Francophone states on to search for new economic links, among others with regional countries.[20] Yet whether or not this should also lead to dissociation (or delinking[21]) from the world economy, as pleaded by dependency theory, can probably not be answered one way or the other. Marginalization actually amounts to *de facto* dissociation in certain areas of economic activity.[22] This process generates numerous political tensions and, if it persists, could lead to fundamental shifts in the relations between the various groups and forces making up African society. While this scenario would probably not unfold solely in peaceful ways, it could throw up new social forces with an ability to better affect the nature of the economic order Africans live in.[23] The rise of informal economic sectors during the 1980s may in this respect be seen as a humble example of individuals falling back on their own energies.[24]

---

18   P. Okigbi, 'The Future Haunted by the Past', in *ibid.*, p 37; P. Economou, M. Gittelman and M. Wubneh, 'Europe 1992 and Foreign Direct Investment in Africa', in Zartman, *Europe and Africa*, pp 115-116; and Ndiaye, 'A Vision', p 122.

19   K. van Walraven, 'Some Aspects of Regional Economic Integration in Africa', in *Hague Yearbook of International Law*, 1991, pp 106-126.

20   Martin, 'Continuity and Change in Franco-African Relations', p 20.

21   S. Amin, *Delinking: Towards a Polycentric World* (London and Atlantic Highlands, NJ, 1990).

22   A. Adedeji, 'Outlook: Africa's Strategic Agenda', in Adedeji, *Africa within the World*, p 218.

23   Also A. Adedeji, 'Marginalisation and Marginality: Context, Issues and Viewpoints' and B. Onimode, 'The Imperatives of Self-Confidence and Self-Reliance in African Development', both in Adedeji, *Africa within the World*, pp 12-13 and 188 respectively.

24   F.i. D. Rothchild and N. Chazan (eds), *The Precarious Balance: State and Society in Africa* (Boulder and London, 1988) and C. Grey Johnson, 'The African informal sector at the crossroads:

It is, however, highly unlikely that Africans could ever discard a Western role, apart from any Western refusal to leave (some) African countries to fend for themselves. The continent's numerous links with the outside world makes the pursuit of autarky utopian and unrealistic. But perhaps it might be possible to adopt a more selective strategy, which would not amount to a blank refusal to interact with the outside world but to a predominance of focus on Africa's internal resources and needs. Like certain African scholars, we would argue that dissociation from the global economic order should mean the subjection of external ties to the logic of internal development. Efforts should be made to achieve greater balance in the structures of economic output, so as to reduce crippling shortages. Inadequate endowments would naturally require imports and, hence, exports. But these would be tied as a necessary supplement to, and not be allowed to thwart, development policies whose contents would be mainly determined by popularly carried objectives.[25]

The fact that the OAU formally professes its faith in self-reliance too might be considered as a hopeful sign. In its treaty for an African Economic Community it does not make clear, however, how it wants to marry self-reliance to co-operation with the rest of the world.[26] Nevertheless, with the experience of three decades of political independence Africa's peoples have little reason to hope that their salvation will come from outside. But as many of their most eloquent spokesmen frequently stress, they cannot afford resignation or pessimism either. So in whatever way the OAU seeks to address the continent's future, what is certain is that any strategy should focus on enhancing the autonomy and self-confidence of Africans — both in and outside the OAU.

---

emerging policy options', in *Africa Development*, 1992, no. 1, pp 65-91.

25   See on this also Amin, *Delinking*, pp 66-67; S. Amin, *La faillite du développement en Afrique et dans le tiers-monde: une analyse politique* (Alençon, 1989), pp 252-267; and Adedeji, 'Marginalisation and Marginality', p 10.

26   See esp. article 93, AEC Treaty. Also *Le Soleil* (Senegal), 12/7/90 (article).

Appendix A

OAU documents

Documents of the OAU can be found in the library and archives of the OAU and ECA in Addis Ababa. There are no complete sets of OAU documents in the West, where they are, in fact, rather sparse and widely scattered. In Europe one should refer to several institutions in London and Paris (Royal Institute of International Affairs, Institute of Commonwealth Studies, London School of Economics, Documentation Française, Centre d'Etudes Africaines) and the Scandinavian Institute of African Studies in Uppsala. Sometimes OAU documents are published in monographs or in (former) periodicals like the *Africa Contemporary Record*.

Our own corpus of documents has been culled from most of the above-mentioned sources. While it is impossible to give the location of each and every document, a copy of our collection has been stored at the library of the African Studies Centre in Leiden, in order to facilitate access and reference.

The following overview of this set of documents has been arranged in chronological order, starting with the OAU's founding conference. Documents of conferences preceding the OAU and cited in chapters 3 and 4 have been omitted. A full listing of Council and Assembly resolutions has also been excluded as these run into more than one thousand documents. They consist of:

- resolutions   (CM/Res.; ECM/Res.; AHG/Res.; EAHG/Res.)
- decisions   (CM/Dec.; AHG/Dec.)
- statements   (CM/St.; AHG/St.)
- declarations (CM/Decl.; AHG/Decl.; EAHG/Decl.)

References to these particular documents can be found in the foot-notes of this study, cited by their official code number.

Proceedings of the Summit Conference of Independent African States: Verbatim Record

Proceedings of the Summit Conference of Independent African States:
- Volume 1, Section 1, Addis Ababa, May 1963
- Volume 1, Section 2, Addis Ababa, May 1963

Draft Protocol for the Commission of Mediation, Conciliation and Arbitration; Council of Ministers, First Session, Dakar: Committee 1, Sub-Committee 2, 7 August 1963

Functions and Regulations of the General Secretariat of the Organization of African Unity; adopted by the Council of Ministers, Dakar, 11 August 1963

Rules of Procedure of the Council of Ministers of the Organization of African Unity; adopted by the Council of Ministers, Dakar, 11 August 1963

DEF.1/29 October 1963: Defence Commission, First Session, Accra, 30 October-2 November 1963

Economic and Social Commission, First Session, Niamey, 13 December 1963: ECOS/12/RES/1 (I); ECOS/16/RES/2 (I); ECOS/17/RES/3 (I); ECOS/18/RES/4 (I); ECOS/19/RES/5 (I); ECOS/20/RES/6 (I)

CM.3 (III): Draft Convention for the Denuclearization of the Continent of Africa; Council of Ministers, Third Session, Cairo, 1964

Health, Sanitation and Nutrition Commission, First Session, Alexandria, 14 January 1964: HSN/17/Res/1; HSN/20/Res/2; HSN/21/Res./3

Educational and Cultural Commission, First Session, Léopoldville, 8 January 1964: EDC/28/Res/1 (I); EDC/29/Res/2 (I); EDC/30/Res/3 (I); EDC/31/Res/4 (I); EDC/32/Res/5 (I); EDC/33/Res/6 (I); EDC/34/Res/7 (I); EDC/35/Res/8 (I)

Scientific, Technical and Research Commission, First Session, Algiers, February 1964: STR/35/Res.1 (I); STR/36/Res.2 (I); STR/37/Res.3 (I); STR/38/Res.4 (I); STR/39/Res.5 (I); STR/40/Res.6 (I); STR/41/Res.7 (I)

Verbatim Record of the Second Extraordinary Session of the Council of Ministers, Dar es Salaam, February 1964

OAU Review, vl. 1, no. 1, May 1964

Commission on the Problem of Refugees in Africa, 4 sessions, Addis Ababa, 1-5 June 1964

CM.33 (III): Memorandum by the Provisional Secretary General on Special Arrangement for Interim Financing of the Secretariat; Council of Ministers, Third Session, Cairo, July 1964

CM.34 (III): The Report of the Secretary General on the Request of the Accra Assembly; Council of Ministers, Third Session, Cairo, July 1964

CM.35 (III): Report of the Provisional Secretary General on His Initial Contacts with UNESCO; Council of Ministers, Third Session, Cairo, July 1964

CM.36 (III): The Work of the Committee of Experts on the Draft Protocol of Mediation, Conciliation and Arbitration; Council of Ministers, Third Session, Cairo, July 1964

Protocol of the Commission of Mediation, Conciliation and Arbitration; approved by the Assembly of Heads of State and Government, Cairo, July 1964

Report of the Rapporteur of Committee II of the Third Session of the Council of Ministers, July 1964

Annex to Report of Rapporteur of Committee II: Extract from Provisional Secretary-General's Progress Report, CM/24 (Part II), paras. 75 to 77, which was adopted by the Third Session of the Council of Ministers (1964)

Rules of Procedure of the Assembly of Heads of State and Government; approved by the Assembly of Heads of State and Government, Cairo, July 1964

Agreement between Ethiopia and the Organization of African Unity, signed at Addis Ababa, 6 July 1965 ["Headquarters Agreement"]

General Convention on the Privileges and Immunities of the Organization of African Unity; adopted by the Assembly of Heads of State and Government, Accra, 25 October 1965

Agreement Between the United Nations and the Organization of African Unity on Co-operation Between the Latter and the United Nations Economic Commission for Africa, 15 November 1965

CAB/LEG/24.4/11: Convention Phytosanitaire pour l'Afrique, Kinshasa, 13 septembre 1967

Report on the OAU Consultative Mission to Nigeria, Nigerian National Press Ltd, Apapa, n.d. (c. November 1967)

Accord entre l'Organisation de l'Unité Africaine et l'Organisation des Nations Unies pour l'Education, la Science et la Culture, Paris, 10 juillet 1968

CM/212 (Part 2): Report of the Administrative Secretary-General Covering the Period from February to September 1968, Algiers, September 1968

Statement by the Liberation Movements to the Assembly of Heads of State and Government of the Organization of African Unity; held in Algiers, September 1968

Nigeria: International Observers Team Reports: Final Report of the first phase from October 5 to December 10 by the Organization of African Unity observers in Nigeria (1968)

Draft Rules of Procedure of the Educational, Scientific, Cultural and Health Commission; approved by the Commission at Addis Ababa, 4 July 1969

CM/270: Introduction to the Report of the Administrative Secretary-General, Covering the Period from February to August 1969, Addis Ababa, August 1969

Manifesto on Southern Africa; approved by the Conference of East and Central African States at Lusaka, 16 April 1969 and adopted by the OAU Assembly of Heads of State and Government at Addis Ababa, 6-10 September 1969

OAU Military Bulletin: A Periodical Review of the Military Activities of African Nationalist Movements, Issue No. 1, June 1970; Executive Secretariat, OAU Liberation Committee, Dar es Salaam

ECM/2 (VII): Report of the Administrative Secretary-General to the 7th Extraordinary Session of the Council of Ministers and the Third Ordinary Session of the OAU Defence Commission held in Lagos on 9 December 1970

CM/351: Report of the Administrative Secretary-General Covering the Period from September 1970 to February 1971, Addis Ababa, February 1971

CM/378: Report of the Administrative Secretary-General Covering the Period from February to June 1971

OAU; Organization of African Unity; Special 8th Summit; OAU General Secretariat Press and Information Service, Addis Ababa, July 1971

The Principles of the OAU Charter, the Lusaka Manifesto, Dialogue and Future Strategy; OAU General Secretariat, Addis Ababa, 1971

ST/2/ECAS/VII: Mogadiscio Declaration; approved by the 7th Summit Conference of East and Central African States, Mogadiscio, 18-20 October 1971; (publ. by) OAU General Secretariat, Addis Ababa

Mémorandum de la Commission des Dix de l'OUA Adressé à Israel et à l'Egypte (novembre 1971) et Réponses du Caire (23 novembre 1971) et de Jérusalem (28 novembre 1971)

CM/412: Report of the Administrative Secretary-General Covering the Period from June 1971 to February 1972

Organization of African Unity - OAU: What it is. How it Works. What it Does; OAU Press Information Division, General Secretariat, Addis Ababa, n.d. (c. 1972)

Organization of African Unity; "Special 9th Summit", September 1972; Press and Information Section, General Secretariat, OAU, Addis Ababa

OAU Ten Years (Tesfa Press), n.d.

OAU 10th Summit Anniversary; OAU Press and Information Section, General Secretariat, Addis Ababa, Ethiopia, 1973

Accra Declaration on the New Strategy for the Liberation of Africa, Liberation Committee, 8-13 January 1973

Nouvelles de l'OUA, Aug.-Sept. 1973

OAU News Bulletin, Oct.-Nov. 1973

OAU News Bulletin, Febr.-March 1974

OAU News, New Series, no. 1, Oct. 1974

OAU Review/OAU News, New Series, no. 2, Jan.-March 1975

ECM/St.15 (IX): Dar es Salaam Declaration on Southern Africa, 7-10 April 1975

Africa and its Refugees: Africa Refugee Day June 20 1975; Bureau for the Placement and Education of African Refugees, Organization of African Unity

Final Communiqué of the Extraordinary Session of the Assembly of Heads of State and Government held in Addis Ababa, 10-12 January 1976 (also CM/Res.490 [XXVII])

Cultural Charter for Africa, Port Louis 1976; Information Division of the OAU General

Secretariat, Addis Ababa, 1976

Convention de l'OUA pour l'Elimination du Mercenariat en Afrique, Libreville, 3 juillet 1977

Resolutions of the Liberation Committee, 30th session, Tripoli, 13-18 February 1978

CM/896 (XXI) Annex III: Financial Rules and Regulations, adopted at Nairobi, 4 March 1979

CM/896 (XXXI) Annexes I and II: Staff Rules and Regulations, adopted at Nairobi, 4 March 1979

CM/977 (XXXIII): Rapport du Comité d'Experts Juridiques sur les Amendements au Protocole de la Commission de Médiation, de Conciliation et d'Arbitrage, mars 1979

CM/977 (XXXIII): Rapport du Secrétaire-Général sur le Comité d'Experts Juridiques sur les Amendements au Protocole de la Commission de Médiation, de Conciliation et d'Arbitrage, 1979

CM/992 (XXXII): Projet de rapport du Comité ad hoc sur la révision du barême des contributions, 11 juillet 1979

Rapport du Comité ad hoc sur la révision du barême des contributions à l'O.U.A., 11 juillet 1979

Functions and Regulations of the Co-ordinating Committee for the Liberation of Africa, n.d., early 1980s

Rules of Procedure of the Co-ordinating Committee for the Liberation of Africa, n.d., early 1980s

CM/Res.814 (XXXV): Règlement Intérieur de la Commission Spéciale sur le Problème des Réfugiés en Afrique (1980)

Règlement Intérieur du Comité de Coordination de l'OUA sur l'Assistance aux Réfugiés (c. 1980)

10th Ordinary Session of the Coordinating Committee of the OAU/BPEAR, Addis Ababa, Ethiopia, March 24-27, 1980: A Compendium of Resolutions on the African Refugees

Acte Final de Lagos, Lagos, 28-29/4/80

Plan d'Action de Lagos pour le Développement Economique de l'Afrique, Lagos, 28-29/4/80

AHG/105 (XVIII) Report of the Good-Offices Committee on Ethiopia/Somalia dispute, Lagos, Nigeria, (18-20 August 1980)

AHG/103 (XVIII)B: Recommendation of the Ad-Hoc Commitee of OAU Heads of State, fifth session, Freetown, Sierra Leone (9-11 September 1980)

CAB/LEG/67/3/Rev.5: OAU Ministerial Meeting on African Charter on Human and Peoples' Rights, January 7-19, 1981, Banjul, The Gambia

PL/SA/39(IV)59.81 Rev.1: Consideration of All Aspects of Sanctions against South Africa: Report Submitted by the Organization of African Unity to International Conference on Sanctions against South Africa, Paris, 20-27 May 1981

Paris Declaration on Sanctions against South Africa, adopted at UN-OAU International Conference on Sanctions aginst South Africa, Paris, 27 May 1981

African Charter on Human and Peoples' Rights; Division of Press and Information, OAU General Secretariat, Addis Ababa, n.d.

20 Questions et Réponses à l'Usage du Réfugié Africain; OAU Bureau for Refugees, Addis Ababa, 1982

OAU Charter & Rules of Procedure; Division of Press and Information of the OAU General Secretariat, Addis Ababa, January 1982

CM/1157 (XXXVIII): Rapport financier de l'O.U.A. pour l'exercice financier 1980/81; Conseil des Ministres, 38ème session ordinaire, Addis Abéba, 28 février 1982

CAB/LEG/97/Draft/Rapt.RPT(III) Rev. 2: Projet de rapport du rapporteur du comité de révision de la Charte de l'OUA, 3ème session ordinaire, Addis Abéba, 10 au 24 mai 1982
Tripoli Declaration of Heads of State and Government, 26 November 1982

(The) African Refugees: (Quarterly) Newsletter published by the Organization of African Unity (OAU Bureau for Refugees, Addis Ababa): no. 2, June 1983; no. 6, February 1985; no. 7, June 1985; no. 8, July 1986; no. 10, July 1987

Linguistic Liberation and Unity of Africa, OAU Bill Publication 6, Inter-African Bureau of Languages, Kampala, 1985

Africa's Priority Programme for Economic Recovery 1986-1990; adopted by the Twenty-First Ordinary Session of the Assembly of Heads of State and Government of the Organization of African Unity 18-20 July 1985; (publ. by) FAO, 1985

Background Paper on the Meetings of the OAU Defence Commission from 1963 to 1986, General Secretariat, Addis Ababa

DEF/4 (IX): Report of the Secretary-General on the Seminar on Peace-Keeping Operations, OAU Defence Commission, Ninth Ordinary Session, 27-30 May 1986, Harare, Zimbabwe

The Special Emergency Assistance Fund for Drought and Famine in Africa: Basic Documents; OAU Press and Information, General Secretariat, Addis Ababa, February 1987

The African Common Position on Africa's External Debt Crisis, Addis Ababa, December 1987

BR/27/ICRSSA/50.87: International Conference on the Plight of Refugees and Displaced Persons in Southern Africa; General Secretariat, Organization of African Unity, Addis Ababa, n.d.

SARRED/88/L.1/Rev.II: Oslo Declaration and Plan of Action on the Plight of Refugees, Returnees and Displaced Persons in Southern Africa (SARRED); General Secretariat, Organization of African Unity, Addis Ababa, n.d.

List of Countries which have signed, ratified or adhered to the African Charter on Human and Peoples' Rights; Organization of African Unity Secretariat, Addis Ababa, 12/4/88

Activity Report of the African Commission on Human and Peoples' Rights; adopted on 27 April 1988

CM/1492 (XLVIII): Report of the 50th Ordinary Session of the OAU Co-ordinating Committee for the Liberation of Africa to the 48th Ordinary Session of the Council of Ministers, 19-24 May 1988 (also *Africa Contemporary Record*, 1988-89, C25-33)

1963: The Year OAU Was Born - Année de la Création de l'OUA; 25th Anniversary; Press and Information Division, OAU General Secretariat, Addis Ababa, 25 May 1988

BR/10/COM/XV/136.89: Number and Location of Refugees in Africa; (as of end October 1988); General Secretariat, Organization of African Unity, Addis Ababa

Brief: General Political Affairs, Defence and Security Division; n.d., c. 1989

BR/10/COM/XV/16.89: Activity Report of the OAU Commission of Fifteen on Refugees to the 50th Ordinary Session of the OAU Council of Ministers; General Secretariat, Organization of African Unity, Addis Ababa, n.d.

BR/27/SARRED/1/89: Brief to the 13th Ordinary Session of the OAU Commission of 15 on Refugees by Ambassador Yilma Tadesse, Assistant Secretary General in Charge of Political Affairs, on the International Conference on the Plight of Refugees, Returnees and Displaced Persons in Southern Africa (30-31 January 1989); General Secretariat, Organization of African Unity, Addis Ababa

CAB/LEG/24.3: OAU Convention Governing the Specific Aspects of Refugee Problems in Africa; General Secretariat, Organization of African Unity, Addis Ababa, 12/4/89

BR/27/SARRED/12.89: Follow-Up Meeting of the Steering Committee of the International Conference on the Plight of Refugees, Returnees and Displaced Persons in Southern Africa (SARRED) and the International Conference on Assistance to Refugees in Africa (ICARA), New York, 7 to 9 June 1989; General Secretariat, Organization of African Unity, Addis Ababa

CM/1546 (L): Council of Ministers, Fiftieth Ordinary Session, 17-21 July 1989, Addis Ababa, Ethiopia

OAU Committee on Southern Africa: Political Declaration, Harare, 21 August 1989

The OAU in a Nutshell; OAU Information Service: Addis Ababa, n.d., early 1990s

Treaty on the African Economic Community, Abuja, Nigeria, 3 June 1991

BR/COM/XV/92: Aide-Memoire: International Conference on the Plight of Refugees, Returnees and Displaced Persons in Southern Africa; General Secretariat, Organization of African Unity, Addis Ababa, n.d.

CM/1710 (LVI) Rev. 1: Report of the Secretary-General on Conflicts in Africa: Prospects for an OAU Mechanism for Conflict Prevention and Resolution (June 1992)

OAU at 30: Reflections on the Past and Prospects for the Future: Address by the Secretary-General, H.E. Dr. Salim Ahmed Salim on the occasion of the 30th Aniversary of the Organization of African Unity, Africa Hall, Addis Ababa, May 25, 1993

Appendix B

Newspaper sources

The search for African newspapers began with the compilation of a list of newspapers and other current affairs periodicals in African states. This was mainly done on the basis of information taken from the annual reference guides *Africa South of the Sahara* and *The Middle East and North Africa*. The list was subsequently used in selecting newspaper publications for research for material on the OAU.

In Europe various libraries and institutes possess collections of African newspapers. However, the largest and most important collections can be found, and were researched, at the newspaper division of the British Library in Colindale, London, and the Documentation Française in Paris. The African Studies Centre in Leiden also has an important corpus of papers, which covers both Anglophone and Francophone countries. At these institutes newspapers are usually kept on microfilm or -fiche and sometimes in their original form.

What follows is, first, a list in alphabetical order (by country) of all the newspapers and other current affairs periodicals that were found and analysed for this study. It includes not only governmental publications, but also some newspapers of opposition parties, independent papers and other non-governmental tracts, whether periodical or incidental. Full titles are given, followed by the years covered by OAU-relevant material found in these publications and some description of their political status or information relevant to their interpretation. This information was derived from the above-mentioned reference guides, the publications themselves or other cited literature.

The second and third list provide an overview of how much material, relevant to the OAU, was collected in terms of years for each country and the inter-African categories discussed in section 1.2 and Appendix D.

I Newspapers and other publications from OAU member states

Algeria

Révolution Africaine
1964-1967; 1971-1973; 1975-1988

El Moudjahid: Organe Central du Front de Libération Nationale
1987
both government party organs

Angola

Jornal de Angola
1976-1979; 1988-1989
government paper; all newspapers nationalized

Benin (Dahomey)

Ehuzu: République Populaire du Bénin. Quotidien d'information. Organe du militantisme révolutionnaire
1988
government paper (contains quotations of presidential speeches)

Botswana

(Botswana) Daily News/Dikgang Tsa Gompieno
1966-1968; 1970; 1972-1978; 1980-1984
government paper

Burkina Faso (Upper Volta)

Carrefour Africain: Hebdomadaire National d'Information du Burkina Faso
1987
government paper

Burundi

Infor-Burundi: bulletin hebdomadaire d'information de l'Office de presse du Burundi
1963
government publication; contains speech by vice-premier to the first extraordinary session of the OAU Council of Ministers, November 1963

Cameroon

E. M'buyinga, *Pan-Africanism or Neo-Colonialism? The Bankruptcy of the O.A.U.*
(London, 1982)
1982
publication of the illegal exile party Union des Populations du Cameroun

Cameroon Tribune: Grand Quotidien National d'Information
1985-1988; 1990-1991
government paper (usually opens with words of the president)

Congo-Brazzaville

La Semaine: Brazzaville. République Populaire du Congo
1966-1967; 1970
Catholic weekly, publ. by Archdiocese of Brazzaville; contains generally phrased
criticism of African governments, but not explicitly directed against the Congolese
government itself. A press censorship committee was established in 1968 (*Africa South
of the Sahara*, 1971, p 239)

Egypt

The Egyptian Gazette
1960-1963; 1968-1970
By presidential decree May 1960 private newspapers and magazines were taken over by
the state. Papers were relatively free to report on domestic news, but had to reflect
government views as far as foreign policy was concerned (*The Middle East and North
Africa*, 1966-67, p 764; 1969-70, p 824; and 1972-73, p 278)

Ethiopia

Ethiopia Observer: Journal of Independent Opinion, Economics, History and the Arts;
editor: Sylvia Pankhurst
1960
non-governmental; contains speeches of Ethiopian and other delegates to the second
Conference of Independent African States (CIAS), Addis Ababa, June 1960

Ministry of Information of the Imperial Ethiopian Government: 'Second Conference of
Independent African States, Addis Ababa, June 24 to 26, 1960' (Addis Ababa, n.d.)
c. 1960
government publication

The Ethiopian Herald
1960-1963; 1976-1985; 1987
government newspaper

Ghana

The Ghanaian Times
1961; 1963-1966; 1979-1983
government-owned

Ghana Today
1963-1964
published by the Information Section of the Ghana Office (embassy), London

Address by Osagyefo the President to the National Assembly on the Occasion of the
Ratification of the Charter of the Organization of African Unity, Friday, 21/6/63
1963
government document

Guinea (Conakry)

Horoya. Travail - Justice - Solidarité: Organe Quotidien du Parti Démocratique de Guinée
1963-1964; 1973-1974
government party organ

Ivory Coast

Fraternité (-hebdo/matin)
1962-1965; 1967-1969; 1971-1979
organ of the governing Parti Démocratique de Côte d'Ivoire; Directeur Politique: Félix
Houphouët-Boigny

Téré: Hebdomadaire du Parti Ivorien des Travailleurs (PIT)
1991
organ of opposition party

Notre Temps
1991-1992
non-governmental/opposition paper

Kenya

East African Standard
1964-1966; 1968-1974
independent; some relative press freedom, while usually very positive on government stand and record in foreign affairs

The Standard
1975-1987
successor to *East African Standard*; independent; some relative press freedom, while usually very positive on the government's stand and record in foreign affairs

Kenya Weekly News
1964-1965; 1967-1968
expresses itself favourably about the government, at least in foreign affairs

Inside Kenya Today
1972-1973
government publication; published by Ministry of Information

Daily Nation
1988
independent; contains non-governmental criticism of OAU member states in general

Libya

Arab Dawn
1977

Jamahiriya Review
1980 and 1982

In 1973 all private newspapers were nationalized and handed over to the Public Press Organization (*The Middle East and North Africa*, 1977-78, p 547)

Madagascar

Nouvelles Malgaches Quotidiennes/Nouvelles Malagasy Quotidiennes: Secrétariat d'Etat à l'Information et au Tourisme. Service Général de l'Information
1963-1966
government paper

Info Madagascar: Publication du Sécretariat d'Etat et au Tourisme de la République Malgache
1966-1973
government paper

Madagascar Renouveau: Magazine d'Information Politique, Economique, Sociale et Culturelle
1978 and 1980
government publication; publ. by the Ministère de l'Information, de l'Animation idéologique et des Relations avec les Institutions; Direction de la Presse et des Publications; Service de production

Malawi

Malawi News
1964-1965; 1967; 1969; 1971
weekly; very positive on the president and the government's stands in foreign affairs

Mali

l'Essor: Organe de l'Union Soudanaise - R.D.A. Hebdomadaire/La Voix du Peuple. Organe de l'Union Démocratique du Peuple Malien
1962-1979; 1981-1985; 1988-1991
organ of the (then) governing party/government

Morocco

Al Istiqlal
1961
organ of the opposition party Istiqlal

l'Opinion: Quotidien National d'Information
1970; 1972-1973; 1984; 1990
organ of the opposition party Istiqlal; pro-government stand as far as the Western Sahara issue is concerned

Le Matin du Sahara
1986
pro-government stand as far as the Western Sahara issue is concerned

Namibia

Die Republikein
1984
organ of the pro-South African Democratic Turnhalle Alliance

The Namibian
1990
non-governmental, independent weekly

Niger

Le Niger: Fraternité - Travail - Progrès
1973
government paper; Directeur Politique: Boubou Hama; editor-in-chief: Ide Oumarou

Sahel-Hebdo: Hebdomadaire d'Informations
1974
government paper

Nigeria

Daily Times
1961-1973; 1975-1980; 1983-1985; 1987-1988
(partly: 60%) government paper since c. 1977 (*Africa South of the Sahara*, 1977-78, p 676); while enjoying some relative press freedom and sometimes critical of African governments in general, it often expresses itself favourably about the government's stands in foreign affairs

O.A.U. '83: Nigeria's Role
1983
published by Department of Information; government document

Senegal

Le Soleil
1981-1987; 1990-1993
government paper

Sierra Leone

Daily Mail
1970-1982
government paper

M. Mustapha, *Big Game in Africa* (n. pl., 1980)
1980
non-governmental diatribe; written by individual who opposed the government, in particular on its decision to host the 1980 OAU summit

Somalia

Somali News: National Weekly
1969
all papers published by the government (*Africa South of the Sahara*, 1987, p 891)

South Africa

Die Burger
1971; 1975; 1977-1980; 1982; 1984-1988
organ of the (then) governing National Party

Weekend/Weekly Mail
1990 and 1992
non-governmental, independent; in orientation close to the United Democratic Front of the 1980s

The Star
1991
non-governmental, independent; expressive of white, conservative-liberal opinion, in orientation close to the Democratic Party

Sudan

Voice of Southern Sudan
1963; 1965; 1969
published outside Sudan by the exiled, southern Sudanese-led opposition party Sudan African National Union

Sudan News
1964
published by the Sudan Embassy, London

The Southern Front Memorandum to O.A.U. on Afro-Arab Conflict in the Sudan, Accra, October 1965
1965
document of temporary legal front of opposition parties inside Sudan, representing southern Sudanese provinces and recognized by exiled southern Sudanese

The Vigilant: An Independent Newspaper
1966
newspaper; non-governmental, pro-southern Sudanese and run by southern Sudanese based in Khartoum

Sudanow
1977-1979; 1981; 1983-1984
government monthly published by the Ministry of Culture and Information, Khartoum

Tanzania

Tanganyika Standard/The Standard
1961; 1966-1971
privately owned by European press group and nationalized in 1972 (D.L. Wilcox, *Mass Media in Black Africa: Philosophy and Control* [New York, 1975], pp 42 and 45); positive on government's stands in foreign affairs

Sunday News
1963
quotes the Tanzanian minister of foreign affairs

The Nationalist
1964-1965
organ of the governing Tanganyika African National Union; merges with *The Standard* in 1972 to form the *Daily-Sunday News* (*Africa South of the Sahara*, 1971, p 840 and 1973, p 920)

External Affairs Bulletin Tanzania: An Official Record of Foreign Policy of the United Republic of Tanzania, vol. 1, no. 2, July 1965
1965
government document

Daily News-Sunday News
1972-1985
government paper; nationalized successor to *The Standard*; editor-in-chief: dr. Julius Nyerere

Togo
Togo Presse: Grand Quotidien d'Information
1975-1977
government paper (front page usually contains a quotation from a presidential speech)

La Nouvelle Marche (successor to *Togo Presse*)
1988
government paper

Tunisia
l'Action: Organe du Parti Socialiste Destourien (fondateur: Habib Bourguiba)
1985 and 1987

Le Renouveau: Organe du Rassemblement Constitutionnel Démocratique (successor to *l'Action*)
1988
both government party organs

Zaire (Congo-Leo.)

Le Courrier d'Afrique: Quotidien Indépendant
1960-1969
(pro-)government paper; based in Leopoldville/Kinshasa; anti-Lumumba (C. Young, *Politics in the Congo: Decolonization and Independence* [Princeton, 1965], p 325); all press nationalized in 1972 (Wilcox, *Mass Media in Black Africa*, p 46)

Epanza: Hebdo d'Opinion et de Formation
1972 and 1974
pro-government; contains sayings by Mobutu; nationalized successor to *Présence Congolaise*

Zaïre-Afrique
1982
pro-government stand on the Western Sahara issue

Zambia

Zambia Daily Mail
1969-1971
government controlled paper

(Sunday) Times of Zambia
1973; 1975-1986
organ of the (then) governing United National Independence Party

Zimbabwe

The Herald
1980-1986
government paper

II Collected data aggregated by OAU member state

Algeria
1964-1967; 1971-1973; 1975-1988
Angola
1976-1979; 1988-1989
Benin (Dahomey)
1988
Botswana
1966-1968; 1970; 1972-1978; 1980-1984
Burkina Faso (Upper Volta)
1987
Burundi
1963
Cameroon
1982; 1985-1988; 1990-1991
Congo-Brazzaville
1966-1967; 1970
Egypt
1960-1963; 1968-1970
Ethiopia
1960-1963; 1976-1985; 1987
Ghana
1961; 1963-1966; 1979-1983
Guinea (Conakry)
1963-1964; 1973-1974
Ivory Coast
1962-1965; 1967-1969; 1971-1979; 1991-1992
Kenya
1964-1988
Libya
1977; 1980; 1982
Madagascar
1963-1973; 1978 and 1980

Malawi
1964-1965; 1967; 1969; 1971
Mali
1962-1979; 1981-1985; 1988-1991
Morocco
1961; 1970; 1972-1973; 1984; 1986; 1990
Namibia
1984 and 1990
Niger
1973-1974
Nigeria
1961-1973; 1975-1980; 1983-1985; 1987-1988
Senegal
1981-1987; 1990-1993
Sierra Leone
1970-1982
Somalia
1969
South Africa
1971; 1975; 1977-1980; 1982; 1984-1988; 1990-1992
Sudan
1963-1966; 1969; 1977-1979; 1981; 1983-1984
Tanzania
1961; 1963-1985
Togo
1975-1977; 1988
Tunisia
1985; 1987-1988
Zaire (Congo-Leo.)
1960-1969; 1972; 1974; 1982
Zambia
1969-1971; 1973; 1975-1986
Zimbabwe
1980-1986

III Collected data aggregated by inter-African classification

A *Collected data by region*

1. North Africa   1960-1973; 1975-1988; 1990

2. West Africa	1961-1993
3. Central Africa	1960-1970; 1972; 1974;
	1976-1979; 1982; 1985-1991
4. East Africa	1960-1988
5. Southern Africa	1964-1986; 1990-1992

B *Collected data by political affiliation*[1]

1. moderate-conservative	
member states	1960-1985
2. radical member states	1960-1985

C *Collected data by linguistic/cultural affiliation*

1. North African member states	1960-1973; 1975-1988; 1990
2. Sub-Saharan member states	1960-1993
3. Anglophone member states	1960-1988; 1990-1992
4. Francophone member states	1960-1993

---

1 This distinction loses its relevance after the mid-1980s.

Appendix C

Interviews

The following list is made up of persons with whom interviews were held during field-work. The persons interviewed were functionaries of the OAU's General Secretariat and officials of embassies in Ethiopia. The list is presented in alphabetical order. For all persons names, as well as first names or initials, are given if known, followed by title and/or function or position, nationality of interviewee (in the case of OAU officials) and the date of the interview. Interviews with OAU functionaries below the professional grade, such as secretaries, typists and receptionists, consisted of informal conversations. The names of Ethiopian general service personnel have been suppressed on request. All interviews were held in Addis Ababa, at the OAU General Secretariat and the respective embassies.

Bah, Ambassador Mamadou, Director of the Political Department, OAU General Secretariat; nationality: Guinean (Conakry); 18 September 1989

Bakwesegha, dr. Chris J., Director of the Bureau for Refugees, OAU General Secretariat; nationality: Ugandan; 2 October 1989

Clerk, OAU General Secretariat, name unknown; nationality: Mozambiquan; 14 September 1989

Dede, Ambassador Brownson N., Assistant Secretary-General for Administration and Finance, OAU General Secretariat; nationality: Nigerian; 22 September 1989

Dualeh, Abdillahi Ali, Chief of the General Political Affairs Section, General Political Affairs, Defence and Security Division, OAU General Secretariat; nationality: Somali; 18 September 1989

Heldring, drs. A., temporary chargé d'affaires at the Netherlands embassy, 15 September 1989

Immaculate,[1] private secretary to Ambassador Brownson N. Dede, Assistant Secretary-General for Administration and Finance, OAU General Secretariat; nationality: Tanzanian; 22 September 1989

Immaculée, secretary to Ambassador Mamadou Bah, Director of the Political Department,

---

1 Most general service staff are known, and were introduced, by their first name, as surnames are considered confusing because of the many nationalities present at the General Secretariat.

OAU General Secretariat; nationality: Rwandan; 15 September 1989

Iskandar, R.S., Ambassador of Egypt, 27 September 1989

Kebe, Amadou, Conseiller at the Senegalese embassy, 3 October 1989

Mainza, David Busiku, First Secretary at the Zambian embassy, 28 September 1989

Member of the general service staff, OAU General Secretariat; nationality: Ethiopian; 15 September 1989

Member of the general service staff, OAU General Secretariat; nationality: Ethiopian; 15 September 1989

Pana, Colonel Zoula Gustave, Chief of the Defence and Security Section, General Political Affairs, Defence and Security Division, OAU General Secretariat; nationality: Congolese (Brazzaville); 19 September 1989

Tesha, dr. J.A., Minister/Counsellor at the Tanzanian embassy, 25 September 1989

Thundu, J.B., Deputy to Ibrahim Dagash, Head of Information Division, Office of the Secretary-General, OAU General Secretariat; nationality: Malawian; 14 September 1989

Appendix D

Classification of OAU member states

As explained in sections 1.2 and 5.6 various cleavages characterize inter-African relations and to a greater or lesser extent affect the functioning of the OAU. These cleavages are:

- the former fissures between radical and moderate-conservative states
- the distinction between English- and French-speaking states
- the division between North African and sub-Saharan countries
- the distinction between member states in terms of one of the continent's regions

Definitions of these categories and assessments of their significance for the OAU are given in the above-mentioned sections. Here the actual classification of individual countries is given in terms of these categories.

First, member states are listed according to the OAU's own regional classification designed for its internal institutional purposes. While Namibia and South Africa were, for long, non-OAU members and target of OAU action, they have also been listed in the Southern Africa category for the period preceding their accession to membership. Morocco is listed in the North Africa category, although it is a non-member country since the mid 1980s. Western Sahara is not included in the regional classification for lack of data. However, as no newspaper material was collected for RASD this does not affect our analysis.

The second classification involves the distinction between North African and sub-Saharan countries. With regard to the North African countries it is based on the North Africa category of the OAU's regional classification. The rationale of Sudan's and Mauritania's listing was discussed in section 1.2.

The third classification is the listing of countries according to the distinction between English- and French-speaking states. The listing of Cameroon, Eritrea, Ethiopia, Somalia, Seychelles and Mauritius is explained in section 1.2.

The last classification is that of radical and moderate-conservative member states. The complexities and partly elusive character of this classification were discussed in section 1.2, as well as the justification for employing it and the approach to its use in this study. As the radical - moderate/conservative divide remained relevant until the mid 1980s the actual listing of countries does not go beyond 1985 and excludes Namibia, South

Africa and Eritrea. Because of changes in political orientation member states are sometimes listed in both the radical and moderate-conservative categories.

As voting does usually not take place in the OAU's policy organs the actual listing of individual member states has to be, and is, mainly based on information of their (general) ideological orientation, especially as it pertains to their foreign policy posture, as derived from various sources of secondary literature cited in this study. The former annual *Africa Contemporary Record*, besides monographs and other sources on individual countries, was of special importance here. These data were combined with data on member state line-up in several major (inter-)African disputes that came before the OAU, such as the Angolan and Western Saharan crises. However, it must be realized that such line-ups at times exposed anomalies.[1] In most cases these were not allowed to affect the actual listing,[2] unless these anomalies could be linked to other data, on the basis of which it could be concluded that the country in question had another — or rather, had significantly altered its — general (foreign policy) orientation. Guinea (Conakry) in the early 1980s is an example.

Identification of most radical member states is usually easier than that of the conservative — and especially moderate — powers, as it is often based on very explicit ideological underpinnings.[3] Thus, the militant member states are listed first. If a country did not possess a radical orientation at independence but began to exhibit this at a later date (often as a result of regime change), the year this occurred is given in brackets. Conversely, if it discarded its militant orientation after some time this is also indicated by mention of the relevant year(s). No year is mentioned if the country in question retained its militant orientation from independence right up to the mid 1980s.

With regard to the list of moderate-conservative countries the following must be said. Most, though not all, conservative member states, were Francophone regimes. However, as was noted in section 1.2 it is not easy to pin down the group of moderate powers. Their ideological underpinnings were usually not very explicit, while internal differentiation made it difficult to treat them as a distinct grouping. They usually adopted postures in between the radical and conservative states and often sided with the conservatives, but in certain cases with the militant group. Thus, while this study frequently referred to them together with the conservative powers, they are here also listed in one group together with those conservative regimes. Rather than pointing out in this listing which member states were moderate and which ones conservative, the true nature of individual regimes is better gauged from the main text of this study, where deconstruction of these orientations by regular mention of examples of countries provides the epithets moderate and conservative with more concrete and distinct meaning. As with the radical listing, years in brackets behind a country's name signify a change in

---

1   For example, in 1976 Chad and Niger — which always exhibited a conservative tendency — lined up with the pro-MPLA powers. See section 6.3.

2   See for example the two countries mentioned in the previous note or the case of Mauritania, which lined up with the radical powers with regard to certain issues during the mid 1960s.

3   Though not always. Thus, Equatorial Guinea during the 1970s tended to line up with the radicals because of its dependence on Eastern bloc aid. It was therefore listed in the radical group, although its ideology was hardly left-wing. Morocco was also listed in this group for 1960-1962/63, because of its membership of the Casablanca group.

orientation — in this case always a switch to or from the radical group. Absence of dates indicates no change.

I Regional categories

North Africa

Algeria
Egypt
Libya
Morocco
Tunisia

West Africa

Benin (Dahomey)
Burkina Faso (Upper Volta)
Cape Verde
Gambia
Ghana
Guinea (Conakry)
Guinea-Bissau
Ivory Coast
Liberia
Mali
Mauritania
Niger
Nigeria
Senegal
Sierra Leone
Togo

Central Africa

Angola
Burundi
Cameroon
Central African Republic
Chad
Congo-Brazzaville

Equatorial Guinea
Gabon
Rwanda
São Tomé and Príncipe
Zaire (Congo-Leo.)

East Africa

Comoros
Djibouti
Eritrea
Ethiopia
Kenya
Madagascar
Mauritius
Seychelles
Somalia
Sudan
Tanzania
Uganda

Southern Africa

Botswana
Lesotho
Malawi
Mozambique
Namibia
South Africa
Swaziland
Zambia
Zimbabwe

II North African and sub-Saharan states

North African states

Algeria
Egypt

Libya
Morocco
Tunisia

Sub-Saharan states

all others

III Anglophone and Francophone states

Anglophone states

Botswana
Eritrea
Ethiopia
Gambia
Ghana
Kenya
Lesotho
Liberia
Malawi
Mauritius
Namibia
Nigeria
Seychelles
Sierra Leone
Somalia
South Africa
Sudan
Swaziland
Tanzania
Uganda
Zambia
Zimbabwe

Francophone states

Benin (Dahomey)
Burkina Faso (Upper Volta)

Burundi
Cameroon
Central African Republic
Chad
Comoros
Congo-Brazzaville
Djibouti
Gabon
Guinea (Conakry)
Ivory Coast
Madagascar
Mali
Mauritania
Niger
Rwanda
Senegal
Togo
Zaire (Congo-Leo.)

IV Radical and moderate-conservative states

Radical states

Algeria
Angola
Benin (Dahomey) (from 1972/74)
Burkina Faso (Upper Volta) (from 1983)
Cape Verde
Congo-Brazzaville (from 1964)
Egypt (until 1972)
Equatorial Guinea (1970s)
Ethiopia (after 1974)
Ghana (until 1966 and from 1982)
Guinea (Conakry) (until early 1980s)
Guinea-Bissau
Libya (from 1969)
Madagascar (after 1972)
Mali
Morocco (1960-1962/63)
Mozambique
RASD
São Tomé and Príncipe
Seychelles (1977-1983)

Somalia (1969-1977)
Sudan (1964 - early 1970s)
Tanzania
Zimbabwe

Moderate-conservative states

Benin (Dahomey) (until 1972/74)
Botswana
Burkina Faso (Upper Volta) (until 1983)
Burundi
Cameroon
Central African Republic
Chad
Comoros
Congo-Brazzaville (until 1964)
Djibouti
Egypt (from 1972)
Equatorial Guinea (from 1980s)
Ethiopia (until 1974)
Gabon
Gambia
Ghana (1966-1982)
Guinea (Conakry) (from early 1980s)
Ivory Coast
Kenya
Lesotho
Liberia
Libya (until 1969)
Madagascar (until 1972)
Malawi
Mauritania
Mauritius
Morocco (from 1962/63)
Niger
Nigeria
Rwanda
Senegal
Seychelles (1976-1977 and from 1983)
Sierra Leone
Somalia (until 1969 and from 1977)
Sudan (until 1963 and from 1970s)
Swaziland

Togo
Tunisia
Uganda
Zaire (Congo-Leo.)
Zambia

Appendix E

OAU Charter[1]

We, the Heads of African States and Governments assembled in the City of Addis Ababa, Ethiopia;

CONVINCED that it is the inalienable right of all people to control their own destiny;

CONSCIOUS of the fact that freedom, equality, justice and dignity are essential objectives for the achievement of the legitimate aspirations of the African peoples;

CONSCIOUS of our responsibility to harness the natural and human resources of our continent for the total advancement of our peoples in spheres of human endeavour;

INSPIRED by a common determination to promote understanding among our peoples and co-operation among our States in response to the aspirations of our peoples for brotherhood and solidarity, in a larger unity transcending ethnic and national differences;

CONVINCED that, in order to translate this determination into a dynamic force in the cause of human progress, conditions for peace and security must be established and maintained;

DETERMINED to safeguard and consolidate the hard-won independence as well the sovereignty and territorial integrity of our States, and to fight against neo-colonialism in all its forms;

---

[1]   Taken from the officially approved text in *Proceedings of the Summit Conference of Independent African States*, vol. 1, section 1, Addis Ababa, May 1963, ch. XIV.

DEDICATED to the general progress of Africa;

PERSUADED that the Charter of the United Nations and the Universal Declaration of Human Rights, to the principles of which we reaffirm our adherence, provide a solid foundation for peaceful and positive co-operation among states;

DESIROUS that all African States should henceforth unite so that the welfare and well-being of their peoples can be assured;

RESOLVED to reinforce the links between our States by establishing and strengthening common institutions;

HAVE agreed to the present Charter.

ESTABLISHMENT

Article 1

1. The High Contracting Parties do by the present Charter establish an Organization to be known as the ORGANIZATION OF AFRICAN UNITY.

2. The Organization shall include the Continental African States, Madagascar and other Islands surrounding Africa.

PURPOSES

Article 2

1. The Organization shall have the following purposes:

a. to promote the unity and solidarity of the African States;
b. to co-ordinate and intensify their co-operation and efforts to achieve a better life for the peoples of Africa;
c. to defend their sovereignty, their territorial integrity and independence;
d. to eradicate all forms of colonialism from Africa; and
e. to promote international co-operation, having due regard to the Charter of the United Nations and the Universal Declaration of Human Rights.

2. To these ends, the Member States shall co-ordinate and harmonise their general policies, especially in the following fields:

a. political and diplomatic co-operation;
b. economic co-operation, including transport and communications;
c. educational and cultural co-operation;
d. health, sanitation, and nutritional co-operation;
e. scientific and technical co-operation; and
f. co-operation for defence and security.

PRINCIPLES

Article 3

The Member States, in pursuit of the purposes stated in Article 2, solemnly affirm and declare their adherence to the following principles:

1. the sovereign equality of all Member States;

2. non-interference in the internal affairs of States;

3. respect for the sovereignty and territorial integrity of each State and for its inalienable right to independent existence;

4. peaceful settlement of disputes by negotiation, mediation, conciliation or arbitration;

5. unreserved condemnation, in all its forms, of political assassination as well as of subversive activities on the part of neighbouring States or any other State;

6. absolute dedication to the total emancipation of the African territories which are still dependent;

7. affirmation of a policy of non-alignment with regard to all blocs.

MEMBERSHIP

Article 4

Each independent sovereign African State shall be entitled to become a Member of the Organization.

RIGHTS AND DUTIES OF MEMBER STATES

Article 5

All Member States shall enjoy equal rights and have equal duties.

Article 6

The Member States pledge themselves to observe scrupulously the principles enumerated in Article 3 of the present Charter.

INSTITUTIONS

Article 7

The Organization shall accomplish its purposes through the following principal institutions:

1. the Assembly of Heads of State and Government;
2. the Council of Ministers;
3. the General Secretariat;
4. the Commission of Mediation, Conciliation and Arbitration.

THE ASSEMBLY OF HEADS OF STATE AND GOVERNMENT

Article 8

The Assembly of Heads of State and Government shall be the supreme organ of the Organization. It shall, subject to the provisions of this Charter, discuss matters of common concern to Africa with a view to co-ordinating and harmonising the general policy of the Organization. It may in addition review the structure, functions and acts of all the organs and any specialized agencies which may be created in accordance with the present Charter.

Article 9

The Assembly shall be composed of the Heads of State and Government or their duly accredited representatives and it shall meet at least once a year. At the request of any Member State and on approval by a two-thirds majority of the Member States, the Assembly shall meet in extraordinary session.

Article 10

1. Each Member State shall have one vote.

2. All resolutions shall be determined by a two-thirds majority of the Members of the Organization.

3. Questions of procedure shall require a simple majority. Whether or not a question is one of procedure shall be determined by a simple majority of all Member States of the Organization.

4. Two-thirds of the total membership of the Organization shall form a quorum at any meeting of the Assembly.

Article 11

The Assembly shall have the power to determine its own rules of procedure.

THE COUNCIL OF MINISTERS

Article 12

1. The Council of Ministers shall consist of Foreign Ministers or such other Ministers as are designated by the Governments of Member States.

2. The Council of Ministers shall meet at least twice a year. When requested by any Member State and approved by two-thirds of all Member States, it shall meet in extraordinary session.

Article 13

1. The Council of Ministers shall be responsible to the Assembly of Heads of State and Government. It shall be entrusted with the responsibility of preparing conferences of the Assembly.

2. It shall take cognisance of any matter referred to it by the Assembly. It shall be entrusted with the implementation of the decisions of the Assembly of Heads of State and Government. It shall co-ordinate inter-African co-operation in accordance with the instructions of the Assembly and in conformity with Article 2 (2) of the present Charter.

Article 14

1. Each Member State shall have one vote.

2. All resolutions shall be determined by a simple majority of the members of the Council of Ministers.

3. Two-thirds of the total membership of the Council of Ministers shall form a quorum for any meeting of the Council.

Article 15

The Council shall have the power to determine its own rules of procedure.

GENERAL SECRETARIAT

Article 16

There shall be an Administrative Secretary-General of the Organization, who shall be appointed by the Assembly of Heads of State and Government. The Administrative Secretary-General shall direct the affairs of the Secretariat.

Article 17

There shall be one or more Assistant Secretaries-General of the Organization, who shall be appointed by the Assembly of Heads of State and Government.

Article 18

The functions and conditions of services of the Secretary-General, of the Assistant Secretaries-General and other employees of the Secretariat shall be governed by the provisions of this Charter and the regulations approved by the Assembly of Heads of State and Government.

1. In the performance of their duties the Administrative Secretary-General and the staff shall not seek or receive instructions from any government or from any other authority external to the Organization. They shall refrain from any action which might reflect on their position as international officials responsible only to the Organization.

2. Each member of the Organization undertakes to respect the exclusive character of the responsibilities of the Administrative Secretary-General and the Staff and not to seek to influence them in the discharge of their responsibilities.

COMMISSION OF MEDIATION, CONCILIATION AND ARBITRATION

Article 19

Member States pledge to settle all disputes among themselves by peaceful means and, to this end decide to establish a Commission of Mediation, Conciliation and Arbitration, the composition of which and conditions of service shall be defined by a separate Protocol to be approved by the Assembly of Heads of State and Government. Said Protocol shall be regarded as forming an integral part of the present Charter.

SPECIALIZED COMMISSIONS

Article 20

The Assembly shall establish such Specialized Commissions as it may deem necessary, including the following:

1. Economic and Social Commission;
2. Educational and Cultural Commission;
3. Health, Sanitation and Nutrition Commission;
4. Defence Commission;
5. Scientific, Technical and Research Commission.

Article 21

Each Specialized Commission referred to in Article 20 shall be composed of the Ministers concerned or other Ministers or Plenipotentiaries designated by the Governments of the Member States.

Article 22

The functions of the Specialized Commissions shall be carried out in accordance with the provisions of the present Charter and of the regulations approved by the Council of Ministers.

THE BUDGET

Article 23

The budget of the Organization prepared by the Administrative Secretary-General shall be approved by the Council of Ministers. The budget shall be provided by contributions from Member States in accordance with the scale of assessment of the United Nations; provided, however, that no Member State shall be assessed an amount exceeding twenty percent of the yearly regular budget of the Organization. The Member States agree to pay their respective contributions regularly.

SIGNATURE AND RATIFICATION OF CHARTER

Article 24

1. This Charter shall be open for signature to all independent sovereign African States and shall be ratified by the signatory States in accordance with their respective constitutional processes.

2. The original instrument, done, if possible in African languages, in English and French, all texts being equally authentic, shall be deposited with the Government of Ethiopia which shall transmit certified copies thereof to all independent sovereign African States.

3. Instruments of ratification shall be deposited with the Government of Ethiopia, which shall notify all signatories of each such deposit.

ENTRY INTO FORCE

Article 25

This Charter shall enter into force immediately upon receipt by the Government of Ethiopia of the instruments of ratification from two thirds of the signatory States.

REGISTRATION OF THE CHARTER

Article 26

This Charter shall, after due ratification, be registered with the Secretariat of the United Nations through the Government of Ethiopia in conformity with Article 102 of the Charter of the United Nations.

INTERPRETATION OF THE CHARTER

Article 27

Any question which may arise concerning the interpretation of this Charter shall be decided by a vote of two-thirds of the Assembly of Heads of State and Government of the Organization.

ADHESION AND ACCESSION

Article 28

1. Any independent sovereign African State may at any time notify the Administrative Secretary-General of its intention to adhere or accede to this Charter.

2. The Administrative Secretary-General shall, on receipt of such notification, communicate a copy of it to all the Member States. Admission shall be decided by a simple majority of the Member States. The decision of each Member State shall be transmitted to the Administrative Secretary-General, who shall, upon receipt of the required number of votes, communicate the decision to the State concerned.

MISCELLANEOUS

Article 29

The working languages of the Organization and all its institutions shall be, if possible African languages, English and French.

Article 30

The Administrative Secretary-General may accept on behalf of the Organization gifts, bequests and other donations made to the Organization, provided that this is approved by the Council of Ministers.

Article 31

The Council of Ministers shall decide on the privileges and immunities to be accorded to the personnel of the Secretariat in the respective territories of the Member States.

CESSATION OF MEMBERSHIP

Article 32

Any State which desires to renounce its membership shall forward a written notification to the Administrative Secretary-General. At the end of one year from the date of such notification, if not withdrawn, the Charter shall cease to apply with respect to the renouncing State, which shall thereby cease to belong to the Organization.

AMENDMENT OF THE CHARTER

Article 33

This Charter may be amended or revised if any Member State makes a written request to the Administrative Secretary-General to that effect; provided, however, that the proposed amendment is not submitted to the Assembly for consideration until all the Member States have been duly notified of it and a period of one year has elapsed. Such an amendment shall not be effective unless approved by at least two-thirds of all the Member States.

IN FAITH WHEREOF, We, the Heads of African State and Government, have signed this Charter.

Done in the City of Addis Ababa, Ethiopia this 25th day of May, 1963.

Bibliography

The following list of literature includes books, articles and (unpublished) conference papers cited in this study and arranged in alphabetical order. Excluded are (often anonymous) articles which were taken from current affairs periodicals as *Jeune Afrique*, *West Africa*, *Africa Report*, *Africa Confidential*, *Africa Research Bulletin*, *New African* etc..

ADAMOLEKUN, L., 'The Foreign Policy of Guinea', in O. Aluko (ed), *The Foreign Policies of African States* (London, 1977), pp 98-117

ADAMSON, W.L., *Hegemony and Revolution: A Study of Antonio Gramsci's Political and Cultural Theory* (Berkeley, Los Angeles and London, 1980)

ADEDEJI, A. (ed), *Africa within the World: Beyond Dispossession and Dependence* (London and Atlantic Highlands, NJ, 1993)

ADEDEJI, A., 'Marginalisation and Marginality: Context, Issues and Viewpoints', in A. Adedeji (ed), *Africa within the World: Beyond Dispossession and Dependence* (London and Atlantic Highlands, NJ, 1993), pp 1-13

ADEDEJI, A., 'Outlook: Africa's Strategic Agenda', in A. Adedeji (ed), *Africa within the World: Beyond Dispossession and Dependence* (London and Atlantic Highlands, NJ, 1993), ch. 19

ADEDEJI, A. and SHAW, T.M. (eds), *Economic Crisis in Africa: African Perspectives on Development Problems and Potentials* (Boulder, 1985)

ADELMAN, H. and SUHRKE, A., *Early Warning and Conflict Management* (Steering Committee of the Joint Evaluation of Emergency Assistance to Rwanda: Odense, 1996)

ADISA, J. and AGBAJE, A., 'Africa's Strategic Relationship with Western Europe: The Dispensability Thesis', in A. Sesay (ed), *Africa and Europe: From Partition to Interdependence or Dependence?* (London, 1986), ch. 8

AGBI, S.O., *The Organization of African Unity and African Diplomacy, 1963-1979* (Ibadan, 1986)

AGGER, B., *The Discourse of Domination: From the Frankfurt School to Postmodernism* (Evanston, 1992)

AJAYI, J.F.A. and CROWDER, M. (eds), *History of West Africa*, 2 vols. (vl.1: New York, 1977; vl.2: London, 1974)

AJAYI, J.F.A. and CROWDER, M. (eds), *Historical Atlas of Africa*, (Harlow, 1985)

AKEHURST, M., *A Modern Introduction to International Law* (London, 1980)

AKINDELE, R.A., 'Africa and the Great Powers: with Particular Reference to the United States, the Soviet Union and China', in *Afrika Spectrum*, 1985, pp 125-151

AKINRINADE, O., 'From Hostility to Accommodation: Nigeria's West African Policy, 1984-1990', in *Nigerian Journal of International Affairs*, 1992, no. 1, pp 47-77

AKINYEMI, B., 'The Organization of African Unity and the Concept of Non-Interference in Internal Affairs of Member-States', in *British Yearbook of International Law*, 1972-73, pp 393-400

ALLISON, G., *Essence of Decision: Explaining the Cuban Missile Crisis* (Boston, 1971)

ALPERIN, R.J., 'The Distribution of Power and the (June, 1979) Zimbabwe Rhodesia Constitution', in *Journal of Southern African Affairs*, 1980, pp 41-54

ALUKO, O., 'Public Opinion and Nigerian Foreign Policy Under the Military', in *Quarterly Journal of Administration*, Apr. 1973, pp 253-269

ALUKO, O., 'Ghana's Foreign Policy', in O. Aluko (ed), *The Foreign Policies of African States* (London, 1977), ch. 5

ALUKO, O., 'Nigerian Foreign Policy', in O. Aluko (ed), *The Foreign Policies of African States* (London, 1977), ch. 9

ALUKO, O. (ed), *The Foreign Policies of African States* (London, 1977)

ALUKO, O., 'Africa and the Great Powers', in T.M. Shaw and S. Ojo (eds), *Africa and the International Political System* (Washington, 1982), ch. 2

ALUKO, O., 'Bureaucratic Politics and Foreign Policy Decision-making in Nigeria', in T.M. Shaw and O. Aluko (eds), *Nigerian Foreign Policy: Alternative Perceptions and Projections* (London and Basingstoke, 1983), pp 77-92

ALUKO, O., 'Alliances within the OAU', in Y. El-Ayouty and I.W. Zartman (eds), *The OAU After Twenty Years* (New York, 1984), pp 67-84

ALUKO, O., 'Nigeria, Namibia and Southern Africa', in O. Aluko and T.M. Shaw (eds), *Southern Africa in the 1980s* (London, 1985), ch. 3

ALUKO, O. and SHAW, T.M. (eds), *Southern Africa in the 1980s* (London, 1985)

AMATE, C.O.C., *Inside the OAU: Pan-Africanism in Practice* (New York, 1986) American Society of African Culture (ed), *Pan-Africanism Reconsidered* (Berkeley and Los Angeles, 1962)

AMIN, S., *La faillite du développement en Afrique et dans le tiers-monde: une analyse politique* (Alençon, 1989)

AMIN, S., *Delinking: Towards a Polycentric World* (London and Atlantic Highlands, NJ, 1990)

ANDEMICAEL, B., *The OAU and the UN: Relations between the Organization of African Unity and the United Nations* (New York and London, 1976)

ANDEMICAEL, B., 'OAU-UN Relations in a Changing World', in Y. El-Ayouty (ed), *The Organization of African Unity After Thirty Years* (Westport and London, 1994), pp 119-138

ANDEMICAEL, B. and NICOL, D., 'The OAU: Primacy in Seeking African Solutions within the UN Charter', in Y. El-Ayouty and I.W. Zartman (eds), *The OAU After Twenty Years* (New York, 1984), pp 101-119

ANDRAIN, C.F., 'Guinea and Senegal: Contrasting Types of African Socialism', in W.H. Friedland and C.G. Rosberg (eds), *African Socialism* (Stanford, 1964), ch. 9

ANSPRENGER, F., *Die Befreiungspolitik der Organisation für Afrikanische Einheit (OAU) 1963 bis 1975* (Grünewald, 1975)

APPIAH, K.A., *In My Father's House: Africa in the Philosophy of Culture* (New York and Oxford, 1992)

APTER, D.E. and COLEMAN, J.S., 'Pan-Africanism or Nationalism in Africa', in American Society of African Culture (ed), *Pan-Africanism Reconsidered* (Berkeley and Los Angeles, 1962), pp 81-120

ARIKPO, O., 'Nigeria and the OAU', in *Nigerian Journal of International Affairs*, 1975, no. 1, pp 1-11

ARNOLD, G., *Aid in Africa* (London and New York, 1979)

ASANTE, S.K.B., *Pan-African Protest: West Africa and the Italo-Ethiopian Crisis, 1934-1941* (London, 1977)

ASANTE, S.K.B., 'Africa and Europe: Collective Dependence or Interdependence?', in A. Sesay (ed), *Africa and Europe: From Partition to Interdependence or Dependence?* (London, 1986), ch. 10

ASIWAJU, A.I. (ed), *Partitioned Africans: Ethnic Relations across Africa's International Boundaries 1884-1984* (London and Lagos, 1985)

ASIWAJU, A.I., 'The Global Perspective and Border Management Policy Options', in A.I. Asiwaju (ed), *Partitioned Africans: Ethnic Relations across Africa's International Boundaries 1884-1984* (London and Lagos, 1985), pp 233-251

ASSO, B., *Le chef d'état africain: l'expérience des états africains de succession française* (Paris, 1976)

AUSTIN, D., *Politics in Ghana, 1946-60* (London, 1964)

AUSTIN, D. and NAGEL, R., 'The Organization of African Unity', in *The World Today*, 1966, pp 520-529

AXELROD, R. (ed), *Structure of Decision: The Cognitive Maps of Political Elites* (Princeton, 1976)

AXELROD, R., *The Evolution of Cooperation* (New York, 1984)

AYOOB, M., 'The Third World in the System of States: Acute Schizophrenia or Growing Pains?', in *International Studies Quarterly*, 1989, pp 67-79

BA, A., KOFFI, B. and SAHLI, F., *l'Organisation de l'unité africaine: de la charte d'Addis-Abéba à la convention des droits de l'homme et des peuples* (Paris, 1984)

BACH, D.C., 'The Politics of West African Economic Co-operation: CEAO and ECOWAS', in *Journal of Modern African Studies*, 1983, pp 605-623

BADIANE, O., 'The Common Agricultural Policy and African Countries', in I.W. Zartman (ed), *Europe and Africa: The New Phase* (Boulder and London, 1993), ch. 6

BAEHR, P.R. and GORDENKER, L., *The United Nations in the 1990s* (London and Basingstoke, 1992)

BAILY, M., *Shell and BP in South Africa* (London, 1978)

BALANDIER, G., 'Contribution à l'étude des nationalismes en Afrique noire', in *Zaïre: revue congolaise*, April 1954, pp 379-389

BANGOURA, D., 'Le rôle juridique, politique et militaire de l'O.U.A. en matière de défense', in *Cahiers de l'IPAG*, no. 10, June 1990, pp 26-73

BARBER, J., *South Africa's Foreign Policy 1945-1970* (London, 1973)

BARNETT, D.L. and NJAMA, K., *Mau Mau from Within* (New York and London, 1966)

BARROWS, W.L., 'Changing Military Capabilities in Black Africa', in W.J. Foltz and H.S. Bienen (eds), *Arms and the African: Military Influences on Africa's International Relations* (New Haven and London, 1985), pp 99-120

BAYART, J.F., 'Civil Society in Africa' in P. Chabal (ed), *Political Domination in Africa: Reflections on the Limits of Power* (Cambridge, 1986), ch. 6

BAYART, J.F., *L'état en Afrique: la politique du ventre* (Paris, 1989)

BAYNHAM, S., 'Somalia: "Operation Restore Hope"', in *Africa Insight*, 1993, pp 17-23

BEDIAKO, K., 'Christian Religion and African Social Norms: Authority, Desacralisation and Democracy'; paper delivered at African Studies Centre: Leiden, 2 April 1992

BEHR, E., *The Algerian Problem* (Harmondsworth, 1961)

BENCHENANE, M., *Les armées africaines* (Paris, 1983)

BENDER, G.J., *Angola Under the Portuguese: The Myth and the Reality* (Berkeley and Los Angeles, 1980)

BENOT, Y., *Idéologies des indépendances africaines* (Paris, 1972)

BENOT, Y., 'l'Unité africaine vue par l'impérialisme (France et U.S.A.)', in *Problèmes actuels de l'unité africaine: colloque d'Alger (25 mars - 12 avril 1971)* (l'Université d'Alger: Algiers, 1973), pp 457-466

BENOT, Y., *Les indépendances africaines: idéologies et réalités*, 2 vls. (Paris, 1975)

BERG, E.J. and BUTLER, J., 'Trade Unions', in J.S. Coleman and C.G. Rosberg (eds), *Political Parties and National Integration in Tropical Africa* (Berkeley and Los Angeles, 1964), pp 342-366

BESHIR, M.O., *Terramedia: Themes in Afro-Arab Relations* (London and Khartoum, 1982)

BLANCHET, G., *Elites et changements en Afrique et au Sénégal* (Paris, 1983)

BOAHEN, A.A. (ed), *General History of Africa, vol. VII: Africa under Colonial Domination 1880-1935* (UNESCO: Paris, London and Berkeley, 1985)

BORELLA, F., 'Le système juridique de l'O.U.A.', in *Annuaire français de droit international*, 1971, pp 233-253

BOUDON, R., *The Analysis of Ideology* (Cambridge and Oxford, 1989)

BOULDING, K.E., *The Image: Knowledge in Life and Society* (Ann Arbor, 1956)

BOUMBA, M., 'l'O.U.A.: le système des contributions financières et la représentation administrative des états membres', in A. Ba, B. Koffi and F. Sahli, *l'Organisation de l'unité africaine: de la charte d'Addis-Abéba à la convention des droits de l'homme et des peuples* (Paris, 1984), pp 515-529

BOUTROS-GHALI, B., *l'Organisation de l'unité africaine* (Paris, 1969)

BOUTROS-GHALI, B., *An Agenda For Peace. Preventive Diplomacy, Peacemaking and Peace-keeping: Report of the Secretary-General pursuant to the statement adopted by the Summit Meeting of the Security Council on 31 January 1992* (New York, 1992)

BOUTROS-GHALI, B., 'The OAU and Afro-Arab Cooperation', in Y. El-Ayouty (ed), *The Organization of African Unity After Thirty Years* (Westport and London, 1994), ch. 10

BOUTROS-GHALI, B., *An Agenda for Peace 1995* (2nd ed.: with the new supplement and related UN documents, New York, 1995)

BOYD, J.B., 'The Origins of Boundary Conflict in Africa', in M.W. Delancey (ed), *Aspects of International Relations in Africa* (Columbia, 1980), pp 159-189

BROWNLIE, I., *African Boundaries: A Legal and Diplomatic Encyclopaedia* (London, 1979)

BROWNLIE, I., *Principles of Public International Law* (Oxford, 1979)

BRUCHHAUS, E.M. (ed), *Afrikanische Eliten zwanzig Jahre nach Erlangung der Unabhängigkeit* (Hamburg, 1983)

BUCHHEIT, L.C., *Secession: The Legitimacy of Self-Determination* (New Haven and London, 1978)

BULL, H., *The Anarchical Society: A Study of Order in World Politics* (London, 1977)

BUSTIN, E., 'The Congo', in G.M. Carter (ed), *Five African States: Responses to Diversity* (Ithaca, 1963), ch. 2

BUTLER, J. and CASTAGNO, A.A. (eds), *Boston University Papers on Africa: Transition in African Politics* (New York, 1967)

BUIJTENHUIJS, R., *Le Frolinat et les révoltes populaires du Tchad, 1965-1976* (The Hague, Paris and New York, 1978)

BUIJTENHUIJS, R., 'The Revolutionary Potential of Black Africa: Dissident Elites', in *African Perspectives*, 1978, pp 135-145

BUIJTENHUIJS, R., *Le Frolinat et les guerres civiles du Tchad (1970-1984): la révolution introuvable* (Paris and Leiden, 1987)

BUIJTENHUIJS, R. and BAESJOU, R., 'Center and Periphery News in Two African Newspapers: Testing some hypotheses on cultural dominance', in *Kroniek van Afrika*, 1974, pp 243-271

BUIJTENHUIJS, R. and RIJNIERSE, E., *Democratization in Sub-Saharan Africa (1989-1992): An Overview of the Literature* (Leiden, 1993)

BUIJTENHUIJS, R. and THIRIOT, C., *Democratization in Sub-Saharan Africa 1992-1995: An Overview of the Literature* (Leiden and Bordeaux, 1995)

CABRAL, A., *Unity and Struggle: Speeches and Writings* (Heinemann African Writers Series: London, 1980)

CALLAGHY, T., 'Politics and Vision in Africa: The Interplay of Domination, Equality and Liberty', in P. Chabal (ed), *Political Domination in Africa: Reflections on the Limits of Power* (Cambridge, 1986), ch. 2

CARTER, G.M. (ed), *African One-Party States* (Ithaca, 1962)

CARTER, G.M. (ed), *Five African States: Responses to Diversity* (Ithaca, 1963)

CERVENKA, Z. (ed), *Land-locked Countries of Africa* (Uppsala, 1973)

CERVENKA, Z., 'The OAU and the Nigerian Civil War', in Y. El-Ayouty (ed), *The Organization of African Unity After Ten Years: Comparative Perspectives* (New York, 1976), pp 152-173

CERVENKA, Z., *The Unfinished Quest for Unity: Africa and the OAU* (London, 1977)

CERVENKA, Z., 'OAU's Year of Disunity', in *Africa Contemporary Record*, 1977-8, A57-65

CERVENKA, Z. and LEGUM, C., 'The Organization of African Unity', in *Africa Contemporary Record*, 1975-76, A66-75

CERVENKA, Z. and LEGUM, C., 'The Organization of African Unity in 1978: The Challenge of Foreign Intervention', in *Africa Contemporary Record*, 1978-79, A25-39

CERVENKA, Z. and LEGUM, C., 'The Organization of African Unity in 1979', in *Africa Contemporary Record*, 1979-80, A58-71

CERVENKA, Z. and LEGUM, C., 'The Organization of African Unity in 1981: A Crucial Testing Time for Peacekeeping', in *Africa Contemporary Record*, 1981-82, A83-96

CERVENKA, Z. and LEGUM, C., 'The OAU in 1982: A Severe Setback for African Unity', in *Africa Contemporary Record*, 1982-83, A42-56

CHABAL, P., 'Introduction: Thinking about Politics in Africa', in P. Chabal (ed), *Political Domination in Africa: Reflections on the Limits of Power* (Cambridge, 1986), pp 1-16

CHABAL, P. (ed), *Political Domination in Africa: Reflections on the Limits of Power* (Cambridge, 1986)

CHAIGNEAU, P., *La politique militaire de la France en Afrique* (Paris, 1984)

CHANDHOKE, N., *The Politics of U.N. Sanctions* (New Delhi, c. 1981)

CHARLES, E., 'Pan-Africanism in French-Speaking West Africa, 1945-1960', *Boston University African Studies Center Working Papers*, no. 59

CHAZAN, N., 'Ghana', in T.M. Shaw and O. Aluko (eds), *The Political Economy of African Foreign Policy* (Aldershot, 1984), ch. 4

CHIME, C., *Integration and Politics among African States: Limitations and Horizons of Mid-Term Theorizing* (Uppsala, 1977)

CHODAK, S., 'Social Stratification in sub-Saharan Africa', in *Canadian Journal of African Studies*, 1973, pp 401-417

CHUKWURA, A.O., 'The Organization of African Unity and African Territorial and Boundary Problems 1963-1973', in *Nigerian Journal of International Studies*, 1975, no. 1, pp 56-81

CLAPHAM, C., 'The Context of African Political Thought' in *Journal of Modern African Studies*, 1970, pp 1-13

CLAPHAM, C. (ed), *Foreign Policy making in developing states: a comparative approach* (Farnborough, 1977)

CLAPHAM, C., 'Sub-Saharan Africa', in C. Clapham (ed), *Foreign Policy making in developing states: a comparative approach* (Farnborough, 1977), ch. 4

CLAPHAM, C., *Transformation and Continuity in Revolutionary Ethiopia* (Cambridge, 1990)

CLARK, J., 'Debacle in Somalia' in *Foreign Affairs*, 1992-93, pp 109-123

CLARK, J.F., 'Patterns of Support for International Organisations in Africa', in T.M. Shaw and K.A. Heard (eds), *The Politics of Africa: Dependence and Development* (London, 1979), pp 319-355

CLAUDE, I.L., *Swords into Plowshares: The Problems and Progress of International Organization* (New York, 1964)

CLAUDE, I.L., *Power and International Relations* (New York, 1966)

CLAUDE, I.L., *The Changing United Nations* (New York, 1967)

COLARD, D., *Le mouvement des pays non-alignés* (Paris, 1981)

COLEMAN, J.S., 'Nationalism in Tropical Africa', in *American Political Science Review*, 1954, pp 404-426

COLEMAN, J.S., *Nigeria: Background to Nationalism* (Berkeley and Los Angeles, 1958)

COLEMAN, J.S. and ROSBERG, C.G. (eds), *Political Parties and National Integration in Tropical Africa* (Berkeley and Los Angeles, 1964)

CONTEH-MORGAN, E., 'ECOWAS: Peace-making or meddling in Liberia?', in *Africa Insight*, 1993, pp 36-41

COOPERSTOCK, H., 'Some Methodological and Substantive Issues in the Study of Social Stratification in Tropical Africa', in T.M. Shaw and K.A. Heard (eds), *The Politics of Africa: Dependence and Development* (London, 1979), ch. 2

COPSON, R.W., 'Peace in Africa? The Influence of Regional and International Change', in F.M. Deng and I.W. Zartman (eds), *Conflict Resolution in Africa* (Washington, 1991), pp 19-41

COPSON, R.W., *Africa's Wars and Prospects for Peace* (New York and London, 1994)

CORNEVIN, M., *Histoire de l'Afrique contemporaine: de la deuxième guerre mondiale à nos jours* (Paris, 1980)

CORNEVIN, R., *Le Togo: des origines à nos jours* (Paris, 1988)

COSGROVE, C., 'The Impact of 1992 on EC-ACP Trade and Investment', in I.W. Zartman (ed), *Europe and Africa: The New Phase* (Boulder and London, 1993), ch. 5

COSSE, J.P. and SANCHEZ, J., *Angola: le prix de la liberté* (Paris, 1976)

COX, R., *Pan-Africanism in Practice. An East African Study: PAFMECSA 1958-1964* (London, 1964)

CRICK, B., 'Philosophy, Theory and Thought', in *Political Studies*, 1967, pp 49-55

CRONON, E.D., *Black Moses: The Story of Marcus Garvey and the Universal Negro Improvement Association* (Madison, 1955)

CROWDER, M., 'Independence as a Goal in French West African Politics: 1944-60', in W.H. Lewis (ed), *French-speaking Africa: The Search for Identity* (New York, 1965), pp 15-41

CROWDER, M., *Senegal: A Study of French Assimilation Policy* (London, 1967)

DADDIEH, C.K., 'Ivory Coast', in T.M. Shaw and O. Aluko (eds), *The Political Economy of African Foreign Policy* (Aldershot, 1984), Ch. 5

DAMIS, J., 'The OAU and Western Sahara', in Y. El-Ayouty and I.W. Zartman (eds), *The OAU After Twenty Years* (New York, 1984), pp 273-296

DAVIDSON, B., *In the Eye of the Storm: Angola's People* (Harmondsworth, 1975)

DAVIDSON, B., *No Fist is Big Enough to Hide the Sky: The Liberation Struggle of Guiné and Cape Verde. Aspects of an African Revolution* (London, 1981)

DAVIDSON, B., *The Black Man's Burden: Africa and the Curse of the Nation-State* (London, 1992)

DE MORAES FARIAS, P.F. and BARBER, K. (eds), *Self-Assertion and Brokerage: Early Cultural Nationalism in West Africa* (Birmingham, 1990)

DE VREE, J.K., 'Politieke integratie en desintegratie', in M.P.C.M. van Schendelen (ed), *Kernthema's van de Politicologie* (Meppel and Amsterdam, 1981), ch. 8

DECALO, S., *Coups and Army Rule in Africa: Studies in Military Style* (New Haven and London, 1976)

DECALO, S., 'The Process, Prospects and Constraints of Democratization in Africa', in *African Affairs*, 1992, pp 7-35

DEDRING, J., 'Multilateral Aspects of Conflict Resolution', in R. Väyrynen (ed), *New Directions in Conflict Theory: Conflict Resolution and Conflict Transformation* (London and New Delhi, 1991), ch. 7

DEI-ANANG, M., *The Administration of Ghana's Foreign Ministers, 1957-1965: A Personal Memoir* (London, 1975)

DELANCEY, M.W. (ed), *Aspects of International Relations in Africa* (Columbia, 1980)

DEN HARTOG, M.J., 'De Organisatie van Afrikaanse Eenheid (OAE): Een Organisatie voor Collectieve Veiligheid?', in *Proceedings: La problématique de sécurité en Afrique subsaharienne* (Centre d'études de défense [Belgium]: no pl., 1995), pp 71-91

DENG, F.M. and ZARTMAN, I.W. (eds), *Conflict Resolution in Africa* (Washington, 1991)

DENG, F.M. and ZARTMAN, I.W., 'Introduction', in F.M. Deng and I.W. Zartman (eds), *Conflict Resolution in Africa* (Washington, 1991), pp 1-15

DEUTSCH, M., *The Resolution of Conflict* (New Haven and London, 1973)

DEUTSCH, M., 'Subjective Features of Conflict Resolution: Psychological, Social and Cultural Influences', in R. Väyrynen (ed), *New Directions in Conflict Theory: Conflict Resolution and Conflict Transformation* (London and New Delhi, 1991), pp 37-50

DEWITTE, PH., *Les mouvements nègres en France 1919-1939* (Paris, 1985)

DIANÉ, C., *Les grandes heures de la F.E.A.N.F.* (Paris, 1990)

DIOP, CH.A., *l'Unité culturelle de l'Afrique noire: domaines du patriarcat et du matriarcat dans l'antiquité classique* (Paris, 1959)

DJAÏT, H., *La personnalité et le devenir arabo-islamiques* (Paris, 1974)

DOORNBOS, M., 'The African State in Academic Debate: Retrospect and Prospect', in *Journal of Modern African Studies*, 1990, pp 179-198

DOS SANTOS, E., *Pan-Africanismo de ontem e de hoje* (Lisbon, 1968)

DRACHLER, J. (ed), *African Heritage: Intimate Views of the Black Africans from Life, Lore, and Literature* (no pl., 1963)

D'SA, R.M., 'The African Refugee Problem: Relevant International Conventions and Recent Activities of the Organization of African Unity', in *Netherlands International Law Review*, 1984, pp 378-97

DUGUÉ, G., *Vers les états-unis d'Afrique* (Dakar, 1960)

DUMONT, R., *l'Afrique noire est mal partie* (Paris, 1962)

DUNN, J., 'The Identity of the History of Ideas', in *Philosophy*, 1968, pp 85-104

EAST, M.A., SALMORE, S.A. and HERMANN, CH.F. (eds), *Why Nations Act* (London, 1978)

ECONOMOU, P., GITTELMAN, M. and WUBNEH, M., 'Europe 1992 and Foreign Direct Investment in Africa', in I.W. Zartman (ed), *Europe and Africa: The New Phase* (Boulder and London, 1993), ch. 7

EKPO, M.U. (ed), *Bureaucratic Corruption in SubSaharan Africa: Toward a Search for Causes and Consequences* (Washington, 1979)

EL-AYOUTY, Y. (ed), *The Organization of African Unity After Ten Years: Comparative Perspectives* (New York, 1976)

EL-AYOUTY, Y., 'Future of the OAU: As Seen from its 19th Summit', in Y. El-Ayouty and I.W. Zartman (eds), *The OAU After Twenty Years* (New York, 1984), pp 327-354

EL-AYOUTY, Y. (ed), *The Organization of African Unity After Thirty Years* (Westport and London, 1994)

EL-AYOUTY, Y. and BROOKS, H.C. (eds), *Africa and International Organization* (The Hague, 1974)

EL-AYOUTY, Y. and ZARTMAN, I.W. (eds), *The OAU After Twenty Years* (New York, 1984)

EL-KHAWAS, M.A., 'Southern Africa: A Challenge to the OAU', in *Africa Today*, 1977, no. 3, pp 25-41

EL-NASSER, G. Abd, *The Philosophy of the Revolution: Book 1* (no pl. or d.)

EL-OUALI, A., '"L'uti possidetis" ou le non-sens du "principe de base" de l'OUA pour le règlement des différends territoriaux', in *Le Mois en Afrique*, 1984-85, nos. 227-228, pp 3-19

ELIAS, T.O., 'The Commission of Mediation, Conciliation and Arbitration of the Organization of African Unity', in *British Yearbook of International Law*, 1964, pp 336-348

ELIAS, T.O., 'The Charter of the Organization of African Unity', in *American Journal of International Law*, 1965, pp 243-267

ELIAS, T.O., 'The Legality of the O.A.U. Council of Ministers' Resolution on Rhodesia in December 1965', in *The Nigerian Law Journal*, 1969, pp 1-12

ELLIS, S., 'Africa after the Cold War: New Patterns of Government and Politics', in *Development and Change*, 1996, pp 1-28

EMERSON, R., *From Empire to Nation: The Rise to Self-Assertion of Asian and African Peoples* (Boston, 1960)

ENGLEBERT, P., *La révolution burkinabè* (Paris, 1986)

ENGO, P.B., 'Peaceful Co-existence and Friendly Relations among States: The African Contribution to the Progressive Development of Principles of International Law', in Y. El-Ayouty and H.C. Brooks (eds), *Africa and International Organization* (The Hague, 1974), pp 31-47

ESEDEBE, P.O., 'Origins and Meaning of Pan-Africanism', in *Présence africaine*, 1970, no. 73, pp 111-127

ESEDEBE, P.O., 'What is Pan-Africanism', in *Journal of African Studies*, 1977, pp 167-187

FANON, F., *Pour la révolution africaine* (Paris, 1964)

FARINGER, G.L., *Press Freedom in Africa* (New York, 1991)

FIELDHOUSE, D., 'Decolonization, Development, and Dependence': A Survey of Changing Attitudes', in P. Gifford and W.R. Louis (eds), *The Transfer of Power in Africa: Decolonization 1940-1960* (New Haven and London, 1982), ch. 17

FIRST, R., STEELE, J. and GURNEY, C., *The South African Connection: Western Investment in Apartheid* (HARMONDSWORTH, 1973)

FISIY, C.F. and GESCHIERE, P., 'Judges and Witches, or How is the State to Deal with Witchcraft?: Examples from Southeast Cameroon', in *Cahiers d'études africaines*, 1990, pp 135-156

FOLTZ, W.J., *From French West Africa to Mali Federation* (New Haven and London, 1965)

FOLTZ, W.J., 'Military Influences', in V. McKay (ed), *African Diplomacy: Studies in the Determinants of Foreign Policy* (London, 1966), pp 69-89

FOLTZ, W.J., 'The Organization of African Unity and the Resolution of Africa's Conflicts', in F.M. Deng and I.W. Zartman (eds), *Conflict Resolution in Africa* (Washington, 1991), ch. 13

FOLTZ, W.J. and BIENEN, H.S. (eds), *Arms and the African: Military Influences on Africa's International Relations* (New Haven and London, 1985)

FOLTZ, W.J. and WIDNER, J., 'The OAU and Southern African Liberation', in Y. El-Ayouty and I.W. Zartman (eds), *The OAU After Twenty Years* (New York, 1984), pp 249-271

FONER, P.S. (ed), *W.E.B. Du Bois Speaks, vl. 1: Speeches and Addresses 1890-1919* (New York, London and Sydney, 1986) and vl. 2: *Speeches and Addresses 1920-1963* (New York, London and Sydney, 1986)

FORTMANN, M. and THÉRIEN, J.PH., 'l'Organisation des états américains: un système de coopération en transition', in *Relations internationales et stratégiques*, summer 1994, pp 187-201

FRANK, A.G., *Capitalism and Underdevelopment in Latin America: Historical Studies of Chile and Brasil* (New York, 1967)

FREDLAND, R.A., 'Service at the Organization of African Unity: Gain or Loss in the Home Polity? (A Tentative Hypothesis about the Domestic Political Benefits for Senior Staff at the OAU'); paper delivered at the International Studies Association Meeting, Los Angeles, March 19-22, 1980

FREDLAND, R.A., 'OCAM: one scene in the drama of West African development', in D. Mazzeo (ed), *African Regional Organizations* (Cambridge, 1984), pp 103-130

FREUND, B., *The Making of Contemporary Africa: The Development of African Society since 1800* (London, 1986)

FRIEDLAND, W.H. and ROSBERG, C.G. (eds), *African Socialism* (Stanford, 1964)

FYFE, C., *Africanus Horton, 1835-1883: West African Scientist and Patriot* (London and New York, 1972)

GALLAGHER, C.F., 'The Death of a Group: Members of the Casablanca Pact Fall Out', *American Universities Field Staff Reports*, North Africa Series, vol. IX (1963), no. 4

GALTUNG, J., 'A Structural Theory of Imperialism', in *Journal of Peace Research*, 1971, pp 81-117

GARIGUE, P., 'The West African Students' Union: A Study in Culture Contact', in *Africa*, 1953, vol. 23, pp 55-69

GAVSHON, A., *Crisis in Africa: Battleground of East and West* (Harmondsworth, 1981)

GEISS, I., *The Pan-African Movement: A History of Pan-Africanism in America, Europe and Africa* (London, 1974)

GELLNER, E., *Encounters with Nationalism* (Oxford and Cambridge, Mass., 1994)

GEORGE, S., 'Uses and Abuses of African Debt', in A. Adedeji (ed), *Africa within the World: Beyond Dispossession and Dependence* (London and Atlantic Highlands, NJ, 1993), ch. 5

GERSHONI, Y., 'From ECOWAS to ECOMOG: The Liberian Crisis and the Struggle for Political Hegemony in West Africa', in *Liberian Studies Journal*, 1993, pp 21-43

GIBSON, R., *African Liberation Movements: Contemporary Struggles Against White Minority Rule* (London, 1972)

GIFFORD, P. and LOUIS, W.R. (eds), *The Transfer of Power in Africa: Decolonization 1940-1960* (New Haven and London, 1982)

GILPIN, R., *War and Change in World Politics* (Cambridge, 1982)

GIRARDET, R., *Mythes et Mythologies Politiques* (Paris, 1986)

GLICKMAN, H., 'Dilemmas of Political Theory in an African Context: the Ideology of Julius Nyerere', in J. Butler and A.A. Castagno (eds), *Boston University Papers on Africa: Transition in African Politics* (New York, Washington and London, 1967), ch. 8

GONIDEC, P.F., *l'OUA trente ans après: l'unité africaine à l'épreuve* (Paris, 1993)

GOOD, R., 'State-Building as a Determinant of Foreign Policy in the New States', in L. Martin (ed), *Neutralism and Nonalignment* (New York, 1962), pp 3-12

GOODRICH, L. and KAY, D.A. (eds), *International Organizations: Politics and Process* (London, 1973)

GORISSEN, P.W. and SCHELTEMA, H.G.,'CVSE, conflictpreventie en crisisbeheersing: Een tussenstand', in *Militaire Spectator*, 1994, no. 4, pp 171-177

GOWA, J., 'Rational Hegemons, Excludable Goods, and Small Groups: An Epitath for Hegemonic Stability Theory?', in *World Politics*, 1989, pp 307-324

GRAHAM, L.G., 'Ideology and the Sociological Understanding', in D.J. Manning (ed), *The Form of Ideology: Investigations into the sense of ideological reasoning with a view to giving an account of its place in political life* (London, Boston and Sydney, 1980), ch. 1

GREY JOHNSON, C., 'The African informal sector at the crossroads: emerging policy options', in *Africa Development*, 1992, no. 1, pp 65-91

GRIECO, J.M., 'Anarchy and the Limits of Cooperation: A Realist Critique of the Newest Liberal Institutionalism', in *International Organization*, 1988, pp 485-507

GRUNBERG, I., 'Exploring the "Myth" of Hegemonic Stability', in *International Organization*, 1990, pp 431-477

GRUNDY, K.W., 'Mali: The Prospects of "Planned Socialism"', in W.H. Friedland and C.G. Rosberg (eds), *African Socialism* (Stanford, 1964), ch. 10

GRUNDY, K.W., 'The 'Class Struggle' in Africa: An Examination of Conflicting Theories', in *Journal of Modern African Studies*, 1964, pp 379-393

GUERNIER, M., *Tiers-Monde: trois quarts du monde* (Paris, 1980)

GURR, T.R.,*Why Men Rebel* (Princeton, 1970)

GURR, T.R., 'Theories of Political Violence and Revolution in the Third World', in F.M. Deng and I.W. Zartman (eds), *Conflict Resolution in Africa* (Washington, 1991), ch. 6

GUTKIND, P.C.W. and WALLERSTEIN, I. (eds), *The Political Economy of Contemporary Africa* (Beverly Hills, 1976)

HAAS, E.B., 'Regime decay: conflict management and international organizations, 1945-1981', in *International Organization*, 1983, pp 189-256

HABTE SELASSIE, B., 'The OAU and Regional Conflicts: Focus on the Eritrean War', in *Africa Today*, 3rd/4th quarters, 1988, pp 61-67

HARBESON, J. and ROTHCHILD, D.(eds), *African International Relations* (Boulder, 1991)

HARDIN, G. and BADEN, J. (eds), *Managing the Commons* (San Francisco and Reading, 1977)

HARRIS, J.E., *African-American Reactions to War in Ethiopia 1936-1941* (Baton Rouge and London, 1994)

HARSH, E. and THOMAS, T., *Angola: The Hidden History of Washington's War* (New York, 1976)

HASSOUNA, H.A., *The League of Arab States and Regional Disputes: A Study of Middle East Conflicts* (New York and Leiden, 1975)

HAUSHOFER, K., *Geopolitik der Pan-Ideeen* (Berlin, 1931)

HAWORTH, G.R., 'The Southern African Customs Union: A Legal and Political Analysis', in Institute of Foreign and Comparative Law, Un. of South Africa: *Alternative Structures for Southern African Interaction* (Pretoria, 1982), pp 5-17

HAYFORD, J.E.C., *Ethiopia Unbound: Studies in Race Emancipation* (2nd ed.: London, 1969 [1st ed. 1911])

HEALY, J. and ROBINSON, M., *Democracy, Governance and Economic Policy: Sub-Saharan Africa in Comparative Perspective* (London, 1992)

HENRIKSEN, T.H., *Revolution and Counterrevolution: Mozambique's War of Independence, 1964-1974* (Westport and London, 1983)

HERMANN, M.G., 'Effects of Personal Characteristics of Political Leaders on Foreign Policy', in M.A. East, S.A. Salmore and Ch.F. Hermann (eds), *Why Nations Act* (London, 1978), ch. 3

HERMANN, M.G., KEGLEY, CH.W. and RAYMOND, G.A., 'The Decay of the Nonintervention Norm'; paper prepared for the Second Pan-European Conference on International Relations, Paris, 13-16 September 1995

HIGGOT, R.A., 'Niger', in T.M. Shaw and O. Aluko (eds), *The Political Economy of African Foreign Policy* (Aldershot, 1984), ch. 7

HILL, R.A. (ed), *The Marcus Garvey and Universal Negro Improvement Association Papers* (Berkeley, Los Angeles and London, 1983-90), 7 vls.

HOBSBAWM, E. and RANGER, T.O. (eds), *The Invention of Tradition* (Cambridge, 1983)

HODGES, T., 'Western Sahara: Edging to the brink of a regional conflagration', in *Africa Contemporary Record*, 1984-85, A80-88

HODGKIN, T., *Nationalism in Colonial Africa* (London, 1956)

HODGKIN, T., 'A Note on the Language of African Nationalism', in K. Kirkwood (ed), *African Affairs, no. 1: St Antony's Papers, no. 10* (London, 1961), pp 22-40

HOLSTI, K.J., *International Politics: A Framework for Analysis* (London, 1974)

HOLSTI, O.R., 'Foreign Policy Formation Viewed Cognitively', in R. Axelrod (ed), *Structure of Decision: The Cognitive Maps of Political Elites* (Princeton, 1976), pp 18-54

HOLSTI, O.R., Siverson, R.M. and George, A.L. (eds), *Change in the International System* (Boulder, 1980)

HOOKER, J.R., *Black Revolutionary: George Padmore's Path from Communism to Pan-Africanism* (London, 1967)

HOOKER, J.R., *Henry Sylvester Williams: Imperial Pan-Africanist* (London, 1975)

HOPKINS, A.G., *An Economic History of West Africa* (London, 1980)

HORNE, A., *A Savage War of Peace: Algeria 1954-1962* (London, 1977)

HOSKYNS, C., 'Pan-Africanism in Accra', in *Africa South*, 1959, no. 3, pp 72-76

HOSKYNS, C., *The Congo Since Independence: January 1960 - December 1961* (London, 1965)

HOSKYNS, C., *Case Studies in African Diplomacy, no. I: The Organization of African Unity and the Congo Crisis, 1964-65* (Dar es Salaam, Nairobi and Addis Ababa, 1969)

HOSKYNS, C., *Case Studies in African Diplomacy, no. II: The Ethiopia-Somalia-Kenya Dispute 1960-67* (Dar es Salaam, Nairobi and Addis Ababa, 1969)

HOUT, W., 'Centres and peripheries: An assessment of the contribution of dependency and world system theories to the study of international relations', in *Acta Politica*, 1992, pp 71-92

HOUT, W., *Capitalism and the Third World: Development, Dependence and the World System* (Aldershot and Brookfield, 1993)

HOWE, R.W., 'Did Nkrumah favour Pan-Africanism?' in *Transition*, 1966, no. 27-4, pp 13-15

HUNTINGTON, S.P., 'The US - Decline or Renewal?', in *Foreign Affairs*, 1988/89, 67, pp 76-96

HYDEN, G., *Beyond Ujamaa in Tanzania: Underdevelopment and an Uncaptured Peasantry* (London, 1980)

HYMANS, J.L., *Léopold Sédar Senghor: An Intellectual Biography* (Edinburgh, 1971)

HYPPOLITE-MANIGAT, M., 'Le groupe de l'Organisation de l'unité africaine à l'ONU', in *Revue française d'études politique africaines*, 1974, no. 104, pp 73-81

ILIFFE, J., *A Modern History of Tanganyika* (Cambridge, 1984)

INGHAM, K. (ed), *Foreign Relations of African States* (London, 1974)

INGRAM, D., 'The OAU and the Commonwealth', in Y. El-Ayouty (ed), *The Organization of African Unity After Thirty Years* (Westport and London, 1994), ch. 11

IYOB, R., 'Regional Hegemony: Domination and Resistance in the Horn of Africa', in *Journal of Modern African Studies*, 1993, pp 257-276

JACKSON, R.H. and ROSBERG, C.G., 'Why Africa's Weak States Persist: The Empirical and the Juridical in Statehood', in *World Politics*, 1982, pp 1-24

JACOBSON, H.K., Reisinger, W.M. and Mathers, T., 'National Entanglements in International Governmental Organizations', in *American Political Science Review*, 1986, pp 141-159

JANOWITZ, M., *Military Institutions and Coercion in the Developing Nations* (Chicago and London, 1977)

JASTER, R., 'A Regional Security Role for Africa's Frontline States', in R. Jaster (ed), *Southern Africa: Regional Security Problems and Prospects* (Aldershot, 1985), pp 89-106

JASTER, R. (ed), *Southern Africa: Regional Security Problems and Prospects* (Aldershot, 1985)

JERVIS, R., *Perception and Misperception in International Politics* (Princeton, 1976)

JERVIS, R., 'Security regimes', in S.D. Krasner (ed), *International Regimes* (Ithaca and London, 1983), pp 173-194

JOHNS, D.H., 'The 'Normalization' of Intra-African Diplomatic Activity', in *Journal of Modern African Studies*, 1972, pp 597-610

JOHNS, D.H., 'Diplomatic Exchange and Inter-State Inequality in Africa: An Empirical Analysis', in T.M. Shaw and K.A. Heard (eds), *The Politics of Africa: Dependence and Development* (London, 1979), ch. 11

JOHNSON, PH. and MARTIN, D. (eds), *Destructive Engagement: Southern Africa at War* (Harare, 1986)

JOSEPH, R., *Le mouvement nationaliste au Cameroun: les origines sociales de l'UPC* (Paris, 1986)

JOUVE, E., *l'Organisation de l'unité africaine* (Paris, 1984)

JULY, R., *The Origins of Modern African Thought: Its Development in West Africa during the Nineteenth and Twentieth Centuries* (London, 1968)

KALCK, P., *Central African Republic: A Failure in De-Colonisation* (London, 1971)

KALE, N.K., 'Crisis in African leadership: OAU's Secretary-General and the Lonrho Agreement', in *The Pan-Africanist*, no. 5, Sept. 1974, pp 12-25

KAMANU, O.S., 'Secession and the Right of Self-Determination: an OAU Dilemma', in *Journal of Modern African Studies*, 1974, pp 355-376

KAMEL, M., *l'Arabisme: fondement socio-politique des relations internationales panarabes* (no pl., 1977)

KAMTO, M., 'Le retrait du Maroc de l'OUA', in M. Kamto, J.E. Pondi and L. Zang (eds), *l'OUA: rétrospective et perspectives africaines* (Paris, 1990), ch. 3

KAMTO, M., 'Les mutations institutionnelles de l'OUA', in M. Kamto, J.E. Pondi and L. Zang (eds), *l'OUA: rétrospective et perspectives africaines* (Paris, 1990), ch. 1

KAMTO, M., PONDI, J.E. and ZANG, L. (eds), *l'OUA: rétrospective et perspectives africaines* (Paris, 1990)

KAPIL, R.L., 'On the Conflict Potential of Inherited Boundaries in Africa', in *World Politics*, 1966, pp 656-673

KAPUNGU, L.T., 'The OAU's Support for the Liberation of Southern Africa', in Y. El-Ayouty (ed), *The Organization of African Unity After Ten Years: Comparative Perspectives* (New York, 1976), pp 135-151

KAUFMANN, J., *United Nations Decision Making* (Alphen aan den Rijn and Rockville, 1980)

KAZEMZADEH, F., 'Pan Movements', in D.L. Sills (ed), *International Encyclopaedia of the Social Sciences* (New York and London, 1972), vl. 11, pp 365-370

KELLER, S., 'Elites', in D.L. Sills (ed), *International Encyclopaedia of the Social Sciences* (no pl., 1968), vol. V, pp 26-29

KEOHANE, R.O., 'The Study of Political Influence in the General Assembly', in L. Goodrich and D.A. Kay (eds), *International Organizations: Politics and Process* (Madison and London, 1973), pp 137-153

KEOHANE, R.O., 'The Theory of Hegemonic Stability and Changes in International Economic Regimes, 1967-77', in O.R. Holsti, R.M. Siverson and A.L. George (eds), *Change in the International System* (Boulder, 1980), pp 131-162

KEOHANE, R.O., *After Hegemony: Cooperation and Discord in the World Political Economy* (Princeton, 1984)

KHAPOYA, V.B., 'Determinants of Support for African Liberation Movements: A Comparative Analysis', in *Journal of African Studies*, 1976, pp 469-489

KHAPOYA, V.B., 'The Politics and the Political Economy of OAU Summitry'; paper presented at the 25th Annual Meeting of the African Studies Association, Washington D.C., Nov. 4-7, 1982

KHAPOYA, V.B., 'Kenya', in T.M. Shaw and O. Aluko (eds), *The Political Economy of African Foreign Policy* (Aldershot, 1984), ch. 6

KI-ZERBO, J., 'Editorial Note: theories on the 'races' and history of Africa', in J. Ki-Zerbo (ed), *General History of Africa*, vl. I: *Methodology and African Prehistory* (UNESCO: London, Paris and Berkeley, 1981), pp 261-269

KI-ZERBO, J. (ed), *General History of Africa*, vl. I: *Methodology and African Prehistory* (UNESCO: London, Paris and Berkeley, 1981)

KINDLEBERGER, CH.P., *The World in Depression 1929-1939* (Berkeley and Los Angeles, 1973)

KIRK-GREENE, A.H.M., *Crisis and Conflict in Nigeria: A Documentary Sourcebook 1966-1970*, 2 vls. (London, 1971)

KIRK-GREENE, A.H.M., 'Diplomacy and diplomats: the formation of foreign service cadres in Black Africa', in K. Ingham (ed), *Foreign Relations of African States* (London, 1974), pp 279-319

KIRKWOOD, K. (ed), *African Affairs, no. 1: St Antony's Papers, no. 10* (London, 1961)

KISANGA, E.J., 'The Organization of African Unity (OAU) and the Liberation Struggle in Southern Africa', in *Taamuli*, 1977, no. 2, pp 32-49

KLINGHOFFER, A.J., *The Angolan War: A Study in Soviet Policy in the Third World* (Boulder, 1980)

KOCH, K., SOETENDORP, R.B. and VAN STADEN, A. (eds), *Internationale betrekkingen: Theorieën en benaderingen* (Utrecht, 1994)

KODJO, E., ... *et demain l'Afrique* (Paris, 1985)

KOHN, H., 'Pan-Movements', in E.R.A. Seligman (ed), *Encyclopaedia of the Social Sciences* (New York, 1958), vl. 11, pp 545-554

KOOIJMANS, P.H., *Internationaal Publiekrecht in Vogelvlucht* (Groningen, 1991)

KOTHARI, R., *Footsteps into the Future: Diagnosis of the Present World and a Design for an Alternative* (New York, 1974)

KOUASSI, E.K. and WHITE, J., 'The Impact of Reduced European Security Roles on African Relations', in I.W. Zartman (ed), *Europe and Africa: The New Phase* (Boulder and London, 1993), ch. 3

KRASNER, S.D. (ed), *International Regimes* (Ithaca and London, 1983)

KRASNER, S.D., 'Regimes and the limits of realism: regimes as autonomous variables', in S.D. Krasner (ed), *International Regimes* (Ithaca and London, 1983), pp 355-368

KRASNER, S.D., 'Structural causes and regime consequences: regimes as intervening variables', in S.D. Krasner (ed),*International Regimes* (Ithaca and London, 1983), pp 1-21

KRASNER, S.D., *Structural Conflict: The Third World against Global Liberalism* (Berkeley, Los Angeles and London, 1985)

KÜHNE, W., 'Looking South After the End of the Cold War', in I.W. Zartman (ed), *Europe and Africa: The New Phase* (Boulder and London, 1993), ch. 2

KUNIG, PH., *Das völkerrechtliche Nichteinmischungsprinzip: Zur Praxis der Organisation der afrikanischen Einheit (OAU) und des afrikanischen Staatenverkehrs* (Baden-Baden, 1981)

KURCZEWSKI, J. and FRIESKE, K., 'Some Problems in the Legal Regulation of the Activities of Economic Institutions', in *Law and Society Review*, 1977, pp 489-505

LAIDI, Z., *Les contraintes d'une rivalité: les superpuissances et l'Afrique* (Paris, 1986)

LANGLEY, J.A., 'Garveyism and African Nationalism', in *Race*, 1969, pp 157-172

LANGLEY, J.A., *Pan-Africanism and Nationalism in West Africa 1900-1945: A Study in Ideology and Social Classes* (Oxford, 1973)

LANGLEY, J.A., *Ideologies of Liberation in Black Africa 1856-1970: Documents on modern African political thought from colonial times to the present* (London, 1979)

LASWELL, H.D., *Power and Personality* (New York, 1948)

LEGUM, C., *Bandung, Cairo & Accra: A Report of the First Conference of Independent African States* (Africa Bureau: n.pl., 1958)

LEGUM, C., *Pan-Africanism: A Short Political Guide* (London and Dunmow, 1962)

LEGUM, C., 'Socialism in Ghana: A Political Interpretation', in W.H. Friedland and C.G. Rosberg (eds), *African Socialism* (Stanford, 1964), ch. 8

LEGUM, C., 'Foreign Intervention in Angola', in *Africa Contemporary Record*, 1975-76, A3-38

LEGUM, C., *Vorster's Gamble for Africa: How the Search for Peace Failed* (London, 1976)

LEGUM, C. and HODGES, T., *After Angola: The War over Southern Africa* (London, 1976)

LEGUM, C. and LEE, B., *The Horn of Africa in Continuing Crisis* (New York and London, 1979)

LEMARCHAND, R., 'On Comparing Regional Hegemons: Libya and South Africa', in R. Lemarchand (ed), *The Green and the Black: Qadhafi's Policies in Africa* (Bloomington and Indianapolis, 1988), pp 167-181

LEMARCHAND, R. (ed), *The Green and the Black: Qadhafi's Policies in Africa* (Bloomington and Indianapolis, 1988)

LeROY BENNETT, A., *International Organizations: Principles and Issues* (5th ed., Englewood Cliffs, 1991)

LE TOURNEAU, R., *Evolution politique de l'Afrique du nord musulmane 1920-1961* (Paris, 1962)

LEVERING LEWIS, D., *W.E.B. Du Bois: Biography of a Race 1868-1919* (New York, 1993)

LEWIN, A., *Diallo Telli: le tragique destin d'un grand Africain* (Paris, 1990)

458

LEWIS, I.M., *A Modern History of Somalia: Nation and State in the Horn of Africa* (London and New York, 1980)

LEWIS, I.M. (ed), *Nationalism and Self-Determination in the Horn of Africa* (London, 1983)

LEWIS, I.M., 'The Ogaden and the Fragility of Somali Segmentary Nationalism', in *African Affairs*, 1989, pp 573-579

LEWIS, W.H. (ed), *French-speaking Africa: The Search for Identity* (New York, 1965)

LEYS, C., *Underdevelopment in Kenya: The Political Economy of Neo-colonialism 1964-1971* (London, 1975)

LEYS, C., 'The "Overdeveloped" Post-Colonial State', in *Review of African Political Economy*, 1976, pp 39-48

LIESHOUT, R.H. and DE VREE, J.K., 'How organizations decide: A systems-theoretic approach to the "behavior" of organizations', in *Acta Politica*, 1985, pp 129-155

LLOYD, P.C., 'Introduction', in P.C. Lloyd (ed), *The New Elites of Tropical Africa* (London, 1970), pp 1-85

LLOYD, P.C. (ed), *The New Elites of Tropical Africa* (London, 1970)

LOHATA, T.O., 'L'idéologie panafricanisme', in *Le Mois en Afrique*, Febr.-Ma. 1987, nos. 253-4, pp 149-161

LONSDALE, J., 'From Colony to Industrial State: South African Historiography as seen from England', in *Social Dynamics*, 1983, pp 67-83

LONSDALE, J., 'Political Accountability in African History', in P. Chabal (ed), *Political Domination in Africa: Reflections on the Limits of Power* (Cambridge, 1986), ch. 7

LONSDALE, J.M., 'Some Origins of Nationalism in East Africa', in *Journal of African History*, 1968, pp 119-146

LOUP-AMSELLE, J. and M'BOKOLO, E., *Au coeur de l'ethnie: ethnies, tribalisme et état en Afrique* (Paris, 1985)

LOW, D.A. and LONSDALE, J.M., 'Introduction: Towards the New Order 1945-1963', in D.A. Low and A. Smith (eds), *History of East Africa*, vl. III (Oxford, 1976), pp 1-63

LOW, D.A. and SMITH, A. (eds), *History of East Africa*, vl. III (Oxford, 1976)

LUMUMBA-KASONGO, T., *Political Re-Mapping of Africa: Transnational Ideology and the Re-Definition of Africa in World Politics* (Lanham, New York and London, 1994)

LYNCH, H.R., *Edward Wilmot Blyden: Pan-Negro Patriot* (London, 1967)

LYSTAD, R.A., 'Cultural and Psychological Factors', in V. McKay (ed), *African Diplomacy: Studies in the Determinants of Foreign Policy* (London, 1966), ch. 5

MACDONELL, D., *Theories of Discourse: An Introduction* (Oxford and New York, 1989)

MAHIOU, A., *L'avènement du parti unique en Afrique noire: l'expérience des états d'expression française* (Paris, 1969)

MAHMUD, K., 'A Short Biography of Duse Mohhamed', in *Nigeria Magazine*, 1986, no. 4, pp 83-92

MALUWA, T., 'The Peaceful Settlement of Disputes Among African States, 1963-1983: Some Conceptual Issues and Practical Trends', in *International and Comparative Law Quarterly*, 1989, pp 299-320

MANGWENDE, W., 'The OAU: An Analysis of the Function, Problems and Prospects of the Organization of African Unity', in *Zambezia*, 1984-/85, no. 12, pp 21-38

MANNING, D.J., 'Introduction', in D.J. Manning (ed), *The Form of Ideology: Investigations into the sense of ideological reasoning with a view to giving an account of its place in political life* (London, Boston and Sydney, 1980), pp 1-11

MANNING, D.J. (ed), *The Form of Ideology: Investigations into the sense of ideological reasoning with a view to giving an account of its place in political life* (London, Boston and Sydney, 1980)

MANNING, D.J., 'The Place of Ideology in Political Life', in D.J. Manning (ed), *The Form of Ideology: Investigations into the sense of ideological reasoning with a view to giving an account of its place in political life* (London, Boston and Sydney, 1980), ch. 5

MARCUM, J., *The Angolan Revolution*, vl. 2: *Exile Politics and Guerrilla Warfare 1962-1976* (Cambridge, Mass., 1978)

MARGARIDO, A., 'l'OUA et les territoires sous domination portugaise', in *Revue française d'études politiques africaines*, 1967, no. 22, pp 82-106

MARKAKIS, J., *National and Class Conflict in the Horn of Africa* (Cambridge, 1987)

MARTENS, L., *1958-1966: 10 jaar revolutie in Kongo: De strijd van Patrice Lumumba en Pierre Mulele* (Berchem, 1988)

MARTIN, D. and JOHNSON, PH., 'Mozambique: To Nkomati and Beyond', in Ph. Johnson and D. Martin (eds), *Destructive Engagement: Southern Africa at War* (Harare, 1986), pp 1-41

MARTIN, D. and JOHNSON, PH., *The Struggle for Zimbabwe: The Chimurenga War* (London and Boston, 1981)

MARTIN, G., 'Africa and the Ideology of Eurafrica: Neo-Colonialism or Pan-Africanism?', in *Journal of Modern African Studies*, 1982, pp 221-238

MARTIN, G., 'Continuity and Change in Franco-African Relations', in *Journal of Modern African Studies*, 1995, pp 1-20

MARTIN, L. (ed), *Neutralism and Nonalignment* (New York, 1962)

MATHEWS, K., 'The African Group at the UN as an Instrument of African Diplomacy', in *Nigerian Journal of International Affairs*, 1988, no. 1, pp 226-258

MATHEWS, K., 'The Organization of African Unity in World Politics', in R.I. Onwuka and T.M. Shaw (eds), *Africa in World Politics: Into the 1990s* (Basingstoke and London, 1989), ch. 2

MATHEWS, K. and MUSHI, S.S. (eds), *Foreign Policy of Tanzania 1961-1981: A Reader* (Dar es Salaam, 1981)

MATTHEWS, R.O., 'Interstate Conflicts in Africa: A Review', in *International Organization*, 1970, pp 335-360

MAYALL, J., *Africa: the Cold War and After* (London, 1971)

MAYALL, J., 'African Unity and the OAU: The Place of a Political Myth in African Diplomacy', in *Yearbook of World Affairs* (London), 1973, pp 110-133

MAYALL, J., 'Self-Determination and the OAU', in I.M. Lewis (ed), *Nationalism and Self-Determination in the Horn of Africa* (London, 1983), pp 77-92

MAZRUI, A.A., *Towards a Pax Africana: A Study of Ideology and Ambition* (London, 1967)

MAZZEO, D. (ed), *African Regional Organizations* (Cambridge, 1984)

M'BOKOLO, E., 'Forces sociales et idéologies dans la décolonisation de l'A.E.F.', in *Journal of African History*, 1981, pp 393-407

M'BUYINGA, E., *Pan-Africanism or Neo-Colonialism? The Bankruptcy of the O.A.U.* (London, 1982)

MCKAY, V. (ed), *African Diplomacy: Studies in the Determinants of Foreign Policy* (London, 1966)

MCKEOWN, TH., 'Hegemonic Stability Theory and 19th Century Tariff Levels in Europe', in *International Organization*, 1983, pp 73-91

MCLELLAN, D., *Ideology* (2nd. ed.: Buckingham, 1995)

MCMASTER, C., *Malawi - Foreign Policy and Development* (London, 1974)

MEARSHEIMER, J.J., 'The False Promise of International Institutions', in *International Security*, 1994/95, vol. 19, no. 3, pp 5-49

MERON, TH., *The United Nations Secretariat* (Lexington and Toronto, 1977)

MEYERS, B.D., 'The OAU's Administrative Secretary-General', in *International Organization*, 1976, pp 509-520

MICHAELS, M., 'Retreat from Africa', in *Foreign Affairs*, 1992-93, pp 91-108

MICHAELSON, M., 'Somalia: The Painful Road to Reconciliation', in *Africa Today*, 1993, no. 2, pp 53-73

MILNER, H., 'International Theories of Cooperation Among Nations: Strengths and Weaknesses', in *World Politics*, 1992, pp 466-496

MINTER, W., *Portuguese Africa and the West* (Harmondsworth, 1972)

MINTER, W. and SCHMIDT, E., 'When Sanctions Worked: The Case of Rhodesia Reexamined', in *African Affairs*, 1988, pp 207-237

MOHAN, J., 'A Whig Interpretation of African Nationalism', in *Journal of Modern African Studies*, 1968, pp 389-409

MOSHI, H.P.B., 'Multinational Corporations and Sanctions in Southern Africa', in *Utafiti*, 1979, pp 183-194

MUDIMBE, V.Y., *The Invention of Africa: Gnosis, Philosophy, and the Order of Knowledge* (Bloomington and Indianapolis, 1988)

MUNGER, E.S., 'All-African People's Conference', in E.S. Munger, *African Field Reports 1952-1961* (Cape Town, 1961), pp 41-90

MUSHI, S.S., 'The Making of Foreign Policy in Tanzania', in K. Mathews and S.S. Mushi (eds), *Foreign Policy of Tanzania 1961-1981: A Reader* (Dar es Salaam, 1981), ch. 1

NAFZIGER, E.W., *The Debt Crisis in Africa* (Baltimore and London, 1993)

NALDI, G.J., *Documents of the Organization of African Unity* (London and New York, 1992)

NAUTA, L., 'Afrika bestaat niet', in *Nieuw Wereldtijdschrift*, 1985, no. 1, pp 71-80

NDIAYE, B., 'A Vision of Shared Responsibilities', in A. Adedeji (ed), *Africa within the World: Beyond Dispossession and Dependence* (London and Atlantic Highlands, NJ, 1993), ch. 9

NEUBERGER, B., 'The African Concept of Balkanisation', in *Journal of Modern African Studies*, 1976, pp 523-529

NEUBERGER, B., *National Self-Determination in Post-colonial Africa* (Boulder, 1986)

N'GANGBET, M., *Peut-on encore sauver le Tchad?* (Paris, 1984)

NICHOLSON, M., 'Negotiation, Agreement and Conflict Resolution: The Role of Rational Approaches and their Criticism', in R. Väyrynen (ed), *New Directions in Conflict Theory: Conflict Resolution and Conflict Transformation* (London and New Delhi, 1991), ch. 3

NICOL, A., 'The Meaning of Africa', in J. Drachler (ed), *African Heritage: Intimate Views of the Black Africans from Life, Lore, and Literature* (no pl., 1963), pp 119-122

NKRUMAH, K., *Neo-Colonialism: The Last Stage of Imperialism* (London, 1965)

NKRUMAH, K., *Axioms of Kwame Nkrumah* (London, 1967)

NKRUMAH, K., *Challenge of the Congo* (London, 1967)

NKRUMAH, K., *Africa Must Unite* (New York, 1984 [1st ed. 1963])

NWABUEZE, B.O., *Presidentialism in Commonwealth Africa* (London and Enugu, 1974)

NWOKEDI, E., 'Le myth d'un leadership nigérian dans les relations inter-africains', in *Etudes internationales* (Quebec), 1991, pp 357-368

NYERERE, J.K., 'A United States of Africa', in *Journal of Modern African Studies*, 1963, pp 1-6

OBERLÉ, PH. AND HUGOT, P., *Histoire de Djibouti: des origines à la république* (Paris and Dakar, 1985)

OFOSU-AMAAH, G.K.A., 'Regional Enforcement of International Obligations: Africa', in *Zeitschrift für ausländisches öffentliches Recht und Völkerrecht*, 1987, pp 80-94

OGBONDAH, C.W., *Military Regimes and the Press in Nigeria, 1966-1993: Human Rights and National Development* (Lanham, New York and London, 1994)

OGUNBAMBI, R.O.A., 'Military Intervention in Independent African States Revisited: A Review 1960-1983', in *Afrika Spectrum*, 3, 1984, pp 291-297

OGUNBAMBI, R.O.A., 'The Administrative Secretary-General in the OAU System: Some Interpretative Observations', in *Nigerian Journal of International Affairs*, 1988, no. 1, pp 189-203

OGUNSANWO, A., 'The Foreign Policy of Algeria', in O. Aluko (ed), *The Foreign Policies of African States* (London, 1977), ch. 2

OHLSON, TH., 'Strategic Confrontation versus Economic Survival in Southern Africa', in F.M. Deng and I.W. Zartman (eds), *Conflict Resolution in Africa* (Washington, 1991), ch. 8

OJO, S., 'The Administration of Nigeria's Foreign Service, 1960-1980', in T.M. Shaw and O. Aluko (eds), *Nigerian Foreign Policy: Alternative Perceptions and Projections* (London and Basingstoke, 1983), ch. 4

OKIGBI, P., 'The Future Haunted by the Past', in A. Adedeji (ed), *Africa within the World: Beyond Dispossession and Dependence* (London and Atlantic Highlands, NJ, 1993), ch. 3

OKOLO, J.E., 'Securing West Africa: the ECOWAS defence pact', in *The World Today*, 1983, pp 177-184

OKONGWU, O., 'The O.A.U. Charter and the Principle of Domestic Jurisdiction in Intra-African Affairs', in *Indian Journal of International Law*, 1973, pp 589-593

OKONKWO, R.L., 'The Garvey Movement in British West Africa', in *Journal of African History*, 1980, pp 105-117

OKOTH, P.G., 'The O.A.U. and the Uganda-Tanzania War'; paper presented to the 27th Annual Meeting of the African Studies Association, Los Angeles, 25-28 October 1984

OKUMU, J., 'Kenya's Foreign Policy', in O. Aluko (ed), *The Foreign Policies of African States* (London, 1977), ch. 8

OLORUNTIMEHIN, B.O., 'African politics and nationalism, 1919-1935', in A.A. Boahen (ed), *General History of Africa,* vol. VII: *Africa under Colonial Domination 1880-1935* (UNESCO: Paris, London and Berkeley, 1985), ch. 22

OLSON, M., *The Logic of Collective Action: Public Goods and the Theory of Groups* (Cambridge, Mass., 1965)

ONIMODE, B., 'The Imperatives of Self-Confidence and Self-Reliance in African Development', in A. Adedeji (ed), *Africa within the World: Beyond Dispossession and Dependence* (London and Atlantic Highlands, NJ, 1993), ch. 16

ONWUKA, R.I., 'CMEA-African Economic Relations', in R.I. Onwuka and T.M. Shaw (eds), *Africa in World Politics: Into the 1990s* (Basingstoke and London, 1989), ch. 4

ONWUKA, R.I. and SHAW, T.M. (eds), *Africa in World Politics: Into the 1990s* (Basingstoke and London, 1989)

OUGAARD, M., 'Dimensions of Hegemony', in *Conflict and Cooperation*, 1988, pp 197-214

OYE, K.A. (ed), *Cooperation Under Anarchy* (Princeton, 1986)

OYE, K.A., 'Explaining Cooperation Under Anarchy: Hypotheses and Strategies', in K.A. Oye (ed), *Cooperation Under Anarchy* (Princeton, 1986), pp 1-24

PADMORE, G., *Pan-Africanism or Communism? The Coming Struggle for Africa* (London, 1956)

PADMORE, G. (ed), *History of the Pan-African Congress* (2nd ed.: London, 1963 [1st ed. 1947])

PALMA, G., 'Dependency and Development: A Critical Overview', in D. Seers (ed), *Dependency Theory: A Critical Reassessment* (London, 1981), pp 20-78

PALMER, R. AND PARSONS, N. (eds), *The Roots of Rural Poverty in Central and Southern Africa* (Berkeley and Los Angeles, 1977)

PARTRIDGE, P.H., 'Politics, Philosophy, Ideology', in *Political Studies*, 1961, pp 217-235

PERSON, Y., 'Les contradictions du nationalisme étatique en Afrique noire', in K. Ingham (ed), *Foreign Relations of African States* (London, 1974), pp 239-257

PETERSON, M.J., *The General Assembly in World Politics* (Boston, 1986)

PETTMAN, J., *Zambia: Security and Conflict* (Lewes, 1974)

PITTMAN, D., 'The OAU and Chad', in Y. El-Ayouty and I.W. Zartman (eds), *The OAU After Twenty Years* (New York, 1984), pp 297-325

PLANK, D.N., 'Aid, Debt, and the End of Sovereignty: Mozambique and its Donors', in *Journal of Modern African Studies*, 1993, pp 407-430

POLHEMUS, J.H., 'The Provisional Secretariat of the O.A.U., 1963-4', in *Journal of Modern African Studies*, 1974, pp 287-295

POLHEMUS, J.H., 'The Birth and Irrelevance of the Commission of Mediation, Conciliation, and Arbitration of the Organization of African Unity', in *Nigerian Journal of International Affairs*, 1977, nos. 1-2, pp 1-20

POMERANCE, M., *Self-Determination in Law and Practice: The New Doctrine in the United Nations* (The Hague, Boston and London, 1982)

PONDI, J.E. and KARIMOU, D.B.A., 'L'évolution de la fonction de "président en exercice" de l'OUA', in M. Kamto, J.E. Pondi and L. Zang (eds), *l'OUA: rétrospective et perspectives africaines* (Paris, 1990), ch. 2

POPITZ, H., *Phänomene der Macht: Autorität-Herrschaft-Gewalt-Technik* (Tübingen, 1986)

PRADHAN, R.C., 'OAU and the Congo Crisis', in *Africa Quarterly*, 1965, vol. V, pp 30-42

PRINCEN, TH., *Intermediaries in International Conflict* (Princeton, 1992) *Problèmes actuels de l'unité africaine: colloque d'Alger (25 mars-22 avril 1971)* (l'Université d'Alger: Algiers, 1973)

RAMBOURG, M., 'Parti unique et administration en Afrique', in *Canadian Journal of African Studies*, 1968, pp 137-146

RASHEED, S., 'Africa at the Doorstep of the Twenty-First Century: Can Crisis Turn to Opportunity?', in A. Adedeji (ed), *Africa within the World: Beyond Dispossession and Dependence* (London and Atlantic Highlands, NJ, 1993), ch. 4

RAVENHILL, J., 'When Weakness Is Strength: The Lomé IV Negotiations', in I.W. Zartman (ed), *Europe and Africa: The New Phase* (Boulder and London, 1993), ch. 4

RAYNER, J.D., 'The Use of Ideological Language', in D.J. Manning (ed), *The Form of Ideology: Investigations into the sense of ideological reasoning with a view to giving an account of its place in political life* (London, Boston and Sydney, 1980), ch. 6

RIDDELL, R.C., 'New Sanctions Against South Africa', in *Development Policy Review*, 1988, pp 243-267

RIDDELL, R.C., 'Aid Performance and Prospects', in I.W. Zartman (ed), *Europe and Africa: The New Phase* (Boulder and London, 1993), ch. 9

RIVIÈRE, C., *Guinea: The Mobilization of a People* (Ithaca and London, 1977)

ROBERTS, A., *A History of Zambia* (London, 1976)

ROBERTS, G.O., 'The Impact of Meeting Sitings of the Organization of African Unity', in *Liberian Studies Journal*, 1980-81, pp 35-46

ROBINSON, M., 'Will Political Conditionality Work?', in *IDS Bulletin*, 1993, no. 1, pp 58-66

ROBINSON, T.J., 'Ideology and Theoretical Inquiry', in D.J. Manning (ed), *The Form of Ideology: Investigations into the sense of ideological reasoning with a view to giving an account of its place in political life* (London, Boston and Sydney, 1980), ch. 4

ROGALLA VON BIEBERSTEIN, J., *Die These von der Verschwörung 1776-1945: Philosophen, Freimaurer, Juden, Liberale und Sozialisten als Verschwörer gegen die Sozialordnung* (Frankfurt, Bern and Las Vegas, 1978)

ROOD, J.Q.TH., *Hegemonie, machtsspreiding en internationaal-economische orde sinds 1945* (The Hague, 1996)

ROOD, J.Q.TH. and SICCAMA, J.G., *Verzwakking van de Sterkste: Oorzaken en Gevolgen van Amerikaans Machtsverval* (The Hague, 1989)

ROPIVIA, M.L., 'Critique des fondements conceptuels de l'unité politique de l'Afrique', in *Cahiers de l'IPAG*, no. 10, June 1990, pp 93-191

ROSBERG, C.G. and CALLAGHY, T.M. (eds), *Socialism in Sub-Saharan Africa: A New Assessment* (Berkeley, 1979)

ROSENAU, J.N., 'The Study of Foreign Policy', in J.N. Rosenau, K.W. Thompson and G. Boyd (eds), *World Politics: An Introduction* (New York and London, 1976), ch. 2

ROSENAU, J.N., THOMPSON, K.W. and BOYD, G. (eds), *World Politics: An Introduction* (New York and London, 1976)

ROTBERG, R.I., 'African Nationalism: Concept or Confusion?', in *Journal of Modern African Studies*, 1966, pp 33-46

ROTHCHILD, D., 'An Interactive Model for State-Ethnic Relations', in F.M. Deng and I.W. Zartman (eds), *Conflict Resolution in Africa* (Washington, 1991), ch. 7

ROTHCHILD, D. and CHAZAN, N. (eds), *The Precarious Balance: State and Society in Africa* (Boulder and London, 1988)

ROTHCHILD, D. and OLORUNSOLA, V.A. (eds), *State versus Ethnic Claims: African Policy Dilemmas* (Boulder, 1983)

ROTHSTEIN, R.L., 'Regime-Creation by a Coalition of the Weak: Lessons from the NIEO and the Integrated Program for Commodities', in *International Studies Quarterly*, 1984, pp 307-328

RUSSET, B. and STARR, H., *World Politics: The Menu for Choice* (New York, 1989)

SAMATAR, S.S., 'The Somali Dilemma: Nation in search of a state', in A.I. Asiwaju (ed), *Partitioned Africans: Ethnic Relations across Africa's International Boundaries 1884-1984* (London and Lagos, 1985), pp 155-193

SCHACHTER-MORGENTHAU, R., *Political Parties in French-Speaking West Africa* (Oxford, 1964)

SCHERMERS, H.G., *Inleiding tot het Internationale Institutionele Recht* (Deventer, 1983)

SCHERMERS, H.G. and BLOKKER, N.M., *International Institutional Law: Unity in diversity* (The Hague, London and Boston, 1995)

SCHNEIDMAN, W.J., 'FRELIMO's Foreign Policy and the Process of Liberation', in *Africa Today*, 1978, no. 1, pp 57-67

SCHRAEDER, P.J., 'U.S. Intervention in the Horn of Africa Amidst the End of the Cold War', in *Africa Today*, 1993, no. 2, pp 7-27

SCHWARZ, A., 'Mythe et réalité des bureaucraties africaines', in *Canadian Journal of African Studies*, 1974, pp 255-284

SCOTT, J.C., *Domination and the Arts of Resistance: Hidden Transcripts* (New Haven and London, 1990)

SEERS, D. (ed), *Dependency Theory: A Critical Reassessment* (London, 1981)

SEGAL, R., *African Profiles* (Harmondsworth, 1962)

SEIDMAN, A., *An Economics Textbook for Africa* (London and New York, 1980)

SENGHOR, L.S., *Nation et voie africaine du socialisme* (Paris, 1961)

SESAY, A., 'The Roles of the Frontline States in Southern Africa', in O. Aluko and T.M. Shaw (eds), *Southern Africa in the 1980s* (London, 1985), ch. 2

SESAY, A. (ed), *Africa and Europe: From Partition to Interdependence or Dependence?* (London, 1986)

SESAY, A., OJO, O. and FASEHUN, O., *The OAU After Twenty Years* (Boulder and London, 1984)

SHAW, T.M., 'African states and international stratification: the adaptive foreign policy of Tanzania', in K. Ingham (ed), *Foreign Relations of African States* (London, 1974), pp 213-233

SHAW, T.M., 'The Actors in African International Politics', in T.M. Shaw and K.A. Heard (eds), *The Politics of Africa: Dependence and Development* (London, 1979), ch. 14

SHAW, T.M., 'Africa in the World System: towards more uneven development', in T.M. Shaw and S. Ojo (eds), *Africa and the International Political System* (Washington, 1982), ch. 5

SHAW, T.M., *Towards a Political Economy for Africa: The Dialectics of Dependence* (New York, 1985)

SHAW, T.M., 'Ethnicity as the Resilient Paradigm for Africa', in *Development and Change*, 1986, pp 587-605

SHAW, T.M., 'Africa in the New World Order: Marginal and/or Central?', in A. Adedeji (ed), *Africa within the World: Beyond Dispossession and Dependence* (London and Atlantic Highlands, NJ, 1993), ch. 7

SHAW, T.M. and ALUKO, O. (eds), *Nigerian Foreign Policy: Alternative Perceptions and Projections* (London and Basingstoke, 1983)

SHAW, T.M. and ALUKO, O. (eds), *The Political Economy of African Foreign Policy* (Aldershot, 1984)

SHAW, T.M. and HEARD, K.A. (eds), *The Politics of Africa: Dependence and Development* (London, 1979)

SHAW, T.M. and NEWBURY, M.C., 'Dependence or Interdependence: Africa in the Global Political Economy', in M.W. Delancey (ed), *Aspects of International Relations in Africa* (Columbia, 1980), pp 39-89

SHAW, T.M. and OJO, S. (eds), *Africa and the International Political System* (Washington, 1982)

SHAW, T.M. and OKOLO, J.E. (eds), *The Political Economy of Foreign Policy in ECOWAS* (Basingstoke and London, 1994)

SHEPHERD, G.W., *Nonaligned Black Africa: An International Subsystem* (Lexington, 1970)

SHEPHERD, G.W., 'The OAU and African Collective Security in the Post Cold War Era: An Editorial', in *Africa Today*, 1988, nos. 3 & 4, pp 3-6

SHEPPERSON, G., 'Notes on Negro American Influences on the Emergence of African Nationalism', in *Journal of African History*, 1960, pp 299-312

SHILLS, E., 'The Concept of Function of Ideology', in D.L. Sills (ed), *International Encyclopaedia of the Social Sciences* (no pl., 1968), vl. 7, pp 66-76

SHIMKO, K.L., 'Metaphors and Foreign Policy Decision Making', in *Political Psychology*, 1994, pp 655-671

SIMON, H.A., *Models of Man* (New York, 1957)

SINGLETON, S., 'Conflict Resolution in Africa: The Congo and the Rules of the Game', in *Pan-African Journal*, vl. 8, 1975, no. 1, pp 1-18

SKINNER, Q., 'Meaning and Understanding in the History of Ideas', in *History and Theory*, 1969, pp 3-53

SKURNIK, W.A.E., *The Foreign Policy of Senegal* (Evanston, 1972)

SKURNIK, W.A.E., 'France and Fragmentation in West Africa: 1945-1960', in *Journal of African History*, 1967, pp 317-333

SMITH, A.D., *State and Nation in the Third World: The Western State and African Nationalism* (Brighton, 1983)

SMITH, S.M., 'Economic Dependence and Economic Empiricism in Black Africa', in *Journal of Modern African Studies*, 1977, pp 116-118

SMITH, T., *The Pattern of Imperialism: The United States, Great Britain, and the Late Industrializing World since 1815* (New York, 1981)

SMITH, T., 'Requiem or New Agenda for Third World Studies?', in *World Politics*, 1985, pp 532-561

SNIDAL, D., 'The Limits of Hegemonic Stability Theory', in *International Organization*, 1985, pp 579-614

SOETENDORP, R.B., 'Analyse van buitenlands beleid', in K. Koch, R.B. Soetendorp and A. van Staden (eds), *Internationale betrekkingen: Theorieën en benaderingen* (Utrecht, 1994), ch. 2

SOHN, L.B. (ed), *Basic Documents of African Regional Organizations*, vl. I (New York, 1971)

SOHN, L.B. (ed), *Basic Documents of African Regional Organizations*, vl. II (New York, 1972)

SOREMEKUN, F., 'Angola', in T.M. Shaw and O. Aluko (eds), *The Political Economy of African Foreign Policy* (Aldershot, 1984), ch. 1

SOUTHALL, A.W., 'The Concept of Elites and their Formation in Uganda', in P.C. Lloyd (ed), *The New Elites of Tropical Africa* (London, 1970), ch. 17

STEDMAN, S.J., 'Conflict and Conflict Resolution in Africa: A Conceptual Framework', in F.M. Deng and I.W. Zartman (eds), *Conflict Resolution in Africa* (Washington, 1991), ch. 14

STEDMAN, S.J., *Peacemaking in Civil War: International Mediation in Zimbabwe, 1974-1980* (Boulder and London, 1991)

STEIN, A.A., *Why Nations Cooperate: Circumstances and Choice in International Relations* (Ithaca and London, 1990)

STRACK, H.R., *Sanctions: The Case of Rhodesia* (Syracuse, 1978)

STRAUCH, H.F., *Panafrika: Kontinentale Weltmacht im Werden? Anfänge, Wachstum und Zukunft der afrikanischen Einigungsbestrebungen* (Zurich, 1964)

STREMLAU, J.J., *The International Politics of the Nigerian Civil War 1967-1970* (Princeton, 1977)

SULLIVAN, M.P., *International Relations: Theories and Evidence* (Englewood Cliffs, 1976)

TARP, F., *Stabilization and Structural Adjustment: Macroeconomic Frameworks for Analysing the Crisis in Sub-Saharan Africa* (London and New York, 1993)

TEKLE, A., 'The Organization of African Unity at Twenty Five Years: Retrospect and Prospect', in *Africa Today*, 3rd/4th quarters, 1988, pp 7-19

TEVOEDJRE, A., *Pan-Africanism in Action: An Account of the UAM* (Harvard, 1965)

THARP, P.A. (ed), *Regional International Organizations: Structures and Functions* (New York, Toronto and London, 1971)

The African Charter on Human and Peoples' Rights: Development, Context, Significance; Papers of a Symposium of the African Law Association held in Maastricht in 1987 (Marburg, 1991)

THIAM, D., *La politique étrangère des états africains* (Paris, 1963)

THOMPSON, V., *West Africa's Council of the Entente* (Ithaca and London, 1972)

THOMPSON, V. and ADLOFF, R., *The Western Saharans: Background to Conflict* (London and Totowa, NJ, 1980)

THOMPSON, V.B., *Africa and Unity: The Evolution of Pan-Africanism* (London and Harlow, 1969)

THOMPSON, W.S., *Ghana's Foreign Policy 1957-1966: Diplomacy, Ideology, and the New State* (Princeton, 1969)

THOMPSON, W.S. and BISSELL, R., 'Legitimacy and Authority in the OAU', in *African Studies Review*, 1972, pp 17-42

THOMPSON, W.S. and ZARTMAN, I.W., 'The Development of Norms in the African System', in Y. El-Ayouty (ed), *The Organization of African Unity After Ten Years: Comparative Perspectives* (New York, 1976), ch. 1

TOSTENSEN, A., *Dependence and Collective Self-Reliance in Southern Africa: The Case of the Southern African Development Co-ordination Conference (SADCC)* (Uppsala, 1982)

TOURÉ, S., *Expérience guinéenne et unité africaine* (Paris, 1959)

TOURÉ, S., *l'Afrique et la révolution* (Paris, 1967)

TOUVAL, S., *The Boundary Politics of Independent Africa* (Cambridge, Mass., 1972)

TOUVAL, S. and ZARTMAN, I.W. (eds), *International Mediation in Theory and Practice* (Boulder and London, 1985)

TOUVAL, S. and ZARTMAN, I.W., 'Introduction: Mediation in Theory', in S. Touval and I.W. Zartman (eds), *International Mediation in Theory and Practice* (Boulder and London, 1985), pp 7-17

TRONCHON, J., *L'insurrection malgache de 1947: essai d'interprétation historique* (Fianarantsoa and Paris, 1986)

UAM documentation (no author, Paris, 1963)

VÄYRYNEN, R. (ed), *New Directions in Conflict Theory: Conflict Resolution and Conflict Transformation* (London and New Delhi, 1991)

VÄYRYNEN, R., 'To Settle or Transform? Perspectives on the Resolution of National and International Conflicts', in R. Väyrynen (ed), *New Directions in Conflict Theory: Conflict Resolution and Conflict Transformation* (London and New Delhi, 1991), ch. 1

VAN BINSBERGEN, W. and HESSELING, G. (eds), *Aspecten van Staat en Maatschappij in Afrika* (Leiden, 1984)

VAN CRANENBURGH, O., *The Widening Gyre: The Tanzanian One-Party State and Policy Towards Rural Cooperatives* (Delft, 1990)

VAN DER MEULEN, J., *Zuid Afrika als Regionaal Machtscentrum* (The Hague, 1986)

VAN HAM, P., 'The lack of a Big Bully: Hegemonic stability theory and regimes in the study of international relations', in *Acta Politica*, 1992, pp 29-48

VAN LIERDE, J., *La pensée politique de Patrice Lumumba* (Brussels, 1963)

VAN ROUVEROY VAN NIEUWAAL, E.A.B., 'Sorcellerie et justice coutumière dans une société togolaise: une quantité négligeable', in *Receuil Penant*, 1989, pp 433-453

VAN SCHENDELEN, M.P.C.M. (ed), *Kernthema's van de Politicologie* (Meppel and Amsterdam, 1981)

VAN WALRAVEN, K., 'Some Aspects of Regional Economic Integration in Africa', in *Hague Yearbook of International Law*, 1991, PP 106-126

VANSINA, J., 'Old and New African Political Traditions'; lecture at the post-doctoral course on African studies, African Studies Centre: Leiden, 9 June 1992

VATIKIOTIS, P.J., *Nasser and His Generation* (London, 1978)

VENTER, D., 'An Evaluation of the OAU on the Eve of South Africa's Accession', in *Africa Insight*, 1994, pp 47-59

VERBEEK, B.J., 'Cognitieve ideeën en internationale politiek', in *Acta Politica*, 1990, pp 95-116

VINAY, B., *Zone franc et coopération monétaire* (Paris, 1980)

VOEGELIN, E., 'The Growth of the Race Idea', in *Review of Politics*, 1940, pp 283-317

VOGT, M.A., 'Nigeria's Participation in the ECOWAS Monitoring Group - ECOMOG', in *Nigerian Journal of International Affairs*, 1991, no. 1, pp 101-121

VOLMAN, D., 'Africa and the New World Order', in *Journal of Modern African Studies*, 1993, pp 1-30

VON ULM-ERBACH, C., *Aethiopiens Beitrag zur Gründung der Organisation für Afrikanische Einheit: Eine Studie zur Rezeption des Pan-afrikanismus in die afrikanische Politik und Anpassung Aethiopiens an diese Entwicklung* (Bern, 1974)

VOVELLE, M., *Ideologies and Mentalities* (Cambridge and Oxford, 1990)

WADE, R., 'East Asia's Economic Success: Conflicting Perspectives, Partial Insights, Shaky Evidence', in *World Politics*, 1992, pp 270-320

WALLERSTEIN, I., 'The Early Years of the OAU: The Search for Organizational Preeminence', in *International Organization*, 1966, pp 774-787

WALLERSTEIN, I., *Africa: The Politics of Unity. An Analysis of a Contemporary Social Movement* (New York, 1967)

WALLERSTEIN, I., 'Dependence in an Interdependent World: The Limited Possibilities of Transformation within the Capitalist World Economy', in *African Studies Review*, 1974, pp 1-26

WALSHE, P., *The Rise of African Nationalism in South Africa: The ANC 1912-1952* (London, 1970)

WALTZ, K.N., *Theory of International Politics* (Reading, Mass., and London, 1979)

WARBURG, G.R. and KUPFERSCHMIDT, U.M. (eds), *Islam, Nationalism, and Radicalism in Egypt and the Sudan* (New York, 1983)

WEBB, M.C. and KRASNER, S.D., 'Hegemonic stability theory: an empirical assessment', in *Review of International Studies*, 1989, pp 183-198

WEILAND, H., 'Wirtschaftssanktionen gegen Südafrika: a never ending story', in *Internationales Afrikaforum*, 1986, pp 83-88

WEISMANN, S., *American Foreign Policy in the Congo 1960-1964* (Cornell, 1974)

WEISS, R., *Zimbabwe and the New Elite* (London and New York, 1994)

WELCH, C.E., *Dream of Unity: Pan-Africanism and Political Unification in West Africa* (Ithaca, 1966)

WELCH, C.E. (ed), *Soldier and State in Africa: a comparative analysis of military intervention and political change* (Evanston, 1970)

WELCH, C.E., 'The Roots and Implications of Military Intervention', in C.E. Welch (ed), *Soldier and State in Africa: a comparative analysis of military intervention and political change* (Evanston, 1970), ch. 1

WEMBOU, M.C.D., 'A propos du nouveau mécanisme de l'OUA sur les conflits', in *Afrique 2000*, February 1994, pp 5-20

WHITAKER, P.M., 'Arms and the Nationalists', in *Africa Report*, May 1970, pp 12-14

WILCOX, D.L., *Mass Media in Black Africa: Philosophy and Control* (New York, 1975)

WILD, P.B., 'Radicals and Moderates in the OAU: Origins of Conflicts and Bases for Coexistence', in P.A. Tharp (ed), *Regional International Organizations: Structures and Functions* (New York, Toronto and London, 1971), pp 36-50

WILLAME, J.C., *L'autonomne d'un despotisme: pouvoir, argent et obéissance dans le Zaïre des années quatre-vingt* (Paris, 1992)

WISEMAN, H., 'The OAU: Peacekeeping and Conflict Resolution', in Y. El-Ayouty and I.W. Zartman (eds), *The OAU After Twenty Years* (New York, 1984), pp 123-153

WISEMAN, J.A., *Democracy in Black Africa: Survival and Revival* (New York, 1990)

WODIE, F., *Les institutions régionales en Afrique occidentale et centrale* (Paris, 1970)

WOLFERS, M., *Politics in the Organization of African Unity* (London, 1976)

WOLFERS, M., 'The Institutional Evolution of the OAU', in Y. El-Ayouty and I.W. Zartman (eds), *The OAU After Twenty Years* (New York, 1984), pp 85-100

WOLFERS, M., 'The Organization of African Unity as Mediator', in S. Touval and I.W. Zartman (eds), *International Mediation in Theory and Practice* (Boulder and London, 1985), ch. 6

WOLFERS, M. and BERGERAL, J., *Angola in the Frontline* (London, 1983)

WOOD, B., 'Preventing the Vacuum: Determinants of the Namibia Settlement', in *Journal of Southern African Studies*, 1991, pp 742-769

WORONOFF, J., *Organizing African Unity* (Metuchen, NJ, 1970)

YABLOTCHKOV, L., 'L'évolution du nationalisme africain', in *Présence africaine*, 1970, no. 74, pp 46-60

YANNOPOULOS, T., 'Aliénation idéologique et unité africaine', in *Problèmes actuels de l'unité africaine: colloque d'Alger (25 mars - 12 avril 1971)* (l'Université d'Alger: Algiers, 1973), pp 487-495

YANSANÉ, A.Y. (ed), *Decolonization and Dependency: Problems of Development of African Societies* (Westport and London, 1980)

YANSANÉ, A.Y., 'Decolonization, Dependency, and Development in Africa: The Theory Revisited', in A.Y. Yansané (ed), *Decolonization and Dependency: Problems of Development of African Societies* (Westport and London, 1980), pp 3-51

YOUNG, C, *Politics in the Congo: Decolonization and Independence* (Princeton, 1965)

YOUNG, C, *The Politics of Cultural Pluralism* (Madison, 1976)

YOUNG, C, *Ideology and Development in Africa* (New Haven and London, 1982)

YOUNG, C, 'Comparative Claims to Political Sovereignty: Biafra, Katanga, Eritrea', in D. Rothchild and V.A. Olorunsola (eds), *State versus Ethnic Claims: African Policy Dilemmas* (Boulder, 1983), ch. 11

YOUNG, C, 'Self-Determination, Territorial Integrity, and the African State System', in F.M. Deng and I.W. Zartman (eds), *Conflict Resolution in Africa* (Washington, 1991), pp 320-346

YOUNG, C. and TURNER, T., *The Rise and Decline of the Zairean State* (Madison, 1985)

YOUNG, D.R., 'Regime dynamics: the rise and fall of international regimes', in S.D. Krasner (ed), *International Regimes* (Ithaca and London, 1983), pp 98-113

ZANG, L, 'L'action économique de l'OUA depuis 1963', in M. Kamto, J.E. Pondi and L. Zang (eds), *l'OUA: rétrospective et perspectives africaines* (Paris, 1990), ch. 7

ZANG, L. and SINOU, D., 'Dynamique des groupes au sein de l'OUA et unité africaine', in M. Kamto, J.E. Pondi and L. Zang (eds), *l'OUA: rétrospective et perspectives africaines* (Paris, 1990), pp 135-181

ZARTMAN, I.W., *International Relations in the New Africa* (Englewood Cliffs, 1966)

ZARTMAN, I.W., 'The OAU in the African State System: Interaction and Evaluation', in Y. El-Ayouty and I.W. Zartman (eds), *The OAU After Twenty Years* (New York, 1984), ch. 2

ZARTMAN, I.W., 'Conflict Reduction: Prevention, Management, and Resolution', in F.M. Deng and I.W. Zartman (eds), *Conflict Resolution in Africa* (Washington, 1991), ch. 11

ZARTMAN, I.W. (ed), *Europe and Africa: The New Phase* (Boulder and London, 1993)

ZARTMAN, I.W., 'Introduction', in I.W. Zartman (ed), *Europe and Africa: The New Phase* (Boulder and London, 1993), ch. 1

ZARTMAN, I.W. and TOUVAL, S., 'Conclusion: Mediation in Theory and Practice', in S. Touval and I.W. Zartman (eds), *International Mediation in Theory and Practice* (Boulder and London, 1985), pp 251-268

ZOLBERG, A., *Creating Political Order: The Party Structures of West Africa* (Chicago, 1966)

ZONIS, M. and Joseph, C.M., 'Conspiracy Thinking in the Middle East', in *Political Psychology*, 1994, pp 443-459

ZOULA, G., 'Perspectives de renforcement des organisations régionales en matière de stabilité et de sécurité: le cas de l'Organisation de l'unité africaine (OUA)', in *Cahiers de l'IPAG*, no. 10, June 1990, pp 75-91

Research Series of the African Studies Centre, Leiden, The Netherlands

1. Dick Foeken & Nina Tellegen
   1994
   Tied to the land. Living conditions of labourers on large farms in Trans Nzoia District, Kenya

2. Tom Kuhlman
   1994
   Asylum or Aid? The economic integration of Ethiopian and Eritrean refugees in the Sudan

3. Kees Schilder
   1994
   Quest for self-esteem. State, Islam and Mundang ethnicity in Northern Cameroon

4. Johan A. van Dijk
   1995
   Taking the waters. Soil and water conservation among settling Beja nomads in Eastern Sudan

5. Piet Konings
   1995
   Gender and class in the tea estates of Cameroon

6. Thera Rasing
   1995
   Passing on the rites of passage. Girls' initiation rites in the context of an urban Roman Catholic community on the Zambian Copperbelt

7. Jan Hoorweg, Dick Foeken & Wijnand Klaver
   1995
   Seasons and nutrition at the Kenya coast

8. John A. Houtkamp
   1996
   Tropical Africa's emergence as a banana supplier in the inter-war period

9. Victor Azarya
   1996
   Nomads and the state in Africa: the political roots of marginality

10. Deborah Bryceson & Vali Jamal, eds.
    1997
    Farewell to farms. De-agrarianization and employment in Africa

11. Tjalling Dijkstra
    1997
    Trading the fruits of the land: horticultural marketing channels in Kenya

12. Nina Tellegen
    1997
    Rural enterprises in Malawi: necessity or opportunity?

13. Klaas van Walraven
    1999
    Dreams of power. The role of the organization of African Unity in the politics of Africa 1963 - 1993

Copies can be ordered at: Ashgate Publishing Ltd.
Gower House
Croft Road
Aldershot
Hampshire GU11 3HR
England